PRACTICAL AUDITING

SPICER AND PEGLER'S

PRACTICAL AUDITING

Fifteenth Edition

by

WALTER W. BIGG, F.C.A.

HFL (PUBLISHERS) LTD
9 BOW STREET, LONDON WC2E 7AL

First published *1911*
Fifteenth Edition *1969*
,,   ,,   *(Second Impression)* *1970*
,,   ,,   *(Third Impression)* *1972*
,,   ,,   *(Fourth Impression)* *1974*

This Edition © H F L (PUBLISHERS) LTD

1972

ISBN 0 372 01640 5

Printed in Great Britain by

THE STELLAR PRESS HATFIELD HERTS

PREFACE TO THE FIFTEENTH EDITION

The major changes brought about by the *Companies Act 1967* have made a new edition essential. I have also taken the opportunity of revising the whole of the text.

My thanks are due to the Institute of Chartered Accountants in England and Wales for their kind permission to include appropriate sections of their recommendations on accounting and auditing principles as an Appendix. In the past these recommendations have been embodied in the text, and it is hoped that this change will simplify the task of the reader.

I have to acknowledge my indebtedness to Mr George H. Forster, F.C.A., A.I.M.T.A., and Mr Noel Cliffe, F.C.A., for their revision of the chapter dealing with the audit of the accounts of local authorities.

I also have to thank Mr E. H. Woolf, A.C.A., for the very great assistance he has given me in the preparation of this edition.

WALTER W. BIGG.

London,
April 1969

TABLE OF CONTENTS

	PAGE
TABLE OF STATUTES	xv
TABLE OF CASES	xvii

Chapter I
THE PRINCIPLES OF AUDITING

§ 1. The Origin of Auditing	1
2. The Nature and Definition of an Audit	2
3. The Objects of an Audit	3
(A) The Report	3
(B) The Detection of Fraud	3
(C) The Detection of Errors	5
4. Various Classes of Audits, and their Advantages	8
(A) Audits under Statute	8
(B) The Audit of the Accounts of Private Firms	11
(C) The Audit of the Accounts of Private Individuals ..	12
(D) The Audit of Trust Accounts	13
5. The Conduct of an Audit	14
(A) Continuous and Final (or Completed) Audits	14
P.E.R.T.	17
(B) Considerations on the Commencement of a New Audit ..	18
Assessment of the System of Internal Control	19
Internal Control Questionnaires	19
Flow Charting	21
Special Matters	27
(C) Audit Programmes	28
(D) Method of Work	30
6. Internal Audits	31
7. The Qualities required of an Auditor	32

Chapter II
THE AUDIT OF CASH TRANSACTIONS

§ 1. Internal Check as regards Cash	35
(A) Receipts	35
(B) Payments	36
2. Vouching Payments	37
(A) General Considerations	37
(B) Missing Vouchers	40
(C) Capital Expenditure	40
(D) Special Payments	43
3. Wages	46
(A) Internal Checks as regards Wages	46
(B) The Auditor's Duty as regards Wages	49
4. Vouching Cash Received	50
(A) General Considerations	50
(B) Credit Sales	51
(C) Cash Sales	52
(D) Special Receipts	52

Chapter II (*continued*)
THE AUDIT OF CASH TRANSACTIONS

PAGE

§ 5. The Bank Statement 54
    (A) Payments into Bank 54
    (B) Payments out of Bank 55
    (C) Reconciliation with Cash Book 56
6. Verification of Cash in Hand and at Bank 56
7. Petty Cash 57
    (A) General Considerations 57
    (B) Internal Check as regards Petty Cash 59
    (C) The Auditor's Duty in relation to Petty Cash 60
8. Vouching 'In Depth' 62
9. The Use of Statistical Sampling Techniques 63

Chapter III
THE AUDIT OF TRADING TRANSACTIONS

§ 1. Purchases 72
    (A) Internal Check as regards Purchases 72
    (B) The Bought Day Book 72
    (C) Vouching Invoices 74
    (D) Forward Purchases 77
2. Purchases Returns 77
3. Sales 78
    (A) Credit Sales 78
    (B) Cash Sales 80
    (C) Goods on Sale or Return 80
    (D) Goods on Consignment 81
    (E) Sales for Future Delivery 83
    (F) Sales under Hire-Purchase Agreements 83
4. Sales Returns 84
5. Containers 85
6. Allowances 86
7. The Journal 86
8. The Bought Ledger 87
9. Sales Ledgers 89
    (A) Internal Check 89
    (B) The Verification of Postings 90
    (C) The Verification of Balances 90
    (D) Bad and Doubtful Debts 91
10. Total (or Control) Accounts and Sectional Balancing 96
11. Loose Leaf and Card Ledgers 97

Chapter IV
THE AUDIT OF MECHANIZED AND ELECTRONIC DATA PROCESSING SYSTEMS

§ 1. Mechanical Systems 98
2. Internal Control 99
    (A) Clerical Organization 100
    (B) Comparison of Records with Evidence Originating outside the Clerical System 100
    (C) Clerical Controls 100
3. Keyboard Accounting Machine Systems 105
    (A) Posting to Accounts Correctly 105
    (B) Proving Data Posted Correctly 106
    (C) Proving Opening Balances Picked up Correctly 107
    (D) Proving Closing Balances Computed Correctly 108

Chapter IV (*continued*)

THE AUDIT OF MECHANIZED AND ELECTRONIC DATA PROCESSING SYSTEMS

PAGE

§ 4. Punched-Card Systems 109
    Proving Accuracy of Input 111
    Proving Accuracy of Processing 112
5. Electronic Data Processing Systems 115
    The Program 116
    Internal Control 118
    Controls on Input 119
    Controls on Computer Processing 120
    Controls on Output 124
    The Client's Use of a Service Bureau 129
    Security 129
    Use of the Computer for Audit Purposes 132

Chapter V

THE AUDIT OF THE IMPERSONAL LEDGER

§ 1. The Impersonal Ledger 136
2. Outstanding Liabilities and Assets 138
    (A) Outstanding Liabilities 139
    (B) Outstanding Assets 144
3. Apportionment of Expenditure between Capital and Revenue .. 146
4. Deferred Revenue Expenditure 147
    (A) Alterations to Plant 148
    (B) Advertising.. 148
    (C) Preliminary Expenditure in Connection with a New Business 149
5. Repairs and Renewals 149
6. Reserves and Provisions 150
    (A) Reserves 151
    (B) Provisions 152

Chapter VI

THE VERIFICATION OF ASSETS

§ 1. General Considerations 156
    (A) Introduction 156
    (B) The Valuation of Assets 157
    (C) Depreciation 162
2. Land and Buildings 167
    (A) Freehold Property 167
    (B) Leasehold Property 169
3. Investments 169
    (A) Registered Stocks and Shares 171
    (B) Bonds to Bearer, and other Securities 171
    (C) Tax Reserve Certificates 172
    (D) Building Society Deposits and Shares 172
    (E) Treasury Bills 173
    (F) Loans to Local Authorities 173
    (G) The Verification of the Values of Investments .. 173
4. Stock-in-Trade 175
    (A) The Auditor's Duty in relation to Stock-in-Trade .. 175
    (B) Method of Stock-taking 178
    (C) Basis of Valuation 179

Chapter VI (*continued*)
THE VERIFICATION OF ASSETS

PAGE

§ 5. Loans on Security 181
    (A) Loans on Mortgage 182
    (B) Loans on the Security of Investments 183
    (C) Loans on Other Security 183
    (D) Loans to Employees 184
    (E) Loans to Subsidiary Companies 185
  6. Bills Receivable 185
  7. Other Assets 186
  8. Events occurring after the Balance Sheet date 192

Chapter VII
THE BALANCE SHEET AUDIT

§ 1. Introduction 194
  2. The Relationship of Balance Sheet and Profit and Loss Account 196
  3. The Programme for a Balance Sheet Audit 197
  4. Audit Working Papers 199
  5. Detailed Checking 204

Chapter VIII
THE AUDITOR OF A LIMITED COMPANY

§ 1. The Appointment and Remuneration of Auditors 206
    (A) Auditors appointed on behalf of the Company 206
    (B) The Qualification Required for Appointment as Auditor of a
        Company 207
    (C) The Auditor's Remuneration 210
    (D) The Removal of Auditors 210
        Disagreement between Directors and Auditors 212
    (E) Joint Auditors 215
    (F) Local Auditors 215
  2. The Status of the Auditor 216
    (A) As Agent of the Members 216
    (B) As an Officer of the Company 216
  3. The Powers of the Auditor 218
  4. The Duties of the Auditor 220
  5. The Auditor's Report 224
  6. The Publication of the Balance Sheet and Auditor's Report .. 227
  7. The Auditor's Lien 229

Chapter IX
THE AUDIT OF A LIMITED COMPANY

§ 1. Considerations on Appointment as Auditor 232
    (A) The Appointment of the Auditor 232
    (B) The Remuneration of the Auditor 232
    (C) Inspection of Books and Documents 233
  2. Share Capital 235
    (A) The Various Classes of Share Capital 235
    (B) Shares issued for Cash 239
    (C) Issue of Warrants to Bearer 240
    (D) Shares Issued for Consideration other than Cash 240
    (E) Shares Issued at a Premium 241
    (F) Shares Issued at a Discount 242

Chapter IX (*continued*)
THE AUDIT OF A LIMITED COMPANY
§ 2. Share Capital (*continued*)
(G) Share Books 243
(H) Share Transfer Audit 243
(I) Forged and Blank Transfers 245
(J) Calls paid in Advance 246
(K) Interest Payable out of Capital during Construction .. 247
(L) Alteration of Rights of Members 247
(M) Increase or Reduction of Capital 248
3. The Prospectus 248
4. Mortgages and Loans 251
5. Debentures 252
(A) Definition of Debenture 252
(B) Issue of Debentures 253
(C) Redemption of Debentures 257
6. Preliminary and Formation Expenses 259
7. Commission on Issue of Shares 260
8. The Statutory Audit 262
9. Adjustment of Accounts with Vendors 264
(A) Purchase of Business 264
(B) Apportionment of Profit or Loss prior to Incorporation .. 265
(C) Receipts and Payments on behalf of Vendors .. 266
10. The Annual Audit 267
(A) The Books of Account 267
(B) The Profit and Loss Account 269
(C) The Balance Sheet 280
(D) Materiality in Accounts 300
(E) The Directors' Report 302
11. The Inclusion of the Balance Sheet in the Annual Return .. 306
12. Directors 306
(A) Liability of Directors to Account 306
(B) Remuneration of Directors 310
(C) Payments to Directors for Loss of Office 314
(D) Director's Qualification 314
(E) Directors' Travelling Expenses 316
(F) Managing Directors 317
(G) Secretary 318
13. Minute Books 318
(A) Directors' Minute Book 318
(B) Members' Minute Book 319
14. Reserve Funds 319
15. Secret or Internal Reserves 323
16. Taxation 324
(A) Distributions 326
(B) Charges 327
(C) Franked Investment Income 327
(D) Unfranked Investment Income 327
(E) Profits 327
(F) Set-off 327

Chapter X
DIVISIBLE PROFITS AND DIVIDENDS
§ 1. Introduction—The Ascertainment of Profits 330
2. Remuneration based on Profits 332
3. Depreciation of Fixed and Current Assets 335
(A) The Legal Decisions 335
(B) The Legal Decisions considered 349

Chapter X (*continued*)
DIVISIBLE PROFITS AND DIVIDENDS

			PAGE
§ 4.	Capital Profits		355
	(A) The Legal Decisions		355
	(B) The Legal Decisions considered		357
5.	Divisible Profits		358
6.	Dividends		359
	(A) Interim Dividends		359
	(B) Final Dividends		361
	(C) Preference Dividends		362
	(D) Arrears of Cumulative Preference Dividends		362
	(E) Dividends paid out of Capital		362
	(F) Scrip Dividends		363
	(G) Vouching Dividends		364
	(H) Unclaimed Dividends		365
	(I) Reserves for the Equalization of Dividends		365

Chapter XI
THE FORM OF ACCOUNTS

§ 1.	The Form of Final Accounts		367
2.	The Profit and Loss Account		367
3.	The Balance Sheet		372
4.	Group Accounts		379
	(A) The Form and Contents of Group Accounts		380
	(B) The Audit of Group Accounts		386
	(C) The Consolidation of Accounts		388

Chapter XII
THE LIABILITY OF AUDITORS

§ 1.	The Sources of Liability		394
2.	Liability for Negligence under the Common Law		394
3.	Liability under Statute		395
	(A) Civil		395
	(B) Criminal		396
4.	Major Legal Decisions		399
	(A) Leeds Estate Building and Investment Co *v.* Shepherd		399
	(B) In *re* London and General Bank (No. 2)		399
	(C) In *re* The Kingston Cotton Mill Co Ltd (No. 2)		402
	(D) The Irish Woollen Co Ltd *v.* Tyson and Others		404
	(E) The London Oil Storage Co Ltd *v.* Seear, Hasluck & Co		406
	(F) Arthur E. Green & Co *v.* The Central Advance and Discount Corporation Ltd		407
	(G) In re The City Equitable Fire Insurance Co Ltd		408
	(H) Rex *v.* Kylsant and Morland		414
	(I) In *re* The Westminster Road Construction and Engineering Co Ltd		417
5.	Consideration of Case Law affecting Auditors		418
	(A) Introduction		418
	(B) Liability for Negligence under Common Law		420
	(C) Civil Liability to Third Parties under Common Law		429
	(D) Relationship between Responsibilities of Directors and Auditors		434
	(E) Civil Liability for Misfeasance under the *Companies Act 1948*		434
	(F) Criminal Liability		439
6.	Unlawful Acts or Defaults by an Accountant's Clients		440

Chapter XIII
SPECIAL POINTS IN DIFFERENT CLASSES OF AUDIT

§ 1. Banks 450
  2. Building Societies.. 451
  3. Estate Agents, Auctioneers, Surveyors etc. 455
  4. Executors' and Trustees' Accounts 455
  5. Insurance Companies 460
  6. Solicitors 464
  7. Stockbrokers 478
      Arbitrage 485
      Option Dealing 486
      Notes for the Guidance of Member Firms and their Accountants 486
  8. Stockjobbers 494
  9. Trust and Finance Companies 496
  10. Unit Trusts 498

Chapter XIV
THE AUDIT OF ACCOUNTS OF LOCAL AUTHORITIES

§ 1. The Classification of Auditors of Local Authorities 500
  2. Borough Audit 500
  3. Professional Audit 501
  4. District Audit 502
  5. Regulations applying to District Audit 503
  6. Internal Audit 506
  7. Preparations for Audit 508
  8. Capital Accounts 508
  9. Loan Indebtedness 509
  10. Stock Issue 510
  11. Consolidated Loans Fund 512
  12. Arrangements for handling Receipts and Payments 513
  13. The Audit of Revenue Income 513
  14. Audit of Expenditure 517
  15. Bank Accounts 518
  16. The Balance Sheet 518
  17. The Auditor's Report 521

Chapter XV
INVESTIGATIONS

§ 1. The Nature of Investigations 524
  2. Investigation on behalf of an Individual or Firm proposing to buy a Business 526
      (A) The Extent of the Investigation 526
      (B) The usual Adjustments necessary 531
      (C) The Report 533
  3. Investigation on behalf of the Promoters of a Proposed Company – Reports in a Prospectus 534
      Legal Requirements 534
      Stock Exchange Requirements 539
  4. The City Code on Take-overs and Mergers 549
  5. Investigation on behalf of an Incoming Partner 552
  6. Investigation on behalf of a Bank for purposes of obtaining Credit 553

TABLE OF CONTENTS

Chapter XV (*continued*)

INVESTIGATIONS

PAGE

§ 7. Investigation on behalf of a Person intending to invest in a Private
Business, Firm or Company 555

8. Investigation for Fraud 558

9. Investigation under the *Companies Acts 1948* and *1967* .. 561

10. Investigations in connection with Taxation Liability 565

APPENDIX – PART A: EXTRACTS FROM STATEMENTS ON ACCOUNTING
PRINCIPLES AND OTHER TECHNICAL STATEMENTS
(*Published by the Institute of Chartered Accountants
in England and Wales*)
Table of Contents 570

PART B: EXTRACTS FROM INTERNAL CONTROL QUESTIONNAIRE 673

INDEX 685

TABLE OF STATUTES

(listed chronologically)

PAGE

Joint Stock Companies Registration
Act 1844 9

Larceny Act
1861 .. 397, 414, 415, 440

Apportionment Act 1870 .. 456

Falsification of Accounts Act 1875 397

Companies Act 1879 216

Bills of Sale Act 1882 184

Companies (Winding-up) Act 1890 400
§ 10 402

Judicial Trustees Act 1896 .. 460

Public Trustee Act 1906 .. 14
§ 13 458

Companies Act 1907 .. 10, 212

Companies (Consolidation) Act
1908 .. .. 10, 349
§ 215 408

Perjury Act 1911
§ 5 309

Bankruptcy Act 1914
§ 154 308

Larceny Act 1916
§ 20 397

Land Charges Act 1925 .. 664

Trustee Act 1925
§ 22 460

Bankruptcy (Amendment) Act 1926 308

Companies Act 1929 10

Children and Young Persons Acts
1933-1963 503

Local Government Act 1933
§ 219-236 .. 500, 503, 504
228 502
237-238 500
239 .. .. 500, 501, 503

Education Act 1944 503

National Health Service Act 1946 503

Children Act 1948 503

PAGE

Companies Act 1948 .. ..
§ 22 247
40 .. .. 250, 251, 640
43 308
44 308
52 322
53 .. .. 260, 262
54 299
56 .. .. 241, 259
57 242
58 .. .. 237, 292
61 .. .. 238, 239, 248
65 247
66-71 248
79 245
83 240
89 258
90 .. .. 256, 258
95 252
104 .. .. 252, 253
110 243
117 245
127 306
130 .. .. 223, 262
145 .. .. 318, 319
147 .. 229, 267, 309, 620
148 .. .. 269, 280
149 392
150 .. .. 379, 380
151 380
152 383
154 380
155 227
156 227
157 302
158 228
159 .. 206, 210, 217, 440
160 .. .. 211, 232
161 .. .. 207, 451
163 .. .. 225, 303
164 .. .. 524, 561, et seq.
165 .. .. 524, 561, et seq.
167 562
168 563
172 .. .. 563, 564
176 306
177 .. .. 306, 318
182 315
184 315
185 315
189 313
190 .. .. 297, 308
191 314
193 .. .. 309, 314

PAGE

Companies Act 1948 (*continued*)

§ 196		272, 275, 277, 317, *et seq.*, 381, 382, 393, 545, 620
197	..	298, 381, 452, 620
198	..	.. 276, 277
199	..	 307
205	..	.. 308, 408, 412
206	..	 247
319	..	 318
328	..	.. 308, 440
329	..	 308
330	..	 440
331	..	.. 268, 308, 440
332	..	 309
333		216, 308, 395, 396, 400, 403, 408, 435, 438, 439
410	..	 297
436	..	.. 135, 319
438	..	308, 309, 396, 397, 537
448	..	.. 308, 395

First Schedule .. 246, 254, 313, 316, 317, 320, 359, 362, 364

Fourth Schedule .. 223, 224, 248 *et seq.*, 534

Fifth Schedule 248

Fifteenth Schedule .. 308, 537

Finance Act 1948 276

National Assistance Act 1948 .. 503

Coast Protection Act 1949 .. 503

Local Government (Miscellaneous Provisions) Act 1953 520

Copyright Act 1956 190

Cheques Act 1957 37

Solicitors Act 1957 .. 464, 469, 473

Adoption Act 1958 503

Children Act 1958 503

Insurance Companies Act 1958 .. 271, 272, 324, 460 *et seq.*

Local Government Act 1958 512, 513

Prevention of Fraud (Investments) Act 1958 309, 394, 398, 498, 535, 537

Building Societies Act 1960 .. 451

Finance Act 1960 .. 447, 448

Trustee Investments Act 1961 .. 457

Building Societies Act 1962 .. 451 *et seq.*, (& *Appendix*)

Finance Act 1963 245

Protection of Depositors Act 1963 398

Stock Transfer Act 1963 244, 246

Police Act 1964 503

PAGE

Finance Act 1965 237, 327, 365, 458

Solicitors Act 1965 .. 469 *et seq.*

Local Government Act 1966 515, 516

Companies Act 1967

§ 2	..	 208
3	..	.. 292, 293
4	..	.. 292, 293, 381
5	..	.. 292, 293
6		276, *et seq.*, 381, 382, 620
7		276 *et seq.*, 381, 382, 620
8	..	.. 277, 382, 620
13	..	 207
14		218 *et seq.*, 224, 268, 386, 387, 396, 449, 619 *et seq.*
16	..	.. 302, *et seq.*
17	..	 303
18	..	 303
19	..	 303
20	..	 303
22	..	 303
23	..	 309
24	..	.. 228, 305, 306
25	..	.. 261, 307
26	..	 307
27	..	.. 307, 309
29	..	.. 307, 309
30	..	 307
31	..	.. 307, 310
32	..	.. 307, 524, 564
33	..	 243
34	..	 243
35	..	 563
37	..	 563
38	..	.. 524, 562
39	..	.. 524, 562, 564
42	..	.. 524, 564
59	..	 461
71	..	 461
72	..	.. 461, 462
73	..	 462
76	..	 462
77	..	 461
78	..	 462
109	..	 564

First Schedule 269

Second Schedule 150, 177, 179, 210, 222, 238, 251, 252, 261, 269, 279, 280 *et seq.*, 287, 295, 296, 323 *et seq.*, 362, 381, 619

Criminal Law Act 1967 441, *et seq.*

General Rate Act 1967 514, 515

Theft Act 1968

§ 15-19 .. 309, 394, 397, 398

TABLE OF CASES

PAGE

A 1 Biscuit Co, *re* 312
Alexandra Palace Co, *re* 363
Allen, Craig & Co (London) Ltd, *re* 228
Ammonia Soda Co. *v.* Chamberlain .. 321, 345 *et seq.* 349, 352, 358
Armitage *v.* Brewer and Knott 423
Arthur E. Green & Co *v.* The Central Advance and Discount Corporation
  Ltd 407
Arthur Francis Ltd, *re* 229
Astley *v.* New Tivoli Co 316
Astrachan Steamship Co Ltd, & others *v.* Harmood Banner & Son .. 426
Attorney-General *v.* Ashton Gas Co 311

Beeton & Co Ltd, *re* 318
Birch *v.* Cropper 237
Bishop *v.* Smyrna and Cassaba Railway 322, 358
Boaler *v.* Watchmakers' Alliance, and others 363
Bodega Co Ltd, *re* 316
Bolivia Exploration Syndicate, *re* 437
Bolton *v.* Natal Land & Colonisation Co Ltd 338, 354
Bond *v.* Barrow Haematite Steel Co 320, 343 *et seq.* 349, 353, 354, 355, 362
Boschoek Proprietary Co *v.* Fuke 312
Bridgewater Navigation Co, *re* 237
Burland *v.* Earle 362
Burleigh *v.* Ingram Clarke Ltd 229

Cairney *v.* Back 318
Candler *v.* Crane, Christmas & Co .. .. 430 *et seq.*, 654
Carr, D. M., & Co Ltd, *re* 231
Catterson, S. P., & Sons Ltd, *re* 438
Chantrey Martin & Co *v.* Martin 229, 230
Charles Fox & Sons *v.* Morrish, Grant & Co 420
City Equitable Fire Insurance Co Ltd, *in re* .. 34, 408, 438, 439
Cox *v.* Edinburgh & District Tramways Co 354
Crabtree, *re*, Thomas *v.* Crabtree 335, 336
Crichton's Oil Co 322
Crittall, Richard Co Ltd (Rex *v.* Hinds, Musgrave & Steven) 535
Cuff *v.* London & County Land & Building Co 218, 219

De Savary *v.* Holden, Howard & Co 430, 431
Dean *v.* Prince and others 558
Dimbula Valley (Ceylon) Tea Co Ltd *v.* Laurie 357
Donoghue *v.* Stevenson 429
Dovey *v.* Cory 341, 349, 352, 355, 363

Edwards *v.* Saunton Hotel Co Ltd 311, 334, 335
Escott *v.* BarChris Construction Corporation 251, 537, 538

Fisher *v.* Black & White Publishing Co 320
Foster *v.* Coles 236
Foster *v.* New Trinidad Lake Asphalte Co Ltd 356, 358
Fox & Sons, Charles *v.* Morrish, Grant & Co 420
Frames *v.* Bultfontein Mining Co 312

Gas Light Improvement Co. *v.* Terrall 312
General Auction Estate Co *v.* Smith 254
Great Eastern Railway Co *v.* Turner 306

PAGE

Hedley Byrne & Co Ltd *v.* Heller and Partners   432 *et seq.*, 645, 654 *et seq.*
Henry *v.* Great Northern Railway Co 236
Henry Squire (Cash Chemists) Limited *v.* Ball, Baker & Co 437
Herschel *v.* Mrupi 655
Hilder *v.* Dexter 261
Hill *re, ex parte* Southall.. 229
Hinds *v.* Buenos Ayres Grand National Tramways Co Ltd 247
Hoole *v.* Great Western Railway Co 364
Howard *v.* Patent Ivory Co 254

Inman *v.* Ackroyd 313
Irish Woollen Co Ltd *v.* Tyson and others 404
Irvine *v.* Union Bank of Australia.. 254
Isle of Thanet Electricity Supply Co Ltd, *re* 237

Johnston *v.* Chestergate Hat Manufacturing Co 311, 334

Kingston Cotton Mill Co Ltd, *in re* (No. 1) 402
Kingston Cotton Mill Co Ltd, *in re* (No. 2) 33, 34, 177, 216, 363, 396, 402, 409,
423, 428, 429, 436, 439, 571, 577
Lee *v.* Neuchatel Asphalte Co Ltd   336 *et seq.* 341, 342 *et seq*, 349 *et seq.*, 354
Leech *v.* Stokes 421, 442
Leeds Estate Building & Investment Co *v.* Shepherd.. .. 312, 399, 409
Leicestershire County Council *v.* Michael Faraday & Partners Ltd .. 230
London & General Bank, *in re* (No. 1) 216, 400
London & General Bank, *in re* (No. 2)   33, 217, 223, 227, 363, 396, 399, 404,
410, 435, 439, 571, 645

London India Rubber Co 236
London Oil Storage Co Ltd *v.* Seear, Hasluck & Co.. .. 61, 406
Looker *v.* Wrigley 254
Lubbock *v.* British Bank of South America 355, 356, 357

Maritime Insurance Co Ltd *v.* William Fortune & Son 421
Martin *v.* Isitt 421
McConnell's Claim 313
McKesson & Robbins Inc. 175, 176, 437
Mead *v.* Ball, Baker & Co 437
Metropolitan Coal Consumers' Association *v.* Scrimgeour 262
Mills *v.* Northern Railway of Buenos Ayres Co 358
Moxham *v.* Grant 363
Myers *v.* Thompson and London Life Insurance Co .. 433, 434

National Bank of Wales, *re* (*see* Dovey v. Cory)
National Funds Assurance Co 363
National Telephone Co, *in re* 236
New British Iron Co, *ex parte* Beckwith, *re* 312
Newspaper Proprietary Syndicate 318
Newton *v.* Birmingham Small Arms Co Ltd 222

Oddy, *re* 460
Ollivant, G. B., & Co Ltd, *re* Agreement of 311
Oxford Benefit Building Society 363

Pendleburys Ltd *v.* Ellis, Green & Co 224
Prudential Assurance Co *v.* Chatterley-Whitfield Collieries Ltd .. 236

PAGE

Rance's Case 361, 363
Regina v. Shacter 217, 398, 440
Regina v. Wake and Stone 398, 536, 537
Rex v. Bates 398, 537
Rex v. Bishirgian and Others 77, 548
Rex v. Hinds, Musgrave & Steven (see Crittall, Richard Co Ltd)
Rex v. Kylsant and Morland (Royal Mail Steam Packet Co Ltd case)
                                                     397, 414, 439
Royal British Bank v. Turquand 254

Salton v. New Beeston Cycle Co 313, 315
Scarborough Harbour Commissioners v. Robinson, Coulson Kirby &
  Co 426, 427
Scottish Insurance Corporation Ltd v. Wilsons and Clyde Coal Co 236, 237
Sharpe, in re 362
Smith v. Sheard 420
Société Générale v. The Tramways Union 245
Spackman v. Evans 216
Spanish Prospecting Co, in re .. .. .. 312, 332 et seq.
Staples v. Eastman Co 236
Stapley v. Read Bros Ltd .. .. .. 347 et. seq., 353
Stringer's Case 363
Swabey v. Port Darwin Gold Mining Co 313

Thomas Gerrard & Son Ltd, re .. .. 75, 178, 406, 427 et. seq., 436
Towers v. African Tug Co 363

Ultramares Corporation v. Touche, Niven & Co 432, 433, 655

Verner v. General and Commercial Investment Trust Ltd 334, 343, 339, 349
                                           et seq., 354, 357, 362, 496

Wakefield Rolling Stock Co, in re 247
Washington Diamond Mining Co, re 312
Webb v. Earle 236
West Yorkshire Derracq Agency Ltd (in Liquidation) v. Coleridge .. 313
Western Counties Steam Bakeries & Milling Co Ltd 217
Westminster Road Construction and Engineering Co Ltd, in re 417, 437
Wheatcroft, in re 230
Whitehall Court, re 312
Wilde and Others v. Cape & Dalgleish 420
Will v. United Lankat Plantations Co 236
William Metcalfe & Sons Ltd, re 236
Williams, re 340, 351, 354
Wilmer v. McNamara & Co Ltd 363, 364
Wood v. Odessa Water Works Co .. ..

Young v. Naval and Military Co-operative Society 317

THE PRINCIPLES OF AUDITING

§ 1. The Origin of Auditing

The practice of auditing had its origin in the necessity for the institution of some system of check upon persons whose business it was to record the receipt and disbursement of money on behalf of others. In the early stages of civilization the methods of account were so crude, and the number of transactions to be recorded so small, that each individual was no doubt able to check for himself all his transactions, but as soon as the ancient States and Empires acquired any coherent organization, systems of check were applied to their public accounts, as evidenced by extant records; the ancient Egyptians, the Greeks, and the Romans, all utilized systems of check and counter-check as between the various financial officials.

The ancient records of auditing are confined principally to public accounts, but there is clear indication that from an early date it was customary for an audit of the accounts of manors and estates to be performed. The person whose duty it was to make such an examination of accounts became known as the auditor, the word being derived from the Latin *audire*, to hear. Originally the accounting parties were required to attend before the auditor who *heard* their accounts.

It was not until the fifteenth century that the great impetus given to trade and commerce generally by the Renaissance in Italy led to the evolution of a system of accounts which was capable of recording completely all kinds of mercantile transactions, and the principles of double entry were first published in 1494 at Venice by Luca Pacioli, although the system had been more or less utilized during the preceding century. It thus became possible to record not only cash transactions, but all transactions involving matters of account, and the duties of the auditor correspondingly increased.

The increase in volume of trading operations, necessitating the use of more capital than was at the disposal of the average trader, induced him to combine in partnership with others for the purpose of obtaining the requisite funds, and this tendency was a potent factor in the evolution of a more perfect system of accounts.

In the same way, no doubt, it had a material effect on the practice of auditing, but the audit of business accounts did not become common until the nineteenth century. The enormous increase in trade in that period, which was fostered by the discovery of steam power and by mechanical inventions generally, led to the formation of numerous joint stock companies, and other corporate undertakings, involving the use of large sums of capital under the management of a few individuals. Under these conditions the advantages to be obtained from utilizing the services of auditors became apparent to the commercial public generally, and a great increase in the practice of auditing resulted; at the present day it forms the most important part of a professional accountant's practice.

§ 2. The Nature and Definition of an Audit

It has been pointed out that an audit was originally confined to ascertaining whether the accounting party had properly accounted for all receipts and payments on behalf of his principal, and was in fact merely a cash audit; but the object of a modern audit, although it includes the examination of cash transactions, has as its ultimate aim the verification of the financial position disclosed by the balance sheet and the profit and loss account of the undertaking.

An audit may, therefore, be said to be such an examination of the books, accounts and vouchers of a business, as will enable the auditor to *report* whether he is satisfied that the balance sheet is properly drawn up, so as to give a true and fair view of the state of the affairs of the business, and that the profit and loss account gives a true and fair view of the profit or loss for the financial period, according to the best of the information and explanations given him, and as shown by the books; and if not, to report in what respects he is not satisfied.

It must not be inferred from the above definition that the whole duty of the auditor is to compare the balance sheet and accounts with the books in order to see that they agree therewith. He must do this, but he must also, by the exercise of reasonable skill and diligence, satisfy himself that the books themselves contain a proper record of the transactions entered into. This will involve a more or less complete examination of the whole of the transactions of the business, and the manner in which they are recorded. How far such an examination must extend will depend upon the individual circumstances of each case, and must be decided by the exercise of the auditor's judgement. It is sufficient here to say that whatever the extent of the examination, it must be such as will satisfy the auditor, having regard to whether he is acting under the direct instructions of his clients or under statute.

§ 3. The Objects of an Audit

(A) THE REPORT

As already stated, the main object of an audit is to give a report on the view presented by the accounts and statements prepared by the client (and his staff), in accordance with the terms of the auditor's appointment. The different considerations which arise on the appointment of an auditor by a private individual, partnership or under statute will be dealt with in the following section. Although of great importance, the detection of fraud and error must be regarded as incidental to this main object.

The prevention of fraud and errors by reason of the deterrent and moral check imposed is also an advantage of considerable importance which is derived from an audit.

(B) THE DETECTION OF FRAUD

In the minds of the public at large, and of many clients, the discovery of fraud is the principal function of the auditor, overshadowing his other duties entirely, and although this is far from correct, there can be no question that it is of great importance.

Fraud may be divided broadly into two classes:

(1) Defalcations, involving either misappropriation of money or goods.

(2) The fraudulent manipulation of accounts not involving defalcation.

As regards the first class, where accounting staff are not subjected to any form of check, the opportunities of committing fraud are so frequent, and the methods necessary to conceal it so comparatively simple, that it is safe to say that no business of any size could be carried on under such conditions for very long without the risk of fraud taking place. In small businesses, where the individual proprietor is in touch with the whole of the detail, and is able to supervise it effectively, the possibilities of concealing fraud may be remote. As soon, however, as the business increases in size and the proprietor is no longer able to do this, if a check is to be maintained at all it must be carried out by members of the staff themselves assisted by an independent auditor. Where the staff is sufficiently large to enable the whole of the work to be subdivided, so that the duties of every member of the staff come under the scrutiny of at least one other member who has had no part in the actual performance of those duties, what is known as an *internal check* comes into operation, and the first business of the auditor should be to examine carefully the system in force, and to ascertain its deficiencies, if any. The strength of a chain is the strength of its weakest link, and the same may be said of a system of internal check.

The auditor, therefore, should pay particular attention to those classes of transactions which offer special facilities for fraud, the principal of which are cash transactions of one kind or another.

As general principles only are under consideration here, the actual way in which these transactions should be verified will be dealt with in due course, but it may be noted that there are two methods by means of which the misappropriation of money may be concealed; the first is by the inclusion of fictitious payments, and the second by the omission of cash received; the latter class being much the more difficult to detect.

The amount of detail checking which the auditor must perform before he can satisfy himself that no fraud exists, will depend on his assessment of the quality of the system of internal check in operation. Where that system is good, collusion between two or more persons must have occurred for fraud to remain undetected. Collusion is not infrequent, and cases of it arise from time to time; but, though certain individuals may not themselves be inherently honest, they see the force of the proverb that 'honesty is the best policy'. Such a person might consider it more to his advantage, when approached by a fellow employee with a view to collusion, to report the matter to his employers than to participate in the fraud, and incur the risk of discovery with its resulting consequences. The necessity for collusion in order that fraud may be perpetrated and concealed is, therefore, a very great safeguard, and one upon which the auditor is entitled to rely. He must not, of course, do this indiscriminately, and assume that because there is a good system of internal check in operation he need perform no detailed checking whatever. Transactions must be tested as exhaustively as the circumstances permit, and should the auditor find anything irregular he must make a complete examination.

The second class of fraud, entailing the falsification of accounts without corresponding defalcations, is naturally considerably less frequent than the class of fraud above mentioned, but when it does occur it may involve very large amounts. It may be done for the purpose of bolstering up a business which is in an insecure condition, in order to maintain the confidence of shareholders, creditors or the public; or it may be done by a manager for the purpose of increasing the apparent profits of the business, thus showing that he has been successful in his management, and possibly increasing the commission on results payable to him; or by directors for the purpose of enabling them to pay dividends which would otherwise not have been possible. Several notable cases of this sort of falsification have occurred. It need only be pointed out here that this form of fraud is often very ingeniously and skilfully concealed, and is in many cases carried out by persons holding positions of the highest trust, and having the entire confidence of directors and shareholders.

(C) THE DETECTION OF ERRORS

An advantage of considerable importance arising from an audit is the detection of errors. What appear to be in the first instance merely clerical errors, are sometimes found ultimately to be due to fraudulent manipulation, and it is therefore important for the auditor carefully to examine the cause of any error, however slight it may appear to be. The vast majority of errors, however, are *bona fide*, and are due either to carelessness or ignorance.

Errors may be classified under the following headings:

(1) errors of omission;

(2) errors of commission;

and these again may be classified as

(3) clerical errors;

(4) errors of principle;

while there is a further type known as

(5) compensating errors.

(1) *Errors of Omission*

An error of omission arises when any transaction is left either wholly or partially unrecorded in the books. If the former, the omission will not affect the trial balance, and will consequently be more difficult to detect. Sometimes it is apparent from an examination of an account that an entry has been omitted, e.g. the rent account may show that rent for three quarters only has been paid, and no entry may have been made recording the quarter outstanding. This would become apparent as soon as the item of rent was compared with that of previous years, or the ledger account was examined, but many other cases can be instanced which are much more difficult to deal with, e.g. an item of purchases may be omitted, with the result that the purchases appear as less than they really are, and the creditors are similarly affected. This would not be disclosed by the trial balance, but might appear from an examination of the ledger account or the creditor's statement. Where only one aspect of the transaction is recorded, the omission will throw out the trial balance. This most frequently arises by reason of items not being posted.

(2) *Errors of Commission*

An error of commission arises when a transaction is incorrectly recorded, either wholly or partially. In the former case the trial balance may not be affected, but the error should be discovered when the transaction is vouched or otherwise checked, e.g. the calculation of the value of the goods being incorrectly extended on a sales invoice. The posting of the incorrect item would be made to the ledger, and the error would not be discovered until either the calculation was checked or notice was received from the customer. If the transaction is partially incorrectly recorded, the result will be to throw the trial balance out to that extent, e.g. where the amount of a sale is posted incorrectly to the ledger.

(3) *Clerical Errors*

A clerical error is one occasioned by an incorrect posting; or by posting an item to a wrong account, but one of the same class as that to which it should have been posted; e.g. an item might be posted to the debit of A instead of to the debit of B. If therefore the trial balance is agreed, all clerical errors of the first kind should have been discovered, unless they are counter-balanced by other errors. Clerical errors of the second kind, even if undetected, should not affect either the amount of profit or the general correctness of the balance sheet.

The following are common instances of clerical errors which the auditor should be on his guard against when engaged on books prior to the trial balance being agreed:

(*a*) An item may be posted to the debit instead of to the credit of an account, or vice versa. This will throw out the trial balance to the extent of double the amount in question, e.g. an item of £3 posted to the debit instead of to the credit will have the effect of making a difference of £6 on the trial balance.

(*b*) An item of £26 9*s* may be posted as £20 6*s* 9*d*. This will make a difference of £6 2*s* 3*d* in the trial balance. This is a common class of error, and if the difference on the trial balance is capable of being explained in this or in a similar manner, all items in respect of which such an error might arise should be re-checked.

(*c*) Although the casts and postings in a ledger account may be correct, the totals of the two sides of the account may not agree, and consequently the balance of the account will be incorrect.

(*d*) Errors often arise in carrying forward totals from one page to another, e.g. £300 10*s* may be carried forward as £310, or £189 as £198.

(4) *Errors of Principle*

An error of principle arises by reason of a transaction being recorded in a fundamentally incorrect manner. This is the most important class of error, and one which the auditor should exercise the utmost care to detect.

Some errors of principle may not affect the ultimate profit, but may arise from revenue items being posted to the wrong class of revenue account, e.g. an item of manufacturing wages posted to trade expenses account, or balance sheet items being posted to the wrong class of asset or liability accounts.

Major errors of principle directly affect the profit, and are occasioned by treating a revenue item as an asset or a liability, or vice versa, e.g. treating rent paid as a debtor instead of as an expense.

(5) *Compensating Errors*

A compensating error is one which is counter-balanced by another error or errors, so that it is not disclosed by the trial balance. This is a dangerous type of error, which is sometimes difficult to detect and it may or may not affect the profit. If the original error and the compensating error both arise in revenue accounts, the profit will not be affected, but if one arises in a revenue account and the other in an asset or liability account, although the trial balance will agree, the profit will be incorrectly stated. Such errors arise in various ways, but most frequently in casting, e.g. the cast of an expenditure account may be £100 too small, and the cast of an asset account £100 too much, the profit and the assets being thereby increased improperly.

§ 4. Various Classes of Audits, and their Advantages

It may be convenient here to indicate the principal classes of audits which are undertaken in practice, and the advantages to be derived therefrom.

(A) AUDITS UNDER STATUTE

Audits are compulsory under statute in the case of a large number of undertakings, chief amongst which are limited companies. The statutory regulations as to the appointment of auditors and their duties in each of these cases will be dealt with in due course; but the considerable advantages to be derived by the shareholders and proprietors of these concerns, from a professional audit, are similar in their nature, and may be dealt with from the general point of view of limited companies.

It has already been noted that trading partnerships arose by reason of the development of trade requiring the utilization of more capital than was at the command of the individual trader; and, in the same way, the concept of joint-stock companies supplied the mechanism for utilizing, under one management, larger amounts of capital than could be provided by either individuals or partnerships. Such companies operated originally under partnership law, and the liability of each of the members was unlimited. It was impossible, however, to obtain efficient management and at the same time to permit each individual shareholder or partner to exercise the rights of an ordinary partner; as a result, committees of management were formed, in whose hands the whole of the operations of the undertaking were placed. Such persons became known as the directors.

As a result of their position, directors found themselves in a fiduciary relationship to the body of shareholders, and liable to account to them for all their dealings on behalf of the company.

The number of companies of this nature having increased very largely, special legislation on the subject was found to be necessary, and in 1844 the *Joint Stock Companies Registration Act* was passed. At this period the liability of each shareholder was unlimited, and it was not until 1855 that the first Act was passed making it possible for shareholders to limit their liability. Several other Acts were passed amending the law on the subject, and in 1862 the law was consolidated in one Act, as a result of which joint-stock enterprise increased very rapidly.

The fact that the whole control of the company was vested in the directors, rendered it necessary that some means should be provided for enabling the shareholders to be assured that the accounts presented to them by the board correctly represented the state of affairs of the company, and that the directors had not utilized their position for the purpose of misappropriating the funds of the company or using them for their private gain. It was impracticable, however, for every individual shareholder to satisfy himself on these points, for as a rule he was not possessed of the requisite technical knowledge, and the right of inspection and enquiry could not be given to one shareholder without being granted to all. Consequently, it became usual for shareholders to appoint one or more of their number to act as auditor or auditors of the company, and to report to the shareholders on their examination of the balance sheet and accounts. Subsequently it was found inadvisable to confine this function to individual shareholders, who might not be possessed of the requisite qualifications, and it became usual to appoint professional auditors to act on behalf of the shareholders generally. Under the *Companies Act 1900* it became legally necessary for the first time for every limited company to appoint an auditor or auditors. The *Companies Act 1907* amended the duties of auditors as defined in the *Companies Act 1900*, and the *Companies (Consolidation) Act 1908* repealed and re-enacted the whole of the statutes relating to limited companies, and consolidated the regulations relating to the audit. These provisions were substantially unaltered by the *Companies Act 1929* but the duties of auditors were extended by the *Companies Act 1948*. The *Companies Act 1967* made the qualifications for the appointment of auditor more stringent, and extended the auditors' duties with regard to the disclosure of certain items of information.

From the point of view of the shareholders the advantages of a professional audit of a company's accounts are manifold. It has already been pointed out that it is impossible for individual shareholders to be familiar with the details of all the various businesses in which they may be interested as shareholders; moreover, the articles of companies do not as a rule permit individual shareholders to have access to the books and accounts; and consequently, the shareholders as a body are entirely dependent on the auditor appointed by them, whose duties are to examine the books and accounts of the company, and report to them on every balance sheet and profit and loss account laid before the company in general meeting. In addition, the audit acts as a check upon the directors, and as a precaution against fraud on the part of the employees. Moreover, the auditor is often able to render valuable assistance, by reason of his expert knowledge of matters of account and finance generally, although it is not within his province to offer advice unless he is asked to do so.

In this connection, the functions of an auditor and those of an accountant should be clearly distinguished. It is commonly the custom, particularly with smaller companies, to arrange for the auditor to prepare the final accounts. If he does this, it should be remembered that he acts in the capacity of accountant, under the instructions of the directors, and not in the capacity of auditor appointed by the shareholders. It may thus be said that the audit commences when the accounting work has been completed.

(B) THE AUDIT OF THE ACCOUNTS OF PRIVATE FIRMS

An audit of the accounts of a partnership is, in the interests of the partners, most desirable, but such an audit is not required by statute, although it may be provided for by the partnership agreement or arranged for by mutual agreement between the partners. There are, therefore, essential distinctions between the audit of a company and the audit of a private firm. The former is obligatory under statute, and the rights and duties of the auditor are defined by statute; he is appointed by the shareholders, or by the directors on their behalf in certain instances, but they cannot limit his statutory duties, though they can, if they wish, extend them. In the case of a private firm the auditor is not appointed under statute, but by agreement between the partners, and his rights and duties are defined by them, and can be subjected to modification or limitation.

In the case of private firms, the auditor frequently acts also in the capacity of accountant, and although it may be possible for him to distinguish accurately between the work he performs in each of these two capacities, this distinction may not be appreciated by his clients. Frequently, where only accountancy work is performed, the client supposes that his books are actually audited, and the responsibility for errors and fraud may in this way recoil upon the accountant. In order to avoid this, the precise duties of the accountant should be carefully defined in writing at the outset, so that no dispute can subsequently arise as to the extent of his responsibility. Similar remarks apply to the professional accountant's work in connection with the accounts of sole traders. This subject is further dealt with in Chapter XII where legal decisions are considered.

In addition to the advantages common to all forms of audit, viz. the verification of accounts and the detection of errors and fraud, the audit of partnership accounts has the following further important advantages:

(1) It affords a convenient means of settling accounts between the partners themselves, and so of avoiding the possibility of future dispute. It is customary to find provisions in partner-

ship agreements arranging for an audit, and making the audited balance sheet, when accepted and signed by them, the final expression of the respective interests of the partners, at the balance sheet date.

(2) The suggestions which the auditor is sometimes able to make with regard to the improvement of the system of accounts in use, and the expert knowledge of accounts at his command, should also prove of advantage to the business.

(3) The settlement of accounts required on the death or retirement of a partner, or the adjustments arising on the admission of a new partner, are much facilitated when audited accounts form the basis upon which to work; and the same remarks apply to the assessment of the firm for taxation, the necessary adjustments relating to the individual partners, and the preparation of their returns of income and gains. The complexities of taxation law make the advantage of professional assistance in this matter particularly noticeable, since an indifferent knowledge of this law may result in considerable loss to the taxpayer.

(4) The sale of the business as a going concern, or the negotiation of loans with banks and others, are considerably facilitated where proper accounts have been prepared and audited.

(5) An audit on behalf of a sleeping partner is highly advisable since such a person, as a rule, has little means of checking the accounts of the business, or of verifying the share of profits due to him.

In the case of individual traders, the arguments in favour of an audit are similar to those already discussed, with the exception of the points applicable only to partnerships. In a business of any size, the absence of partners and the impossibility of one man being assured of the correctness of all the details of his business, render it all the more essential that he should employ professional accountants for this purpose.

(C) THE AUDIT OF THE ACCOUNTS OF PRIVATE INDIVIDUALS

Many persons whose incomes are considerable and derived from numerous sources, and whose expenditure is heavy, have their private accounts audited. Frequently the auditor in such cases also acts as accountant, and actually writes up the books.

The advantages to be derived from an audit of this nature are, in the first place, that the individual is assured of having his accounts properly kept and his expenditure vouched. These considerations apply particularly where the expenditure is incurred in respect of landed property, or the upkeep of large establishments, when it is practically impossible for the proprietor to control personally the payments made. He is obliged to place his trust in individual agents or servants, and to give them the control of money, and unless an efficient check is exercised over their actions the risk of fraud may be considerable. Secondly, the presentation of accounts prepared on a uniform basis affords a valuable means of comparison of the various classes of expenditure between one year and another, and where such expenditure exceeds the limits of prudence, it is possible immediately to ascertain the origin of the increase, with the result that steps may be taken to rectify the position. The preparation of tax returns etc. is also greatly facilitated.

In addition to the cases above-mentioned, there are many other instances where agents are appointed for the purpose of controlling business operations, and the value of an audit to the principal concerned is particularly apparent when he has no effective check on the agent's accounts. Instances of this class of audit are the audit of the accounts of rent collectors, estate managers etc.

If private books of account have been kept, they will, on the death of the person concerned, be of great assistance to his executors or administrators in their task of preparing the estate duty account and computations of any liability to capital gains tax. Such books will naturally be of even greater value if their accuracy has been confirmed by a regular audit. As a result of the failure of a person of substance to keep proper records during his lifetime, great difficulty is often experienced on his death in compiling a complete list of all his assets and liabilities.

(D) THE AUDIT OF TRUST ACCOUNTS

The accounts of executors and trustees furnish the occasion for another class of audit.

In the majority of cases executors and trustees are private persons, sometimes possessing considerable business capacity, but sometimes none at all. The law relating to the administration of trusts is very complex, particularly in relation to matters of account. The two classes of beneficiaries – tenants for life and remaindermen, to whom the accuracy of trust accounts is of supreme importance – are often widows and minors, who cannot criticize the accounts in any effective manner. In some cases also, the trustees present no accounts at all until forced to do so, and even then such accounts are sometimes incorrect. In other cases the trustees keep no proper accounts, and this omission can serve to conceal misappropriations of trust frunds.

For these reasons the advantages of a professional audit of trust accounts, and of a strict verification of the securities composing the trust are apparent, but until the *Public Trustee Act 1906* came into force, it was very difficult to obtain such an audit, except with the consent of the trustees themselves. The increasing number of scandals, some of great magnitude, arising from the defalcation of trust moneys, led to the passing of this Act, and the institution of a Public Trustee. The only point of the Act which need be emphasized here is that which provides machinery for the audit of the accounts of any trust, whether commenced before or after the passing of the Act, and whether the Public Trustee is or is not connected with it. An auditor appointed in such a case must either be a solicitor or a public accountant.

It may be noted that banking companies, insurance companies, and certain other corporate bodies have taken power to act as executors and trustees, and recognizing the advantages of a professional audit to the beneficiaries, they usually stipulate that this shall be performed as one of the conditions on which they are parepared to undertake the trust.

Private trustees also recognize the advantages of an audit in their own interest, since any erroneous treatment in the accounts for which they might be personally liable will be pointed out by the auditor, and can then be rectified. Further, they are able to consult the auditor on points of difficulty before action is taken.

§ 5. The Conduct of an Audit

(A) CONTINUOUS AND FINAL (OR COMPLETED) AUDITS

An audit may involve the whole of the transactions in the books being checked, or it may entail checking only some of the transactions. The auditor must satisfy himself as to the correctness of the accounts he is asked to verify, and it is for him to decide the extent to which details should be checked. In most businesses of any size, however, the amount of detail is so voluminous, and the time occupied in checking the whole of it would be so excessive, that reliance for the accuracy of the detail is, to a large extent, placed upon the system of internal check in operation in the business itself, and the auditor, after making such tests of the detail work as commend themselves to his judgement, is then able to devote his attention to questions of principle. It must be stressed, however, that the great volume of detailed transactions does not of itself entitle the auditor to reduce the amount of detail checking to be executed. This decision must rest upon his assessment of the quality of the system of internal check in operation.

In any case, the audit may be carried out either continuously, at fixed or indefinite interim dates, or wholly after the completion of the period under review.

(1) Continuous Audits

A continuous audit is one where members of the auditor's staff are occupied continuously on the accounts the whole year round, or where they attend at frequent intervals, fixed or otherwise, during the currency of the financial year, in order to perform an interim audit; such audits are adopted where the work involved is considerable, and have many points in their favour, although they are subject to certain disadvantages.

The following are the advantages of a continuous audit:

(1) More detail checking may be performed.

(2) The work is checked sooner than would be the case otherwise; errors can be rectified more quickly; and if any fraud has taken place it may be discovered sooner. In the latter event there is less time for the defrauding party to operate, with the result that the amount involved may be considerably less than would have been the case if the audit had not taken place until after the end of the financial period.

(3) The final audit can be completed more quickly, and the accounts presented at the end of the financial year sooner than would otherwise have been possible.

(4) The frequent attendance of the auditor has the effect of causing the staff to keep their work well up to date.

(5) Where the auditor's attendance is at uncertain intervals, the moral check involved is considerably strengthened, as members of the staff are not aware, from day to day, when the auditor will attend.

The following are the disadvantages of a continuous audit:

(1) It is possible for figures to be altered, either innocently or fraudulently, after the auditor has checked them.

(2) The audit, not being carried on consecutively to a finish, it may be possible for the audit clerk to lose the thread of the work, and omit to follow up completely transactions which were left open at the date of his last visit.

These disadvantages, however, can be guarded against in order to minimize the risk involved. A strict rule should be instituted, that no alteration may be made in any figures after the auditor has once passed them, and that, if necessary, adjusting entries should be made to rectify any error discovered. The fraudulent alteration of figures is somewhat difficult to provide against, and it is advisable for the auditor to use a special 'tick' where he checks figures that have been erased or otherwise altered, and actually to insert (inset on the account or book of prime entry) the figures he has accepted, so that on a subsequent occasion he can see that the amended figures are those previously seen by him.

Fraudulent manipulations in personal accounts can most easily be concealed by making compensating false entries in impersonal accounts. It is of the utmost importance, therefore, in the case of a continuous audit, for the auditor to make certain that no 'juggling' can take place with the impersonal accounts which he has already checked; and for this reason, where, as in most cases, the impersonal accounts are not voluminous, it may be wise to postpone checking them until the final trial balance has been extracted. The work done during the interim period is usually best confined to the vouching of cash, casting of subsidiary books, and work on the personal ledgers etc.

In some cases it may be inconvenient to leave the impersonal ledger work in this way until the end of the period, and, in that event, unless the impersonal ledger is balanced off at the interim periods (which is unusual), the auditor should take a note of all the totals in the impersonal ledger up to the date to which he has checked it, and verify these totals on the occasion of his next visit, in order to see that no manipulation has taken place.

The disadvantage arising from the lack of continuity in the work, and the possibility of points being overlooked in consequence, can therefore be remedied by the exercise of proper care and supervision in the conduct of the work, aided by the judicious use of notes.

(2) *Final (or Completed) Audits*

A final audit is commonly understood to be an audit which is not commenced until after the end of the financial period, and is then carried on until completed. This is the most satisfactory form of audit from the auditor's point of view, and is usually adopted wherever practicable, particularly in the case of small concerns. In large businesses, however, a completed audit is rarely practicable, as the time occupied by the audit after the completion of the accounts would, normally, be so considerable, that the presentation of the audited accounts would be delayed beyond a reasonable period.

The proprietors are usually anxious for the audit to be completed as soon as possible after the financial year, and this is essential in the case of limited companies, in order that annual general meetings may be held and final dividends declared.

So crucial has the close planning of large audits become, in order to avoid delays in placing annual accounts before shareholders, that some firms have adapted certain Operational Research techniques, long established in other fields, to use for audit purposes. One such technique is P.E.R.T., or *Programme Evaluation and Review Technique*. This is a system of pre-planning any task in chart form, in sequence, so as to demonstrate the time expected to be taken at each stage of the work. The sum of the estimated times for successive tasks (each of which is dependent upon the completion of the previous task) gives the total time required. Supplementary tasks not delaying these tasks are charted on parallel lines. The line which traces the *successive* tasks is known as the 'critical path'.

This technique may be of considerable use to the auditor in planning more audits efficiently, enabling him to reduce, as far as possible, the perennial difficulties of recruiting the most suitable staff for particular audits at all times, and the problem of acute pressures of work building up shortly after the more 'popular' accounting dates, e.g. March 31st and December 31st. Thus P.E.R.T. may assist in enabling final accounts to be available for publication as soon as possible after the accounting date.

(B) CONSIDERATIONS ON THE COMMENCEMENT OF A NEW AUDIT

On undertaking a new audit, the first care of the auditor should be to ascertain the precise nature and scope of his duties. In the case of audit under statute this question does not, of course, arise since his duties and powers are defined in the statute itself, but in other cases the line between accountancy work and audit work proper is sometimes so uncertain, any rate in the minds of clients, that it is advisable for the auditor to ascertain in the first instance exactly what his client requires, and to take care that this is formulated in writing, especially where the audit is to be other than a complete one.

This information having been obtained, the next step should be to ascertain the precise nature of the business carried on, in order to obtain a picture of the information which the books should contain. The auditor should then obtain a complete list of all books in use and the names of the principal officials, together with particulars of the work controlled by each, and the scope of their authority. Where there is a definite system of internal check in operation, the auditor should ask for a written statement regarding it.

It is appropriate here to quote the essential features of an audit, as given by the Institute of Chartered Accountants in the statement entitled 'General Principles of Auditing', which is reproduced in the Appendix.

The essential features of an audit are:

(a) to make a critical review of the system of book-keeping, accounting and internal control,

(b) to make such tests and enquiries as the auditors consider necessary to form an opinion as to the reliability of the records as a basis for the preparation of accounts,

(c) to compare the profit and loss account and balance sheet with the underlying records in order to see whether they are in accordance therewith, (*d*) to make a critical review of the profit and loss account and the balance sheet in order that a report may be made to the members stating whether, in the opinion of the auditors, the accounts are presented and the items are described in such a way that they show not only a true but also a fair view and give in the prescribed manner the information required by the Act.

When referring to this statement in the Appendix, it is important that particular note should be taken of the distinction between the terms 'internal check' and 'internal control', since they are frequently confused.

Assessment of the System of Internal Control

A review of the system of internal control (including internal check) usually presents little difficulty in the case of small, or even medium-sized, businesses, since by making judicious enquiries, and using his own powers of observation, skill and experience, the auditor will be able, in a relatively short period of time, to appreciate the system in operation and to assess its efficiency in practice. However, in the case of large concerns, enquiry into the system of internal control must, of necessity, take on a new dimension, and a haphazard form of enquiry would be both wasteful of time and ineffectual. In order to assist in acquiring an appreciation of the system of accounting and internal control in operation, many auditing firms have in recent years adopted certain aids, the most common of which is the 'internal control questionnaire', or I.C.Q.

An abbreviated form of I.C.Q. will be found in the Appendix, but the features of this method which are particularly to be noted are as follows:

(1) Answers which are entered are not to be regarded as conclusive if they are based simply on the verbal reply of a company official, i.e. answers must be corroborated by actual observation by the audit staff.

(2) It is advisable that clients' staffs should not be given the forms to fill in at their convenience. More revealing replies are usually received during verbal interrogation, the auditor filling in the replies, and this method allows the auditor's experience and intuition full scope.

(3) Only senior officials, e.g. heads of department and directors, should be interviewed for the purpose of completing the I.C.Q., and only professionally qualified audit staff should be entrusted with the interviews, which will usually be by appointment.

In view of the fact that the persons being questioned should be in a position to readily provide information on the departments under their control, any undue hesitancy during I.C.Q. interviews, or the obvious appearance of a head of a section being out of touch with those for whose activities he is responsible, might indicate to the auditor areas of the organization where additional checking will be required. This insight is extremely difficult to achieve when the questionnaires are given to the client's own staff for completion.

(4) The form of I.C.Q. which is usually adopted allows for questions to be answered simply in the affirmative or negative; furthermore the questions are phrased in such a way that the answer 'yes' is to be regarded as an indication that the system is satisfactory in the particular regard being considered, while the answer 'no' is to be interpreted in one of two ways: either a definite weakness (real or potential) exists, or else the system of internal check in operation succeeds in overcoming the apparent weakness revealed by the answer 'no', by some other means. Therefore it is imperative that every answer 'no' should be referenced to an explanatory memorandum giving details of the particular circumstances. This feature has the distinct advantage of attracting the attention of the partner and senior audit staff to those aspects of the system where additional detail checking may be needed before a conclusion can finally be reached on the adequacy of the system.

(5) An I.C.Q. which has been constructed and filled in with requisite care and attention, should continue to be effective for a period of three to five years, on average, although a radical alteration in the system of accounting, e.g. the transition from semi-mechanized accounting techniques to electronic processing, might well render an I.C.Q. (which had been prepared prior to the change) obsolete in a much shorter period. However, it is essential that on the conclusion

of each audit a certain amount of time be devoted to a review of the I.C.Q., and any changes which have taken place since the last review should be entered in the appropriate sections. When these changes become particularly numerous or extensive, the preparation of a fresh I.C.Q. ought to be undertaken.

Although each auditing firm will design its I.C.Q.s according to its own particular requirements and preference, the fundamental purpose underlying their use will in each case be as described above.

Flow charting

In recent years the techniques for describing and assessing the systems operated by clients have become progressively more sophisticated, particularly in the case of firms with strong American connections, and, while it is outside the scope of this volume to make a special study of these methods, one further technique which has proved its usefulness, and in some instances its superiority, over the exclusive use of I.C.Q.s is the use of flow charts. These are sometimes used in isolation, and at other times in conjunction with an I.C.Q.

A flow chart may be simply described as a map of inter-related operations, specially arranged to indicate the sequence and type of these operations as part of a larger unit. It is, of course, also possible to prepare a chart of the larger unit itself, or, in fact, of the entire accounting system. Descriptions of accounting procedures presented in diagrammatic form have the advantage of imparting essential information in considerably less time than is possible with detailed verbal descriptions, even where these are kept to a minimum, as in the case of a well-designed I.C.Q. Moreover, in many instances weaknesses in internal control systems become more readily apparent when represented on a flow chart than when described verbally. Of course, a certain skill is required both in preparing the charts and in interpreting them, and until members of the auditing staff have acquired this skill it is advisable not to rely on flow charts exclusively for the purpose of assessing the quality of the internal control procedures. The first essential is to view the basic operations of the system, and to relate these to each other showing the logical sequence of events through the system. The various controls which should apply at respective stages in the operations must be incorporated in the chart; these will usually take the form of checking, approving and initialling, comparing with an independent source of information etc. It is, of course, essential that the symbols used in flow charts should be understood by all audit staff concerned. Uniformity in the use of symbols is therefore important, although universal agreement has not as yet been achieved. Although the British Standards Institute has prescribed uniform symbols for use in connection with data processing generally, symbols used in systems analysis by auditors are still subject to a certain amount of variation; however, those in most frequent use may be regarded as standard throughout the profession.

The example of a flow chart which follows (concerned with the physical verification of work in progress) demonstrates the advantages of economy and clarity which are afforded by the use of a constructed picture, which leaves no room for incomplete descriptions and ambiguous writing. It has the additional advantage of having arisen from the system operated by a *particular* client, whereas the I.C.Q. used by most firms follows a standard form which emerges as more or less applicable to the peculiar features of each individual client.

This flow chart also demonstrates that no particular symbols are necessary in order to achieve the full benefits of this form of representation.

AUTOS LTD.
CHART F – FLOWCHART OF PHYSICAL VERIFICATION OF W.I.P.

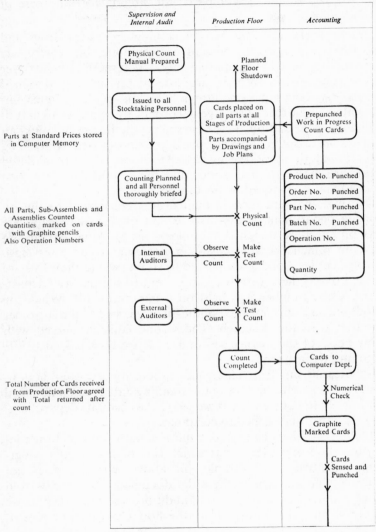

The value of flow charting in simplifying the task of understanding the operation of a client's system may be further dem-
onstrated by the following example of a large mail order drug

supplier. The flow chart is given after a narrative description and the two should be compared for *intelligibility* and *ease of assimilation*.

Narrative Description: Most incoming orders for drugs and medicines are received by mail or telephone, but emergency orders are received by telephone only. Upon receipt by the order department orders by mail are entered on specially designed forms. The telephone operator advises out-of-stock items immediately in the case of emergency orders, by reference to an up-dated daily tabulation. If the emergency items are in stock, an order is made out in duplicate, one copy being passed to invoicing department, the second being passed to stores, where the ordered items are made up. The goods and the second copy are then packed and despatched to the customer.

Normal (non-emergency) mail orders are passed to the invoicing department where invoices are processed in triplicate sets on specially designed stationery, the standing data being held on punched cards (customer names and addresses etc.). Invoice copies 1 and 2 are passed to stores, where the items are made up and then, with the goods, sent to the packing department. Copy number 3 is held on a temporary file. When the goods are packed, copy no. 1 of the invoice is sent to the customer together with the despatch. The second copy is merged with copy no. 3 of the invoice set, and both are then passed to the accounts department.

Invoices arising from emergency orders are processed in duplicate as a separate run, using the standing data filed on punched cards, as before. One copy is passed to the accounts department, and the other despatched to customer.

(*Note:* The chart cannot give more detailed information concerning procedures than that which is contained in the underlying narrative For example, the above narrative does not indicate what happens to the order documents, nor are we told of any internal check or internal audit procedures. Much as we would require this information, the flow chart cannot give it, unless we make further enquiries into the system details.)

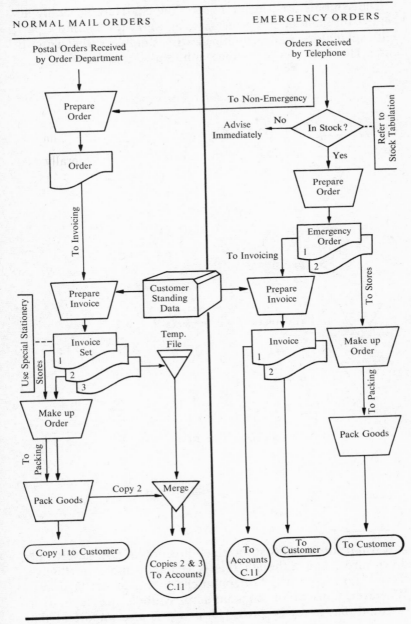

NORMAL MAIL ORDERS

EMERGENCY ORDERS

Postal Orders Received
by Order Department

Orders Received
by Telephone

Prepare Order

To Non-Emergency

Order

To Invoicing

Prepare Invoice

Customer Standing Data

Use Special Stationery

Invoice Set
1
2
3

Stores

Temp. File

Make up Order

To Packing

Pack Goods

Copy 2

Merge

Copy 1 to Customer

Copies 2 & 3
To Accounts
C.11

Advise Immediately

No

In Stock?

Refer to Stock Tabulation

Yes

Prepare Order

Emergency Order
1
2

To Invoicing

To Stores

Prepare Invoice

Invoice
1
2

Make up Order

To Packing

Pack Goods

To Accounts
C.11

To Customer

To Customer

Title: Order & Invoice Processing
Originator: P. Stevens
Reference: Chart C.12

Date: 29th Jan. 1970
Client: Drug Supply Co. Ltd.
Year: Ended 31st Mar. 1970

The symbols used in the above flow chart are generally accepted throughout the profession, and are, for the most part, self-explanatory when combined with suitable verbal descriptions. However, the key to the symbols used is as follows:

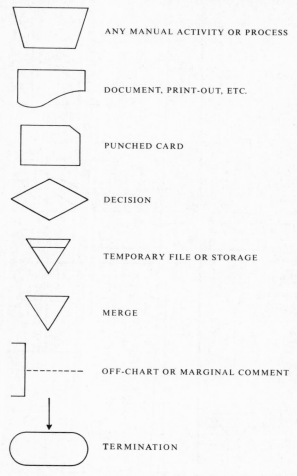

ANY MANUAL ACTIVITY OR PROCESS

DOCUMENT, PRINT-OUT, ETC.

PUNCHED CARD

DECISION

TEMPORARY FILE OR STORAGE

MERGE

OFF-CHART OR MARGINAL COMMENT

TERMINATION

It will be observed that the chief direction of flow is vertically downwards, and although this is generally more intelligible, there is no reason why horizontal charts should not be drawn. Wherever unusual or non-standard symbols are used, it is essential that a key be provided, and it is also important that each chart should be correctly referenced and titled etc. Cross-references to other charts must be clearly indicated by use of a 'connector' symbol, thus:

Although many different symbols are currently in use by auditing firms, the above illustrations show how a flow chart may be effectively drawn with the use of very few symbols. The illustrations also demonstrate how, in order to achieve greater clarity, the chart may be divided vertically into columns in order to separate different areas of activity.

A recent development in flow charting technique is the combination, in one set of documents, of flow chart, I.C.Q. and audit programme, placed alongside each other for easy reference, so that the advantages of each method of systems portrayal may be fully utilized.

Special Matters

Considering the instance of a manufacturing business further, examples of the special matters which would occupy a considerable proportion of the relevant sections of an I.C.Q., are as follows:

(1) The regulations in force relative to the receipt and payment of cash, and the cashier's duties; and particularly whether he is concerned with the writing-up of other books of prime entry.

(2) The methods employed in the preparation of the wages sheets, and the manner of payment.

(3) The regulations in force with regard to the passing and checking of invoices and statements. (This will be dealt with extensively in the next chapter.)

(4) The method of keeping and controlling the petty cash.

(5) The manner in which the entries in the personal ledgers are checked, and the balances agreed; the intervals at which the balancing is effected; and, in the event of each ledger being

balanced separately, whether the total accounts are kept beyond the control of the ledger clerks concerned.

The opening balance sheet will be examined by the auditor, who should ensure that all of the balances at the start of the period now under review, commenced with the balances shown therein. If the accounts have been subject to prior audit, the previous auditor's report should be seen, as it may contain material information.

In the event of the business concerned being of a technical nature with which the auditor is unfamiliar, he must acquaint himself as far as possible with the technical details. It is clear that no audit can be effective unless the auditor himself grasps the nature and meaning of the transactions recorded, and it is essential, therefore, for him to make himself intimately acquainted with the procedure, by following through representative transactions of each class until he has succeeded in acquiring the necessary knowledge.

Where an auditor is appointed to supersede another auditor, before accepting the appointment enquiry should be made as to the reason for the change, and the retiring auditor should be communicated with in order to ascertain whether there is any professional reason why the audit should not be accepted. Such a step is, in any event, a matter of professional etiquette.

Special considerations arising on the occasion of the first audit of a limited company will be dealt with in Chapter IX.

(C) AUDIT PROGRAMMES

There is some difference of opinion among practising accountants as to the advantages to be derived from the use of programmes for audits of varying size and complexity. In a properly organized office, it is essential that the principals should be perfectly familiar with the work performed on each audit, so that in the event of the clerk in charge being away or leaving the firm, no difficulty need be experienced in carrying on that particular matter.

It is therefore desirable that some definite record should be kept of the work performed at each audit. In order to ensure uniformity, and to make certain that all the work is done which should be done, it is advisable to make out a programme of work, and for the clerk responsible for each portion of the work to initial it as it is performed. In this way the progress of the audit can be ascertained immediately by the principal, and in the event of work being left undone, or errors being passed or made, the responsibility can be allocated to the clerk concerned.

On the occasion of the first audit it is not advisable to draw up a hard-and-fast programme, as the work to be done can really only be decided on as the audit proceeds. Careful note should, however, be taken of the work performed, and this will afford material for the preparation of an audit programme to be followed in the future.

The principal argument advanced against this procedure is, that by laying down a definite plan of work, the initiative of the clerk in charge is to a large extent stifled, and the audit is apt to become too automatic in its nature. There is no reason, however, why this should be so, as there is nothing to prevent the clerk in charge from making suggestions for amending the programme, and he should be *encouraged* to do so where his experience shows the amendments to be desirable.

As long as the audit is not allowed to become too stereotyped and the programme is changed or revised from time to time according to circumstances, the system suggested has so many advantages that in a practice of any size it can hardly be dispensed with in one form or another. Great care must, however, be taken to ensure that the programme does not become obsolete.

Clearly, a definitive audit programme can only be finalized when the system of internal control is thoroughly understood by the audit staff, and the most effective programme will therefore be the logical outcome of an enquiry based on the use of an I.C.Q. or flow chart, or a combination of both methods. (Of course, these techniques would only be employed where the client's business is of a size which warrants it – in the case of smaller businesses, a programme could be simply and effectively prepared on the basis of observations and tests freshly devised by the auditor.) It is therefore most important to appreciate that fundamental changes in the system operated by the client will invariably have their effect on the audit programme, and it should thus be impressed on audit managers that alterations in I.C.Q. details should not be made in isolation from the programme of work, and that when the I.C.Q. undergoes general revision, this task should incorporate a similar treatment of the audit programme.

The practice of making notes during the progress of the audit, apart from a record of the work done, should not be extended further than is absolutely necessary. It is infinitely preferable to settle a query and thereby get rid of it, than to make a note of it for future settlement. Those points, however, which cannot immediately be cleared up *must* be noted, as in the case of missing vouchers, duplicates of which may have to be obtained.

Points of importance also, which require to be remembered from one audit to another, but which are not apparent on the face of the accounts, should also be recorded.

On the occasion of the first audit of a business, an understanding of which requires a technical knowledge, and where special considerations apply, it is very convenient to make explanatory notes of all transactions of technical difficulty, so that these can be referred to by others who may have to take up the work subsequently.

(D) METHOD OF WORK

The method of work to be adopted on any audit will naturally vary with the individual training and experience of the auditor, and with the circumstances of each case. There are, however, one or two points which may conveniently be noted here.

Special 'ticks' should be adopted for each class of transaction checked, and the following are the usual classes of 'ticks': (1) posting, (2) casting, (3) carry forward, (4) vouching, (5) bank statement, and (6) contras. The same kind of 'tick' is not used by every firm for the same transaction, nor is this necessarily desirable, but a rule should be made in every office that the system of 'ticks' adopted must be closely adhered to, and not explained to a client's staff. It is usual for the auditor to use some coloured ink, or indelible pencil in order to distinguish his 'ticks' from those utilized by the business itself and usually colours are changed to distinguish periods.

Each section of the work should be completed, as far as practicable, and cleared definitely to a certain point. The habit of leaving 'loose ends', which is a common failing with some audit clerks is a very dangerous practice, as it may lead to points being ultimately forgotten or overlooked, or even possibly to fraudulent alterations being made. Fraud has been known to occur where the ledger balances had been checked one day and not cast till the next, the schedules having in the meantime been handed back to the ledger clerk, who had taken the opportunity of altering the figures already checked by the auditor. If the casts had been checked in the first instance this could not have occurred.

In the case of continuous audits, the work should only be performed up to a fixed date to which the books have been completed. In no case should pencil figures be accepted. The practice of making pencil entries or casts is extremely undesirable, and the auditor should insist that all such entries are inked in before he commences to work on the books concerned. In checking balances, unless these are brought down in ink, the auditor should require the amount of each balance to be noted at the side of the ledger account in ink, which preferably should be of some other colour than that used in the body of the ledger. If this is not done, the auditor must himself note such balances in ink, in order to avoid the risk of items being inserted afterwards which would affect the balance.

It is not the business of an auditor to balance the books, although he is often requested to do so. If the auditor undertakes this work, he does so in the capacity of accountant, and not of auditor, and it should be subject to a separate arrangement with the client. The question often arises whether it is advisable for the auditor to commence the audit before the books are balanced. Sometimes it is found necessary to do so in order that the audit may be completed within a required period; but it is not desirable, since it increases very materially the risk of passing errors, as the books have not, in the first instance, been subjected to the clerical test provided by the trial balance. In the case of many small companies, however, who have no skilled accounting staff, the auditor has no alternative but to deal with some accountancy work.

Where necessary, the auditor should make clear to his client the exact nature of the responsibility assumed, having regard to the nature of the work undertaken.

§ 6. Internal Audits

It has been suggested that the most desirable form of audit is to have an interim or continuous audit performed by one auditor supplemented by a final audit performed by another, but this is normally impracticable owing to the expense involved. The principle, however, is carried out by many large concerns by means of an internal audit staff.

The members of the internal audit staff, who are employees of the business, devote their time to reviewing the operations and records of the undertaking and in the course of their duties check much of the detail work. Even if an efficient internal audit exists, the need for an independent audit by external professional auditors remains, although the amount of detail checking which they must do may be reduced. The notes on the 'Field of Relationship between Independent and Internal Auditor' issued by the Council of the Institute of Chartered Accountants in England and Wales are reproduced in the Appendix.

§ 7. The Qualities required of an Auditor

The general principles of auditing having been indicated, it may be profitable to point out the essential characteristics which an auditor must possess if he is to perform his duties efficiently.

In the first instance it is imperative that the auditor should have a wide knowledge of the theory and practice of accountancy, and should be so familiar with the underlying principles thereof, that he can apply them without difficulty to transactions of which he has had no direct previous experience. It is impossible for a person to audit accounts properly unless he is capable of preparing those accounts himself. The lack of this fundamental requirement is the principal cause of inefficient auditing, and it cannot be too strongly emphasized that the only safe rule to adopt is never to pass a transaction if its precise meaning is not understood. Unfortunately this principle is often transgressed by those who, not having the requisite experience or knowledge, are afraid to ask the necessary questions, and consequently pass items blindly, trusting to luck that they are in order. Such a habit – for it is apt to become a habit – involves very heavy risks, and is certain to end sooner or later in disaster.

It is impossible for everyone to have experience in every class of business, and therefore occasions must from time to time arise when the auditor is presented with transactions of a technical nature, of which he has no knowledge. The proper course for the auditor to pursue in such circumstances is to ask intelligent questions of his clients or their staff, and thus place himself in possession of the requisite information to enable him to view the transaction critically. The exercise of a certain amount of tact is required, and caution is needed to avoid putting questions which, owing to ignorance of technicalities, might appear ridiculous; but, assuming this to be done, greater respect will be gained by an honest admission of unfamiliarity with the transaction, than by the assumption of knowledge which is not possessed, and lack of which will be almost certainly discovered.

Lord Justice Lindley said: 'An auditor must be honest – that is, he must not certify what he does not believe to be true and he must take reasonable care and skill before he believes that what he certifies is true.' (*In re London and General Bank* (No. 2) (1895) 2 Ch. 682.)

If there is a difference of opinion between the auditor and his clients on a matter of importance, he must have the courage of his convictions. He must possess, in some considerable degree, that characteristic of genius – an infinite capacity for taking pains; he should possess tact and patience; he must be conscientious, and must not be hurried into signing a certificate or report until he has received the whole of the evidence which he requires; nor should he sign under a promise that the evidence required will be forthcoming the next day.

An auditor must exercise constant vigilance; he must not allow his work to become automatic, or to lapse into a mechanical routine. He must be accurate, since his function is to detect the mistakes of others; he must be methodical, in order that no detail of his work may be omitted; he must be cautious, but he need not be unduly suspicious. As Lord Justice Lopes said: 'It is the duty of an auditor to bring to bear on the work he has to perform that skill, care, and caution which a reasonably competent, careful, and cautious auditor would use. What is reasonable skill, care and caution must depend on the particular circumstances of each case. . . . If there is anything calculated to excite suspicion he should probe it to the bottom; but in the absence of anything of that kind he is only bound to be reasonably cautious and careful. . . . The duties of the auditors must not be rendered too onerous. Their work is responsible and laborious, and the remuneration moderate. . . .' (*In re Kingston Cotton Mill Co.* (No. 2), (1896) 2 Ch. 279), and he must never relax his high standard. 'If an auditor has, even in one instance, fallen short of the strict duty of an auditor, he cannot, I apprehend, be excused merely because in general he has displayed the highest degree of care and skill' (per Romer, J., *In re The City Equitable Fire Insurance Co Ltd* (1924) Acct. L.R. 53 and 81).

If asked to give advice on matters of financial policy, or to suggest improvements in the accounts, although not strictly within his sphere as auditor, he must be prudent, and, above all things, practical. Theoretical knowledge can often be pushed to extremes, and thus it must be tempered with a nice appreciation of practical possibilities.

Last, but not least, the auditor should have a full share of that most valuable commodity – common sense.

CHAPTER II

THE AUDIT OF CASH TRANSACTIONS

§ 1. Internal Check as regards Cash

Before commencing the audit of the cash transactions of a business, it is most important that the auditor should, by the means described in the previous chapter, make himself familiar with the system of internal check in operation under this heading, since the majority of frauds arise in connection with cash.

A system of internal check is an arrangement of staff duties whereby no one person is allowed to carry through and to record every aspect of a transaction, so that, without collusion between two or more persons, fraud is prevented and at the same time the possibilities of error are reduced to a minimum.

It is not intended to set out here any complete system of internal check as regards cash, but merely to indicate the main points to which an auditor should direct his attention.

The duties of the cashier must be ascertained, particularly as to whether he has charge of any ledgers or books of prime entry other than the cash book. In large businesses, the cashier will be fully employed with his proper duties, but in smaller concerns it is not usually possible for the whole of one man's time to be occupied in the performance of the duties of a cashier. In such cases, the opportunities for the concealment of fraud by the cashier may be considerably enlarged.

(A) RECEIPTS

The relevant section of the I.C.Q. reproduced in the Appendix should be examined for full details of the enquiries which should be made in this connection, but the following points represent the major lines of enquiry:

(1) Whose duty is it to open letters containing remittances?

(2) Are all cheques, postal orders etc., immediately crossed, by means of a rubber stamp, to the firm's bankers, and for the firm's account?

(3) Are the remittances entered in a rough cash diary, and checked and initialled by at least two persons, neither of

whom is the cashier; and are the daily totals of the diary subsequently compared with the entries in the cash book, and if so, by whom?

(All sums received should be listed, preferably by some person other than the cashier. Where printed and numbered receipts are issued, these should not be prepared by the cashier, or by anyone connected with entering remittances in the rough cash diary. Unused receipt books should be kept in safe custody.)

(4) Whose duty is it to enter up the counterfoil of the paying-in book? (Preferably, the cashier should enter up the slip to be retained by the bank, while the clerk who makes out the counterfoil receipts should complete the counterfoil portion of the paying-in book.)

(5) Are all receipts banked daily, and is the clerk, whose duty it is to take money to the bank, otherwise engaged in connection with the cash transactions?

(6) What is the method of recording and checking cash sales (if any)?

(7) Do travellers have authority to collect debts, and if so, under what conditions?

(8) How frequently is the bank statement checked with the cash book and reconciliation statements prepared, and is this done by anyone other than the cashier?

(9) What are the arrangements for the custody and treatment of any bills receivable?

(B) PAYMENTS

The auditor's attention should be directed along the following lines of enquiry:

(1) Are all payments made by cheque, with the exception of those dealt with through petty cash; who has authority to sign cheques, and is any counter-signature required?

(2) Are cheques made payable to 'bearer' or 'order', and are they crossed 'a/c payee only – not negotiable' before being sent out?

(3) Are proper regulations in force for checking statements with invoices before cheques are drawn, and for invoices to be

stamped 'paid' when the cheques are signed in order to preclude the possibility of the same invoices being paid more than once?

(4) Are the paid cheques filed in numerical order after they are received back from the bank, or are they attached to the relative invoices and/or statements?

(5) What regulations are in force to sanction payments of a special nature? (This authority should be exercised only by principals or directors.)

(6) What system is in operation as regards petty cash?

(7) What system is in operation as regards the preparation and payment of wages?

§ 2. Vouching Payments

(A) GENERAL CONSIDERATIONS

Vouching may be defined as the examination by the auditor of all documentary evidence which is available to support the authenticity of transactions entered in the client's records. In relation to payments, it will be primarily concerned with the ascertainment of *cost* (distinguishing between capital and revenue cost), and the requisite *authority* for the payment.

It is provided by Section 3, *Cheques Act 1957*, that an unendorsed cheque which appears to have been paid by the banker on whom it is drawn is evidence of the receipt by the payee of the sum payable by the cheque. Paid unendorsed cheques may, therefore, be accepted by the auditor as evidence that the payee named therein has received the amount in question, but a paid cheque does not provide evidence of the consideration for which the payment was made, as is the case with a formal receipt.

Where payments for goods or services supplied are debited to a personal account for the supplier, the auditor's only interest in such payments lies in ensuring that the supplier did, in fact, receive the amount of the remittance, because the transaction in respect of which the payment arises will have been recorded in some book of prime entry or its equivalent, which record he will vouch in the course of his audit. If all cheques issued by the firm are crossed 'not negotiable, account payee only', the recipients of such cheques cannot negotiate them to third parties and the paid unendorsed cheques can, therefore, be accepted by the auditor as evidence that the payments have been made to the persons named. Where, however, cheques are not crossed restrictively, and can, therefore, be negotiated by the payee to third parties, it may be necessary for the auditor to insist on a proper receipt being obtained for a payment made where he finds that the cheque drawn therefor has been endorsed.

In recent years, many firms have discontinued the use of bought ledgers and bought day books in order to reduce clerical labour. In such cases, all invoices from suppliers for goods or services are filed until payment is due, so that no accounting entries in respect thereof are made until cheques are drawn in settlement and entered in appropriate columns in analysed or special cash payments books. In these circumstances, the auditor has a twofold duty in respect of payments made, viz.

(*a*) to verify the consideration for which each cheque has been drawn, and

(*b*) to see evidence that the proceeds of the cheques have been received by the payees thereof.

Under these conditions, the auditor's work will be greatly facilitated if the paid cheques are attached or referenced to the invoices or statements to which the payments relate.

The auditor should always insist on the production of specific receipts for payments of an exceptional nature, e.g. loans, settlements of claims, disputed accounts etc., and where, in his view, it is essential that the payment made be linked with some specific transaction.

Where unendorsed paid cheques are accepted as evidence of payment, the auditor should take care to see that the names of the payees and the dates on the cheques agree with the names and dates in the cash book.

When vouching payments it is necessary for the auditor to verify the nature of the consideration therefor by reference to invoices etc., and he should pay particular attention to the following points when examining the relevant vouchers:

(1) the name of the party to whom the voucher is addressed;

(2) the date of the invoice or statement, in order to ensure that it lies within the period under consideration;

(3) the nature of the payment;

(4) whether, and by whom, the payment has been passed as in order;

(5) the account to which the item is posted, in order to ensure that it has been correctly allocated.

It is important for the auditor to observe the name of the party to whom an invoice is addressed. The fact of its being addressed directly to the business concerned is *prima facie* evidence that the payment relates to the business, but in some cases it may be found that vouchers are addressed to an individual, such as a partner, director, or manager. When this is so, care must be taken to ascertain that the payment is a proper business one, and the auditor should make certain of this by referring to the original invoice to which the payment relates, and seeing that the goods are of such a kind as would be required by the business; he should also refer to the goods received book or the suppliers' advice and delivery notes, to see that the goods have actually been received by the business. If the payment does not relate to goods, it is still more necessary for the auditor to make sure that it is actually connected with the business, and he will do this by examining whatever evidence is available. If, however, there are any items which are properly chargeable to individuals, the auditor should ensure that such payments are debited to the personal accounts concerned and not treated as expenses of the business.

The auditor will have ascertained whether there is an efficient system of internal check as regards the examination and checking of invoices and statements for payment, and he should also ascertain the names of the parties whose duty it is to perform this work, and to initial the documents as having been checked. In examining the vouchers, therefore, it should be seen that the items have been properly checked and initialled by the parties responsible, and particular care should be taken, where the payment is of a special nature, to see that it has been duly authorized.

After each voucher has been passed by the auditor he should cancel it, preferably by the use of a rubber stamp bearing the name or initials of his firm, in order to prevent the same voucher being produced on a subsequent occasion in support of another transaction.

It will be appreciated that the foregoing remarks regarding receipts apply only to payments made by cheque. The auditor must inspect proper receipts for all payments made by cash, and when doing so he must pay particular attention to the following matters in addition to those referred to above in connection with invoices and other documents supporting cheque payments:

(*a*) the date on the receipt and whether it is properly stamped;

(*b*) if the statement states that only the firm's official receipts will be recognized, that the official form has been used;

(*c*) that the figures on the receipt do not appear to have been altered.

Where a bought ledger is kept, cash discount allowed by trade credoitrs is usually entered in a special column on the credit side of the cash book reserved for discount, the entry being made opposite the payment to which it relates. The auditor should question any apparent failure of his client to take advantage of discounts available to him. (The gross sum may have been paid and the discount shared with an employee of the payee.) If no bought ledger is kept, payments to creditors are normally entered net in the cash payments book.

(B) MISSING VOUCHERS

As soon as the auditor has completed his examination of the vouchers, he should extract a list of items which remain un-vouched because of missing evidence, and, where necessary, ask for duplicates to be obtained.

Vouchers for certain items will not be found in the ordinary voucher file, but these payments may usually be verified by reference to other books and documents.

(C) CAPITAL EXPENDITURE

The vouching of payments made on account of capital, and posted direct from the cash book to the asset accounts, is of great importance, since any erroneous treatment may affect the amount of profit or loss disclosed. Capital expenditure is all expenditure incurred for the purpose of acquiring, extending, or improving assets of a permanent nature, by means of which the business may be carried on, or for the purpose of increasing the earning capacity of the business.

The subject of the distinction between capital and revenue expenditure demands separate treatment, and it is only proposed to deal here with the vouching of cash payments on capital account, and to indicate the procedure to be adopted in dealing with the usual classes of payments of this nature.

(1) *Freehold and Leasehold Property*

The completion statement from the firm's solicitors must be examined. This statement will show the amount payable for the property, the amount of the deposit paid and the apportionments between the vendor and purchaser of rates, insurance etc. Legal charges and stamp duties payable may also be embodied in this statement but, if not, will be the subject of a separate account from the solicitors. The auditor must take care to see that the apportionments of unexpired rates etc., have been correctly charged or credited to the appropriate impersonal accounts and not included in the asset account. The legal costs and stamp duties incurred on the acquisition of capital assets may properly be regarded as part of their cost.

(2) *Buildings*

Where the building is being erected under contract, the actual contract should be examined and also the accounts for extras, if any. Payments under the contract will usually be made on a surveyor's or architect's certificate, and this should be seen by the auditor, in addition to the paid cheque or receipt given by the builder. The surveyor's fees should be vouched by reference to his account; such items form part of the cost of building and can be charged to capital. In certain cases, the buildings may be wholly or partially erected by the staff of the business, in which event allocation of materials and wages will be necessary. Such division, however, will not usually be made through the cash book, but will be dealt with through the journal and the entry therein will be vouched. In some instances cash purchases may be debited direct to the asset account, and the auditor will then examine the invoices, in order to ascertain that the items are of a capital nature, and to see that they have been properly examined and passed by an authorized person.

(3) *Plant and Machinery*

Similar considerations apply here as in the case of buildings, and all payments debited direct to the plant account will be examined in the same manner. Care must be taken to see that the expenditure is properly chargeable to capital.

(4) *Patents*

The letters patent should be examined. If the patent has been purchased, the assignment should also be seen, together with the receipt for the purchase consideration. Patent agents' fees in connection with the acquisition can be charged to capital, and will be vouched with the agent's account. Fees for renewal of patents must not be charged to the patent account, as they represent revenue expenditure.

(5) *Payments under Hire-Purchase and Instalment Agreements*

The actual hire-purchase agreement, or agreement to pay by instalments, should be examined, and the vouchers for the payment of instalments seen. A proportion of each instalment will represent interest, which should be charged to revenue, and care must be taken to see that the interest is not debited to the asset account, or, if this is done in the first instance, that it is afterwards transferred to profit and loss account. If the amount of the interest is not shown on the statements rendered by the vendors the rate of interest should be ascertained, and the appropriate adjustment made. It is essential that the method of apportioning instalments between capital and interest is consistently applied in successive accounting periods, and in respect of all agreements.

(6) *Investments*

For the purchase of investments the broker's bought note will be examined. The proper vouching of this item will also include the inspection of the securities; but this is not usually done in the course of vouching the cash book. It will be dealt with when the verification of assets is considered.

(7) *Loans*

The receipt given by the borrower should be inspected. If the loan is on mortgage, the mortgage deed will state the amount of the loan, and should be examined, together with the title deeds or endorsed land registry certificate. It should be seen that there is proper authority for the loan.

(8) *Office Furniture, Fixtures and Fittings*

Similar considerations apply as in the case of plant and machinery, and all payments debited direct to the furniture account will be examined in the same manner.

Where the fixtures form landlord's fixtures, this fact should be considered in providing the necessary amount of depreciation.

(D) SPECIAL PAYMENTS

Certain payments found in most classes of business are subject to special considerations in vouching, and the more important of these are dealt with below. Special payments, particularly those relating to companies, will be considered in Chapter IX.

(1) *Agents' and Travellers' Commission*

The agreements should be examined to ascertain the actual basis on which the commission is to be calculated and the arrangements, if any, regarding expenses. If the travellers are paid by cheque the paid cheques should be seen, but where payment is made in cash receipts signed by the travellers should be inspected. The commission records should be examined and the calculations tested.

(2) *Travelling Expenses*

Travellers' expenses, when payable by the business, are frequently computed on some fixed basis, and when this is the case, it should be seen that the basic amount is not exceeded. In other cases, the voucher for travelling expenses should specify the details of the expenditure and the auditor should ascertain that the amount has been passed as in order by a responsible official.

(3) *Insurance Premiums*

The insurance company's receipts or paid cheques will be in evidence for such payments. In the case of first premiums, where interim receipts have not been issued, the auditor should examine the policies, which will contain a note of the premium paid.

(4) *Bank Charges*

Bank charges for commission, cheque books, interest on overdrafts and loans etc., should be vouched by inspection of the bank statement and where necessary the calculations should be tested.

(5) *Salaries*

Salaries books should be in use, containing particulars of weekly and monthly salaries. These should be cast by the auditor, and cheques drawn for salaries vouched therewith. Any changes in the salary list should be verified with an official source. The national insurance cards and income tax deduction cards should be tested with the entries in the salaries books. The payment of wages is dealt with separately in § 3.

(6) *Petty Cash*

Cheques drawn on account of petty cash should be vouched by ascertaining that they are properly entered on the receipts side of the petty cash book, care being taken to see that the dates correspond. The vouching of the petty cash book itself is dealt with in § 7.

(7) *Bills Payable*

The returned bills, duly cancelled, will be in evidence as vouchers.

(8) *Bills Receivable Dishonoured*

If a bill receivable has been discounted through the bank, but is dishonoured on presentation, the amount of the bill will appear as a payment in the bank statement, and will also be entered in the cash book, being posted therefrom to the debit of the person from whom the bill was received.

Where the bill has not been discounted, but has been deposited with the bank for collection it is common to find the amount thereof credited by the bank on the date it becomes due, it being subsequently debited if the bill is dishonoured.

The auditor should examine the dishonoured bill, if it has not since been met or retired. The expenses of noting will appear in the bank statement (in cases where the bill has been presented through the bank), and should be debited to the person from whom the bill was received.

The expenses of discounting a bill will be vouched with the bank statement, if the bill has been discounted with the bank, and should be charged to the discounting charges account. In vouching the charge for discount it should be remembered that it is based on the nominal amount of the bill, and not on the money advanced by the bank. Thus the real interest charged is at a higher rate than would appear from the discount quotation.

(9) *Freight and Carriage*

Freight and carriage accounts require careful examination. Where the accounts are voluminous, payments are sometimes made on account throughout the month, and a final statement rendered. Such a statement should be checked with the carriage accounts, and the payments on account vouched thereto, ensuring that all of these have been brought into account.

In railway accounts where rates charged include cartage, a rebate is often allowed for cartage, if this is performed by the customer or his agent. The auditor should ascertain whether such rebates have been allowed, and see that the actual cash payment made corresponds with the net amount payable. Rebates are also afforded by shipping companies in some cases.

(10) *Customs Duties*

Where Customs duties are paid by a railway or forwarding agents on behalf of a customer, they will render monthly accounts, which should be examined by the auditor. Where the transactions are numerous, such accounts will follow the same principle as the freight accounts above mentioned.

Where duty is paid direct in cash, receipts are not always issued, but an acknowledgement can be obtained from the Custom House on the occasion of each payment, if it is asked for. Where such receipts are not produced, the auditor should request that they be obtained.

Payment is made in cash or by a transfer on the Bank of England. The latter is the usual mode for payment of large sums, and the auditor will then see no voucher except the returned transfer, which is, in effect, a cheque payable. It is important, therefore, that the auditor should see that there is a proper system of internal check in operation in respect of such payments.

In special cases, the Customs authorities will accept a guaranteed cheque, in which case they will issue receipts for the payments made.

As the sums involved are sometimes very large, and special opportunities exist for fraud in connection therewith, the auditor should vouch the duty account thoroughly.

In the case of purchase tax, Customs receipts are issued, and the payments should be verified therewith.

(11) *Income Tax and Corporation Tax*

In regard to the clients' own liability to these taxes, the official receipts should be compared with the relevant demands, and the entries in the cash book vouched therewith.

Income tax deducted from employees' remuneration under 'Pay-as-you-earn' must be remitted to the collector of taxes monthly, and the official receipts should be seen. The auditor should also check the amount of each remittance with the total of the deductions during the month in question.

(12) *Partners' Drawings*

It is not usual for specific vouchers to be available in respect of partners' drawings, but where the payment is in the form of a cheque payable to the partner concerned, the paid cheques should be examined to ensure that the sum was in fact received by the partner concerned. Where payments are made to third parties on behalf of partners, it is not always possible to obtain receipts, and such items should be vouched by direct reference to the partner concerned. Where partners' drawings are numerous, each partner should be asked to initial his drawings account as being correct.

§ 3. Wages

(A) INTERNAL CHECK AS REGARDS WAGES

The vouching of wages is a very important part of the auditor's duties in the case of a concern employing a considerable number of workers, owing to the numerous possibilities of fraud in this direction. It may be said that no auditor can vouch this item satisfactorily unless there is a proper system in force as regards the preparation of the wages sheets and the payment of employees. The first care of the auditor, therefore, will be to examine the methods adopted, and if he finds that the internal check in this connection is inadequate, he should advise his clients of the risks likely to result from this fact and suggest to them the alterations he considers to be advisable. Should his recommendations not be adopted, the auditor would be wise to disclaim any responsibility for errors or fraud which can be attributed to the lack of system, in order to protect himself from any subsequent charge of negligence.

The best system to be adopted in any particular case will naturally vary with the circumstances, but the principal dangers which any system should be designed to counteract are as follows:

(1) Inadequate time records, resulting in employees receiving pay for time not devoted to the business.

(2) Inadequate piece-work records, enabling pay to be received for work not executed.

(3) Errors in the preparation of the wages sheets.

(4) Fraudulent manipulation of the wages sheets, enabling cash to be drawn in excess of amounts due, or fictitious names to be inserted.

In order to counteract these dangers, a system should be in operation which will necessitate collusion between two or more officials before any fraud can remain undetected for any length of time. It is essential that any such system should be strictly adhered to, and supervised by those responsible for the control of the business, who should at all times be prepared to introduce such variations as experience proves to be advisable.

The following is an outline of a system of preparing wages sheets and paying the wages of a manufacturing concern, which, if properly carried out, should effectually minimize the risk of fraud:

(1) There should be a properly organized wages office under the control of a responsible person who should not be the cashier.

(2) A record card showing, e.g. date of birth, marital status, terms of employment, name of previous employer etc., should be kept for each employee.

(3) Rates of pay and alterations thereto should be set out in writing and duly authorized.

(4) The times of employees entering or leaving the works should be recorded, either by a gatekeeper or time-recording clock. In order to avoid loitering in the works, and to act as a check on the original record, the foreman of each department

should take the times of entering and leaving the shops, or departmental time clocks should be utilized.

(5) Where pay is based on the actual work performed, and not on the time occupied, an efficient system of recording piece-work is essential. When the work is given out it should be entered on the piece-worker's card. On completion, this card should be initialled by the piece-work viewer as soon as the work has been examined and checked by him, and where possible, also by the stock-keeper.

(6) Overtime should be separately recorded and passed by the foreman and by the works manager.

(7) Separate wages sheets or books should be used for time-workers and piece-workers respectively, and should be ruled to record all the essential particulars, special columns being provided for the gross amount payable, deductions for national insurance and graduated pension contributions, income tax, holiday and sports funds etc., payments on account, and the net amount payable. Columns should also be provided showing the employer's contributions under the National Insurance Acts.

The gate records and departmental time records should be compared by two clerks in the wages office, and any discrepancies enquired into. A third clerk should enter on the wages sheets the names of the employees, rates of pay, number of hours worked, and particulars of any deductions, and these entries should be checked by another clerk. A separate clerk should work out and enter up the net amount due to each worker, and cast the sheets, the calculations being independently checked by another clerk. Similar work should be performed in connection with the piece-workers' wages. Each wages clerk should initial for that portion of the work performed by him, and the whole should be counter-signed by the works manager, a partner, or a director.

(8) Wages should be paid by a person, or persons, who have not performed any part of the work detailed above. An analysis of the wage payments should be prepared so that the proper amount of change can be obtained from the bank. A separate cheque should then be drawn for the precise amount of the wages, and each person's wages placed in an envelope en-

dorsed with details showing the make-up of the contents. Preferably, where adhesive national insurance stamps are used these should be paid for by a separate cheque drawn in favour of the Postmaster General. Many firms, however, use a franking machine for national insurance stamps or, if the number of their employees warrants it, obtain a permit from the Ministry of Social Security to remit contributions direct to the Ministry, in which case the insurance cards will be neither stamped nor franked.

The workers should attend personally to receive their wages, the foreman of each department being present when those in his shop are being paid, in order to avoid the possibility of substitution. Special arrangements should be made for the payment of wages of persons who are absent, and the wages of one person should only be paid on his behalf to another on production of written authority from the absentee.

As a general rule it is not found possible to obtain the signature of each employee for wages, and where such a system as the above is in force, it is not necessary to do so. The payment should be attested by the signatures of the person who has made the payment, the foreman, and the works manager, if present.

The occasional attendance, without prior warning, of a partner or director whilst the wages are being paid, also adds considerably to the effectiveness of the check imposed.

(B) THE AUDITOR'S DUTY AS REGARDS WAGES

The auditor will ascertain the precise particulars of the methods employed in preparing and paying wages, and will pay special attention to any portion of the system which he considers to be defective. Where such a system as the one described above is in force, the auditor will ascertain that it is consistently and properly carried out, and that the signatures and initials of those responsible are duly appended to the wages sheets. He will vouch the cheques drawn for wages and insurance with the totals shown by the sheets, and check the casts and extensions of a certain proportion of the items. The national insurance cards and income tax deduction cards should be called for and extensively tested with the names and particulars appearing in the wages sheets. This precaution should minimize the possibility of fraud by the inclusion of 'dummy' names in the wages sheets. If adhesive stamps are used the auditor must take care to see that the national insurance cards are stamped up to date, or, where this is not so, that the stamps or cash drawn for this purpose are in hand. Where the number of employees is considerable it is more usual to find that insurance cards are either franked by means of an approved franking machine or that a permit has been obtained from the Ministry of Social Security for contributions to be remitted direct to them by cheque. If a franking machine is used the auditor must check the consumption by reference to the register readings on the machine. Where contributions are remitted to the Ministry of Social Security the auditor should vouch the payments made with the wages records and test the copy of the annual summary, which shows the names of the employees and the denominations of the stamps applicable to each case. In such cases the auditor must check the consumption by reference to the register readings on the machine.

It is a good plan for the auditor to attend personally on occasions, without notice, at the time of payment of wages.

§ 4. Vouching Cash Received

(A) GENERAL CONSIDERATIONS

From the auditor's point of view the operation of vouching receipts is often more difficult than that of vouching payments, since only indirect evidence can as a rule be obtained.

The system of internal check should be carefully enquired into by the auditor, and he should direct special attention to any part he considers inadequate. In order to ensure that the system is properly carried out, he should test each portion of the check and observe the procedures in operation, and if discrepancies are found he should carry his examination further. If the transactions he has examined are in order, he is entitled to assume that the remainder can be safely passed. Where a rough cash book or diary is kept, such book should be tested thoroughly with the cash book proper, since if amounts received are entered in the former but misappropriated by the cashier, and not entered in the cash book, the auditor might be held responsible if he failed to detect the fraud, owing to his omission to examine the records available. This point is one of some importance, as there can be no doubt that where memoranda books are kept which provide corroboration of the books of account, an auditor would be held negligent if he failed to examine them. This point emphasizes the necessity of the auditor obtaining a list of *all* books in use.

It is also essential that the auditor should test exhaustively the counterfoils of the bank paying-in book with the debit side of the cash book, noting particularly in the case of each lodgment that the separate items making up the total are the same in both cases.

(B) CREDIT SALES

Apart from checking the sales ledgers, the auditor cannot specifically verify receipts on account of credit sales, particularly where it is not the custom of the business to issue printed counterfoil receipts to its customers. Where counterfoil receipts are in use, the auditor should ascertain the regulations in force regarding them, and vouch a certain number of the counterfoils with the cash book.

It cannot be contended that in a large business which issues receipts it is the duty of the auditor to check the whole of the counterfoils. There is nothing to prevent a smaller amount being entered on the counterfoil than the sum actually received. Further, unless unused counterfoil receipt books are kept in safe custody, there is nothing to prevent receipts being issued from unused books. On the other hand, if the counterfoil is properly filled in, but the entry in the cash book is incorrect, and the auditor fails to discover the fraud by entirely omitting to check the counterfoil receipts, he might find himself in a position of some difficulty. An appropriate sample should therefore be selected for checking, based on the efficacy of the internal check system for sales as a whole. All spoilt receipts should be attached to the counterfoils, and cancelled by the auditor, as far as his examination extends. It should be seen that the dates on the counterfoils correspond with those in the cash book.

Where no official receipts are issued for sums received by cheque, the daily lists of such receipts, showing the amount and nature of each transaction and the name of the payer, should be verified with the entries in the cash book.

Where travellers are authorized to collect money from customers, the regulations in force should be ascertained, and it should be seen that they are sound and regularly adhered to. If the travellers issue counterfoil receipts, the counterfoils should be tested. The travellers' returns, giving particulars of the amounts received, should also be examined and compared with the actual receipts in the cash book.

Discount allowed to debtors is usually entered in a special column on the debit side of the cash book against the receipt to which it relates. The auditor should ascertain the terms on which discount is allowed, and test a certain number of the entries to ascertain whether the discount is in order. This is important, as defalcations in respect of receipts may be concealed by means of fictitious entries of discount. The discount columns should be cast, and the total checked to the debit of the discount payable account in the impersonal ledger.

(C) CASH SALES

The opportunities for fraud in this connection are very numerous, and no amount of checking by the auditor will be of much avail unless an efficient system of internal check is in operation.

Assuming a proper system to be in force, the auditor will test its operation by checking the counterfoils of the cash sales books with the salesmen's summaries or abstracts. Each salesman's abstract should agree with the analysis of the cash received by the receiving cashier, the details of which can again be checked with the cash sales counterfoils. The daily totals of the receiving cashiers' memorandum cash books should be vouched into the main cash book.

Where automatic cash registers are employed, the daily totals entered in the cash book should be checked with the till rolls.

(D) SPECIAL RECEIPTS

Certain receipts of common occurrence are subject to special considerations in vouching, and the more important of these are dealt with below. Special receipts relating particularly to companies will be dealt with in Chapter IX.

(1) *Income from Investments*

A separate ledger account should be kept for each investment, and where a large number of investments is held, an investment ledger will usually be found. In the case of fixed interest stocks the dates when dividends or interest payments are due should be noted at the head of the account. The auditor should ascertain that all dividends and interest receivable have been properly accounted for. Where the rate is fixed, the amount of the dividend or interest can be verified by checking the calculation on the nominal value of the stock held. In other cases, the counterfoils of the dividend warrants should be seen. Where investments are sold *ex div.*, it should be seen that the dividends are subsequently received, and similarly when a purchase is made *cum div.*

(2) *Rents Receivable*

In order to vouch the income derived from this source, the auditor should inspect counterparts of leases and agreements, noting the rent payable, and the provisions as to repairs and allowances. He should then ascertain that all rents that should have been received have been received, and vouch deductions made by the tenants. Enquiry should be made into arrears outstanding for any length of time, in order to ascertain whether they are genuine. Similar precautions must be taken in respect of properties which are shown as unlet. Where counterfoil rent receipt books are utilized, the counterfoils should be checked with entries in the cash book. When rents are collected by agents, their accounts should be examined and vouched.

(3) *Interest on Loans and Bank Deposits*

If the loan is secured by a mortgage, the deed will be consulted for the rate of interest and the dates when it is payable. If the loan is unsecured, whatever other evidence is available will be inspected, and it should be seen that the interest is duly received. Interest on deposit will be verified by reference to the bank statement or deposit account pass book, and the correctness of the amount there credited can be tested by checking the calculations in accordance with the terms allowed by the bank.

(4) *Bad Debt Dividends*

These items should be vouched by examining the counterfoils of the dividend warrants or other documents, which will state the amount of the debt and the rate of the dividend.

(5) *Sales of Investments*

The amounts received should be vouched by reference to the broker's sold notes.

(6) *Bills Receivable*

The bills receivable book will be examined to ascertain the due dates of the various bills. The proceeds of those discounted will be received prior to maturity, and should be vouched by reference to the bills book, or bills discounted books, and the rate of discount charged. Those held till maturity should be received in full on the due dates. If not so received, they will either have been retired and new bills given, or dishonoured.

(7) *Miscellaneous Receipts*

Other special receipts, such as receipts from the sale of fixed assets, receipts from insurance companies in respect of claims etc., will be vouched by reference to the correspondence, and any other documents relating to the matter.

§ 5. The Bank Statement

(A) PAYMENTS INTO BANK

The desirability of paying all receipts into the bank daily has already been emphasized, and the auditor should check the amounts paid in as shown by the bank statement with the entries in the cash book. Note should be taken of the dates of lodgments, to see that they correspond with the dates of receipt. This is important, since cases have been known where the cashier has continuously delayed his bankings for a few days, thereby placing himself in a position to manipulate regularly the current receipts.

The auditor should test a representative number of entries with the counterfoil paying-in book and he should refer to this book particularly for the purpose of vouching money received and paid into the bank prior to the date of closing the accounts, but not credited by the bank till the next period. As the paying-in book will show the actual date on which the items were paid in, and will be initialled by the receiving cashier, the record will be sufficient evidence that the money was paid in prior to the date of closing the accounts, if supplemented by an examination of the bank statement for the subsequent period, to see that the amount has been credited in due course.

In certain businesses it is the custom to enter remittances received after the close of the balancing period, as if they had been received and paid into the bank on the last day of the period, in order that these transactions may be recorded in the books before the close of the period, and so reduce the outstanding debtors. Such treatment cannot be regarded as in order, since it will have the effect of increasing the cash appearing in the balance sheet, and decreasing the outstanding debtors correspondingly. In this way the accuracy of the balance sheet is affected, but this can be remedied by adjusting the cash and debtors to the extent of the items in question. As, however, the trial balance will include these items as having been received, the auditor must vouch the receipt thereof as if they had actually been received during the period and require the necessary adjustment to be made on the final accounts.

(B) PAYMENTS OUT OF BANK

Where the bank statement has not already been agreed with the cash book, it will be necessary for the auditor to check the payments in detail with the statement, and he should be careful to observe that all bank charges, dishonoured bills, returned cheques etc., have been properly recorded in the cash book.

Where, however, the payments are numerous, and a reconciliation statement has been prepared and presented to the auditor, it may not be necessary for him to check the payments with the bank statement in detail, assuming an appropriate sample of those payments to have been vouched, and the credit side of the cash book to have been cast. The statement should, however, be checked in detail with the cash book for a representative period. Contras appearing in the statement but omitted from the cash book must be examined carefully and their nature ascertained, particular attention being paid to the dates of the entries. They are occasionally due to errors on the part of the bank, rectified by contra entry, or more often to cheques paid in and returned on account of a technical irregularity. The latter are not usually put through the cash book as returned, and the contra entry in relation to them will therefore not appear in that book. Similarly, great care must be taken to ensure that contras appearing in the cash book, but not in the statement, are in order. Fictitious contras have sometimes been made to cover up defalcations.

Cheques drawn before the close of the period, and appearing as payments in the cash book, but debited in the bank statement in the succeeding period, should be checked through into that period by the auditor as far as possible. Where the method of treating as receipts items received in the succeeding period is adopted, as referred to above, it will usually be found that the same principle is applied as regards payments, with the result that the cash balance is reduced, and the creditors decreased correspondingly. In this case, a similar adjustment should be made to that described as regards receipts, in order that the balance sheet may reflect the true position. For the purpose of reconciling the cash book balance with the bank statement balance, however, such items must be regarded as outstanding cheques.

(c) RECONCILIATION WITH CASH BOOK

A reconciliation statement should be prepared and submitted to the auditor, showing how the cash book and bank statement balances are agreed, and the auditor should check the details thereof with the bank statement. If no such reconciliation statement is submitted, he will be obliged to prepare one himself, which he will do by taking the balance as shown by the bank statement, adding thereto cheques paid in but not yet credited by the bank, and deducting therefrom outstanding cheques drawn but not yet presented for payment. Differences caused by bank charges or standing orders etc., not appearing in the cash book, should be immediately rectified.

In large concerns separate cash books are normally used for cash receipts and cash payments respectively. If this is done, the auditor should check the totals therefrom to the main cash book in which the balancing is effected, or to a total cash account in the impersonal or private ledger, which is sometimes employed in order to prevent the staff from knowing the bank balance.

The reconciliation of the bank statement with the cash book where there is an overdraft follows the same lines, but the cheques not credited will, of course, be deducted from the overdraft, and the cheques not cleared added thereto.

§ 6. Verification of Cash in Hand and at Bank

Where all receipts are not banked, and all payments are not made by cheque, the balance appearing on the cash book will be composed of cash in hand and at the bank, and will be divided accordingly, if separate columns have been utilized for cash and bank transactions, as should always be done.

In such an event, it is sometimes arranged that the cash balance in hand at the close of the period be paid into the bank on that day, and where this is done, the auditor will be able to vouch the asset through the bank statement. Where this procedure is not adopted, the auditor should, if possible, attend on the day of closing the accounts, and verify the balance in hand by actual inspection. This, however, is not always convenient, and the auditor must then check the entries in the cash book up to the date of his attendance, and verify the existence of the balance in hand as at that date. Where there are two or more cash accounts all should be checked up to the same date, and all the balances produced to the auditor at the same time in order to prevent the substitution of one for another.

The inspection of the bank statement is not sufficient evidence for the verification of the bank balance, since it is not unknown for fictitious statements to have been presented to auditors in the past. It is therefore essential that the balance as shown by the bank statement should be verified by a certificate from the bank sent direct to the auditor. The bank should be asked to specify the balances on all the accounts of the client if more than one is maintained.

Cash on deposit should be verified in a similar manner, and if deposit receipts have been issued these should be examined.

§ 7. Petty Cash

(A) GENERAL CONSIDERATIONS

The treatment of petty cash payments is often regarded as an unimportant matter, and it is common to find in the case of businesses which have not been subject to audit, that the petty cash arrangements are very inadequate, and afford numerous opportunities for manipulation. Under these circumstances it is essential for the auditor to direct particular attention to this subject, and he should recommend the adoption of a proper system. This is the more important as vouchers cannot be obtained for a large number of petty cash payments. Moreover, in most businesses of any size, the individual payments, though small in amount, are very numerous, and it will not be possible for the auditor to satisfy himself by the usual method of vouching that all the payments are in order.

In small businesses, cheques drawn for petty cash are often posted to a petty cash account in the impersonal ledger, and the details of the petty cash payments themselves recorded in a rough cash book. In such cases, the auditor will usually find on enquiry that there are no vouchers worth speaking of to support the payments, and the book is not subject to the examination of anyone other than the petty cashier. The expenditure made will probably not be analysed, but the total debited to the petty cash account in the impersonal ledger, less the balance in hand, will be written off to profit and loss account.

Such a system should be strongly discouraged by the auditor, and he should recommend the adoption of a columnar petty cash book, containing on the debit side a column for receipts, and on the credit a column for total payments, with subsidiary columns for the various classes of expenditure usually incurred. Each item of expenditure should be extended into its appropriate column, and the book balanced at least once a month. A column should be provided for the voucher number, and the vouchers should be numbered and filed in order. It is advisable to provide an additional column, into which to extend items for which there is no specific subsidiary column and from which each item will be posted to the debit of the account to which it relates.

There are two methods of regulating payments to the petty cashier, the first being to draw cheques as and when required for petty cash purposes, these being entered in the receipts column of the petty cash book.

The second method is known as the *imprest system*, under which the petty cashier receives a starting sum, the amount of which will be determined by the normal demand on the petty cash. When the petty cash requires replenishing, a cheque is drawn for the precise amount of the payments that have been made, thus restoring the balance to the amount of the imprest. This system has certain advantages in most cases, since it necessitates the petty cash book being kept regularly written up, as the petty cashier should be required to furnish an analysis of the payments made each time that he requires a further cheque. It is particularly applicable where the petty cash relates to a branch, or when it is inconvenient to draw petty cash cheques at short notice. In other cases, it might be disadvantageous, since it might result in placing a larger balance in the hands of the petty cashier at the commencement of each period than is necessary. On the other hand, the imprest system is convenient for checking purposes, since at any moment the cash in the hands of the petty cashier, plus any vouchers for payments made since his balance was last replenished, should be equivalent to the amount of the imprest.

(B) INTERNAL CHECK AS REGARDS PETTY CASH

It has been pointed out that it is not usually possible for the auditor to verify the petty cash transactions in detail, and therefore it is advisable that, in addition to a good system of account, there should exist an efficient internal check, by means of which the petty cash can be kept effectively under control.

The points to which such a system should be applied are as follows:

(1) The petty cashier should be a reasonably responsible official, but should not himself be the cashier.

(2) The only receipts paid into petty cash should be cheques drawn for that purpose. Sundry cash receipts are often entered in the petty cash book, but this is inadvisable, and the rule should be enforced that all receipts, however small, should pass through the cashier's hands, and be paid into the bank in due course.

(3) No payment should be made unless a proper voucher is obtained. Many payments are, however, of such a nature that no receipt is available, and to enable a proper record thereof to be obtained, petty cash slips or dockets should be provided, and the person making the payment should be required to insert the necessary particulars, and initial for the sum received, the docket being counter-initialled by a responsible official where necessary. In this way either an actual receipt or a docket will be in evidence for each payment.

(4) At frequent intervals the petty cash book should be checked in detail with the vouchers, and the balance in hand verified by some responsible official, who should initial the petty cash book accordingly.

(5) No employee should be allowed to borrow from the petty cash – except under special circumstances, with the authority of a senior official.

(C) THE AUDITOR'S DUTY IN RELATION TO PETTY CASH

Where a good system of petty cash, supported by an efficient internal check, is in force, the auditor will not, as a rule, find it necessary to perform much detailed work. He should ascertain that the system is regularly carried out, vouch the cheques drawn for petty cash from the credit side of the cash book to the debit side of the petty cash book, and cast the receipts and total payments columns of the latter. The totals of the subsidiary columns should be cross-cast, and agreed with the total payments.

The vouchers should be tested, either by taking a certain consecutive period, or by examining all vouchers over a certain amount. When examining vouchers the auditor should take great care to see that the amounts thereon have not been altered or, if they have, that the alterations have been signed by a responsible person.

Most firms whose expenditure on postages is considerable, use approved franking machines. In such cases cash will not be required for the purchase of postage stamps so that neither cash nor stamps will be available for misappropriation. The franking machine is set by the postal authorities for the number of frankings purchased, for which payment will be made by cheque, and meters show the number of frankings used and the balance in hand. A postage book may be kept as a record of the dispatch of letters, but in the majority of cases today, such a record is dispensed with.

Where postage stamps are used, the cash for their purchase will, normally, be provided out of petty cash and the amounts so drawn must be checked from the petty cash book to the postage book. It should be seen that the postage book has been regularly checked, and it may be advisable to count the balance of stamps in hand where this is considerable. The main point, however, is for the auditor to see that a proper system of check on the postage is in force, since otherwise the opportunities to commit fraud may prove too tempting to be resisted.

Where the petty cash book is kept on the columnar principle, it may be made to form part of the double entry, and, in that event, there will be no petty cash account in the impersonal ledger, and the balance of the petty cash book will feature in the trial balance. The totals of the columns will, in such a case, be posted direct from the petty cash book to the impersonal ledger, and should be checked by the auditor. Otherwise a petty cash account will be opened in the impersonal ledger, which will be debited with all cheques drawn for petty cash, and credited with the analysis of the various payments, either through the journal, or by way of direct transfer to the ledger accounts involved. The auditor should vouch such transfers with the analysis of the petty cash, and see that the balance brought down on the petty cash account in the impersonal ledger agrees with the balance as shown on the petty cash book.

Where the petty cash system is not adequate, there being no effective internal check, the auditor should examine the transactions carefully, and vouch them as fully as he considers necessary. Where the evidence of payments is not sufficient, he must report to his clients the facts of the case, and inform them that he cannot hold himself responsible for the accuracy of petty cash transactions, owing to the lack of available evidence.

In any event, the auditor should verify by actual inspection the balance in hand. Where possible this should be done without previous warning and need not necessarily take place on the day of the balance sheet. The petty cash book must be vouched to date and the petty cashier called upon to produce his cash balance. It will sometimes be found that such balance consists in part of IOU's. Due note should be taken of these by the auditor and, if necessary, he should report the matter to his clients.

Where two or more petty cash accounts exist, the balances should be verified simultaneously, in order to avoid substitution of one balance for another.

In the case of the *London Oil Storage Co Ltd* v. *Seear, Hasluck & Co* (Acct. L.R. 30, p. 93), it was found that the auditors had committed a breach of duty in not vouching the existence of the petty cash balance, which was shown by the books to be £796, but was in fact only £30. The mere size of the alleged balance should, of itself, have aroused the auditor's suspicions.

§ 8. Vouching 'In Depth'

It is again necessary to consider the difference in approach required by the auditor when engaged in the audit of concerns of varying size. 'Horizontal' vouching, or the selection of a substantial batch of exactly similar operations for checking (e.g. postings from cash book to sales ledger) may give entirely satisfactory results in the case of small or even medium-sized concerns. However, in view of the vast number of transactions (and hence of accounting entries) with which the auditor is faced when auditing the accounts of large concerns, it is necessary for a precise and comprehensive technique in vouching to be applied to a relatively small sample of transactions, without in any way diminishing the effectiveness of the examination. The technique which is most frequently used in this connection is known as 'depth checking', or 'examination in depth'. It involves the selection of an extremely small sample of transactions of a particular type (e.g. purchases), and the tracing of these through their various stages, from initiation to conclusion. In relation to purchases, depth checking might involve an examination of goods requisitions, purchase orders, and invoices, noting that due authority has been given at each stage, and watching for evidence of details of goods and prices etc. having been checked internally. The auditor would continue his examination by reference to entries in the cash book and bank statements regarding payment for these purchases, and the returned cheques would be examined. Of course, the postings would be checked from the prime records to the ledgers, or their equivalent. Finally, details of the goods purchased should be seen to have been correctly entered in the stock records, which should also reflect movements out of stock, if the goods have been sold. (The vouching of purchases will be more fully dealt with in the next chapter.)

It will be seen that this procedure is extremely flexible and may be applied in varying circumstances and to different departments within the client's organization. Moreover, the examination may be focused on a particular period within the financial year, or it may be spread out over a larger period of time without necessarily increasing the overall sample size. As the examination of successive stages reveals results which satisfy the auditor as to the accuracy of recording and the operation of the internal check, he may progressively reduce the number of items to be examined at subsequent stages. Conversely, should examination at any stage disclose a proportion of errors greater than 'acceptance level', a more detailed check will be indicated. The auditor should continue in this way, until his assessment is complete.

As a result of applying this technique, which is virtually an *enactment* of the flow-chart described earlier, the auditor is ideally situated to make recommendations to the client regarding the improvement of those aspects of the system where this is felt to be necessary, and in the majority of cases the management will be found to be highly co-operative. Where, however, the auditor encounters resistance to proposals which he regards as essential to the provision of an adequate system of internal check, he will be obliged to refer to the matter in his final report.

It is the great thoroughness of depth checking which constitutes its chief advantage, and it must always be borne in mind by those adopting this technique that each item selected, regardless of amount or other 'stratifying' features which have been incorporated in the sample selected, must be treated with the same attention to detail, and apparently insignificant items, such as a cancelled cheque, should under no circumstances be brushed aside, but should be fully investigated and understood.

§ 9. The Use of Statistical Sampling Techniques

In the previous subsection frequent reference was made to the selection of samples by the auditor for checking purposes. It is therefore necessary to consider briefly the techniques, involving the use of statistical tables or graphs, by which the most appropriate sample sizes in varying circumstances may be determined with reasonable and ascertainable accuracy, and selected without bias.

The chief object governing the use of statistical sampling is to achieve a suitable balance between the following two extremes: a complete check of all items (probably quite unnecessary, and unduly costly), on the one hand, or a sample check which is so small as to run the risk of overlooking a material number of errors (which could turn out to be equally costly, if not more so, and which could by far outweigh the savings achieved by a reduced check). A practical illustration of what is known as 'percentage' sampling may be considered.

Transactions are easily classified into months, the first and last months of any period in any event requiring special consideration on the part of the auditor. The problem of test-checking thus refers to the remaining ten months. Assume that during these ten months 10,000 entries are made recording the sale of goods to customers. If a random selection of 1,000 of these is taken for detailed checking, a measure of the reliability of this sample is ascertained by applying the statistical rule which states that the reliability of a sample is proportionate to the square root of its size. Thus, the index of reliability of the 10 per cent. sample of 1,000 entries is represented by the square root of 1,000, or approximately 31·6. Now, should the auditor wish to double the reliability of his check, he will have to undertake a random selection of 4,000 items (*not* 2,000), the square root of 4,000 being 63·6. It is thus seen to be necessary to do *four* times as much work in order to achieve *twice* the reliability. (It will be appreciated that in practice it is highly unlikely that the auditor will consider it necessary to check such a large proportion of items: the figures are given merely to indicate the operation of statistical law.) The following table illustrates fully the relationship between the amount of audit work necessary for different sample sizes, and the reliability secured thereby:

Number of entries examined	Work involved (percentage of total volume)	Reliability index
1,000	10	31·6
2,000	20	44·7
3,000	30	54·8
4,000	40	63·3
5,000	50	70·7
6,000	60	77·5
7,000	70	83·6
8,000	80	89·6
9,000	90	94·9
10,000	100	100·0

It should be clear from this table that there is *some* sample which provides a suitable balance between:

(a) the amount of worked involved, and

(b) the reliability of the corresponding results.

If the table is represented graphically the problem of selecting this optimum point is somewhat simplified:

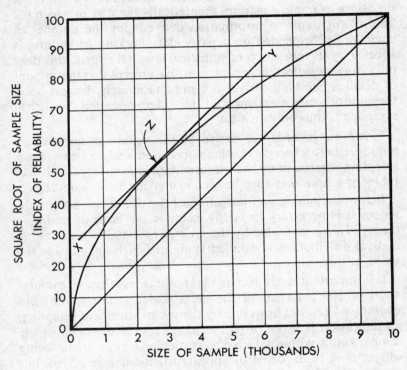

In this graph the straight line from the lower left-hand corner to the upper right-hand corner represents the amount of work involved for various sized samples. The curve represents the reliability of the respective sample sizes. A sharp increase in reliability will be noticed towards the left-hand side of the graph, while the increase at the right-hand side is noticeably less. If we now draw a tangent (XY) to the curve parallel with the diagonal, the point where the tangent meets the curve indicates the size of sample which achieves a balance between the amount of auditing work and the reliability derived therefrom. This point is located at approximately 2,500, meaning that if the auditor were to check a sample comprising 2,500 entries, the index of reliability is roughly 50, and any work in excess of this is subject to severely diminishing returns.

'Percentage sampling' is somewhat impractical, since it tempts the auditor to carry out far more checking than is necessary, but the above example illustrates theoretically the way in which the 'return' (in terms of information derived) for the number of 'audit-hours' expended on a particular checking procedure, is affected by the operation of statistical law. (Of course, this does not in any way affect the incontrovertible precept that the amount of detailed checking carried out must ultimately depend upon the auditor's own assessment of the system operated. Statistical sampling is thus only an aid.)

However, in order to arrive at the optimum sample size appropriate to a *specific* checking operation, and hence to plan a sampling scheme, more basic information is necessary; statistical tables or graphs may then be used in arriving at the sample size.

Before examining an illustration of the use of sampling techniques it is necessary to briefly examine the basis of sampling theory. This is provided by the laws of probability and mathematical distribution, a detailed study of which lies outside the scope of this volume.

It is important to appreciate that nothing less than an examination of 100 per cent. of the items under scrutiny will yield guaranteed results; however, by the use of statistical sampling, an indication is given of (i) the margins on either side of the sample result within which the particular characteristic being sought may be expected to appear; (ii) the degree of risk implicit in drawing a particular sample; (iii) mathematical proof of the evaluation of the test, provided this is correctly expressed.

When discussing sampling for audit purposes it is imperative that the allied concepts of (*a*) statistical estimation and (*b*) random selection should initially be treated separately. Statistical estimation has two basic purposes in the audit field: these are respectively known as 'sampling for attributes', and 'sampling for variables' (otherwise known as value estimation). An example of an expression of an evaluated test for attributes is as follows:

'The population error rate is 2 per cent. ± 1.5 per cent. at a confidence level of 95 per cent'; similarly, a conclusion on the entire value of a particular population (value estimation) may be given expression in the following way:

'The total value of the population is £250,000 ± £19,000 at a confidence level of 90 per cent.'

Great care must be taken when expressing the results of any test after employing statistical means for the purpose of evaluation, since incorrect expression may have the effect of rendering the conclusion meaningless.

The concept of 'confidence level' mentioned above is complementary to that of 'risk', i.e. a confidence level of 90 per cent. means that there is one chance in ten that the sample selected will not be representative of the whole population (or 'universe'). It will also have been noticed from the above evaluations that sampling results are expressed within certain limits (e.g. ± 2 per cent.). These limits – or margins – are generally known as the degree of 'precision', bearing in mind, once again, that only a 100 per cent. examination carries no margin of error (assuming the examination itself to be reliable). Precision and confidence levels should be related to accounting principles and concepts, not the least important of which is the question of materiality. Clearly the precision limits selected for a test should be such that if the errors discovered lie within these limits, there is no danger of the validity of the accounts as a whole being materially affected. The auditor must clearly use his own judgment in selecting both precision and confidence levels. When sampling for attributes such as errors, the auditor must decide upon the *Maximum Acceptable Error Rate* (which is the *anticipated* error rate *plus* the precision margin). The results of the sampling tests, however, are expressed in terms of *Maximum Potential Error Rate* (which is the *actual* error rate *plus* precision). In determining precision limits it should be remembered that it is generally highly uneconomic to increase sample sizes in order to give greater precision, since for all practical purposes sample sizes are independent of the size of the population. Similarly, the confidence level is also determined by the auditor according to his own judgment. The normal range of confidence levels for auditing purposes lies between 90 per cent. and 99 per cent.

The chief considerations in the determination of confidence levels and precision limits will, of course, be based upon the auditor's own evaluation of the client's system of internal con-

trol, and this aspect of auditing remains of paramount importance. Statistical sampling, or any other technique, should thus
be regarded merely as an aid, and not as an end it itself. The
auditor's evaluation of the client's system will in turn be based
upon his experience of examining the client's records during
previous audits, his interviews with key personnel, investigation
of weaknesses made apparent through use of the I.C.Q., and any
other means of systems appraisal adopted. It is also worth noting
that any conscientiously executed audit test may be statistically
evaluated after it has been completed: it is therefore not essential
that the sample size be statistically determined *before* any testing
is carried out. If the subsequent evaluation indicates that an
inadequate sample was selected, or that the number of errors
discovered would appear to materially affect the view presented
by the accounts, the sample may be enlarged.

When the particular attribute of concern to the auditor is
errors (as is usual), it is most important that he should be clear
as to what, in each context, constitutes an 'error'. Clearly there
are any number of aberrations which may be discovered while
engaged on normal audit testing; some of these are serious while
the effect of others is minimal. The effect of each *type* of error
must be independently assessed, since not all error-types (even
though errors by definition) give rise to or require the same confidence level and margin of precision. Furthermore, it is usually
also necessary for the auditor to quantify the degree of tolerance
which he will allow when errors of a relatively small amount are
discovered: two errors may be the same error-type, but one may
have an overwhelming effect on, say, the total of a schedule of
outstanding balances, while others may involve merely a few
shillings.

The actual procedure for selecting sample sizes for the purpose
of attributes sampling may be summarized in the following way:

(*a*) The population *category* and the population *unit* should be
clearly defined. All units within a total population must be
of the same type (e.g. petty cash vouchers) ,and the population must be complete. Where there have been changes in
the system operated during the period under review, separate
populations exist on either side of the date of change, and
separate tests must be devised.

(*b*) The population size must be determined. This is simplified if all items within the population are pre-numbered, but in other circumstances it may be difficult to estimate, in which event the largest estimate should be adopted, bearing in mind that the effect of the population on the sample size is minimal.

(*c*) Examine the way in which the population is constituted and consider whether *stratification* is necessary. This step is usually taken where the population is made up of both large and small items; it is then suitably stratified and separate tests are carried out on each stratum.

(*d*) Define 'errors' and 'error-types'. The anticipated error rate in the population should then be estimated. This estimate is arrived at as a result of the auditor's previous experience of that particular department or section of the client's organization, or as a result of other means of systems appraisal such as interviews, I.C.Q.s, flow charts etc. If necessary a 'pilot' sample test may be carried out in order to assist in determining the anticipated error rate. (Of course, different error-types will be separately tested.)

(*e*) The precision limits and the level of confidence required for the particular population being sampled should be determined. The precision margin is added to the anticipated error rate in order to arrive at the Maximum Acceptable Error Rate.

(*f*) Refer the data thus determined to specially prepared tables or graphs in order to discover the appropriate sample size, and random-number tables should then be used for selecting individual items constituting the sample.

(*g*) The test should now be evaluated, comparing the number of errors discovered in the sample with the predetermined acceptance level, in order to discover whether or not the test has been satisfactory.

(*h*) Ensure that the final expression of the conclusion of the test is valid, and if the test has been unsatisfactory the next course of action must be positively decided.

The correct use of random-number tables, as indicated above, is most important. A random starting point should be selected anywhere in the tables and items may be chosen for testing simply by moving up or down the list of random numbers in the table. Of course, this is only feasible if each number in the tables is capable of being freely translated into a particular population item. It is essential that items should not be dropped from the test simply because they are not available at the time, or because to test them may involve considerable inconvenience. Alternatively, systematic selection may be adopted. Once again, a random starting point is selected (e.g. by reference to the seconds hand on a wrist-watch) and thereafter every nth item is selected for examination, the interval being determined by dividing the population size by the sample size.

In view of the fact that the auditor may be called upon to justify the samples selected by him it is essential that comprehensive and intelligible working papers are compiled and maintained for each test executed.

The technique of sampling for attributes described above may be simply illustrated by the following example. A company's inventory of work in progress comprises 10,400 items which may be broadly stratified into two distinct groups, viz. relatively large items, totalling 1,900 (group A) and the balance of 8,500 items, all relatively small (group B). It is estimated that the rate of errors as defined (valuation errors, clerical errors etc.) will not exceed 2 per cent. and 5 per cent. in groups A and B respectively, and the auditor is prepared to accept a precision margin of ± 1.75 per cent. in the case of group A, and ± 2.5 per cent. in the case of group B, at a level of confidence of 95 per cent. for both groups.

Reference to the tables shows that the appropriate sample size for group A is 217 items, and that for group B is 282 items, a total of 499 items to be checked out of the total of 10,400. Provided the proportion of errors found in the group A sample does not exceed 3.75 (2+1.75) per cent., and that in the group B sample does not exceed 7.5 (5+2.5) per cent., the inventory may be passed by the auditor. (In practice it would be possible, by the use of value estimation techniques – variously known as sampling for variables, survey sampling or estimation sampling – to determine the total value of the inventory, within defined precision limits, by examining a suitable sample; the characteristics displayed by the sample are taken together with the standard deviation and projected onto the population as a whole.) In practice, variations of the acceptance technique are frequently used when appropriate. Where a 'double' sample is used, the sample is divided into two parts, and the second part is checked only in circumstances where the examination of the first part fails to yield a clear result. This technique has the advantage of keeping checking to a minimum in those cases where there is no need to examine the second part. Of course, the predetermined acceptable rate of errors in the first part would have to be much lower than where a single sample is used, as in the illustration described above.

Variations and refinements of these techniques are constantly being devised, and there is every indication that auditors will make fuller use of statistical sampling methods in future years. In fact, as the size of audits increases, and auditors are virtually compelled to eliminate all but essential audit tests, the use of statistical sampling will act as a positive influence, enabling auditors to prove mathematically, and hence objectively, the definable degree of accuracy afforded by the tests which they have executed.

CHAPTER III

THE AUDIT OF TRADING TRANSACTIONS

§ 1. Purchases

(A) INTERNAL CHECK AS REGARDS PURCHASES

It is highly important that a proper system should be in force for the purpose of checking the receipt of goods and the accuracy of invoices in order to prevent fraud and errors, and to ensure that the business only pays for the goods which it actually receives.

Before entering on an examination of the purchases the auditor should ascertain what system, if any, is in force, and the following are the principal points to which his attention will have been directed in the course of his initial enquiry:

(1) Which officials are authorized to sanction the ordering of goods?

(2) Is a goods inwards book kept by the gate-keeper, in which particulars of all goods received are entered?

(3) Are the invoices, when received, checked by the invoice clerk with the order book, and the number of the order entered on them? The invoices should also be checked with the goods inwards book, to ascertain whether the goods have been actually received, and a reference made both in the goods inwards book and on the invoices. This should prevent the entering of fictitious invoices or the treatment of duplicates as originals. The invoice clerk should initial each invoice, to indicate that he has checked the calculations and verified the items as above described.

(4) Is each invoice then passed to the particular department from which the goods were ordered, and initialled by the manager who thus makes himself responsible for the correctness of the price and quality of the goods?

(B) THE BOUGHT DAY BOOK

As stated in the previous chapter, many firms now dispense with bought day books and bought ledgers by dealing with purchases on a cash basis. Invoices received from suppliers, after they have been checked, are filed in 'unpaid accounts' files until they are due to be paid. When the cheques are drawn in settlement, the invoices are marked 'paid' by means of a rubber stamp and then filed in appropriate files for paid accounts. The cheques are sent to the suppliers together with their statements, or with remittance slips made out by the paying firm, and the amounts thereof entered in a purchases column in the cash payments book. If the cheques are made out by means of an accounting machine, a carbon copy is taken which forms a subsidiary cash payments book, the total of which is entered in the purchases column of the general cash payments book. The discontinuance of the use of bought day books and ledgers is frequently effected by the introduction of a system of mechanized or electronic accounting, and a full treatment of this subject appears in the next chapter, in conjunction with the statement of the Institute of Chartered Accountants, which is reproduced in the Appendix.

Where bought day books are still utilized, it is often found that invoices for services etc., as well as those for goods purchased, are entered therein, as accounts for all creditors are kept in the bought ledger. In these circumstances a columnar day book is generally employed, the book providing a separate column for each class of expenditure, or for departmental analysis.

The amount of each invoice will be entered in the day book, and the invoices numbered consecutively. Where the system of internal check is adequate, it will be sufficient for the auditor to test the casts and cross-cast of the subsidiary columns to see that they agree with the grand total. The postings of the totals of the subsidiary columns will be checked to the accounts in the impersonal ledger to which they relate.

Where the number of columns required is too large to be dealt with conveniently in one book, the bought day book should be divided into two or more sections. In such cases it is usual to find an expenses day book in operation, recording all invoices relating to expenses other than purchases of goods.

It will be appreciated that if purchases of goods and expenditure on services etc., are dealt with on a cash basis, the auditor, when vouching the payments made to creditors, will be concerned also with the nature of the consideration for such pay-

ments and the accuracy of the postings made in respect thereof
to the relevant impersonal ledger accounts. The following remarks on vouching invoices, therefore, are as equally applicable
to the auditor's examination of invoices entered in a bought day
book as to his inspection of invoices in corroboration of cheque
payments where no day book is kept.

(C) VOUCHING INVOICES

When vouching invoices, the following are the most important
considerations:

 (i) The auditor should see that the invoices are initialled by the
     clerk whose business it is to check them.

 (ii) Each invoice relating to goods should have attached to it a
      docket signed by the gate-keeper acknowledging receipt of
      the goods, or bear a reference to a goods inwards book, to
      which the auditor should refer to see that the goods stated
      in the invoice have actually been received.

(iii) Care should be taken to see that the invoices are made out
      in the name of the firm, and appear to be of a nature
      relating to the business carried on.

(iv) It should be seen that each item is extended into its proper
     subsidiary column in the bought day book or cash pay-
     ments book, and if any column is provided for capital
     expenditure, such as plant and machinery, the items con-
     tained therein should be checked to see that they are strictly
     of a capital nature.

 (v) All such items should be passed and initialled by some com-
     petent official.

(vi) The details relating to discounts and purchase tax and the
     various calculations and extensions should be examined.

(vii) It should be seen that the date of the invoice falls within the
      accounting period under review.

In some businesses it is the practice to allow members of the
staff to order goods for themselves and to obtain the benefit of
trade discounts. Unless special care is exercised in relation to
such goods there is the possibility of their not being correctly
charged out to the recipients, and the auditor should take care
to see that each such invoice has a corresponding sales invoice.

At the close of the balancing period it is important for the auditor to ascertain, as far as possible, whether all goods received prior to the date of closing the books are included in the purchases, since, if they are included in the stock but omitted from the purchases, the profit will be over-stated to that extent. Profits can be inflated deliberately by manipulating the purchases in this manner, and where no proper system for dealing with the receipt of goods is in force, it may be difficult for the auditor to detect fraud or errors of this nature.

The procedure in operation which is aimed at ensuring that such accord exists between the purchases records and the stock inventories at the year-end, is sometimes known as 'cut-off' procedure. (Of course, similar considerations apply to sales, and it must be seen that goods which have been sold, and included in sales in the trading account, have been omitted from stock even though still on the premises.) In the case of *re Thomas Gerrard and Son Ltd* (1967) the auditors were found guilty of negligence for failing to investigate thoroughly alterations of the dates of purchases invoices at the company's year-end, once these alterations had come to their notice. These alterations had been made fraudulently in order to inflate the company's profits.

Where, however, the gate-keeper's records are referenced to the suppliers' invoices, there should be no difficulty in ascertaining whether or not the liability for all goods received prior to the date of the balance sheet has been correctly dealt with.

In the absence of adequate gate-keeper's records, it may be necessary for the auditor to refer to the suppliers' delivery notes received with the goods.

Errors occasionally arise in this connection owing to the system sometimes adopted in certain trades of post-dating invoices. This is done for the purpose of giving an extended period of credit – all goods ordered, say, after the 20th of each month being post-dated to the 1st of the following month, in order to extend the term of the two or three months' credit that may be allowed. For the convenience of the ledger clerk, it is usual to make the entries relating to these invoices as at the 1st of the month, although the goods themselves have been received in the previous month; and care must be taken at balancing periods to ascertain that all goods of this nature brought into stock have been properly dealt with as purchases.

Where the firm has dispensed with a bought day book and bought ledger, the invoices in the 'unpaid' accounts files should represent the outstanding liabilities at the balance sheet date. The auditor must call for the list of such invoices, prepared at the close of the financial period, and vouch therefrom the adjustments made on the relevant impersonal ledger accounts and the closing balances on these accounts. Each item on the list, or a representative number thereof, must be vouched by reference to the appropriate invoices, which will probably have been paid before the audit is completed. The auditor must also take the normal precautions to ensure that the list of outstanding liabilities is complete, bearing in mind the fact that the absence of a bought day book has possibly increased the risk of omissions.

It is customary in many businesses to allow *trade discount*. This discount is an allowance made by one firm to another in the same trade, and takes the form of a percentage of the recommended selling price of each article. It varies greatly in different trades, and even on different articles in the same trade, and bears no relation to the payment of cash. The deduction is made from the invoice at the time it is rendered, and in vouching the invoices the auditor should see that only the *net* figure is entered.

Cash discount, on the other hand, is an allowance made by the seller to the purchaser in consideration of the latter paying his account at once, or within the period of credit allowed. Such discount, as affecting purchases, is usually recorded in a discount column on the credit side of the cash book, the discount being entered therein, and posted to the debit of the account in the bought ledger. Where such discount is regularly taken advantage of, it is sometimes deducted from the invoice before the entry is made in the day book. Such treatment cannot be recommended, however, as the ledger account with the creditor will not agree with the statement rendered by him.

Where purchases are dealt with on a cash basis, the debits to purchases account from the totals of the appropriate columns of the cash payments book will represent the net cost of purchases, as the cheques drawn will be for the net amounts payable after deduction of cash discounts. If the firm desires to show the amount of discounts received as a separate item in its profit and loss account, it will be necessary to record discounts taken in a special column in the cash payments book and for the total of such column to be posted to the debit of purchases account and to the credit of discount account. It is doubtful, however, whether the information so obtained would justify the clerical labour involved.

(D) FORWARD PURCHASES

In many businesses forward contracts are placed for the purchase of commodities, and in such cases it will be necessary to decide whether provision should be made in the accounts for any potential loss which may arise from a fall in the market price of commodities contracted to be purchased but not yet delivered. Practice is not consistent on this point, but it would seem that so long as a company is merely following its usual procedure in entering into such contracts, and market fluctuations are not abnormal, no special provision need be made for the difference between the contract price and the market price at the date of the balance sheet. If, however, *exceptional* forward commitments have been entered into, the outcome of which may adversely affect the financial position of the company, suitable disclosure should be made in the balance sheet, and the auditor should qualify his report if it is not made (*Rex* v. *Bishirgian and Others*; the 'Pepper Pool' case). Even though the commitments are not abnormal, if it appears that a substantial loss will probably arise in connection therewith, the auditor should refer to the matter in his report unless the prospective loss is fully provided for.

§ 2. Purchases Returns

The auditor should ascertain that a proper system is in force with regard to the treatment of purchases returns, so as to ensure that full credit is obtained for all goods returned. The department concerned should advise the accounts department of all goods returned, and this advice note should be checked with the original invoice, and the proper entry made in the purchases return book. If the invoice has not already been paid, the advice note will be attached thereto in order that it may not be overlooked when payment is made. If the original invoice has been paid, a credit note should be obtained from the creditor, and placed with the invoices not yet paid, so that it can be seen that the proper deduction is made from the next payment.

The form of the purchases returns book may be of a columnar nature, and similar to that of the bought day book. Where bought day books are dispensed with, the advice notes or credit notes will be attached to the invoices in the 'unpaid' accounts files.

§ 3. Sales

(A) CREDIT SALES

The auditor should ascertain the system in force relating to the record of sales from the time that the order is received until the invoice therefor is rendered to the customer. The system adopted will naturally vary with each class of business, but a proper record must be kept of all goods sent out. Much saving of labour is effected by the adoption of a system whereby three copies of each invoice are obtained simultaneously by the use of carbon paper. The first copy will be sent to the customer, the second used as a delivery note, and the third filed in a suitable manner.

In the majority of businesses, the copy of the invoice sent to the customer will be used as the medium for posting the sale to his account in the sales ledger. If this system is adopted only the date, invoice number and the amount need be entered in the sales day book which can, of course, be provided with analysis columns if it is desired to analyse sales between different commodities or geographical areas. In many cases, however, a sales day book is dispensed with, the copies of the invoices rendered being totalled daily or weekly by an adding and listing machine to provide the credit to be made to the sales account.

In some businesses, where the number of invoices rendered to each customer within the period of credit granted is small, and such customers, in the main, pay their accounts regularly in full, even sales ledgers are dispensed with. Where such a system is operated, the copies of the invoices rendered are filed in a suitable folder for each customer until they are paid, when they will be removed and filed in numerical or other convenient order. If credit notes are issued, copies thereof will be inserted in the appropriate folders which will thus contain a record of all amounts due by trade debtors. To guard against the danger of unpaid invoices being lost or removed from the folders with fraudulent intent, control accounts must be kept, the balances on which should, at any time, equal the aggregate of the unpaid invoices, less credit notes, to be found in the customers' folders. The control accounts will be written up from the daily totals of invoices rendered, credit notes issued and cash received from debtors.

The auditor's work in connection with credit sales must, therefore, be determined by the method of accounting in operation and the view which he takes of the system of internal check in force. In all cases, however, it is clear that to follow through a representative number of transactions from the primary records as part of a series of tests 'in depth', e.g. the tracing of a sample of customers' orders to the ultimate receipt of cash, is of greater value than the mechanical checking of a large number of postings from a sales day book, or the automatic acceptance of carbon copies of sales invoices.

If a sales day book is kept, a representative number of the entries should be vouched with the carbon copies of the sales invoices and a suitable proportion of the postings checked to the sales ledgers. The casts of the book should also be tested and the totals transferred to the sales account.

Where the sales day book has been dispensed with, the carbon copies of the sales invoices being listed and added by machine, a number of the machine lists should be checked with the relevant copies of the invoices and the totals checked to the sales account.

If sales ledgers are not kept, the auditor should test thoroughly the control accounts and agree the balances thereon with the aggregate of the unpaid invoices and credit notes in the relevant customers' folders, which he should ask to be listed for this purpose. The auditor will examine the lists of unpaid accounts extracted at the date of the balance sheet and:

(a) agree the totals with the relevant control accounts;

(b) test the subsequent payment of a representative number of items;

(c) enquire carefully into any amounts cleared after the balance sheet date by what appear to be unduly large credits for returns, allowances etc.

Where the business is that of a manufacturer or wholesaler, and the goods sold are subject to purchase tax, the amount of the purchase tax must be disclosed separately on the relevant sales invoices, and should be entered in the sales day book in a separate column or listed separately on machine lists, for posting to the purchase tax account in the impersonal ledger, which in effect represents a personal account for the Customs and Excise authorities. The auditor should take care to see that all purchase tax has thus been segregated from the sale price of the goods themselves.

Occasionally sales will be made of old plant and machinery, or other assets of a capital nature. The auditor must take care to see that the amounts derived from such sales have not been included in general sales.

A representative number of sales invoices should always be checked with the goods outwards records, to ascertain that the goods in question have actually left the premises. This test is particularly useful towards the close of the accounting period, in order to discover whether sales really belonging to the succeeding period have been treated as sales for the current period, although the goods themselves may not have been despatched, and may also have been included in stock, thus creating a fictitious profit. An examination of the company's cut-off procedure will be essential in order to assess the likelihood of such instances arising.

(B) CASH SALES

It has already been pointed out that it is essential that there should be an efficient method of recording transactions of this nature. Where the book-keeping system is indifferent, it will frequently be found that the cash sales are merely entered as cash is received, and that there is no method by which the auditor can verify their accuracy. In such cases, he should disclaim any responsibility in connection with the item, and suggest that a proper system be introduced. The vouching of cash sales, where an efficient system is in force, has already been dealt with in Chapter II, 4 (c).

(C) GOODS ON SALE OR RETURN

Where goods have been sent to customers on sale or return, the auditor should ascertain that unsold goods in the hands of customers at the date of the balance sheet are not treated as sales, but are brought into account as stock in the hands of customers, at cost price, a percentage being deducted where necessary for damage. It is a primary rule that no credit should be taken for profit on a sale until the sale is actually effected.

It may be found that transactions of this nature are not properly recorded, but are included in the ordinary records of sales, the sale price being debited to the customers' accounts in the sales ledger and corresponding credit given if the goods are returned. In such a case, the debtors' balances will include goods in the hands of customers at selling price, and the sales will have been correspondingly increased. The auditor should require a schedule of goods in the hands of customers to be prepared, and if it is inconvenient to adjust the individual debtors' accounts in the sales ledgers, he should see that an appropriate adjustment is made in the sales account so that sales and debtors are reduced to their correct figures. The stock in the hands of customers should then be valued at cost or under, and brought to the credit of trading account together with the other closing stock, and shown on the balance sheet as an asset.

(D) GOODS ON CONSIGNMENT

(1) *Consignor's Books*

Following the principle that no profit should be taken until the sale is actually effected, where goods are sent on consignment, the auditor should ascertain that credit has only been taken for profit in respect of goods actually sold prior to the date of the balance sheet. Where it is desired to show the profit or loss on each consignment, a separate consignment day book is normally used, the goods sent out being passed through this book at cost, and debited to a consignment account. Any freight, insurance, or other expenses incurred by the consignor are also debited to the consignment account and on receipt of the account sales from the consignee an entry will be made, crediting the consignment account and debiting the consignee's personal account with the *gross* proceeds. The latter account will be credited with the consignee's commission and charges, the consignment account being debited. The balance on the consignment account will then represent either profit or loss, unless some portion of the goods remains unsold, in which event they should be valued at cost, or under, as the case may be, brought down as a debit balance on the consignment account, and appear as an asset on the balance sheet.

Where consignments are treated in this way, each consignment account will represent a trading account in respect of the goods sent on consignment, and consequently the sales in connection therewith will not go to the credit of sales account. The auditor should ascertain that the goods have been actually debited to the consignment account at cost, and inspect the account sales rendered by the consignee, and any account current he may have furnished, which will afford respectively an indication of the sales made, the stock-in-hand, if any, and the balance of the consignee's personal account.

Although the system above described is the best where it is desired to ascertain the result of each consignment, it is not always adopted in practice. Goods are not, as a rule, invoiced at cost price, but at an estimated selling price, sometimes for the purpose of insurance, and sometimes in order that the consignee shall not be aware of the actual cost of the goods consigned to him. In such cases, it is common to find the goods consigned treated as ordinary sales, a personal account for the consignee in the sales ledger being debited therewith. If the goods remain unsold, or if the consignment is not closed at the date of the balance sheet, and the necessary adjustments are not made, this treatment will be incorrect, as credit will have been taken for sales not actually made, and the consignee will appear as a debtor, whereas in fact he is liable only to account for the proceeds of the goods or the goods themselves. In such a case, the auditor should see that the accounts are properly adjusted, and that consigned stock remaining unsold is brought in at a proper valuation, according to the circumstances.

(2) Consignee's Books

In auditing the accounts of a business which receives goods on consignment for sale on behalf of a principal, the auditor should ascertain that such sales are kept entirely distinct from the ordinary sales effected by the business. A separate record of such sales should be kept, the total thereof being posted to the credit of the personal account of the consignor, and not to sales account. In the same way, care must be taken to see that no stock which is the property of a consignor is included as part of the stock belonging to the consignee's business. For these reasons, it is desirable that no entries should be made in the consignee's books (except the stock record in a consigned stock book) until sales are actually effected, when the various debtors concerned will be debited, and the consignor's personal account credited. Commission and charges will be debited to the consignor, and credited to the respective nominal accounts. The auditor should ascertain by the inspection of contracts, correspondence etc., the terms of the arrangement, and in cases of importance, a signed copy of the consignor's account should be obtained for the purpose of verifying the balance. It is usually necessary to reconcile the balance of such an account with the balance as shown by the consignee's books, owing to the existence of items so far dealt with by one of the parties only.

(E) SALES FOR FUTURE DELIVERY

In certain businesses contracts are entered into for forward sales, delivery being made, either at stipulated times, or as and when called for within a certain period. Although a valid contract may exist, it is not desirable that any profit should be taken in advance in connection with transactions of this nature, and the auditor should ascertain that only those goods which have been actually delivered at the date of the balance sheet have been treated as sales. This applies particularly where the goods are not yet ready for delivery, and all the necessary expenditure has not yet been incurred. Even where the goods under contracts of this nature are ready for delivery at the date of the balance sheet, they should be treated as stock and valued at cost price. Cases will sometimes be met where the purchaser pays cash for a quantity of goods, but does not take delivery of the whole, leaving a portion with the seller until the goods may be required. In such an event, it may validly be argued that the whole sale has taken place, and that profit can properly be taken in respect thereof, the goods undelivered at the date of the balance sheet not being brought into stock, but being treated as belonging to the purchaser, and held for his account. The auditor must take all the circumstances into consideration in deciding whether this treatment may be permitted.

(F) SALES UNDER HIRE-PURCHASE AGREEMENTS

Where hire-purchase trading is conducted, it is sometimes the practice to take credit for the full cash selling price of the goods in the year in which the contract is entered into and to treat the hirer as a debtor for the instalments not yet due at the date of the balance sheet. In other cases, sales account is credited only with each instalment payable under the contract as and when it becomes due, so that the profit on the contract is spread over the whole period during which the instalments are payable. The latter method is strictly the more correct, as it results automatically in no credit being taken for profit not yet realized. Where this method is followed the auditor must, however, be careful to see that the amount of the unpaid instalments, reduced by the unearned profit estimated to be included therein, is credited to the trading account and brought into the balance sheet as stock out on hire. Where credit is taken at the outset for the full selling price of the goods, provision should be made at the date of the balance sheet for an amount equal to the unrealized profit included in the unpaid balances on hire-debtors' accounts, such provision being deducted from the total of such balances in the balance sheet. Where the total of the instalments represents the cash selling price plus interest on the diminishing balance of principal outstanding, the auditor should see that credit is taken in each year only for such interest as has actually accrued during the accounting period.

§ 4. Sales Returns

The method of recording goods returned by customers should be enquired into by the auditor. Appropriate records should be kept by the gate-keeper, recording the necessary particulars, which should furnish the basis of the credit notes issued. If a sales returns day book is kept the auditor should check the casts and the postings to the impersonal ledger. A certain number of the entries should be tested with the gate-keeper's records, and in the case of large items, it may be desirable to refer to correspondence on the matter. It should be seen that all credit notes are approved and initialled by a responsible official before being issued. Where stock records are kept, the larger entries should be checked therewith to see that the goods were actually received back.

If the postings to the sales ledger are made direct from the copies of the credit notes issued, a sales returns day book will probably be dispensed with. In such circumstances, the copies of the credit notes will have been listed and added by machine at appropriate intervals to provide the totals to be posted to the debit of sales account. The machine lists should be tested by the auditor with the carbon copies of the credit notes and the totals checked to the impersonal ledger. A representative number of credit notes must be tested with the gate-keeper's records to confirm that the goods were in fact returned.

§ 5. Containers

Some firms deliver their products in cases, bags or other forms of container which are returnable by the customer. The auditor must ascertain the exact terms on which such containers are issued and give careful consideration to the method of accounting for them.

Where no charge is made to customers for containers provided that they are returned within a stated time, the auditor should satisfy himself that the records kept of issues and returns are adequate and that there is a proper system in force for invoicing customers for containers they have failed to return within the stipulated time. The records should show the numbers of each class of container in the hands of customers at the date of the balance sheet and the auditor must satisfy himself that the value placed on this stock is reasonable, having regard to normal deterioration arising from usage. The charges made to customers for containers not returned must be tested and the possibilities of bad debts, disputed accounts etc., given careful consideration.

In those cases where customers are charged with containers issued and given credit in full for the amounts charged when the containers are returned, the auditor must take care to see that normal sales and trade debtors are not inflated by such charges and that due regard is had for the liability to give credit in due course for containers in customers' hands at the date of the balance sheet. It will be appreciated that the fact that a customer has paid his account in full does not necessarily mean that he will not return containers at a later date and demand the appropriate credit note.

When the charge made to a customer for a container is higher than the credit he will be given on its return, the excess represents a profit for which immediate credit may be taken. The auditor should, therefore, satisfy himself that the accounting entries segregating the excess from the total charged are made correctly.

The provision made for the liability to accept returns from customers may be deducted from the total of trade debtors for balance sheet purposes or it may be included therein as a liability with other provisions.

§ 6. Allowances

It will be appreciated that cash defalcations may be concealed by putting through fictitious entries under the heading of 'allowances', and it is therefore of the utmost importance that the auditor should examine the allowances recorded, in order to ascertain that they are in order.

A separate allowances or credit book may be kept, which will be written up from the counterfoils or duplicates of the credit notes sent to the customers. Alternatively, the carbon copies of the credit notes may be listed by machine, the lists then becoming the equivalent of an allowances book. Credit notes or counterfoils should be initialled by the manager of the department concerned, and the auditor should test entries of any consequence, where necessary referring to the correspondence, or to any other evidence available. The totals of the allowances book or machine lists should be checked to the impersonal ledger, and the casts of the allowances book tested.

§ 7. The Journal

The use of the journal is principally confined to recording adjusting entries and all entries of a special nature for which no separate subsidiary book or record is kept.

The auditor should check the postings to the respective ledger accounts, and ascertain that each entry is in order. It is necessary that narratives should accompany the entries, explaining their nature, and referring to whatever evidence may be available for the purpose of substantiating them. Such evidence will take the form of correspondence, contracts, minutes, resolutions etc., and should be examined by the auditor.

Vouching the journal is as important as vouching cash, since journal entries may be made which have a material bearing on the accounts. Entries of a complicated nature are frequently found in this book, and these must be considered most carefully by the auditor before they are passed.

The auditor should check the casts of journal entries composed of more than one item. In some cases, both columns of the journal are cast throughout the book, for the purpose of sectional balancing, in order that the analysis of the entries relating to each ledger can be proved. Where this is done, it may be advisable for the auditor to test the casts.

In those continental countries where the Code Napoleon is in force, the use of the journal is compulsory, and all entries, of whatsoever nature, have to pass through this book in one form or another. In this way proper accounts can be prepared at any time from the material embodied in the journal.

§ 8. The Bought Ledger

As already stated, many firms have dispensed with bought ledgers by treating purchases on a cash basis. If, however, such records are kept and the auditor considers it necessary to check the details of the bought ledger, the purchases will be checked from the bought day book, the returns from the returns book, and the cash and discount from the cash book. Entries of a special nature should have been passed through the journal, and will be checked therefrom. The ledger accounts should be examined, to ascertain that every item within the sample tested has been examined by the auditor, including the balances brought forward at the commencement of the period. The ledger casts will then be tested, and the balances checked with the schedule of creditors.

Where it is not considered necessary to verify the whole of the detail the auditor will exercise his judgement in determining how far his examination should extend. Where the balances on the bought ledger can be separately proved, as referred to in § 10 below, the auditor should check the total account representing the bought ledger, and see that the balance thereon agrees with the total of the individual balances.

In examining the balances on the bought ledger, the auditor should see that the composition of each balance represents some definite item or items. If this is not apparent, and the account is of a complicated nature, it is desirable to obtain the last statement rendered by the creditor, and to compare this with the ledger account, in order to see whether there are any items in dispute, in respect of which deductions or provision ought to be made.

It has already been pointed out in § 1 that profits may be inflated by including in stock goods for which the purchase invoice has not been entered in the bought day book prior to the balance sheet date.

As stated in § 1 (c), the auditor should ascertain that invoices have been correctly dealt with for all goods which, according to the gate-keeper's or other records, were received during the last few days of the accounting period. As an additional precaution, the auditor should check the schedule of creditors' balances with their statements. If the client will agree, it is a good plan, at least once every few years, for a circular letter to be sent to all firms with whom the client deals, asking them to send direct to the auditor a statement showing the balance, if any, due to them at the balance sheet date. If this is done, the list of firms to whom the letter is to be sent must be prepared by the auditor and, obviously, such list must not be confined to firms whose accounts appear to show outstanding balances. It will normally be found that a number of firms to whom the letter is sent ignore the request but, if the check is to be effective, these must be followed up until a reply is received. The auditor will check the statements so received with the schedule of balances and enquire carefully into any discrepancies revealed.

Debit balances will occasionally be found on the bought ledger and these should be enquired into carefully. They may represent returns made after the goods have been paid for, in which case, if the item has been outstanding for any length of time and no further dealings have taken place, the auditor should ascertain whether the amount is recoverable, and does not represent items in dispute. If it does, provision should be made accordingly. Where the debit balance is occasioned by the payment of cash, the presumption is that the corresponding credit representing the invoice for the goods has not been passed through the books. Enquiry should be made to ascertain if this is the case, and if so, the outstanding liability should be entered and the goods taken into stock. Where the goods not delivered at the date of the balance sheet have been paid for in advance, a credit entry should be passed through the bought ledger account if the property in the goods resides in the purchaser, the goods being taken into stock as in transit, or as in the hands of the seller. Where the property in the goods has not passed, the item may remain as a debit balance. If the total of the debit balances in the bought ledger is material it should not be deducted from creditors but should be included in the balance sheet under the heading of sundry debtors.

When mutual dealings take place between two parties, it is usual to find an account in the bought ledger for purchases, and one in the sales ledger for sales effected. If each account is separately settled for cash, no difficulty will arise, but where the bought ledger account is settled by contra, the auditor should check the entry, and examine the voucher acknowledging the contra settlement.

If bought ledgers are not kept the auditor will verify the amounts due to creditors at the date of the balance sheet in the manner explained in § 1 (C), of this chapter.

§ 9. Sales Ledgers

(A) INTERNAL CHECK

It is important for the auditor to ascertain whether there is an efficient system of internal check in operation as regards the sales ledgers. Particular reference should be made to the following points:

(1) Whether the cashier has any control over the sales ledgers, or any books of prime entry relating thereto, other than the cash book. If this is so, the opportunities for the concealment of fraud on the part of the cashier are considerable, and the auditor should exercise additional caution accordingly.

(2) Whether the sales ledger balances are capable of separate proof, by means of total accounts as described in § 10 below. If so, the total accounts should not be under the control of the ledger clerks.

(3) Whether the ledger clerks take any part in checking their own work. Where there is a sufficient number of clerks, no one should be permitted to do this, but in small businesses such an arrangement may be unavoidable.

(4) Whether monthly or periodical statements are sent regularly to customers.

(5) The arrangements that are in force with regard to the collection of overdue accounts.

(6) Regulations relating to the passing of credit notes for returns, allowances, empties etc. These have been dealt with above.

(B) THE VERIFICATION OF POSTINGS

The extent to which the auditor may find it necessary to verify the postings to the sales ledgers will depend on the circumstances of each case. Where the system of internal check in operation is not entirely satisfactory and the transactions are not too numerous, it may be necessary to check the whole of the postings from the books of prime entry to the ledgers. Where this is not practicable, special attention should be directed to the credit postings, since any attempt to conceal defalcations will more usually take the form of fictitious credit entries. The cash and discount postings should be checked from the debit of the cash book, and this is a convenient occasion for testing discounts allowed, enquiry being made into any discounts which appear to be excessive and into cases where discount has been allowed although the term of credit has expired. The entries from the returns and allowances books should also be checked, and the auditor should go through each account to see that every item is ticked.

Where the sales ledgers are numerous, and there is a good system of internal check in operation, it will be sufficient for the auditor to test an appropriate number of postings. This can be done by checking thoroughly an individual ledger, or by taking individual accounts in different ledgers. It is preferable to check accounts that are selected completely, rather than to rely upon testing individual entries. Note should be taken of the ledgers selected for testing, so that in the course of a period of years, the whole of the ledgers may come under review in this manner. This method is often referred to as 'rotation' testing.

(C) THE VERIFICATION OF BALANCES

However good the system of internal check may be, and although total accounts may be in operation, it is necessary that a representative number of the individual balances on the sales ledgers should be examined by the auditor and checked to the schedules.

From the auditor's point of view, it is most convenient if the balances on the sales ledgers are brought down at the date of the balance sheet but this is not always done, since it is sometimes found more convenient to balance off each account at the time of settlement, rather than at any given date. Although the auditor may prefer that the balances should be brought down, he is not usually in a position to insist upon this being done, but he is entitled to request that the balance of each account at the date of balance sheet be inserted in ink at the side of the account, according to whether it is a debit or a credit balance.

When examining the accounts the auditor should ascertain the composition of each balance, it being noted whether it represents specific items of goods, or is an accumulated balance. In the latter case enquiries should be made as to the reason why the account is open as this may be due to errors or disputes in respect of which adjustments or provisions should be made. This examination of the composition of balances is particularly important where the sales ledgers are mechanized, for the reasons expressed in Chapter IV.

Balances representing goods out on sale or return, goods on consignment etc., require careful attention, and have already been dealt with in § 3. The position which arises when sales ledgers have been dispensed with was considered in § 3 (A), of this chapter.

As mentioned in § 8 above in connection with the accounts of creditors, direct confirmation of balances is frequently resorted to; in the case of sales balances, a selection of debtors would be approached for confirmation of the amounts shown against them as outstanding, using either the negative or positive method. In the former case, the balance is stated in the letter to the debtor, and he is asked to reply only if he disagrees with the amount of it; in the latter case, debtors are requested to reply positively, stating the amount which they owe in respect of items purchased. One of the most important requirements of this technique is the satisfactory composition of the sample selected, which should be fully representative of the ledger as a whole. It is also of the utmost importance for the auditor to control and supervise the operation and the follow-up procedure. The Institute of Chartered Accountants has issued a recommendation on this subject, the substance of which is reproduced in the Appendix.

(D) BAD AND DOUBTFUL DEBTS

It is not sufficient for the auditor merely to satisfy himself of the correctness of the balances on the sales ledgers. It is also his duty to ascertain, from the evidence at his disposal, whether any of the individual balances represent debts which are irrecoverable, or of such doubtful nature that some provision for possible loss should be made.

In very many cases the period of credit granted to the customers who were debtors at the date of the balance sheet will have expired by the time the final audit is commenced and the majority of the outstanding accounts will, therefore, have been paid before the auditor makes his examination of the balances. In such circumstances, the auditor will note on the schedules of balances the accounts which have since been paid in full and concentrate his attention on those still outstanding, or in respect of which only part of the amount due has since been received, or against which credits have been made for returns or allowances. In some cases, however, the period of credit granted will not have expired before the audit is completed and the auditor will, therefore, be compelled to examine a much larger number of accounts, the actual number depending upon his view of the adequacy of the system of internal check in operation.

In examining these balances, the following points should be taken into consideration:

(1) The term of credit allowed by the business.

(2) The age of the debt.

(3) Whether the account is regularly settled within the term of credit, and advantage taken of any cash discount offered.

(4) Whether payments are being made on account, and if so, whether the balance has tended to increase.

(5) Whether an old balance is being carried forward to be paid off by instalments, new goods being supplied for cash.

(6) Where bills of exchange are received, whether any bills have been dishonoured or retired.

(7) Whether any cheques have been dishonoured.

(8) Whether any notes have been made on the ledger account relating to suspension of payment, deeds of arrangement, bankruptcy, liquidation, receivership, or of the placing of the account in the hands of solicitors or debt collectors.

The auditor, before commencing his examination of the ledger balances, should ask that a schedule of bad and doubtful debts be prepared and presented to him. This schedule should be certified by the manager, secretary or other responsible official, as representing, in his opinion, a complete list of all doubtful debts for which provision should be made. Having obtained such a schedule, the auditor, as he checks the balances, will be in a position to see whether all those debts which appear to him to be bad or doubtful are included therein, and it will only be necessary for him to make further enquiries in respect of any other debts which in his view should have been included in the schedule. These should be marked on the schedule of ledger balances, and discussed by the auditor with the appropriate official. If no certified list of bad and doubtful debts is presented to the auditor, he should mark on the schedule of ledger balances all those against which he considers provision should be made.

It is impossible to lay down any hard-and-fast rule as to the valuation of book debts. The term of credit allowed in different businesses varies considerably, and may vary even in the same business for different classes of goods; moreover, in certain cases, the terms of credit are not strictly adhered to, or special terms may be granted to individual customers. The auditor, therefore, will require to exercise considerable judgement in arriving at an opinion, and each case must be taken on its merits. Where the average term of credit is, say, three months, but certain accounts are settled half-yearly or yearly, so long as the settlement is regularly effected, there may be no reason why the debt should be considered doubtful. Statute-barred debts, although they may in fact be good, should be provided for in full, as there is no legal right to recover them.

If payments have been made on account, and the balance against the debtor continues to increase, the auditor should enquire into the circumstances of the debt, and for this purpose it may be useful for him to consult any reports from credit agencies and others, as to the amount of credit that can be safely allowed, and where the amount of the debt is within such limit, and the report is of comparatively recent date, the account may be passed. The payment of an old balance by instalments, while new goods are paid for by cash, is nearly always a sign of weakness, and the old balance should, in such cases, be regarded as doubtful, and provided for accordingly. If the debtor has an arrangement of this sort with one firm, he probably has a similar arrangement with several of his other creditors, and default in payment of the agreed instalment in any one instance may result in pressure being put upon him, and cause subsequent insolvency.

The fact that bills have been dishonoured or renewed is evidence of weakness. If a provision is considered necessary, and any bills are outstanding on the account, they will, unless discounted, form part of the balance of the bills receivable account, and provision should be made against them accordingly. Where such bills have been discounted, a provision should be made in respect of the contingent liability.

Returned cheques are not necessarily a sign that the account is doubtful, as the return may be due to errors in drafting or otherwise. Where, however, the cheque has been dishonoured for lack of funds, and especially where it was in the first instance post-dated, the account should be considered doubtful.

Notes of insolvencies etc., are usually made at the head of the account concerned for the convenience of the credit controller, and the information to be derived from them is of material assistance to the auditor. In cases where the debt is of any consequence, the papers relating to the matter should be examined, and the auditor will probably be able to form an opinion from the reports of the trustees, liquidators etc., as to the proper amount of the provision which should be made. Where final dividends have been received, the balance of the account should be written off.

The fact that an account has been placed in the hands of solicitors or agents for collection, does not necessarily mean that the debt is bad or doubtful. The omission to pay may have been due to an oversight or neglect, and not to financial difficulty. The auditor should ascertain the date when the account was put into such hands, and, if any considerable period has elapsed since that time without payment being received, the account should be regarded as doubtful.

Debts should not be written off so long as there is any possibility, however remote, of some payment being obtained. If debts are written off prematurely the account may be overlooked and any opportunity that may subsequently present itself of recovering the whole, or a portion, of the debt, lost irrevocably.

Further, in the event of such debts being eventually paid, or dividends received in respect of them, the misappropriation of such sums is facilitated by the fact that no debits appear therefor in the ledger. In order to avoid this possibility, and at the same time to prevent a considerable number of bad debts remaining on the current ledgers, a bad and doubtful debts ledger is sometimes utilized, to which accounts are transferred as soon as they become doubtful. In this way a check can be kept on the bad debts, and the ultimate loss in respect of each account ascertained.

Bad debts should not be written off without the sanction of some responsible official, in order to prevent the possibility of misappropriations being concealed by the creation of fictitious bad debts. Bad debts written off during the period should be passed through the journal, the entries being initialled by the authorizing official.

As regard the amount of the provision to be made in respect of bad and doubtful debts not actually written off, this should cover the full extent of those debts regarded as bad, while the doubtful debts should be provided for according to their estimated value, having regard to the circumstances of each case.

Where the debts are very numerous and of an average amount, the provision for doubtful debts may be made by way of a percentage on the outstanding debtors, the rate of which will be arrived at from previous experience; but this should be supplemented by specific provisions, if necessary.

Where the auditor, after careful investigation, is of opinion that the provision for bad debts is insufficient, he should endeavour to induce his clients to make the additional provision which he considers necessary. If, however, he is unsuccessful, his only course is to refer to the matter in his report, stating to what extent he considers the provision is inadequate. The question is one of material importance, since it directly affects the accuracy of the profit and loss account and the balance sheet.

If sales ledgers are not kept, the unpaid invoices, dated on or before the date of the balance sheet, which are still in the customers' folders when the auditor comes to verify the balances due by trade debtors, will represent the accounts into which he must enquire. In addition, however, owing to the lack of ledger accounts, he should pay particular attention to any credits made since the date of the balance sheet (but before his inspection of unpaid accounts) which have resulted in eliminating, or reducing substantially, balances which were outstanding at the end of the financial period. Such items as returns, large allowances, bad debts written off etc., must be scrutinized carefully and the auditor must consider whether, in fact, these appear to be in order.

§ 10. Total (or Control) Accounts and Sectional Balancing

In a business of any magnitude employing handwritten records, the difficulty experienced in balancing the books may be considerable, unless some method is adopted by means of which the balances of the sales and bought ledgers can be respectively proved. This can be done by the construction of total debtors and creditors accounts, the total debtors account containing the totals of all items posted in detail to the debit and credit of the sales ledgers, and the total creditors account the totals of all items posted to the debit and credit of the bought ledgers. The balance on the total debtors account should, at the end of any given period, equal the total of the individual debit balances on the sales ledgers, less any credit balances; and correspondingly, the balance of the total creditors account should equal the net balances on the bought ledgers.

Control accounts are, of course, essential if sales ledgers are dispensed with, in order that a check be imposed on the aggregate of the unpaid invoices, less credit notes, filed in the customers' folders.

In small businesses, where there are only a few ledgers, the system of compiling total accounts for debtors and creditors respectively is sufficient for all practical purposes, but, as the number of ledgers increases, some further extension of the principle becomes necessary if balancing is to be effected accurately and promptly. Where, for instance, there are five sales ledgers, only one total debtors account being compiled representing the whole of these ledgers, and it is found that a difference exists, there will be no means of locating the difference to a particular ledger. In order to overcome this difficulty, a *separate* total account should be compiled for each ledger.

Where control accounts are in use, the auditor should check or test the postings to the total accounts and should see that the balances thereon agree with the net balances on the personal ledgers. It should be arranged that the clerks who take out the ledger balances are not concerned with the posting of those particular ledgers, or with the control accounts applicable thereto.

§ 11. Loose Leaf and Card Ledgers

Where the ledgers used are in loose leaf or card form the auditor must bear in mind the possibility of sheets or cards being accidentally lost or destroyed, and the risk of fraudulent substitution of one sheet or card for another, in order to conceal defalcations.

CHAPTER IV

THE AUDIT OF MECHANIZED AND ELECTRONIC DATA PROCESSING SYSTEMS

§ 1. Mechanical Systems

At one time all accounting records were handwritten, and after the primary documents were prepared, the details thereof were copied into day books and then again into ledger accounts. Several records were thus made of the same transaction, with the result that there was unnecessary duplication and the clerical work involved was laborious and monotonous. The increase that has taken place in the number of commercial transactions during this century and the decrease in the number of persons prepared to devote their lives to writing up a day book or sales ledger have combined to make it necessary to eliminate all records which are not absolutely essential and, where practicable, to produce two or more records by one operation.

The first step in this direction was made possible by the typewriter, with the aid of which documents could be prepared more rapidly than by hand and, by the use of carbon paper, copies of such documents provided automatically. Once sales invoices were typed and copies taken, it became apparent that to enter full details thereof in a sales day book and to repeat these details in the customer's account in the sales ledger was wasting time, as the copy of the invoice was always available for reference when required. The information recorded in the day book was, therefore, reduced to the date and number of the invoice, the customer's name and the amount chargeable to him. In the customer's account in the sales ledger only the date, number and amount of the invoice were shown. Further consideration showed that the information recorded in the day book could be reduced still more by the elimination of the customer's name if the posting to the sales ledger were made direct from the carbon copies of the sales invoices. The day book then became a mere record of invoice numbers and amounts, its sole purpose being to provide figures of total sales. The introduction of adding and listing machines has now, in many cases, resulted in the final elimination of the sales day book in its old form. The carbon copies of the sales invoices are listed and added by the machine and the list so prepared is suitably bound or filed to form the equivalent of a sales day book.

Some of the further changes in the process of eliminating, or reducing, the entries in books of prime entry have been:

(a) Typing all cheques drawn and using the carbon copy as a cash payments book, the totals of which are entered in a general cash book.

(b) Printing official receipts in such a form that the carbon copies thereof, totalled by machine, form a receipts cash book and the media for posting the amounts received to the credit of the customers' accounts. By reason of the *Cheques Act 1957* many firms no longer issue receipts and in such cases remittances received are listed by machine, such lists forming the cash receipts book and posting media.

(c) The elimination of bought day books and bought ledgers by dealing with purchases and accounts for services etc., on a cash basis.

(d) The elimination of sales ledgers by filing all invoices rendered in suitable folders until they are paid.

Each of these changes has brought new problems to the auditor by reason of the elimination of records, but the principles of auditing are not affected thereby. The auditor has, however, been compelled to change his methods of verifying transactions and to give much more attention to primary documents owing to the absence of day books but, in the main, this has improved the value of his audit.

The mechanization of accounting records by the use of book-keeping machines, punched-card systems, or electronic computers represents merely one further step in the evolution of accounting. The auditor has again, as a result of such systems, to vary his procedures but the purposes of his audit remain the same.

§ 2. Internal Control

Before he reports on an accounting statement an auditor is concerned to satisfy himself that the system of record-keeping maintained by an organization (whatever that method may be) is adequate to ensure that all transactions are correctly recorded, allocated and summarized and that accounting statements prepared from the records are in agreement with such records and correct in accounting principle.

In order to assess the efficiency of an accounting system the auditor must make a detailed study of the methods by which the accounting data are originated and of their flow through the system, including the internal controls that are incorporated into the procedures. The internal control questionnaires already described are helpful in this connection.

The most common principles of internal control are:

(A) CLERICAL ORGANIZATION

(i) the separation of the functions of record-keeping from physical control of assets, and

(ii) the breakdown of the clerical functions in a manner which ensures that the work of one clerk is regularly reviewed by another and that no clerk performs the whole of the clerical steps involved in a transaction, e.g. the ledger clerk is not permitted to write up the day books or cash books.

(B) COMPARISON OF RECORDS WITH EVIDENCE ORIGINATING OUTSIDE THE CLERICAL SYSTEM

(i) Physical checks; constant checking of the records against physical quantities, for example:

    (a) comparison of the stores ledger with physical stocks, and

    (b) inspection of machinery and comparison with plant ledger.

(ii) Comparison of records with documents originating outside the organization, e.g. comparison of suppliers' statements received with the suppliers' accounts in the purchase ledger.

(C) CLERICAL CONTROLS

(i) *Proving the data entering the system*

Whenever a transaction gives rise to two or more documents originating at different points in the system, a reconciliation may be attempted, e.g.

    (a) the clock card of each employee contains details of the number of hours worked by him; if time sheets are prepared, the hours entered on the time sheets may be proved against those on the clock cards;

(*b*) a comparison of invoices received with a copy of the original order to the supplier.

(ii) *Proving that original data are a true record*

This check ensures that the data entering the system have been reviewed by a responsible person within the organization and been passed by him as being an accurate and true record of a transaction, e.g. the authorization of an allowance for damaged goods or the writing off of a bad debt.

(iii) *Proving that data once entered into the system are processed through the system consistently*

These checks ensure that once data enter the system they pass through all stages consistently, e.g. that items entered into the sales day books are posted correctly both to the customers' accounts and the sales analysis. Checks which ensure this in manual systems are:

(*a*) pre-listing of amounts to be posted and proof against the totals posted. (This control feature is also widely used in mechanized accounting.);

(*b*) the cross casting of analyses and comparison of the total analysed with the account or total which required analysis;

(*c*) maintenance of total accounts.

The auditor should satisfy himself that:

(*a*) all transactions which take place are properly recorded;

(*b*) all items recorded are valid records of actual transactions of the organization;

(*c*) once recorded they are processed through the organization's records accurately, according to sound accounting principles.

It is difficult to appreciate the pattern of a system and the controls built into it without pictorial assistance and, as described in Chapter I, it is now standard practice for the auditor to draw a flow chart which depicts in graphical form the progress of a transaction through the system, showing the points at which checks take place. Another typical flow chart, illustrating the progress of a purchase invoice through a system, is given on page 102.

PURCHASES DOCUMENT FLOW AND CONTROLS EXTERNAL TO ACCOUNTS DEPT.

Stages of Routine	1 PURCHASING DEPT. (Issue of Order)	2 SUPPLIER	3 RECEIVING AND INSPECTION	4 STORES	5 ACCOUNTS	6 PURCHASING DEPT.	7 ACCOUNTS
	ORDER TOP / 2ND / 3RD	INVOICE / DELIVERY NOTE	GOODS INWARDS NOTE 1 / 2 / 3				
Procedure	Order made out in triplicate. Top Copy to Supplier 2nd Copy to Stores 3rd Copy retained	(1) Invoice rec'd passed to Accounts (2) Delivery Note accompanies goods	(1) Goods rec'd (2) Goods Inwards Note made out in triplicate.		Invoice received and passed to Purchasing Dept.	Invoice, Delivery Note, and Goods Inwards Note received	Certified Invoice received
Internal Control	(1) Orders all on printed Serial numbered forms. (2) Strict control of blanks properly authorised. (3) Departmental Requisition required before order placed.		(1) Delivery Note checked against goods and initial'd. (2) Goods Inwards Notes prepared. 1st and 2nd copies to Stores with Delivery Note. 3rd retained by inspection as reference.	(1) Goods rec'd and stored. (2) Goods Inwards Notes initialled. 1st copy passed to Purchasing Dept. with Delivery Note. 2nd copy retained as reference.	Internal Serial No. inserted for control purposes	(1) Agree all documents with copy Order and initial after checking quantity, price, and quality. (2) Pre-List and pass Invoices to Accounts	(1) Batch and agree no Invoices missing (2) Pre-list invoice totals and agree with Purchasing Dept. total.

The object of the flow chart is to enable the auditor to determine the efficiency of the system of internal control and its points of weakness, and hence the amount of detailed checking which is required. The auditor will then test the system by his audit procedures to see that it is actually enforced and working satisfactorily. The chart also enables him to determine the 'audit trail', i.e. the flow of the transaction through the records. Once he has a clear audit trail the auditor may select any transaction and follow it through the records from any point until it reaches its final entry, e.g. in the purchases account or a supplier's account. Similarly the auditor can select any item and trace it backwards through the system to its original source document.

Mechanized accounting does not alter in any way the aims of the auditor; he is still concerned to see that the system of record-keeping is adequate for the organization's purpose. It does, however, mean that in most systems the techniques and procedures adopted by the auditor may require modification. It is a feature of mechanized systems that they handle a large volume of transactions, and it is impracticable, and indeed unnecessary, for an auditor to check every item. The auditor must, therefore, rely on the system of internal control and ensure that a sound system is operated which will enable him to dispense with detailed checking and to use sampling procedures.

A large section of the report of the Institute of Chartered Accountants on mechanized accounting and the auditor is given in the Appendix, to which reference should be made.

Mechanized systems are advantageous when a large number of similar transactions is recorded. By treating all similar transactions in a uniform manner, an accounting machine is able to operate at speed, bringing benefits of economy of effort, clarity of printing, automatic balancing of accounts and accuracy. All mechanized systems demand a clearly laid out routine for each major type of transaction, e.g. purchases, cash receipts, sales, cash payments etc., covering the detailed procedures laid down concerning the flow of documents to the machine, and the machine operations performed. That part of the routine covering the machine processing operations is normally prepared by the manufacturers of the machine and 'built in' to a programme panel which is attached to the machine. In keyboard accounting machine systems, it is unusual for the machine operator or supervisor to know how to alter the programme of the machine apart from changing printing positions. The assistance of the manufacturer's staff would be required for other alterations. In punched-card installations many supervisors are trained in programming the equipment and do, therefore, know how to alter the machine's programme. The auditor should satisfy himself that the changes made are strictly controlled and do not seriously weaken the internal control procedure. He must therefore be informed of all changes, preferably in advance of their coming into effect.

The detailed procedures laid down are of great assistance to the auditor in his task as he is able to follow the passage of transactions through the system stage by stage. The difficulty from the auditor's point of view is that in many systems it is difficult or even impossible for him to trace an audit trail for particular transactions. The report on mechanized accounting issued by the Institute (substantially reproduced in the Appendix) dealt with many of these difficulties and suggested remedies. The section entitled 'Specific Audit Difficulties' should be referred to in this connection.

Although suffering from many of the disadvantages mentioned in the Institute's report, mechanized systems do provide the auditor with safeguards which are not present in manual systems. Mechanization itself calls for clearly defined routines which are not always present in manual systems, and arithmetical checks are usually built into the machine programmes.

Machine systems may be analysed into two parts:

(*a*) that part of the system which is outside the machine, i.e. the receipt of source documents and their progress through the system to the machine, together with that part of the system controlling the progress and use of the figures and reports prepared by the machine, and

(*b*) that part of the system directly concerned with the operation of the accounting machines.

The first part of the system, although designed to fit into the mechanized system and subject to time limitations laid down by the machine processing schedule, is similar to that of a manual system and subject to the same internal control and audit routines.

The second part of the system, e.g. ledger posting, analysis and report producing is subject to machine capabilities and limitations.

§ 3. Keyboard Accounting Machine Systems

The errors that arise in such systems fall into one or other of the following categories:

(a) Posting data to the wrong account.

(b) Posting data incorrectly.

(c) Picking up the opening balance incorrectly.

(d) Calculating the new balance wrongly.

Many controls have been devised to eliminate these sources of error and the auditor must examine each system carefully to ensure that adequate controls are operated, distinguishing carefully between those which are human controls and those which are programmed into the machines. It will be appreciated that the mechanical controls are normally more reliable than those performed by staff.

The main controls operated are first to batch and pre-list all source documents entering the machine room to obtain a control total, which is subsequently used to ensure that all documents have been processed accurately through the system, and then to adopt the following additional controls:

(A) POSTING TO ACCOUNTS CORRECTLY

The accounts to be posted are selected for the machine operator by another member of the staff. The reason for this is primarily to speed up the posting operation but it also serves as a measure of clerical internal check by subdividing the process. This work is usually done by a junior who will either 'stuff' the invoices in the appropriate part of the card ledger, 'pull' the ledger cards from the ledger or 'off set' the ledger accounts to be posted.

If the organization is a large one it may have coded the personal ledger accounts which will enable the accounting machine to operate an arithmetical check on the account number. Under this system the account numbers to be posted are endorsed on the source documents or posting media. On each ledger account card, the account number is added to the closing balance (or the closing balance is deducted from the account number) to achieve a 'hash' total which is entered by the machine on the account card. The machine will then be programmed to compare the account number on the posting medium with that included in the 'hash' total and if they do not agree will reject the entry. (See 'prior proof' below.) Although this proof is mechanical, and therefore accurate, the auditor must bear in mind that it depends on how accurately the medium is coded, and he should therefore test this process thoroughly.

Audit checks

The auditor can test the efficiency of the method of control adopted by testing the purchase ledger with supplier's statements for mis-postings, or sales ledger accounts with remittances, and by scrutinizing ledger accounts for adjusting entries.

(B) PROVING DATA POSTED CORRECTLY

During the posting operation the accounting machine will store a total of all items which have been posted and print it out at the bottom of the proof sheet (i.e. copy of items posted). The proof total should agree with the total of the pre-list. The supervisor should initial the pre-list and proof sheet and enter the totals in a control book. The total will then be posted to a control account for the particular ledger affected. Should the total not agree it is a simple and speedy process to check the pre-list against the proof sheet. This check will in most cases ensure that data have been correctly posted to the ledger. It must be borne in mind, however, that the check does not locate compensating errors (which are very infrequent) nor does it prove that items have been posted to the correct account. In some cases, however, it does prove that opening balances have been picked up correctly.

Audit checks

The auditor should examine the supervisor's control book, pre-lists and proof sheets to see that they have been agreed and initialled by the supervisor. The auditor should insist that a correction journal be kept and examination of this will reveal the frequency of errors and their type and cause.

(C) PROVING THAT OPENING BALANCES HAVE BEEN PICKED UP CORRECTLY

In order that the accounting machine may calculate the new balance it is essential that the opening balance be entered into the machine accurately. There are various way of ensuring the accuracy of the opening balance, the most common being the following:

(i) '*Double pick up proof*' – which depends on the old balance being picked up twice, once before the posting is made and once after. The machine will in effect deduct one from the other and they should thus cancel out leaving the amount posted in the machine. The machine will then print out the posting, or better still a zero, which indicates that the two balances picked up have agreed. This is a fairly good check, but it occasionally fails as the operator can twice pick up the opening balance incorrectly. This error does not, however, occur with any frequency.

(ii) '*Visual proof*' – in this case the machine prints the old balance picked up on the ledger card and the operator can then check the 'pick up' with the old balance visually. This, however, is not a very satisfactory method of proof and if the auditor finds it in use he should give due consideration to its obvious weaknesses.

(iii) '*Prior Proof*' – In both of the above methods, if there has been a mistake in picking up the old balance an incorrect entry will have been made on the statement and ledger card. To avoid this a method of prior proof has been developed by which a verification figure is incorporated on the ledger card. The verification figure may be, for example, twice the account balance, or the account number less the account balance.

Example 1 – Verification figure – twice the account balance:

Account Balance	..	£112·81
Verification Figure ..	..	£225·63

The operator first enters £225·63 the verification figure, and then £112·81, the old balance. The machine doubles the old balance entered and so computes a second figure £225·63 which it compares with that originally entered. If the account balance has been correctly entered the two verification figures will agree.

Example 2 – Verification figure – account number less the account balance.

Account No. 9765		
Account Balance	..	£112·81
Verification Figure ..	..	£9,652·19

The operator first enters the verification figure of £9,652·19 and next the old balance of £112·81 which the machine will add to the verification figure. The operator will then enter the account number from the posting media and the machine will compare this entry with the number it has computed. If these agree then the opening balance has been correctly entered and the correct account selected; the machine will print a zero and tabulate to the posting position. If the figures do not agree the machine will print something other than a zero – or automatically clear the incorrect information and return to the start position.

The methods of proof described in (i) and (iii) above are programmed into the machine operations and the auditor may rely on them unless the machine is found to be faulty. He should, however, bear in mind that the following errors may still arise:

(i) *'double pick up proof'* – errors due to double incorrect pick up of the opening balance.

(ii) *'visual proof'* – errors passing unnoticed by the operator.

(iii) *'prior proof'* – the item will be posted to the wrong account if the posting medium is itself incorrectly coded.

(D) PROVING THAT CLOSING BALANCES HAVE BEEN COMPUTED CORRECTLY

Proving new balances is not considered necessary after each posting as machines have now achieved an extremely high degree of mechanical accuracy. If the opening balance and posting are correct, the new balance should also be correct. Periodical checks are obtained, however, by the maintenance of control accounts. The totals of each batch of entries are posted to these accounts, the balances of which can be compared with the total of the balances on all accounts comprised in one control. This is normally done at the month end, proving:

(*a*) that all accounts with balances have been listed and are in the ledger;

(b) that all accounts (including those with 'nil' balances) have had their closing balances correctly computed.

In installations where the majority of the accounts are posted daily a check on closing balances may be maintained by:

(a) listing the closing balances on all accounts; and

(b) deducting the pre-list total of items posted that day.

The balance then remaining should be the previous balance on the control account, thus proving that closing balances have been correctly computed.

Audit checks

The auditor should examine the supervisor's control book and confirm that the extraction sheets of monthly balances have been agreed with the control account totals.

Error routines

It is essential that errors by machine operators should be adjusted under the control of the supervisor and initialled. Special routines for error correction will have been laid down and the auditor should check the adjustment journal through which all errors and adjustments should be passed. As mentioned above, this journal is a useful guide to the efficiency of the installations.

Changes in Audit Procedures

If the auditor is satisfied that the many arithmetical and other controls included in the accounting system are adequate and are being operated properly he may safely reduce the amount of detail checking which is performed, and devote more time to the systems audit, matters of accounting principle and the verification of assets and liabilities.

§ 4. Punched-Card Systems

The records maintained by keyboard machines are in the main very similar to manual records in that a visual audit trail is available – even keyboard analysis machines print out a tally roll of all entries made and the auditor can, if he wishes, check the entries.

Punched-card records, however, appear less like conventional records and the auditor therefore has to study the system very carefully. Many stages of the operation, e.g. sorting, will take place without the machine tabulating each individual card as it is entered. It is, therefore, more difficult for the auditor to distinguish an audit trail and he must be content to check the analysis by total controls and test checking.

The auditor of a punched-card system must investigate the system used very thoroughly, paying particular attention to the checks programmed into the machines. He will be relying on the accuracy of the system itself more than when auditing keyboard machines, on the principle that if the system is adequate and the input verified as correct, the results should also be correct.

The auditor's approach should be:

(i) to satisfy himself that the source data are correct by means of:
   (a) reviewing the internal control procedures governing the preparation of documents internally and the receipt of documents from external organizations; and
   (b) ensuring that the controls built into the system relating to the conversion of source data into punched cards are adequate and working effectively.

(ii) to examine the system of processing the data to ascertain that adequate safeguards are built in to ensure that:
   (a) data are processed accurately;
   (b) no data are mislaid or altered during processing.

(iii) to examine the intermediate or final tabulations and compare them with the source data to ensure that the processing has been accurately performed.

The audit of a punched-card installation is, therefore, concerned to a large extent with proving the accuracy of the source data and its conversion into punched cards. The flow of information before it enters the machine room is similar to that in any manual system and is subject to the same controls, but is also subject to the processing time schedule of the punched-card department, i.e. all information must be in the hands of the punched-card installation before processing starts.

The specific audit difficulties encountered, apart from finding the audit trail, are that punched-card machines operate on numerical code systems and, therefore, all accounts have number references instead of alphabetic descriptions; narrative detail is abbreviated to avoid waste of column capacity on the punched cards. The cards themselves are unintelligible to the auditor unless the 'field' headings are printed on the face of the card and the punchings in the card interpreted by being passed through an interpreter machine (which is not usual). The results of punched-card processing are tabulated on long sheets which in many cases are not ruled and headed thus being meaningless to the auditor until he has familiarized himself with the numerical codings.

Codes

The operation of a punched-card system depends upon the coding of much of the information that is to be recorded on cards, the most obvious example being the use of account numbers. Other examples are the assignment of numbers to branches, departments, employees (for payroll and costing), expense classifications etc., according to the nature of the business. The chief object of coding is to facilitate sorting, and for this reason most codes are numerical only, although an *alpha/numeric* code may be used where the number of available columns is limited.

All codings in current use must be recorded in schedules or registers (i.e. manuals) which are available to those members of the office staff who either originate or interpret them. In practice, codes tend to be amended and extended fairly frequently and unless the auditor makes special requests, he may find that code changes are not reported to him. He should examine the system for altering codes and advise that all changes be authorized by a responsible member of the accounting staff and amendment slips passed to each holder of the manual immediately.

PROVING ACCURACY OF INPUT

All documents passed to the punched-card department should be batched and pre-lists made by the department concerned of all material data, i.e. accounts, numbers, codes and amounts, and the batch totals must be entered in a register. The documents should already have been coded by a responsible person.

On receipt by the machine room the batches will be passed to a punch operator who will punch holes in cards to represent the information contained on the source documents. This is an important task as, if the data punched on to the cards is incorrect the error will pass through the whole of the system. The punch operator will therefore pass the batch of documents and the punched cards to a verifying operator who will re-punch the cards as verification. There are two types of verifications in common use.

Under the first system the verifying punch locks if the key depression made by the verifying operator is different from that required. The operator then knows that something is wrong, since, if on re-checking the data on the source document it is found that the key indexed is the correct one it follows that the card is wrongly punched and must be corrected. This system does, however, depend on the accuracy and intelligence of the operator and it sometimes happens that a verifying operator will pass an incorrect card if in a hurry. The auditor should be aware of this possibility although it should rarely arise in well conducted installations.

The second system of verification uses a verifying punch which causes the holes originally punched to be ovalized. The cards are then passed through a mechanical verifier which rejects all cards containing a hole which is not oval. This system takes the onus of rejecting cards away from the operator.

The batch of verified cards may then be run through the tabulator set at 'non print' to obtain control totals which can be agreed with the original pre-lists. This proof ensures that no source document has been omitted from the punching process and no errors made in punching. It is better, however, from the auditor's point of view if the tabulator prints a list, which is safely filed, as he can then check the list against the batch of source documents in detail.

PROVING ACCURACY OF PROCESSING

The totals provided by the listing should then be entered into a machine room control book which will provide total controls for all subsequent processing. If a portion only of the cards is actioned the balance of the cards should be listed and the combined totals agreed with the controls to ensure that no cards are omitted. This is not a long job as cards can be listed at speeds of around 400 per minute and faster.

The final results of punched-card processing represent printed tabulations of information which should contain the information contained on the cards. If the auditor insists that the original batch number and document control number be punched into the card as part of the original data it will be possible for him to check the tabulations against the individual source documents. In some cases the auditor may have to refer for the detailed make up of items to subsidiary tabulations, but in all cases there should be a sound system of cross-referencing, with references punched into the cards and of control totals entered in registers which the auditor should check. The example given on page 114 illustrates these controls:

(1) The invoices received are verified in the usual way, i.e. they are agreed with the original copy order and delivery note, passed for payment and initialled by the competent authorities. The invoices will be coded for expense classification and supplier number and then passed to a clerk who batches the documents and makes a pre-list of all the important information, i.e. supplier's account number, expense classification numbers, quantity and value.

(2) The totals are entered into a departmental control register and the pre-list passed to the machine room with the documents. .

(3) The machine room punches a card for each item on each invoice for analysis purposes and a supplier's payment card for the total of each invoice. The cards are verified and then tabulated; the analysis cards being totalled and agreed with the supplier's card for each invoice and the supplier's cards listed to provide an invoice register, the total of which is agreed with the pre-list and posted to the total creditors account. The documents should then be filed in batch order. The punched cards should, where possible, contain a reference to the original invoice and batch number.

(4) The supplier's cards are sorted into customer account order and then merged in the outstanding card file until their due date of payment.

(5) On the payment date the cards due for payment are sorted out and listed to provide total payments due to each creditor. A remittance advice and cheque may then be prepared by

SPECIMEN PURCHASES ACCOUNTING ROUTINE
BY PUNCHED CARD

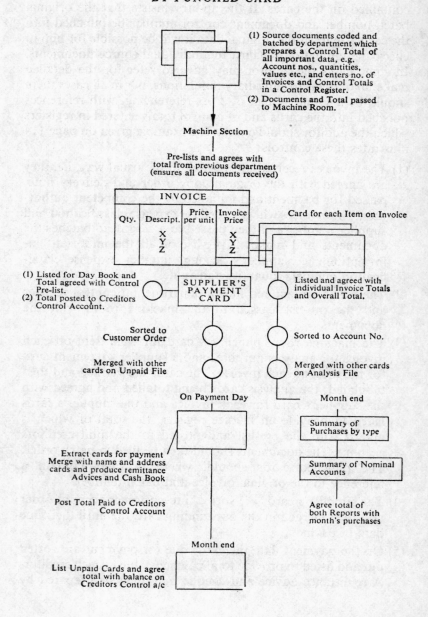

(1) Source documents coded and batched by department which prepares a Control Total of all important data, e.g. Account nos., quantities, values etc., and enters no. of Invoices and Control Totals in a Control Register.
(2) Documents and Total passed to Machine Room.

Machine Section

Pre-lists and agrees with total from previous department (ensures all documents received)

INVOICE			
Qty.	Descript.	Price per unit	Invoice Price
	X Y Z		X Y Z

Card for each Item on Invoice

(1) Listed for Day Book and Total agreed with Control Pre-list.
(2) Total posted to Creditors Control Account.

SUPPLIER'S PAYMENT CARD

Listed and agreed with individual Invoice Totals and Overall Total.

Sorted to Customer Order

Sorted to Account No.

Merged with other cards on Unpaid File

Merged with other cards on Analysis File

On Payment Day

Month end

Extract cards for payment Merge with name and address cards and produce remittance Advices and Cash Book

Summary of Purchases by type

Summary of Nominal Accounts

Post Total Paid to Creditors Control Account

Agree total of both Reports with month's purchases

Month end

List Unpaid Cards and agree total with balance on Creditors Control a/c merging the creditor's name and address cards with the payment cards. A copy of this tabulation serves as a cash payments sheet and copies of the remittance advice as a visual ledger record.

(6) The total of the payments will then be deducted from the creditors control account.

(7) The cards remaining in the unpaid file should agree in total with the balance on the control account. These cards are tabulated at least once a month and agreed with the control account.

(8) The analysis cards are sorted into nominal account and stock account numbers and filed until the end of a period when they are tabulated to provide statistics of nominal expenses incurred and purchases made. These tabulations serve as subsidiary records to the nominal ledger.

(9) The totals of the analyses should be agreed with the periodical totals of suppliers' cards to ensure that all analysis cards have been processed.

The auditor should check each stage of the system operated to ensure that the controls included therein are in fact carried out. The supervisor's control sheets should be examined and the initialling of the tabulations checked. The auditor may require a tabulation of the unpaid file to be made at odd intervals to ensure that it agrees with the control account total.

The system of cross-referencing should enable the auditor to test the final tabulations against the source documents as each item should be referenced to the batch number and invoice concerned.

§ 5. Electronic Data Processing Systems

(*Note: In order to avoid confusion between audit 'programmes' and computer 'programs', particularly when dealing with 'computer audit programs', throughout this section the now conventional spelling of 'program' as related to a set of computer instructions, has been adopted.*)

This term applies to the processing of data by means of electronic computers. Digital computers – the type used for business purposes – are controlled by a program of instructions, stored in the equipment, which enables them to store information, perform complete processing routines upon that information and any new data fed into the machine, and to print out final results in readable form without human intervention.

A computer operates by passing electric impulses through complicated circuits which have been constructed in such a way as to enable the computer to add, subtract, multiply, divide, move data from one position to another and to compare two or more quantities and determine which is the largest or smallest. All data must, therefore, be converted to a form readable by the machine.

THE PROGRAM

The processing within the computer and the operation of subsidiary equipment, i.e. input and output devices are controlled by means of the program, i.e. a detailed list of instructions to be followed in performing each step in the processing. The program is contained on punched cards, punched paper tape or magnetic tape and is fed into the computer before each processing operation.

The program is designed and constructed by programmers skilled in the operation of the particular model of computer being used, under instruction from the systems analysts. The programmers analyse the process to be performed and construct a set of coded instructions to the computer. The program must cover every possible situation arising in the proposed routine – including errors – and also control the input and output equipment. As programming is such a complex operation the process is first set out in the form of a flow chart (or 'block diagram') describing the broad outlines of the procedure to be followed. Once this outline of the procedure has been agreed, a flow chart of the detailed procedure within the computer in readable, although abbreviated, form is constructed. The programmer will then prepare a draft program in machine code which will be tested and amended until a workable program is obtained. A readable flow chart of the revised computer procedure will then be prepared, setting out the tests and checks included in the program.

At first sight electronic data processing presents the auditor with grave difficulties, because:

(a) all information must be presented to the computer in machine-sensible form;

(*b*) the program of instructions is in machine-sensible form;

(*c*) all processing within the computer is performed electronically, and, therefore, there is no visible evidence of the processing for the auditor to examine.

This problem will be aggravated in the future as means of direct ('on-line') input to the computer are developed, i.e. the development of machines which enable an operator to index information on to a keyboard which will cause electronic impluses to be fed into the computer.

The absence of a visible audit trail does not, however, mean that a trail does not exist. Instead of checking the detail of individual transactions through the various stages of the accounting routine the auditor must examine the routine itself. Computers have proved in practice to be extremely reliable and if a computer failure does occur it is generally caused by a failure of a part of the circuitry. To prevent this the computer engineer will deliberately operate the computer on very low voltage in order to reveal any circuits which are in need of replacement, thus avoiding breakdowns during processing. Auditors can, therefore, largely rely upon their accurate functioning. If an adequate routine is laid down, the auditor may be assured that each transaction processed through it has been dealt with in accordance with that routine. It follows, therefore, that once he has proved the effectiveness of the routine the auditor has, in fact, checked the processing of every item subjected to that routine.

Clearly, internal control is extremely important in computer systems. The data processing department itself will usually be centralized and operated as a service to the other departments, which in itself serves as a measure of clerical internal control, as the custody of assets and the preparation of original documents is not within the control of the computer operators. Fraud would thus normally require the collusion of members of the programming and operating staff. Computers, however, operate only according to the instructions and data given to them and cannot trace errors in data in the same way as a person can. If the data conforms to the instructions given in its program a computer will accept and process it. Great care, therefore, must be taken to ensure that all data provided to the computer is both accurate and complete. 'Reasonableness' and other checks on input are, however, commonly incorporated in machine programs, so that certain invalid data is rejected before processing.

The internal control routines which are applied to the receipt and preparation of documents within the firm must clearly be strict. Errors may not be detected by the computer and, even if they are, valuable computer time will be lost as incorrect data will be referred back to its original source for correction.

INTERNAL CONTROL

The internal control procedures incorporated into the data processing system will cover three major aspects:

(1) the preparation of *input* data, and its transfer to the computer;

(2) the *processing* of data within the computer;

(3) the preparation of *output* and its distribution.

These controls will consist of:

(a) *clerical* controls similar to those found in manual and mechanical systems;

(b) overall *administrative* controls, arising chiefly from the risks implicit in

  (i) concentration of power in the E.D.P. department;

  (ii) carrying a large number of files of important data centrally stored; and

  (iii) storing data in a form which is highly inflammable, concentrated, sensitive to temperature and atmospheric conditions, and dependent for processing on machinery which is susceptible to breakdown;

(c) controls 'built into' the computer circuitry by the manufacturers to ensure accuracy;

(d) *procedural* controls over processing and operating, which may be inserted in the program by the programmers in conjunction with the auditors when the program is written, or which simply codify the operating routines to be followed by the E.D.P. and the user departments in their relations with each other; and

(e) *systems development* controls, intended to ensure a valid system of processing whenever new applications are devised, meeting the requirements of management and user departments. These aims are achieved by

  (i) the use of standard documentation;

  (ii) the use of standard procedures, wherever possible;

  (iii) specifying rigid authorization procedures whenever new applications are envisaged, or existing programs amended or extended;

  (iv) the adoption of adequate testing routines prior to implementation;

  (v) instituting a comprehensive system of program and document security.

Controls on Input

The controls over input preparation should ensure that input is:

(*a*) a valid record of an actual transaction;

(*b*) authorized by a responsible official;

(*c*) correctly allocated to an account; and

(*d*) correctly translated into machine-sensible codes.

At present most computer input is initially on documents which are:

 (i) raised by persons authorizing transactions; or

 (ii) received from outside organizations.

These documents should be subjected to the same control procedures as in manual systems, batched and pre-listed for quantity, value, account codes etc. The number of transactions should also be recorded before being transferred to the input preparation section. The input preparation section will translate the data into machine-sensible form, i.e. into punched card, punched paper tape or magnetic tape. In order to prove accurate translation the equipment will total the data as it is processed and provide totals to be agreed with the pre-list. The pre-list figures can be in the form of a 'hash' total, i.e. a combined total of account numbers, quantities and values which serves no purpose other than its control function. The number of transactions will also be counted to provide a 'a record count' which is used to ensure that no items are omitted during subsequent processing. Both the totals and the record count will be entered as input.

Many types of input preparation equipment provide a printed list of all items which have been included in the input, thus providing the auditor with a visible record against which he can check the original documents.

The validity of account and code numbers can be checked during input preparation by adding a check digit as an integral part of each account and code number to make each such number comply with a simple formula. The input machinery will then subject each account code number to a simple test in order to prevent incorrect data being fed to the computer.

Many forms of computer input are at present prepared as a by-product of a control routine, e.g. the creation of punched paper tape by cash registers. The auditor should examine the machine controls very carefully.

Controls on Computer Processing

(I) The *clerical and procedural controls* over computer processing consist mainly of:

(a) segregating the systems analysts and programmers, who design and construct the programs, from the operation of the computer and storing of the programs;

(b) segregation of input preparation and control from the operation of the computer;

(c) keeping a close check on the use of the computer by recording in a log book the programs run and the time started and finished, to prevent unauthorized processing;

(d) controlling the storage of the programs (and their issue to the computer operators and programmers), storage of the working files of input data, and storage of applications not being processed currently;

(e) strict control over input and output files which it is desired to retain for rebuilding of current files should they be damaged;

(f) supervision of all test operations on the computer by programmers.

The above controls, if operated, should ensure that no unauthorized alterations to programs or data are made nor any unauthorized processing of data performed.

The computer operator is able through the console of the computer to monitor the processing operation, stop and start the hrutine and enter data manually. The auditor should ascertain utat an adequate control system is enforced to ensure that no onauthorized data is processed.

(II) *'Built in' processing controls* consist of the following:

Input Section of Computer

The computer may have controls built into the circuitry to ensure correct reading of input. The reading equipment may read the data twice and compare the result, ensuring that data is transmitted to the storage section of the computer only when it has been proved accurate.

The computer may also be built to operate on an odd or even parity code. When the input machinery is preparing data it will insert an extra 'bit' (binary digit) if necessary, in order to make the number of digits for each character odd or even as the case may be. When the computer is reading data in, it will reject any character that does not conform to the parity codes, thus signalling errors. This check is useful in ensuring that dust or atmospheric conditions have not caused a digit to be obscured.

Processing Section of Computer

Controls built into central processing equipment include the duplication of certain circuits in order to repeat calculations separately and compare the result, thus proving the accuracy of the calculation. Some processors are designed so that the complements of the true figures are used in repeating the calculation, which is then compared with the original calculation. This method allows a different combination of machine components to be used.

The computer engineer will also test the computer regularly by using a test program on specially prepared data. Most failures are preceded by a loss of efficiency and by running the machine at low voltage the engineer is able to locate faulty circuits and replace them before they fail.

The computer will also conduct parity checks on data as it is moved from one location to another inside the computer.

Output Section of Computer

The computer may be designed in such a way that as it prints out data, punches cards or tape, the printers or punches activated cause electric impulses which are compared with those already prepared by the computer, to ensure that the output section is functioning accurately. Magnetic tape output equipment will be equipped with a reading and a writing head. As the data is written on to the tape it will be read simultaneously by the reading head and compared by the computer with the data which should have been written, thus ensuring accurate output.

(III) *Programmed procedural controls*, which are built into the programs, are designed to ensure that:

(*a*) only data relevant to the application is processed, so as to prevent tapes of other applications or old input tapes being read-in as input by mistake;

(*b*) magnetic input tapes cannot be inserted in the output deck by mistake, thus eliminating the risk of data being lost (new entries on tape automatically erase the old records);

(*c*) tapes are not destroyed prematurely by re-use;

(*d*) all items are processed;

(*e*) all data is processed accurately.

The input tapes will include an identifying label which will contain details of the application, the date the tape was made and its sequence. The computer will check each tape to ensure that it belongs to the application being processed and is the next in sequence. This prevents irrelevant data being processed and destroying other records.

In order to prevent input tapes being erroneously fitted to the output deck the label may also include a date before which the tape must not be re-used.

In addition to these controls mechanical checks may also be incorporated. If a specially coloured disc is required to be attached to output tapes in order that they can be inserted on to the output tape deck, the fact that an input tape does not have one should serve as a control.

A record count contained as part of each input tape should ensure that all items on the tape are, in fact, processed. The computer program will contain instructions to add the number of items processed and agree with the record count on the tape. Should any error have occurred, the computer will signify this and either stop or go into an error routine, depending on its programmed instructions. The computer may repeat this test at various control points during the processing to ascertain that all items are passing through the processing properly.

Controls to ensure accuracy of processing include:

(a) *The use of 'hash' totals.* The data read into the computer will be added to make a grand total which will be checked against that encoded into the tape or cards by the input preparation equipment. This control ensures that no item has been omitted and that all descriptive figures, account numbers etc., have been correctly read into the machine.

(b) *Check digits.* The addition of a check digit to descriptive codes such as account numbers to make them conform to a simple formula. The computer may then test the validity of the codes during processing. These checks can help to eliminate transposition and transcription errors from descriptive numbers.

(c) *Tolerance or 'reasonableness' checks.* This check is the setting of a limit for totals of calculations or data fed into the computer. The computer then checks to see that all data read-in conforms to the limits and tests calculations to see that they are reasonable, e.g. if no items of data read-in should exceed £20 the computer will reject any item in excess of this; similarly, if the result of any particular calculation should not exceed £45, the computer will signal apparent errors for checking.

Sequence Checks

Many small computer installations have no direct-access facilities (i.e. it is not possible to refer directly to information recorded on the middle of a reel of magnetic tape) and processing is therefore done sequentially. Input data must be sorted into sequential order either on punched card equipment outside the computer or by the computer itself before processing begins. Sequence checks are built into the program which ensure that the input data is processed in the same sequence as on the master file being updated.

The magnetic disc storage devices on larger installations do, however, allow direct-access facilities by the use of an 'address' system for locating a particular item of information, e.g. the number of spare machine parts in stock.

Controls on Output

Third generation computers operate at electronic speeds which are faster than any methods of printing out information that have yet been devised. In order to avoid delay in processing – through the computer having to wait until, say, the printer has finished one job before it can commence the next – output is first transferred to magnetic tape by the computer. Speeds of writing magnetic tape are extremely fast and thus the computer is not delayed by printing speeds.

Special printing units are then used away from the computer – 'off line'– to prepare any written reports which are required. It is important that the off line printers are accurate, and this is ensured by a system which produces electric signals when the printer is operated. These signals are compared with the data being read into the printer and should they not agree the printer will re-read the data and should they still disagree will stop. The fault can then be corrected by an engineer.

AUDIT APPROACH AND PROCEDURES

The auditor should examine the data processing system in force very carefully, particularly the controls which are incorporated into the equipment or included in the programs. In new installations it is better if this examination takes place immediately before the programs are finalized. The auditor then has an opportunity to make suggestions for improving the controls and of reviewing the final system. Furthermore, he is thus able to ensure the provision of adequate audit trails whereby the sequence of accounting procedures may be traced through the system and checked. To examine the programs earlier would be wasteful, as alterations would probably be made necessitating a further review, and to do so later, when the programs are already being operated, would be inconvenient and impracticable.

The clerical procedures up to the translation of the data into machine sensible form are subject to the same internal control conditions as a manual system and the auditor should have little difficulty in appraising them.

The computer processing system itself can be appraised by examining the detailed flow chart of the procedures which have been incorporated into the programs. Alterations to the programs should be strictly controlled; they should be authorized in writing by a person in authority, preferably the E.D.P. manager, and a control book initialled when the alteration has been correctly carried out and tested by someone other than the programmer concerned.

The auditor should build up an audit control file containing full details of the system including:

(1) Copies of all the forms which source documents might take, and details of the checks that have been carried out to ensure their accuracy.

(2) Details of physical control over source documents, and any control totals of numbers, quantities or values, including the names of the persons keeping these controls.

(3) Full description of how the source documents are to be converted into input media, and the checking and control procedure.

(4) A detailed account of the clerical, procedural and systems development controls contained in the system, e.g. separation of programmers from operators; separation of control of assets from records relating thereto.

(5) The arrangements for retaining source documents and input media for suitable periods. This is of great importance, as they may be required for reconstructing stored files in the event of error or mishap.

(6) A detailed flow diagram of what takes place during each routine processing run.

(7) Details of all tapes and discs in use, including their layout, labelling, storage and retention arrangements.

(8) Copies of all the forms which output documents might take, and details of their subsequent sorting and checking.

(9) The auditor's comments on the effectiveness of the controls.

Once he has appraised the system the auditor will, as usual, decide on the amount of detailed checking to be undertaken.

There are two broad audit approaches – 'round the machine' and 'through the machine'. The 'round the machine' audit ignores the detailed procedures within the computer and concentrates on proving the initial input and checking its validity;

that it is properly authorized and described, that it has been properly coded and that it has been correctly translated into computer input; and the finished reports.

The output from the computer will be compared exhaustively with the source documents and control totals as a check on accurate processing. This approach is familiar to auditors and can be adopted in some audits but, where the input information has been much changed during processing, it may be impossible to identify individual items of source data with the end product, unless unduly large samples are taken. Again, where changes have been made in programs during the period under review, the results of the sample traced would not be applicable to all the data processed. A reduction in the amount of 'hard copy' printed out will also have the effect of making it difficult to trace a clear audit trail.

The 'through the machine' approach concentrates on proving the input data and a thorough examination of the processing procedures to:

(i) ensure –

    (*a*) that all input is actually introduced into the computer;

    (*b*) that unusual conditions in the input cannot cause mis-processing; and

    (*c*) that the computer and operators cannot cause undetected irregularities in the final reports, and

(ii) study the effect of any alterations to programs.

This approach calls for an extremely wide and expert knowledge of data processing routines in general and of the characteristics of the particular type of equipment under audit. Shortage of audit staff able to undertake such an audit usually requires that both the above approaches be combined in practice.

Where procedural controls are based strongly in the user departments, the audit approach is fundamentally the same as in the case of manual systems. The detailed audit work, of necessity, must be adapted to the E.D.P. system, chiefly because,

(*a*) the volume of data involved will necessitate a considerable degree of batching, and hence greater reliance will have to be placed on total accounts;

(b) considerable advantage is invariably taken of the facility of most computer configurations to print detailed reports covering a wide range of information, much of which is often found to be superfluous. Print-outs of exception and rejection routines will, however, be of concern to the auditor;

(c) standing data is held collectively on master files, and updating of this information (e.g. price catalogues, rates of pay, customer addresses etc.) must be the subject of carefully controlled processing, unlike conventional systems, where amendments to standing data are often made manually as and when they arise.

The above features tend to have an exaggerated effect on audit procedures in cases where the E.D.P. department participates in the implementation of internal controls, or where the major controls are included in the programs themselves, such as special exception reports and reasonableness checks.

The auditor should, above all, adopt a flexible attitude to audits of E.D.P. systems, since each configuration will have its own peculiar features which he must discover by examining each facet objectively, keeping an open mind. Where he finds that overall procedural controls are weak greater emphasis must inevitably be placed on systems advancement and organizational controls. The use of specially designed I.C.Q.s for E.D.P. systems will in many instances be found to be invaluable. Furthermore, despite the reluctance of certain managements to provide the auditor with sufficient 'hard-copy' to re-create an audit trail, where he considers it necessary he should persist in his requests for this data. A certain amount of conventional detailed audit work is usually advisable, preferably on a rotation basis, simply to ensure that programmed controls are functioning correctly; detailed checking of this nature should not be avoided even though it is occasionally met with derision on the part of the E.D.P. staff. In any event, it may be necessary in some circumstances to re-create the audit trail manually (e.g. by casting subtotals or checking postings) where no other method is possible.

The above considerations are of particular importance in the light of the contemporary shift away from the production of hard copy, towards the dominance of 'management by exception' (the emphasis being on exception and rejection reporting). Inevitably, auditors are being forced to work in parallel with current processing, as opposed to 'historical' auditing; apart from a dearth of visible print-out, accounting input media and source documents are retained for a limited period only, after which they are either destroyed or re-sorted for an entirely different purpose. The following brief quotation from a paper by the Chief Organizing Accountant of the National Coal Board, and published in *The Accountant*, admirably assesses the position in which the auditor may find himself:

'It should also be borne in mind that a data-processing centre is not, in popular terms, an "electronic office", but is more akin to a factory. There is a planned production cycle, a flow-line of successive operations, and any idea of these processes being interrupted or halted for audit purposes cannot be entertained. The continuous, and in some cases automatic, inspection and control processes in a factory with a production belt must be simulated by the auditor in applying his own techniques. Indeed, it may well be that the auditor, while preserving his independence will nevertheless have to subjugate his methods to the needs of the process, and may have to accept some disciplines in operation.'

It should be pointed out, however, that there is no question of the auditor inevitably having to acquiesce in the process of eliminating visible print-out if he feels that it is in any way undermining the ability of management itself to adequately fulfil its obligations. The auditor should therefore give consideration to the information which is regularly passed to management, in order to assess its adequacy for this purpose. A deficiency in this area represents one of the most fundamental and, regrettably, most frequently encountered internal control weaknesses.

The amount of detailed audit work is, as always, governed by the degree of confidence which the auditor has in the controls operated by his client, and in many ways E.D.P. systems facilitate audit work on the final accounts through their ability to provide more immediate and effective control over company assets and liabilities. For example, reconciliation between individual debtor and creditor account balances and total accounts may be effected monthly, weekly or even daily, if desired and necessary. By the use of exception reporting, debts of doubtful value may be noted without delay and any necessary action taken immediately to recover the sums due. Similar controls may be exercised over slow-moving and obsolete stocks and regular reconciliations between physical and book stocks facilitated. With many manual systems it is found that these controls and tests are only applied half-yearly, or even annually. Computers may assist in the preparation of monthly or other interim accounts by the use of files of standing data, such as price lists and depreciation rates on all items of plant. Indeed, it is quite feasible for the entire plant inventory, with full details of costs, additions, disposals, accumulated depreciation charges, allowances for taxation purposes etc. in respect of each item of plant to be held on one such file.

The Client's Use of a Service Bureau

Concern for security is sometimes caused where the client is using the facilities of a computer service bureau in cases where many of the controls are at the bureau and therefore not under the client's direct supervision. It is most important that this consideration should be given due weight at the time the system is being designed, preferably in consultation with the auditor, so that the minimum reliance requires to be placed upon the controls at the bureau.

In many ways, however, audit problems are lessened when processing is executed by a bureau. Managements often wish to reduce the 'gap' between the bureau and themselves by requesting more detailed print-out, and input is data frequently retained for longer periods. If the auditor is able to demonstrate to his client that the evidence required for audit purposes is equally advantageous for the purposes of management control and general security, little difficulty will be experienced in obtaining the necessary information. Hence, in practice it is rare for bureau-oriented systems to be computer-controlled.

Security
(a) Files

The security of files containing current transaction data and standing data is clearly an important consideration from both the management and the audit viewpoint. Files may become unreadable because of some machine malfunction, physical damage, accidental or even wilful destruction etc. and certain standard security measures have been almost universally adopted.

Where information is stored serially such as on magnetic tape (it being necessary to run the tape from the beginning in order to reach information stored further on), the most usual security precaution is that generally known as 'grandfather/ father/son'. When a new file ('father') is created by updating an existing one ('grandfather') the latter is retained until the new file has, in turn, been updated and the data transferred to a third file ('son'). Should the 'son' file be found to be defective in some way, it can be reconstructed by re-running the source data against the 'grandfather' or 'father' files which have been re-tained. This procedure is illustrated by the following diagram:

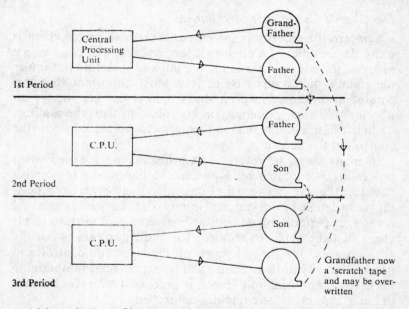

Although three file-generations are normally regarded as adequate, it is held in some quarters that yet another generation ('grandson') should be included in the arrangement.

Where magnetic tape files are in use the above security technique may conveniently be employed owing to the fact that new tapes are created by the updating process. On the other hand, where data is stored in a random or direct access organization such as on magnetic discs, updating takes place *in situ*, no further copies being created by processing. In such cases file security is facilitated by a process known as 'dumping', whereby copies of file information are made at regular intervals. These copies may consist of the whole or any part of a file, but in practice only those 'addresses' which are to be updated will usually require to be dumped. Information may be dumped either on to another magnetic disc or on to magnetic tape, as illustrated:

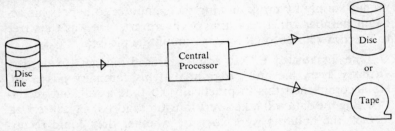

(b) General

The problem of general security clearly takes on mammoth proportions in the case of large computer configurations, and the multitude of aberrations, major and minor, which have arisen and been publicized from time to time are now legion. Nevertheless, this is a matter with which auditors are deeply concerned, and their duty to assess the adequacy or otherwise of E.D.P. security is by no means the least onerous of their tasks. An article in the *Harvard Business Review* of November/December 1968 highlights the hazards to which E.D.P. complexes are subject, by quoting several actual cases where catastrophe (or near-catastrophe) was attributable to security weaknesses in the computer area. The examples given below are drawn from these cases and give an indication of the scale on which the results of such weaknesses operate, and demonstrate the need for organizations which are E.D.P. – bound to appoint a team of specialists in computer security, who would act independently of the computer management and whose function it would be to plan, implement and supervise the various control procedures which they consider necessary in all circumstances. The auditor should strongly encourage the appointment of such a group if his investigations lead him to believe in its necessity.

'1. The E.D.P. manager of a large airline noted that data losses were occurring in the company's procedures, and he found the answer one evening during a spur-of-the-moment visit to the computer facility. He discovered that the night operators were "speeding up" operations by by-passing an automatic safety device on the tape drives during rewind. They got away with it when they were careful, but occasionally they broke tapes and consequently lost data.

'2. A programmer in a bank managed to steal large amounts of money simply by programming the computer to bypass his account number when reporting on overdrafts. He was then free to overdraw his account by any amount he pleased.

'3. One dissatisfied E.D.P. employee used magnets to destroy virtually every file and program that his company possessed. He accomplished this in practically no time at all, but reconstructing the data will take a very long time indeed. At last report, in fact, the auditors were not sure whether they could reconstruct enough information to keep the company in business. In this particular case, the consequences of poor security in the E.D.P. area may have been not merely serious, but fatal.

'4. A large insurance company gave a ladies' garden club a tour of its E.D.P. facilities. The spinning tapes and blinking lights impressed one visitor so much that she felt she had to have a souvenir of the occasion. She later said, "I hope I didn't do anything wrong. There were all those boxes of cards on the table, and I just reached into the middle of a box and took one." Perhaps this lady only caused a program to be re-run. A more serious possibility is that the card may not have been missed at all, and the centre is still trying to correct the resulting confusion.'

Use of the Computer for Audit Purposes

The auditor should consider the extent to which he can use the computer during his audit. He may devise a test set of transactions (known as an audit *'test pack'*) covering every type of entry, including errors, which he can process through the computer, and compare the results obtained with pre-calculated answers to determine whether or not the programs contain the necessary controls.

The devised test-pack input is converted into machine-readable form, and then processed by normal means, using existing programs, although the amendment of master file data may be involved. Since this processing is usually executed by the client's operators, according to their standing instructions, it is necessary for the auditor (who should actually observe the processing) to be reasonably familiar with the work of the operatives. He should be capable of ascertaining whether the 'edit' checks are operating as intended, and of interpreting error reports arising from the deliberate input of invalid data. After processing, the results will be compared with his already determined solutions.

The auditor may request that print-outs be made from the magnetic tape files so that he may compare detail entries with documents or control totals. The nominal ledger, if kept on magnetic tape, should be printed out to enable the auditor to undertake detailed checking.

Apart from their usefulness in testing the controls built into programs, such as the printing of exception reports, test packs are invaluable where there is almost complete loss of an audit trail. The data used in test packs need not necessarily be contrived, but may consist of actual out-of-date information, such as a payroll relating to an earlier week or month. Certain invalid data may be deliberately included in order to test the effectiveness of 'reasonableness' controls, e.g. specially programmed print-out of all employees shown as having worked more than 50 hours of overtime in one week. The test-pack output would then be compared with the anticipated results.

Test packs have the disadvantage of giving an indication of correct or incorrect functioning of controls *only at the time of the test*, and results cannot be regarded by the auditor as applicable to every computer run, past and future. Notorious cases have been publicized in which operators deliberately caused the machine to by-pass certain major control routines included in the program, merely in order to save time! (Presumably, the the auditors were unaware of the by-pass facility, also included in the program). It will thus be appreciated that these audit tests must be supplemented by other tests, particularly on clerical and administrative controls.

Another way in which the auditor may use the computer is by designing his own computer audit programs for processing on his client's computer. Such programs can be used as a check on procedural controls by selecting individual transactions for detailed tests, and may thus be conveniently incorporated in statistical sampling schemes. Both 'transaction' data and 'standing' data may be tested in this way, the auditor taking full advantage of the computer's ability to read large files of data at great speed. Exceptional items may be singled out by the auditor's program, e.g. by reading a current customer file and printing exception reports on all balances over, say, £500, and all balances outstanding for more than three months. Clearly this technique is more satisfactory than requiring from the client a complete print-out of the entire ledger and then commencing detailed audit tests in conventional fashion.

In view of the effort and expense which is necessarily involved in the creation of such audit programs, the auditor will not infrequently encounter a reluctance on the part of the management and the E.D.P. department to co-operate with him in implementing them. Furthermore, the insertion of additional programs into an already 'tight' schedule may cause normal processing runs to be delayed. It is therefore preferable that computer audit programs should be built into the client's own programs wherever possible, preferably when the latter are being written. In any event, few auditors at present possess the necessary skill to write their own computer programs, and they are thus dependent for this function upon the client's own programming staff. However, it is observable and noteworthy that the unprecedented technological strides in hardware development over the past fifteen years are now likely to be transferred to the field of software, particularly in the form of

(a) manufacturer's 'packages' (programs for particular applications, e.g. stock control) which may be purchased together with the computer or at any later stage; and

(b) high-level programming languages, the most sophisticated of which are almost indistinguishable from straightforward English, which enable users to write their own programs after a very short training period. This is made possible by the use of special 'compiler' programs, which, by being run together with the high-level language programs (which are held on punched cards or paper tape or other machine-sensible device) translate the latter into machine language (binary).

In America, computer audit programs are being mass-produced as packages, and are designed to cover a wide range of normal audit testing routines.

Major advances are also to be witnessed in the efficiency and ingenuity of computer peripherals. Some of these carry implications which auditors will not be able to ignore, e.g. 'on-line' cathode ray output, which provides virtually instantaneous output responses to input keyed in. The general development in on-line, 'real-time' configurations is bound to cause the auditor to carry out much of his work in parallel with actual processing, as is mentioned above in the section dealing with the general audit approach.

The auditor is required by the *Companies Act 1967* to carry out such investigations as will enable him to form an opinion as to whether proper books of account have been kept by the company. In this connection Section 436, *Companies Act 1948*, states *inter alia* that:

(1) any book of account required by this Act to be kept by a company may be kept either by making entries in bound books or by recording the matters in question in any other manner;

(2) where any such book of account is not kept by making entries in a bound book, but by some other means, adequate precautions shall be taken for guarding against falsification and facilitating its discovery.

If the system of internal control and visible control records is adequate the auditor should have no difficulty in reporting that proper records have been kept notwithstanding that most of the detailed records are kept on magnetic tape or disc storage; however, in view of the degree of concentration of information in a relatively small area, and the occupational hazards of electronic processing equipment (atmospheric sensitivity, breakdown, fire etc.) the auditor should be entirely satisfied with the security and 'back-up' arrangements in force before signing his report.

CHAPTER V

THE AUDIT OF THE IMPERSONAL LEDGER

§ 1. The Impersonal Ledger

In previous chapters, the duties of the auditor in relation to the examination of cash transactions and matters affecting the personal ledgers of a trading business have been considered, and it is now proposed to deal with the impersonal ledger, and the points that should be considered by the auditor in connection therewith. The verification of assets is a subject of great importance, and is dealt with in the succeeding chapter. Similarly, questions particularly affecting limited companies will more properly be considered in the chapters dealing with company audits. There remain, however, a large number of questions common to most classes of accounts, which particularly affect the ascertainment of profit or loss, and involve the consideration of important principles.

Ledger accounts may be divided primarily into two classes – *personal* and *impersonal*.

Personal accounts record dealings with persons, and, in the case of a trading business, consist principally of the accounts of persons from whom goods are bought, or to whom goods are sold, being recorded in the bought and sales ledgers respectively, or their equivalents. There remain, however, a certain number of personal accounts which will be found in the impersonal ledger, such as loan accounts, partners' capital and current accounts etc.

Impersonal accounts record the aspect of transactions as they affect the business, and not as they affect persons. The impersonal ledger, therefore, should contain the whole of the accounts affecting the composition of the trading and profit and loss account and all accounts representing assets and liabilities, other than those contained in the personal ledgers. The impersonal ledger is variously known in common usage as the private ledger, general ledger or nominal ledger, these terms generally being interchangeable although in many businesses a private ledger is utilized to contain only accounts of an essentially private nature. Such variations of detail will be determined according to the convenience of each particular business, and the term impersonal ledger is here employed to cover all those accounts not included in the personal ledgers.

Except in very large businesses, the amount of detail in the impersonal ledger is not excessive, and the auditor will be able to check the whole of the entries therein. This is important, because, if the auditor is able to verify the correctness of the impersonal accounts, this fact in itself will go a long way towards proving the accuracy of the personal accounts, at any rate in total; one of the commonest methods of concealing manipulations in personal accounts being to make a corresponding fictitious entry in an impersonal account.

The entries in the impersonal ledger will come either from the totals of books of prime entry or their equivalents, the journal or from the cash book. The casts of the various books of prime entry or machine lists, having been verified, the totals thereof should be checked to the accounts in the impersonal ledger to which they relate. Where the totals have been subjected to analysis, the analysis should be cast and proved, and the individual items checked to their respective accounts in the impersonal ledger. Where batches of invoices replace day books, details of postings will frequently appear on the invoices themselves, and this may take the form of a rubber stamp imprint of suitably spaced squares, with the impersonal ledger account codes entered in ink by a clerk. It is therefore essential that the auditor should have an up-to-date list of all such codes so that he may verify the accuracy of the allocations.

Many important transactions of an impersonal nature are recorded through the journal. The vouching of such entries has already been dealt with, and when this is being performed by the auditor, he should see not only that there is sufficient evidence supporting the entry, but that the entry itself properly records the transaction. If this has been done, the actual checking from the journal into the impersonal ledger becomes a matter of routine. In order to avoid a multiplicity of entries in the journal, it is common to find many transactions recorded by means of a mere transfer from one account to another in the impersonal ledger. No serious objection can be taken to this practice where the nature and reason for the transfer are apparent, but where transactions of an important or complicated nature have to be recorded direct transfers between accounts are to be deprecated. The auditor must examine and vouch direct transfers in the same manner as if they had been passed through the journal. The postings from the cash book to the impersonal ledger should be tested exhaustively, as the auditor must satisfy himself, from the nature of the evidence available, that the accounts to which the items have been posted are the correct ones. Frequently, however, the particulars recorded in the cash book are insufficient to indicate the account to which the item should be posted. In such cases, when he examines the vouchers in support of the payments, the auditor should note against the entry sufficient particulars to enable him to ensure that when the posting is checked, the item has gone to the correct account. It will be appreciated that payments should be vouched before postings are checked.

Where the books are presented to the auditor balanced, and accounts have been prepared for submission to him, it is advisable that he should leave the examination of the impersonal ledger until the whole of the entries have been completed, the necessary adjustments made and the accounts closed off. He can then check the balances direct to the trading and profit and loss account, the balance sheet and its schedules. In many cases, however, the auditor is called upon to act in the capacity of accountant, and make the necessary adjusting entries, draft the final accounts for submission to his clients and close the impersonal ledger when these have been approved. Where this is so, the auditor will check the balances of the impersonal ledger to the trial balance that is produced to him, and utilize that as a basis from which to make the necessary adjusting entries and prepare the final accounts.

The distinction between audit and accountancy work has already been referred to in Chapter I, and need not again be discussed here; but whether the auditor makes the adjusting and closing entries, or merely audits them, he must satisfy himself that those entries are correct, and that all the necessary adjustments, of which he has knowledge, have been made.

§ 2. Outstanding Liabilities and Assets

In a business of any size, there is always a considerable number of adjustments to be made at each balancing period, for the purpose of properly recording outstanding liabilities and assets, which for some reason or other have not already been brought into the accounts. Adequate schedules of such outstandings should be prepared and these will form the basis of the adjusting entries to be made.

The normal practice is to carry an outstanding liability down as a credit balance on the impersonal account concerned and in a similar manner to carry an outstanding asset down as a debit balance. Care should be taken to see that such balances are treated as liabilities and assets respectively in the balance sheet. The auditor should compare the items on the schedules of outstandings with the corresponding schedules for the previous year and satisfy himself as to the reasons for any material differences. It is also essential that the auditor should ensure that the outstandings brought forward at the beginning of the year have been cleared during the year. A liability for which provision was made, or an amount recoverable brought down at the end of the previous year, may still remain unsettled and if attention is not paid to this point, the balance on the relevant impersonal account for the year under review will be inflated or deflated if the item is not again carried forward.

(A) OUTSTANDING LIABILITIES

The inclusion of all known liabilities in the accounts is of great importance, inasmuch as it directly affects the correctness of the profit and loss account and the balance sheet. It is therefore one of the duties of the auditor to ascertain that all outstanding liabilities are dealt with. This is not always an easy matter, as a liability may be suppressed or concealed and the books and vouchers may contain no indication of its existence. There are, however, certain classes of outstanding liabilities which are common to most businesses, and the existence of these, though not recorded in the books, should be apparent to the auditor from the nature of the transactions. The existence of other liabilities, though not so apparent, may be suggested to the auditor by his experience. The more usual of these will now be dealt with.

(1) *Purchases*

In some instances invoices relating to purchases of goods that have been taken into stock are received too late to be included in the purchases day book, if any, before the accounts are closed, and may consequently have been entered in the succeeding period. A schedule of these should be prepared, and the total debited to the purchases account, and carried down as an outstanding liability. Where the precise amount of the liability cannot be ascertained, an estimate should be made by some responsible official.

(2) *Wages*

In the case of a manufacturing business, where the date of the balance sheet happens to fall in the middle of the wages week, the proportion of wages accrued, if material, should be calculated and brought in as a liability.

(3) *Rent and Rates*

It should be seen that all rents which are payable in arrear have either been paid to the last due date, or that the outstanding rent is brought in as a liability. Where the date on which the accounts are closed falls between the dates at which the rent is payable, the rent accrued to date must also be calculated and brought into account. The same remark applies to rates, though, as these are usually payable in advance, the adjustment necessary will be to carry forward the prepayment as an outstanding asset, as will also be the case with rents payable in advance.

(4) *Freight*

Carriage and freight accounts may not be rendered till some time after the period to which they relate, and it is often necessary to close the accounts before they are received. In such a case, the amount outstanding must be estimated, and a comparison with the corresponding items in the previous year will afford a useful indication of the probable amount outstanding, if the business is of a regular nature. Payments for freight are usually posted direct to the impersonal account, and the auditor should be able to ascertain, from his examination of the freight account, the period in respect of which any liability is outstanding.

(5) *General Expenses*

A schedule of the expenses outstanding should be prepared, and the total brought down as a liability on the general expenses account. It will be found, usually, that certain classes of expenditure are outstanding, particularly where no personal accounts are kept for the creditors concerned.

(6) *Legal Expenses*

Solicitors often allow some time to elapse before sending in accounts to their clients, and consequently legal expenses may be outstanding, which should be provided for. Where no account has been received from the solicitor, an estimate of the amount of his costs up to the date of the balance sheet should be obtained from him.

(7) *Audit Fee*

In some cases the audit may not even have been commenced till after the date at which the accounts were closed, in which event it could be said that the fee was not a liability at the date of the balance sheet. On the other hand, the work involved relates to the period covered by the accounts, and it is therefore certainly advisable that the audit fee should be treated as an outstanding liability. Similar remarks apply to accountancy charges for the preparation of the accounts etc. In cases where the fee has not yet been agreed, but is dependent on the amount of work involved, an estimated amount should be brought in as outstanding.

(8) *Travelling Expenses*

A schedule should be compiled of all travelling expenses due to travellers and others up to the date of the balance sheet, and these can be verified by the auditor, since they will probably have been paid early in the succeeding period.

(9) *Travellers' Commission*

The travellers' commission account in the impersonal ledger should be examined and tested with the commission statements relating to each traveller. It will be found, usually, that the commissions in respect of sales for the closing month of the period will not have been paid till the succeeding month, and the amounts due must therefore be brought in as outstanding. If any sums have been paid to individual travellers on account, only the balance of the commission due should be brought in as outstanding. Sometimes it is found that the advances exceed the amount of commission payable, and in that case the excess of the amount advanced over the amount due is in effect a loan, and should be brought down as an outstanding asset and treated in the balance sheet as a debtor, provision being made where necessary for any doubtful debts.

In some cases a traveller is not paid commission until the goods ordered through his agency have been paid for; in other cases only part of the commission is paid on execution of the order, and the balance when the goods are paid for. Where arrangements of this nature are in force, the auditor should ascertain that proper provision has been made for outstanding commissions that will become payable in respect of goods sold prior to the date of the balance sheet.

Sometimes the arrangement with the traveller provides that returns, allowances and bad debts in respect of orders upon which commission has already been paid are to be brought into account in arriving at the current commission. If this is so, the auditor should ascertain that the proper deductions have been made.

(10) *Interest on Loans*

All interest due or accrued should be calculated at the proper rate, and brought in as an outstanding liability.

(11) *Taxation*

As the exact income tax liability of a partnership is affected by the personal allowances and other reliefs claimed by the individual partners, it is often found that no provision for the tax payable by the firm appears in the partnership balance sheet, the partners' current accounts being debited with their due proportions when the tax is paid. Unless the auditor deals with the personal taxation affairs of each partner he will have no direct knowledge of the allowances and reliefs to which they are individually entitled and he must, therefore, obtain confirmation from each partner of the accuracy of the charge made to his account for his share of the income tax paid by the firm.

It is often felt desirable, however, to create a provision for the taxation liabilities arising from the profits earned to date by a partnership in order to ensure that each partner leaves in the firm sufficient profit to meet his share of such liabilities when they fall due. It will often be found that the personal and other allowances to which a partner will be entitled for the year of assessment can only be estimated, so that the amount debited to each partner and credited to a provision for taxation account must, in such circumstances, be regarded as only approximate. When the exact liability is ascertained the auditor must take care to see that the correct adjustments have been made if the actual personal allowances granted are different from the estimates made when the taxation provision was created.

It will usually be found that no provision for income tax is made in the accounts of a sole trader. When, however, the tax payable is considerable, it is suggested that the auditor should recommend to his client that provision be made for the estimated liability, in order that the trader shall be in no doubt as to his future financial commitments.

The question of providing for taxation liabilities in the accounts of companies is a matter of considerable importance and is dealt with in Chapter IX.

(12) *Contingent Liabilities*

The auditor should ascertain whether there are any transactions outstanding at the date of the balance sheet which might involve the payment of money at some subsequent date. Such outstandings are termed 'contingent liabilities', and may be of two classes: the one involving a loss should the liability accrue, and the other involving the acquisition of an asset of corresponding value.

It is sufficient for the amount of the contingent liability to be stated on the face of the balance sheet by way of a note, unless there is a definite probability that a loss will materialize, when specific provision should be made therefor. The most familiar instance is the contingent liability on bills receivable which have been discounted. If at the date of the balance sheet any of the bills that have been discounted are outstanding, there will be a contingent liability in respect thereof, since, if the acceptors do not meet the bills on maturity, the holders will have a right of recourse against the drawer or any prior indorser. As it may not be known at the date of the balance sheet whether all these bills will be met, a note of the amount of the contingent liability must be appended. Where, however, it is anticipated that any bills will be dishonoured, and that a loss will subsequently be incurred, provision should be made accordingly. In many cases, by the time the audit is completed some of the bills will have matured, and it will be only in respect of those still outstanding that the auditor should consider the advisability of a provision being made.

Other instances of contingent liabilities which might involve a loss, should they accrue, would be damages and costs in the case of an action pending, forward contracts, guarantees for third parties, and speculative transactions on the Stock Exchange still undecided. The last-mentioned will be considered in Chapter XIII.

In cases where, should a liability accrue, it will involve the acquisition of a corresponding asset, it is usual to make no reference thereto on the balance sheet. Instances of this are contingent liabilities under trade contracts, or under agreements for service, though where the amount involved is considerable, it is advisable to note it. Where partly paid shares in other companies are held, there is a contingent liability for the amount uncalled. Since, however, the payment of the calls will result in the acquisition of an asset of equivalent value, it may be considered unnecessary to refer to them in the balance sheet. If, however, the company in which the shares are held is insolvent, the payment of the calls may involve a loss for which provision should be made. In the case of companies, the *Companies Act 1967* requires, where practicable, the aggregate amount or estimated amount, if material, of contracts for capital expenditure, so far as not provided for, and the aggregate or estimated amount of capital expenditure authorized by the directors which has not been contracted for, to be shown as a note on the balance sheet or in a statement or report annexed thereto.

(B) OUTSTANDING ASSETS

There are two classes of outstanding assets which may require to be dealt with: firstly, items accruing or due, not recorded in the books, which will ultimately be received in cash; and, secondly, expenditure already incurred, some portion or the whole of which relates to a period subsequent to the date of the balance sheet. Items coming within the latter class are usually named *payments in advance* or *prepayments* and should be shown in the balance sheet in one total under such a heading. In order that the profit or loss may be correctly stated, it is important that on the one hand only expenditure relating to the period under review is included, and that on the other hand all income accruing, that is reasonably certain to be received, is brought into account.

Expenditure which is not strictly apportionable in respect of time, but the benefit of which has not been entirely received during the period under review, may in many cases be properly carried forward in suspense, and written off over a period of years. The treatment of such items will be dealt with in § 4.

The following are the more usual classes of outstanding assets:

(1) *Rents Receivable*

All rents receivable due or accrued to the date of the balance sheet should be calculated and brought into account, provision being made for doubtful or irrecoverable arrears, allowances for repairs etc.

(2) *Interest and Dividends*

Interest receivable on loans accrued to the date of the balance sheet should be brought into account in all cases where the interest is regularly paid on the due dates. If the interest is in arrear, the amount accrued should either be omitted, or brought into account, and a corresponding provision made against it.

Dividends on stocks bearing a fixed rate of interest, which it is known will be received in due course, may be calculated and brought into account, in so far as they have accrued at the date of the balance sheet. Dividends on ordinary shares, however, should not be brought into account unless they have been received subsequently, when the amount so received could be apportioned, although this would be unusual.

(3) *Commission Receivable*

Commissions due or accrued should be brought into account, but before passing the item the auditor should examine the basis on which the calculation is made, and satisfy himself of the amount due to be received.

(4) *Rents and Rates paid in Advance*

Rent is sometimes payable in advance, and the amount so paid relating to the period subsequent to the date of the balance sheet should be carried forward. Rates are usually payable in advance, and where paid prior to the date of the balance sheet, similar considerations apply. The auditor should examine the demand notes to ascertain the period to which the rates apply.

(5) *Insurance Paid in Advance*

Insurance is payable in advance, and in the case of a large business the premiums payable may be considerable. The proportion thereof applicable to the period subsequent to the date of the balance sheet should be calculated, and brought down as an outstanding asset. The last premium receipts will have been inspected in the course of vouching, and the auditor should refer to the actual policies if he considers it desirable.

Certain types of insurance, e.g. public liability, floating stock policies etc., require a premium adjustment at the end of the year and care must therefore be taken to see that provision is made for any liability or amount recoverable.

(6) *Advertising*

Payments are frequently made in advance under advertising contracts, and the proportion thereof relating to any period subsequent to the date of the balance sheet should be carried forward. Stock of advertising material, such as posters, signs, samples etc., if not obsolete, may be valued at or under cost, and carried forward as an asset, depreciation, where necessary, being allowed for. This subject is further considered in § 4 (B).

§ 3. Apportionment of Expenditure between Capital and Revenue

The distinction between capital and revenue is of vital importance as it affects the amount of profit or loss, and the correctness of the balance sheet.

Capital expenditure may be said to be all expenditure incurred for the purpose of acquiring, extending or improving assets of a permanent nature, by means of which to carry on the business, or for the purpose of increasing the earning capacity of the business.

Revenue expenditure is all expenditure incurred in the actual running of the business, and in maintaining the capital assets in a state of efficiency.

The allocation of expenditure as between capital and revenue calls for the auditor's careful examination. Where the expenditure is directly incurred for capital purposes, it can be vouched by the auditor in the course of his examination of the cash book and his duties in this connection have already been dealt with. In many cases, however, the expenditure takes the form of wages of the firm's own workmen, either wholly or partially employed on capital improvements and extensions, whose wages are included in the general wages account. Unless, therefore, a transfer is made from the wages account to the debit of the asset account concerned, revenue will be charged with wages which should properly be capitalized. Before passing any such transfer the auditor should examine the basis upon which it has been calculated. In these cases general estimates are unreliable and insufficient; precise particulars should be furnished of the number of men employed, the nature of their work, rates of pay etc., and the proportion thereof applicable to capital. Such an analysis should be certified by the wages clerk as to calculations, and by the foreman as to the nature of the work done and the time taken by each employee engaged, and finally by the works manager as being correct and properly chargeable against capital. Expenditure in the form of wages on repairs or renewals should be charged to the repairs and renewals account, and not left in wages account.

Similar considerations apply to expenditure on materials which cannot be directly allocated to capital purposes at the time of purchase. Schedules of all goods taken from store for such purposes should be prepared by the storekeeper and certified by the works manager, the values being calculated at cost price.

Where obsolete plant is replaced it is prudent to write off the cost of dismantling the old plant, although this could be considered to be part of the total expenditure on the new installation.

§ 4. Deferred Revenue Expenditure

Reference has already been made to certain classes of expenditure which are primarily of a revenue nature but the benefit of which is not exhausted during the period covered by the profit and loss account. Such expenditure may be conveniently termed deferred revenue expenditure, and may be carried forward and written off within the period likely to benefit from it, in order to avoid an unduly heavy charge being made against the profits of any one year.

Where it is proposed to carry forward expenditure of this nature, the auditor should enquire into all the facts of the case before he passes this treatment, since it could be resorted to for the sole purpose of inflating the profits of the current financial period.

The following are examples of expenditure which can be carried forward in this manner.

(A) ALTERATIONS TO PLANT

Heavy expenditure may be incurred for the purpose of improving plant and machinery, or in adapting it to altered conditions of trade. Whilst the bulk of such expenditure may be regarded as capital expenditure a proportion may in fact represent repairs and must be written off. If the expenditure on repairs is unduly heavy it may be carried forward, and written off over a short period of years, where no provision for future repairs exists against which it may be debited. The nature of the expenditure should be clearly stated in the balance sheet, and, if material, the auditor should draw attention to the treatment of it in his report.

Similar considerations may apply in the case of heavy renewals occasioned by scrapping obsolete plant.

(B) ADVERTISING

Abnormally heavy expenditure on advertising is frequently incurred in the course of establishing a new business. Where such expenditure is on a large scale, it is in fact a form of capital expenditure, and may actually be capitalized under the heading of development expenditure or advertising goodwill. Goodwill of this nature, however, cannot be maintained unless considerable advertising is continued in subsequent years, and a certain proportion should therefore be written off to the profit and loss account. The balance may be carried forward permanently as an asset, though it is preferable to write it off over a period.

Where the expenditure on advertising is not incurred for the purpose of creating an entirely new business, but is nevertheless of an abnormal nature owing to the marketing of a new product or the opening of a new department, the average annual charge for advertising should be estimated, and such amount written off to profit and loss account, the balance being carried forward and shown separately in the balance sheet as advertising suspense. The auditor should ascertain that the amount written off is adequate, and that the suspense account balance is not carried forward over an unreasonable length of time.

Similar considerations apply to businesses where the advertising is not continuous, but heavy expenditure is incurred from time to time. In seasonal trades, expenditure may be made in connection with a new season, the benefit of which may not be felt before the accounts are closed. In such cases a proper proportion of the expenditure may be carried forward, but a consistent treatment should be employed in successive financial periods.

(c) PRELIMINARY EXPENDITURE IN CONNECTION WITH A NEW BUSINESS

Heavy preliminary expenditure may be incurred in connection with the commencement of a business, or the institution of a new department, before it can reach a revenue-earning stage. Such expenditure may take the form of rent, rates, salaries, wages and general charges; and in order to avoid unduly burdening the profit and loss account of the first period, it may properly be carried forward, and written-off over a short period of years. In such a case the auditor should ascertain that all current expenditure incurred after the revenue-earning stage has been reached is charged to the profit and loss account.

§ 5. Repairs and Renewals

Repairs and small renewals should in all cases be charged against revenue, and the auditor should ascertain whether this has been done. The distinction between small renewals, which should be charged to revenue, and replacements which can be treated as additions to capital, provided the rate of depreciation has been sufficient to eliminate the old asset, is sometimes difficult to define. It is essential for the auditor to examine carefully all amounts debited to the asset account, and, by selecting certain items for enquiry, to satisfy himself that the treatment is a proper one.

Where the expenditure on repairs is of a variable nature and considerable in amount, the estimated average annual charge under this heading may be debited to revenue, and credited to a provision for maintenance account, the actual repairs in each year being debited to this account, the balance of which should be carried forward, and stated separately in the balance sheet.

If such a balance becomes a debit balance, there is no reason why it should not be carried forward, so long as it is likely to be recouped by subsequent instalments; but the auditor should satisfy himself on this point, since the fact of a debit balance being created may be due to the inadequacy of the annual charge, which in such cases should be increased. In any event, the amount of the annual charge will require to be carefully watched, and adjusted from time to time.

§ 6. Reserves and Provisions

The aggregate amounts respectively of reserves and provisions are required by the Second Schedule to the *Companies Act 1967* to be disclosed. These are defined in the following way:

(a) The expression 'provision' means any amount written off or retained by way of providing for depreciation, renewals or diminution in value of assets or retained by way of providing for any known liability of which the amount cannot be determined with substantial accuracy.

(b) The expression 'reserve' shall not, subject as aforesaid, include any amount written off or retained by way of providing for depreciation, renewals or diminution in value of assets or retained by way of providing for any known liability. Nor shall a reserve include any sum set aside for the purpose of its being used to prevent undue fluctuations in charges for taxation; such sums should be separately disclosed.

Where a provision is, in the opinion of the directors of the company, in excess of that which is reasonably necessary for the purpose, the excess must be treated as a reserve and not as a provision.

Although these requirements of the Companies Acts are applicable only to limited companies, it is most desirable, in order to avoid confusion, that the same meanings should be given to these terms in the accounts of all undertakings.

It will thus be seen that the term 'reserve' should be used to describe amounts set aside out of profits and other surpluses which are not designed to meet any liability or contingency or diminution in value of assets known to exist at the date of the balance sheet, and which thus remain part of the capital employed in the business. Reserves are thus available for distribution as dividends. The term 'provision' should be used to describe amounts set aside out of profits to meet specific liabilities the amounts whereof cannot be estimated closely, and also to meet any diminution in the values of assets existing at the date of the balance sheet. The creation of a provision thus reduces the net assets employed in the business.

Prior to the passing of the *Companies Act 1967*, the division of reserves between capital reserves and revenue reserves had to be shown. Capital reserves were previously defined in the Eighth Schedule to the 1948 Act as not including any amount regarded as free for distribution through the profit and loss account, any other reserves being revenue reserves. The creation of capital reserves by the directors for specific purposes may still arise, of course, but these may now be included under the general heading of 'reserves'.

(A) RESERVES

It is not the duty of the auditor to concern himself with the adequacy or otherwise of amounts of profits set aside to reserve, since this is a matter of financial policy. Frequently, however, he may be called upon to advise as to the amount that should be carried to reserve, and as to whether it is preferable to retain the corresponding assets in the business, or to invest the amount outside the business. Where additional working capital may be usefully and profitably employed in the business, it is sound financial policy to leave such profits in the business, since the amount so utilized will probably earn a far higher return than if it were invested in marketable securities. Where, however, it is desired to retain more than can be profitably employed in the business, a specific investment in securities should be made, to the extent of such excess. In this manner realizable assets can be utilized at any moment, should there be a sudden call upon the business. A reserve so invested is therefore a source of considerable strength. The fact, however, that the reserve is not invested in this manner, but is retained in the business, is not by any means a sign of weakness, since it may imply that the business is progressing, and consequently requires further working capital. At the same time the existence of such a reserve depends entirely upon the valuations placed on the assets, and if these are excessive, owing to the omission of proper provision for depreciation, or other causes, the reserve may be considerably smaller in fact than the figure at which it appears in the balance sheet.

Where a reserve is invested outside the business, it is called a *reserve fund*. It is often found in practice that this term is loosely applied to reserves not represented by specific investments outside the business. In order to avoid misconception, it is preferable to use the term reserve account rather than reserve fund in these circumstances, and this view has been endorsed by the Council of the Institute of Chartered Accountants in England and Wales.

(B) PROVISIONS

(1) *General*

A provision is made where a loss or expense is anticipated, but the amount thereof being unascertained, it cannot be finally dealt with. As, however, the loss will have been incurred before the date of the balance sheet, the profit and loss account should be debited accordingly, a provision account being credited.

Such provisions may be made to provide for losses likely to be sustained on the realization of certain assets, or for accruing liabilities, the precise amount of which is not known, and which will not result in the acquisition of corresponding assets.

Instances of the former class are provisions for bad debts, discounts etc., and it is the auditor's duty to satisfy himself that all estimated losses have either been written off or provided for in this manner.

The following are instances of unascertained liabilities in respect of which provisions will be made: loss resulting from a fire, not fully covered by insurance; loss on bills discounted likely to be dishonoured; costs or damages under legal action pending; claims not admitted. The auditor should ascertain that due provision has been made for all contingencies of this nature of which he is aware.

(2) *Provision for Bad Debts*

The question of bad or doubtful debts from the auditor's point of view has been fully dealt with in Chapter III, 9 (D). Having ascertained, in the manner there described, what provision he considers should be made under this heading, the auditor should check the provision for bad debts account in the impersonal ledger, and see that the necessary entries have been made.

It has been pointed out that it is not the duty of the auditor, as auditor, to make the provisions he considers to be necessary, nor has he power to do so unless so instructed by his client, in which case he acts in the capacity of accountant. Where, however, the provisions made are, in his opinion, materially inadequate and he cannot persuade his client to increase them, he should make express reference thereto in his report.

(3) *Provisions for Discounts*

The necessity of providing for cash discount on outstanding debtors, and the anticipation of cash discount in respect of outstanding creditors, is a matter of opinion; but the auditor should see that whatever principle is adopted is applied consistently. The argument in favour of such a provision is that it is desirable that the book debts should appear in the balance sheet at the amount which it is expected they will ultimately realize, and that, as the proportion upon which cash discount will probably be allowed can be ascertained from previous experience, this should be taken into account.

The argument against the necessity for such a provision is that as cash discount is an allowance made in consideration of the debtor paying his account within a given term of credit, the liability to allow such discount is conditional, and does not accrue until the debtor pays. Moreover, as the discount is granted for the purpose of inducing the debtors to pay their accounts as soon as possible, it may be regarded as an expense attendant thereon. The more rapidly the debts can be realized, the less will be the working capital required, and the more frequently can that capital be turned over in the course of the trading period. From this point of view, therefore, it may very well be argued that the expense of discount should be charged against the period which receives the use of the money.

It might be added that for taxation purposes discounts will only be allowed as charges against the profits of the period during which they are granted. As, therefore, provisions for prospective discounts are not allowable deductions for taxation, this fact may have considerable influence on the decision whether or not to make them.

The auditor, therefore, can point out the arguments in favour of making such a provision, but it cannot be regarded as essential, and the omission to do so cannot be said to affect materially the accuracy of the balance sheet.

The amount of the provision necessary will be calculated either on each individual debt, or, more usually, by way of a percentage on the outstanding *good* debtors, the rate of which will be based on the discount allowed in relation to the turnover of previous years.

The anticipation of discount in respect of outstanding creditors should not be permitted, unless provision is made against discount on outstanding debtors. Similar principles will apply as to its calculation.

(4) *Provision for Fall in Value of Investments*

Where the market value at the date of the balance sheet of investments held as current assets is less than the book value, it is essential to provide for the fall that has occurred. Where, however, the investments are held as fixed assets, provision for such a loss is not essential unless it appears to be permanent. The most convenient method of providing for the loss is to create a provision for depreciation of investments account, debiting profit and loss account with the difference between the total market value of the investments and their book value.

If this method is adopted, it will be unnecessary to amend the book value of each investment at the date of each balance sheet, the provision account being adjusted from time to time according to circumstances. In the event of any loss arising on realization, this will be debited to the provision account instead of to profit and loss account. In the balance sheet the provision account should be deducted from the book value of the investments.

Where no provision is made and the fall in value is considerable, the auditor should refer to the matter in his report.

In the case of an investment-holding company, provided the current income of the company is unaffected by the fall, no provision for fall in value is necessary, even though it may appear to be permanent.

(5) *Provision for Obsolete and Slow-moving Stock*

This is fully dealt with in § 4 of the next chapter.

CHAPTER VI

THE VERIFICATION OF ASSETS

§ 1. General Considerations

(A) INTRODUCTION

One of the most important of the auditor's duties is the verification of the assets appearing in the balance sheet. If all transactions have been correctly recorded in the books, evidence will appear therein of all the assets that have been acquired in the course of business; but it is not sufficient for the auditor merely to verify the correctness of the balance sheet as shown by the books – he must go further, and verify, by actual inspection or otherwise, the *existence* of the assets. The fact that there is an entry in the books recording the asset does not prove that the asset itself exists, even though the auditor may have vouched the accuracy of the entry. The entry only goes to prove that the asset ought to exist, and it is the duty of the auditor to satisfy himself that it actually does; and if his inspection or examination of evidence takes place after the date of the balance sheet, he must satisfy himself that the asset existed at the date of the balance sheet.

In the case, however, of those assets which continually change in the ordinary course of business, such as cash, bills receivable, and, in some cases, investments, an inspection should be made either at the close of business on the day of the balance sheet or as soon thereafter as possible. If transactions have occurred subsequent to the date of the balance sheet and prior to the date of examination, these must be vouched in order to ascertain the position at the date of the balance sheet.

When verifying cash balances or other assets of an easily negotiable character, the auditor must take every precaution to guard against the possible substitution of assets, e.g. where there are several cash balances, he must call for the production of all of them at the same time, since, if he examines them on different days, a portion of one balance may be used to make good a deficiency in another. In a similar manner, where there is a large number of investments, care must be taken to see that all are produced at the same time. Unless proper precautions are taken, there is always the risk that assets that have already been verified by the auditor could be used to free others that have been pledged. The auditor must take all possible steps to ensure that all the assets he examines are free from any charge upon them which is not properly recorded in the books of the business.

The verification of assets also serves to guard against the improper inflation of values, or the creation in the books of the record of an asset which does not exist or which in fact never has existed. The object of this form of manipulation is in most cases to inflate the profits, and correspondingly to increase the value of assets, thus making the position of the business shown by the balance sheet appear stronger than it actually is. A common instance of this is the inflation of the value of stock-in-trade, either by over-valuation or by the inclusion of fictitious items.

Misappropriation of assets, inflation of profits, and falsification of the balance sheet, may not be detected by the auditor if he is negligent in the performance of his duties in this connection, and he may find himself liable for heavy damages in consequence.

Documents of the title deposited with bankers and others for safe custody, or for the purpose of reference or sale, should actually be inspected by the auditor where possible. In any case, he should obtain a certificate from the holder stating that the assets are held free from charge; and where he is forced to rely solely upon such a certificate, he may feel it necessary to state in his report that he has done so.

The verification of assets should include not only the verification of their existence, but also the values at which they appear in the books, as far as it is possible for the auditor to satisfy himself of this.

(B) THE VALUATION OF ASSETS

It may be convenient here to indicate the general principles which should be applied to the valuation of assets in a balance sheet. The legal aspect of the subject as affecting limited companies will be dealt with in Chapters IX and X.

(a) *Fixed Assets*

Fixed Assets are those of a permanent nature, by means of which the business is carried on, and which are held for the purpose of earning income, and not for the purpose of sale, e.g. land, buildings, plant and machinery etc.

Such assets are shown in the balance sheet at cost and the total of the provisions made to date for depreciation shown as a deduction therefrom. Depreciation is normally calculated on such a basis as will spread the cost equitably over the effective life of the assets, so that the profit and loss account of each accounting period may be charged with the proper proportion of the cost.

The changes which have taken place in recent years in the purchasing power of money, however, have resulted in:

(a) fixed assets appearing in balance sheets at values far below their current replacement values, and

(b) where depreciation has been provided on such book values, profits being distorted because turnover is in terms of depreciated sterling, and

(c) inadequate amounts being accumulated out of profits for replacement.

The result of (a) is that shareholders do not obtain a true picture of the present value of the assets of the companies in which they have invested their money, whilst as a result of (b) they do not appreciate that when fixed assets have to be replaced, much higher depreciation charges will follow and that, as a consequence, profits will be reduced. Furthermore, the ratio of net earnings (expressed in terms of depreciated sterling) to capital employed (expressed in terms of sterling values of earlier years) is also rendered highly inaccurate, since like is not being compared with like.

It is sometimes contended, therefore, that fixed assets should be written up to their current replacement values, capital reserve being credited with the surplus, and that depreciation should be provided on such amended values. These suggestions have received the serious attention of the professional accountancy bodies and extracts from their pronouncements on the subject are reproduced in the Appendix. The recommendations of the Institute of Chartered Accountants are summed up in the following extract:

'Any amount set aside to finance replacements (whether of fixed or current assets) at enhanced costs should not be treated as a provision which must be made before profit for the year can be ascertained, but as a transfer to reserve. If such a transfer to reserve is shown in the profit and loss account as a deduction in arriving at the balance for the year, that balance should be described appropriately.

'In order to emphasize that as a matter of prudence the amout set aside is, for the time being, regarded by the directors as not available for distribution, it should normally be treated as a specific capital reserve for increased cost of replacement of assets.

'For balance sheet purposes fixed assets should not, in general, be written up on the basis of estimated replacement costs, especially in the absence of a measure of stability in the price level.'

It will be seen from the above pronouncements and those in the Appendix that the leading professional bodies recommend that provision for depreciation should continue to be made on the basis of historical cost, but that where it is anticipated that the cost of replacing a fixed asset will be greatly in excess of its original cost an additional amount should be set aside to provide the further funds which eventually will be required for replacement. However, these recommendations were made some years ago, and owing to the continued escalation of inflation and its results, certain companies have now adopted the practice of revaluing their assets periodically, usually by reference to published indices, and recalculating the accumulated depreciation thereon; the idea being to counteract the illusory effect on the accounts of loss of purchasing power. Unless this is done, a substantial understatement of the real capital resources employed will result. The longer the physical life of a company's assets, the greater the understatement will be. This understatement can result in the erroneous conclusion that the company's assets are more profitable than they really are, and it is primarily for this reason that there has been widespread adoption amongst large companies of what is now known as 'purchasing power accounting', as opposed to conventional historical cost accounting. There are several other major considerations which favour the adoption of purchasing power accounting, but a treatment of these lies outside the scope of this volume. It will be appreciated that where assets are revalued and written up in the company's books, depreciation must be charged on the basis of the revised values. Of course, details of the revaluation and the creation of reserves thereby should be disclosed on the company's balance sheet, and the profit and loss account must disclose the change in the basis of providing depreciation.

In August 1968 The Research Foundation of the Institute of Chartered Accountants in England and Wales published a paper entitled 'Accounting for Stewardship in a Period of Inflation', which aimed to clarify the nature of the calculations required to be made in order to assess the effects of inflation on accounts prepared on the basis of historical cost. The first four paragraphs of this paper are of considerable interest in relation to the views expressed above, and are here reproduced:

'1. In May 1952 The Institute of Chartered Accountants in England and Wales issued its Recommendation on Accounting Principles entitled 'Accounting in relation to changes in the purchasing power of money'. This statement emphasised that not the least of the limitations on the significance of accounts prepared on the basis of historical cost was the fact that the monetary unit in which they are expressed is not a stable unit of measurement. It pointed out that the ascertainment of profits involved bringing together into one account monetary amounts for transactions which had taken place at various times, and that, if the value of the monetary unit (as measured by its purchasing power) had changed between the time when a transaction was entered into and the date as on which the accounts were prepared, it could be said that the currency in which the transaction took place was different from that in use at the date of the accounts. The statement drew the conclusion that, for the purpose of accounting for stewardship, historical cost should continue to be the basis on which accounts are prepared; but it recommended, in effect, that the consequences of changes in the value of the currency should be quantified and disclosed (e.g. in the directors' report) and that, in so far as these had inflated the profits as conventionally determined, the amount of this inflation should be recognised by a corresponding appropriation of those profits.

'2. It is now more than sixteen years since that statement was issued and in that time the domestic value of the pound has fallen by close on one-third. Its recent devaluation in the international currency market will tend to cause a further fall in its domestic value. Nevertheless, the majority of companies in the United Kingdom have made no attempt in their published annual statements to measure the extent to which their reported profits have been attributable to the progressive decline in the value of the currency in which they are measured, and those few which have done so have generally confined their calculations to one aspect only of this change, namely its bearing on the charges against profits for the amortization of long-term expenditure on fixed assets.

'3. This disinclination on the part of business undertakings to quantify the effects, or the full effects, of inflation on their stewardship accounts may have been due in part to doubts whether the value of this information would justify the extra trouble and expense of ascertaining it. The fall in the value of the pound since 1952, though progressive, has been gradual; it could therefore have been expected that for any one year the effects of inflation would be small except perhaps in relation to any substantial writing off of capital expenditure incurred much earlier. Moreover, in so far as the consequences of inflation have a bearing on the financing of a business and on the amount which can prudently (as distinct from legally) be distributed in dividend, it is well recognised that accounts of past stewardship have a much less important part to play than have budgets and programmes which, looking to the future will properly take account not merely of the current value of money as reflected in the general price-level, but of (a) the actual and prospective prices of the particular goods (whether fixed assets or stock-in trade) and services on which expenditure will be incurred or from which revenue will be derived, and (b) the cash flow which fulfilment of these budgets and programmes may be expected to generate.

'4. Nevertheless, over a period of years even a gradual fall in the value of money will, if progressive, have significant consequences. Unless these are quantified, comparisons of results and net assets for a number of years fail to indicate to investors the real growth (or lack of it) in the business, and management remains ill-informed, if not uninformed, of the extent to which their policies have procured benefits or the reverse from the general effect of inflation as distinct from the circumstances inherent in the particular business or trade.' (The recommendation referred to in paragraph 1 above is included in the Appendix.)

(b) Wasting Assets

Wasting assets are those of a fixed nature which are gradually consumed or exhausted in the process of earning income, e.g. a mine, cemetery etc.

It will be seen that wasting assets are in effect a subdivision of fixed assets, but include only those which decrease in value through the operation of being worked, and therefore are not subject to depreciation through wear and tear.

The question as to the value at which wasting assets should appear in the balance sheets of limited companies is particularly important and involves legal considerations which are considered in Chapter X.

From a general point of view, it may be remarked here that in order to replace the exhausted capital out of revenue, it is necessary to reduce the book value of the wasting asset to the extent of the estimated amount by which it has diminished in value.

(c) Current Assets

Current assets are those in which the business deals, and which are acquired for the purpose of sale, and the subsequent stages of their conversion into cash, e.g. stock, book debts, cash etc.

The valuation of current assets should be made at cost or realizable value, whichever is the lower at the date of the balance sheet. The object of the business being to convert current assets into cash, and to make a profit from dealing in them, it becomes a matter of the utmost importance that the valuation placed on these assets at the date of the balance sheet shall be such that any loss sustained in connection therewith is taken into account.

(C) DEPRECIATION

(a) General Considerations

One of the most important points which an auditor has to consider is whether sufficient provision has been made in the accounts for depreciation.

Depreciation may be defined as the measure of the exhaustion of the effective life of an asset from any cause during a given period. If an asset has been acquired for the purpose of being utilized to earn income, and in the course of such process it becomes worn out or obsolete, such expired capital outlay is a loss which should be set off against the income derived from working the asset, before the balance of divisible profit can be ascertained. If this is not done, the profit and loss account will not show the correct profit for the period, and the balance sheet cannot be said to represent a true and correct view of the state of the affairs of the business, inasmuch as the assets will remain at their original cost, notwithstanding the fact that depreciation has taken place. Moreover, the profits for the period will not have been charged with the proportion of the original cost which has been absorbed within that period.

The question of setting aside sums from profits to provide for depreciation cannot be isolated from the considerations dealt with in the previous section, relating to the need to provide for increased replacement costs as a result of inflation.

Where objection is taken by clients to the proper provision for depreciation, and the auditor advances theoretical arguments in support of his view, these do not always receive sufficient consideration, owing to the fact that the practical bearing of the question of depreciation upon the financial position of the business is not sufficiently emphasized. It cannot be too strongly pointed out that if the whole of the profits of a business are withdrawn without providing for the loss arising through depreciation, no funds will be accumulated out of revenue during the life of the asset for the purpose of replacement. When such replacement becomes necessary, fresh capital will have to be provided for the purpose.

In this connection it may be remarked that where large sums will be required at some subsequent period for the renewal of assets, it may be advisable for the funds provided out of revenue to be invested outside the business, in order that they may be readily available. If the amount so set aside is left in the business, it will in due course form part of the working capital, and may be locked up in stock or other assets which may not be capable of ready realization when it is necessary for the replacement to be made.

Before the auditor can satisfy himself that the provision made for depreciation is adequate, he must have some knowledge of the considerations which are necessary to determine the rate of depreciation in connection with any particular class of asset.

Depreciation may be said to arise from two causes – internal and external. Internal depreciation is that arising from the operation of any cause natural to, or inherent in, the asset itself, e.g. wear and tear in the case of plant and machinery. External depreciation is that arising from the operation of forces outside the asset itself, e.g. obsolescence in the case of plant; effluxion of time in the case of a lease. Unfortunately, in practice it is unusual for obsolescence and wear and tear to be (correctly) considered separately. Nevertheless it is important to appreciate that each is caused by the working of entirely different factors, and that the interplay of these factors will have vastly different effects on business concerns of varying natures. Examples of businesses where the obsolescence factor is high would be those which make extensive use of the products of advanced technology, such as computers, aircraft etc., where vast technological improvements take place in relatively short periods of time. The questions of fashion and prestige play an important role in creating obsolescence, in addition to the obvious causes, such as the provision of greater efficiency at lower cost made possible by the latest improvements. Assets rendered thus obsolete may have incurred little internal depreciation, and will have to be disposed of although much of their effective life still remains. At the other end of the scale are those concerns which have employed similar manufacturing techniques for lengthy periods of time, without any substantial technical advances, such as those companies operating certain processes in textile production in the north of England. The techniques used in some cases are virtually unchanged since the early years of this century. It will thus be seen that the managements of businesses operating at different points on this scale will be faced with widely differing factors to consider when determining depreciation policy.

In order to fix the rate of internal depreciation, the effective operating life of the asset must be determined or estimated, and before this can be done the various forms of depreciation to which it may be subject should be considered. It is usually possible, given some knowledge and experience of the business concerned, to estimate the rate of wear and tear with reasonable accuracy. The loss occasioned by effluxion of time can be calculated exactly, but other forms of external depreciation are often so variable that the amount cannot be estimated accurately, and in many instances complete provision is not made until the actual loss occasioned thereby has arisen.

The term 'depreciation' should not be confused with 'fluctuation', which connotes *temporary* change in realizable value, quite distinct from depreciation of a permanent character.

Where the auditor is of the opinion that insufficient provision has been made for depreciation, and he is unable to induce his clients to adopt his point of view, he *must* deal with the matter in his report.

In considering the basis of the provision for depreciation, it should be remembered that in the course of years conditions may alter materially, and thus affect the accuracy of the original calculations. It is therefore advisable that the rates should be reconsidered from time to time.

(b) *The Principal Methods of Providing for the Depreciation of Different Classes of Assets*

The following are the principal methods of providing for depreciation, where it is desired that the amount set aside should be accumulated in the business:

(i) THE FIXED INSTALMENT SYSTEM, OR 'STRAIGHT LINE' METHOD whereby a *fixed* rate per cent. on the original cost of the asset is set aside each year. This is the most suitable method for general application.

(ii) THE REDUCING INSTALMENT SYSTEM, whereby a fixed rate per cent. on the *diminishing* value of the asset is set aside each year.

(iii) THE ANNUITY SYSTEM, whereby the asset is regarded as earning a certain rate of interest, and each year such fixed amount is provided for depreciation as, after debiting the asset account with interest at a fixed rate per cent. (upon the diminishing value), will equal the amount at which the asset, plus the interest added to the original cost, stands in the books at the end of its life.

Where it is desirable to accumulate funds outside the business, the following are the principal methods utilized:

(iv) THE DEPRECIATION FUND SYSTEM whereby an equal amount is debited to the profit and loss account each year, and credited to a depreciation fund account, and an equivalent amount of cash is invested outside the business. The investment is usually made in a fixed interest bearing security with a redemption date as near as possible to the date on which the funds will be required; the interest, as received, will be reinvested.

(v) THE INSURANCE POLICY SYSTEM whereby an endowment policy is taken out for the life of the asset, so as to produce the amount required at the end of the particular period.

(vi) In cases where the nature of the asset renders it difficult to provide for depreciation on a mathematical basis, REVALUATION should be resorted to. In this case, the asset will be revalued each year and the loss disclosed on book value written off to revenue.

(vii) THE DEPLETION UNIT SYSTEM, applicable to wasting assets such as mines and quarries, whereby such a sum is set aside each year out of profits, as represents the expired capital outlay, on the basis of a comparison of the amount of the produce extracted during the period with the estimated total workable deposits of the mine or quarry.

(viii) THE MACHINE HOUR SYSTEM, whereby the estimated total number of working hours of a machine during the whole of its effective life is divided into the cost of the machine to arrive at an hourly rate of depreciation. The profit and loss account of each period is then charged with depreciation, calculated at the hourly rate, for the number of hours during which the machine has been worked during the period.

The recommendations of the Council of the Institute of Chartered Accountants on the subject of depreciation are reproduced in the Appendix. The depreciation of patents and copyrights, however, calls for some additional comment.

Patents

Patents suffer depreciation through effluxion of time, since a patent is only granted for a period of sixteen years, though it may be subject to extension in certain cases. It is desirable, therefore, that the value of the patent should be written off over a period not longer than its official life, although in many cases a residual value remains in the shape of goodwill, built up during the continuance of the patent. Sometimes the master patent is so protected by subsidiary patents that the asset remains of considerable value.

Other causes of depreciation affecting patents are obsolescence, the impracticability of working the patent at a profit, or failure to induce the public to buy the patented article. It by no means follows, therefore, that a patent remains of value during the whole of its life, and consequently revaluation in such cases should be resorted to. In no case should the value be written up, even though it proved to be much in excess of the cost price.

Fees incurred in taking out the patent are of a capital nature, but renewal fees for maintaining the patent must be charged to revenue, and not debited to the patent account.

It is preferable to adopt the fixed instalment system when it is desired to write-off the whole cost of the patent over a term of years.

Copyrights

Similar considerations apply to copyrights as to patents, except that the term of copyright is considerably longer, being, with certain exceptions, the life of the author and a period of fifty years after his death. As the vast majority of copyrights do not retain any value during the greater part of their legal life, depreciation cannot be based on that period, and provision by way of revaluation of each copyright is the only really satisfactory method. Further remarks on patents, copyrights and trade-marks will be found in § 7 below.

The verification of the different classes of assets common to most balance sheets will now be considered. Assets of a special nature affecting particular businesses will be dealt with in Chapter XIII, which is devoted to the audits of different undertakings.

§ 2. Land and Buildings

(A) FREEHOLD PROPERTY

The title deeds should be examined by the auditor, but he cannot, however, make himself responsible for the validity of the title. It is the duty of the purchaser's solicitor to verify the validity of the title acquired by his client, and it is sufficient if the auditor ascertains that the title deeds appear to be genuine and in order, that they refer to the property the existence of which he desires to verify, and that the sequence of the various deeds composing the title appears to be complete. He should examine the last conveyance, and see that it duly vests the property in his clients or their trustees.

If the property has been mortgaged, the title deeds will be in the possession of the mortgagee, from whom a certificate to that effect should be obtained.

If the land has been registered under the Land Transfer Acts, a land registry certificate will be issued, which the auditor should inspect. This certificate states that the land described therein is registered with an absolute, qualified, good leasehold, or possessory title (as the case may be) and the auditor should see that his client is described thereon as the owner of the property.

The owner of freehold property may create a leasehold interest therein, whereby he reserves to himself the right to receive from the lessee an annual ground rent during the period of the lease and the reversion of the property to himself at the end thereof. The asset representing the interest of the freeholder in such property is called a freehold ground rent. The title deeds or land registry certificate relating to the property must be examined by the auditor, together with the counterpart of the lease which has been granted. The auditor should also see that all ground rents receivable during the period have been properly accounted for. In view of the right to the ultimate reversion of the property, freehold ground rents increase in value annually and no question of providing for their depreciation therefore arises.

Subject to any provision for depreciation that may be necessary in respect of buildings, freehold property should appear in the balance sheet at cost. It is not usual to write up this asset, even though its value may have increased, but where this course is followed, the method adopted must be clearly shown in the accounts. On the other hand, it is not usual to take account of any fall in the market value until realization, when the loss can be accurately ascertained.

The auditor should ensure that adequate insurance cover has been arranged for the property, and that premiums have been paid whenever due, either by his clients or by the lessees, if any, according to the terms of the lease. Where it is discovered that the company's buildings are under-insured, or are totally un-insured, the auditor's position may be somewhat difficult: in a management audit, where the auditor reports to principals rather than to shareholders, he would naturally criticize this fact strongly. In a statutory audit, however, there is no clear duty on the auditor to comment on directorial policy in this connection, particularly where the buildings in question are simply under-insured. It may nevertheless be said that where the asset values involved are substantial, and there is no insurance cover whatever, the auditor would be within his rights to require an explanatory note to be placed on the face of the accounts or to acquaint the members with the circumstances by referring to the matter in his report.

(B) LEASEHOLD PROPERTY

The lease and, where the client is not the original lessee, the assignment thereof, should be inspected, and the auditor should ascertain that all conditions, the non-fulfilment of which might involve forfeiture of the lease, such as prompt payment of ground rent, maintenance of fire insurance etc., have been duly complied with. If the property is registered, the land registry certificate will be examined.

Where leasehold property has been sublet, the counterpart of the tenant's agreement should also be examined.

It should be seen that proper provision has been made for depreciation of leases and for any possible claims for dilapidations arising thereunder.

§ 3. Investments

Where investments are numerous, the auditor should have produced to him a schedule showing the nominal amount and full title of each investment, the book value, and the market value thereof, as at the date of the balance sheet.

The whole of the investments should be produced at the same time, and where they are registered in the names of individuals, as nominees for a company or corporation, a deed of trust should be produced. Where no such deed is in existence, the auditor should obtain a letter from the parties, stating that they hold the investments on behalf of the company, free from any charge, and he should advise that a deed of trust be executed. In all cases the auditor should see that the particulars of the investments correspond with those entered on the schedule, especially where different classes of stock or shares are issued by the same company.

Where the actual securities are not examined, but the auditor obtains a certificate from bankers or other parties, the certificate should state the names in which the securities are registered and that they are held free of any charge or encumbrance.

In recent years, many companies have raised additional capital by offering new shares to their shareholders *pro rata* to their existing holdings, on terms which compare favourably with the current market value of the company's shares. A provisional renounceable allotment letter (often called a 'rights' letter) is issued to each shareholder for the number of new shares he is entitled to take up. A shareholder who does not wish to acquire his new shares may renounce the allotment letter in favour of a third party and, in view of the favourable price at which the new shares can be acquired, the 'rights' are normally quoted on the market at a premium. When a company makes an issue of bonus shares to its shareholders, the normal practice is for renounceable allotment letters or share certificates to be sent to the shareholders for the shares so allotted. If the shareholder wishes to keep the new shares allotted him, he will retain the renounceable share certificate, or, if allotment letters were issued, he will in due course receive the appropriate definitive certificate but, within a specified period from the date of the allotment, he has the right to sell the new shares in the market, his title thereto being transferred to the purchaser by delivery of the allotment letter or share certificate, duly renounced.

It will be appreciated that the fact that bonus shares, or 'rights' to take up new shares, *should* have been received will not be apparent from the relevant investment accounts, and that, therefore, these are matters into which the auditor must make the closest enquiries. Not only must he make sure that the correct holding of each investment is recorded, but he must bear in mind the comparative ease with which, in certain cases, allotment letters or share certificates could be renounced and the proceeds of sale misappropriated. Where necessary, the auditor should ask his own stockbroker to furnish him with details of bonus and 'rights' issues made by particular companies or should himself refer to the appropriate cards issued by an agency which provides a daily statistical service.

As the number of bonus shares issued to each shareholder is calculated *pro rata* to his existing holding, fractions of shares will frequently arise. It is usual for the shares representing these fractions to be sold by the company and for the proceeds to be divided between the persons entitled thereto. The auditor should, therefore, ensure that the cheques for any fractions due to his client have been properly accounted for.

(A) REGISTERED STOCKS AND SHARES

The term 'registered' implies that the name of the holder has been entered in the register of members of the company, and that a certificate has been issued in his name. The certificate will be examined, and the auditor should see that it appears to be properly executed and sealed.

Where registered stocks or shares have been sold prior to the date of the balance sheet, but delivery has not been effected by that date, the certificate will not have been handed over, and should be produced to the auditor, together with the broker's sold note; or if the certificate has been sent to the broker his receipt should be seen. If delivery has been effected, it should be seen that the proceeds of sale have been duly received.

Where part of a holding has been sold, and the certificate for the total holding has been delivered, but no new certificate has yet been issued, the auditor should call for a certificate from the stockbrokers who effected the sale stating that they are due to deliver a certificate for the balance unsold.

Where shares have been purchased, but the new certificate has not been issued at the date of the audit, the auditor should ask for a certificate from the stockbrokers who effected the purchase stating that they are due to deliver the relevant share certificate.

(B) BONDS TO BEARER, AND OTHER SECURITIES

It is compulsory to lodge all bearer bonds and share warrants to bearer with authorized depositaries which include bankers, members of recognized stock exchanges, insurance companies, solicitors and others. A certificate must, therefore, be obtained by the auditor from the depositary concerned that the bonds are held by them for safe custody and that the coupons for the future payments of interest or dividend are attached.

Where stock has only recently been issued, and all the instalments or calls have not been paid, definitive certificates will not as a rule be available. The document of title will then consist of the letter of allotment, with bankers' receipts attached for the sums paid on application and allotment, calls or instalments. Fully paid allotment letters for bonus shares received, will also be examined if, at the balance sheet date, they have not been exchanged for definitive certificates.

(C) TAX RESERVE CERTIFICATES

The certificates in hand should be inspected, it being seen that they are in the name of the client and not out of date. If the certificates are held by the client's bankers for safe custody, a certificate should be obtained from the bank setting forth the date and amount of each tax reserve certificate so held.

Where certificates have been surrendered in payment of taxation since the date of the balance sheet but before the attendance of the auditor, the Inland Revenue receipts must be examined and the calculation of the interest claimed on surrender checked.

It is recommended that tax reserve certificates should be shown separately on the balance sheet and grouped with the current assets. The interest allowed on certificates surrendered in payment of taxation should be treated as interest received, and not as a reduction of the taxation charge in the accounts. It is inadvisable to take credit for interest accrued on certificates held at the date of the balance sheet, unless the certificates have been surrendered before the balance sheet is signed, in payment of tax which was due at the accounting date.

(D) BUILDING SOCIETY DEPOSITS AND SHARES

It is customary for building societies to issue pass books for money received on deposit and also for investments in its shares. The auditor should examine the pass books but, in addition, should obtain a certificate from the building society confirming the balance which was standing to the credit of his client's deposit or shares account at the date of the balance sheet.

(E) TREASURY BILLS

These securities, which are payable to bearer, are normally held by the client's bankers for safe custody. A certificate should, therefore, be obtained from the bank setting forth the date and face value of each bill held by them and certifying that they have no charge thereon.

If Treasury bills are actually in the possession of the client, they should be examined by the auditor who should see that they are not out of date. If, before the auditor attends to verify securities, the Treasury bills have matured, he will vouch the proceeds from the bank statement and collection advice received from the client's bankers.

Treasury bills should be grouped in the balance sheet with the current assets and be stated at cost or at their face value discounted at the market rate.

(F) LOANS TO LOCAL AUTHORITIES

The documents issued by the local authority, acknowledging receipt of the loan and the terms on which the money has been borrowed, must be inspected. In some cases the only document will be a letter signed by the borough treasurer, and in such circumstances the auditor should obtain a certificate from the local authority confirming the amount of its indebtedness to the client as at the date of his balance sheet.

(G) THE VERIFICATION OF THE VALUES OF INVESTMENTS

Investments should appear in the balance sheet at cost or under, and brokers' bought notes will be sufficient evidence of the price paid. The necessity or advisability of providing for depreciation can only be considered in relation to the present value of the investments, and the auditor should therefore ascertain this as far as he is able to do so.

In the case of stocks and shares quoted on a recognized stock exchange, the Official List published at the date of the balance sheet should be consulted and the middle price taken. Stocks and shares not officially quoted may nevertheless be quoted by financial papers, and if so, the mean of the various markings should be taken.

Where no market quotation exists, considerable difficulty is sometimes experienced in arriving at a fair estimate of the value.

Enquiries can be made of the secretary of the company concerned, as to the prices at which shares have recently been transferred; but this is not necessarily a true criterion of the value, inasmuch as, where no free market exists, the purchase consideration does not always represent the actual value. In any case, such information is not sufficient, and the auditor should ascertain what dividends have been paid recently on the shares, and inspect a copy of the last audited balance sheet of the company concerned.

In the case of investments in subsidiary companies, special considerations may arise which are dealt with in Chapter XI.

Investments should not be written up except in special circumstances, as in the case where changes in a partnership require that the partnership assets should be recorded at their true present values; but on a revaluation of all the investments a rise in the value of some may be set off against a fall in the value of others.

In the case of limited companies, the aggregate amounts respectively of the company's quoted and unquoted investments must be shown under separate headings in the balance sheet. It is also necessary to show on the balance sheet or in a statement or report annexed thereto the aggregate market value of the company's quoted investments where it differs from the amount of the investments as stated, and the stock exchange value of any investments of which the market value is shown (whether separately or not) and is taken as being higher than their stock exchange value. The auditor must see that these and other requirements of the Companies Acts relating to investments have been complied with. The disclosure requirements will be more fully dealt with in Chapter IX.

Investments which have been made for the purpose of securing some trading advantage from the companies or firms in which the investments are held or for the purpose of protecting the goodwill of the investor's business are usually known as 'trade' investments; for example, an investment made by a manufacturing company in the shares of one of its principal suppliers of raw materials, for the purpose of having some control over dates of delivery, prices etc. It will be appreciated that such an investment must represent a substantial proportion of the capital of the company in which it is made if it is to have any trading advantage to the investor. Such investments are usually classed as fixed assets on the balance sheet.

§ 4. Stock in Trade

(A) THE AUDITOR'S DUTY IN RELATION TO STOCK-IN-TRADE

As the correctness of the profits of a trading concern depends, to a large extent, on the accuracy of the valuation of the stock in trade at the date of the balance sheet, the verification of this asset forms a very important part of the auditor's duties. This verification, however, is attended by many more difficulties than is the case with other assets, inasmuch as no entries will usually appear in the financial books, showing what stock in trade should be on hand at any particular time. Where accurate stock records are kept evidence is available which will materially assist the auditor to satisfy himself as to the correctness of the stock figures, but in the majority of businesses the maintenance of such detailed accounts is not practicable. The auditor cannot normally be expected to verify the existence of each and every item of stock by actual inspection. He is not a valuer, and the limited technical knowledge of the trade concerned which he may or may not possess, will not as a rule be sufficient to enable him to form an accurate assessment of the correct valuation of the stock. He is usually unable, therefore, to assure himself of the accuracy of its value by the methods which are available in the case of other assets, such as investments. Accordingly, the auditor is compelled to rely extensively upon an examination of the available stock records, making such tests of the accuracy of the inventory sheets as are possible in the particular circumstances, together with appropriate tests of stock-taking procedures whilst stock-taking is in progress.

The execution of audit tests on stocktaking procedures by physical inspection has very recently been recommended in this country by the Institute of Chartered Accountants, whereas for over thirty years the accountancy profession in the United States of America has, mainly as a result of the disclosures in the *McKesson & Robbins* case in 1939, formally acknowledged the physical testing of inventories to be part of normal auditing practice, and for many years prior to the Institute's recommendation (July 1968) it was argued by sections of the profession that a similar procedure should be officially adopted in this country.

The facts of the above case were that the president of McKesson & Robbins, Incorporated (Maryland), in collusion with certain other of the company's high officials, fabricated and presented to the auditors a completely fictitious set of records of purchases, sales, stock inventories and debtor balances, which resulted in the assets being overstated in the balance sheet by approximately 21,000,000 dollars.

In a summary of their findings and conclusions on the case, published in 1941, the Securities and Exchange Commission (of which, at present, there is no exact counterpart in this country) stated that they found that a difference of opinion existed among accountants as to the auditor's duties and responsibilities in connection with the physical verification of quantities, quality and condition of stocks. The auditors of the company, in common with a substantial section of the profession took the position that the verification of inventories should be confined to the records. On the other hand, a body of equally authoritative opinion supported the view, which the Commission endorsed, that auditors should gain physical contact with the inventory, either by test counts, or by observation of the taking of the inventory, or by a combination of these methods. The judgment of the Commission contained the following verbatim statement, referring to the auditors: 'Their failure to discover the gross overstatement of assets and of earnings is attributable to the manner in which the audit work was done. In carrying out the work they failed to employ that degree of vigilance, inquisitiveness and analysis of the evidence available that is necessary in a professional undertaking and is recommended in all well known and authoritative works on auditing.'

The auditors of companies registered in this country which are subsidiaries of American companies have been expected to conform to the American procedure in this matter, and for the most part, it is their influence that has led to the formal recommendation of the Institute in England and Wales that this be adopted in the U.K. However, it is obvious that in the case of certain businesses such technical knowledge is necessary in connection with stock quantities and values, that the scope and effectiveness of physical tests applied must, of necessity, be limited. Nevertheless, it is the auditor's duty to observe a part of the stock-taking, in order to satisfy himself that the procedure laid down is being followed by those involved.

The extent to which the auditor is responsible for the accuracy of the amount at which the stock-in-trade is stated in the balance sheet was considered in the case of the *Kingston Cotton Mill Co.* (No.2, 1896, 2 Ch. 279), which is fully discussed in Chapter XII. It was decided in this case that, in the absence of suspicious circumstances, the auditor is entitled to rely upon the certificate of a responsible official of the company, regarding the valuation of stock, and that it was no part of the duty of the auditor to check the physical stocks himself.

When considering this case it must be remembered that it was decided more than seventy years ago, when the standard of skill and care required of an auditor was not so exacting as it is now, and it would be most imprudent to rely on this decision today, particularly in the light of contemporary thought and practice as reflected in the Institute's recommendations. The *Companies Act 1948* requires the auditor of a company to report whether the balance sheet shows a true and fair view of the state of the company's affairs, and, as has been shown, in order to do this he must verify the continued existence and values of the various assets disclosed therein. Moreover, the *Companies Act 1967* requires that if the amount carried forward for stock in trade or work in progress is material for the appreciation by its members of a company's state of affairs, or of its profit or loss for the financial year, the manner in which that amount has been computed shall be stated by way of note on the company's balance sheet, or in a statement or report annexed, if not otherwise shown.

The auditor thus cannot confine himself to seeing that the stock is duly certified by the directors or proprietors; he must, in addition, impose such tests upon the stock-sheets as are practicable in all the circumstances, including physical tests on a suitable selection of inventory items. The nature and scope of tests to be executed must depend upon the nature of the business and the records which are kept. If a proper costing system is in operation, stores and stock accounts will be maintained, and the auditor will be entitled to rely on the quantity balances shown thereby at the date of the balance sheet after relatively little detailed checking. In some businesses it is possible to ascertain the total quantities purchased and sold during the year, so that, after adjusting for the opening stock, the approximate quantity which should be in hand at the end of the period can be determined without difficulty. In other businesses it is possible to associate each item sold with its purchase, e.g. a dealer in second-hand motor cars, so that by the process of elimination the unsold items representing the closing stock can be ascertained. In the majority of businesses, however, the verification of stock is not facilitated by the nature of the business or by the records maintained, and the auditor must rely on such tests as are possible in the circumstances. In the 1967 case of re *Thomas Gerrard and Son Ltd*, the company's auditors were held to have been negligent in carrying out their audit, because they did not fully investigate and report on invoices which had been fraudulently altered, even though the alterations had come to their notice. The amounts at which stocks were stated in the accounts were also considerably affected by these alterations. This case is dealt with more fully in Chapter XII.

The 1968 recommendations of the Council of the Institute of Chartered Accountants, referred to above, together with their other and more general recommendations are reproduced in the Appendix, to which reference should now be made.

The tests to be made in various circumstances must be determined by the auditor's assessment of the quality of the system operated and the records available, but such tests as those described in the recommendations referred to, though not of themselves proving the correctness of the stock, will serve to protect the auditor against any charge of negligence, should errors or fraud afterwards be discovered.

(B) METHOD OF STOCK-TAKING

Whenever practicable, stock should be taken immediately after the close of business on the last day of the financial period, one person calling out the quantities and description of the goods, and another entering them on the stock sheets. The price at which each item of stock is to be valued will be entered later by a responsible official and the total values will be calculated and extended. The calculations and casts should be checked by someone who has taken no other part in the stock-taking and each person should initial for the work he has performed. The completed stock sheets should be certified by a manager, partner, or director.

The 'cut-off' procedure must be examined, and in this connection it should be seen that all goods not on the premises, but which form part of the stock of the business, and in respect of which invoices have been passed through the books, are included. Instances of this class are stock in transit, at the docks, in the hands of agents or customers, or at branches.

On the other hand, no item should be taken into stock in respect of which invoices have not yet been passed through the books, unless the property therein resides in the purchaser at the date of the balance sheet, when it should be seen that the corresponding liability is also included. It should be ascertained that no goods are taken into stock which have been sold and already treated as sales, although not yet delivered to the customers, and in the same way no goods held on behalf of third parties, by way of consignment or agency, should be included.

In some businesses it may be necessary to spread the work of stock-taking over several days. In such cases, special precautions must be taken to ensure that goods received after the date of the balance sheet are not taken into stock and that due allowance is made for goods which were, in fact, in stock at the close of the financial period but have been sold and delivered before that particular stock is taken.

Unless great care is exercised, errors are almost certain to arise in connection with stock-taking. In many cases the people employed to take stock are not competent to distinguish between one class of stock and another, or to realize how seriously errors of this nature may affect the accuracy of the accounts. Consequently, active and efficient supervision on the part of responsible officials is essential.

(C) BASIS OF VALUATION

Stock should be valued at cost or net realizable value (or replacement price), whichever is the lower at the date of the balance sheet. The *Companies Act 1967* requires that disclosure shall be made of the manner of computation of the amount carried forward for stock-in-trade or work in progress, if this amount is material for the appreciation by the members of the company's state of affairs or of its profit or loss for the financial year.

The recommendations on the treatment of stock-in-trade and work in progress in financial accounts which were made by the Council of the Institute of Chartered Accountants are given in the Appendix, to which reference should be made.

The operation of the *base stock* method mentioned therein may be explained as follows: where base (or standard) quantities of materials are essential to the proper functioning of a business, the initial stock at the commencement or first adoption of the scheme is valued at actual cost at that date, and all replacements of that stock up to (but not exceeding) the initial quantity are valued at the same prices. (In effect, the original stock is thus regarded as a fixed asset.) All additions to the respective quantities of stock, after deducting the consumption or disposals during the accounting period, are valued at the average cost of those additions. The cost of the additions thus ascertained is added to and averaged with the 'base' stock to form a moving average price of the entire stock of each of the respective kinds of goods. If, at any accounting date, cost or net realizable value of stock is lower than the value determined by the base stock method, the lower value would be substituted and that lower value would then be adopted as the opening figure for the next accounting period. The method has the advantage of minimizing the fluctuations in stock values caused by changing price levels and was recommended by the Royal Commission on Taxation of Profits and Income in their final report but has not been accepted by the Inland Revenue for taxation purposes. There are, in practice, many variations of the base stock method, but the above explains the more general application of the system.

Other classes of stocks may be on hand at the date of the balance sheet in addition to normal stock in trade, e.g. stores for the upkeep and maintenance of plant and machinery, fuel etc. Where these are of any consequence, it is desirable that a valuation thereof should be taken, in order that the amount charged against revenue may represent the actual quantity consumed during the period under review. In order to effect this, such stock should be brought down as a debit balance on the expenditure account to which it relates, and not included in the general total of stock-in-trade taken to the credit of the trading account.

§ 5. Loans on Security

The verification of loans on security involves not only an examination of the loan account in the ledger, but also of the security lodged, in order that the auditor can satisfy himself that the loan is properly secured, and that there is a reasonable margin between the amount of the loan and the value of the security.

The fact that interest is regularly charged up and paid on the due dates is additional evidence of the existence of the loan. Interest in arrear for any length of time may indicate that the account is doubtful, and where it is added to the amount of the debt, it should be seen that, if necessary, further security is lodged.

When the auditor does not consider the debt fully secured and particularly in cases where the interest is accumulating without further security being lodged, he should see that proper provision is made to cover any possible loss. Where interest has not been paid, it is sometimes left out of account altogether. This prevents the possibility of irrecoverable interest being credited to revenue, and distributed as profit. On the other hand, this treatment does not record the actual state of the loan account, and in the case of banks and other concerns whose business it is to advance money, it is usual to find that interest is regularly charged up, but when its recovery is doubtful the amount thereof is either fully provided against or taken to the credit of an interest suspense account and carried forward, and not treated as profit until actually received.

Where lending money is not part of the normal business of the concern it is suggested that the auditor should obtain confirmation from the borrower of the amount outstanding at the balance sheet date.

The nature of the security lodged against loans varies with each class of business transaction. A loan on the security of land, or any estate therein, is secured by way of a mortgage, which may either be *legal*, when an actual title to the land will be conveyed, or *equitable*, which may be effected either by a written instrument termed a memorandum of deposit, or by the mere deposit of the title deeds.

Where the loan is secured by the transfer of possession of movable assets or by the deposit of securities, the transaction is called a pledge.

The auditor's duties in connection with the verification of the more usual classes of loans on security will now be considered.

(A) LOANS ON MORTGAGE

On the occasion of the first audit, the mortgage deed should be examined in detail, the following points being noted:

(1) The name of the party to whom the mortgage is granted. If a nominee of the client has been named as the lender (i.e. as mortgagee) the auditor must obtain a certificate from such nominee acknowledging that he has no beneficial interest in the mortgage.

(2) The particulars of the property mortgaged, which should correspond with the title deeds of such property.

(3) The amount of the loan, and date thereof.

(4) The rate of interest payable.

The above details are usually endorsed on the back of the mortgage, and if the auditor has verified them on the first occasion, it will not be necessary for him to examine the deed in detail at subsequent audits.

The title deeds deposited with the mortgage deed should be examined, the same considerations applying as with the verification of freehold and leasehold properties, referred to in § 2 of this chapter.

If the title to the property has been registered under the Land Transfer Acts, particulars of the mortgage will be entered in the charges section of the land registry certificate, which should be examined by the auditor.

The last receipt for the fire insurance premium should be produced, in order that it may be seen that the property is protected against fire, and in the case of leaseholds the last receipt for ground rent.

In order to verify the value of the property, and to see that there is sufficient margin of security, the auditor should inspect the valuer's certificate. Where the loan has been outstanding for some time, and there is any possibility that the value of the property has diminished, a further valuation should be made.

In the case of a second mortgage, the mortgage deed should be examined, and this should recite the prior charge. The title deeds will be in the possession of the first mortgagee, and the auditor will therefore not be able to inspect them, but an acknowledgement should be obtained from the first mortgagee, or his solicitors, stating that he has received notice of the second charge.

Where, as in the case of building societies, there is a large number of mortgage deeds, special considerations apply, and these are dealt with in Chapter XIII.

(B) LOANS ON THE SECURITY OF INVESTMENTS

The auditor should examine the schedule of investments deposited as security for the loan, and verify the investments in the manner already described in § 3.

In the case of registered stocks, the auditor should see that the stocks have actually been transferred into the name of the lender or his nominee.

The deposit of the certificate issued to the borrower, accompanied by a blank transfer signed by him, which is not completed and registered on issue, though it may constitute an equitable charge, will not of itself afford complete security.

The values of the securities deposited should be tested by the auditor in the manner previously indicated, in order that he may ascertain whether there is sufficient margin to secure the loan fully; and he should ascertain that the usual undertakings have been lodged to repay the loan on demand, or at a fixed date with interest, or to deposit further security in the event of that held depreciating by reason of a fall in market values during continuance of the loan.

(C) LOANS ON OTHER SECURITY

Goods are frequently pledged for advances. Where the goods are in transit, the complete set of bills of lading, duly endorsed in favour of the lender, will be deposited, together with the insurance policy. Where the goods are at the docks, or in bonded or other warehouses, the dock warrants or warehouse certificates, endorsed in favour of the lender, will be lodged. Where warrants or certificates have not been issued, delivery orders in favour of the lender will be lodged. Delivery, however, will not be made on such orders until all the rent and other charges accrued on the goods have been paid; and the extent of any liability outstanding in this respect should be ascertained, as it may materially affect the value of the security. The auditor should test the value of the goods by reference to market quotations, invoices and any other evidence available.

In order to verify a loan on personal guarantee, the guarantee should be seen. Under the Statute of Frauds it is necessary that this should be evidenced in writing and duly stamped. In order to ascertain whether the loan is secured, the auditor should satisfy himself that the guarantor is good for the amount involved.

Loans on the security of life policies, though they may be fully covered in the event of the immediate death of the assured, should only be regarded as secured to the extent of the surrender value of the policies. The auditor should require the production of a statement from the insurance company, showing the surrender value, and ascertain that due notice of assignment has been given to the company. The last premium receipt should be inspected.

A loan on the security of a bill of sale will be verified by inspection of that document. It should be seen that the bill has been duly registered, and that all the requirements of the *Bills of Sale Act 1882* have been complied with.

(D) LOANS TO EMPLOYEES

Loans are often made by firms to their employees to assist them to purchase houses or meet other exceptional expenditure. The loan agreements or other documents signed by the employees acknowledging such loans must be inspected and the terms in respect of interest, if any, and repayment noted.

If the loans are secured the securities must be examined in the usual manner. Many loans of this description, however, are unsecured and the auditor must give due consideration to the possibility of bad debts arising.

If it has been arranged with the employee that the loan shall be repaid over a period by the deduction of a fixed weekly or monthly sum from his salary, the auditor should see that the appropriate adjustments have been made. A certificate must be obtained from each employee setting forth his indebtedness to the firm on loan account at each balance sheet date.

The requirements of the Companies Acts in regard to loans made to officers of a company are dealt with in Chapter IX.

(E) LOANS TO SUBSIDIARY COMPANIES

If the auditor of the holding company is also the auditor of the subsidiary company to whom a loan has been made, he will be able himself to verify from the books of the latter company the amount outstanding at the date of the balance sheet. If, however, the auditor of the holding company is not the auditor of the subsidiary company he must obtain a certificate as to the balance outstanding according to the books of the subsidiary company. In view of the close relationship between a holding company and its subsidiary, it is considered that the certificate required should be obtained from the auditor of the subsidiary company, rather than from a director of that company, who may also be a director of the holding company.

As many loans of this nature are made without security, it will frequently be necessary for the auditor to consider the possibility of a loan proving to be wholly or partially irrecoverable. The auditor should call for the last audited accounts of the subsidiary and make a personal assessment of the value of the debt.

§ 6. Bills Receivable

The balance of the bills receivable account in the impersonal ledger will represent bills on hand at the date of the balance sheet, and if the auditor attends on that date he should inspect the actual bills. In most cases, however, the verification will take place after the date in question, and consequently, the bills that have been met subsequently will be verified by vouching the cash received. In the case of bills discounted since the date of the balance sheet, the receipt of the proceeds will be verified.

In examining the bills the auditor should see that they are properly drawn and stamped, and that they are not overdue. Where there is any doubt as to whether the bills will be met, enquiries should be made, and it should be seen that sufficient provision has been made for any loss likely to be sustained. Where a bill has been retired since the date of the balance sheet, the new bill should be seen; and where part of the original bill has been paid, it should be seen that the proceeds have been received, and that a new bill has been obtained for the balance.

Where transactions in bills are numerous, it is usual to place them in the hands of bankers or other agents for collection, and, in such cases, certificates should be obtained from them detailing the bills they held at the balance sheet date. It is essential that such certificates should give details of the charge, if any, the bankers or others have on the bills so held.

The auditor should see that a note of the contingent liability in respect of bills discounted outstanding appears on the balance sheet, and that proper provision has been made in respect of any anticipated loss.

§ 7. Other Assets

(1) *Book Debts*

The verification of book debts has already been dealt with at length in Chapter III, § 9 (c).

(2) *Cash at Bank and in hand*

The verification of cash in hand and at bank on current or deposit account, and of the petty cash balance has been dealt with in Chapter II, §§ 6 and 7.

(3) *Endowment Policies*

Endowment policies taken out for the redemption of leases, or sinking fund policies for the redemption of debentures, and other policies of a similar nature, should be verified by inspection of the policies, and the auditor should ascertain that the last premium has been duly paid. Where such policies are shown in the balance sheet at values other than their surrender values the auditor should see that the surrender values are shown as a note.

(4) *Assets abroad*

Where the documents of title relating to assets abroad are not in this country, a certificate should be obtained from the agent, or other party holding the documents, or in the case of land, a certified extract from the local land registry should be submitted, and the auditor should state in his report what evidence has been produced, if the amount involved is material.

(5) *Plant and Machinery*

In most manufacturing businesses expenditure on plant and machinery is charged to one account under that heading, irrespective of the effective life of the machines. It will be appreciated, therefore, that to provide for depreciation on the basis of the balance on the plant and machinery account, without regard for the nature, age and cost of each machine comprising such balance, would often result in an inaccurate provision being made. In order that the asset account shall remain at cost, and the total amount of the accumulated provision for depreciation be readily ascertainable, provisions for depreciation should be credited to a provision for depreciation of plant and machinery account, the balance on which will represent the total accumulated provision to date. Very considerable research, however, will normally be necessary to ascertain how much of the total accumulated provision for depreciation relates to any particular machine, unless a plant register is kept.

The plant register will show the cost of each machine purchased and the amount accumulated for its depreciation, and suitable entries will be made therein in respect of machines sold or scrapped. When vouching the entries made in the financial books for purchases of machinery, the auditor should also vouch the corresponding entries in the plant register and, in due course, he should test the arithmetical accuracy and the adequacy of the provisions made therein for depreciation.

At each balance sheet date a list should be extracted from the plant register, showing in respect of each machine:

(a) its description or number;

(b) its cost;

(c) the provision made in the year under review for its depreciation; and

(d) the accumulated provision for its depreciation.

The auditor should test a representative number of the entries on this list with the plant register and agree the total of (b) with the balance on the plant and machinery account, and the total of (d) with the balance on the provision for depreciation of plant and machinery account. The total of (c) will be reconciled with the debit for depreciation in the accounts for the year. The list should be certified by a director and the works manager or other competent person as representing a complete record of all plant and machinery owned at the date of the balance sheet.

When machines are sold or scrapped, the auditor must satisfy himself that appropriate entries have been made to remove the cost thereof from the asset account, and the accumulated provision for their depreciation from the provision for depreciation of plant and machinery account. Some profit or loss is almost certain to arise from the sale or scrapping of a machine and the auditor must ensure that this is dealt with correctly. In cases where provisions for depreciation are credited to the asset account and no plant register is kept, it may be found that the only entry made when a machine is sold is a credit to the plant and machinery account for the proceeds, with the result that the balance left on the account either includes a loss incurred or has been deflated by a profit made on a machine no longer owned, and does not therefore represent the true written down value of the machinery still on hand.

The preparation of taxation computations is greatly facilitated if there are recorded in the plant register details of capital allowances and written-down values for taxation purposes.

Where plant is revalued, either for fire insurance purposes or otherwise, the valuation should be examined by the auditor, and if it is below the book value he should ascertain the cause of the difference.

In the case of loose tools and plant, it is usual for a valuation to be taken each year, and the item treated in the same manner as stock. Where this is done, the auditor should examine the valuation sheets, and ascertain that they are properly certified.

(6) *Furniture, Fittings and Office Equipment*

The remarks made above in connection with plant and machinery also apply in many respects to furniture, fittings etc. Few firms, however, keep a furniture etc., register recording all of such assets, but many keep a record of the more expensive items, e.g. accounting machines, comptometers, adding machines and typewriters. If such a record is kept, it is advisable for the items recorded therein to be dealt with in a separate account in the financial books and not merged in the general furniture and fittings account, in order that the cost of the assets and the provision for their depreciation as shown by the register can be reconciled with the balances on the relevant accounts at the balance sheet date.

In view of the varied nature of the items coming within the general heading of furniture, fittings and equipment, the auditor must pay particular attention to the adequacy of the provision made for depreciation. It will be appreciated that the life of an accounting machine will not compare with that of a desk and that, therefore, the adoption of one rate of depreciation for all items would normally be unsatisfactory.

Many firms make a complete inventory of all furniture and fittings once every few years in order to satisfy themselves that their insurance cover is adequate. Where a recent inventory is available, the auditor should list a representative number of major items shown to have been purchased during the last few years and confirm that they are included in the inventory.

As in the case of plant and machinery, the auditor must pay particular attention to the treatment of profits or losses arising from the sale of furniture and other equipment.

(7) *Motor Vehicles*

Where the number of vehicles owned is considerable, it is desirable that a register, similar to a plant register, be kept of these assets. If such a register is not used, it is essential that the make up of the balance brought down on the motor vehicles account should be clearly shown thereon by indicating the registration number and cost of each vehicle comprising such balance.

The auditor will examine the registration book for each vehicle, noting that the registration number and description recorded therein agree with the particulars shown in the ledger account or vehicles register. If it is found that a vehicle is not registered in the client's name, the auditor must ascertain the reason for this and obtain written confirmation from the person named in the registration book that the vehicle is the property of the client and that no charge is claimed thereon. The payment of road fund tax is no longer recorded on the vehicle registration books and there is thus no conclusive evidence that the payment of an amount of tax relates to a particular vehicle. However, the auditor may submit a list of selected vehicles to the local licensing department where they are registered, and request full details of the up-to-date licensing position of each of them.

The auditor must verify the adequacy of the provision made for depreciation and the adjustments arising from the sale or scrapping of vehicles in the same manner as outlined above in connection with plant and machinery.

(8) *Patents*

In order to verify the existence of a patent, the actual patent should be examined and it should be seen that it has been duly registered. Where the patent has been purchased, the assignment as well as the patent should be inspected. Patents taken out by companies are, in the first instance, registered in the name of the company and of an individual, who is technically the inventor, since patent law requires that an invention can be protected only upon the application of an *individual*. In most cases the individual is only an employee of the company but in all such cases the auditor should inspect a registered assignment to the company by the individual. Where a considerable number of patents is held, a schedule should be presented to the auditor, containing in the case of each patent its registered number, date, description and number of years unexpired. The last renewal certificate should also be examined, as unless this is taken out at the prescribed time, the patent will lapse. Where patents are held by a company, a resolution should be passed by the directors in respect of all patents allowed to lapse.

The question of the valuation of patents for balance sheet purposes has been considered in § 1 above.

(9) *Copyrights*

The *Copyright Act 1956* protects authors and others from infringement of their exclusive right to publish, reproduce, broadcast or in other ways to deal with their literary, dramatic, musical or artistic works. The Act also deals with the copyright in sound recordings, cinematograph films, television and sound broadcasts. In the cases of literary works the copyright subsists until the end of the period of fifty years from the end of the calendar year in which the author dies. In other cases the copyright expires at the end of the period of fifty years from the end of the calendar year in which the recording, film etc., was first published.

When a copyright has been purchased, the auditor will examine the written assignment and vouch therewith the price paid. Where, however, the client is the original author no value would, normally, be placed upon the copyright in his books and no documents of title are available for inspection. The auditor must examine all licences or assignments granted by his client and satisfy himself that all royalties, fees etc., due thereunder have been properly accounted for. The question of the valuation of copyrights has been dealt with in § 1 above.

(10) *Trade Marks*

Trade marks are registered at the Patent Office and the auditor should examine the certificate issued by the registrar. Where a trade mark has been acquired by assignment, the amount paid therefor will be vouched with the assignment and will represent capital expenditure. Where the trade mark has been registered by the proprietor, the auditor must vouch the amounts treated as capital expenditure, e.g. registration fees, payments to artists etc., and satisfy himself that any sums capitalized in respect of staff salaries, overheads etc., for the time devoted to the design of the mark are reasonable. Fees paid for the renewal of trade marks must be charged to revenue and the auditor must examine the last renewal receipt to ensure that the mark has not been allowed to lapse.

The *Companies Act 1967* requires the amount of goodwill, patents and trade marks to appear under a separate heading in the balance sheet of a limited company (in so far as not previously written off) if the amount is shown as a separate item in the books, or is otherwise ascertainable.

(11) *Goodwill*

Goodwill is an intangible asset and an account therefor will, normally, only be found in the books of a business which has made some payment for goodwill purchased from some other firm or individual. In such circumstances, the vending agreement will be examined to ascertain the amount paid for goodwill which will be either a specified sum or the excess of the total price paid for the business acquired over the book value of the net assets taken over. The real value of the goodwill of any business can be said to fluctuate almost daily and it is not part of an auditor's duty to consider whether this value is greater or smaller than its book value at a balance sheet date.

In partnerships the book value of goodwill may be written up or down at will, provided that all the partners are in agreement with the adjustment made. The auditor, in such circumstances, should satisfy himself that the implications of the entries made have been fully understood by all the partners and he should inspect a minute or other document signed by all parties in which they formally agree thereto.

§ 8. Events occurring after the Balance Sheet date

The interval which elapses between the date of the balance sheet and the completion of the audit naturally varies considerably, but during this period events may take place which have some bearing on the values placed on the assets or the amounts of the liabilities included in the balance sheet. It must be remembered, however, that the purpose of a balance sheet is to show the financial position of the business *as at the date of such balance sheet* and that, therefore, matters which arise after that date, however important they may be, cannot be dealt with in the balance sheet unless they are such as to show that the first draft was, in fact, incorrect. Thus, if a property owned by a company was destroyed by fire on 15th February – a date prior to the completion of the audit – this would not justify any amendment of the balance sheet dated the preceding 31st December, even though the property was uninsured and a substantial loss had resulted. Such a matter would be the concern of the directors who should communicate the facts to the shareholders in their report or in the chairman's statement accompanying the accounts.

Many matters may arise, however, before the audit is completed, which show that estimates or valuations made at the balance sheet date were wrong *at that date*. Regard must be had for events of this nature and the auditor should see that the appropriate adjustments have been made in the balance sheet. Examples of such matters are:

(*a*) Provision for liabilities, the precise amount of which cannot be ascertained, must normally be made at a balance sheet date. Such provisions are estimates and subsequent events may prove them to have been inadequate or excessive. The after-acquired information must be used to adjust the amount of the provision if the difference is material.

(*b*) Changes in legislation affecting taxation may take place after the date of the balance sheet, which in turn affect the provisions for taxation made therein. The provisions should be adjusted to give effect to the new taxation position.

(c) The provision at a balance sheet date for bad and doubtful debts must necessarily be made on an estimated basis. It may be, however, that before the audit is completed certain debts which were regarded as bad are paid in full, whilst others, deemed to be good, prove to be irrecoverable. These events show the real value of the debts in question *at the balance sheet date* and the necessary adjustments must be made to the provision created.

The recommendations of the Council of the Institute of Chartered Accountants on this matter are given hereunder.

Events which, at the time of preparing annual accounts, are known to have occurred after the balance sheet date, should not normally be taken into account in preparing accounts unless:

(a) they assist in forming an opinion as to the amount properly attributable, in the conditions existing on the balance sheet date, to any item the amount of which was subject to uncertainty on that date; or

(b) they arise from legislation affecting items in the accounts, for example changes in taxation, or are required by law to be shown in the accounts, for example appropriations and proposed appropriations of profits.

The foregoing recommendation concerns the extent to which events occurring after the balance sheet date need to be dealt with in the accounts for the period ended on that date but events which are properly excluded from those accounts may nevertheless be of such importance that they need to be disclosed to shareholders through some other medium.

CHAPTER VII

THE BALANCE SHEET AUDIT

§ 1. Introduction

The method of auditing which has been described in the preceding chapters can be summarized as follows:

(1) Original entries in day books and cash books are vouched and the casts of such books tested.

(2) The postings from the books of prime entry to the appropriate ledger accounts are tested.

(3) Ledger balances are checked and, in the cases of sales and bought ledgers, or their equivalents, agreed with schedules of debtors and creditors, and with the trial balance in the cases of the private and impersonal ledgers.

(4) Sales ledger balances are examined from the viewpoint of possible bad or doubtful debts and the balances on the bought ledger confirmed by reference to creditors' statements, and circularization where necessary.

(5) The provisions made for outstandings at the balance sheet date are subjected to careful scrutiny.

(6) The items appearing in the trading and profit and loss account and balance sheet are agreed with the trial balance and the schedule of any adjustments which are required.

(7) The ownership and continued existence of the assets appearing in the balance sheet are verified and due regard is paid to the adequacy of the provisions made for depreciation.

A detailed audit thus starts with the books of prime entry and ends with the balance sheet, the sequence of checking following the order in which the entries are made.

This procedure is satisfactory when applied to the audit of the accounts of small and medium sized concerns, especially when the books are kept by hand-written methods. In larger cases, however, particularly when the records are mechanized, the 'vouch and post' audit is often unsatisfactory, if not impracticable, for the following reasons:

(a) A large volume of transactions requires a considerable amount of summarization and posting of totals to other summaries, with the result that it is frequently difficult to appreciate the ultimate effect of the entry under examination.

(b) Links in the chain of records which extends from prime entry to private ledger may either be missing entirely or be presented in a very attenuated form, e.g. by means of a mechanized list summarizing an accompanying file of documents.

(c) If the financial and cost accounts are integrated, it will be impossible to trace expenditure on materials, wages and overheads directly to the impersonal ledger. In these circumstances it will be found that almost all expenditure is posted to one or more control accounts and that the vast majority of entries in the impersonal ledger are made from costing abstracts which are based on materials requisitions, wage allocations and summaries of overhead expenses. The link between outgoings on the one hand and the ultimate ledger accounts on the other will be provided by the following records:

   (i) *Purchases of raw materials:* the stores ledger, materials requisitions and the costing summaries.

   (ii) *Wages:* the wages control account, time sheets or clock cards and the wages allocations.

   (iii) *Overhead Expenses:* the overhead expenses control account (which may be divided so as to provide separate control accounts for works, selling and administrative expenses) and summaries and abstracts of expenditure.

(d) In large companies, the system of internal check, coupled possibly with an internal audit, is often sound enough to make the exhaustive checking of original entries unnecessary.

In any event the volume of transactions may be so great that it is impossible for more than a small proportion of the routine accounting entries to be checked by conventional methods, if the audit is to be completed in a reasonable time and at a reasonable fee.

For the reasons enumerated above, and an increasing realization of the fact that the importance of checking arithmetical accuracy must be kept in its right perspective, there has been a growing tendency in recent years to carry out what is usually termed a 'Balance Sheet Audit'. This type of audit *starts* with the verification of the items appearing in the balance sheet and involves only such an examination of original entries and vouchers as the auditor feels to be necessary in the circumstances.

§ 2. The Relationship of Balance Sheet and Profit and Loss Account

It will be appreciated that every transaction has an ultimate effect on the balance sheet. Some transactions affect both the balance sheet and the profit and loss account but others merely result in a variation in certain balance sheet items, thus:

(*a*) The payment of a liability reduces the *asset* 'cash at bank' and the *liability* 'creditors' by the same amount.

(*b*) The collection of a sum due results in a reduction in the *asset* 'debtors' and a corresponding increase in the *asset* 'cash at bank'.

(*c*) The purchase of a fixed asset increases the appropriate 'fixed *asset*' account and either reduces the *asset* 'cash at bank' or increases the *liability* 'creditors'.

(*d*) The issue of debentures for cash results in an increase in the *asset* 'cash at bank' and a similar increase in fixed '*liabilities*'.

The majority of transactions, however, affect both the balance sheet and the profit and loss account as will be seen from the examples of the ultimate effect of normal trading transactions given below.

(*a*) The sale of goods on credit at a profit increases the *asset* 'debtors' by the selling price, reduces the *asset* 'stock' by the cost price and increases the balance on the profit and loss account by the profit earned.

(*b*) The payment of salaries reduces the *asset* 'cash at bank' and the balance on the profit and loss account.

(*c*) Provisions made for depreciation of fixed assets reduce the net values at which such assets appear in the balance sheet and the balance on the profit and loss account, but do not reduce the liquid resources of the business.

(*d*) The receipt of bank interest increases the *asset* 'cash at bank' and the balance to the credit of profit and loss account.

It must also be realized that any under- or over-statement of an asset or liability will normally have a corresponding effect on the balance of the profit and loss account. For example, an over-valuation of stock results in an overstatement of profit; an excessive provision for an outstanding liability deflates profit; the omission from trade creditors of a supplier's invoice for goods taken into stock inflates profit.

It should therefore be appreciated that the verification of the accuracy of the assets and liabilities appearing in the balance sheet, coupled with a careful analysis of the changes which have taken place therein since the previous balance sheet, also does much to prove the accuracy of the profit and loss account.

§ 3. The Programme for a Balance Sheet Audit

If the auditor is satisfied that the system of internal check in operation is adequate, and it has been shown to be working satisfactorily by the tests he has made of the detailed entries, he may feel justified in carrying out a balance sheet audit. The following are the principal items to be included in the programme for such an audit. It will be seen that each is of such a nature that it can only be performed by a skilled accountant; work of this description cannot be delegated to clerks who do not possess the technical knowledge and experience required to make the appraisals which are called for.

(1) Compare each item in the trading and profit and loss account with the corresponding item for the previous year and ascertain the reasons for any material variations.

(2) Consider whether increases or decreases in wages, materials consumed and variable expenses appear to be proportionate to the increase or decrease in turnover. Ascertain the quantities of turnover where the monetary value thereof has been inflated or deflated by price changes, alterations in rates of purchase tax, customs duties etc.

(3) Obtain a satisfactory explanation for any material change in the rate of gross profit earned.

(4) Ascertain the reason for any substantial increase or decrease in the net profit for the period compared with that recorded for the previous period.

(5) Scrutinize any exceptional transactions or items of a nonrecurring nature which have resulted in charges or credits of a material amount to the revenue of the period.

(6) Consider the effect of the recorded profit on the position disclosed by the balance sheet. For example, does this reveal increased liquidity, a reduction in capital or long-term liabilities or increases in fixed assets?

(7) Compare the value of stocks on hand with the cost of turnover and enquire into any material change in this ratio, which indicates the average rate at which stocks have been turned round in the year. Compare such values with those adopted for insurance purposes.

(8) Examine the schedules showing the composition of each item appearing in the balance sheet and compare such items with the corresponding figures for the previous period. Consider carefully all material changes.

(9) If the total due by trade debtors is disproportionate to turnover, as compared with the corresponding figures for the previous year, ascertain the reason for this. If it is found that longer credit appears to have been taken by customers, pay particular attention to the provisions for bad and doubtful debts and the possibility that remittances have not been accounted for. If sales of an exceptional amount are recorded towards the end of the period, make certain that the sales in question are properly attributable to that period, and examine the returns for the ensuing period.

(10) Consider the total shown to be due to trade creditors in relation to the purchases for the period, the value of stocks on hand and the period of credit normally taken.

(11) Compare the schedules of outstandings and provisions with those for the previous period and enquire into any material changes.

(12) Scrutinize the minute books for any references to matters affecting the accounts, e.g. capital commitments, litigation, commissions payable under service agreements, capital issues etc.

(13) Consider the values placed on current assets, with particular attention to the basis of valuation of stock and work in progress.

(14) Consider the reasonableness of all provisions made for depreciation and, where appropriate, compare them with the capital allowances granted for taxation. Consider the creation of a taxation equalization account, if such a comparison reveals substantial differences.

(15) Ascertain whether there have been any changes in the basis of accounting which have resulted in a material increase or decrease in the recorded profit.

(16) Make all necessary enquiries to determine the amounts and nature of any contingent liabilities and commitments for capital expenditure not provided for in the accounts, and ascertain the extent of any contracts for forward purchases or sales. In cases of forward contracts, consider whether any provision for anticipated losses is required at the balance sheet date.

(17) Examine carefully the adjustments made in the taxation computations. See that any amounts added back which come within (5) above have been properly dealt with.

(18) Where appropriate, compare with the accounts concerned the figures shown by certificates and returns made to trade associations, insurance companies and government departments in respect of wages and salaries paid, declarations for insurance purposes, returns to the customs and excise authorities and similar documents.

(19) Verify in the usual manner the other assets and liabilities not already dealt with.

It must, of course, be emphasized that where such a programme is followed it must not be overlooked that an apparently satisfactory position in relation to a particular line of enquiry may, in fact, be the result of compensating factors.

§ 4. Audit Working Papers

In addition to his permanent file and audit programme, it is essential in the case of a balance sheet audit for the auditor to prepare a full set of detailed schedules forming a fully documented summary of the books of account. For each class of asset and liability a separate schedule should be prepared, each of which should be supported by supplementary schedules reconciling the particular asset or liability under consideration with the corresponding figure in the previous balance sheet and thus providing an epitome of the transactions affecting the account during the period.

The entries in the schedule should be carefully cross indexed so that it can readily be seen, for example, that the amount credited to the provision for depreciation account is the same as that charged in the profit and loss account, or, if it is not, how the difference is explained. An example of typical working papers, covering fixed assets, depreciation and debtors is given below:

PQR LTD.

AUDIT WORKING PAPERS

Year to 31st December, 19......

Fixed Assets at Cost   *Schedule A*

	LAND AND BUILDINGS	PLANT	VEHICLES
	£	£	£
Balance per previous balance sheet ..	17,500	24,000	16,000
Additions at cost per Schedule A.1 ..	2,400	6,000	1,800
	19,900	30,000	17,800
Less: Cost of assets sold etc., per Schedule A.2	700	1,100	400
	£19,200	£28,900	£17,400

Schedule of Assets purchased   *Schedule A.1*

Land and Buildings

(a) Deposit on land (authorized by Minute of 15th November, 19......)		£400
(b) Purchase of house (Minute 24th September, 19......) ..		2,000
Per Schedule A		£2,400

(a) Completion of land purchase to be made 15th January, 19......
Balance per schedule of capital commitments (R3) £3,600.
Contract inspected by J.B.

(b) Purchase of house:
    Contract and completion statement inspected and adjustments for accruals verified by J.B.
    Fire insurance policy inspected by J.B.
    Deeds inspected at bank by L.M.R.

Plant and Machinery
Per Capital orders (wages, materials and works overheads):

C.O. 72.	New machine (Minute 14th January, 19......) ..	£4,800
73.	Extension to Machine 24 (Minute 15th February, 19......)	1,000
74.	Foundation for new P machine	200
	Per Schedule A	£6,000

Note: P machine is expected to cost £1,700
Ordered 15th December, 19...... .. ..
This item requires the approval of the Board.
Balance per schedule of Capital Commitments (R.3) £1,700

Checked with Plant Register by J.B.

Motor Vehicles

New van AB 9999 (purchased 30th June ......)		£1,100
New car AB 8888 (purchased 1st January ......)		700
Per Schedule A		£1,800

Checked with Vehicles Register by J.B.
Registration books inspected by J.B.

Schedule of Assets Sold, Scrapped etc   *Schedule A.2*

Land and Buildings

Claim for destruction by fire	£650
Loss (transferred to depreciation, Schedule D.1)	50
Per Schedule A	£700

Insurance claim and settlement examined by L.M.R.

Plant and Machinery

Sale of machine 21 (cost £1,100)	£800
Accumulated depreciation written back from provision for depreciation account (Schedule R.2)	250
Loss (Schedule D.1)	50
Per Schedule A	£1,100

Checked with Plant Register by J.B.

Motor Vehicles

Sale of van AB 7777 (cost £400)	£225
Accumulated depreciation written back (Schedule R.2) ..	200
	425
Profit on sale (Schedule D.1)	25
Per Schedule A	£400

Checked with Vehicles Register by J.B.

Depreciation and Obsolescence   *Schedule D.1*

On assets 31/12/19......

Land and buildings	nil
Plant: 10% on cost	£2,400
Vehicles: 25% on cost	4,000

On additions during the year (A.1):

Land and buildings	nil
Plant C.O. 72. 10% for 6 months	240
73. 10% for 3 months	25
74. —	nil

Motor Vehicles (A.1):

AB 9999 25% for 6 months	137
AB 8888 25% for 12 months	175
Per Schedule R.2	6,977
Loss on fire claim (A.2)	50
Loss on sale of Machine 21 (A.2)	50
	7,077
Less: Profit on sale of van AB 7777	25
Per profit and loss account ..	£7,052

Provision for Depreciation   *Schedule R.2*

	TOTAL £	PLANT £	VEHICLES £
Balance per last balance sheet	16,500	7,500	9,000
Charge for the year (D.1)	6,977	2,665	4,312
	23,477	10,165	13,312
Less: Accumulated depreciation on assets displaced	450	250	200
Per balance sheet	£23,027	£9,915	£13,112

Checked with Plant and Vehicles Registers by J.B.

Schedule of Capital Commitments   *Schedule R.3*

Purchase of Land (A.1)	£3,600
New P. Machine (A.1)	1,700
Per note to balance sheet.. ..	£5,300

Debtors   *Schedule C.1*

Sales ledger accounts (per summary D.2)	£75,000
Debit balances on bought ledger (per summary D.3)	290
Prepayments (per summary P.1)	1,400
	76,690
Less: Provision for bad debts (unchanged since previous year) ..	1,500
Per balance sheet	£75,190

Notes:

  (i) The balances of Ledger A-C checked to schedule by A.B.

 (ii) All debts appearing bad have been written off.

(iii) All sales ledger debtors circulated with audit statement. No material discrepancies revealed.

Notes:

  (i) Schedules D.2, D.3 and P.1 are not given.

 (ii) The sales and bought ledger control accounts might be included in the working papers in summary form so that the causes of the variation in sales and bought ledger balances during the period under review are clearly revealed.

It will be observed that a perusal of the working papers will bring the transactions into focus so that the content of the items appearing in the accounts can be understood.

If the additions to plant are fabricated in the company's own workshops, each capital order will consist of labour, materials and overhead allocations, based on wages abstracts, requisitions and overhead expense summaries. Although the auditor can, and should, test a proportion of these documents, noting the code number and the certification of each, he will not obtain such a clear picture of the nature and purpose of the expenditure as by the method of 'working backwards' indicated above. Each capital order can be substantiated by board minute or by engineer's certificate, and the auditor can call for the various internal documents making up the total.

The principles of valuation of assets are unchanged under the balance sheet audit and each must be verified in the normal way. In fact this method of approach places greater emphasis on verification.

§ 5. Detailed Checking

It cannot be too strongly emphasized that a careful consideration of the adequacy of the system of internal check is of paramount importance in determining the programme to be followed in the audit of large undertakings and the auditor should obtain a written statement of the procedures adopted. If there is an internal audit department, the auditor should obtain copies of their programme and periodical reports. In the light of these, the auditor will be able to appraise the effectiveness of the system of internal check and plan his own audit programme accordingly.

If the auditor is satisfied that the system of internal check ensures that errors are brought to light and rectified and that it provides an adequate safeguard against fraud, it would clearly be absurd for him to check every posting and cast and vouch every entry in the books. It will be appreciated, however, that the quantity of detailed checking carried out is the auditor's own responsibility and that, therefore, the accuracy of his appraisal of the effectiveness of the internal check is a matter of the greatest importance.

When the auditor decides to confine his checking of details to a series of tests, he must ensure that a representative number of transactions are checked through from the primary records to their final destination in the accounting system by the method of 'depth checking', dealt with earlier. For example, all purchases for a short period may be vouched in detail, the receipt of the goods being traced to the goods inwards books and stores ledger accounts, if any. The invoices should be compared with the copy orders and the prices tested with tenders, quotations or price lists. A batch of requisitions should be checked to the stores ledger and enquiries made as to the certification thereof. These requisitions should be traced to the materials abstracts, particular attention being paid to the codings appearing on the forms. The method of allocating overhead expenses should be investigated, the loading for overheads added to capital and service orders being noted.

For the same period, the system of invoicing should be examined and attention paid to any reconciliations of quantities of raw materials purchased with the quantities of finished products sold. The allowances for wastage should be examined and comparisons made, if possible, between one factory and another or between one period and another.

The method of authorizing the dispatch of goods from the premises must be ascertained and the danger of goods being dispatched without being invoiced (either fraudulently or by error) should be assessed. The wage system should be investigated and a proportion of the time sheets or clock cards examined and used as vouchers for the earnings recorded for the employees. The safeguards against the inclusion of 'dummy men' should be examined and the extent of the collusion which would be necessary to perpetrate this type of fraud considered. Periodically the names on the payroll should be compared with the file of new and discharged employees kept in the personnel department and with the register of the superannuation scheme if one is in force. Any discrepancies should be carefully enquired into.

The detailed examination of the transactions of a comparatively short period will give the auditor a greater insight into the methods and procedures and the personnel employed than would a more superficial check of a longer period. Where the 'depth' procedure, as exemplified above, is followed through its various stages in respect of the *same* selected transactions, a continuity is achieved which is impossible in cases where the audit programme merely specifies the length of period to be checked at a particular stage of recording, e.g. postings from cash book to sales ledger. Furthermore, the so-called 'random' selection of, say, two months for detailed checking may *increase* the possibility of fraud if it is the auditor's practice to omit an examination of those two months in the subsequent year, and the client's staff have become aware of this practice through its consistent application over a number of years.

CHAPTER VIII

THE AUDITOR OF A LIMITED COMPANY

§ 1. The Appointment and Remuneration of Auditors

The majority of the audits undertaken by professional accountants are those of limited companies and it is, therefore, essential
that the auditor should be fully conversant with the provisions of
the *Companies Acts 1948* and *1967* relating to his appointment,
duties and rights.

(A) AUDITORS APPOINTED ON BEHALF OF THE COMPANY

The appointment of auditors is dealt with in Section 159,
Companies Act 1948, the provisions of which are as under:

(1) Every company shall at each annual general meeting appoint an
auditor or auditors to hold office from the conclusion of that, until the conclusion of the next, annual general meeting.

(2) At any annual general meeting a retiring auditor, however appointed,
shall be reappointed without any resolution being passed unless –

(*a*) he is not qualified for reappointment; or

(*b*) a resolution has been passed at that meeting appointing somebody instead of him or providing expressly that he shall not be reappointed; or

(*c*) he has given the company notice in writing of his unwillingness to be
reappointed:

Provided that where notice is given of an intended resolution to appoint
some person or persons in place of a retiring auditor, and by reason of the
death, incapacity or disqualification of that person or of all those persons,
as the case may be, the resolution cannot be proceeded with, the retiring
auditor shall not be automatically reappointed by virtue of this subsection.

(3) Where at an annual general meeting no auditors are appointed or reappointed, the Board of Trade may appoint a person to fill the vacancy.

(4) The company shall, within one week of the Board's power under the
last foregoing subsection become exercisable, give them notice of that
fact, and, if a company fails to give notice as required by this subsection,
the company and every officer of the company who is in default shall be
liable to a default fine.

(5) Subject as hereinafter provided, the first auditors of a company may
be appointed by the directors at any time before the first annual general
meeting, and auditors so appointed shall hold office until the conclusion of
that meeting:

Provided that—

(a) the company may at a general meeting remove any such auditors and appoint in their place any other persons who have been nominated for appointment by any member of the company and of whose nomination notice has been given to the members of the company not less than fourteen days before the date of the meeting; and

(b) if the directors fail to exercise their powers under this subsection, the company in general meeting may appoint the first auditors, and thereupon the said powers of the directors shall cease.

(6) The directors may fill any casual vacancy in the office of auditor, but while any such vacancy continues, the surviving or continuing auditor or auditors, if any, may act.

(B) THE QUALIFICATION REQUIRED FOR APPOINTMENT AS AUDITOR OF A COMPANY

The auditor of a company must possess the qualification required by Section 161 (1) *Companies Act 1948*, as amended by Section 13 (4) *Companies Act 1967*.

Section 161 (1) of the 1948 Act is as follows:

(1) A person shall not be qualified for appointment as auditor of a company unless either:

(a) he is a member of a body of accountants established in the United Kingdom and for the time being recognized for the purposes of this provision by the Board of Trade; or

(b) he is for the time being authorized by the Board of Trade to be so appointed either as having similar qualifications obtained outside the United Kingdom or as having obtained adequate knowledge and experience in the course of his employment by a member of a body of accountants recognized for the purposes of the foregoing paragraph or as having before the sixth day of August, nineteen hundred and forty-seven, practised in Great Britain as an accountant.

However, application to the Board of Trade in this connection must have been made before 27th January, 1968 (Section 13 (4), *Companies Act 1967*).

The following bodies of accountants established in the United Kingdom have been recognised by the Board of Trade for the purposes of Section 161 (1) of the *Companies Act 1948*:

The Institute of Chartered Accountants in England and Wales.
The Association of Certified and Corporate Accountants.
The Institute of Chartered Accountants of Scotland.
The Institute of Chartered Accountants in Ireland.

A member of any of the above bodies is accordingly qualified, as far as this provision is concerned, for appointment as auditor of a company.

In view of the repeal, under Section 2 of the 1967 Act, of the status of exempt private company, the exceptions to the qualification requirements previously available to auditors of exempt private companies no longer have any effect. However, provisions which deal with the situation of such auditors are included in Section 13, and these may be summarized as follows:

(1) A person shall be qualified for appointment as auditor of a private company or unquoted public company provided he has been authorized by the Board of Trade as having been in practice as an accountant throughout the twelve months to 3rd November, 1966, and on that date was the duly appointed auditor of a company which was an exempt private company under the principal Act. In all cases such a company's holding company must also be a private company or unquoted public company.

(2) A person who is the auditor of an exempt private company may continue in office until the expiration of twelve months from 27th January, 1968, provided that none of that company's shares or debentures, or those of its holding company, have been quoted on a stock exchange or offered to the public (Section 13 (1) and (2)).

Apart from the disqualifications from appointment as auditor on the grounds of lack of professional competence as explained above, the following persons are not qualified to act as auditors of a company:

(a) An officer or servant of the company;

(b) A person who is a partner of or in the employment of an officer or servant of the company;

(c) a body corporate;

(d) A person who, for one of the reasons given above, is disqualified from acting as auditor of any other body corporate which is that company's subsidiary or holding company or a subsidiary of that company's holding company or would be so disqualified if the body corporate was a company.

Prior to the coming into effect of the 1967 Act, the disqualification provided by (b) above did not apply to the auditor of an exempt private company. It is now provided under Section 13 (3) that a person shall not be disqualified from acting as auditor of a company which was an exempt private company, on the grounds expressed in (b) above, at any time during the period of three years from 27th January, 1968, on condition that on that date he was the duly appointed auditor thereof, and that none of the company's shares or debentures (or those of its holding company) have been quoted on the stock exchange or offered to the public.

Any body corporate which acts as auditor of a company is liable to a fine not exceeding £100.

In view of the uncertainty as to whether some of the duties often undertaken by accountants on behalf of a company might disqualify them or their partners from acting as the company's auditors, the Institute of Chartered Accountants obtained counsel's opinion as to the position where an accountant acts in any of the following capacities. The opinion is summarized hereunder:

(i) *Registrar.* A registrar is not an officer of the company provided that his contract with the company is 'for services' and not 'of service'.

(ii) *Financial Adviser.* A financial adviser or consultant is not a servant of the company unless the company has the right to control his services.

(iii) *Employee of Auditor.* An accountant is not disqualified from appointment as auditor of a company by reason of the fact that his employee acts as a director, secretary or otherwise as an officer of the company. (The employer of an officer or servant of a building society, however, may not act as the society's auditor.)

(iv) *Liquidator or Receiver.* The appointment of an accountant as liquidator or receiver of a company does not disqualify him or his partner from appointment as auditor of a subsidiary, holding company or fellow subsidiary of that company or, in the case of a receiver, as auditor of the company itself. If, however, an accountant is appointed *receiver and manager* of a company, he will be an officer of the company and the disqualification will, therefore, apply.

(C) THE AUDITOR'S REMUNERATION

By Section 159 (7) *Companies Act 1948*, the remuneration of the auditors of a company—

(*a*) in the case of an auditor appointed by the directors or by the Board of Trade, may be fixed by the directors or by the board, as the case may be;

(*b*) subject to the foregoing paragraph, shall be fixed by the company in general meeting or in such manner as the company in general meeting may determine.

For this purpose the expression 'remuneration' includes sums paid by the company in respect of the auditor's expenses, and the amount thereof must be shown separately in the company's profit and loss account (Second Schedule, *Companies Act 1967*). In those cases where the exact remuneration and expenses cannot be determined at the date when the accounts are completed, the Council of the Institute of Chartered Accountants recommend that 'an estimated amount should be included in the accounts, and any subsequent adjustment, if material in relation to the estimated amount previously disclosed should be shown in the accounts of the following period'.

In many cases in practice, auditors charge an inclusive fee for auditing the company's books and other work, e.g. secretarial, taxation and accountancy matters. In these circumstances it is recommended by the Council of the Institute that the remuneration, shown separately in the company's profit and loss account, 'should be limited to or specified separately as the remuneration for the auditor's duties under the Acts. The fees for other professional services should be treated as a general expense of the business'.

(D) THE REMOVAL OF AUDITORS

As explained above, when the first auditors of a company are appointed by the directors prior to the first annual general meeting, such auditors may be removed by the members in general meeting. Where it is desired to appoint a person other than the retiring auditor as auditor of the company at an annual general meeting, notice of the intention to move such a resolution must be given to the company by a shareholder not less than fourteen days before the annual general meeting in the case of the first auditor, and *special* notice of twenty-eight days in all other cases. On receipt of such a notice the company must forthwith send a copy to the retiring auditor.

If he wishes to do so, the retiring auditor, after receipt of the notice intimating that a resolution is to be moved appointing another person in his place or that he shall not be reappointed auditor of the company, may make representations to the company in writing (not exceeding a reasonable length) and ask for such representations to be sent to the members of the company (Section 160 (3) *Companies Act 1948*). On receipt of such representations the company must, unless it is too late to do so –

(*a*) state the fact that such representations have been made in any notice of the resolution sent to members; and

(*b*) send a copy of the representations to every member of the company to whom notice of the meeting is sent (whether before or after receipt of the representations by the company).

If a copy of the representations is not sent to the members, either because it was received too late to do so, or because of default by the company, the auditor may insist that the representations shall be read out at the meeting. The Act provides, however, that copies of the representations need not be sent out, and the representations need not be read out at the meeting if, on the application either of the company or of any other person who claims to be aggrieved, the Court is satisfied that the rights conferred upon the auditor by Section 160 are being abused to secure needless publicity for defamatory matter. In these circumstances the Court may order the company's costs on an application to be paid in whole or in part by the auditor, notwithstanding that he was not a party to the application. The first auditor of a company has a similar right to make representations when notice is given of an intention to remove him at a general meeting.

It must, of course, be remembered that in addition to his right to make written representations, the retiring auditor has the power to attend the annual general meeting at which his removal is to be proposed and to address the members.

The right to make written representations was conferred upon the retiring auditor for the first time by the *Companies Act 1948*.

It will be observed that although the directors have power to appoint the first auditors before the first annual general meeting, such auditors can be removed by resolution of the company in general meeting, and in this way the ultimate right of appointment rests with the members in every instance, with the exception of a casual vacancy. This emphasizes the fact that the auditor is responsible to the members, and acts on their behalf, and not on behalf of the directors. In actual practice, as the directors are agents for the members in conducting the affairs of the company, the auditor will naturally come into personal contact with them in the course of his duties, and he will sometimes meet directors who seem to consider that the auditor exists merely to seal with his official approval the accounts presented by the board; but it must be remembered that the auditor is the representative of the members, and his statutory duties are owed to them.

Special provisions for the appointment of an auditor, other than a retiring auditor, were first introduced by the *Companies Act 1907* owing to the method, sometimes adopted by directors where there was a difference of opinion between the retiring auditor and themselves, of nominating another auditor without notifying the retiring auditor of their intention so to do, and carrying the appointment of the new auditor by means of the proxies at their disposal. Such procedure was in many cases detrimental to the general interests of the members, and was certainly a very poor reward for the auditor who had too faithfully discharged his duties to them. The fact that notice must be sent to the retiring auditor, and to all members prior to the general meeting, in the event of any auditor other than the retiring auditor being nominated, prevents any alteration in the appointment without the knowledge of all the members.

The situation arising as a result of an irreconcilable difference of opinion between the director of a company and its auditors was exemplified in the case of the accounts of The City of London Real Property Company Limited for the year ended April 12th, 1963, where the directors and auditors could not agree on the amount at which shares in subsidiary companies ought to be stated on the balance sheet. The directors sought the opinion of counsel, who supported their view, but the auditors were not swayed in their own opinion as to the correct treatment of this item. The directors, in order to avoid the inclusion in the accounts of a qualified auditors' report, finally agreed to the publication of the balance sheet in conformity with the views of the auditors, but proposed that owing to the loss of mutual confidence between the directors and auditors, the latter should be replaced by another firm. In this connection, the following important announcement was made by the Institute of Chartered Accountants in England and Wales in June 1963:

DISPLACEMENT OF AUDITORS
STATEMENT BY THE INSTITUTE OF CHARTERED ACCOUNTANTS IN ENGLAND AND WALES

(1) In view of the important responsibilities of auditors towards the investing public, the Institute considers that the proposal, contained in the report of the directors of The City of London Real Property Company Limited for the year ended 12th April, 1963, that the auditors at present in office shall be replaced by another firm, raises issues of general importance which render it necessary for a statement to be made by the Institute on the principles which are involved in relation to such a displacement. The reason given by the directors for this proposal is set out in the chairman's review, the relevant paragraph of which is reproduced as a footnote hereto.*

(2) The auditors of a company are appointed to represent the shareholders in accordance with the requirements of the Companies Act and have a statutory duty to make a critical review of the accounts submitted by the directors and to report to the shareholders whether those accounts show a true and fair view and comply with the requirements of the Act.

(3) If the auditors disagree with such accounts to any material extent their duty is to say so in their report and to specify the material respects in which they disagree.

(4) The fact that the auditors disagree, if they do so, is not a justification for their displacement unless the reasons for their disagreement are such that the shareholders no longer have confidence in the judgment, competence or conduct of the auditors as their representatives.

(5) Confidence between directors and auditors, whilst obviously desirable, is not indispensable for the adequate performance by the auditors of their onerous duties on behalf of the shareholders; indeed in some circumstances the performance of those duties may lead inevitably to difference of opinion between the directors and auditors and to a report to this effect by the auditors to the shareholders.

(6) The existence of such a possibility is among the reasons why auditors are appointed. The work of auditors and their freedom to perform it with a sense of complete independence can only continue as long as it is generally accepted that the issue by auditors of a report expressing disagreement with the directors of a company of which they are the auditors

does not of itself provide a reason for the removal of the auditors from office. The purpose implicit in the appointment of auditors under the Companies Act would be defeated if there were to grow up a practice of displacing auditors whenever a disagreement between them and the directors of a company occurs on a matter of accounting principle.

(7) The displacement of auditors who represent and report to the shareholders is, therefore, a serious matter and is of great importance to shareholders. The principles set out in this statement are of the greatest significance and the Institute considers, therefore, that it has a duty to draw attention to them.

---

*EXTRACT FROM THE CHAIRMAN'S REVIEW

'AUDITORS

As indicated in the Notice of the Annual General Meeting and the Directors' Report a change of Auditors is to be proposed. This arises out of a difference of opinion between the Board and the Auditors in regard to which the view of the Board is supported by the advice of Counsel. The Auditors were not prepared to give an unqualified certificate unless the Balance Sheet reflected their view, so it is presented in accordance therewith. As, however, the all important mutual confidence between the Board of a Company and its Auditors no longer exists a change is in the opinion of the Board in the interests of the Stockholders.'

It is not surprising to note that the proposed change did not, in fact, materialize.

Before allowing himself to be nominated as auditor in place of a retiring auditor, a person must communicate with the retiring auditor to ascertain whether he knows of any reason why the nomination should not be accepted. Failure to do this is regarded as a breach of professional etiquette, and is liable to evoke disciplinary action by the governing bodies of the accountancy profession.

Clients may seek professional and consultancy services from accountants other than those presently acting as auditors, and accountants who are introduced to such clients for this purpose should, as a matter of etiquette, contact the firm's auditors in order to keep them informed as to the work which they have been invited to undertake, and their progress while executing it. The Institute of Chartered Accountants, in their newsletter of June 1968, recommended the following approach to such a relationship:

Whatever the nature of the introduction the consultant should, in so far as it is practicable, ensure that the existing accountant is kept informed as to the general nature of the work which the consultant is doing. This may be done either by the consultant himself or, if the client so requests, by the client. The existing accountant for his part should keep in touch with the consultant so as to give him any assistance within his power. From time to time the consultant may be asked by the client to undertake additional work of a type which is clearly distinct from that originally undertaken. In such cases the consultant should regard this as a separate request to provide advice or services and should communicate with the existing accountant as indicated in the previous paragraph.

A member called upon to render service of whatever kind to the client of another accountancy practitioner who is continuing in his relationship with that client has not merely the negative duty of refraining from soliciting any work which is being performed by that other practitioner but the positive duty of taking all steps reasonably open to him to support the other practitioner in retaining his relationship. The latter has an equivalent duty to his professional colleague to support the relationshp between the client and the consultant.

Failure to observe the standards of conduct set out in this statement could render a member liable to disciplinary action.

(E) JOINT AUDITOR

Two or more auditors are sometimes appointed, particularly in the case of large concerns, such as banking or insurance companies, or where the regulations of the company so require. In such cases each auditor is jointly responsible; but where the work performed by the auditors is divided by mutual agreement, it may be desirable for each auditor to avoid responsibility for work he has not performed, by a specific statement in the report as to the extent of the audit carried out by him.

(F) LOCAL AUDITORS

Companies carrying on business abroad, such as those possessing foreign branches or mines, frequently employ a local auditor or auditors, who audit the accounts locally and report upon them before their transmission to the head office. Such auditors may be appointed by the main board of directors or by the local board, or their appointment may be made by the members in general meeting. The latter course is preferable, as it renders the local auditors more independent, and they become directly responsible to the members.

Where a local audit of this nature is performed, the company's auditor will not examine the returns rendered in detail, but will confine himself to questions of principle, and to ascertaining that the accounts are properly incorporated in the head office books.

In his report he should state that he has accepted the foreign returns as passed by the local auditor.

§ 2. The Status of the Auditor

(A) AS AGENT OF MEMBERS

The question as to how far the auditor is the agent of the members was discussed in *Spackman* v. *Evans* (3 H.L. 236), when Lord Chelmsford expressed the view that although auditors may be the agents of the shareholders, the latter could not be deemed to be precluded from objecting to any actions of the directors or others merely on the grounds that the auditors were aware of such actions.

Lord Cranworth stated in the course of the same case: 'The auditors may be agents of the shareholders, so far as relates to the audit of the accounts. For the purposes of the audit, the auditors will bind the shareholders.'

(B) AS AN OFFICER OF THE COMPANY

The question as to whether an auditor is an officer of the company is of particular importance, as it is only in his capacity as officer that he has been held liable, under Section 333 of the *Companies Act 1948*, to contribute to the company in the event of winding-up, any loss occasioned by misfeasance or breach of trust on his part. In the case of the *London & General Bank* (No. 1, 1895, 2 Ch. 166) it was held that the auditor of a banking company, registered under the *Companies Act 1879*, is an officer of the company. Lindley, L.J., read the section of that Act relating to auditors, and said: 'It seems impossible to deny that for some purposes, and to some extent, an auditor is an officer of the company. He is appointed by the company, he is paid by the company, and his position is described in the section as that of an officer of the company. He is not a servant of the directors. On the contrary, he is appointed by the company to check the directors, and for some purposes, and to some extent, it seems to me quite impossible to say that he is not an officer of the company.' The articles of this particular company frequently referred to the auditor as an officer of the company, and thus further influenced the decision.

In the case of the *Kingston Cotton Mill Co Ltd* (1896, 2 Ch. 279), the articles of the company relating to the audit of the accounts were, in substance, the same as the audit clauses of Table 'A' to the *Companies Act 1862*; but the articles did not specifically refer to the auditors as officers of the company. Notwithstanding this, it was held that there was no specific distinction between this case and that of the *London & General Bank*, and that the auditor, in the event of a winding-up, was an officer.

An auditor who has never been properly appointed is not an officer of the company (*Western Counties Steam Bakeries & Milling Co Ltd* (1897), 1 Ch. 617).

In *Regina* v. *Shacter* (1960, 1 All E.R. 61) the Court of Criminal Appeal held that an accountant appointed by a company to fill the office of auditor (as distinct from an appointment for a *particular* purpose) is an officer of the company and can therefore be charged under the *Companies Act 1948* and the *Larceny Act 1861* (under the provisions dealing with frauds and defaults by officers of a company) with publishing fraudulent statements and falsifying books of account. This case is dealt with more fully in Chapter XII.

It will therefore be seen that the auditor has in the past been held liable as an officer in both civil (Section 333) and criminal (Sections 328 to 332) cases under the *Companies Act 1948*.

There has been no further decision on the subject, but it would in any event appear that since Section 159 of the *Companies Act 1948* refers to the 'office of auditor' in terms similar to the Act of 1879, an auditor would be held to be an officer of the company, in so far as his duties as auditor are concerned.

There are numerous sections of the *Companies Act 1948*, under which, if default is made in complying with the requirements thereof, the company, and every director, manager, secretary, or other officer of the company, who is knowingly a party to the default, is liable to fines varying in amount according to the offence; and it is interesting to consider whether an auditor who, in the course of his duties, becomes aware of a default of this nature, might be held liable as an officer of the company. The point has not yet come before the courts, but it is one of some practical importance, as from time to time the auditor does become aware of such defaults. The question then arises as to his duty in these circumstances, particularly where the default is persisted in. Probably it would be sufficient for him to give the company notice in writing of his knowledge of the default, pointing out the consequences thereof, and dissociating himself from any responsibility in connection with it. If he has done this, it can hardly be said that he continues to be knowingly a party to the default. In any event, it could hardly be maintained that an auditor is an officer of the company for the purposes of, say, making returns to the Registrar of Companies.

The course which the professional accountant should adopt when he becomes aware of unlawful acts by his client, is fully discussed in Chapter XII.

§ 3. The Powers of the Auditor

Section 14 (5), *Companies Act 1967*, provides that every auditor of a company shall have a right of access at all times to the books and accounts and vouchers of the company, and shall be entitled to require from the officers of the company such information and explanation as he thinks necessary for the performance of his duties. The auditor can, therefore, inspect the company's records when he chooses: in practice, however, an auditor will arrange with the company a convenient date on which to commence his work, although he will usually exercise his statutory power to attend without notice for the purposes of verifying cash balances, negotiable securities etc., and should certainly do so where he suspects fraud or any other irregularity.

The phrase 'books and accounts and vouchers' will include, not only the financial books of the company, but all the books, whether statutory, statistical, or memorandum. In a similar manner the term 'vouchers' will include all or any of the correspondence of the company which may in any way serve to vouch for the accuracy of the accounts.

In a case where negligence was alleged against the auditors by the directors of a company who refused them access to the books for the purposes of the audit, the Court refused to make an order on the application of the auditors for access to the books, it being the practice of the Court, in cases affecting internal management, to direct that a meeting of members be summoned to determine their wishes in the matter (*Cuff* v. *London and County Land and Building Co* (1912), 1 Ch. 440). The auditors are the servants of the company, and if the company does not desire them to act, no Court will, by mandatory injunction, force them upon it. However, this decision must be seen in the context of the particular circumstances prevailing. The directors of the company were about to institute proceedings against the auditors for negligence, and had informed the auditors that in any event their services were no longer required.

The power entitling the auditor to require from the directors and officers of the company such information and explanations as he thinks necessary for the performance of his duties as auditor, is a most important one. The power is very wide and the decision as to what information and explanation is necessary is left entirely to the discretion of the auditor. If information or explanation is refused on the ground that the directors consider it is not necessary for the performance of the duties of the auditor, the auditor should report to the members that he has not obtained all the information and explanations he has required (Section 14 (6), *Companies Act 1967*).

The auditor is required to report to the members on the accounts examined by him. It is the duty of the directors to prepare the accounts for presentation to the auditor. It is not the duty of the auditor to balance the books, nor should he undertake to do so, unless specially requested by the directors, when he will be acting in the capacity of accountant, and not as auditor. Any additional work of this nature should be subject to a separate agreement and specially remunerated.

Where the company's accounts are kept on a system of which the auditor does not approve, he cannot *require* the directors to amend their system, but he can *request* them to do so, and in the majority of cases the auditor's advice will be followed. Where, however, the suggestions are not carried out, he should refer the matter to the members, if in his opinion the system employed is detrimental to their interests. Should the method of accounting be so inadequate that the auditor is unable to satisfy himself as to the accuracy of the accounts he must state in his report to the members that, in his opinion, proper books of account have not been kept by the company.

Under Section 14 (7) of the 1967 Act, the auditor has power to attend any general meeting of the company and to receive all notices of, and other communications relating to, any general meeting which any member of the company is entitled to receive. The auditor also has the right to be heard at any general meeting which the members attend, on any part of the business of the meeting which concerns him as auditor. This power to make explanations at the meeting does not absolve the auditor from making a clear and unambiguous report in the usual manner under Section 14 (1), see *infra*. Thus, the auditor cannot avoid liability for failure to report omissions or inaccuracies in the accounts merely by making a verbal explanation to such members of the company as are present at the annual general meeting.

§ 4. The Duties of the Auditor

Section 14 (1), *Companies Act 1967*, provides that the auditors shall make a report to the members on the accounts examined by them, and on every balance sheet, every profit and loss account and all group accounts laid before the company in general meeting during their tenure of office.

Section 14 (2) provides that the auditors' report shall be read before the company in general meeting and shall be open to inspection by any member.

Under Section 14 (3) the report must state whether in the auditor's opinion the company's balance sheet and profit and loss account and (if it is a holding company submitting group accounts) the group accounts have been properly prepared in accordance with the provisions of the Acts of 1948 and 1967, and whether in their opinion a true and fair view is given:

(i) in the case of the balance sheet, of the state of the company's affairs as at the end of its financial year;

(ii) in the case of the profit and loss account (if it be not framed as a consolidated profit and loss account), of the company's profit or loss for its financial year;

(iii) in the case of group accounts submitted by a holding company, of the state of affairs and profit or loss of the company and its subsidiaries dealt with thereby, so far as concerns members of the company.

It is further provided under Section 14 (4) that it shall be the duty of the auditors of a company, in preparing their report under this section, to carry out such investigations as will enable them to form an opinion as to the following matters, that is to say:

(*a*) whether proper books of account have been kept by the company and proper returns adequate for their audit have been received from branches not visited by them; and

(b) whether the company's balance sheet and (unless it is framed as a consolidated profit and loss account) profit and loss account are in agreement with the books of account and returns;

and if the auditors are of opinion that proper books of account have *not* been kept by the company, or that proper returns adequate for their audit have *not* been received from branches not visited by them, or if the balance sheet and (unless it is framed as a consolidated profit and loss account) profit and loss account are *not* in agreement with the books of account and returns, they shall state that fact in their report.

It will be observed that the auditor must report whether the profit and loss account gives a true and fair view of the profit or loss *for the financial year*. Para. 14 (6) of the Second Schedule to the 1967 Act provides that if not otherwise shown in the accounts the following matters shall be stated by way of a note:

Any material respects in which any items shown in the profit and loss account are affected –

(a) by transactions of a sort not usually undertaken by the company or otherwise by circumstances of an exceptional or non-recurrent nature; or

(b) by any change in the basis of accounting.

In some businesses, e.g. builders, contractors and civil engineers, owing to the time which usually must elapse before final accounts, claims for increased costs etc., can be agreed with surveyors and government departments, the profit of an accounting period may often be augmented by the addition of claims settled in respect of contracts completed in earlier years for which provision was not made at the time. If such amounts are material, they must be shown separately in the profit and loss account, otherwise the auditor must qualify his report on the grounds that the profit disclosed does not represent the profit *for the financial year*. If in such cases the auditor is of the opinion that further material sums will be received in respect of completed contracts for which no provision has been made in the accounts, he must mention this matter in his report unless an adequate note covering the position has been made on the accounts by the directors.

There are certain exemptions in the case of banking or discount companies, insurance companies and shipping companies, regarding the matters which have to be disclosed in the

financial accounts, and these exemptions are detailed in Part III
of the revised Eighth Schedule (now the Second Schedule to the
1967 Act). Section 14 of the 1967 Act requires that in the case of
these companies, the auditors' report shall state whether in
their opinion the company's balance sheet and profit and loss
account and (if it is a holding company submitting group
accounts) the group accounts have been properly prepared in
accordance with the provisions of the Companies Acts.

No limitation can be placed upon the duties of the auditor
under Section 14 of the 1967 Act, either by the articles of the
company or by any resolution of the members.

In the case of *Newton* v. *Birmingham Small Arms Co.* (1906) 2
Ch. 378), the articles of the company provided:

(*a*) That the directors should have power to form an *internal*
reserve fund which was not to be disclosed in the balance
sheet, and which should be utilized in whatever way the
directors thought fit.

(*b*) That the auditors should have access to the accounts relating
to such reserve fund, and that it was their duty to see that the
reserve fund was applied to the purposes of the company as
specified in the special articles, but that they should not disclose any information with regard thereto to the shareholders
or otherwise.

These provisions were held to be *ultra vires* as being a limitation of the statutory duties of the auditors.

Buckley, J., said: 'Any regulations which precluded the
auditors from availing themselves of all the information to
which under the Act they are entitled, as material for the report
which under the Act they are to make as to the true and correct
state of the company's affairs, are, I think, inconsistent with the
Act.'

The auditor is not required to *certify* the correctness of the
balance sheet; all he is required to do is to *report* to the members
whether in his opinion it is correct. The auditor will not be held
responsible if he has acted on information and explanations
which he believes to be *bona fide*, but which are as a matter of
fact untrue or incorrect, provided he has exercised reasonable
skill and diligence in testing the information supplied to him.
On the other hand, the balance sheet may be correct as shown by

the books of the company, but there may be information at the disposal of the auditor which would indicate that the books themselves were incorrect, and he cannot report to the members in the terms of the Act unless he takes account of such knowledge.

The auditor cannot be held reponsible for transactions which are omitted from the books, unless by the exercise of reasonable skill and diligence he *could* have discovered them. At the same time the duty of the auditor is not confined to comparing the balance sheet with the books to see that it agrees therewith. On this point the remarks of Lindley, L.J., *In re London & General Bank* (No.2 (1895), 2 Ch. 673), are pertinent:

' . . . The auditor's business is to ascertain and state the true financial position of the company at the time of the audit, and his duty is confined to that. But then comes the question: How is he to ascertain such position? The answer is: By examining the books of the company. But he does not discharge his duty by doing this without inquiry, and without taking any trouble to see that the books of the company themselves show the company's true position. He must take reasonable care to ascertain that they do. Unless he does this, his duty will be worse than a farce . . . The auditor, however, is not bound to do more than exercise reasonable care and skill in making the inquiries and investigations. He is not an insurer; he does not guarantee that the books do correctly show the true position of the company's affairs . . . His obligation is not so onerous as this . . . He must be honest – that is, he must not certify what he does not believe to be true, and he must take reasonable care and skill before he believes that what he certifies is true. What is reasonable care in any particular case must depend upon the circumstances of that case . . .'

Further duties falling upon the auditor under the *Companies Act 1948* are referred to in Section 130, under which the auditor, if appointed before the statutory meeting of a *public* company, must certify the statutory report issued to the members, so far as it relates to cash received in respect of shares allotted and to the receipts and payments by the company on capital account. Private companies are not required to hold a statutory meeting and, therefore, no statutory report has to be filed. Section 130 has little application in practice, since the great majority of public companies were originally incorporated as private companies.

The Fourth Schedule, Part II, to the 1948 Act, requires a report by the auditor on the profits and losses, assets and liabilities, and dividends paid by the company to be included in a prospectus.

There is also a special obligation imposed upon the auditor to ascertain that information with regard to loans to officers of the company and particulars regarding the emoluments etc., of directors and certain employees are correctly exhibited in the accounts to be laid before the company, otherwise he must, as far as possible, include in his report a statement giving the required particulars. These matters are more fully considered in Chapter IX.

It is sometimes assumed that because the great bulk of the shares in a private company are held by one or two individuals, who may be directors, such persons have the right to vary the duties of the auditor, and place restrictions upon what he shall or shall not do. It need hardly be pointed out that any such attempt to limit the rights and duties of the auditor is *ultra vires*.

In *Pendlebury's Ltd* v. *Ellis Green & Co* (1936), 80 Acct. L. R. 29), however, it was held that where the directors of a private company are the sole shareholders, a report by the auditor made personally to the directors to the effect that he has been unable to verify to his complete satisfaction the entries in the company's cash book, owing to the inadequacy of the system in force, will be sufficient to relieve the auditor from liability for not including the relevant information in his report attached to the balance sheet. Although in this case the auditors were relieved from liability, it is still considered necessary that their report attached to the balance sheet should contain all essential qualifications, irrespective of the number of shareholders and who such shareholders may be, particularly when it is remembered that debenture-holders are also entitled to receive copies of the accounts and notes, reports etc., attached thereto, and that audited accounts are frequently displayed to third parties with a view to obtaining finance from such parties, who should therefore be be informed of any reservations made by the auditors in giving their opinion.

§ 5. The Auditor's Report

The following is the recommendation of the Institute of Chartered Accountants regarding the form of an unqualified audit report required under Section 14 of the *Companies Act 1967*:

Companies not submitting group accounts

Auditors' report to the members of . . .

(*See note* (*a*) *below*). In our opinion, the accounts set out on pages . . . to . . . (*see note* (*b*)) give a true and fair view of the state of the company's affairs at . . . and of its profit (*or loss*) (*see note* (*c*)) for the year ended on that date and comply with the *Companies Acts 1948* and *1967*.

Companies submitting group accounts

Auditors' report to the members of . . .

(*See note* (*a*).) In our opinion, the accounts set out on pages . . . to . . . (*see note* (*b*)) together give, so far as concerns members of the holding company, a true and fair view of the state of affairs at . . . and of the profit (*or loss*) (*see note* (*c*)) for the year ended on that date and comply with the *Companies Acts 1948* and *1967* (*see note* (*d*)).

Banking, discount, insurance and shipping companies

In the case of a company which is entitled to avail itself and has availed itself of any of the provisions of Part III of Schedule 2 to the *Companies Act 1967*, the auditors are not required to report whether, in their opinion, the accounts give a true and fair view. This dispensation, however, applies only to the consequences of the exemptions from disclosure which are permitted by Part III and does not extend to other matters (for example, the overstatement of assets or the omission of liabilities) which, in the auditors' opinion, prevent the disclosure of a true and fair view in the generally accepted sense. In the absence of qualifications the following form of auditors' report is considered appropriate by the Council:

Auditors' report to the members of the . . . Bank (*or the . . . Insurance Co etc.*)

(*See note* (*a*).) In our opinion, the accounts set out on pages . . . to . . . (*see note* (*b*)) comply with the provisions of the *Companies Acts 1948* and *1967* applicable to (*banking or insurance etc.*) companies.

Notes of variations to suit particular circumstances

The following are the notes referred to in the forms of audit report set out above:

(*a*) If it is desired to refer to the auditors' examination, each of the forms of auditors' report may appropriately commence as follows:

'We have examined the accounts set out on pages . . . to . . . and report that, in our opinion, they . . .'

(*b*) The documents to which the auditors' report relates should be clearly identified by reference to the page numbers, or if the pages are not numbered, the word 'accounts' should be replaced by a description, e.g. 'the annexed balance sheet, profit and loss account and notes'. If it is necessary for the auditors to make reference to information included in the directors' report (for example, if the directors have taken advantage of the proviso to section 163 of the *Companies Act 1948* to include in their report certain matters which the Act requires to be included in the accounts), the auditors' report should clearly specify the paragraphs of the directors' report which fall within its scope.

(c) In certain circumstances, for example, where the consolidated accounts disclose a profit but the holding company incurs a loss, it may be convenient to use the word 'results'.

(d) If the consolidated accounts incorporate the accounts of material subsidiaries which the auditors of the holding company have not themselves audited, it is usually desirable for them to include a reference to the fact in their report for the information of the members. This may be done by adding an appropriate sentence at the end of the report on the accounts of companies submitting group accounts above.

If the accounts on which the auditor is reporting are not self-contained because material information is given in the directors' report or in other documents annexed to the accounts, reference to the specific documents which must be read as part of the accounts must be made by the auditor in his report in terms which identify clearly the source to which the reference is made.

The balance of the recommendations of the Institute on auditors' reports, including those on group accounts and qualifications in audit reports, are reproduced in the Appendix.

Where the auditor is of opinion that the balance sheet does not give a true and fair view of the state of the company's affairs, or, that the profit and loss account does not give a true and fair view of the profit or loss for the year, he must qualify his report accordingly. The most common reasons for the qualification of the report are where the auditor has been unable to verify to his satisfaction the existence or values of certain assets; where, in his opinion, there has not been sufficient provision for depreciation, or where he is not satisfied that adequate provision has been made for certain liabilities. It may sometimes happen that the auditor does not agree with the treatment of certain material items in the balance sheet presented to him for audit, and the directors do not agree to such alterations as the auditor may suggest. In such a case the auditor must qualify his report.

The following is an illustration of a qualification in an auditor's report:

'I have not inspected the title deeds to freehold and leasehold properties, all of which are registered or held abroad. The profit disclosed for the year includes the sum of £5,000, received in settlement of claims in respect of work completed in previous years. Subject to the foregoing, in my opinion . . .'

Strong pressure is sometimes put upon the auditor to induce him to refrain from making certain comments in his report, on the ground that the fact of his doing so will be detrimental to the interests of the members, and he is sometimes asked whether he cannot indicate in more or less general terms the point at issue without specifically stating the facts. The auditor who allows himself to be persuaded to do this runs the very serious risk of being held to have failed in discharging his duty to the members.

Lindley, L.J., said, *In re London & General Bank* (No.2 (1895) 2 Ch. 673):

'A person whose duty it is to convey information to others does not discharge that duty by simply giving them so much information as is calculated to induce them or some of them to ask for more. Information and means of information are by no means equivalent terms . . . An auditor who gives shareholders the means of information instead of information in respect of a company's financial position, does so at his peril, and runs the very serious risk of being held judicially to have failed to discharge his duty.'

§ 6. The Publication of the Balance Sheet and Auditor's Report

Section 155, *Companies Act 1948*, provides that:

(1) Every balance sheet of a company shall be signed on behalf of the board by two of the directors of the company, or if there is only one director, by that director.

(2) In the case of a banking company registered after the fifteenth day of August, eighteen hundred and seventy nine, the balance sheet must be signed by the secretary or manager, if any, and where there are more than three directors of the company by at least three of those directors, and where there are not more than three directors by all the directors.

(3) If any copy of a balance sheet which has not been signed as required by this section is issued, circulated or published, the company, and every officer of the company who is in default shall be liable to a fine not exceeding fifty pounds.

Section 156 provides that:

(1) The profit and loss account and, so far as not incorporated in the balance sheet or profit and loss account, any group accounts laid before the company in general meeting, shall be annexed to the balance sheet, and the auditor's report shall be attached thereto.

(2) Any accounts so annexed shall be approved by the board of directors before the balance sheet is signed on their behalf.

(3) If any copy of a balance sheet is issued, circulated or published without having annexed thereto a copy of the profit and loss account or any group accounts required by this section to be so annexed, or without having

attached thereto a copy of the auditor's report, the company and every officer of the company who is in default shall be liable to a fine not exceeding fifty pounds.

It is important to observe that the auditor's report must be *attached* to the balance sheet. The report must be read before the members in general meeting and is open to inspection by any member.

Although it is considered that it is not the duty of the auditor to see that the balance sheet is signed by the required number of directors, it is customary for the auditor to obtain the directors' signatures before attaching and signing his report.

The rights of members and others to receive copies of the balance sheets etc., are as follows (Section 158, *Companies Act 1948*):

(*a*) A copy of every balance sheet, including every document required by law to be annexed thereto, which is to be laid before the company in general meeting; and

(*b*) a copy of the auditor's report shall be sent to:

  (1) every member of the company (whether he is or is not entitled to receive notices of general meetings); and

  (2) every debenture holder;

not less than twenty-one days before the meeting.

The above provisions do not apply, in the case of a company not having a share capital, to members and debenture holders who are not entitled to receive notices of general meetings.

There is no distinction for this purpose between public and private companies or between the holders of ordinary and preference shares.

Section 24 of the Act of 1967 requires that Section 158 of the 1948 Act shall have effect as if references to the auditors' report included references to the directors' report.

In re Allen Craig & Co (London) Ltd (1934) 50 T.L.R. 301), it was held that the duty of the auditors, after having affixed their signatures to the report annexed to a balance sheet, is confined to forwarding that report to the secretary of the company, leaving the secretary or the directors to convene the general meeting and send the balance sheet and report to the members entitled to receive it. It is no part of the duty of the auditors to send a copy of their report to each member individually.

§ 7. The Auditor's Lien

It is considered that an accountant has a particular lien on account books for charges incurred in the writing-up of such books (*Re Hill, Ex parte Southall* (1848) 17 L.J.R. (Bankruptcy 21); *Burleigh* v. *Ingram Clarke Ltd* (1901) 27, Acct. L.R. 65).

In *re Arthur Francis Ltd* (1911, 44, Acct. L.R. 61) a lien was claimed by accountants on books and documents in their possession on the ground that they had worked upon them and had not been paid either their audit fees or accountancy charges. Swinfen Eady, J., made an order that the books should be produced to the liquidators of the company without prejudice to the lien, if any, of the respondents.

In view of the fact that Section 147, *Companies Act 1948*, requires that the books of account of a registered company be kept at the registered office of the company, or at such other place as the directors think fit, and be at all times open to the inspection of the directors, there was some doubt as to whether an accountant could exercise a lien over such books. In the opinion of counsel, obtained by the Institute of Chartered Accountants, however, where books of account are entrusted to an accountant by the authority of the directors there is no statutory provision which deprives the accountant of his lien over such books. In counsel's opinion an accountant claiming such a lien would have to give reasonable facilities to the directors to inspect the books. Counsel has also advised that in his opinion the accountant's lien is not affected by the appointment of a receiver for debenture holders or a liquidator.

In *Chantrey Martin & Co* v. *Martin* ([1953] 3 W.L.R. 459), it was held that working papers prepared by an accountant for the purpose of producing a balance sheet on behalf of a client for audit purposes belonged to the accountant and not to the client. The Court held on the other hand that correspondence between an accountant and the Inland Revenue concerning a client's taxation liabilities belonged to the client, since the accountant was acting in the capacity of agent for his client.

Extracts from a statement published in 1953 by the Council of the Institute of Chartered Accountants on the subject of the ownership of records are given hereunder. This statement embodied the opinion given to the Institute by counsel, and emphasized that such opinion applies whether the accountant is acting as an accountant or as auditor (whether under a private arrangement or under the Companies Acts) or as receiver but is, of course, subject to any special contract made between the accountant and his client or to any special facts or circumstances in a particular case.

Working papers

(1) An accountant's working papers are his own property and he is entitled to retain them. His right to retain his working papers is not altered by the state of his client's records. The expression 'working papers' is used here to mean any document that the accountant or his staff may prepare in order to help him carry out the work which he is engaged to do; for example, draft profit and loss accounts and draft balance sheets, schedules prepared from incomplete records in order to enable such draft accounts to be prepared, memoranda and draft reports. These documents are clearly prepared for the accountant's own purposes and a client can have no claim to them.

(2) The above opinion is in accordance with the decision of the Court of Appeal in *Chantrey Martin & Co* v. *Martin* ([1953] 3 W.L.R. 459), where the Court held that the following documents were the property of the firm of accountants who acted as auditors of a company: working papers and schedules relating to the audit, draft accounts of the company, the accountants' office copy of the final typed accounts of the company, notes and calculations relating to these draft accounts made by a partner of the firm of accountants, and the draft tax computation prepared by an employee of the firm of accountants.

Correspondence with clients

(3) Letters received by the accountant from his client are the accountant's property and may be retained by him. So may the accountant's copies of his letters to his client. Clearly, when the accountant writes to his client he is not writing on his client's behalf or anyone's behalf but his own. Equally clearly, the accountant's copies of such letters are made solely for his own purposes (*In re Wheatcroft* (6 Ch.D. 97)).

Communications with third parties

(4) In *Chantry Martin & Co* v. *Martin* the Court of Appeal held that correspondence between the accountants and the Inland Revenue in regard to the company's accounts and tax computations thereon (both the copies of letters sent and the originals of letters received) were the property of the client. This decision was on the basis that the accountants had been acting as agents for the client for the purpose of settling with the Inland Revenue the client's tax liability; and accordingly the Court followed the principle expressed by Lord Justice Mackinnon in *Leicestershire County Council* v. *Michael Faraday & Partners Ltd* ([1941]) 2 K.B. 216) that if an agent brings into existence certain documents whilst in the employment of his principal, they are the principal's documents and the principal can claim that the agent should hand them over.

(5) Having regard to the basis on which the Court of Appeal reached its decision regarding correspondence with the Inland Revenue, it is considered that the Courts would hold that communications with third parties and copies of communications by the accountant to third parties are the property of the accountant where the relationship is that of client and professional man and not, as in the case of communications with the Inland Revenue, that of principal and agent. It is considered, for example, that certificates of bank balances, certificates of the custody of securities, statements confirming or otherwise the balance of an account between a third party and the client, and other documents which the accountants have obtained for their own use in carrying out their duties in a professional capacity would be held to be the property of the accountants, notwithstanding that they have been brought into existence in connection with work done for the client.

Compliance with clients' requests

(6) Where there is any doubt as to the legal ownership of communications with third parties, it would generally be wise for the accountant, whilst keeping copies for his own protection, to supply the client with any documents the client may require (unless the accountant desires the doubtful distinction of giving his name to a leading case).

Further amplification regarding liquidation and bankruptcy

An accountant is not deprived of his lien over a company's books by the appointment of a liquidator. In a compulsory liquidation, however, the court has power under Section 268 (3) of the *Companies Act 1948* to require him to produce any books and papers in his custody or power and where he claims any lien the production shall be 'without prejudice to that lien and the court shall have jurisdiction in the winding-up to determine all questions relating to that lien'. The court would have similar power in a voluntary liquidation in the event of the liquidator applying to the court under Section 307.

The Council has approved the inclusion of the following addendum:

'On November 15th, 1962, in the Companies Court in the Chancery Division of the High Court, on a summons by the liquidator of a company (*D. M. Carr & Company Limited* [Chancery Division, No. 1172 of 1961]) for the delivery by the auditor of the company of the company's books of accounts and other documents which were in the possession of the auditor, the Registrar ordered:

(a) that the auditor should produce to the liquidator all the books and papers of the company in his possession, without prejudice to the lien claimed by him;

(b) that the liquidator should pay out of the assets of the company in priority to his own remuneration but after all creditors ranking above the liquidator so much of the fees claimed by the auditor as related to work carried out before the commencement of winding-up (in this case the whole sum);

(c) that the auditor's taxed costs on the liquidator's summons should be paid out of the assets of the company.'

CHAPTER IX

THE AUDIT OF A LIMITED COMPANY

References to the 'principal Act' are to the Companies Act 1948

§ 1. Considerations on Appointment as Auditor

The general considerations on the commencement of a new audit have been dealt with in Chapter I, § 5 (B), and the importance of obtaining a list of the books in use and a statement of the system of internal check (if any) in operation has been emphasized. In the case of a limited company, there are further points which the auditor should consider at this stage.

(A) THE APPOINTMENT OF THE AUDITOR

If the company is a new one, the directors will probably have exercised their power to appoint the auditor prior to the first annual general meeting, and if the auditor is so appointed, he should obtain from the secretary of the company a copy of the directors' minute recording his appointment. If appointed by the company in general meeting, in succession to a previous auditor, he should obtain a copy of the resolution, and ascertain that due notice of his intended nomination was given to the company in the first place, and subsequently to the members and the retiring auditor in accordance with the provisions of Section 160, since if this has not been done his appointment will be invalid.

It has already been pointed out that professional etiquette requires that the retiring auditor be approached to ascertain whether, in his opinion, any reasons exist which would make it undesirable or improper for the office to be accepted by the new nominee.

In the case of a casual vacancy in the office of auditor, occasioned either by the death or retirement of the auditor during his term of office, the directors have power to appoint a new auditor, and the auditor so appointed should obtain a copy of the directors' minute appointing him.

(B) THE REMUNERATION OF THE AUDITOR

The amount of the auditor's fee is generally based on the time occupied by the audit, regard being had to the responsibility involved. The auditor is sometimes asked to quote the fee he requires to perform the audit, but it is often very difficult to do this with any degree of accuracy, and where the auditor is appointed by the directors before the first annual general meeting, it is usually arranged that his remuneration will be agreed with the directors after the audit is completed. .

In succeeding years the remuneration is voted either in advance or retrospectively by the company in general meeting, whilst in some cases a resolution is passed authorizing the directors to agree the remuneration with the auditor.

As has already been stated the amount of the auditor's remuneration must be shown separately in the company's profit and loss account. For this purpose the term remuneration includes the auditor's expenses.

In cases where the books of the company are not balanced prior to the audit, or where draft accounts are not prepared by the company's officials and presented to the auditor, he should make it clear to the directors that it is no part of his duty to perform work of this nature, and if it is desired that he should do this, it will be in his capacity as accountant. A separate fee should be arranged for additional work of this kind.

(C) INSPECTION OF BOOKS AND DOCUMENTS

In addition to obtaining a list of all the books in use and inspecting these, the auditor should examine the following documents:

(1) *The Memorandum and Articles of Association*

The auditor should peruse the memorandum, and particularly the objects clauses, since occasionally the question may arise as to whether certain transactions are *intra vires* the company. If transactions have been entered into which are not within the scope of the company's objects, the auditor should draw attention to the fact in his report to the members. Owing to the comprehensive nature of most objects clauses, however, this contingency rarely arises.

The articles of association call for careful scrutiny by the auditor upon his appointment, and special attention should be paid to the following points:

(*a*) The regulations as to the issue of capital, payment of underwriting commission etc.

(b) Making calls, interest on calls in arrear, and on calls paid in advance.

(c) Forfeiture and lien.

(d) Directors: their number, remuneration, qualification, disqualification and removal.

(e) Appointment and powers of managing directors.

(f) Proceedings and powers of the board.

(g) Dividends and reserves.

(h) Extent of borrowing powers.

(i) Rights of members *inter se*.

Any special resolutions passed subsequently which alter any provision of the articles should also be carefully noted.

(2) *The Prospectus*

Where a prospectus has been issued, the auditor should examine this, with particular reference to the following points:

(a) The amount of capital proposed to be issued, the different classes of shares to which it relates, and the rights of members *inter se*.

(b) The amounts payable on application and allotment, the dates fixed for future calls, and the amounts thereof, if any.

(c) Particulars of any contract entered into with the vendors for the purchase of any property, and the amount payable in cash, shares or debentures in respect of such purchase consideration. The amount, if any, payable for goodwill must be specified separately.

(d) The amount payable for underwriting commission, or for commission on placing shares or debentures. The rate of commission in respect of shares must not exceed 10 per cent. of the issue price, or such lower rate as may be allowed by the articles.

(e) The amount, or estimated amount, of the preliminary expenses.

(f) Particulars of any material contracts entered into within two years of the date on which the prospectus is issued.

(g) The amount specified as the minimum subscription.

(3) *Contracts*

The auditor should examine all contracts with vendors or other persons relating to the purchase of property, payment of commission, or preliminary expenses.

(4) *Balance Sheet, Accounts and Reports*

When he has been appointed in place of a retiring auditor, the new auditor should examine the last balance sheet and accounts, as these will contain the opening entries for the period under review. The late auditor's report should also be examined, as this may contain material information of which it is important the new auditor should be aware.

The last report of the directors to the members should be seen, as this will contain the recommendations of the directors in respect of the appropriation of the previous year's profits. The members' minute book should be examined, in order to ascertain whether such recommendations have been approved.

It is the usual practice for the auditor to make a record of the information he has obtained with regard to the books, documents and other matters set out above. These constitute what are known as permanent audit notes, which are kept separate from the notes relating to each annual audit, and obviate constant reference to the documents themselves. It is of the greatest importance that these permanent notes should be kept up-to-date.

§ 2. Share Capital

(A) THE VARIOUS CLASSES OF SHARE CAPITAL

The share capital of a company is frequently divided into different classes, of which the following are the most usual:

(1) *Preference Shares*

Preference Shares may be either *cumulative* or *non-cumulative*. The latter only carry a right to a fixed dividend out of the profits of any year, and if there are insufficient profits in that year to pay the full amount of dividend, they have no right to have such arrears made up out of future profits. They may or may not carry the right to repayment of capital in priority to other classes of shares in the event of liquidation.

Cumulative preference shares entitle the holders to a fixed rate of dividend in the same way as non-cumulative preference shares, but with the additional right that any arrears of dividend for a particular year shall be made up out of future profits, in priority to any dividends on other classes of shares.

The rights of preference shareholders are governed by the memorandum and articles of association, and there are other varieties than the two enumerated above; such as, for example, participating preference shares, which have a right to further dividends after the ordinary shares have received a certain rate.

Where it is stated that preference shares are entitled to a preferential dividend at a specified rate per cent., such dividend is *prima facie* cumulative (*Webb* v. *Earle*, 1875, L.R. 20 Eq. 556; *Henry* v. *Gt N. Rly Co*, 1 de G. & J. 606; *Foster* v. *Coles*, 22 T.L.R. 555). If the intention is that the preference shares should be non-cumulative, the clause defining their rights must clearly express this. A declaration that the preference dividend is to be paid out of the profits *of each year*, has been interpreted as not giving cumulative rights (*Staples* v. *Eastman Co*, 1896, 2 Ch. 303).

In the absence of specific provision, preference shares entitled to a fixed cumulative dividend are not entitled to share in any surplus profits after such dividend has been paid (*Will* v. *United Lankat Plantations Co*, 1914, 83 L.J. Ch. 195).

A preference shareholder is not entitled to preference in respect of return of capital, unless specific rights are attached in this connection (*London India Rubber Co*, 1861, 5 Eq. 519).

The question as to whether preference shareholders are entitled to share with the ordinary shareholders in the distribution of any surplus assets after the ordinary shares have been repaid is dependent upon a true construction of the company's articles.

The correct principle of construction is that 'either with regard to dividend or with regard to the rights in a winding-up, the express gift or attachment of preferential rights to preference shares is *prima facie* a definition of the whole of their rights in that respect' (*per* Sargant, J., in *Re National Telephone Co* (1914) 1 Ch. 755, approved by the House of Lords in *Scottish Insurance Corporation Ltd* v. *Wilsons & Clyde Coal Co* (1949), A.C. 462 and *Prudential Assurance Co* v. *Chatterly–Whitfield Collieries Ltd* (1949), A.C. 512, over-ruling *Re William Metcalfe & Sons Ltd* (1932), W.N. 205). If the articles give the preference shareholders the right to priority as to the return of capital in a winding-up, the presumption is that they are not entitled to any further share in the assets. Even though, on a true construction of the articles, they may be entitled to share in a surplus, they could nevertheless not claim to participate in any part thereof which arises from profits which by the express terms of the articles the ordinary shareholders could, prior to the liquidation, have distributed amongst themselves (*Re Bridgewater Navigation Co No. 2.* (1891), 2 Ch. 317, approved by the House of Lords in *Scottish Insurance Corporation Ltd* v. *Wilsons & Clyde Coal Company, supra*). There may, however, be other surplus assets in which preference shareholders could participate (*re Bridgewater Navigation Co; Birch* v. *Cropper* (1889), 14 App. Cas. 525) but the burden of proof that they are entitled to do so is on them (*Re Isle of Thanet Electricity Supply Co Ltd* (1949), 2 All E.R. 1060).

(2) Redeemable Preference Shares

Redeemable preference shares may be issued in accordance with the provisions of Section 58, *Companies Act 1948*, subject to authorization by the articles. The redemption can only be effected out of profits available for dividends or out of a fresh issue made for the specific purpose. The shares cannot be redeemed unless they are fully paid. When the shares are redeemed out of divisible profits, a sum equal to the nominal value of the shares redeemed must be transferred therefrom to a 'capital redemption reserve fund,' which for the purposes of the provisions of the Act relating to the reduction of share capital must be regarded as if it were paid-up share capital of the company. Any premiums payable on redemption must be provided out of profits, or out of any share premium account, before the shares are redeemed. Such a premium represents a distribution for taxation purposes and the company must account for income tax on the gross equivalent (*Finance Act 1965*).

Where shares are redeemed out of the proceeds of an issue made for the specific purpose, no additional *ad valorem* duty will be payable on the new issue, if the redemption is effected within one month after such new issue.

The redemption of preference shares is not to be taken as reducing the amount of the company's authorized capital.

The capital redemption reserve fund may only be applied in paying up unissued shares of the company to be issued as fully paid bonus shares to the members.

The Second Schedule to the *Companies Act 1967* requires disclosure of the earliest and latest dates on which the company has power to redeem its redeemable preference shares, and such disclosure must also state whether those shares must be redeemed in any event, or are liable to be redeemed at the company's option, and whether any (and, if so, what) premium is payable upon redemption.

(3) *Ordinary Shares*

Ordinary shares are those taking the surplus profits remaining after satisfaction of prior interests (if any).

These may be divided between preferred and deferred ordinary shares, the former having a preferential right to a fixed rate of dividend over the latter, while the latter frequently have a right to the whole, or a proportion of the surplus after the payment of dividends on other classes of shares.

(4) *Founders' or Deferred Shares*

Founders' or deferred shares are usually limited in number and of small nominal value. They are generally issued fully paid to the original vendors or their nominees, in consideration either of part of the purchase price or of services connected with the formation of the company. Generally, they only rank for dividend after other classes of shares have received certain rates of dividend, when they are entitled to the whole or a portion of the surplus profits. In some instances shares of this nature are termed *management shares*. Shares of this nature are rarely issued today.

(5) *The Distinction between Stock and Shares*

The chief differences are as follows:

(*a*) Stock must be fully paid up; whereas shares need only be partly paid up.

(*b*) Stock may be issued or transferred in fractional parts; a fraction of a share cannot be transferred.

Substantial numbers of fully paid shares may be 'bonded together' in units of stock of a much larger denomination, e.g. each block of one hundred fully paid shares of £1 each may be converted into single stock units of £100 each.

Under Section 61, *Companies Act 1948*, a company can, by ordinary resolution, convert all or any of its paid up shares into stock, and reconvert that stock into paid up shares of any denomination.

The issued capital of a company, other than capital represented by shares whose rights to participation in profits and capital are restricted, is known as the equity share capital.

In the majority of cases, the equity share capital is represented by ordinary shares, but where there are deferred or founders' shares and the participation in profits by ordinary shareholders is limited, it will be the deferred or founder shareholders who have the equity.

(B) SHARES ISSUED FOR CASH

In order to vouch shares issued for cash, the following procedure will be necessary:

(1) Check the applications with the application and allotment sheets.

(2) Check the shares allotted and the amounts payable on application and allotment, from the application and allotment sheets into the share register.

Reference should be made to the schedule of split and renounced allotment letters, as the names of the original allottees may in many cases not be the same as those ultimately entered in the registers.

(3) Check cash received on application and allotment with the bank statement; check the special cash book or machine lists in detail to the share register, and in total to the application and allotment accounts.

(4) Where application money has been returned owing to allotment not being made, vouch repayment of cash with the application and allotment sheets.

(5) Examine the directors' minute book to see that all allotments have been made the subject of a minute, and where only the total number of shares allotted on any day is referred to in the minutes, see that the application and allotment sheets have been initialled by a director up to the point referred to in the minutes.

(6) A similar procedure should be adopted to verify the proceeds of calls.

(7) See that the issue is within the limits authorized by the memorandum and articles of association.

(8) See that the provisions with regard to the minimum subscription (if any) have been complied with.

(9) Vouch the journal entries relating to the issue, and check the postings.

(10) Check the balances on the shares registers, and see that the total agrees with the total capital issued.

If it was stated in the prospectus that application had or would be made for permission to deal in, and for a quotation of the shares on any stock exchange, see that:

(11) All money received on application is kept in a separate banking account so long as liability to refund such money exists.

(12) Permission to deal has been granted by the stock exchange or, if this has been refused, that application monies have been repaid to the applicants.

(c) ISSUE OF WARRANTS TO BEARER

The company may have issued share warrants to bearer under the provisions of its articles, and in accordance with Section 83, *Companies Act 1948*. Such warrants can only be issued in respect of fully-paid shares. A private company cannot take power to issue such warrants, since they are transferable to bearer, and there can therefore be no effective restriction on transfers. The auditor should check the cancelling entries in the register of members with those in the register of share warrants, and the aggregate of the balances on both should be agreed with the total of the issued share capital.

(d) SHARES ISSUED FOR CONSIDERATION OTHER THAN CASH

The issue of shares to a vendor of the business in part payment of the purchase consideration will be vouched by reference to the contract between the company and the vendor, and the minutes recording the allotment. Such contracts must be filed with the Registrar of Companies within one month after allotment, and the auditor should ascertain whether this has been done.

Where the contract has not been reduced to writing, particulars of it must be filed, duly stamped. The effect of non-registration of a contract, or of particulars thereof in the circumstances mentioned, within the prescribed period or such extended time as may be allowed by the Court, is the liability to a penalty of £50 a day for every day during which the default continues, on every director or other officer who is knowingly a party to the default, but the title of the allottee is not affected so long as the contract itself is valid.

Frequently shares are issued to the nominees of the vendor, either by virtue of a supplementary agreement or under a written nomination by the vendor in favour of his nominees. The issue of such shares will be vouched by reference to these documents.

Shares are sometimes issued as fully paid to persons in consideration of the payment by them of part or the whole of the preliminary expenses of the company; the issue of such shares will be vouched in the same manner as the vendor's shares.

Payment of underwriting commission, or commission on placing shares, is usually made in cash, but it is sometimes discharged by the issue of fully paid shares. The auditor's duties in connection with the vouching of payments of this nature are considered in § 7 below, and assuming the issue of such shares to be in order, the vouching of the issue will be carried out in the same manner as that described above.

The auditor should vouch the journal entries relating to shares issued for a consideration other than cash with the contracts and the minute book. The shares allotted should be checked into the register of members.

(E) SHARES ISSUED AT A PREMIUM

Shares may be issued at a premium, and the auditor should see that the amount received in respect of the premium, whether in cash or otherwise, is placed to the credit of a share premium account, which must be shown as a separate item in the balance sheet.

Under the provisions of Section 56, *Companies Act 1948*, the balance on the share premium account may only be used for the following purposes:

(*a*) In paying up unissued shares of the company to be issued to the members as fully paid bonus shares.

(*b*) To write off preliminary expenses.

(*c*) To write off the expenses of, or the commission paid or discount allowed on, any issue of shares or debentures.

(*d*) In providing for the premium payable on redemption of any redeemable preference shares or debentures.

(F) SHARES ISSUED AT A DISCOUNT

The right to make an issue of shares at a discount is rarely exercised in practice, because the mere fact that the shares are to be issued at less than par casts doubt on their true value and acts as a deterrent to the potential investor.

The conditions imposed by Section 57, *Companies Act 1948*, must be complied with if shares are to be issued at a discount. These conditions are:

(1) The new issued must be of a class of shares already issued.

(2) The issue must be authorized by ordinary resolution of the company, and sanctioned by the Court.

(3) The resolution must specify the maximum rate of discount at which the shares are to be issued.

(4) There must have been an interval of at least one year between the date upon which the company was entitled to commence business, and the issue of the shares.

(5) The shares must be issued within one month after the date on which the issue was sanctioned by the Court, or within such extended time as the Court may allow.

(6) Every prospectus of the issue must show particulars of the discount or so much as has not been written off at the date of the prospectus.

Every balance sheet subsequently issued must show as a separate item the amount of discount not written off to date.

Where shares have been so issued, it will be the duty of the auditor to ascertain that due effect has been given to the statutory provisions. There does not appear to be any obligation to write off the discount, but the same principles will apply to this item as to preliminary expenses, underwriting commission etc., and it is advisable that provision be made for the elimination of the item over a short period of years.

(G) SHARE BOOKS

Under Section 110, *Companies Act 1948*, every company is obliged to keep a register of members. It will occasionally be found that a register of transfers is kept, recording particulars of all transfers registered by the company, but usually this book is dispensed with, all postings being made direct from the transfer forms to the register of members, thus avoiding duplication.

As already stated, on the occasion of any issue of share capital, the auditor must check the entries relating thereto into the register of members, since it is his duty to report upon the balance sheet of the company, for which purpose he must ascertain that the issued capital as stated therein is correct. Once this has been done, however, it is immaterial to the auditor by whom the shares are held and he need not, therefore, check share transfers in detail. He should, however, check the balances on the register of members on the occasion of each audit, in order to see that the total agrees with the issued capital as shown in the balance sheet.

Furthermore, under Sections 33 and 34 of the *Companies Act 1967*, every person who becomes interested in shares carrying unrestricted voting rights in a quoted company, of an amount equal to at least one-tenth of the nominal value of the voting share capital of the company, must notify the company in writing of the existence of the interest, and must supply information regarding subsequent changes in that interest. The company must maintain a register of the identities of shareholders who fall into this category, and this register must disclose:

(*a*) the amount and class of shares in which the holders are interested; and

(*b*) any change in the number of such shares.

(H) SHARE TRANSFER AUDIT

It does not form part of the auditor's duties in the ordinary course to check the share transactions in detail, but he is frequently employed by the directors to perform this work at a special fee. Such an audit is termed a share transfer audit, and its object is the prevention of clerical errors, and the improper issue of duplicate share certificates or certified transfers, whether fraudulently or otherwise. The necessity for such an audit has often been emphasized, particularly where the duties of registrar for groups of companies are carried out by a separate company under the control of the dominant directors of the groups.

Unless the Stock Exchange has waived the rule requiring such notices (on the grounds that adequate insurance cover has been effected against claims arising from forged transfers) the auditor must satisfy himself that all transferors have been notified of the lodgment of transfers, and enquire as to whether any objections have been received. It should be noted that under the *Stock Transfer Act 1963*, it is no longer necessary for the signature of the transferor to be witnessed or for the transferee to sign the transfer. The transfer itself need not be in the form of a deed and execution by the transferor may be under-hand, except where the transferor is a body corporate having a common seal, in which case execution under seal is necessary.

Apart from the above, the following are the major steps in the programme of the audit of share transfers:

(1) Inspect each transfer as to consideration, stamp, date and signatures of transferors. If the consideration does not appear sufficient, inquiry will be necessary unless the adjudication stamp of the Revenue Stamp Office appears on the transfer.

(2) Check transferors' names etc., and class, number and distinctive numbers of shares (if any) as stated in the transfers, with the old certificates and see that these have been cancelled.

(3) Check particulars of balance receipts (if any) issued, and compare with counterfoils.

(4) See that any stop notices have been duly observed, and that notice of the lodgment of the transfer has been given to the mortgagee.

(5) Verify postings from transfers to register of members; check counterfoils of new certificates.

(6) Check the stock of unused share certificates, balance tickets and transfer receipts, paying particular attention to the serial numbers.

On the occasion of his next visit the auditor should examine the minute book to ascertain whether the board have passed all transfers previously examined by him, and, if so, he should check the postings from the transfer forms to the register of members.

(I) FORGED AND BLANK TRANSFERS

When a company certifies a transfer, such certificate may be taken as a representation by the company to any person acting on the faith of the certificate that there have been produced to the company such documents as *prima facie* show the transferor to have a title to the shares or debentures which are the subject of the transfer. The certificate is not, however, a representation that the transferor has, in fact, a title. If any person acts on the faith of a false certification which has been made by the company negligently, the company will be under the same liability to such person as if the certification had been made fraudulently (Section 79, *Companies Act 1948*).

Under Section 117, *Companies Act 1948*, no notice of any trust may be entered on the register; but if the directors are aware that a transfer is being made in breach of trust or for the purpose of defrauding any person having equitable rights in the shares, they may become personally liable if they pass the transfer without notifying the person interested, although the company is under no liability (*Société Générale* v. *The Tramways Union*, 1885, 14 Q.B.D. 424).

A blank transfer is sometimes deposited by way of security for an advance, accompanied by a share certificate. The transfer is signed by the transferor, but the name of the transferee and the date of execution are not inserted until it is desired to register the transfer, if this becomes necessary.

Under Section 67, *Finance Act 1963*, where a blank transfer giving effect to a sale has been delivered to the purchaser or his agent, or to his order, it must not be passed on to any other person or taken outside Great Britain before the transferee's name has been inserted. The person whose name is to be inserted as transferee must be one of the following:

(a) The purchaser. This means the person who is the purchaser at the time of delivery of the transfer: it would not include a subsequent purchaser;

(*b*) A person entitled to a charge on the stock or securities for money lent to that purchaser;

(*c*) A nominee holding as bare trustee for that purchaser or for a person within (*b*) above;

(*d*) A person acting as agent of that purchaser for the purpose of the sale.

The section applies equally to gifts, subject to the modification that references to the purchaser are to be taken as references to the donee.

This provision is designed to prevent the avoidance of stamp duty on transfers which might have become possible as a result of the simplified transfer procedure laid down by the *Stock Transfer Act 1963*.

The fact that most companies note on their share certificates that no transfer will be registered without production of the certificate, does not apparently prevent a company issuing duplicate certificates in place of those lost or defaced, and most companies take power under their articles to issue such duplicates, a letter of indemnity from the holder usually being required. It would not be a difficult matter for the transferor who has signed a blank transfer and deposited his share certificate as security for an advance, to obtain from the company a duplicate certificate, under a misrepresentation that he had lost his original certificate, and then to execute a fresh transfer, selling the shares on the faith of the duplicate certificate so issued.

Persons lending money on the security of share certificates or certified transfers should, therefore, to prevent the possibility of loss, take immediate steps to have the transfers completed, and registered in the names of themselves or their nominees. Alternatively, they may serve upon the company a stop notice. When such a notice is served, the company cannot transfer the stock or shares without giving eight days' notice to the mortgagee or other person filing the affidavit, within which time an injunction can be applied for to restrain the transfer.

(J) CALLS PAID IN ADVANCE

Directors may receive money from shareholders in advance of calls. Under Table A power is given to pay interest at a rate not exceeding 5 per cent. on amounts so advanced, and such interest is a charge against the profits, but can be paid out of capital. Calls paid in advance do not strictly form part of the share capital, and should be shown separately in the balance sheet. In the event of winding-up, they are repayable with interest before any return is made in respect of called-up capital. (In re *Wakefield Rolling Stock Co*, 1892, 3 Ch. 165).

(K) INTEREST PAYABLE OUT OF CAPITAL DURING CONSTRUCTION

Under Section 65, *Companies Act 1948*, where shares are issued for the purpose of raising money for the construction of works, buildings, or plant which cannot be made profitable for a lengthened period, a company may pay interest at the rate of 4 per cent. per annum, or at such other rate as may be prescribed by order of the Treasury, on so much of such capital as is for the time being paid up, and charge such interest to capital as part of the cost of construction. The payment must be authorized by the articles or by special resolution, and must receive the previous sanction of the Board of Trade. The payment must not extend beyond the close of the half-year next after the half-year during which the works or buildings have been actually completed or the plant provided. The accounts of the company must show the share capital on which, and the rate at which, interest has been paid out of capital.

Interest on debentures issued for a similar purpose can be charged to capital during the period of construction (*Hinds* v. *Buenos Ayres Grand National Tramways Co, Ltd*, 1906, 2 Ch. 654).

(L) ALTERATION OF RIGHTS OF MEMBERS

The rights attaching to any class of shares may be altered in accordance with power which may be contained in the memorandum, subject to the provisions of Section 22 as to the rights of minorities, or alternatively under Section 206, *Companies Act 1948*, when a compromise or arrangement is proposed.

The auditor should satisfy himself that the appropriate resolution has been duly passed, and that, where required, the approval of the Court has been obtained. This will enable him to vouch the necessary journal entries recording the alteration. Where the scheme involves an alteration in the number of shares held by each member, or in the nominal amount of such shares, or the conversion of one class of shares into another class, the auditor should check the necessary entries in the books and also the alterations in the register of members.

(M) INCREASE OR REDUCTION OF CAPITAL

An increase of capital, if authorized by the articles, may be effected by an ordinary resolution of the company (Section 61, *Companies Act 1948*).

A reduction of capital must be in accordance with the provisions of Sections 66-71 of the 1948 Act. The power to reduce, which is exercisable by a special resolution, must be contained in the articles and the sanction of the Court must be obtained.

The auditor must, therefore, satisfy himself that the statutory procedure has been properly carried out, that due effect has been given thereto in the books of account, and, in the case of reduction, that the necessary alterations have been made in the register of members.

Where effect has been given to the resolution to increase the capital of the company, the procedure outlined in § 2 (B) of this chapter would be followed.

§ 3. The Prospectus

Where a company seeks to obtain the whole or part of its capital by public subscription, a prospectus must be issued, the preparation of which is a matter for the promoters or directors.

The work of the auditor in connection with a prospectus is dealt with in detail in Chapter XV.

Where a public company does not issue a prospectus, it must file with the Registrar of Companies a *statement in lieu of prospectus* in the form, and containing the particulars, prescribed by the Fifth Schedule to the *Companies Act 1948*.

The Fourth Schedule, Parts II and III, requires that the prospectus shall contain a report by the auditors of the company with respect to:

(1) (*a*) profits and losses and assets and liabilities, in accordance with subparagraph (2) or (3) of this paragraph, as the case requires; and

(*b*) the rates of the dividends, if any, paid by the company in respect of each class of shares in the company in respect of each of the five financial years immediately preceding the issue of the prospectus, giving particulars of each such class of shares on which such dividends have been paid and particulars of the cases in which no dividends have been paid in respect of any class of shares in respect of any of those years;

and, if no accounts have been made up in respect of any part of the period of five years ending on a date three months before the issue of the prospectus, containing a statement of that fact.

(2) If the company has no subsidiaries, the report shall—

(a) so far as regards profits and losses, deal with the profits or losses of the company in respect of each of the five financial years imme-- dietely preceding the issue of the prospectus; and

(b) so far as regards assets and liabilities, deal with the assets and liabilities of the company at the last date to which the accounts of the company were made up.

(3) If the company has subsidiaries, the report shall—

(a) so far as regards profits and losses, deal separately with the company's profits or losses as provided by the last foregoing sub-paragraph, and in addition, deal either—

(i) as a whole with the combined profits or losses of its subsidiaries, so far as they concern members of the company; or

(ii) individually with the profits or losses of each subsidiary, so far as they concern members of the company;

or, instead of dealing separately with the company's profits or losses, deal as a whole with the profits or losses of the company and, so far as they concern members of the company, with the combined profits or losses of its subsidiaries; and

(b) so far as regards assets and liabilities, deal separately with the company's assets and liabilities as provided by the last foregoing sub-paragraph and, in addition, deal either—

(i) as a whole with the combined assets and liabilities of its subsidiaries, with or without the company's assets and liabilities; or

(ii) individually with the assets and liabilities of each subsidiary;

and shall indicate as respects the assets and liabilities of the subsidiaries the allowance to be made for persons other than members of the company.

Where a business is to be bought directly or indirectly out of the proceeds of the issue, accountants, who must be named in the prospectus, must report upon—

(a) the profits or losses of the business in respect of each of the five financial years immediately preceding the issue of the prospectus; and

(b) the assets and liabilities of the business at the last date to which the accounts of the business were made up.

If the proceeds, or any part of the proceeds, of the issue of the shares or debentures are or is to be applied directly or indirectly in any manner resulting in the acquisition by the company of shares in any other body corporate, and if by reason of that acquisition or anything to be done in consequence thereof or in connection therewith that body corporate will become a subsidiary of the company, the prospectus must contain a report by accountants named therein upon—

(i) the profits or losses of the other body corporate in respect of each of the five financial years immediately preceding the issue of the prospectus; and

(ii) the assets and liabilities of the other body corporate at the last date to which the accounts of the body corporate were made up.

The said report shall—

(*a*) indicate how the profits or losses of the other body corporate dealt with by the report would, in respect of the shares to be acquired, have concerned members of the company and what allowance would have fallen to be made, in relation to assets and liabilities so dealt with, for holders of other shares, if the company had at all material times held the shares to be acquired; and

(*b*) where the other body corporate has subsidiaries, deal with the profits or losses and the assets and liabilities of the body corporate and its subsidiaries in the manner provided by sub-paragraph (3) of paragraph 19 of this Schedule in relation to the company and its subsidiaries (Fourth Schedule, Part II).

The reports to be made by accountants named in the prospectus must be made by accountants who are qualified under the Act to be auditors of a company and such accountants must not themselves be officers or servants, or partners of or in the employment of officers or servants, of the company or the company's subsidiary or holding company, or of a subsidiary of the company's holding company. The term 'officer' for this purpose includes a proposed director but not an auditor.

In some cases a company will raise capital by allotting shares or debentures to an issuing house who will then offer such shares or debentures for sale to the public. The document by which the *offer for sale* is made is for all purposes deemed to be a prospectus issued by the company.

The accountant giving the report referred to above is an expert within the meaning of Section 40, *Companies Act 1948*, and the prospectus may not be issued until he has given his written consent to the issue thereof, and a statement that he has given and has not withdrawn his consent appears in the prospectus.

It has been recently held in the American case of *Escott, et al.* v. *BarChris Construction Corporation, et al.* (U.S. District Court, Southern District, N.Y. 1968) that a company's auditors were guilty of negligence for having failed to report a material worsening of the company's position which took place *after* the time of signing their prospectus report, but *before* the date when the prospectus registration actually became effective. Under U.S.A. law, the burden of proof in such cases alleging negligence is on the auditors, who must show that they had been neither negligent nor fraudulent, by proving that they had reasonable grounds to believe, and did believe, that the statements were true not only as at the date when they signed the statements, but at the time the statements became effective, which in the above case was almost three months later. British statute law has no exact parallel to these onerous stipulations. Even the provisions of Section 40 mentioned above do not demand that experts reporting in prospectuses should consider the validity of the information contained in their reports as at the *time of the registration* of the prospectus.

Where a statement in lieu of prospectus is filed, if it is proposed to use any unissued shares or debentures of the company for the purchase of a business, the statement must contain a report by accountants named therein, in the same form as would be required in a prospectus. It is not necessary to include in a statement in lieu of prospectus a report by the auditors of the company as to the profits etc., of that company.

It cannot be too strongly emphasized that an auditor should refrain from giving in his report for inclusion in a prospectus any forecasts as to future profits, or any opinion as to the prospects of the company; his duty is confined to facts as required by statute.

§ 4. Mortgages and Loans

A *mortgage* is a transfer of an interest in property for the purposes of securing repayment of a loan with interest at a given rate. Until default is made in the terms of the deed, either as regards the payment of interest or repayment of principal, or in any other way, the mortgagor (i.e. the borrower) retains possession and the use of the property, and the mortgagee (the lender) has no right to deal with it.

Mortgages affecting the property of a company, as defined in Section 95, *Companies Act 1948*, must be registered with the Registrar of Companies in the same manner as in the case of debentures referred to below.

The auditor should vouch the receipt of the loan, and examine the register of charges in which particulars of the loan must be inserted under Section 104, *Companies Act 1948*.

Bank loans (and overdrafts) must be separately disclosed on a company's balance sheet. In addition, the Second Schedule to the *Companies Act 1967* requires separate disclosure on the balance sheet of loans which are repayable wholly or in part more than five years from the date of the balance sheet, showing the terms of repayment and the rate of interest in respect of each loan. (If this information will result in a statement of excessive length it shall be sufficient to give a general indication of the terms on which the loans are repayable, and the rates at which interest is payable thereon.) Where the loans are secured, a note to that effect must be added. For the purposes of the above requirements, the term loans is taken to include debentures (see § 5 below).

In a company's profit and loss account, the amount of interest on bank loans, overdrafts and other loans repayable *within* five years from the balance sheet date, must be shown separately from interest on all other loans (i.e. those repayable wholly or in part *more* than five years from the balance sheet date). It is therefore not necessary to show interest paid on debentures and other fixed loans separately (Schedule 2, para. 12 (1) (*b*), *Companies Act 1967*).

§ 5. Debentures

(A) DEFINITION OF DEBENTURE

A *debenture* is a written acknowledgment, usually under seal, of a debt due by a company, containing provisions as to payment of interest and repayment of principal. It may be either a simple or naked debenture, carrying no charge, or a debenture carrying either a fixed or floating charge on some or all of the assets of the company.

Under Section 95, *Companies Act 1948*, all mortgages and charges affecting the property of the company, as defined in that section, must be registered with the Registrar of Companies within 21 days after the date of creation, otherwise they will be void against the liquidator and any creditor of the company, so far as the security comprised by the charge is concerned. If so rendered void, the principal sum will immediately become repayable.

Under Section 104 of the 1948 Act, the necessary entries must be made in the register of charges kept by the company.

Debentures either take the form of bonds to bearer, or they may be registered in the names of the holders, transmission being by transfer. In the latter case, although there is no direct statutory obligation to do so, it is usual to keep a register of debenture holders.

Debenture stock may also be issued, the distinction between debentures and debenture stock being similar to that between shares and stock. Usually, debenture bonds cannot be divided and must be transferred entire; but debenture stock can be transferred in whole or in part, subject to any fractional limitations imposed at the time of issue.

On the issue of a series of debentures by a company, it is usual for two or more persons or a trustee corporation to be appointed as trustees for the debenture holders for the purpose of acting generally on their behalf.

(B) ISSUE OF DEBENTURES

Where a series of debentures is issued, the procedure is similar to that in the case of an issue of shares, and the work to be performed by the auditor in vouching the issue will be of the same character.

When debentures are issued for cash, the receipt of the cash must be vouched. Frequently debentures are issued to vendors of the business as fully paid in part payment of the purchase consideration, and in such cases the auditor must examine the contracts under which the issue is made.

The auditor should examine a copy of the debentures, or the trust deed under which they are issued, in order to ascertain the terms and conditions of issue.

The memorandum and articles of association should be examined to ascertain the borrowing powers of the company. Where no such provision is made, a company has no power to borrow unless borrowing can be regarded as properly incidental to the carrying on of the business. A trading company has an implied power to borrow and give security, even without any specific powers to do so (*General Auction Estate Co* v. *Smith*, 1891 3 Ch. 432).

Under Clause 79 of Table A directors may exercise all the powers of the company to borrow money and they may mortgage or charge the undertaking and property of the company or any part thereof. The clause also gives the directors power to issue debentures, debenture stock and other securities, whether outright or as security for any debt, liability or obligation of the company or of any third party. The amount so borrowed by the directors by virtue of this power must not, without the previous sanction of the company in general meeting, exceed the nominal amount of the company's share capital for the time being issued. In calculating this maximum, however, temporary loans obtained from the company's bankers in the ordinary course of business need not be taken into consideration.

Where a company has no borrowing powers, or where the memorandum fixes a limit, any loan in the former case, or any loan in excess of the limit in the latter, is *ultra vires* the company. It is, in consequence, absolutely void, and any securities given are inoperative (*Howard* v. *Patent Ivory Co*, 1888 38 Ch. D. 1956). If the loan is *ultra vires* the directors it is invalid, and the security given is inoperative, except in so far as the company is estopped from denying its validity, under the rule in *Royal British Bank* v. *Turquand* (1856, 6 El. and Bl. 327). This rule is that persons dealing with a company are not bound to enquire whether all the necessary steps have been taken so long as the particular act appears to conform to the provisions of the memorandum and articles. Thus, if a company may only borrow up to a limit of £2,000 without the prior consent of the members in general meeting, a *bona fide* lender may lend £2,000 without enquiring if there are other loans outstanding. If other loans are outstanding, the company is estopped from denying the validity of this loan. Where directors have acted *ultra vires* their borrowing powers, the company may elect to ratify their acts (*Irvine* v. *Union Bank of Australia*, L.R. 2 A.C. 366). An overdraft at a bank must be taken into account where limited powers of borrowing are involved (*Looker* v. *Wrigley*, 1880, 9 Q.B.D. 397).

The auditor should ascertain that the debentures have been duly registered with the Registrar of Companies, and should examine the entries relating thereto in the register of charges.

Debentures may be issued at par, at a discount, or at a premium; and may be repayable at par or at a premium. Special points arise in each case, which demand consideration.

(1) *Debentures issued at a Premium*

Although the *Companies Act 1948* does not prescribe the manner in which premiums received on an issue of debentures should be dealt with, it is considered that they should be regarded as capital profits and credited to capital reserve. Alternatively, they may be utilized to form the nucleus of a debenture redemption fund; or, if not employed in this manner, they may be used to write off fictitious assets. It is usual to charge the expenses of issuing the debentures against the premium received.

In the balance sheet the debentures will appear as a liability at their *nominal* value.

(2) *Debentures issued at a Discount*

Debentures may be issued at a discount, and the discount can be regarded as a lump sum allowance to the lenders when taking up the debentures, in consideration of their accepting a lower rate of interest than would have been payable had the debentures been issued at par. The financial position of the company and the state of the money market at the date of issue are important factors in determining the price of issue.

The debentures will appear in the balance sheet as a liability at their *nominal* value, and the discount will be written off over a period of years, the balance remaining at any date being carried forward as a separate item in the balance sheet. Any sums paid by way of commission in respect of the issued debentures, or allowed by way of discount, must be stated in the annual return.

As this discount is not represented by any value it is advisable that it should be written off as soon as possible. It cannot be said, however, to be incorrect to write off the discount over the full term of the debentures; and in that case, when no sinking fund is formed for the purpose of repaying the debentures, and the debentures are repayable at the end of a given period, an equal amount of the discount should be written off each year. If the debentures are repayable by annual drawings, without the provision of a sinking fund, the discount should be written off in relative proportion to the amount of debentures outstanding each year, in order that the periods enjoying the use of the greater portion of the debentures may be charged with the greater portion of the discount.

Where the redemption of the debentures is provided for by annual charges against profit and loss account, such charges will include provision for the discount, and, consequently, the discount can be written off against the credit balance of the redemption account when the debentures have been redeemed.

(3) *Debentures repayable at a Premium*

These debentures will appear in the balance sheet as a liability at their nominal amount, with a note of the amount at which they are repayable, any discount or premium on issue being treated in one of the ways described above.

If a sinking fund is formed to provide for repayment, this should include provision for the payment of the premium on redemption. If no sinking fund is formed, the premium should be provided for out of profits over the term of the debentures.

(4) *Debentures issued as Collateral Security for a Loan*

It is a common practice for companies to issue debentures as collateral security against a loan or overdraft from a bank or other parties. Section 90 (3), *Companies Act 1948*, expressly refers to this procedure, and provides that such debentures shall not be deemed to have been redeemed by reason only of the account of the company having ceased to be in debit whilst the debentures remained so deposited.

The term collateral security means a security which can be realized by the party holding it, in the event of the original loan in respect of which the security was given not being repaid at the proper time, or in any other specific cases, according to the agreement between the parties. As soon as the loan is repaid, the collateral security is automatically released.

When debentures are issued in this manner a note to this effect should be shown on the balance sheet. The loan against which they are issued will appear as a liability in the usual way.

(C) REDEMPTION OF DEBENTURES

Debentures may be redeemable according to the terms of issue, at specified dates, by annual or other drawings, or at the option of the company, after due notice has been given of intention to repay.

The auditor should examine the provisions of the trust deed or the debenture bonds relating to the redemption, and ascertain that they are duly complied with.

Where the debentures are redeemable at the end of a given period, it is usual to find provision made in the trust deed for a sinking fund to be raised out of profits for this purpose.

The operation of such a fund entails a charge against profit and loss account each year of an amount which, if invested at compound interest, will produce the required sum at the end of a given period. The investments so made are usually held in the names of the trustees for the debenture holders. When redemption takes place, the investments will be sold and the debenture holders paid off. The amounts standing to the credit of the redemption or sinking fund will then represent accumulated profit, but in place of being invested in specific assets, will be represented by the general assets of the business which had previously been subject to the charge of the debentures. The amount of such fund should therefore be transferred to reserve. It cannot, as a rule, be used for the payment of dividends, since it may not be represented by available cash; but there would be no legal objection to its being utilized in this way if the liquid funds were available, since it has been built up out of revenue.

Where debentures have been redeemed by purchase in the open market at a discount, but the full nominal amount has been provided for by the operation of a sinking fund, the profit on the redemption can be taken to the profit and loss account, as it represents an amount previously provided in excess of that actually required for redemption. It is, however, preferable to place the amount to a capital reserve. Where no sinking fund has been provided, any profit on redemption should be similarly treated.

In vouching the redemption of debentures, the auditor should examine the cancelled debenture bonds or stock certificates, and inspect the directors' minute authorizing the redemption.

Instead of investing the redemption fund in securities, it is a common practice to effect an endowment policy with an insurance company, under which annual premiums are paid, the insurer undertaking to provide the capital sum required at the end of a given period. Such policies will be assigned to the trustees for the debenture holders, if any, but the premiums will be paid by the company, the annual amount thereof being debited to the profit and loss account and credited to the redemption account, while the premiums paid will be debited to the policy account. The only distinction between this method and that of making specific investments is that accruing interest will not be received in cash or require to be invested. Unless, however, some account is taken of accruing interest, the book value of the policy will ultimately be less than its surrender value. If it is desired to maintain the policy in the books at its surrender value, the necessary adjustments will be made through the redemption account.

Where debentures are redeemable by annual drawings on the principle of a sinking fund, although it is necessary to debit profit and loss account and credit the redemption account with the amount required for the annual drawing, it will not be necessary to invest such amount, as the money represented thereby is immediately paid out in discharge of the drawn debentures. The amount standing to the credit of the redemption account will, as soon as the debentures have been drawn and paid off, be transferred to reserve.

Debentures may also be irredeemable or perpetual, and specific provision is made for the legality of such debentures by Section 89, *Companies Act 1948*.

Power is granted to re-issue redeemed debentures in certain cases by Section 90, *Companies Act 1948*. Under this section, where either before or after the commencement of the Act, a company has redeemed any debentures previously issued, then, unless any provision to the contrary is contained in the articles, or in any contract entered into by the company, or the company has passed a resolution, or by some other act indicates its intention that the debentures shall be cancelled, the company shall have, and shall be deemed always to have had, power to re-issue the debentures, either by re-issuing the same debentures, or by issuing other debentures in their place.

Where a company has power to re-issue debentures which have been redeemed, particulars with respect to the debentures which can be so re-issued must be included in every balance sheet of the company issued subsequent to the redemption and up to the date of re-issue.

§ 6. Preliminary and Formation Expenses

This is the term given to the expenses incidental to the creation and flotation of a company. The following items are usually included under this heading:

(1) Stamp duties and fees on the nominal capital, and stamps on the contracts transferring the assets.

(2) The legal costs of preparing the prospectus, memorandum and articles of association and contracts, and of the registration of the company.

(3) Accountants' and valuers' fees for reports, certificates, etc.

(4) Cost of printing the memorandum and articles of association, and printing, advertising, and issuing prospectuses.

(5) Cost of preparing and printing letters of allotment, and share certificates.

(6) Cost of preparing, printing and stamping debentures and debenture trust deed (if any).

(7) Cost of the company's seal and statutory books.

These preliminary and formation expenses are sometimes borne entirely by the company, and sometimes by the promoters or the vendors of the business, or apportioned between these parties. Care must be taken to see that the company is only charged with expenses properly payable by it, and the auditor must examine the contracts relating to these expenses, and vouch the payments made. This expenditure is of a capital nature, but as it is not represented by available assets, it is advisable that it should be written off as soon as possible.

Where a premium is received on shares issued, it is common to find the preliminary expenses charged against such premium, and power to do so is given by Section 56, *Companies Act 1948*.

Expenditure in connection with preliminary expenses, so far as it has not been written off to date, must be shown as a separate item in the balance sheet of the company, and any expenses incurred in connection with the issue of share capital or debentures must also be shown separately.

Underwriting commission and commission on placing shares must not be included under the general heading 'Preliminary Expenses', but must be shown separately on the balance sheet, until written off.

§ 7. Commission on Issue of Shares

Underwriting commission is the amount payable to persons who undertake to subscribe for a certain number of shares, in the event of the public not taking up the whole of the shares for which they are invited to apply. An underwriting contract is therefore in the nature of a speculation. If the public subscribe for the total of the shares available, the underwriters receive their commission, and do not have to take up any shares. If the public do not subscribe for the issue in full, the underwriters have to take up the shares not subscribed for, in proportion to their respective contracts, if more than one underwriter is involved. It is usual for the underwriters to make formal application for the shares they underwrite, on the understanding that allotments to them will be made only to the extent to which the public do not apply.

Commission on placing shares is an amount payable to parties who introduce to the company persons who are willing to become members, and to take up shares accordingly. This commission therefore differs from underwriting commission, in that it does not arise from a speculative transaction, and is only paid in the event of capital being introduced.

Section 53, *Companies Act 1948*, empowers companies to pay commission of this nature under certain conditions. The amount or rate per cent. of the commission must be authorized by the articles and must not exceed 10 per cent. of the price at which the shares are issued, or the amount or rate authorized by the articles, whichever is the lower. This amount must be disclosed in the prospectus or in the statement required to be filed with the Registrar in lieu thereof, and in any invitation to subscribe for shares, not being a prospectus. The number of shares which persons have agreed for a commission to subscribe for absolutely must also be disclosed in the same manner.

This commission is usually payable in cash, but sometimes it is satisfied by the issue of fully paid shares, or partly in cash and partly in shares.

In some companies, in place of paying commission, an option is given to the underwriters to subscribe within a specified period for a certain portion of the company's unissued shares at par or at a fixed premium, and where such shares are likely to go to a high premium, this option may be of considerable value. It was held by the House of Lords (*Hilder* v. *Dexter*, 1902, A.C. 474) that such an arrangement is not an application of shares in payment of commission within the meaning of Section 53 as quoted above. Where such an option has been given, the auditor must see that a note thereof appears on the accounts or in a statement or report annexed thereto giving particulars of the period during which the option is exercisable, and the price to be paid for the shares subscribed under it (Second Schedule, Part I, (11) (2), *Companies Act 1967*). An option cannot, however, be given to a director of the company or to the spouse or infant children of a director (Section 25, *Companies Act 1967*).

In order to vouch the payment of underwriting commission, the auditor should examine the articles of association, to ensure that power is given to make payments of this nature, and should ascertain that the provisions of Section 53 have been duly complied with. The underwriting contract and the application letters signed by the underwriters should be seen. The amount or rate per cent. paid must not exceed that authorized, and where payment has been made in shares, it should be seen that the contracts have been properly filed.

Should the auditor find that the underwriter's calls or payments on allotment are in arrear, he should mention this fact in his report to the members.

The vouching of commission on placing shares is somewhat more difficult, as it is not easy for the auditor to satisfy himself that commission paid to any person is in respect of applications actually introduced by such person. No commission should be paid unless the application form on which the shares have been allotted was initialled by the party claiming the commission before being sent into the company, and the auditor should examine the application forms in respect of which such commission is payable, to ascertain whether this has been done.

All commission of this nature should be referred to in the minutes, and a resolution passed by the directors for the payment thereof.

Brokerage on placing shares is an amount payable to brokers and other agents whose clients have subscribed for shares in the company, on application forms stamped with the agent's stamp.

Such a brokerage, not exceeding $2\frac{1}{2}$ per cent., has been held to be *intra vires* the company (*Metropolitan Coal Consumers Association* v. *Scrimgeour*, 1895, 2 Q.B. 604), and the payment thereof is not subject to the restrictions imposed by Section 53. In order to vouch items of this nature, the auditor should examine the application letters, ensuring that these are stamped by the agents concerned.

The total of any sums paid or allowed by way of commission in respect of any shares, or so much thereof as has not been written off, must be stated separately in every balance sheet. The annual return must disclose the total amount of the sums (if any) paid by way of commission in respect of any shares since the date of the last return.

There is nothing in the Acts to prevent the payment of such commissions out of revenue, should the articles give power to do so; and such transactions are not subject to the restrictions imposed by Section 53.

§ 8. The Statutory Audit

This is a term commonly applied to the audit required to be performed by the auditor, if appointed prior to the *statutory meeting* of the company. Under Section 130 of the *Companies Act 1948*, every *public* company must hold a general meeting not less than one month, nor more than three months, after the date on which the company is entitled to commence business, and such meeting is called the statutory meeting.

At least fourteen days before the date on which this meeting is to be held, the directors must forward a report, called the *statutory report*, to every member of the company. This report must be certified by not less than two of the directors, and must state:

(*a*) The total number of shares allotted, distinguishing shares allotted as fully or partly paid up otherwise than in cash, and stating in the case of shares partly paid up the extent to which they are so paid up, and in either case the consideration for which they have been allotted;

(*b*) The total amount of cash received by the company in respect of all the shares allotted, distinguished as aforesaid;

(*c*) An abstract of the receipts of the company, and of the payments made thereout, up to a date within seven days of the date of the report, exhibiting under distinctive headings the receipts of the company from shares and debentures and other sources, the payments made thereout, and particulars concerning the balance remaining in hand, and an account or estimate of the preliminary expenses of the company.

(*d*) The names, addresses and descriptions of the directors, auditors (if appointed), managers (if any), and secretary of the company.

(*e*) The particulars of any contract, the modification of which is to be submitted to the meeting for its approval, together with the particulars of the modification or proposed modification.

So much of the report as relates to the shares allotted by the company and the cash received in respect of such shares, and the receipts and payments of the company on capital account, must be certified by the auditors (if appointed) of the company.

The work to be performed by the auditor in connection with the shares allotted and cash received in respect thereof, will follow the lines laid down for the audit of the issue of share capital in § 2 (B) and (C) of this chapter.

The manner in which the section is worded makes it clear that a summarized cash account must be supplied, although apparently there is no necessity for revenue receipts and payments to be shown in any detail, nor is the auditor concerned therewith at this stage, since his certificate is only designed to cover the receipts and payments of the company on capital account.

The auditor must examine the contracts with the vendors, and vouch all payments; the work necessary in connection with the vouching of payments for the preliminary and formation expenses and commission on the issue of shares has already been discussed.

A *private* company is *not* required to hold a statutory meeting or prepare a statutory report. It is unusual today for a company to be incorporated initially as a public company, the normal practice being to register the company as a private company in the first instance and subsequently to convert it into a public company. As a result of this procedure, the company is not required to hold a statutory meeting or issue a statutory report, as it is a private company on the date it becomes entitled to commence business.

§ 9. Adjustment of Accounts with Vendors

(A) PURCHASE OF BUSINESS

Where a company acquires a business, the auditor should vouch the journal entries recording the assets acquired and liabilities taken over (if any), with the contracts between the vendors and the company. Where a prospectus has been issued, the amount payable for goodwill must be specified therein, and will be equivalent to the difference between the value of the tangible assets acquired and the amount of the consideration payable to the vendors, plus the liabilities taken over (if any).

Where the purchase consideration is less than the value of the tangible assets acquired, there will be no goodwill, but on the other hand a surplus will be shown representing a book profit. The cost of such assets to the company is only the amount paid therefor, and consequently any apparent surplus should preferably be utilized in adjusting the values of the assets acquired. Where, however, such treatment is not desired, the amount should be placed to the credit of capital reserve, which will not be available for distribution.

Where a reconstruction has taken place, and a new company has been formed to take over from the liquidator of the old company all the assets of that company, and possibly also to undertake certain of its liabilities, the old company receiving the purchase consideration either wholly or partly in shares of the new company, the auditor of the reconstructed company should examine the contract under which the assets are acquired, and ascertain that all such assets are duly brought into account. In some cases the liabilities of the old company may be wholly or partly satisfied by the issue of shares or debentures, and where this is so, the auditor should vouch the issue of such shares or debentures, and ascertain that it is in accordance with the contract.

(B) APPORTIONMENT OF PROFIT OR LOSS PRIOR TO
INCORPORATION

Frequently a company takes over a business as from a date prior to the incorporation of the company itself. In such an event any profits earned prior to the date of incorporation, to which the company may be entitled, cannot be regarded as profits available for dividend, but are of a capital nature, since the company cannot earn profits before it comes into existence. When the vendors are not entitled to take such profits, they are usually entitled to interest on the purchase consideration from the date when the business was taken over to the date when the purchase consideration is discharged. If that is so, the interest payable to the vendors for the period from the date of taking over the business until the date of incorporation can be charged against the profits earned during that period, any interest payable in respect of any period after the date of incorporation being charged against the profit and loss account. The remaining balance of profit earned prior to incorporation (if any) should either be written off the goodwill, or, if there is no goodwill, carried forward as a capital reserve not available for revenue purposes.

If stock is not taken at the date of incorporation, and the exact profit, prior thereto cannot consequently be ascertained, it is necessary to arrive at the approximate proportion of profits applicable to the period prior to incorporation. This may be done by apportioning the whole of the profit earned according to the time covered by the respective periods, or in proportion to the turnovers of those periods. A more accurate division of profit will, however, be obtained by apportioning the *gross* profit and the expenses which vary with turnover, between the two periods on the basis of their respective turnovers, and all other expenses on the basis of time.

The date of the division, in these cases, should be the date of incorporation, and not, in the case of a public company, the date of the certificate entitling it to commence business, since once that certificate has been issued the company's power to legally carry on business relates back to the date of incorporation.

The auditor must take care to see that an equitable division of profit has been made between the two periods, and that the period subsequent to incorporation (the profits of which are available for dividends) has not been favoured at the expense of the prior period.

In the event of a loss in the first period it is not usual to make any apportionment in respect of the period prior to incorporation, but to carry forward the debit balance against future profits. However, there is nothing to prevent the proportion of the loss relating to the period prior to incorporation being added to the goodwill account as it represents, in fact, an increase in the price paid for that asset.

(C) RECEIPTS AND PAYMENTS ON BEHALF OF VENDORS

In most instances the company does not acquire the book debts from the vendors, but, for the purposes of convenience, undertakes to collect them on their behalf. In such cases the company does not, as a rule, take over the liabilities, but for similar reasons arranges to pay these liabilities out of the proceeds of the book debts. Where this is so, the assets and liabilities concerned should be brought into the books of the company for the purposes of recording what ought to be collected and paid away on behalf of the vendors, the book debts being credited to the vendors and the liabilities debited. The auditor should see that the cash received from the debtors, or the payments made to the creditors, are duly apportioned as between the company and the vendors. Any discount or bad debts relating to the vendors' book debts must be borne by the vendors.

Sometimes the company takes over the book debts, their value being guaranteed by the vendors. Any bad debts incurred relating to such debts will therefore be charged to the vendors. It is an open point whether cash discount allowed on payment of such debts within the usual term of credit can be so charged; but this will depend on the precise wording of the contract with the vendors. The auditor should take care to ascertain that all losses properly chargeable against the vendors are debited to them.

The contract should be consulted to ascertain whether there are any provisions other than those above referred to affecting the adjustment of the accounts between the vendors and the company. It is sometimes arranged that the vendors shall account for all money withdrawn from the business between the date from which the company acquires it and the date when the company takes it over, and in the same manner any sums paid into the business during that period by the vendors may be repayable to them.

§ 10. The Annual Audit

As indicated in § 4 of Chapter VIII, it is the duty of the auditors to make a report on the accounts examined by them, and on every balance sheet, every profit and loss account and all group accounts laid before the company in general meeting during their tenure of office.

(A) THE BOOKS OF ACCOUNT

Under Section 147 of the *Companies Act 1948*, every company shall cause to be kept proper books of account with respect to—

(*a*) all sums of money received and expended by the company and the matters in respect of which the receipt and expenditure takes place;

(*b*) all sales and purchases of goods by the company;

(*c*) the assets and liabilities of the company.

The section further provides that such books must be kept as will give a true and fair view of the state of the company's affairs and explain its transactions.

The necessary books must be kept at the registered office of the company, or at such other place as the directors may think fit, and shall at all times be open to inspection by the directors.

If books of account are kept at a place outside Great Britain, returns and accounts which disclose with reasonable accuracy the financial position of that business must be sent to and kept in Great Britain, at intervals not exceeding six months. The returns and accounts must be in such a form as will enable the company to prepare its balance sheet and profit and loss account and any documents required by the Acts to be annexed thereto.

Failure to take all reasonable steps to comply with the requirements of Section 147 will, if the Court considers the offence to have been committed wilfully, involve a director in a liability to imprisonment for a term not exceeding six months. The section also provides an alternative penalty of a fine of £200. It will be a defence to any action brought against him for the director to prove that he had reasonable ground to believe and did believe that a competent and reliable person was charged with the duty of seeing that the requirements of the Act were complied with in this regard.

Under Section 331 of the 1948 Act it is provided that if proper books of account are not kept throughout the period of two years immediately preceding the commencement of the winding-up of a company (or the period between the incorporation of the company and the commencement of the winding-up, if shorter), every officer of the company who was in default is liable to imprisonment for a term not exceeding one year, or on summary conviction, six months, unless he can show that he acted honestly and that in the circumstances in which the business was carried on the default was excusable. For the purposes of this section, such books and accounts must be kept as are necessary to exhibit and explain the transactions and financial position of the trade or business of the company, so as to contain entries from day to day in sufficient detail of all cash received and paid, and where dealings in goods are involved, statements of the annual stock-takings, and (except in the case of goods sold by way of ordinary retail trade) of all goods sold and purchased, showing the goods and the buyers and sellers thereof in sufficient detail to enable those goods and those buyers and sellers to be identified.

These provisions are analogous to those contained in Section 147, but it will be observed that in the event of liquidation, failure to keep stock-taking statements will render the officers liable to penalties.

It will be remembered that under Section 14, *Companies Act 1967*, the specific duty is imposed upon auditors, in preparing their report, to carry out such investigations as will enable them to form an opinion as to whether proper books of account have been kept by the company and proper returns adequate for their audit have been received from branches not visited by them.

It is emphasized that this duty must be discharged irrespective of the size of the company – there is no distinction for this purpose between a large public company and a small private company. However, reference to these requirements need be made in the auditors' report only in the event of some qualification being necessary.

(B) THE PROFIT AND LOSS ACCOUNT

The directors of every company shall at some date, not later than eighteen months after the incorporation of the company, and subsequently once at least in every calendar year, lay before the company in general meeting a profit and loss account, (or in the case of a non-trading company, an income and expenditure account) for the period, in the case of the first account, since the incorporation of the company, and in any other case, since the preceding account, made up to a date not earlier than the date of the meeting by more than nine months, or in the case of a company carrying on business or having interests abroad, by more than twelve months. These periods may be extended in special circumstances by the Board of Trade (Section 148, *Companies Act 1948*).

The Eighth Schedule, *Companies Act 1948*, as amended by the First Schedule to the *Companies Act 1967*, sets forth the items and information which must be shown in the profit and loss account. These provisions, now contained in Part I of the Second Schedule to the 1967 Act, are set out hereunder:

12. (1) There shall be shown—

(*a*) the amount charged to revenue by way of provision for depreciation, renewals or diminution in value of fixed assets;

(*b*) the amount of the interest on loans of the following kinds made to the company (whether on the security of debentures or not), namely, bank loans, overdrafts and loans which, not being bank loans or overdrafts,—

　(i) are repayable otherwise than by instalments and fall due for repayment before the expiration of the period of five years beginning with the day next following the expiration of the financial year; or

　(ii) are repayable by instalments the last of which falls due for payment before the expiration of that period;

and the amount of the interest on loans of other kinds so made (whether on the security of debentures or not);

(*c*) the amount of the charge to revenue for United Kingdom corporation tax and, if that amount would have been greater but for relief from double taxation, the amount which it would have been but for such relief, the amount of the charge for United Kingdom income tax and the amount of the charge for taxation imposed outside the United Kingdom of profits, income and (so far as charged to revenue) capital gains;

(*d*) the amounts respectively provided for redemption of share capital and for redemption of loans;

(e) the amount, if material, set aside or proposed to be set aside to, or withdrawn from, reserves;

(f) subject to sub-paragraph (2) of this paragraph, the amount, if material, set aside to provisions other than provisions for depreciation, renewals or diminution in value of assets or, as the case may be, the amount, if material, withdrawn from such provisions and not applied for the purposes thereof;

(g) the amounts respectively of income from quoted investments and income from unquoted investments;

(ga) if a substantial part of the company's revenue for the financial year consists in rents from land, the amount thereof (after deduction of ground-rents, rates and other outgoings);

(gb) the amount, if material, charged to revenue in respect of sums payable in respect of the hire of plant and machinery;

(h) the aggregate amount (before deduction of income tax) of the dividends paid and proposed.

(2) The Board of Trade may direct that a company shall not be obliged to show an amount set aside to provisions in accordance with sub-paragraph (1) (f) of this paragraph, if the Board is satisfied that that is not required in the public interest and would prejudice the company, but subject to the condition that any heading stating an amount arrived at after taking into account the amount set aside as aforesaid shall be so framed or marked as to indicate that fact.

(3) If, in the case of any assets in whose case an amount is charged to revenue by way of provision for depreciation or diminution in value, an amount is also so charged by way of provision for renewal thereof, the last-mentioned amount shall be shown separately.

(4) If the amount charged to revenue by way of provision for depreciation or diminution in value of any fixed assets (other than investments) has been determined otherwise than by reference to the amount of those assets as determined for the purpose of making up the balance sheet, that fact shall be stated.

12A. The amount of any charge arising in consequence of the occurrence of an event in a preceding financial year and of any credit so arising shall, if not included in a heading relating to other matters, be stated under a separate heading.

13. The amount of the remuneration of the auditors shall be shown under a separate heading, and for the purposes of this paragraph, any sums paid by the company in respect of the auditors' expenses shall be deemed to be included in the expression 'remuneration'.

13A. (1) The matters referred to in sub-paragraphs (2) to (4) below shall be stated by way of note, if not otherwise shown.

(2) The turnover for the financial year, except in so far as it is attributable to the business of banking or discounting or to business of such other class as may be prescribed for the purposes of this sub-paragraph.

(3) If some or all of the turnover is omitted by reason of its being attributable as aforesaid, the fact that it is so omitted.

(4) The method by which turnover stated is arrived at.

(5) A company shall not be subject to the requirements of this paragraph if it is neither a holding company nor a subsidiary of another body corporate and the turnover which, apart from this sub-paragraph, would be required to be stated does not exceed £50,000.

14. (1) The matters referred to in the following sub-paragraphs shall be stated by way of note, if not otherwise shown.

(2) If depreciation or replacement of fixed assets is provided for by some method other than a depreciation charge or provision for renewals, or is not provided for, the method by which it is provided for or the fact that it is not provided for, as the case may be.

(3) The basis on which the charge for United Kingdom Corporation Tax and the United Kingdom Income Tax is computed.

(3A) Any special circumstances which affect liability in respect of taxation of profits, income or capital gains for the financial year or liability in respect of taxation of profits, income or capital gains for succeeding financial years.

(5) Except in the case of the first profit and loss account laid before the company after the commencement of this Act the corresponding amounts for the immediately preceding financial year for all items shown in the profit and loss account.

(6) Any material respects in which any items shown in the profit and loss account are affected—

(a) by transactions of a sort not usually undertaken by the company or otherwise by circumstances of an exceptional or non-recurrent nature; or

(b) by any change in the basis of accounting.

The above provisions do not apply to banking or discount companies, with the exception of paragraphs 12 (1) (ga) and (h), 12A, 13 and 14 (1) and (5). In the case of such companies, however, if in the balance sheet reserves or provisions (other than provisions for depreciation, renewals or diminution in value of assets) are not stated separately, any heading stating an amount arrived at after taking into account a reserve or such a provision must be so framed or marked as to indicate that fact, and the profit and loss account must indicate by appropriate words the manner in which the amount stated for the company's profit or loss has been arrived at.

Insurance companies to which the *Insurance Companies Act 1958* applies shall not be subject to the requirements of paragraphs 12, other than 12 (1) (b), (c), (d) and (h)) and 14 (2) set out above, but are subject to the same requirement as banking and discount companies with regard to disclosure of the manner in which the company's profit or loss has been arrived at, and of the fact that movements on provisions and reserves have taken place.

Shipping companies are likewise exempt from certain disclosure requirements in the profit and loss account, viz. paragraphs 12 (1) (a), (1) (e), (1) (f), (3), (4), and paragraph 13 A.

The special provisions of the Acts dealing with the consolidated accounts of holding companies and subsidiaries are dealt with in Chapter XI.

In addition to the aforementioned requirements, Section 196, *Companies Act 1948*, provides for the disclosure in the accounts of directors' emoluments, pensions etc. This section is very comprehensive and is given in detail hereunder:

(1) In any accounts of a company laid before it in general meeting, or in a statement annexed thereto, there shall, subject to and in accordance with the provisions of this section, be shown so far as the information is contained in the company's books and papers or the company has the right to obtain it from the persons concerned—

(a) the aggregate amount of the directors' emoluments;

(b) the aggregate amount of directors' or past directors' pensions; and

(c) the aggregate amount of any compensation to directors or past directors in respect of loss of office.

(2) The amount to be shown under paragraph (a) of sub-section (1) of this section—

(a) shall include any emoluments paid to or receivable by any person in respect of his services as director of the company or in respect of his services, while director of the company, as director of any subsidiary thereof or otherwise in connection with the management of the affairs of the company or any subsidiary thereof; and

(b) shall distinguish between emoluments in respect of services as director, whether of the company or its subsidiary, and other emoluments;

and for the purposes of this section the expression 'emoluments', in relation to a director, includes fees and percentages, any sums paid by way of expenses allowance in so far as those sums are charged to United Kingdom income tax, any contribution paid in respect of him under any pension scheme and the estimated money value of any other benefits received by him otherwise than in cash.

(3) The amount to be shown under paragraph (b) of the said subsection (1)—

(a) shall not include any pension paid or receivable under a pension scheme if the scheme is such that the contributions thereunder are substantially adequate for the maintenance of the scheme, but save as aforesaid shall include any pension paid or receivable in respect of any such services of a director or past director of the company as are mentioned in the last foregoing subsection, whether to or by him or, on his nomination or by virtue of dependence on or other connection with him, to or by any other person; and

(b) shall distinguish between pensions in respect of services as director, whether of the company or its subsidiary, and other pensions;

and for the purposes of this section the expression 'pensions' includes any superannuation allowance, superannuation gratuity or similar payment, and the expression 'pension scheme' means a scheme for the provision of pensions in respect of services as director or otherwise which is maintained in whole or in part by means of contributions, and the expression 'contribution' in relation to a pension scheme means any payment (including an insurance premium) paid for the purposes of the scheme by or in respect of persons rendering services in respect of which pensions will or may become payable under the scheme, except that it does not include any payment in respect of two or more persons if the amount paid in respect of each of them is not ascertainable.

(4) The amount to be shown under paragraph (c) of the said subsection (1)—

(a) shall include any sums paid to or receivable by a director or past director by way of compensation for the loss of office as director of the company or for the loss, while director of the company or on or in connection with his ceasing to be a director of the company, of any other office in connection with the management of the company's affairs or of any office as director or otherwise in connection with the management of the affairs of any subsidiary thereof; and

(b) shall distinguish between compensation in respect of the office of director, whether of the company or its subsidiary and compensation in respect of other offices;

and for the purposes of this section references to compensation for loss of office shall include sums paid as consideration for or in connection with a person's retirement from office.

(5) The amounts to be shown under each paragraph of the said subsection (1)—

(a) shall include all relevant sums paid by or receivable from—

(i) the company; and

(ii) the company's subsidiaries; and

(iii) any other persons;

except sums to be accounted for to the company or any of its subsidiaries or, by virtue of section one hundred and ninety-three of this Act, to past or present members of the company or any of its subsidiaries or any class of those members; and (*b*) shall distinguish, in the case of the amount to be shown under paragraph (*c*) of the said subsection (1), between the sums respectively paid by or receivable from the company, the company's subsidiaries and persons other than the company and its subsidiaries.

(6) The amounts to be shown under this section for any financial year shall be the sums receivable in respect of that year, whenever paid, or, in the case of sums not receivable in respect of a period, the sums paid during that year, so, however, that where—

(*a*) any sums are not shown in the accounts for the relevant financial year on the ground that the person receiving them is liable to account therefor as mentioned in paragraph (*a*) of the last foregoing subsection, but the liability is thereafter wholly or partly released or is not enforced within a period of two years; or

(*b*) any sums paid by way of expenses allowance are charged to United Kingdom income tax after the end of the relevant financial year;

those sums shall, to the extent to which the liability is released or not enforced or they are charged as aforesaid, as the case may be, be shown in the first accounts in which it is practicable to show them or in a statement annexed thereto, and shall be distinguished from the amounts to be shown therein apart from this provision.

(7) Where it is necessary so to do for the purpose of making any distinction required by this section in any amount to be shown thereunder, the directors may apportion any payments between the matters in respect of which they have been paid or are receivable in such manner as they think appropriate.

(8) If in the case of any accounts the requirements of this section are not complied with, it shall be the duty of the auditors of the company by whom the accounts are examined to include in their report thereon, so far as they are reasonably able to do so, a statement giving the required particulars.

(9) In this section any reference to a company's subsidiary—

(*a*) in relation to a person who is or was, while a director of the company, a director also, by virtue of the company's nomination, direct or indirect, of any other body corporate, shall, subject to the following paragraph, include that body corporate, whether or not it is or was in fact the company's subsidiary: and

(*b*) shall for the purposes of subsections (2) and (3) be taken as referring to a subsidiary at the time the services were rendered, and for the purposes of subsection (4) be taken as referring to a subsidiary immediately before the loss of office as director of the company.

This section is of particular importance to a company's auditors in view of the requirement expressed in subsection (8), i.e. that it shall be the duty of the auditors to supply the required particulars (in so far as they are able to do so) if the accounts themselves do not.

It will be observed that a distinction must be drawn between emoluments paid to a director as director and those paid for management services, and that the directors may make any necessary apportionment of sums paid to them in order to give the requisite information. In view of the doubt which may sometimes arise as to how the distinction between 'director' and 'management' services is to be interpreted, the Institute of Chartered Accountants obtained the following opinion from counsel:

'In our opinion, Section 196, *Companies Act 1948*, is intended to draw a distinction between service as a director and service as manager or executive. The conception seems to be that directors control the policy of the company, whereas managers carry out the decisions of the directors and take the action necessary to give effect to those decisions. The distinction is not easy to work out logically, since the directors are inherently managers. In subsection 196 (2) (*b*), both directorial and managerial functions are referred to: the directorial functions by the words "in respect of his services as a director" and the managerial functions by the words "or otherwise in connection with the management of the affairs of the company."

' In our opinion, emoluments in respect of services " as director " are those fees which are paid to directors in their capacity as such and not in any managerial or executive capacity. Normally these would be fees fixed either by the articles or by the company in general meeting but they would, we think, include remuneration paid to directors for special services, e.g for going or residing abroad or for serving on committees.

'Emoluments paid in connection with the management of the affairs of the company in our opinion mean remuneration paid to a director for services in a managerial or executive capacity, e.g. as managing director, manager, secretary or as a departmental head. Such remuneration would normally be paid under a service contract.

'The power given to the directors by Section 196 (7) to apportion is expressed as being permissive; but if it is necessary to exercise the power in order that the accounts may give the information required by the section of a true and fair view of the state of the company's affairs, then the directors must exercise the power. Thus if a managing director were paid say, £5,000 a year inclusive of directors' fees, it would necessary to apportion the sum between the directorial and managerial functions. If he were paid £5,000 plus directors' fees no question of apportionment would arise. If he were paid £5,000 a year as managing director and had no right under the articles to directors' fees, again no apportionment would be necessary.'

Section 196 (2) provides that the expression 'emoluments' in relation to a director includes 'the estimated money value of any other benefits received by him otherwise than in cash'. The question as to what constitutes a benefit and the assessment of the monetary value thereof presents considerable difficulty for the auditor. Examples of benefits which a director may derive from the company are: the free use of living accommodation, the free use of motor cars, goods and services supplied by the company without charge or at less than normal prices, regular luncheons, etc. Very similar provisions were enacted by the *Finance Act 1948*, under which benefits or facilities in kind are regarded for taxation purposes as perquisites of the office of director. The position for taxation purposes provides a useful guide to directors and auditors as to the benefits which must be disclosed in the accounts under the *Companies Act 1948*.

An extract from the opinion of counsel obtained on this matter by the Institute of Chartered Accountants is reproduced hereunder:

'In our opinion it is the duty of the auditor to make enquiry from the company and from the directors in order that he may verify the benefits obtained by the directors otherwise than in cash. Section 196 (2) requires the aggregate of the directors' emoluments to be shown in the accounts or in a statement annexed thereto, and subsection (8) imposes a direct obligation on the auditor to supplement the information in his report, if it is deficient. The auditor must assess the value of the benefits to the best of his ability and satisfy himself that the value of benefits has been shown at a fair figure.

'We do not think that an auditor could place himself in a position to perform his duties unless he obtained an assurance from the directors that no benefits had been received otherwise than in cash or alternatively a statement of such benefits.

'In our opinion the fact that an independent quorum of the board passes a resolution to the effect that some particular expense is incurred for the benefit of the company and not for the benefit of a director is in no way conclusive of the facts. The two things are not necessarily in opposition. An expense, although incurred for the benefit of the company, may nonetheless benefit a director, e.g. the managing director of an hotel lives with his family in a flat in the hotel free of charge. This would no doubt be a benefit to the company but it is also a benefit to the director and its value would be an emolument.'

Sections 6 and 7 of the *Companies Act 1967* stipulate the additional information which must be disclosed regarding the emoluments of directors, and this is summarized as follows:

(1) The chairman's emoluments, attributable to the period during which he was chairman, unless his duties as chairman were wholly or mainly discharged outside the United Kingdom.

(2) The number of directors in any of the following categories:

    (*a*) receiving nil to £2,500 per annum,

    (*b*) receiving £2,500 per annum to £5,000 per annum – and so on in brackets of £2,500 per annum each time (unless their duties as directors were wholly or mainly discharged outside the United Kingdom).

(3) The emoluments of the highest paid director, where he is not also the chairman, unless his duties as director were wholly or mainly discharged outside the United Kingdom (Section 6).

(4) The numbers of directors who have waived their rights to receive emoluments, and the aggregate amount of emoluments so waived (Section 7).

Sections 6 and 7 do not apply in cases where the aggregate amount of directors' emoluments, shown *in the accounts* as required by Section 196, does not exceed £7,500, and the company is neither a holding nor a subsidiary company.

For the purpose of Section 6, emoluments are to include those receivable from subsidiary companies and are as defined by Section 196 of the 1948 Act, except that contributions paid under pension schemes are excluded.

Under Section 8 it is necessary to state the number of persons (except those wholly or mainly employed outside the United Kingdom, and other than directors) whose emoluments are £10,000 a year or more – bracketed in groups rising by £2,500 a year each time.

It is important to note that if the requirements of Sections 6, 7 and 8 are not complied with, it shall be the duty of the auditors of the company to include the required particulars in their report, so far as they are reasonably able to do so.

Under Section 198 (1) of the *Companies Act 1948*, it shall be the duty of any director to give notice to the company of such information required under Section 196 (details of emoluments, pensions, compensation and benefits) as relate to himself, and in this connection the Council of the Institute of Chartered Accountants issued the following recommendation:

'Where the notice to be given by each director under Section 198 (1) is not given in writing in the form of a statement of pensions, compensation and emoluments, including all benefits received otherwise than in cash approved by the Board and recorded in the minutes, the auditor should require such a statement in writing approved by a resolution of the Board.'

The disclosure required under Section 198 (1) of the 1948 Act is to be construed as also including information to be shown under Sections 6 and 7 of the 1967 Act, and the following is an outline of the form of statement which, it is suggested, an auditor could ask each director of a large company to complete, if the director has not already submitted a statement to the company.

To...Ltd.

....
.... } *Registered Office*
....

STATEMENT OF DIRECTORS' EMOLUMENTS, PURSUANT TO THE COMPANIES ACTS 1948 AND 1967, FOR THE YEAR ENDED ....19...........

	From the Company £ s. d.	From the Company's Subsidiaries £ s. d.	From any other person (*see note 1*) £ s. d.
1. REMUNERATION			
(*a*) as a director			
(*b*) as a managing director; as a general or departmental manager; as secretary or accountant or in any other capacity.			
2. OTHER EMOLUMENTS			
(*c*) any part of an expense allowance charged to United Kingdom income tax during the year.			
(*d*) the contribution on my behalf to any pension scheme.			
(*e*) estimated money value of any benefits in kind.			
3. PENSIONS			
(*f*) received for services as a director ..			
(*g*) received for services outlined in (*b*) above.			
4. COMPENSATION FOR LOSS OF THE OFFICE			
(*h*) of director			
(*i*) of any office defined in (*b*) above ..			
5. AGGREGATE EMOLUMENTS WHILE CHAIRMAN			
6. AGGREGATE AMOUNT OF EMOLUMENTS WAIVED			

I certify that the above statement is correct and complete.

Date... *Signed*..

Notes.

(1) The amounts shown under the heading 'any other person' will comprise sums or benefits received from other companies (not including subsidiary companies), associations, partnerships or persons because of the director holding office in this Company.

(2) Compensation for loss of office includes sums received on retirement from office.

(3) Remuneration includes fees, salary, commissions and bonuses.

(4) Pensions in (*f*) and (*g*) above do not include pensions received under a scheme the contributions to which were substantially adequate to maintain it, but do include those received by any person nominated by the director.

In the case of small companies a statement in respect of each director on the lines of that given below would normally be adequate.

To..Ltd.

....⎫
....⎬ *Registered Office*
....⎭

STATEMENT OF DIRECTORS' EMOLUMENTS, PURSUANT TO THE COMPANIES ACTS 1948 AND 1967, FOR THE YEAR ENDED ....19.........

	In respect of services as a director £　s.　d.	For services in a managerial or executive capacity £　s.　d.
1. EMOLUMENTS		
Fees　.. 　.. 　.. 　.. 　..		
Salary　.. 　.. 　.. 　.. 　..		
Special remuneration .. 　.. 　..		
Commissions　.. 　.. 　.. 　..		
Percentage or share of profits.. 　..		
Expense aowances (chargeable to U.K. tax)　.. 　.. 　.. 　..		
Contributions paid under any pensions scheme .. 　.. 　.. 　.. 　..		
Estimated value of any benefits receive otherwise than in cash .. 　.. 　..		
2. PENSIONS　.. 　.. 　.. 　..		
3. COMPENSATION FOR LOSS OF OFFICE　.. 　.. 　.. 　..		
4. AGGREGATE EMOLUMENTS WHILE CHAIRMAN　.. 　..		
5. AGGREGATE AMOUNT OF EMOLUMENTS WAIVED ..　..		

I certify that the above statement is correct and complete.

Signed...

Date...

Paragraph 14 (6) of the Second Schedule to the *Companies Act 1967*, imposes upon the directors an obligation to disclose in the accounts or by way of a note any material respects in which any items shown in the profit and loss account are affected by—

(*a*) transactions of a sort not usually undertaken by the company or otherwise by circumstances of an exceptional or non-recurrent nature; or

(*b*) any change in the basis of accounting.

In this regard the following recommendation has been made by the Council of the Institute of Chartered Accountants:

'The disclosure of the results of the period implies substantial uniformity in the accounting principles applied as between successive accounting periods, any change of a material nature, such as a variation in the basis of stock valuation or in the method of providing for depreciation or taxation, should be disclosed if its effect distorts the results. The account should disclose any material respects in which it includes extraneous or non-recurrent items or those of an exceptional nature, and should also refer to the omission of any item relative to, or the inclusion of any item not relative to, the results of the period.'

It will also be remembered that it is the auditor's duty to state in his report whether in his opinion the profit and loss account gives a true and fair view of the company's profit or loss *for its financial year*, and that paragraph 12 A of the Second Schedule requires that the amount of any charge arising in consequence of an event in a *preceding financial year* (and of any credit so arising) shall, if not included in a heading relating to other matters, be stated under a separate heading.

(C) THE BALANCE SHEET

(1) *Disclosure Requirements*

Under Section 148 (2) of the *Companies Act 1948* a balance sheet must be made out in every calendar year as at the date to which the profit and loss account (or income and expenditure account) is made up, and default in so doing will involve penalties similar to those enforceable in the event of failure to keep proper books of account.

The balance sheet, which must be signed on behalf of the Board by two directors, or if there is only one director by that director, must give a true and fair view of the state of affairs of the company at the end of its financial year and comply with the requirements of the Eighth Schedule to the 1948 Act, the revised form of which is set out in the Second Schedule to the 1967 Act. These requirements are given in detail hereunder:

(Paragraph (1) is a preliminary introduction to the Schedule.)

2. The authorized share capital, issued share capital, liabilities and assets shall be summarized, with such particulars as are necessary to disclose the general nature of the assets and liabilities, and there shall be specified—

(a) any part of the issued capital that consists of redeemable preference shares the earliest and latest dates on which the company has power to redeem those shares, whether those shares must be redeemed in any event or are liable to be redeemed at the option of the company and whether any (and, if so, what) premium is payable on redemption;

(b) so far as the information is not given in the profit and loss account, any share capital on which interest has been paid out of capital during the financial year, and the rate at which interest has been so paid;

(c) the amount of the share premium account;

(d) particulars of any redeemed debentures which the company has power to reissue.

3. There shall be stated under separate headings, so far as they are not written off—

(a) the preliminary expenses;

(b) any expenses incurred in connection with any issue of share capital or debentures;

(c) any sums paid by way of commission in respect of any shares or debentures;

(d) any sums allowed by way of discount in respect of any debentures; and

(e) the amount of the discount allowed on any issue of shares at a discount.

4. (1) The reserves, provisions, liabilities and assets shall be classified under headings appropriate to the company's business:

Provided that—

(a) where the amount of any class is not material, it may be included under the same heading as some other class; and

(b) where any assets of one class are not separable from assets of another class, those assets may be included under the same heading.

(2) Fixed assets, current assets and assets that are neither fixed nor current shall be separately identified.

(3) The method or methods used to arrive at the amount of the fixed assets under each heading shall be stated.

5. (1) The method of arriving at the amount of any fixed assets shall, subject to the next following sub-paragraph, be to take the difference between—

(a) its cost or, if it stands in the company's books at a valuation, the amount of the valuation; and

(b) the aggregate amount provided or written off since the date of acquisition or valuation, as the case may be, for depreciation or diminution in value;

and for the purposes of this paragraph the net amount at which any assets stand in the company's books at the commencement of this Act (after deduction of the amounts previously provided or written off for depreciation or diminution in value) shall, if the figures relating to the period before the commencement of this Act cannot be obtained without unreasonable expense or delay, be treated as if it were the amount of a valuation of those assets made at the commencement of this Act and, where any of those assets are sold, the said net amount less the amount of the sales shall be treated as if it were the amount of a valuation so made of the remaining assets.

(2) The foregoing sub-paragraph shall not apply—

(a) to assets for which the figures relating to the period beginning with the commencement of this Act cannot be obtained without unreasonable expense or delay; or

(b) to assets the replacement of which is provided for wholly or partly—

(i) by making provision for renewals and charging the cost of replacement against the provision so made; or

(ii) by charging the cost of replacement direct to revenue; or

(c) to any quoted investments or to any unquoted investments of which the value as estimated by the directors is shown either as the amount of the investments or by way of note; or

(d) to goodwill, patents or trade marks.

(3) For the assets under each heading whose amount is arrived at in accordance with sub-paragraph (1) of this paragraph, there shall be shown—

(a) the aggregate of the amounts referred to in paragraph (a) of that sub-paragraph; and

(b) the aggregate of the amounts referred to in paragraph (b) thereof.

(4) As respects the assets under each heading whose amount is not arrived at in accordance with the said sub-paragraph (1) because their replacement is provided for as mentioned in sub-paragraph (2) (b) of this paragraph, there shall be stated—

(a) the means by which their replacement is provided for; and

(b) the aggregate amount of the provision (if any) made for renewals and not used.

5A. In the case of unquoted investments consisting in equity share capital (as defined by subsection (5) of section 154 of this Act) of other bodies corporate (other than any whose values as estimated by the directors are separately shown, either individually or collectively or as to some individually and as to the rest collectively, and are so shown either as the amount thereof, or by way of note), the matters referred to in the following heads shall, if not otherwise shown, be stated by way of note or in a statement or report annexed:

(a) the aggregate amount of the company's income for the financial year that is ascribable to the investments;

(b) the amount of the company's share before taxation, and the amount of that share after taxation, of the net aggregate amount of the profits of the bodies in which the investments are held, being profits for the several periods to which accounts sent by them during the financial year to the company related, after deducting those bodies' losses for those periods (or *vice versa*);

(c) the amount of the company's share of the net aggregate amount of the undistributed profits accumulated by the bodies in which the investments are held since the time when the investments were acquired, after deducting the losses accumulated by them since that time (or *vice versa*);

(d) the manner in which any losses incurred by the said bodies have been dealt with in the company's accounts.

6. The aggregate amounts respectively of reserves and provisions (other than provisions for depreciation, renewals or diminution in value of assets) shall be stated under separate headings:

Provided that—

(a) this paragraph shall not require a separate statement of either of the said amounts which is not material; and

(b) the Board of Trade may direct that it shall not require a separate statement of the amount of provisions where they are satisfied that that is not required in the public interest and would prejudice the company, but subject to the condition that any heading stating an amount arrived at after taking into account a provision (other than as aforesaid) shall be so framed or marked as to indicate that fact.

7. (1) There shall also be shown (unless it is shown in the profit and loss account or a statement or report annexed thereto, or the amount involved is not material)—

(a) where the amount of the reserves or of the provisions (other than provisions for depreciation, renewals or diminution in value of assets) shows an increase as compared with the amount at the end of the immediately preceding financial year, the source from which the amount of the increase has been derived; and

(b) where—

(i) the amount of the reserves shows a decrease as compared with the amount at the end of the immediately preceding financial year; or

(ii) the amount at the end of the immediately preceding financial year of the provisions (other than provisions for depreciation, renewals or diminution in value of assets) exceeded the aggregate of the sums since applied and amounts still retained for the purposes thereof;

the application of the amounts derived from the difference.

(2) Where the heading showing the reserves or any of the provisions aforesaid is divided into sub-headings, this paragraph shall apply to each of the separate amounts shown in the sub-headings instead of applying to the aggregate amount thereof.

7A. If an amount is set aside for the purpose of its being used to prevent undue fluctuations in charges for taxation, it shall be stated.

8. (1) There shall be shown under separate headings—

(a) the aggregate amounts respectively of the company's quoted investments and unquoted investments;

(b) if the amount of the goodwill and of any patents and trade marks or part of that amount is shown as a separate item in or is otherwise ascertainable from the books of the company, or from any contract for the sale or purchase of any property to be acquired by the company, or from any documents in the possession of the company relating to the stamp duty payable in respect of any such contract or the conveyance of any such property, the said amount so shown or ascertained so far as not written off or, as the case may be, the said amount so far as it is so shown or ascertainable and as so shown or ascertained, as the case may be;

(c) the aggregate amount of any outstanding loans made under the authority of provisos (b) and (c) of subsection (1) of section fifty-four of this Act;

(d) the aggregate amount of bank loans and overdrafts and the aggregate amount of loans made to the company which—

(i) are repayable otherwise than by instalments and fall due for repayment after the expiration of the period of five years beginning with the day next following the expiration of the financial year; or

(ii) are repayable by instalments any of which fall due for payment after the expiration of that period;

not being, in either case, bank loans or overdrafts;

(e) the aggregate amount (before deduction of income tax) which is recommended for distribution by way of dividend.

(2) Nothing in head (b) of the foregoing sub-paragraph shall be taken as requiring the amount of the goodwill, patents and trade marks to be stated otherwise than as a single item.

(3) The heading showing the amount of the quoted investments shall be subdivided, where necessary, to distinguish the investments as respects which there has, and those as respects which there has not, been granted a quotation or permission to deal on a recognized stock exchange.

[N.B. This clause means that a distinction must be drawn between investments which are quoted on a recognized stock exchange in this country and those quoted on a stock exchange of repute outside Great Britain.]

(4) In relation to each loan falling within head (*d*) of sub-paragraph (1) of this paragraph (other than a bank loan or overdraft), there shall be stated by way of note (if not otherwise stated) the terms on which it is repayable and the rate at which interest is payable thereon:

Provided that if the number of loans is such that, in the opinion of the directors, compliance with the foregoing requirement would result in a statement of excessive length, it shall be sufficient to give a general indication of the terms on which the loans are repayable and the rates at which interest is payable thereon.

9. Where any liability of the company is secured otherwise than by operation of law on any assets of the company, the fact that that liability is so secured shall be stated, but it shall not be necessary to specify the assets on which the liability is secured.

10. Where any of the company's debentures are held by a nominee of or trustee for the company, the nominal amount of the debentures and the amount at which they are stated in the books of the company shall be stated.

11. (1) The matters referred to in the following sub-paragraphs shall be stated by way of note, or in a statement or report annexed, if not otherwise shown.

(2) The number, description and amount of any shares in the company which any person has an option to subscribe for, together with the following particulars of the option, that is to say—

(*a*) the period during which it is exercisable;

(*b*) the price to be paid for shares subscribed for under it.

(3) The amount of any arrears of fixed cumulative dividends on the company's shares and the period for which the dividends or, if there is more than one class, each class of them are in arrear, the amount to be stated before deduction of income tax, except that, in the case of tax free dividends, the amount shall be shown free of tax and the fact that it is so shown shall also be stated.

(4) Particulars of any charge on the assets of the company to secure the liabilities of any other person, including, where practicable, the amount secured.

(5) The general nature of any other contingent liabilities not provided for and, where practicable, the aggregate amount or estimated amount of those liabilities, if it is material.

(6) Where practicable the aggregate amount or estimated amount, if it is material, of contracts for capital expenditure, so far as not provided for and, where practicable, the aggregate amount or estimated amount, if it is material, of capital expenditure authorized by the directors which has not been contracted for.

(6A) In the case of fixed assets under any heading whose amount is required to be arrived at in accordance with paragraph 5(1) of this Schedule (other than unquoted investments) and is so arrived at by reference to a valuation, the years (so far as they are known to the directors) in which the assets were severally valued and the several values, and, in the case of assets that have been valued during the financial year, the names of the persons who valued them or particulars of their qualifications for doing so and (whichever is stated) the bases of valuation used by them.

(6B) If there are included amongst fixed assets under any heading (other than investments) assets that have been acquired during the financial year, the aggregate amount of the assets acquired as determined for the purpose of making up the balance sheet, and if during that year any fixed assets included under a heading in the balance sheet made up with respect to the immediately preceding financial year (other than investments) have been disposed of or destroyed, the aggregate amount thereof as determined for the purpose of making up that balance sheet.

(6C) Of the amount of fixed assets consisting of land, how much is ascribable to land of freehold tenure and how much to land of leasehold tenure, and, of the latter, how much is ascribable to land held on long lease and how much to land held on short lease.

(7) If in the opinion of the directors any of the current assets have not a value, on realization in the ordinary course of the company's business at least equal to the amount at which they are stated, the fact that the directors are of that opinion.

(8) The aggregate market value of the company's quoted investments where it differs from the amount of the investments as stated, and the stock exchange value of any investments of which the market value is shown (whether separately or not) and is taken as being higher than their stock exchange value.

(8A) If a sum set aside for the purpose of its being used to prevent undue fluctuations in charges for taxation has been used during the financial year for another purpose, the amount thereof and the fact that it has been so used.

(8B) If the amount carried forward for stock in trade or work in progress is material for the appreciation by its members of the company's state of affairs or of its profit or loss for the financial year, the manner in which that amount has been computed.

(9) The basis on which foreign currencies have been converted into sterling, where the amount of the assets or liabilities affected is material.

(10) The basis on which the amount, if any, set aside for United Kingdom corporation tax is computed.

(11) Except in the case of the first balance sheet laid before the company after the commencement of this Act, the corresponding amounts at the end of the immediately preceding financial year for all items shown in the balance sheet.

When the company is a holding company, the following items must be shown separately in the balance sheet or, where appropriate, by way of a note or in a statement annexed thereto. References are to Part II of the Second Schedule, *Companies Act 1967*.

15. (1) This paragraph shall apply where the company is a holding company, whether or not it is itself a subsidiary of another body corporate.

(2) The aggregate amount of assets consisting of shares in, or amounts owing (whether on account of a loan or otherwise) from the company's subsidiaries, distinguishing shares from indebtedness, shall be set out in the balance sheet separately from all the other assets of the company, and the aggregate amount of indebtedness (whether on account of a loan or otherwise) to the company's subsidiaries shall be so set out separately from all its other l'abilities and—

(a) the references in Part I of this Schedule to the company's investments (except those in paragraphs 11 (6B) and 12 (4)) shall not include investments in its subsidiaries required by this paragraph to be separately set out; and

(b) paragraph 5, sub-paragraph (1)(a) of paragraph 12, and sub-paragraph (2) of paragraph 14 of this Schedule shall not apply in relation to fixed assets consisting of interests in the company's subsidiaries.

(3) There shall be shown by way of note on the balance sheet or in a statement or report annexed thereto the number, description and amount of the shares in and debentures of the company held by its subsidiaries or their nominees, but excluding any of those shares or debentures in the case of which the subsidiary is concerned as personal representative or in the case of which it is concerned as trustee and neither the company nor any subsidiary thereof is beneficially interested under the trust, otherwise than by way of security only for the purposes of a transaction entered into by it in the ordinary course of a business which includes the lending of money.

(4) Where group accounts are not submitted, there shall be annexed to the balance sheet a statement showing—

(a) the reasons why subsidiaries are not dealt with in group accounts;

(b) the net aggregate amount, so far as it concerns members of the holding company and is not dealt with in the company's accounts, of the subsidiaries' profits after deducting the subsidiaries' losses (or vice versa)—

(i) for the respective financial years of the subsidiaries ending with or during the financial year of the company; and

(ii) for their previous financial years since they respectively became the holding company's subsidiary;

(c) the net aggregate amount of the subsidiaries' profits after deducting the subsidiaries' losses (or vice versa)—

(i) for the respective financial years of the subsidiaries ending with or during the financial year of the company; and

(ii) for their other financial years since they respectively became the holding company's subsidiary;

so far as those profits are dealt with, or provision is made for those losses, in the company's accounts;

(d) any qualifications contained in the report of the auditors of the subsidiaries on their accounts for their respective financial years ending as aforesaid, and any note or saving contained in those accounts to call attention to a matter which, apart from the note or saving, would properly have been referred to in such a qualification, in so far as the matter which is the subject of the qualification or note is not covered by the company's own accounts and is material from the point of view of its members;

or, in so far as the information required by this sub-paragraph is not obtainable, a statement that it is not obtainable:

Provided that the Board of Trade may, on the application or with the consent of the company's directors, direct that in relation to any subsidiary this sub-paragraph shall not apply or shall apply only to such extent as may be provided by the direction.

(5) Paragraphs (b) and (c) of the last foregoing sub-paragraph shall apply only to profits and losses of a subsidiary which may properly be treated in the holding company's accounts as revenue profits or losses, and the profits or losses attributable to any shares in a subsidiary for the time being held by the holding company or any other of its subsidiaries shall not (for that or any other purpose) be treated as aforesaid so far as they are profits or losses for the period before the date on or as from which the shares were acquired by the company or any of its subsidiaries, except that they may in a proper case be so treated where—

(a) the company is itself the subsidiary of another body corporate; and

(b) the shares were acquired from that body corporate or a subsidiary of it;

and for the purpose of determining whether any profits or losses are to be treated as profits or losses for the said period the profit or loss for any financial year of the subsidiary may, if it is not practicable to apportion it with reasonable accuracy by reference to the facts, be treated as accruing from day to day during that year and be apportioned accordingly.

(6) Where group accounts are not submitted, there shall be annexed to the balance sheet a statement showing, in relation to the subsidiaries (if any) whose financial years did not end with that of the company—

(a) the reasons why the company's directors consider that the subsidiaries' financial years should not end with that of the company; and

(b) the dates on which the subsidiaries' financial years ending last before that of the company respectively ended or the earliest and latest of those dates.

16. (1) The balance sheet of a company which its a subsidiary of another body corporate, whether or not it is itself a holding company, shall show

the aggregate amount of its indebtedness to all bodies corporate of which it is a subsidiary or a fellow subsidiary and the aggregate amount of indebtedness of all such bodies corporate to it, distinguishing in each case between indebtedness in respect of debentures and otherwise, and the aggregate amount of assets consisting of shares in fellow subsidiaries.

(2) For the purposes of this paragraph a company shall be deemed to be a fellow subsidiary of another body corporate if both are subsidiaries of the same body corporate but neither is the other's.

The special provisions applicable to group accounts are dealt with in Chapter XI.

It is to be noticed that assets should be grouped as 'fixed', 'current', and those which fall into neither of these categories. It is usually sufficient to indicate the latter class by exception, being those assets not labelled either 'fixed' or 'current'. Examples of this class might be preliminary expenses, discount on debentures, debts due more than one year from the balance sheet date, or inter-company accounts with an indefinite date of settlement.

The terms 'provision', 'reserve' and 'liability' are defined by Part IV to the amended Eighth Schedule as follows:

(a) the expression 'provision' shall, subject to sub-paragraph (2) of this paragraph, mean any amount written off or retained by way of providing for depreciation, renewals or diminution in value of assets or retained by way of providing for any known liability of which the amount cannot be determined with substantial accuracy;

(b) the expression 'reserve' shall not, subject as aforesaid, include any amount written off or retained by way of providing for depreciation, renewals or diminution in value of assets or retained by way of providing for any known liability or any sum set aside for the purpose of its being used to prevent undue fluctuations in charges for taxation;

and in this paragraph the expression 'liability' shall include all liabilities in respect of expenditure contracted for and all disputed or contingent liabilities.

Where any amount written off or retained by way of providing for depreciation, renewals or diminution in value of assets, not being an amount written off in relation to fixed assets before the commencement of the *Companies Act 1967*, or any amount retained by way of providing for any known liability, is in excess of that which in the opinion of the directors is reasonably necessary for the purpose, the excess must be treated in the accounts as a reserve and not as a provision.

The following are the recommendations of the Council of the Institute of Chartered Accountants regarding the use of the word 'provision':

(a) The word 'provision' should cease to be used to denote amounts set aside to meet specific requirements the amounts whereof can be estimated closely; such amounts should be grouped with creditors since they represent liabilities or accruals.

(b) Amounts set aside to meet deferred repairs the execution of which is a contractual or statutory obligation (e.g. under a dilapidations clause of a lease) should be treated as liabilities if the amounts can be determined with substantial accuracy and as provisions if the amounts cannot be so determined.

(c) Other amounts set aside to meet deferred repairs because they are regarded as charges necessary for the correct computation of profits should be treated as provisions, on the footing that they are closely analogous to amounts provided for renewals (which are specifically required to be treated as provisions) and differ from these in degree rather than in character.

An amount set aside out of profits to meet future corporation tax is not a liability and it should not, therefore, be treated as a provision. Such an amount is now commonly shown as a separate item in the balance sheet, and it is recommended by the Institute of Chartered Accountants that the due date for payment be shown.

It will have been noticed that sums set aside for the purpose of equalizing taxation charges are not to be regarded as reserves, and the Schedule (paragraph 7 A) requires such amounts set aside to be separately stated.

Where additions to or withdrawals from reserves and provisions have been made during the year and such transfers affect the profit and loss account, the amounts involved, if material, must be shown separately in that account or by way of a note. Where, however, the additions or withdrawals are of a capital nature which do not affect the profit and loss account, e.g. a transfer to reserve of a capital profit arising on a revaluation of the company's assets, such transactions should appear clearly on the face of the balance sheet or in a statement or report annexed thereto. The source from which the increase has been derived or the manner in which the decrease has been applied must be shown.

It will be observed that the Schedule requires the aggregate of provisions (other than provisions for depreciation, renewals or diminution in value of assets) to be stated. The following is the recommendation of the Council of the Institute of Chartered Accountants on this point:

'On a proper grouping of the balance sheet some provisions will not be suitable for aggregation; for example, where some provisions are current liabilities and others are not. In such cases, an "aggregate" should be regarded as a minimum requirement intended to avoid the unnecessary disclosure of separate items which individually have no significance; it should not be treated as a restriction operating against the presentation of a true and fair view.'

Although the Eighth Schedule, Part IV, as amended by the 1967 Act, requires the aggregate amount of reserves to be stated, no distinction being necessary between capital and revenue reserves, there would seem to be no reason why the two kinds of reserves should not continue to be distinguished in appropriate cases. The question of whether reserves are legally distributable, or whether the directors wish to regard them as such, is quite distinct from the question of disclosures; moreover, the law relating to distributability of reserves, particularly those arising as a result of unrealized surpluses on asset revaluations, is by no means settled. A distinction in the balance sheet based upon *source* rather than *destination* would therefore seem to be more reliable and, in many cases, more meaningful, since it is important that the balance sheet should reveal the extent to which net assets have arisen from ordinary retentions, from capital profits which have been realized and from those which have not. (The question of the divisibility of profits and dividends will be dealt with fully in the following chapter.) Prior to the amendments brought about by the *Companies Act 1967*, the 1948 Act defined a capital reserve as *not* including 'any amount regarded as free for distribution through the profit and loss account', and this negative description should continue to be the basis of classification. The term will therefore continue to include amounts which because of their origin or the purpose for which they are retained, are regarded by the directors as not being free for distribution through the profit and loss account, e.g. a sum received as compensation for damage to goodwill, a profit made on the sale of a fixed asset, to the extent that such profit is not due to past excessive provision for depreciation.

Of course, the obligation to show separately such statutory

reserves as share premium account and capital redemption reserve fund (and any other reserves which have to be maintained under the articles) is quite unaffected by these considerations. The amended Eighth Schedule, paragraph 2 (*c*), requires the amount of share premium account to be separately disclosed, while a correct construction of Section 58 of the principal Act shows that the amount of the capital redemption reserve fund requires similar treatment.

Capital and revenue reserves should therefore be combined only in cases where the true distinction, as outlined above, has been lost or become meaningless, as where their origins are beyond recollection, the funds themselves having become completely absorbed in the company's working capital.

A debit balance on profit and loss account should be shown as far as possible as a deduction from the aggregate of revenue reserves. If the profit and loss account debit balance exceeds the revenue reserves, the excess may be shown as a deduction from the paid up capital, the balance of which would then represent the net book value of the shareholders' interest in the assets. Alternatively, the debit balance on profit and loss account may be shown on the assets side of the balance sheet.

In addition to the information detailed above, Sections 3, 4 and 5 of the *Companies Act 1967* specify the following information which must be disclosed in relation to certain investments and subsidiary companies:

(1) If, at the end of its financial year, a company holds:

(i) more than one-tenth in nominal value of any class of equity shares of another company (not being its subsidiary company; or

(ii) shares in another company (not being its subsidiary) the amount of which exceeds one-tenth of the investing company's total assets, there shall be stated:

(*a*) the name of the company and the country (if other than Great Britain) of its incorporation; and

(*b*) each class of shares held and the proportion of nominal value of the issued shares of that class represented by the shares held (Section 4).

Certain exemptions are specified for companies incorporated or trading outside the U.K., if the Board of Trade agrees that disclosure could be harmful to the business.

(2) Holding companies are obliged to disclose each subsidiary company's name and specify details in relation to the country of incorporation, the classes of shares held in the subsidiary and the proportion of the nominal value of the issued shares of each class held, distinguishing between subsidiary company shares held directly by the parent company and shares held in one subsidiary through another (Section 3).

(Subject to Board of Trade agreement the Act specifies certain exemptions for subsidiaries incorporated or trading outside the U.K. if disclosure is considered by the directors of the holding company to be harmful.)

(3) A subsidiary company is required to state the name of the company regarded by the directors as being the subsidiary company's ultimate holding company at the end of the financial year, and the country of the holding company's incorporation, unless the subsidiary company carries on business outside the U.K. and the disclosure is considered by the directors to be harmful to any company in the group and the Board of Trade agrees to the non-disclosure (Section 5).

As pointed out §10 (B) above in connection with the profit and loss account, Part III of the amended Eighth Schedule specifies exemptions from disclosure for certain classes of companies, and the following balance sheet exemptions apply:

(a) Banking and discount companies shall not be subject to any of the requirements of Part I, other than those of paragraphs 2, 3, 4 (so far as it relates to assets), 8 (except sub-paragraphs 1(d) and (4)), 9, 10 and 11 (except sub-paragraphs (6A), (6B), (6C), (8) and (8A)).

(b) Insurance companies to which the *Insurance Companies Act 1958* applies shall not be subject to the requirements of paragraphs 4 to 7 inclusive, 8 (1) (a) and (3), and 11 (4) (5) and (6A) to (8) inclusive, of Part I.

(c) Shipping companies shall not be subject to the requirements of paragraphs 4 (except so far as it relates to assets), 5, 6, 7, and 11 (6A) and (6B), of Part I.

(2) *The Valuation of Fixed Assets*

The normal basis on which fixed assets should be shown in the balance sheet is arrived at by taking the difference between:

(*a*) the cost of the asset or, if it stands in the company's books at a valuation, the amount of the valuation; and

(*b*) the aggregate amount provided or written off for depreciation or diminution in value since the date of acquisition or valuation, as the case may be.

The amount arrived at in this way will be the net amount extended in the balance sheet, but the aggregate of (*a*) and the aggregate of (*b*) must also each be shown thereby.

There are cases, however, where the normal basis cannot be adopted because the company's records do not provide sufficient information to enable the cost and provision for depreciation of assets acquired prior to July 1st, 1948, to be ascertained without unreasonable expense or delay. In such cases, the Acts provide that the net amount at which the assets stood in the company's books at July 1st, 1948, shall be treated as if it were the amount of a valuation of those assets made at that date. This method of valuation is known as the '*net book amount basis*'.

If, however, the amount at which any of the fixed assets have been stated has been arrived at by reference to a valuation, the years in which the assets were severally valued and the several values must be disclosed. If assets have been valued during the financial year, the names or the qualifications of the valuers, as well as the basis of valuation employed by them, must be given.

In addition, there must be disclosed the aggregate amounts respectively of fixed assets acquired and disposed of or destroyed during the year, as determined for the purpose of making up the balance sheet. (Although not statutorily required, the aggregate depreciation which had been provided on fixed assets disposed of during the year, is often stated.)

The amount of fixed assets consisting of land must be subdivided between land of freehold tenure and land of leasehold tenure, and in relation to the latter, it must be stated how much is ascribable to land held on long lease (fifty or more years) and how much to land held on short lease.

The following is a suggested method of showing the information described above, in the balance sheet (usually in the form of a detailed note):

FIXED ASSETS

	Plant and other Equipment £	Freehold Land and Buildings £	Leasehold Properties		Total £
			Long Lease £	Short Lease £	
Cost and valuations at 1st January	....	....	....	....	....
Additions during year at cost ..	....	....	....	....	....
Amount added on revaluation of certain freehold property ..	....	....	....		
Less: Cost of disposals and items scrapped during year	....	....	....	....	....
Cost and valuations at 31st December	£	£	£	£	£
Comprising:					
Valuation in 1961	....	....	....	....	....
Valuation in 1963	....	....	....	....	....
Valuation during the year (*see note (a)*)	....	....	....	....	....
Cost	....	....	....	....	....
	£	£	£	£	£
Aggregate depreciation at 1st January	....	....	....	....	....
Amount provided during year	....	....	....	....	....
Less: eliminated in respect of disposals	....	....	....	....	....
Aggregate depreciation at 31st December	£	£	£	£	£
NET BOOK VALUE at 31st December	£	£	£	£	£
NET BOOK VALUE at previous 31st December ..	£	£	£	£	£

Notes.

(*a*) During the year a freehold factory was valued on the basis of current use, by a chartered surveyor.

(*b*) Long leases are for terms of not less than fifty years unexpired.

(*c*) No provision has been made for depreciation of certain freehold properties, included above at an amount of £

(*d*) Future capital expenditure:

Amounts contracted for but not provided for in the accounts   £———

Amounts authorized by the directors but not contracted for   £———

(*e*) In addition to providing for depreciation of certain plant, included above at a cost of £—— separate provision of £—— is also made towards renewal.

It will be observed that notes (*d*) and (*e*) above are appended in compliance with paragraphs 11 (6) and 12 (3) respectively, of the Second Schedule. The former requires disclosure of the amount of capital expenditure authorized by the directors but not contracted for, and the aggregate or estimated amount of contracts for capital expenditure (so far as not provided for). Paragraph 12 (3) requires that any amount charged for provision for renewal assets for which there has also been a depreciation charge, shall be disclosed. (This item might more properly be shown as a note to the profit and loss account.)

It will be appreciated that in order to comply with the above-mentioned requirements of the Acts, it is essential, where the items of plant and machinery are numerous, that a company should maintain a plant register in order that adjustments for plant sold can be made correctly. Annual provisions for depreciation should not be credited to the asset account but to a provision for depreciation account which will show automatically the cumulative figure required for balance sheet purposes. When a machine is sold, the depreciation applicable thereto will be written back from the provision for depreciation account and any profit or loss adjusted.

Where a company purchases a number of assets for a lump sum without separate values being assigned to each, it is recommended by the Council of the Institute of Chartered Accountants that—

'a value should be allocated to each asset or class of asset by the directors or other competent person in such a manner as to enable the various assets or classes of assets to be shown in the balance sheet at "a valuation" and depreciation provided thereon. Otherwise it will not be possible during the useful life of these assets to conform to the intentions of paragraph 5 (1), Part I, Eighth Schedule [now Second Schedule].'

If depreciation or replacement of any fixed asset is provided for by some method other than a depreciation charge or provision for renewals, the profit and loss account must show or state the method adopted. If no depreciation charge or provision for renewals is made for any asset or class of assets, this fact must be stated in the profit and loss account, and this is so, even though it may not normally be regarded as necessary to provide for depreciation of the asset in question, e.g. freehold land.

Provisions for renewals should be shown separately in the balance sheet and not as a deduction for the assets concerned.

Amounts set aside to meet the *increased cost* of replacing assets are reserves and not provisions.

Oversea companies, i.e. companies incorporated outside Great Britain but which have a place of business within Great Britain must, by virtue of Section 410, *Companies Act 1948*, make out a balance sheet and profit and loss account in every calendar year, and, if the company is a holding company, group accounts, in such form, and containing such particulars and including such documents, as under the provisions of the Acts (subject, however, to any prescribed exceptions) it would, if it had been a company within the meaning of the Acts, have been required to make out and lay before the company in general meeting, and deliver copies of those documents to the Registrar of Companies.

If any such document as is mentioned above is not written in the English language, there must be annexed to it a certified translation thereof.

(3) *Loans to Officers of the Company*

Section 190, *Companies Act 1948*, prohibits a company from making loans to a director of the company or to a director of its holding company or from entering into any guarantee or providing any security in connection with a loan to such director made by some other person. This prohibition does not apply, however, to a loan:

(*a*) made by a subsidiary company to the holding company which is its director;

(*b*) made to a director for the purpose of providing him with funds to meet expenditure incurred or to be incurred by him for the purposes of the company or to enable him properly to perform his duties as an officer of the company;

(*c*) made by a company whose ordinary business includes the lending of money, provided such loan is made in the ordinary course of business.

A loan can only be made to a director under (*b*) above if:

(i) it has received the prior approval of the company in general meeting at which the purposes of the expenditure and the amount of the loan or the extent of the guarantee or security, as the case may be, are disclosed; or

(ii) it is on condition that, if the approval of the company is not given at or before the next following annual general meeting, the loan shall be repaid or the liability under the guarantee or security shall be discharged, as the case may be, within six months from the conclusion of that meeting.

Where the approval of the company is not given as required by any such condition, the directors authorizing the making of the loan, or the entering into the guarantee, or the provision of the security, will be jointly and severally liable to indemnify the company against any loss arising therefrom.

A company may make loans to its officers, other than directors, but by Section 197 details thereof must be given in the accounts to be laid before the company in general meeting showing:

(a) The amount of any loans made during the company's financial year to:

  (i) any officer of the company; or

  (ii) any person who, after the making of the loan, became during that year an officer of the company;

  by the company or a subsidiary thereof or by any other person under a guarantee or on a security provided by the company or a subsidiary thereof (including any such loans which were repaid during that year); and

(b) the amount of any loans made in manner aforesaid to any such officer or person as aforesaid at any time before the company's financial year and outstanding at the expiration thereof.

The above information need not be given in the accounts in the case of:

(a) a loan made in the ordinary course of its business by the company or a subsidiary thereof, where the ordinary business of the company or, as the case may be, the subsidiary, includes the lending of money; or

(b) a loan made by the company or a subsidiary thereof to an employee of the company or subsidiary, as the case may be, if the loan does not exceed two thousand pounds and is certified by the directors of the company or subsidiary, as the case may be, to have been made in accordance with any practice adopted or about to be adopted by the company or subsidiary with respect to loans to its employees;

not being, in either case, a loan made by the company under a guarantee from or on a security provided by a subsidiary thereof or a loan made by a subsidiary of the company under a guarantee from or on a security provided by the company or any other subsidiary thereof.

If the requisite information regarding loans to officers of the company is not given in the accounts, it is the duty of the auditors of the company to include in their report a statement giving the particulars required, so far as they are reasonably able to do so.

It may be difficult to determine in all cases what payments to or indebtedness by officers will come under this provision as to 'loans'; in many instances, particularly in the case of private companies, officers of the company may have a current account with the company, or may purchase goods from the company for which they do not pay for some considerable time. It is suggested that where officers discharge obligations incurred in the ordinary course of trading with the company, within the usual term of credit allowed to other persons, any amounts of this nature outstanding could be grouped with other sundry debtors, but every other case should be carefully scrutinized by the auditor, especially in view of the obligation upon him to supply in his report any information not sufficiently disclosed.

The auditor must never overlook the fact that it is illegal for a company to lend money or provide security etc. to enable the borrower to purchase shares in the company or in its holding company, except when:

(a) lending money is part of the ordinary business of the company and the loan is made in the ordinary course of business; or

(b) the loan is made to trustees to enable them to purchase shares to be held for the benefit of employees, including salaried directors; or

(c) the loan is made to employees of the company, other than directors, to enable them to acquire shares as beneficial owners (Section 54).

It should be noted that there is no legislation to prevent the making of loans to members of a director's family, his associates, or to other companies in which he is a controlling shareholder.

It would appear, on the other hand, that directors are not permitted to avail themselves of loan facilities for the benefit of employees.

(D) MATERIALITY IN ACCOUNTS

The Second Schedule to the *Companies Act 1967* contains no fewer than thirteen references to materiality in relation to the accounts; the various factors which ought to be considered when assessing the materiality, or otherwise, of items in accounts being audited have been set out in a recomendation of the Institute of Chartered Accountants, which is reproduced in the Appendix. Its most important aspects, however, are summarized below:

(1) In an accounting sense, an item is material if its 'non-disclosure, misstatement or omission would be likely to distort the view given by the accounts or other statements under consideration.'

(2) The principle of materiality arises in relation to the preparation and presentation of *any* type of accounts, both statutory and non-statutory, where the object is to present a true and fair view of the results for a period, and a position at a particular date.

(3) The question of materiality can arise in relation to:

    (i) disclosure (including manner of disclosure, e.g. inclusion in a conglomerate total, separately, or specific mention with appropriate emphasis);

    (ii) correction of errors or omissions;

    (iii) methods of computation, i.e. whether the particular method gives due regard to all relevant factors.

(4) Once an item is adjudged material, consideration will be presumed to have been given to:

    (i) its amount in relation to the overall view of the accounts; the total of which it forms a part; associated items in the final accounts; and the corresponding amount in the previous year;

    (ii) description, emphasis, presentation and context, and statutory requirements for disclosure.

(5) Materiality is essentially a relative factor, and those responsible for preparing and auditing accounts must decide which facts of the many available to them have a real bearing on the true and fair view. Percentage differences are useful (if properly used) guides to materiality, but should never be applied indiscriminately.

(6) In assessing the latitude permitted in arriving at the amount of a particular item, regard must be had to its nature, distinguishing between those items capable of precise and accurate determination, and those whose amount is determined by assumption and the exercise of informed judgment. In the latter category, the charge for depreciation is a prime example, whereas the charge for directors' fees and the audit fee, for example, are items which may be of particular interest to shareholders, and no latitude is permissible, especially as they are normally capable of precise expression.

(7) Miscellaneous factors affecting considerations as to materiality, are as follows:

(i) The degree of approximation which is implicit in ascertaining the amount of an item may be a factor in deciding its materiality.

(ii) Losses or low profits tend to vitiate the use of the profit figure as a point of comparison.

(iii) Inaccuracies or omissions not normally considered to be material, may affect the view given by the accounts, inasmuch as the *trends* of profit, turnover, or certain expense items may be especially significant in certain circumstances.

(iv) Items of small amount are not necessarily insignificant, especially where they might have been expected to be larger.

(v) Care should be exercised before offsetting items of opposite effect where each on its own might have been regarded as material, e.g. a non-recurring loss against a profit arising from a change in the basis of accounting; moreover, several individually insignificant items might represent a material amount in total.

It is interesting in this context to contrast the words 'true' and 'fair', bearing in mind that the concept of 'fairness' was introduced into company legislation as recently as 1948: earlier Companies Acts required that the view presented by accounts be 'true and correct'. Clearly, the whole question of materiality bears directly on the constitution of the true and fair view. Arithmetic accuracy, although fundamentally important in accounting, is not of itself sufficient to satisfy the legal requirements – the widest possible appreciation must be made, and considerations of 'materiality' must serve the truth and fairness of the view presented. Section 149 of the *Companies Act 1948* clearly makes this the over-riding criterion, by providing that the powers of the Board of Trade to modify any requirements of the Act on the application of a company's directors, shall *not* extend to 'true and fair' requirement laid down in sub-section (1) of that section.

(E) THE DIRECTORS' REPORT

Under Section 157 (1) of the principal Act, a report by the directors of a company must be attached to every balance sheet of the company laid before it in general meeting. The subsection also requires there to be disclosed the state of the company's affairs, the amount, if any, which the directors recommend to be paid by way of dividend, and the amount, if any, which they propose to carry to reserves.

Copies of the directors' report must be sent to every member of the company, debenture holders, and any other person so entitled, together with copies of every balance sheet and auditors' report (Section 24, *Companies Act 1967*).

Sections 16 to 22 of the *Companies Act 1967* specify the additional information to be included in the report of the directors to the members, and those matters which are essentially of financial concern may be summarized as follows:

(1) An indication of the difference between the market value and the book value of land, where these differ substantially (Section 16 (1) (*a*)).

(2) Details of classes of shares or debentures issued during the year under review, the reasons for the issue, and the consideration received by the company for any such issue (Section 16 (1) (*b*)).

(3) The turnover and profit or loss (before taxation) of each class of business carried on by the company, where these

classes differ substantially. (Where the company is neither a holding nor a subsidiary company, and its total turnover does not exceed £50,000, it is exempted from this provision). (Section 17 (1)).

(4) (a) A statement of the average number of persons employed by the company (including subsidiaries, if any) in each week in the financial year, and

   (b) the aggregate remuneration paid or payable in respect of that year to the persons by reference to whom the number stated under (a) above is ascertained.

This provision does not apply to companies with less than 100 employees, or to companies which are wholly owned subsidiaries of a company incorporated in Great Britain (Section 18).

(5) The amount of contributions (if these exceed £50) given for political and/or charitable purposes, and identification of the political party which is the recipient. In a group, these particulars are to relate to contributions by the holding company and the subsidiaries between them, and therefore they need not be given by a wholly owned subsidiary of a company incorporated in Great Britain (Section 19).

(6) The amount of turnover during the financial year arising from the export of goods by the company (if its total turnover exceeds £50,000) or by the group (if the total group turnover exceeds £50,000). If no goods were exported, there shall be a statement of the fact (Section 20).

(7) Where items are shown in the directors' report instead of in the accounts (advantage being taken of the proviso to Section 163 of the principal Act), corresponding amounts for the immediately preceding year must also be shown (Section 22).

Other information of a more general nature, which must be disclosed, may be summarized thus:

(1) Names of persons who were at any time during the financial year directors of the company (Section 16 (1)).

(2) The principal activities of the company during the year and of its subsidiaries, and any changes therein (Section 16 (1)).

(3) If at the end of the year there subsists a significant contract with the company in which a director has or at any time during the year had a material interest, a statement of the fact with the names of the parties to the contract, the name of the director, and an indication of the nature of the contract and of the director's interest therein (Section 16 (1) (c)). (It is for the directors of the company to determine whether or not the contract is significant and the director's interest material.)

(4) Details of any arrangements whereby the company enables directors to acquire benefits by means of acquisition of shares or debentures of the company or of any other body corporate, explaining the effect of the arrangements and giving the names of the directors who at any time during the year were directors and held, or whose nominees held, shares or debentures acquired as a result of the arrangements (Section 16 (1) (d)).

(5) A statement for each director as to whether or not he had an interest in any shares or debentures of the company or of any other body corporate within the group, specifying the number and amount of shares and debentures held at the beginning and end of each financial year, or if he was not a director at the beginning of the year, the details when he became a director (Section 16 (1) (e)).

(6) Particulars of any other matters so far as they are material for the appreciation of the state of the company's affairs the disclosure of which will not, in the opinion of the directors, be harmful to the business of the company or of its subsidiaries (Section 16 (1) (f)).

While the *Companies Act 1967* does not require the auditor to report on matters to be contained in the directors' report, since these are now so extensive and include information which is of an essentially financial nature, the auditor may take the view that he cannot confine his responsibility solely to matters contained in the accounts themselves, but will wish to be satisfied that the accounts give a true and fair view of the profit or loss and state of affairs *within the context* in which they are placed before the members.

The degree of the auditor's concern with information contained in the directors' report, is a matter regarding which widely differing views are held within the profession. On the one hand, it is believed that checking of such information should be confined to an examination for any figure or statement inconsistent with anything in the accounts themselves, such inconsistencies usually giving rise to audit queries; and that in any event it should be pointed out clearly to the directors that no responsibility is assumed for the contents of the report.

On the other hand, some members of the profession have taken the view that sight of the final form (not necessarily signed) of the directors' report should be insisted on, prior to releasing a copy of the accounts with a signed audit report. It is further held that figures given in the report should be checked from all available information, and it should be ensured that the directors have adequate grounds for making the statements and quoting the figures that are featured. No inconsistencies, either real or apparent, should exist as between items in the directors' report and in the accounts. Adherents of this view maintain that if after due enquiries have been made, the auditor is dissatisfied regarding the accuracy or reasonableness of some information in the report, or considers that the report is itself misleading in some way, the directors should be requested to make the necessary alterations. Should the directors not accede to the wishes of the auditor, it will be necessary for him to consider what form of disclaimer regarding the directors' report is advisable for inclusion in his own report.

Until the acceptable professional approach to this matter has been conclusively evolved, or legal guidance given, it would seem that the auditor should attempt to persuade the directors that any financial information included in the directors' report which may equally acceptably be included in the accounts or in a note annexed thereto, should be so included, so that the auditor may report thereon in the normal way. It would, furthermore, appear to be prudent for the auditor to include in his own report a statement to the effect that he assumes no responsibility for the financial contents of the directors' report, if the directors do not agree to make any amendments which he considers necessary.

In the light of the above comments, it should be particularly noted that under Section 24 of the 1967 Act, copies of the directors' report must be distributed, in exactly the same way as the accounts and auditor's report, to members, debenture holders, and other persons so entitled. The former requirement was merely that the report should be available at the annual general meeting.

§ 11. The Inclusion of the Balance Sheet in the Annual Return

By Section 127, *Companies Act 1948*, companies are obliged to include in their Annual Return a written copy, certified by a director and by the secretary of the company to be a true copy, of every balance sheet, including every document required by law to be annexed thereto, laid before the company in general meeting during the period to which the return relates. There must also be included with the return a certified copy of the auditor's report on, and of the report of the directors accompanying, such balance sheet.

§ 12. Directors

Every company, other than a private company, registered after November, 1st 1929, must have at least two directors, and every company registered before that date, and every private company must have at least one director (Section 176). Every company must have a secretary, and where there is only one director such director cannot also be the secretary (Section 177).

(A) LIABILITY OF DIRECTORS TO ACCOUNT

The relation between the directors of a company and the company itself has been defined by Lord Selbourne, in *G.E. Rly Co* v. *Turner* (1872 8 Ch. 149), when he said: 'The directors are the mere trustees or agents of the company – trustees of the company's money and property; agents in the transactions which are entered into on behalf of the company.' As such, directors are liable to account to the company for the assets which have come into their hands or are under their control.

Directors therefore occupy a fiduciary position, and cannot make any profit out of the company beyond the remuneration to which they are entitled.

If a director is in any way, whether directly or indirectly, interested in a contract or proposed contract with the company, he must disclose the nature of his interest at a meeting of the directors (Section 199).

The auditor should note carefully any contracts entered into by the company with its directors and he should satisfy himself that any requirements of the articles in connection therewith have been complied with.

Every company must maintain details of directors' service contracts, or variations thereof, or a memorandum setting out the terms of contracts, unless:

(i) the director concerned is employed wholly or mainly outside the United Kingdom; or

(ii) the contract has less than twelve months to run or can be terminated by the company within twelve months without payment of compensation (Section 26, *Companies Act 1967*).

Under Sections 25 and 30 of the *Companies Act 1967*, a director of a company is guilty of an offence if he (or his spouse or infant child) purchases options to buy or sell the right to quoted shares or debentures of the company, or companies in its group.

Furthermore, a director must notify the company of his (or his spouse's or infant children's) interest in any shares or debentures in the company or other companies in its group, and continue to keep the company informed of any alterations in his interest during his period of office. A register for this purpose must be maintained by the company (Sections 27, 29 and 31). Should circumstances arise which suggest that contraventions may have occurred in relation to the requirements described in this and the previous paragraph, the Board of Trade may appoint an inspector to investigate the share (or debenture) dealings concerned (Section 32).

Where the auditor performs a share transfer audit he should see that all transactions by the directors in the company's shares as disclosed by the audit, are properly recorded in the prescribed register. It is not considered necessary, however, in the course of the ordinary audit of the company's accounts that the auditor should attempt to check the accuracy of the entries made in the register.

In the event of any loans having been made to directors, it should be seen that these transactions are *intra vires* the company and are within the limitations prescribed by Section 190 of the principal Act, and that the security is adequate; otherwise the auditor should consider the necessity to refer to the matter in his report.

Directors may sustain liability for misfeasance or breach of trust under Section 333 of the *Companies Act 1948*. Where a claim is made, or there is reason to believe that a claim will be made against him for misfeasance or breach of trust, a director may apply to the Court for relief under Section 448 of the 1948 Act.

It used at one time not to be unusual for a clause to be included in the articles indemnifying directors and other officers (including auditors) from the consequences of negligence, not amounting to wilful negligence, in the performance of their respective duties, but under Section 205 of the principal Act such provisions are void. Nothing in Section 205 will, however, operate to deprive any person of any exemption or right to be indemnified in respect of anything done or omitted to be done by him whilst any such provision was in force; and a company may still indemnify a director or other officer against any liability incurred by him in defending any proceedings, whether civil or criminal, in which judgment is given in his favour, or in which he is acquitted, as the case may be, or in connection with a successful application for relief under Section 448.

Directors may, in addition, be liable for offences committed in the following circumstances:

(1) Under Section 43 and 44, *Companies Act 1948*, for authorizing the issue of a prospectus containing untrue statements.

(2) Under Section 438, *Companies Act 1948*, for wilfully making false statements in reports, certificates, balance sheets etc., and other matters specified in the Fifteenth Schedule.

(3) Under Section 329 of the same Act, for destruction, mutilation, falsification etc., of books, papers or securities of a company being wound up.

(4) Under Section 328, for various offences analogous to those applicable to a debtor under Section 154 of the *Bankruptcy Act 1914*, as amended by the *Bankruptcy Act 1926*.

(5) Under Section 331, where proper books of account have not been kept by the company throughout the period of two

years immediately preceding the commencement of the liquidation of the company or the period between incorporation and the commencement of winding up, whichever is the shorter.

(6) Under Section 147, for failure to keep the necessary books of account for the purpose of recording the prescribed information.

(7) Under Section 332, where any business of the company has been carried on with intent to defraud creditors.

(8) Under Section 193, for failure to disclose payment for loss of office etc.

(9) Under Section 5 of the *Perjury Act 1911*, for making false statements in accounts, balance sheets, reports etc.

(10) Under Sections 17 and 19 of the *Theft Act 1968*, for false accounting and publication of false statements with intent to deceive.

(11) Under Section 15, 16 and 18 of the *Theft Act 1968*, for obtaining property and pecuniary advantage by deception.

(12) Under Section 13 of the *Prevention of Fraud (Investments) Act 1958*, where criminal liability may result from *recklessly* making a false statement in a prospectus. (This should be compared with Section 438 of the *Companies Act 1948*, referred to in (2) above, under which it must be established that the false statement was *wilfully* made with intent to deceive.)

(13) Under Section 23, *Companies Act 1967*, for failure to secure compliance with the disclosure requirements of the Acts regarding the directors' report.

(14) Under Section 27, *Companies Act 1967*, for failure to notify the company of his interest in its shares or debentures, or those of its associated companies, or for making a false statement recklessly or wilfully in connection therewith. Such interests include those of a director's wife and infant children.

(15) Under Section 29 of the same Act, for failure to produce and leave open for inspection the register of directors' interests required under Section 27, for the duration of each annual general meeting.

(16) Under Section 31, for failure to notify the grant (or exercise of such grant) to his or her spouse or infant child, of a right to subscribe for the companys' shares or debentures.

(B) REMUNERATION OF DIRECTORS

Directors are not entitled to remuneration unless the articles of the company provide for the payment thereof, or the members in general meeting resolve to pay such remuneration. The auditor should therefore examine the articles to ascertain whether the remuneration is fixed thereby, and, if not, he must ascertain by reference to the members' minute book whether any resolution has been passed under which the directors are entitled to remuneration.

It is usual to find that a company's articles provide for the payment of a fixed director's fee, with an additional fee for the chairman, and permit the directors themselves to fix the emoluments of those who are appointed to executive offices. Frequently, executive directors have service agreements with the company which provide for their emoluments, and, where these are to be calculated as a percentage of profits, define the basis upon which the profits are to be calculated.

Alternatively, the articles of the company may provide that:

(1) a fixed lump sum shall be divided between the directors in the proportions they themselves shall decide; or that

(2) the directors shall be paid a fixed fee for each meeting attended; or that

(3) the remuneration of directors shall be fixed by the company in general meeting.

The auditor will verify the remuneration paid by reference to the company's articles, the members' minute book or the directors' service agreements, as the case may be.

Where fees are based on attendances at meetings, the auditor should examine the Directors' Attendance Book, and see that fees paid to each director are properly calculated according to the number of his attendances.

Where directors are entitled to a percentage of profits, the auditor must examine the articles or service agreements in order to ascertain the basis on which profits are to be calculated for this purpose. Unfortunately, in many cases this is not clearly defined, and it may be advisable for the definition to be amplified by resolution of the company in general meeting. Where the directors are entitled to a percentage on the *net profits* of the company, the question arises as to whether the term 'net profits' means the profits after or before charging such remuneration. Although such percentage is a charge so far as the members are concerned, it is an appropriation of the profits so far as the directors are concerned, and should, in the absence of a clear indication in the articles to the contrary, be based on the profits *before* charging the percentage. This view was confirmed by the Court in *Edwards* v. *Saunton Hotel Ltd* (1942, T.R. 359).

A further point arises in connection with the treatment of corporation tax. Corporation tax is considered to be an appropriation of profits, and is treated as such in the accounts of the company. It was decided that where a manager of a company was entitled to a percentage of net profits, income tax on the company's profits should *not* be charged before arriving at the sum upon which the commission was to be calculated (*Johnston* v. *Chestergate Hat Manufacturing Co*, 1915, L.J. 8 4,Ch. 914). It was held in this case that income tax was part of the net profits available for dividends, and the phrase 'net profits' in the particular case in question was defined in the agreement to mean 'the net sum available for dividends as certified by the auditors . . .' The Court followed the earlier ruling in *Attorney-General* v. *Ashton Gas Company* (1906, A.C. 10) where it was held that income tax was part of the profits, viz., such part as the Revenue was entitled to take of the profits.

It will be noted that the agreement provided that the auditor's certificate of the amount upon which the commission was to be paid was to be taken as final, but the Court held that where such a certificate is based on a wrong principle, it is not conclusive and binding on the parties.

Although income tax was not a proper deduction in arriving at the net profits, it was held in *Re Agreement of G. B. Ollivant & Co Ltd* (1942, 2 All E.R. 528), that 'for the purpose of drawing up the profit and loss account of a trading company, excess profits tax must be deducted, if ordinary commercial practice is to be followed.' Although the point has not yet received judicial consideration, the normal practice is to regard corporation tax as an appropriation of profits in the same way as was income tax.

Any provisions made for anticipated losses must be charged before arriving at the amount of profits on which the percentage is calculated; but appropriations to general reserve, or reserves for equalizing dividends should not be charged.

Where the remuneration is to be based on the 'net trading profits' losses or expenses not arising in the ordinary course of trading, corporation tax or other appropriations of profit should not be debited, but on the other hand, interest and dividends received on investments, or any profit *not* arising in the ordinary course of trading, should not be credited.

Remuneration based on a percentage of profits does not include a percentage of the profits made on the sale of the whole undertaking of the company (*Frames* v. *Bultfontein Mining Co*, 1891 1 Ch. 140); but in the absence of special stipulations to the contrary, 'profits,' in cases where the rights of third parties are involved, means actual profits, and not necessarily the profits as shown by the profit and loss account (*In re Spanish Prospecting Co*, 1911, 1 Ch. 92).

Where the remuneration is voted by the members in general meeting, the auditor must examine the members' minute book.

It is a misfeasance on the part of a director to take remuneration in excess of the amount that is payable, and any directors who are parties to such payments are jointly and severally liable to refund the amount (*Leeds Estate Co* v. *Shepherd*, 1887 36 Ch. D 787; *re Whitehall Court*, 1887, 56 L.T. 280). The company, however, can ratify the payment of remuneration in excess of that prescribed by the articles by altering the articles or by passing a special resolution (*Boschoek Proprietary Co* v. *Fuke*, 1906 1 Ch. 148).

Directors are ordinary creditors for remuneration due to them and can rank as such with outside crecitors (*Re New British Iron Co ex parte Beckwith*, 1898 1 Ch. 324; *re A1 Biscuit Co*, 1899, W.N. 115); but they may not pay themselves fees in priority to outside creditors when the funds are not sufficient to pay everyone in full (*Gas Light Improvement Co* v. *Terrall*, 1870, 10 Eq. 168); or in the case of the insolvency of the company pay up their calls and utilize the money so obtained to pay their own fees (*Re Washington Diamond Mining Co*, 1893 3 Ch. 95).

The question as to whether a director is entitled to any remuneration if he vacates office during the currency of a year has been before the courts on a number of occasions. Where the directors were entitled to a lump sum, no apportionment was allowed to a director who vacated office during the year (*Salton v. New Beeston Cycle Co*, 1898 1 Ch. 775); and where the provision was that each director should be paid the sum of £300 per annum, no apportionment was allowed (*McConnell's Claim*, 1901, 1 Ch. 728); and again, no apportionment was allowed where the words were 'The sum of £300 per annum per director' (*Inman* v. *Ackroyd*, 1901 1 K.B. 613). These decisions, however, followed that of the Court of Appeal in *Swabey* v. *Port Darwin Gold Mining Co* (1889, 1 Meg. 385), which apparently was erroneously reported, and they cannot, therefore, be regarded as final. It would appear that if the provision is 'at the rate of £—— per annum', apportionment would be allowed. Owing to the uncertainty involved, it has become customary, since these cases were decided, to provide in the articles that the remuneration shall be apportionable. Table A of the *Companies Act 1948*, provides that directors' remuneration shall be deemed to accrue from day to day.

Sometimes directors waive the whole or a portion of their fees. In such a case the minute book would contain a resolution of the board to that effect, although all the directors would require to be present at the meeting, and to vote on the resolution. A verbal agreement between the liquidator of a company and the directors, and by the directors mutually with each and all the others to forego directors' fees is valid (*West Yorkshire Darracq Agency Ltd* (in Liqdn.) v. *Coleridge*, 1911, 80 L.J. K.B., 1122). Disclosure of the number of directors who have waived emoluments, and the aggregate sum so waived, requires to be made in a company's profit and loss account (Section 7, *Companies Act 1967*).

The general provisions of the Act regarding the disclosure in the accounts of remuneration paid to directors and what is regarded as emoluments, were dealt with in §10 (B) of this chapter. Tax free payments to directors are prohibited by Section 189 of the principal Act, which provides as follows:

(1) It shall not be lawful for a company to pay a director remuneration (whether as director or otherwise) free of income tax or of income tax

other than surtax, or otherwise calculated by reference to or varying with the amount of his income tax or his income tax other than surtax, or to or with the rate or standard rate of income tax, except under a contract which was in force on the eighteenth day of July, nineteen hundred and forty-five, and provides expressly, and not by reference to the articles, for payment of remuneration as aforesaid.

(2) Any provision contained in a company's articles, or in any contract other than such a contract as aforesaid, or in any resolution of a company or a company's directors, for payment to a director of remuneration as aforesaid shall have effect as if it provided for payment, as a gross sum subject to income tax and surtax, of the net sum for which it actually provides.

It will thus be observed that if a director is voted remuneration of, say, £1,000 free of income tax, the words 'free of income tax' must be ignored and the amount of £1,000 will represent the gross sum payable to the director from which income tax under the rules of P.A.Y.E. will be deducted in the usual way.

Power is usually given in the articles for the directors, by resolution, to vote additional remuneration to any director who is called upon to travel on business for the company. The auditor should see that any such payments are properly authorized as prescribed in Section 190 of the 1948 Act.

(c) PAYMENTS TO DIRECTORS FOR LOSS OF OFFICE

A company may not make a payment to a director as compensation for loss of office or in consideration of his retirement from office, unless particulars thereof are disclosed to and approved by the members of the company (Section 191).

If a company transfers the whole or part of its undertaking, no payment in connection with such transfer may be made to a director as compensation for loss of office or as consideration for his retirement, unless particulars of the proposed payment are disclosed to the members and approved by them. If a director receives such a payment without the requisite approval of the company, he is deemed to hold the amount in trust for the company (Section 193).

These provisions do not of course apply to a payment made to a director as compensation for the cancellation of his service agreement with the company.

(d) DIRECTOR'S QUALIFICATION

Unless the articles provide that he shall do so, a director need not hold any share qualification, but, where this is required, the auditor should ascertain that the director has duly acquired the shares within two months after appointment, or such shorter time as may be fixed by the articles, as required by Section 182, *Companies Act 1948*. If the qualification is not so acquired, the office of director is vacated. A director who acts without acquiring his qualification shares may be entitled to his remuneration up to the date at which the office becomes vacated (*Salton* v. *New Beeston Cycle Co*, 1899 1 Ch. 775).

The company may by ordinary resolution remove a director before the expiration of his period of office. Special notice must be given to the members of any resolution to remove a director, and the director has similar rights to make written representations to the members as those given to auditors who are to be removed or replaced (Section 184).

Section 185, *Companies Act 1948*, provides that no person shall be capable of being appointed a director of a company if at the time of appointment he has attained the age of seventy. The section also provides that any director reaching the age of seventy shall vacate his office at the conclusion of the annual general meeting commencing next after he attains the age of seventy. The provisions of this section do not apply to a private company unless such company is a subsidiary of a public company.

Notwithstanding the above provisions, a person over seventy years of age may be appointed a director or may continue to act as such after reaching that age if:

(*a*) his appointment was made or approved by the company in general meeting and special notice was given of the resolution, the notice stating the director's age; or

(*b*) in the case of a company registered after January 1st, 1947 the articles exclude the provisions; or

(*c*) in the case of a company registered prior to January 1st, 1947, a special resolution is passed to alter the articles and to exclude the provisions.

Any person appointed or proposed to be appointed a director of a company which is subject to the above provisions, must give notice to the company when he attains the retiring age applicable to him under the Act or the articles of the company.

Any person failing to comply with this section will be liable to a fine not exceeding five pounds a day for every day in which failure to notify continues, or in which he acts as director after his appointment has been terminated or become invalid by reason of his age.

The Act makes no provision for vacation of office in any other circumstances, but Table A and the articles of most companies make specific regulations on this point. Vacation of office takes place automatically upon the specified event occurring and remuneration will cease accordingly (*Bodega Co, Ltd*, 1904 1 Ch. 276). Subject to the articles, a director may not hold any other office or profit under the company, and the acceptance of such an office will vacate the directorship; the appointment of a director as trustee for debenture holders, receiving a remuneration for his services, is sufficient to disqualify him (*Astley* v. *New Tivoli Co*, 1889 1 Ch. 151).

Clause 84, Table A provides:

(3) A director may hold any other office or place of profit under the company (other than the office of auditor) in conjunction with his office of director for such period and on such terms (as to remuneration and otherwise) as the directors may determine and no director or intending director shall be disqualified by his office from contracting with the company either with regard to his tenure of any such other office or place of profit or as vendor, purchaser or otherwise, nor shall any such contract, or any contract or arrangement entered into by or on behalf of the company in which any director is in any way interested, be liable to be avoided, nor shall any director so contracting or being so interested be liable to account to the company for any profit realized by any such contract or arrangement by reason of such director holding that office or of the fiduciary relation thereby established.

(4) A director, notwithstanding his interest, may be counted in the quorum present at any meeting whereat he or any other director is appointed to hold any such office or place of profit under the company or whereat the terms of any such appointment are arranged, and he may vote on any such appointment or arrangement other than his own appointment or the arrangement of the terms thereof.

(5) Any director may act by himself or his firm in a professional capacity for the company, and he or his firm shall be entitled to remuneration for professional services as if he were not a director; provided that nothing herein contained shall authorize a director or his firm to act as auditor to the company.

(E) DIRECTORS' TRAVELLING EXPENSES

Unless the articles specifically provide, a director is not entitled to travelling expenses incurred in attending board meetings, which are presumably covered by his remuneration

(*Young* v. *Naval and Military Co-operative Society*, 1905 1 K.B. 687). It is, however, common to find a provision in the articles entitling directors to their travelling expenses incurred in attending board meetings, and power to make such payments is given by clause 76 of Table A, which also authorizes the payment by the company of expenses incurred by directors in travelling on the business of the company.

Where lump sum allowances are made to directors for travelling and entertaining expenses, the auditor must examine the minute of the directors authorizing such allowances or the service agreements providing therefor. In such cases the auditor will not be concerned with the manner in which a director has expended the allowance given to him but he must see that the payment is within the dispensation granted by the Inspector of Taxes or, if not, that income tax has been deducted from the allowance under the P.A.Y.E. regulations. The auditor must also ascertain whether any part of the allowance has been charged to income tax in the hands of a director as, if it has, this part must be included in the total of directors' emoluments required to be shown separately in the company's accounts under Section 196 of the principal Act.

Amounts paid to a director in reimbursement of specific expenses incurred by him on the company's behalf, must be vouched with receipts, signed by the director, and any supporting vouchers which are available. Here also the auditor must ascertain that dispensation has been granted by the Inspector of Taxes for such payments to be made without deduction of income tax.

(F) MANAGING DIRECTORS

Table A gives power to the directors to appoint one or more of their number as managing directors and to fix their remuneration, which may be by way of salary, or commission, or participation in profits, or partly in one way and partly in another, and the articles of most companies make similar provision. Where a managing director has been appointed under such powers, the resolution of the board appointing him and fixing his remuneration must be examined by the auditor, and the remuneration vouched according to the basis on which it is payable.

A managing director is not a clerk or servant of the company within the meaning of Section 319, *Companies Act 1948*, and consequently is not entitled to preferential treatment in respect of arrears of salary or commission in the event of winding-up (*Newspaper Proprietary Syndicate* 1900 2 Ch. 349). A secretary of the company, however, who devotes the whole of his time to the services of the company, can claim preferential rights (*Cairney* v. *Back*, 1906 2 K.B. 746); and so also can a director in respect of employment where he is authorized by the articles to accept such employment in the company (*Re Beeton & Co, Ltd*, 1913 2 Ch. 279).

(G) SECRETARY

Every company must have a secretary, and a sole director shall not also be secretary (*Companies Act 1948*, Section 177). Table A provides that the secretary shall be appointed by the directors for such term, at such remuneration, and upon such conditions as they may think fit, and any secretary so appointed may be removed by them.

§ 13. Minute Books

(A) DIRECTORS' MINUTE BOOK

Under Section 145, *Companies Act 1948*, every company must cause minutes of all proceedings at meetings of directors or managers to be entered in a minute book. Any minute purporting to be signed by the chairman of the meeting, or by the chairman of the next succeeding meeting, is evidence of the proceedings.

The auditor should peruse the minute book and should see that all minutes which he is utilizing as evidence of transactions are duly signed, and that the names of the directors present at the meeting have been inserted. The auditor should refer to the minute book in vouching all transactions other than those involving the usual trading operations.

The following are instances of transactions of a special nature:

(1) Allotment of shares.

(2) Adoption of contracts.

(3) Authorizing the use of the company's seal.

(4) Making calls.

(5) Forfeiting shares.

(6) Appointment and remuneration of managing director, manager, secretary, or other officials.

(7) Appointment of auditors prior to the first annual general meeting, or to fill a casual vacancy, and fixing their remuneration.

(8) Authorization of capital expenditure.

(9) Resolution to pay interim dividends, where such are *intra vires*.

(10) Payment of travelling expenses or special remuneration to directors.

(11) Adoption of accounts.

(12) Adoption of directors' report to the members and recommendations as to division of profits.

(B) MEMBERS' MINUTE BOOK

Section 145 also requires minutes to be made of all proceedings and resolutions at members' meetings, and entered in the members' minute book. The auditor should examine the minutes of each meeting, particularly with reference to the following matters:

(1) Adoption of accounts.

(2) The declaration of dividends.

(3) Remuneration voted to directors.

(4) The remuneration of auditors and, where appropriate, their election.

(5) Any resolutions affecting the accounts.

The minute books of most companies are in the form of bound books, but by Section 436, *Companies Act 1948*, any other system may be adopted, provided that adequate precautions are taken to guard against falsification and to facilitate its discovery.

§ 14. Reserve Funds

The nature of reserves and the distinction between reserves and provisions have been discussed in Chapter V, § 6, where the question as to whether a general reserve should be retained in the business or invested specifically outside the business is considered; and it is there pointed out that although the term 'reserve fund' is frequently employed when the reserve is not represented by specific investments outside the business, it is preferable to designate such a reserve as 'reserve account,' and to confine the use of the term 'reserve fund' to those cases where there are specific investments representing the fund.

Most companies have power to put profits to reserve before payment of any dividend, and clause 117 of Table A provides that the directors may, before recommending any dividend, set aside out of the profits of the company such sums as they think proper as reserve or reserves, which shall, at the discretion of the directors, be applicable for any purpose to which the profits of the company may be properly applied, and pending such application, may be employed in the business of the company, or invested in such investments as the directors may think fit.

If the articles provide that a fixed percentage of the profits must be retained each year and placed to reserve until a certain sum has been accumulated the auditor should see that the provision is duly carried out. Such compulsory provision, however, is unusual, and normally the articles leave the matter to the discretion of the directors. Where such discretion is given, it is a matter for the directors to determine how much of the profits of any one year they shall put to reserve before recommending the payment of a dividend, even though the result of their action may be to prevent payment of any dividend on founders' shares (*Fisher* v. *Black and White Publishing Co*, 1901 1 Ch. 174), or preference shares (*Bond* v. *Barrow Hæmatite Steel Co*, 1902 1 Ch. 358).

In addition to appropriations of profits, exceptional profits may be placed direct to reserve. Where a sinking fund has been provided for the redemption of debentures, the amount standing to the credit of this account, when the redemption of the debentures has been accomplished, should be transferred to the credit of reserve or back to profit and loss account, and will be represented by the assets formerly subject to the charge contained in the debentures.

A reserve accumulated out of profits may be utilized in any manner in which the profits of the company may be applied and can be drawn upon for payment of dividends or to meet exceptional losses. Where a loss has been incurred on revenue account, such loss can be made good by a transfer from the reserve so long as the transfer is disclosed in the profit and loss account. Any loss arising from diminution in value of the fixed or capital assets of the company may be written off against the reserve account.

Where the book value of the fixed assets is less than their real value and it is desired to write up the value of such assets in the balance sheet, the increase should be placed to the credit of a capital reserve account, since it will not be available for revenue purposes, but any subsequent loss in connection with these assets may be charged against such reserve. Before passing any entries recording the appreciation in value of assets in this manner the auditor should ascertain by whom the revaluation has been made, and satisfy himself that it is *bona fide*. Under no circumstances should such an appreciation be taken to the credit of revenue, unless it can be shown to have risen by reason of excessive provisions for depreciation in the past; even then it may be more desirable to transfer the amount to the credit of reserve. It would appear, however, that a *bona fide* increase in the value of fixed assets can be utilized to extinguish the debit balance on profit and loss account, thus leaving current profits available for the payment of dividend (*Ammonia Soda Company* v. *Chamberlain*, 1918, 1 Ch. 266). This decision is more fully considered in Chapter X.

Many prosperous companies have accumulated large reserves, which are used permanently in the business, and thus form part of the real capital employed. The rate of dividend paid on the issued share capital, however, does not represent the rate actually earned on the capital employed, and in many cases it has been thought desirable to bring the issued capital more into line with the capital employed, by capitalizing a portion of the reserves by the issue of bonus shares to shareholders *pro rata* to their existing holdings.

In the majority of cases bonus shares are allotted by means of renounceable allotment letters or share certificates thus enabling shareholders, within a specified time, to sell their new shares, if they so desire, by renunciation in favour of the buyers, free of stamp duty.

Where a bonus issue is contemplated, it should be seen that the articles of the company permit such a capitalization of profits and, if not, they should be altered by special resolution. The company must have sufficient unissued shares to enable the operation to be performed, otherwise it will be necessary to increase its authorized capital.

If the members do not have an unconditional right to take their dividends or bonuses in cash, should they wish to do so, the bonus issue will require a contract to be filed with the Registrar of Companies, constituting the title of the allottees to the shares, under Section 52, *Companies Act 1948*.

A resolution having been passed by the company authorizing the capitalization of reserves, the directors should pass a resolution appropriating the amount of the capitalization to the shareholders in proportion to their shareholdings, and applying it on their behalf in paying up in full the new shares to be alloted to them. Arrangements are usually made for the sale of fractions of shares arising from the *pro rata* allotment and for the distribution of the proceeds amongst the shareholders entitled thereto.

Sometimes a bonus is satisfied by applying the amount thereof to discharging wholly or partly the uncalled liability on shares already issued. In this case the procedure is to declare the bonus out of reserve, and at the same time to make a call on the shares to a corresponding amount.

A reserve accumulated out of profits retains its revenue nature in the event of liquidation, and is divisible amongst the members in the proportion in which they are entitled to share the profits. If the articles provide that the preference shareholders are entitled to profits in certain proportions and there are any arrears of preference dividend, preference shareholders will be entitled to such arrears out of the reserve (*Bishop* v. *Smyrna & Cassaba Railway*, 1895 2 Ch. 596); but where the right of such preference shareholders to dividends only accrues after a resolution to pay such dividend has been passed by the directors, and the company goes into liquidation before any such resolution is passed, the preference shareholders will have no claim against the reserve in respect of arrears of dividend (*Crichton's Oil Co*, 1901 2 Ch. 184; 1902 2 Ch. 86).

The ultimate distribution of surplus assets after repaying to members the nominal amount of their capital, whether such surplus is represented by a reserve or not, must depend upon the rights of the respective classes of members as defined in the articles.

§ 15. Secret or Internal Reserves

A secret reserve may be described as a reserve, the existence and/or amount of which is not disclosed on the face of the balance sheet.

Prior to the coming into operation of the *Companies Act 1948*, many companies created such secret or internal reserves, and in some cases the practice was abused by the directors, with the result that shareholders were presented with most misleading financial statements.

By virtue of the provisions of the *Companies Acts 1948 and 1967*, however, the subject of secret reserves is now largely one of academic interest. If there has been an appreciation in the value of fixed assets which is unrecorded, or goodwill has been written down below its true value, the company has to this extent a secret reserve, but apart from such exceptions, for all practical purposes secret reserves can no longer legally be created. The methods formerly adopted for the creation of secret reserves are no longer possible in view of the following provisions, now embodied in the Second Schedule to the *Companies Act 1967*:

(*a*) The amount, if material, set aside or proposed to be set aside to, or withdrawn from reserves must be shown in the profit and loss account, [paragraph 12 (1) (*e*)].

(*b*) The amount, if material, set aside to provisions other than provisions for depreciation, renewals or diminution in value of assets or, as the case may be, the amount, if material, withdrawn from such provisions *and not applied for the purposes thereof* must be shown in the profit and loss account [paragraph 12 (1) (*f*)].

(*c*) The aggregate amount provided or written off since the date of acquisition or valuation of fixed assets must be shown separately on the balance sheet [paragraph 5 (*b*)].

(*d*) The aggregate amounts respectively of reserves and provisions must be shown separately on the balance sheet [paragraph 6].

(e) Where any amount written off or retained by way of providing for depreciation, renewals or diminution in value of
assets (not being an amount written off in relation to fixed
assets before January 27th, 1968) or any amount retained by
way of providing for any known liability is in excess of that
which in the opinion of the directors is reasonably necessary
for the purpose, the excess must be treated as a reserve and
not as a provision and the amount of such excess thus disclosed [paragraph 27 (2)].

The fact that secret reserves are essential in the case of certain
types of companies is, however, recognized by the Acts, which
provide that items (a) to (d) above, shall not apply to banking
and discount companies, or to insurance companies within the
meaning of the *Insurance Companies Act 1958*, while items (c)
and (d) shall not apply to shipping companies. The Board of
Trade also have power, on the application or with the consent
of a company's directors, to modify in relation to the company
any of the above requirements, and in particular the Board of
Trade may direct that they shall not require a separate statement of the amount of provisions where they are satisfied that
it is not required in the public interest and would prejudice the
company.

§ 16. Taxation

It is not within the province of this work to consider in detail
the question of taxation, either from a legal point of view, or
from the practical aspect as affecting accounts.

It is not the duty of the auditor to prepare computations for
taxation purposes and to submit them to the Inland Revenue,
although he frequently is called upon to do so in practice. The
preparation of such computations should be undertaken by
competent officials of the company, but where the auditor is
asked to do such work, it will be performed by him as an accountant and not as auditor.

The auditor must, however, check the taxation computations
in order to satisfy himself that the charge for taxation shown in
the profit and loss account is correct. It must be remembered
that the amount of the charge for United Kingdom corporation
tax (together with a note of the amount it would have been but

for double taxation relief), the amount of the charge for United Kingdom income tax, and the amount of overseas taxation on profits, income and (so far as charged to revenue) capital gains, must be respectively disclosed in the profit and loss account. It is also necessary to disclose by way of note (if not otherwise shown) the basis on which these charges (other than in respect of capital gains) are computed, and any special circumstances which affect liability in respect of taxation of profits, income or capital gains for the financial year, or which will affect it in succeeding years (Schedule Two to *Companies Act 1967*, paragraphs 12 (1) (*c*), 14 (3) and (3A)).

These stipulations would appear to be met by the following presentation in the profit and loss account of a company whose adjusted taxable profits from all sources for corporation tax purposes is £100,000, and whose overseas taxation covered by double tax relief is £30,000, of which £5,000 is unrelieved:

	£	£
United Kingdom corporation tax (45 per cent.) ..		15,000
Overseas taxation:		
For which double tax relief against United Kingdom corporation tax is obtained ..	30,000	
Not thus relieved	5,000	
		35,000
Total charge		£50,000

Note: The corporation tax charge is arrived at thus:

	£
45 per cent. on assessable profits	45,000
Less: Overseas tax relieved under double tax arrangements ..	30,000
	£15,000

It will readily be appreciated what a misleading impression could be created by a balance sheet in which there was an inadequate or grossly excessive amount set aside for taxation, and as the auditor is required to report on whether the balance sheet shows a true and fair view of the state of the company's affairs, this duty cannot be discharged without proper consideration being given to the taxation liabilities included therein.

Where it appears that the company is entitled to make a claim or claims for the recovery of tax, the auditor should satisfy himself that these have been or will be made, and vouch the receipt of the refund in due course.

The year of assessment commences on April 6th and extends to the following April 5th, but the assessment is based on the profits of an accounting period, and the tax is payable, in the case of a company, on January 1st after the year ended April 5th in which the company's financial period ended, e.g.:

(i) Company's year ends February 28th, 1969: corporation tax payable January 1st, 1970;

(ii) Company's year ends April 30th, 1969: corporation tax payable January 1st, 1971.

Provision must, therefore, be made when preparing the accounts, for the company's estimated corporation tax liability based on the adjusted profits of the financial period.

A rate of corporation tax for each 'financial year' (which for this purpose commences on April 1st in one year and ends on March 31st the next) will be fixed by the Government in the budget. Thus, the financial year '1969' commences on April 1st, 1969 and ends on March 31st, 1970. The profits of a company may have to be apportioned into financial years for the purpose of computing the tax payable, if there has been a change in the rate from one financial year to the next.

However, a limited company's involvement with taxation does not end with corporation tax (which is assessed on the company's adjusted profits and chargeable gains arising in its financial year); the law requires companies to deduct income tax at the standard rate when paying dividends, debenture interest, royalties, and other standing charges. These sums deducted have then to be paid over to the Inland Revenue, although amounts suffered on investment income received may be set-off, as explained below.

In order to be in a position to verify transactions involving the deduction of tax, familiarity with the following technicalities is an important prerequisite:

(A) DISTRIBUTIONS

These normally comprise dividends paid (of either a capital or revenue nature), payments out of company assets in specie, bonus issues of redeemable preference shares or debentures, and

the premium payable on the redemption of redeemable preference shares. (A full list is included in the *Finance Act 1965*).

(B) CHARGES

These are fixed payments made by a company (other than
distributions) from which income tax must be deducted at
source; which tax is subsequently assessed on the company, to
the extent that it has not been set-off against tax suffered on
income, under Section 170 of the *Income Tax Act 1952*. Examples of such payments are debenture interest, mortgage and loan
interest, royalties, etc.

(C) FRANKED INVESTMENT INCOME

This is represented by dividends and other distributions (as
defined in (a) above) *received* from a company resident in the
United Kingdom, under deduction of income tax.

(D) UNFRANKED INVESTMENT INCOME

Such income comprises charges (as defined in (B) above)
received in the form of loan interest etc., income on government securities, local authority loans, building society deposits
etc., all after deduction of income tax.

(E) PROFITS

This term includes trading profits and other income received
without deduction of tax (e.g. rents, interest on $3\frac{1}{2}$ per cent.
War Loan, Defence Bonds, and other government securities
paid without deduction of tax) and chargeable capital gains.

(F) SET-OFF

(i) *Temporary*

In the income tax account for each income tax year (from
April 6th to the following April 5th) debit entries, representing
income tax suffered by deduction, may be set-off indiscriminately against credit entries, representing income tax recouped on payments. Companies must balance off their income
tax accounts on the 5th day of each month: credit balances will
be paid over to the Inland Revenue by the 19th of the month,
while debit balances may be reclaimed to the extent that tax has
actually been paid over previously; income tax deducted by
other persons cannot be reclaimed

(ii) *Permanent*

On April 5th in each year permanent set-off must be applied in accordance with the following rules:

(*a*) Income tax suffered on franked investment income received must be set-off against tax recouped on distributions paid in the same period. Any excess of tax suffered must be *either* carried forward and set-off against tax deducted from distributions payable in the following accounting period, *or* written off to profit and loss account. (Since the amount thus written off will still be available for set-off against tax deducted from future distributions, it is in the nature of a secret reserve, and the auditor should recommend that the amount thereof, if material, be disclosed by way of note to the accounts.)

Any excess of tax deducted from distributions over tax suffered on franked investment income, must be paid over to the Revenue.

(*b*) Tax suffered on unfranked investment income received must be set-off against:

  (i) tax deducted from charges paid;

  (ii) corporation tax on profits of the financial period.

Any remaining excess will be repaid by the Inland Revenue.

An excess of tax recouped by deduction from annual charges must be paid over to the Inland Revenue.

Separate accounts are normally opened for (i) corporation tax, and (ii) each income tax year, e.g. income tax account 1969–70, and income tax account 1970–71.

It is recommended by the Institute of Chartered Accountants that the rate of corporation tax at which the charge for the year has been computed should be disclosed. Under or over provisions in respect of previous years should be deducted from, or added to, as appropriate, the profits brought forward from previous years in the appropriation account.

Corporation tax payable in respect of the profits for the year should be shown on the balance sheet as a deduction from current assets less current liabilities, before ascertaining the working capital; or, if the balance sheet has been drawn up horizontally, it should be stated immediately before current liabilities. The date of payment should also be stated. In all cases, corporation tax due in respect of *previous* accounting periods should be shown separately as a current liability, the date of payment also being shown.

CHAPTER X

DIVISIBLE PROFITS AND DIVIDENDS

§ 1. Introduction – The Ascertainment of Profits

The proper ascertainment of profits in the case of a company is a matter of very great importance, affecting the rights and interests of various parties in different ways. If the profits shown in the accounts have been arrived at incorrectly, and are in excess of the actual profits, and further, if they have been distributed in dividend, the effect may be that the dividend will have been paid out of capital in whole or in part, and that the capital fund contributed by the members will not have remained intact.

Similarly, such a proceeding might affect the rights of debenture holders, since the dividend so paid away would have the result of depleting the assets which form their security.

If the improper distribution of dividends has so depleted the funds of the company that the remaining assets are insufficient to provide for the payment of ordinary creditors, the interests of the latter are obviously affected; while the directors of the company may make themselves personally liable to account for any dividends paid out of capital.

Further, there may be third parties entitled to a share of the profits, such as directors, managers, or others, who receive a percentage thereof.

If the total assets of a business are valued at the commencement of the year, the difference between this sum and the total of liabilities and capital at that date represents a surplus or deficiency, as the case may be. If a similar valuation is made at the end of the year and the surplus is found to have increased, or the deficiency decreased, such difference, subject to any appropriations of profit for specific purposes, or adjustments of capital, is the profit for the period, while if the surplus has decreased, or the deficiency increased, such difference is the measure of the loss for the period.

It is clear that the amount of profit so arrived at is dependent upon the method employed in determining the value of the assets.

If all the assets were valued at the amounts they are expected to realize if the business were closed down, a loss would possibly be shown and this method is therefore not adopted, the valuation being made on the basis of a going concern. It is necessary, however, to distinguish between the various classes of assets, since if fixed assets representing capital expenditure, such as freehold land, rise in value and this increase is taken into account, it represents an unrealized increment which may never materialize into a tangible profit.

Fixed assets, therefore, are generally valued at their cost price, less proper allowances for the depreciation which has arisen as a result of their being utilized in carrying on the business, and any obsolescence which has taken place.

Similarly, current assets should not be valued above cost, as this would involve taking credit for a profit before it is realized, the proper basis of valuation being cost or realizable value, whichever is the lower.

In effect, therefore, the profits for a given period may be said to be the excess of current income over current expenditure applicable to that period, after making good any loss on fixed or current assets sustained in the process of earning such income.

It does not follow, however, in the case of a company, that profits so arrived at are necessarily divisible profits, and the courts have held in certain instances that it may not be necessary to make good expired capital expenditure before arriving at the profits out of which dividends may be payable; in each case the provisions of the memorandum and articles of association and their validity must be considered. It may be found, on the other hand, that various appropriations must be made from the profits before any balance is available for distribution.

It is most important, when considering the effect of these legal cases, to bear in mind the period of time which has elapsed since many of the decisions were reached; and although, strictly, they are still binding under the doctrine of precedent, there are two major reasons why many of them are chiefly of academic interest at this time. Firstly, legal decisions are reached within the context of, and by reference to, the prevailing climate of opinion during that period. This climate is frequently given substance by statute law which, in its turn, is largely a reflection of contemporary thought and theory. For example, cases concerning limited companies are bound to be decided within the framework of company law operative at the particular time, and by this token any cases concerned with the subject of divisible profits which might arise today will inevitably be decided by reference to a legal framework which was certainly no part of the law thirty, sixty or eighty years ago. The recommendations on company law reform made by the committee under Lord Jenkins, published in 1962, have also been an important influence in the courts since that time, despite the fact that no more than about half of these recommendations were actually incorporated in the *Companies Act 1967*.

Secondly, the fact that each decision arises from the circumstances of that particular case makes any attempt to formulate in general terms the principles arising therefrom for future application, extremely hazardous. Although outwardly the features of certain cases bear a strong similarity, it is the subtle differences between them which may be considered by the judge to justify a departure from an opinion previously expressed. This is not to suggest that decided points of law having a bearing on a case under consideration will not be taken into account by the judge. Indeed, previous judgments may provide an invaluable means of sifting relevant evidence from irrelevant and may also illuminate issues which would otherwise be cloudy and confused. It is the circumstances of a case, viewed *as a whole* that lead to a particular decision.

Some of the more important decisions dealing with the ascertainment of divisible profits are summarized below.

§ 2. Remuneration based on Profits

(1) *The Spanish Prospecting Co Ltd* (1911, 1 Ch. 92).

In this case the company had entered into an agreement with two men, A and B, who were to receive a salary at the rate of £41 13s 4d per month each, subject to the proviso that they should not be entitled to draw their salary 'except only out of profits', if any, arising from the business of the company, which might from time to time be available for such purpose. Any such salary was to be cumulative, and any arrears thereof payable out of succeeding profits.

The business of the company included the purchase and sale of shares; and certain debentures which had been acquired stood in the books at no value.

The company went into liquidation while the debentures were still unsold, but they were subsequently realized by the liquidator and it was claimed that the proceeds should be credited to the profit and loss account, in order to enable A and B to receive their salaries out of the profits arising therefrom. Swinfen Eady, J., decided that a surplus on realized assets in winding-up, over and above the subscribed capital, was not a profit arising out of the business of the company; but the Court of Appeal reversed the decision, and indicated that the proceeds could be properly credited to profit and loss account.

Fletcher Moulton, L.J., said:

' . . . We start therefore with this fundamental definition of "profits", viz. if the total assets of the business at the two dates be compared, the increase which they show at the later date as compared with the earlier date (due allowance, of course, being made for any capital introduced into or taken out of the business in the meanwhile) represents in strictness the profits of the business during the period in question. But the periodical ascertainment of profits in a business is an operation of such practical importance as to be essential to the safe conduct of the business itself. To follow out the strict consequences of the legal conception in making out the accounts of the year would often be very difficult in practice. Hence the strict meaning of the word "profit" is rarely observed in drawing up the accounts of firms or companies. These are domestic documents designed for the practical guidance of those interested, and, so long as the principle on which they are drawn up is clear, their value is diminished little, if at all, by certain departures from this strict definition which lessen greatly the difficulty of making them out. Hence certain assumptions have become so customary in drawing up balance sheets and profit and loss accounts that it may almost be said to require special circumstances to induce parties to depart from them. For instance, it is usual to exclude gains and losses arising from causes not directly connected with the business of the company – such for instance, as a rise in the market value of land occupied by the company. The value assigned to trade buildings and plant is usually fixed according to an arbitrary rule, by which they are originally taken at their actual cost and are assumed to have depreciated by a certain percentage each year, though it cannot be pretended that any such calculation necessarily gives their true value either in use or in exchange. These, however, are merely variations of practice by individuals. They rest on no settled principle. They mainly arise from the sound business view that it is better to underrate than to overrate the profits, since it is impossible for you to foresee all the risks to which a business may in future be exposed.

For instance, there are many sound business men who would feel bound to take account of depreciation in the value of business premises (or in the value of plant specially designed for the production of a particular article), although they would not take account of appreciation in the same arising from like causes . . . But though there is a wide field for variation of practice in these estimations of profit, this liberty ceases at once when the rights of third persons intervene . . . In the absence of special stipulations to the contrary "profits" in cases where the rights of third parties come in mean actual profits, and they must be calculated as closely as possible, in accordance with the fundamental conception or definition to which I have referred.'

This judgment is an extremely able appreciation of the methods usually put into practice in business circles for the ascertainment of profits. While it is true that the method adopted is not a mere single entry process, nevertheless the end is to ascertain the net gain shown by the balance sheet over its predecessor, after allowing for depreciation on the various assets.

This case, however, was concerned with the ascertainment of profits in which third parties are interested, and not with the question of profits available for dividend. In fact the learned judge went on to say:

'I would have it clearly understood that these remarks have no bearing upon the vexed question of the fund out of which dividends may be legally paid in limited companies. Cases such as *Verner* v. *General and Commercial Investment Trust* and *Lee* v. *Neuchatel* show that this fund may in some cases be larger than what can rightly be regarded as profits, and the decisions in these cases depend largely on the fact that there is no statutory enactment which forbids it to be so.'

(The two cases mentioned in the above quotation are considered in the following section.)

(2) *Johnston* v. *Chestergate Hat Manufacturing Co* (1915, L.J. 84, Ch. 914).

The manager of the company was entitled to a percentage of the net profits, and it was held that income tax was *not* to be charged before arriving at the sum upon which the remuneration was to be calculated. Income tax was to be regarded as part of the net profits available for dividend and such 'net profits' were defined in this particular agreement as 'the net sum available for dividends as certified by the auditors'.

(3) *Edwards* v. *Saunton Hotel Co, Ltd* (1942, T.R. 359).

Where a director of the company was entitled to 20 per cent. of the profit 'available for distribution each year', such profit was to be arrived at after charging normal depreciation on the company's fixed assets, the further direction being made that the depreciation should be calculated on the fixed instalment method, and not on the reducing instalment system, which would cause a disproportionate charge to be made against profits in the early years of the life of an asset.

It was also confirmed that in ascertaining the profits income tax should *not* be deducted, and that the commission should be computed on the profits *before* deducting the commission itself.

No judicial decision has been given as to whether corporation tax should be deducted for such purposes, but it is considered that it should be treated in the same way as income tax.

§ 3. Depreciation of Fixed and Current Assets

The terms 'fixed', 'current' and 'wasting' assets have already been defined in Chapter V, and the treatment of depreciation on such assets from a general point of view has been considered. The legal aspect of the subject as affecting limited companies is of great importance in determining divisible profits, and has been the subject of some notable decisions. It is proposed first of all to summarize these cases, and from the consideration thereof to draw such general conclusions as may be possible.

(A) THE LEGAL DECISIONS

(1) *Re Crabtree, Thomas* v. *Crabtree* (1912, 106, L.T. 49).

Held – THAT NORMAL CHARGES IN RESPECT OF DEPRECIATION OF FIXED ASSETS OUGHT PROPERLY TO BE MADE PRIOR TO THE ASCERTAINMENT OF PROFITS FOR DISTRIBUTION.

A testator gave his trustees authority to carry on his business during the lifetime of his wife, and directed that the profits arising from the said business should be paid to her. The trustees, before arriving at the profits, had charged an annual sum for depreciation of machinery at the rate of $7\frac{1}{2}$ per cent. on its original value in addition to the cost of repairs, and the tenant for life contended that this ought to be disallowed. The Court of Appeal held that following Swinfen Eady, J., such depreciation had been properly charged.

In the course of his judgment Cozens-Hardy, M.R., said:

'But in the ordinary course of ascertaining the profits of a business where there is power machinery and trade machinery which is necessary in order to perform the work of the business, it is, in my opinion, essential that, in addition to all sums actually expended in repairing the machinery, or in renewing parts, that there should be also written off a proper sum for depreciation, and that sum ought to be written off before you can arrive at the net profits of the business, or at the profits of the business, and it is not profit until a proper sum, varying with the class of machinery, with the nature of the business, and the life of the machinery, has been written off for depreciation.'

During the argument the case of *Lee* v. *Neuchatel Asphalte Co* was referred to (see (2) below), and in the course of his remarks Buckley, L.J., said:

'The only authorities referred to were those of companies formed to work a wasting property, and in such a case all profit arising from the wasting property is divisible without any deduction for the depreciation in value of the wasting property. That is because the object of the company was to acquire a wasting property and to divide all the profits. That is not so here. The profits of this business are not ascertained until a sufficient sum has been deducted to meet the depreciation of the machinery. One of the witnesses in his affidavit referred to the "saleable value" of this machinery. That is not the right standard. Here it is the value of the machinery for the purposes of this business, not the saleable value.'

It must be remembered that the business concerned in the *Crabtree Case* was not carried on by a limited company.

(2) *Lee* v. *Neuchatel Asphalte Co Ltd* (1889, 41 Ch. 1).

Held – THAT A COMPANY, EMPOWERED TO DO SO BY ITS ARTICLES OF ASSOCIATION, MAY DISTRIBUTE DIVIDENDS WITHOUT MAKING GOOD THE DEPRECIATION OF WASTING ASSETS.

This action was brought by Mr Lee on behalf of himself and all the ordinary shareholders of the Neuchatel Asphalte Company, with the object of obtaining an injunction to prevent the directors of that company from distributing a dividend to the preference shareholders until depreciation of the company's property had been provided for. The articles of the company provided that the directors should not be bound to reserve money for the renewal or replacement of any lease, or of the company's interest in any property or concession; though as a matter of fact the company did from time to time write off considerable amounts, but had not made any such provision in the year during which the profit which it was proposed to distribute had arisen.

It may be remarked that in the case of a leasehold mine which cannot be exhausted during the term of the lease, the loss is continuous whether the mine be worked or not, and is a question of time as well as of output; while in the case of a freehold mine the loss is one of output only. The learned judge, in the remarks quoted below on this point, did not refer to the element of time.

Lindley, L.J., in the course of his judgment said (Acct. L.R. 1889, 26):

'The respondent company was formed for the purpose of working certain asphalte mines of which it had got a lease. It was quite obvious that with respect to such a property, every ton of stuff got out of that which was bought with capital represented a portion of capital. It was said that a division of the profit arising from the sale of such was a return of capital. If that was so, it is not, at all events, such a return of capital as is prohibited by the Companies Acts. There is nothing in any of the Companies Acts prohibiting anything of the kind. . . . It has been very judicially and properly left to the commercial world to settle how the accounts were to be kept. The Acts do not say what expenses are to be charged to capital account and what to revenue account. Such matters were left to the shareholders: they may or may not have a sinking fund or a deterioration fund, the articles of association may or may not contain regulations on these matters; if they do, the regulations must be observed; if they do not, the shareholders can do as they like, so long as they do not misapply their capital. In this case one of the articles provides that the directors shall not be bound to reserve moneys for the renewal or replacing of any lease or of the company's interest in any property or concession. . . . Now, the *Companies Act 1862* does not require the capital to be made up if lost, and it does not prohibit payment of dividends so long as the assets are of less value than the capital called up, nor does it make loss of capital a ground for winding-up. But if a company is formed to acquire or work property of a wasting nature, e.g. a mine, quarry, or patent, the capital expended in acquiring the property may be regarded as sunk and gone, and if the company retains assets sufficient to pay its debts, any excess of money obtained by working the property over the cost of working it may be divided amongst the shareholders; and this is true, although some portion of the property itself is sold, and in one sense the capital is thereby diminished. If it is said that such a course involves payment of dividends out of capital, the answer is that the Acts nowhere prohibit such a payment as here supposed. The proposition that it is *ultra vires* to pay dividends out of capital is very apt to mislead, and must not be understood in such a way as to prohibit honest tradings. It is not true, as an abstract proposition, that no dividends can be properly declared out of moneys arising from the sale of property bought by capital. But it is true that if the working expenses exceed the current gains, profits cannot be divided, and that if in such a case capital is divided and paid away as dividend, the capital is misapplied, and the directors implicated in the misapplication may be compelled to make good the amount misapplied . . . '

(3) *Bolton* v. *Natal Land and Colonisation Co Ltd* (1892, 2 Ch. 124).

Held – THAT A COMPANY MAY DECLARE A DIVIDEND OUT OF CURRENT PROFITS WITHOUT NECESSARILY MAKING GOOD LOSS OF CAPITAL.

The Natal Land Company, in 1882, had charged against revenue £70,000 in respect of a bad debt which had been incurred, and, at the same time, adjusted the profit and loss account by crediting to it practically the same sum in respect of an increase in value attributed to lands held by them.

In 1885 a profit was made and a dividend subsequently declared, and the plaintiff thereupon brought this action for restraining the payment of the dividend. His argument was that the book value of the land was now in excess of the true value, and that the difference between the 1882 book value and the acutal value should be written off against profits before anything could be appropriated for the purposes of dividend.

The Court held that, assuming a part of the capital had in fact been lost, and not subsequently made good, no sufficient ground was thereby afforded for restraining the payment of the dividend; that the fact of the company having written-up the value of the land in 1882, and credited the increase to the profit of that year in the manner described, did not place it under any obligation to bring into account in every subsequent year the increase or decrease in the value of its lands: and that, having regard to the case of *Lee* v. *Neuchatel Asphalte Company Limited*, it was not correct, in estimating the profits of a year, to take into account the increase or decrease in the value of the capital assets of the company.

It might appear that this case supported the suggestion that a company might write-up the value of its capital assets to conceal a revenue loss without being obliged to charge against revenue any decrease subsequently found to have occurred owing to excessive appreciation in the past; but it should be remembered that the Court did not have before it the question as to whether the bad debt should have been charged against revenue or not, the judge specifically stating that this point was not raised in the pleadings.

(4) *Verner* v. *General and Commercial Investment Trust Ltd,* (1894, 2 Ch. 239).

Held – THAT, SUBJECT TO ITS ARTICLES, A TRUST COMPANY MAY DISTRIBUTE A DIVIDEND OUT OF THE EXCESS OF CURRENT INCOME OVER CURRENT EXPENDITURE, WITHOUT MAKING GOOD LOSS OF CAPITAL.

This trust company had issued share capital to the extent of £600,000, and had borrowed £300,000 on the security of debenture stock. The proceeds of these issues had been invested in various securities authorized by the memorandum of association. The market value of such securities at the date of the accounts was £654,776, depreciation having thus occurred to the extent of about £240,000, of which it was estimated that about £75,000 represented an amount which there was no prospect of recovering within any reasonable period of time. During the company's last financial year the current income from investments had exceeded the current expenditure by more than £23,000, and the question for the Court to decide was whether such excess could be utilized for the purposes of dividend without taking into account the loss of capital to the amount of £75,000.

Lindley, L.J., in the course of his judgment, said:

'The broad question raised by this appeal is whether a limited company which has lost part of its capital, can lawfully declare or pay a dividend without first making good the capital which has been lost. I have no doubt it can – that is to say, there is no law which prevents it in all cases and under all circumstances. Such a proceeding may sometimes be very imprudent, but a proceeding may be perfectly legal and may yet be opposed to sound commercial principles. We, however, have only to consider the legality or illegality of what is complained of . . . There is no law which prevents a company from sinking its capital in the purchase or production of a money-making property or undertaking, and in dividing the money annually yielded by it without preserving the capital sunk so as to be able to reproduce it intact, either before or after the winding-up of the company. A company may be formed upon the principle that no dividends shall be declared unless the capital is kept undiminished, or a company may contract with its creditors to keep its capital or assets up to a given value. But in the absence of some special article or contract there is no law to this effect, and, in my opinion, for very good reasons. It would, in my judgment, be most inexpedient to lay down a hard-and-fast rule which would prevent a flourishing company either not in debt or well able to pay its debts from paying dividends, so long as its capital sunk in creating the business was not represented by assets which would, if sold, reproduce in money the capital sunk. Even a sinking fund to replace lost capital by degrees is not required by law . . . But, although there is nothing in the statutes requiring even a limited company to keep up its capital, and there is no prohibition against payment of dividends out of any other of the company's assets, it does not follow that dividends may be lawfully paid out of other assets, regardless of the debts and liabilities of the company. A dividend presupposes a profit in some shape, and to divide as dividend the receipts, say, for a year, without deducting the expenses incurred in that year in producing the receipts, would be as unjustifiable in point of law as it would be reckless and blameworthy in the eyes of business men. The same observation applies to the payment of dividends out of borrowed money. Further, if the income of any year arises from a consumption in that year of what may be called circulating capital, the division of such income as dividend without replacing the capital consumed in producing it will be a payment of a dividend out of capital within the meaning of the prohibition which I have endeavoured to explain . . . Perhaps the shortest way of expressing the distinction which I am endeavouring to explain is to say that fixed capital may be sunk and lost, and yet that the excess of current receipts over current payments may be divided, but that floating or circulating capital must be kept up, as otherwise it will enter into and form part of such excess, in which case, to divide such excess without deducting the capital which forms part of it, will be contrary to law. . . . .

(5) *Wilmer* v. *McNamara & Co Ltd* (1895, 2 Ch. 245).

Held – THAT A COMPANY CAN DECLARE A DIVIDEND OUT OF CURRENT PROFITS, WITHOUT MAKING GOOD DEPRECIATION OF FIXED ASSETS.

This company made a profit for the year ended June 30th, 1894, of £5,816 12s 6d, before making any provision for depreciation in respect of the value of the leases, goodwill, or plant. Depreciation had been provided on these assets to a considerable extent in earlier years, but no provision was made during the year in question. A resolution was passed by the company to distribute the above-mentioned profit in payment of a dividend to the preference shareholders. This action was taken on behalf of the ordinary shareholders to restrain the directors from giving effect to the resolution, on the ground that until the loss of capital had been made good no dividends ought to be paid.

Stirling, J., in the course of his judgment, refusing the injunction asked for, said:

'Clause 117 of the company's articles of association provides that "no dividend shall be payable except out of the profits arising out of the business of the company". What are these profits? . . . . . Apart from the use of the word "profits" in clause 117, there is nothing in the articles to show that the capital of the company (or, rather, assets of the value of those acquired by the company at its formation) must be kept up. Further, the articles appear to contemplate "profits" as the excess of receipts over all expenditure properly attributable to the year. It is necessary, however, to consider whether the depreciation in goodwill and leaseholds is to be treated as loss of "fixed" capital or of "floating" or "circulating" capital, and on this point I am of opinion that it is to be treated as loss of "fixed" capital. It very closely resembles the loss which a railway company may be said to suffer if it be found that their line, which was made, say, ten years ago at a certain cost, could now be made at a much smaller cost. Having regard to the remarks of Lindley, L.J., in *Lee* v. *Neuchatel Asphalte Company* (*supra*) I think that the balance sheet cannot be impeached simply because it does not charge anything against revenue in respect of goodwill. I feel much more doubt whether £200 is a sufficient sum to allow in respect of depreciation of leaseholds, but I do not think under the circumstances that a case has been made out for an injunction.'

(6) *Dovey* v. *Cory* (*National Bank of Wales case*, 1901, A.C. 477).

Held – THAT A DIRECTOR, IF HE ACTS IN GOOD FAITH, IS ENTITLED TO RELY ON THE OFFICERS OF THE COMPANY TO PREPARE TRUE AND HONEST ACCOUNTS.

This was an appeal from the decision of the Court of Appeal. It was sought to make the director liable in respect of alleged misfeasance for paying dividends out of capital.

Wright, J., had previously ordered the respondent to pay £54,787, being £37,000, the aggregate amount of dividends paid to the shareholders in 1887, 1888, 1889, and part of the dividend of 1890, and as to the balance, interest at 5 per cent. per annum on each of the dividends, holding that these dividends were in fact paid out of capital. Such dividends had been paid without making proper provision for bad debts; had these bad debts been written off there would have been no profits available for dividend. The Court of Appeal had relieved the respondent of liability on the ground that he had been deceived by persons he was entitled to trust, and that the dividends were not in fact paid out of capital utilizing for the latter point the arguments advanced in the *Lee* v. *Neuchatel* series of cases.

The House of Lords decided the case purely on the question

as to whether the director concerned was or was not justified in reposing confidence in the officials of the company, and did not feel themselves called upon to deal with the question as to whether the dividends had or had not in fact been paid out of capital.

Although, however, the House of Lords did not actually give their decision on this point, remarks were made by the Lord Chancellor (Lord Halsbury) and Davey, L.J., in the course of their judgments, which clearly showed that they were not at all inclined to agree with the deductions drawn in the Court of Appeal from the *Lee* v. *Neuchatel* and other cases; and consequently doubts have been cast upon the finality of those decisions.

The Lord Chancellor said:

'If I assume, as I do, that Mr Cory acted upon representations made to him which he believed, and which as coming from the officers of the bank to whom he was, in my judgment, justified in giving credit, the discussion of whether the dividends actually paid were or were not properly divisible, has no bearing on Mr Cory's liability, and I am very reluctant to give any opinion upon it, inasmuch as the question may arise when it may be necessary to decide it. I deprecate any premature judgment. My Lords, I am, as I have said, very reluctant to enter into a question which for the reasons I have given does not arise here, and into which the Court of Appeal has entered at some length. The only reason why I refer to it at all, is lest by silence I should be supposed to adopt a course of reasoning as to which I am not satisfied that it is correct. I doubt very much whether such questions can ever be treated in the abstract at all. The mode and manner in which a business is carried on, and what is usual or the reverse, may have a considerable influence in determining the question what may be treated as profits and what is capital. Even the distinction between fixed and floating capital, which in an abstract treatise like Adam Smith's "Wealth of Nations" is appropriate enough, may with reference to a concrete case be quite inappropriate. It is easy to lay down as an abstract proposition that you must not pay dividends out of capital, but the application of that very plain proposition may raise questions of the utmost difficulty in their solution. . . . On the one hand, people put their money into a trading concern to give them an income, and the sudden stoppage of all dividends would send down the value of their shares to zero, and possibly involve its ruin. On the other hand, companies cannot at their will and without the precautions enforced by the statute reduce their capital; but what are profits and what is capital may be a difficult and sometimes an almost impossible problem to solve. When the time comes that these questions come before us in a concrete case we must deal with them, but until they do, I, for one, decline to express an opinion not called for by the particular facts before us, and I am the more averse to doing so because I foresee that many matters will have to be considered by men of business which are not altogether familiar to a Court of Law.'

Davey, L.J., said:

'I desire to express my dissent from some propositions of law which were laid down in the Court of Appeal, and upon which your Lordships thought it right to hear the respondent's counsel. The learned judges seem to have thought that a joint stock company, incorporated under the Companies Acts, may write off to capital, losses incurred in previous years, and may in any subsequent year, if the receipts for that year exceed the outgoings, pay dividends out of such excess without making up the capital account. If this proposition be well founded it appears to me that a company whose capital is not represented by available assets need never trouble itself to reduce its capital, with the leave of the Court and subject to the other conditions imposed by the Act of 1877, in order to enable itself to pay dividends out of current receipts. My Lords, it may be that I have misapprehended the statement of law intended to be made by the learned judges in the Court of Appeal. I think that is possible, because I find that in *Verner* v. *General and Commercial Investment Trust* (1894, 2 Ch. 124), "Perhaps," Lord Lindley says, " the shortest way of expressing the distinction which I am endeavouring to explain is to say that fixed capital may be sunk or lost, and yet that the excess of current receipts over current payments may be divided, but that floating or circulating capital must be kept up, as otherwise it will enter into and form part of such excess, in which case to divide such excess without deducting the capital which forms part of it will be contrary to law." I reserve my opinion as to the effect of an actual and ascertained loss of part of the company's fixed capital. . . . But, subject to this observation, I think that the statement of law in the passage I have quoted is not open to objection, and it is only because the learned judge appears to me to have departed from it in his judgment in the present case that I have troubled your Lordships with these remarks.'

(7) *Bond* v. *Barrow Hæmatite Steel Co Ltd* (1902, 1 Ch. 353).

Held – THAT WHERE THE ARTICLES GIVE POWER TO PUT SUMS TO RESERVE BEFORE THE PAYMENT OF A DIVIDEND, PREFERENCE SHAREHOLDERS CANNOT COMPEL DIRECTORS TO DECLARE A DIVIDEND WITHOUT MAKING SUCH RESERVES AS THE DIRECTORS CONSIDER NECESSARY.

The profit and loss account of this company for the year 1900 showed a balance of £157,605 12s 11d, which was provisionally carried forward. No depreciation had been written off land, buildings, works, fixed plant, and mining leases for some years, and on a revaluation being made it appeared that a considerable loss had been sustained, and application was made to the Court for a reduction of capital. This was dismissed on the ground that the alleged loss was not proved to the satisfaction of the Court, and an action was subsequently taken by certain preference shareholders to compel the company to pay their dividends out of the credit balance on profit and loss account, without making good the loss stated to have been sustained.

Farwell, J., gave judgment for the company, on the ground that the preference shareholders could not compel directors to declare a dividend without making such reserves as they considered necessary, but he added some further remarks on the question of the application of the *Lee* v. *Neuchatel* series of cases, which are of some importance.

He said:

'It has been proved to my satisfaction . . . that the company has sustained an actual ascertained and realized loss of capital to an amount exceeding £200,000, and has also lost capital by estimate and valuation to an amount exceeding £50,000. The various sums claimed by the plaintiffs as available to pay their dividends amount to about £240,000. If, therefore, these ascertained and estimated losses have to be made good before any dividend can properly be paid, there are obviously no funds out of which to pay dividends. The defendants allege and the plaintiffs deny that the company are bound to make good these losses before paying any dividend. The question is one of very considerable difficulty on the authorities, but the result of these authorities is, in my opinion, that there is no hard-and-fast rule by which the Court can determine what is capital and what is profit. . . . The real question for determination, therefore, is whether there are profits available for distribution, and this is to be answered according to the circumstances of each particular case, the nature of the company, and the evidence of competent witnesses. . . . Now in the present case the £200,000 realized loss arises by the surrender of the leases of certain mines, by the pulling down of certain furnaces, and on the sale of certain cottages. The company is a smelting company on a very large scale, and for the convenience of its works and by way of economy they acquired the leases of the surrendered mines in order to supply themselves with their own ore instead of buying it as required. The ore was used exclusively for the purposes of the company's works. The mines were drowned out and the cost of pumping them out was prohibitive. The company, therefore, surrendered the leases, pulled down the blast furnaces, and sold the cottages connected therewith. Now the evidence before me is all on one side. The plaintiffs called none, and Sir David Dale and the defendants' other witnesses all agree that in a company of this nature these items ought to come into the account before any profit can be said to be earned, and my own opinion coincides with theirs, inasmuch as I think that the money invested in those items is properly regarded in this company as circulating capital. Suppose the company had bought enormous stocks of ore sufficient to last for ten years, it could hardly be said that the true value of so much of this as remained from time to time ought not to be brought into the balance sheet, and I can see no difference for the purpose of the account between ore *in situ* and ore so bought in advance. The blast furnaces and cottages are mere accessories to the ore, and resemble a building for burning the stores bought in advance already mentioned. There is more difficulty about the remaining £50,000. I think that the onus is on the plaintiff to show that it is fixed capital, and that in a company of this nature such fixed capital may be sunk or lost. They have not done this, and the evidence, so far as it goes, is the other way. But this is not an actual loss, but depreciation by estimate. The plaintiffs really relied on *Lee* v. *Neuchatel Asphalte Company* as an authority for this proposition as a universal negative – viz. "that no company owning wasting property need ever create a depreciation fund". In my opinion that is not the true result of the decision. It must be remembered that in that case there had been no loss of assets. The company's assets were larger than at its formation, and the Court decided nothing more than the particular proposition that some companies with wasting assets need have no depreciation fund. For instance, I cannot think that it would be right for the defendant company to purchase out of capital the last two or three years of a valuable patent and distribute the whole of the receipts in respect thereof as profits, without replacing the capital expended in purchase. It is for the Court to determine in each case on evidence whether the particular company ought, or ought not, to have such a fund. There is not doubt as to the opinion of the witnesses in this case, and further, the opinion of the directors cannot be altogether disregarded. The Courts have, no doubt in many cases, overruled directors who proposed to pay dividends, but I am not aware of any case in which the Court has compelled them to pay when they have expressed their opinion that the state of the accounts does not admit of any such payment. In a matter depending on evidence and expert opinion it would be a very strong measure for the Court to override the directors in such a manner.'

(8) *Ammonia Soda Co* v. *Chamberlain* (1918, 1 Ch. 266).

Held – THAT IT IS NOT NECESSARILY ILLEGAL FOR DIRECTORS OF A COMPANY TO PAY DIVIDENDS OUT OF THE PROFITS OF THE COMPANY DURING A CURRENT YEAR WITHOUT MAKING GOOD EXISTING DEFICIENCIES IN PAID-UP CAPITAL, OR WITHOUT WRITING OFF A DEBIT TO THE COMPANY'S PROFIT AND LOSS ACCOUNT, OCCASIONED BY LOSSES IN PREVIOUS YEARS.

The profit and loss account of this company in the year 1911 showed a debit balance of £19,028. This amount arose by debiting to that account certain sums for depreciation of buildings, plant and machinery, and for directors' fees and mortgage and debenture interest, at a time when the company's gross trading profit was insufficient to provide for the purpose

In 1908, a boring made by the company to reach water for use in the company's works, failed in that purpose, but showed a new bed of rocksalt of which the existence was previously unknown. This discovery was considered to increase the value of the company's property, and the directors obtained a report from two of their number which advised that their land should be valued at the increased figure of £79,166, and its value was raised in the balance sheet of July 31st, 1911, from £63,246 to £83,788 by the addition of a sum of £20,542. This sum was credited to a reserve account and used to cancel £12,990 of the debit of £19,028 on the profit and loss account, the remainder being written-off out of net profits. For the thirteen months ended January 31st, 1912, the net profit made by the company was £13,030, and for the twelve months ended January 31st, 1913, £15,669. From September 1912, to April 1915, dividends amounting to £13,116 were paid on the preference shares of the company. In so far as these dividends were paid before providing for the £12,990 (the proportion of the debit balance on the profit and loss account referred to above) it was claimed that they were paid out of capital and that the directors were liable to repay them. The Court of Appeal held that the re-valuation of the property was *bona fide* and that the directors were not liable to refund any of the dividends. The facts were not, in any way, concealed from the shareholders, and the treatment adopted had been clearly drawn to their attention by the auditors in their report.

In the course of this judgment, Swinfen Eady, L.J., said:

'The plaintiffs contend that, although net profits were earned during the period they were not available for dividend, and cannot really be considered "profits," as in the earlier period of the company's history, a loss had been incurred, and they contend that until such loss has been first made good there cannot be any profits in the real true sense of the word. In my judgment, this argument is unsound and has been exposed again and again. The Companies Acts do not impose any obligation upon a limited company nor does the law require it, that it shall not distribute as dividend the clear net profit of its trading unless its paid-up capital is intact, or until it has made good all losses incurred in previous years. . . . Counsel for the appellants invited the Court to lay down that wherever there was a debit to the profit and loss account, irrespective of the way in which it arose, of the stage in the company's operations, and of the nature and business of the company, it was illegal to divide profits subsequently earned without first writing off out of those profits the amount of the debit. To do so would be to fall into the error which Lord Macnaghten pointed out should be avoided, and would only serve to harass and embarrass business men, and impose upon companies a burden which Parliament has abstained from casting upon them. The directors in this case were of opinion that no capital had been really lost, and they were of opinion that the value of the land and works as a going concern had been increased, as a result of their boring and exploratory work, to a considerably greater amount than £19,028. . . . The result of increasing the value at which the land stood was to give a credit which would have enabled the debit of £19,028 to be written-off. Part of it was, however, actually written-off out of subsequent net profits. Now, the debit consisted in part of a nominal depreciation in the fixed assets of the company, buildings, plant and machinery, and as regards the balance, it consisted of sums paid out of the subscribed capital of the company for mortgage and debenture interest, and directors' fees, there not being sufficient trading profits to provide these amounts. The transaction was carried out with the full approval of the shareholders in general meeting, and in all honesty and good faith. The dividends complained of, paid out of net earnings in the subsequent years, were not paid out of capital, but out of profits, and the defendants are, in my opinion, under no liability whatever to repay the same, or any part. . . . '

Warrington, L.J., said:

'There is, however, one accepted restriction on the powers of companies incorporated under the Companies Acts, namely, that they must not, under the guise of dividends or in any other way, return to their shareholders money subscribed for their shares, unless it be with the sanction of the Court under the appropriate statutory provisions. It has been asserted in this case, not for the first time, that there is a further restriction – suggested to be a corollary of the rule I have just mentioned – which would make it illegal for a company to pay dividends out of the profits of a current year, unless it first makes good deficiencies in paid-up capital occasioned by losses in previous years; or, to put the contention in a broader form, no dividends can properly be paid out of profits so long as there are losses previously incurred and not made good. In my opinion this alleged restriction has no foundation in law. . . . I am, of course, far from saying that in all such cases dividends can properly be paid without making good the previous loss; the nature of the business and the amount of the loss may be such that no honest and reasonable man of business would think of paying dividends without providing for it. In such a case, I apprehend the Court would take the view that a payment which no honest and reasonable man of business would think it right to make could not properly be made by directors.'

(9) *Stapley* v. *Read Bros Ltd* (1924 – 40, T.L.R. 442).

Held – THAT A COMPANY IS NOT PRECLUDED FROM PAYING DIVIDENDS OUT OF CURRENT PROFITS WHERE A DEBIT BALANCE ON PROFIT AND LOSS ACCOUNT HAS

BEEN WRITTEN-OFF BY THE RESTORATION OF GOODWILL
AS AN ASSET AT AN AGREED FAIR VALUE, GOODWILL
HAVING PREVIOUSLY BEEN COMPLETELY WRITTEN-OFF
OUT OF PROFITS.

In 1918 the company wrote-off the balance of goodwill
account which was then standing at £51,000 against a reserve
account which had been built up out of profits. In 1921 and
1922 there were losses resulting in a debit balance on profit and
loss acount of £25,500.

In 1923 a profit of £13,430 was made, but this was not sufficient to pay the dividend on the preference shares for 1923, and
the arrears for 1921 and 1922. The directors proposed to re-
debit goodwill account with £40,000 on the ground that this
was a conservative value to be placed on goodwill, and to credit
this sum to a reserve account. The reserve account was then
to be utilized for writing-off the debit balance of £25,500 on
profit and loss account, the remainder, with the profit for 1923,
to be used for payment of the dividends on the preference
shares.

A shareholder thereupon applied for an injunction to restrain
the directors from treating as profits available for distribution
any profits previously used for writing-down the company's
assets and subsequently written back.

In the course of his judgment, Russell, J., said:

'. . . If they had retained goodwill as an asset in their balance sheet, and
if, instead of writing-off its value out of profits, they had carried those
profits to a goodwill depreciation reserve fund, they would have been at
liberty at any time to distribute those profits, at all events to the extent by
which the amount of such a reserve fund exceeded the amount of the actual
depreciation . . .

'Does it make any difference that they have kept their accounts in another form, and that, instead of placing the profits to a reserve account,
they have purported to apply them in writing-off a corresponding amount
of the value of the goodwill? The answer seems to me to depend upon the
further question: Have the company finally and irrevocably capitalized
those profits so as to disentitle themselves for ever afterwards from restoring them to reserve and from dealing with them as profits? No doubt
the accounts showing the particular methods adopted were approved every
year by the shareholders in general meeting; but I am not satisfied that the
shareholders thereby intended, or bound themselves, for all time and in all
circumstances to give up their claims to these profits and to treat them as
capital only.'

'In my opinion, unless there is anything in the *Companies (Consolidation) Act 1908*, or in the constitution of the company to prohibit it, the shareholders may, if they think fit, write back to profit account so much of the depreciation written off goodwill as has proved to have been in excess of proper requirements.'

(B) THE LEGAL DECISIONS CONSIDERED

The authority of the judgments of the Court of Appeal in the *Lee* v. *Neuchatel* series of decisions was regarded as somewhat shaken by the remarks of Lord Halsbury and Lord Davey in the House of Lords Appeal in *Dovey* v. *Cory*, quoted above; and the remarks of Farwell, J., in the *Bond* v. *Barrow Hæmatite* case further indicate that these decisions must be taken as applying to the specific cases concerned, and that in future each case must be taken in connection with the particular circumstances surrounding it. In the case of *Ammonia Soda Co* v. *Chamberlain*, the Court of Appeal strongly confirmed the principles laid down by its predecessors in the *Lee* v. *Neuchatel* series of cases, and clearly indicated that if these were to be disturbed, it must be done by some higher Court than the Court of Appeal.

Accordingly it becomes a matter of some difficulty to attempt to summarize the legal position as regards the necessity of providing depreciation in respect of fixed or wasting assets.

Before considering how far it is wise to rely upon the authority of the judgments in actual practice, it is desirable to note the financial distinction between the result of the judgment in the *Neuchatel* case, and that in the *Verner* case. The latter followed the former from a legal point of view, but the financial position of a trust company is fundamentally different from that of a mining company, although the Court took no cognisance of this distinction.

In the *Neuchatel* case the principal property of the company consisted of a leasehold mine, which was gradually exhausted in the process of earning income. The capital contributed by the shareholders was sunk in acquiring this particular property, and the question was whether it was necessary to make good the waste before distributing a dividend out of the excess of current income over current expenditure. The articles of the company gave power to distribute dividends without so making good, and from the judgment of the Court, and subsequent decisions, it is clear that this article was not regarded as *ultra vires* the Companies Acts. The contention that any company in similar circumstances desiring to act in this manner must first have power under its articles to do so, thus falls to the ground, since had the Neuchatel Company's article been *ultra vires*, as was held by the plaintiffs, it could have afforded no authority to the company to distribute dividends without providing for the depreciation.

In the case of a company formed for the express purpose of working a leasehold mine, it is probable that the shareholders of the company would expect it to go into liquidation on the exhaustion of its principal asset. If this were so and a sufficient balance of working capital maintained, any money retained out of profits representing provision for depreciation could not be utilized by the company, but would necessarily have to be invested in outside securities. These investments would gradually accumulate, and if the calculations on which the depreciation was based were correct, on the final exhaustion of the asset the company would be in possession of funds sufficient to pay back in full to the shareholders the nominal value of capital contributed by them. Though this may be considered as theoretically desirable, shareholders might not necessarily wish this course to be taken, but might prefer to receive larger dividends during the life of the mine. In a case of this sort, where the company is expected to wind-up on the exhaustion of its principal asset, the matter becomes one of policy, and there would seen to be no reason, financial or otherwise, why the general body of shareholders should not receive the bulk of their proportion of capital by way of dividends, should they desire to do so, provided sufficient funds are retained at all times for the repayment of liabilities.

The *Verner* case, however, although it was decided on the precedent of the *Neuchatel* case, presents a totally different aspect from the practical point of view.

The company was a trust company, and the market value of the investments had very largely depreciated. Although the Court held that the investments of a trust company are to be regarded as fixed assets, they cannot be called wasting assets, and therefore are not in the same category as, say, a leasehold mine or a cemetery.

The shareholders of a trust company do not anticipate that the securities in which the bulk of their capital has been invested are assets of a wasting nature. The company is not expected to wind-up within any definable period; and no doubt the majority of the shareholders would expect their capital to be returned to them in full on liquidation. On the other hand, shareholders in companies of this nature rely upon obtaining regular income, and to be deprived of dividends for a long period while capital loss is made good, would prove a tremendous hardship in many cases.

This case, therefore, cannot be regarded as similar to the *Neuchatel* case from a financial point of view, notwithstanding the fact that the Court treated the question of depreciation in the same manner. Lindley, L.J., said that although a proceeding might be perfectly legal, it might be opposed to sound commercial principles, but that the Court had only to consider the legality or illegality of the company's action.

The same judge made some important remarks on the distinction between 'fixed' and 'current' assets, when he said that 'fixed' capital might be sunk and lost, and yet the excess of current receipts over current payments might be divided, but that 'floating' or 'circulating' capital must be kept up, as otherwise it will enter into and form part of such excess, in which case, to divide such excess without deducting the capital which forms part of it, would be contrary to law.

The term 'floating' (or 'circulating') capital here used is equivalent to that portion of the capital represented by 'current' assets.

From the *dicta* of Lindley, L.J., in both the *Neuchatel* and *Verner* cases it is clear that the Court will protect the interests of creditors and that even in a case where it may not be necessary to make good depreciation on wasting assets before paying a dividend sufficient assets must be retained to pay the company's liabilities.

In *Wilmer* v. *McNamara & Co Ltd* (*supra*), the Court followed the *Neuchatel* case, Stirling, J., stating that depreciation of goodwill and leaseholds was in his opinion to be treated as a loss of 'fixed' capital, and accordingly it was not obligatory on the company to provide for such loss out of revenue before paying any dividend. Some doubt, however, was expressed by him with reference to the adequacy of the provision made for the depreciation of the leaseholds, and it would seem prudent to regard such provision as necessary in ordinary cases.

As already indicated, doubt was thrown upon this series of decisions by the remarks of the Law Lords in *Dovey* v. *Cory* (*supra*). The Court of Appeal in the *National Bank of Wales* case had implied by their judgment that the payment of dividends without making provision for bad debts was not equivalent to paying dividends out of capital, and although the House of Lords was not required to express an opinion on this point, the Lord Chancellor stated that the only reason why he referred to it at all was lest by silence he should be supposed to adopt a course of reasoning which he was not satisfied was correct. He doubted whether such a question could ever be treated in the abstract at all, and expressed his opinion that distinction between 'fixed' and 'floating' capital might be appropriate enough in an abstract treatise but might be quite inappropriate when applied to a concrete case. His remarks clearly indicate that the House of Lords held their opinion on these matters in suspense, and did not desire it to be thought that they necessarily upheld the opinions expressed by the Court of Appeal in the *Lee* v. *Neuchatel* series of cases.

Since, however, the decisions in these cases have not been challenged or overruled by the House of Lords during the long period which has elapsed since the *obiter dictum* in the *National Bank of Wales* case was pronounced these decisions must now be regarded as representing the established law on the subject, but bearing in mind the reservations on this point mentioned earlier in this chapter.

In *Ammonia Soda Co* v. *Chamberlain*, the Court of Appeal took the view that it was not necessary in all cases to make good a debit balance on profit and loss account before paying dividends out of current profits, but regard must be had to the way in which such debit balance had been arrived at, the nature of the company's operations, and to all the facts of the case. The circumstances in which the dividend is paid must not be such that 'no honest and reasonable man of business' would think it right to make the distribution. The payment of dividends out of current profits without making good prior losses is not necessarily a payment of dividends out of capital. It is clear, however, that each case must still be considered on its merits, and it is very difficult to lay down any fixed rule, particularly since the

Jenkins Committee on company law reform categorically dissented from this view in 1962. The committee held that a company's profits should be viewed continuously rather than as having been earned in separate financial periods.

The decision in *Stapley* v. *Read Bros. Ltd* followed the *Ammonia Soda Co* case in determining that dividends might be paid out of current profits, although the debit balance on the profit and loss account had not been made good out of subsequent profits. Russell, J., held that profits which had been utilized to write off goodwill in the first instance had not become irrevocably capitalized; that the company could place a proper valuation upon the existing goodwill and re-debit the account with that value, crediting the reserve account, and that such reserve could be utilized so far as might be necessary to write off the existing debit balance on profit and loss account or for distribution as profits available for the payment of dividends.

It is apparent, however, that this course would only be permitted where the assets concerned had been previously written off or written-down out of divisible profits to a figure below their true value. Clearly, too, it would be difficult to justify a high valuation on goodwill after a period of successive trading losses, since goodwill is commonly regarded as the capitalized value of future super-profits.

In *Bond* v. *Barrow Hæmatite Steel Company*, the company had sustained an actual ascertained and realized loss exceeding £200,000, and a further estimated loss exceeding £50,000. Had these losses been written-off no dividend could have been paid.

Farwell, J., said that the question was one of very considerable difficulty on the authorities, but in his opinion the result of these authorities was that there was no hard-and-fast rule by which the Court could determine what is capital and what is profit. The loss in this case arose in connection with certain assets which had been acquired in order to enable the company to produce its own ore instead of purchasing ore in the market, and the judge expressed the view that such expenditure was equivalent to expenditure on large stocks of ore bought in advance, and as such, any loss arising thereon should be treated as a loss of circulating capital, which ought to be made good before paying a dividend. It is apparent, therefore, that the classification of assets in any particular case as between 'fixed' and 'current' is a question of fact which will be decided by the Court, having regard to all the circumstances, and to the opinions of experts and business men, and further that the Courts are strongly disinclined to lay down any general rule on the subject.

As regards the question of depreciation of fixed assets similar remarks apply. Farwell, J., said in the case quoted above, that the *Neuchatel* case was no authority for the proposition that no company owning 'wasting' property need ever create a depreciation fund. In his opinion the Court decided nothing more than that some companies with 'wasting' assets need have no depreciation fund. It was for the Court to determine in each case on evidence whether the particular company ought or ought not to have such a fund.

In this connection the decision of the Scottish Courts in *Cox* v. *Edinburgh & District Tramways Co* (*Glasgow Herald*, June 17th, 1898) may be noted. The company had incurred a heavy loss in converting their system from horse to mechanical traction, and the Court held that such a loss need not be made good before the payment of a dividend, on the ground that it might be assumed that the additional expenditure enhanced the value of the undertaking as a whole.

It is clear, however, that a distinction must be drawn between a fixed asset which is held as the company's principal object and one, such as plant and machinery, which is merely incidental to the company's main purpose. When plant and machinery is exhausted it *must* be replaced and it would, therefore, be commercially imprudent to fail to provide for its depreciation.

The legal position as regards depreciation may therefore be summarized as follows:

(1) Depreciation of 'current' assets must be made good before the payment of a dividend (*Verner* v. *General and Commercial Investment Trust Ltd; Bond* v. *Barrow Hæmatite Steel Co*).

(2) Depreciation of 'fixed' or 'wasting' assets need not necessarily be made good before the payment of a dividend, though sufficient assets must be retained to pay liabilities (*Lee* v. *Neuchatel Asphalte Co Ltd; Bolton* v. *The Natal Land Co; Verner* v. *General and Commercial Investment Trust; Wilmer* v. *McNamara & Co*); but as to whether such

provision is necessary or not is a question of fact to be determined by the Court, having regard to the circumstances of each particular case and the memorandum and articles of the company concerned (*Dovey* v. *Cory; Bond* v. *Barrow Hæmatite Steel Company*).

The auditor should therefore consider each case in practice according to the circumstances, but in all cases where loss of fixed assets has not been written-off he should report the fact to the members, if the accounts themselves do not disclose the true position. Where, by not making such provision, the financial position of the company is likely to be seriously affected and its creditors prejudiced, the auditor should draw the attention of the directors and the members to this point of view, and recommend that the necessary provision should be made. Where the omission to provide depreciation will only affect the members when the company is wound up, the matter is more of a domestic nature for the members themselves to decide, and as long as the auditor places them in possession of the facts, he will have absolved himself from any responsibility in connection with the matter.

§ 4. Capital Profits

The question as to whether capital profits are available for the payment of dividends, and if so, under what circumstances, is a particularly important one, and there have been two cases decided which will now be summarized, and from which it will be possible to draw some general conclusions.

(A) THE LEGAL DECISIONS

(1) *Lubbock* v. *The British Bank of South America* (1892, 2 Ch. 198).

Held – THAT A PROFIT MADE ON THE SALE OF A PART OF THE UNDERTAKING OF A COMPANY IS AVAILABLE FOR DIVIDEND, IF THE ARTICLES SO PERMIT.

This company, under the name of the English Bank of Rio de Janeiro, had sold to another bank its goodwill and property in Brazil for a sum of £875,000, agreeing, upon the payment of that sum, to discontinue the use of its name, and to adopt a name not indicating a bank doing business in Brazil, and also contracting to refrain from carrying on business in Brazil. Subsequently this restraint was released on payment by the defendant bank of £75,000. It was then proposed to distribute £205,000, which consisted of the original consideration for the Brazilian business, less the paid-up capital of the company (£500,000), the £75,000 referred to above, and sundry other payments for outgoings and compensations in reference to the sale of the Brazilian Bank.

Chitty, J., held that the £205,000 was plainly profit on capital, and not part of the capital itself, for that sum was the surplus ascertained after the liabilities and capital were placed on one side of the account and the assets on the other. Under the articles of the company the directors were justified in carrying over the £205,000 to the profit and loss account; and having appropriated to the reserve fund so much of the sum as they thought fit, they could distribute the remainder as dividends after an ordinary meeting, called in pursuance of the articles, had passed the requisite resolution.

(2) *Foster* v. *The New Trindad Lake Asphalte Company Ltd* (1901, 1 Ch. 208).

Held – THAT A REALIZED APPRECIATION IN THE VALUE OF A BOOK DEBT TAKEN OVER BY A COMPANY AT ITS FORMATION IS NOT PROFIT AVAILABLE FOR DIVIDEND, UNLESS SUCH SURPLUS REMAINS AFTER A REVALUATION OF THE WHOLE OF THE ASSETS.

This company at its formation had taken over amongst other assets a debt of $100,000, secured by promissory notes. This debt was not then regarded as of any value, but subsequently it was paid in full, together with interest accrued, realizing £26,258 16s. As no value was placed on this asset in the company's books, the amount received was treated as a profit, and it was proposed by the directors to regard it as available for dividend, and to distribute it accordingly, without taking into account any decrease in the value of other assets.

Byrne, J., in the course of his judgment *restraining the distribution*, said:

'It appears to me that the amount in question is *prima facie* capital and that I have no evidence which would justify me in saying that it has changed its character because it has turned out to be of greater value than had been expected. . . . I must not, however, be understood as determining that this sum or a portion of it may not properly be brought into profit and loss account or be taken into account in ascertaining the amount available for dividend. That appears to me to depend upon the result of the whole account for the year. It is clear, I think, that an appreciation in total value of capital assets, if duly realized by sale or getting in of some portion of such assets, may in a proper case be treated as available for purposes of dividend. This, I think, is involved in the decision in the case of *Lubbock* v. *British Bank of South America* (1892, 2 Ch. 198), cited with approval by Lord Lindley in *Verner* v. *General and Commercial Investment Trust* (1894, 2 Ch. 239, at page 265), where he says: "Moreover, when it is said and said truly, that dividends are not to be paid out of capital the word 'capital' means the money subscribed pursuant to the memorandum of association, or what is represented by that money. Accretions to that capital may be realized and turned into money, which may be divided amongst the shareholders, as was decided in *Lubbock* v. *British Bank of South America*." If I rightly appreciate the true effect of the decisions, the question of what is profit available for dividend depends upon the result of the whole accounts fairly taken for the year, capital, as well as profit and loss, and although dividends may be paid out of earned profits, in proper cases, although there has been a depreciation of capital, I do not think that a realized accretion to the estimated value of one item of the capital assets can be deemed to be profit divisible amongst the shareholders without reference to the result of the whole accounts fairly taken.'

(B) THE LEGAL DECISIONS CONSIDERED

From a consideration of the above cases taken in conjunction with one another, it may be said that capital profits are not available for dividend unless:

(1) the articles of association permit such distribution;

(2) the surplus is realized; and

(3) such surplus remains after a proper valuation of the whole of the assets has been fairly taken.

It should be noted, however, that in the case of *Dimbula Valley (Ceylon) Tea Co Ltd* v. *Laurie* (1961, 1 All E.R. 769) Buckley, J., expressed the view that a surplus on capital account resulting from a *bona fide* revaluation made by competent valuers was available for paying up bonus shares to be issued to the members even though it was *not* realized. The judge did, however, point out that a distribution from such a source would not, normally, be regarded as wise commercially. The Jenkins Committee dissented from this decision, moreover, maintaining that capital distributions should be permitted only out of surpluses which had been realized.

In the *New Trinidad* case the company were not apparently prepared to revalue the whole of their assets; had they been willing to do so, and had they been able to prove to the satisfaction of the Court that a capital profit was finally shown, there is no doubt that the Court would have permitted such a profit to be distributed as dividend.

Where expenditure of a capital nature has been charged to revenue, a company can subsequently reimburse revenue out of capital; and the same procedure can be followed where an estimated loss on capital account has been charged to revenue, but the assets have subsequently appreciated in value (*Mills* v. *Northern Rly. of Buenos Ayres Co*, 1870, 5 Ch. 621; *Bishop* v. *Smyrna and Cassaba Rly. Co* (No. 2), 1895, 2 Ch. 596).

It has been seen that a capital profit arising on a *bona fide* revaluation of fixed assets can be utilized to write off a debit balance on profit and loss account arising in prior periods, thus enabling dividends to be paid out of current profits (*Ammonia Soda Co* v. *Chamberlain, supra*).

§ 5. Divisible Profits

Having regard to the fact that the legal decisions which have been given on the question of divisible profits depend to a very large extent on the circumstances of each particular case, it is somewhat hazardous to attempt to lay down in general terms any definition of divisible profits. From the auditor's point of view, however, it is desirable that some general rule should be formulated. Subject, therefore, to the qualifications above-mentioned and to the memorandum and articles of the company concerned, the divisible profits of a company may be said to be –

(1) The excess of current income over current expenditure after making good depreciation of current assets and retaining sufficient funds to pay liabilities, but without necessarily in all cases taking into account depreciation of fixed assets.

(2) Realized capital profits may be divisible if a surplus remains after making good any capital losses, and if it is within the powers of the company to distribute such capital profits.

(3) Revenue losses must be made good before revenue profits can be distributed, and capital losses must be made good

before capital profits can be distributed; but capital losses need not necessarily be made good before revenue profits are distributed.

It is not, however, necessarily illegal for dividends to be paid out of current revenue profits without making good existing deficiencies in paid-up capital, or without writing-off a debit on the companys' profit and loss account occasioned by losses in previous years.

§ 6. Dividends

The divisible profits of a company having been considered, there remain a number of points which require to be dealt with in connection with the declaration and payment of dividends.

(A) INTERIM DIVIDENDS

Under clause 115 of Table 'A', *Companies Act 1948*, the directors may from time to time pay to the members such interim dividends as appear to the directors to be justified by the profits of the company, and where this Table applies, or the operation of this clause is not excluded, the directors will have this power. Most companies having articles of their own empower the directors to pay interim dividends.

The question as to whether a company is justified in paying an interim dividend, and, if so, to what extent, is a most important one, and the advice of the auditor is frequently requested. In such circumstances, he should suggest that interim accounts be prepared for the purpose of ascertaining what profits have been made. Many companies have half-yearly accounts prepared for this reason. Assuming such accounts to have been prepared, and that a profit is shown after making all the necessary adjustments and proper provision for depreciation, bad debts etc., the question will arise as to what proportion of such profit should be applied in payment of an interim dividend. Certain considerations must be taken into account before it is possible to arrive at a decision as to the rate of dividend to be paid. Where the dividend is in respect of preference shares, and is expressed as being payable half-yearly, and there is ample margin of profit, the full half-yearly dividend may be paid; but in the case of ordinary shares it is advisable that the interim dividend should be declared at a lower rate than that of the estimated dividend for the whole year.

It must be remembered that an interim dividend is only a payment on account of the dividend for the whole year and, consequently, if an interim dividend is declared in respect of profits earned during a portion of the year, and during the remainder of the year a loss is made resulting in a loss for the whole year, the interim dividend will have been paid out of capital or past accumulations of profit.

The general conditions and prospects of the trade carried on by the company must therefore be taken into account in this connection. The financial aspect of the matter also requires consideration. If the liquid position of the company is not strong, and the whole of the funds in hand are required for carrying on the business, it is not advisable to reduce the resources further by distributing an interim dividend, but this general principle may be subject to special considerations which will be referred to subsequently.

In the case of a company carrying on business of a regular and stable nature, where the rate of gross profit earned is subject to little, if any, variation, it may be possible to arrive at a sufficiently accurate estimate of the profits without taking stock or preparing complete accounts. The gross profit for the period can be estimated by reference to the turnover at the average percentage earned in previous years; and the actual expenses incurred by the company can be ascertained. After all the necessary allowances have been made for outstandings, provisions etc., the net profit can be estimated with sufficient accuracy, although in such cases a greater margin for contingencies should be allowed in fixing the rate of dividend than when annual accounts have been prepared.

It is sometimes thought by persons unacquainted with the fundamental principles of accounts, that if there is a considerable cash balance, this fact is in itself sufficient to justify the payment of an interim dividend, and that the preparation of a receipts and payments account is an adequate substitute for an interim profit and loss account. This idea is entirely fallacious, and, if acted upon, might easily result in the dividend being paid out of capital, and in the serious depletion of the company's resources. The receipts and payments account might include receipts on account of capital or loans, the proceeds of which have not yet been expended, with the result that a large balance remains in hand. On the other hand, considerable capital payments might have been made with the result that the balance in hand might be less, rather than more than the actual profit earned.

The receipts and payments account takes no account of fluctuation in the amounts of stock, debtors or creditors. Stock and debtors might be materially less than at the commencement of the period, and, consequently, the cash balance might be increased, or the creditors might be greater, with a similar result; in neither case might any profit have been earned. No account is taken of the provisions necessary for bad debts, depreciation, or other losses which may not have arisen through cash transactions. In other words, there is not necessarily any direct correlation between the availability of cash resources and profits; and, therefore, no reliance can be placed upon a receipts and payments account for the purpose of determining whether or not an interim dividend should be paid.

Where a bonus was improperly declared on the faith of a surplus shown by a receipts and payments account, without the preparation of a profit and loss account and balance sheet, and without making due allowance for outstandings, the Court ordered a director who had participated in the bonus to refund the amount received by him (*Rance's Case*, 1870, L.R. 6 Ch. App. 104).

(B) FINAL DIVIDENDS

The articles usually give the directors power to declare and pay final dividends on preference shares, but not on ordinary shares, a resolution of the members in general meeting being required to authorize the latter.

In no case should a final dividend be declared until the accounts of the year have been prepared and the actual divisible profits ascertained. The considerations which will guide the directors in recommending to the members the amount of the final dividend are similar to those discussed above; and it has already been pointed out that in most cases no dividends can be declared unless previously recommended by the directors, and that they usually have absolute discretion as to the amount they consider it advisable should be distributed, having regard to the actual profits earned by the company, and to their power to place to reserve any amount they may think necessary before recommending the payment. In *Bond* v. *Barrow Hæmatite Steel Co* (1902, 1 Ch. 353), Farwell, J., said that the Court would be very reluctant to compel directors to divide more than they thought proper; and the Courts will not compel a division of profits up to the hilt, as they regard it as perfectly proper and lawful for a company to carry forward a portion of the year's profits to the credit of next year's profit and loss account (*Burland* v. *Earle*, 1902, A.C. 93).

Clause 118 of the present Table 'A' provides that subject to the rights of persons, if any, entitled to shares with special rights as to dividends, all dividends shall be declared and paid according to the amounts *paid* on the shares. Apportionment on a time basis may also take place in respect of shares issued within the financial period.

(c) PREFERENCE DIVIDENDS

The rights of preference shareholders to dividends will be defined in the articles, and the question as to whether such shareholders are entitled to simple or cumulative dividends in the absence of express provisions has been considered in Chapter IX, § 2.

(d) ARREARS OF CUMULATIVE PREFERENCE DIVIDENDS

There must be shown as a note or in a statement or report annexed to the accounts the amount of any arrears of preference dividends before deduction of income tax, and the period for which the dividends or, if there is more than one class, each class of them are in arrear. In the case of tax-free dividends, the amount shall be shown free of tax and the fact that it is so shown shall be stated (Second Schedule, paragraph 11 [3] *Companies Act 1967*).

(e) DIVIDENDS PAID OUT OF CAPITAL

Dividends must only be paid out of profits and cannot be paid out of capital, and if the memorandum or articles of association give power to the company to do so, such power is invalid (*Verner* v. *General & Commercial Investment Trust, Ltd* 1894, 2 Ch. 239; *re Sharpe*, 1892, 1 Ch. 154).

Where it is alleged that a dividend has been paid out of capital, the onus of proof is on the plaintiff.

Directors who knowingly pay dividends out of capital are personally liable to make good the amount of such dividends to the company (*Oxford Benefit Building Society*, 1886, 35 Ch. D. 502; *re London & General Bank*, 1895, 2 Ch. 673; *re Kingston Cotton Mill Company* (No. 2), 1896, 2 Ch. 279); but where such payment was made on the faith of a *bona fide* valuation of a company's assets, which subsequently proved to be an over-estimate, the directors were not liable (*Stringer's Case*, 1869, 4 Ch. 475; *Rance's Case*, 1870, 6 Ch. 104); although if the articles state that dividends are only payable out of realized profits, the directors may be responsible for a dividend paid out of estimated profits (*Oxford Benefit Building Society*, 1886, 35 Ch. D. 502).

Directors are entitled to rely upon reports and valuations of trusted officers of a company, unless there is ground for suspicion (*Re Kingston Cotton Mill Co* [No. 2], 1896, 2 Ch. 279; *Dovey* v. *Cory*, 1901, A.C. 477).

If dividends are received by members who know that they have been paid out of capital, the directors may have a right of indemnity against such members to the extent that they have respectively received dividends, although they have no such right of indemnity if they represented that the dividend was paid out of profits (*Moxham* v. *Grant*, 1900, 1 Q.B. 88); but the directors will primarily be liable to the company (*Re Alexandra Palace Co*, 1882, 21 Ch. D. 149; *National Funds Assurance Co*, 1878, 10 Ch. D. 118). Where an interim dividend has been paid out of capital owing to a *bona fide* mistake, and the directors propose to recoup such dividend out of profits before distributing any further dividends, a member who has received such dividend cannot maintain an action against the directors (*Towers* v. *African Tug Co*, 1904, 1 Ch. 558); and when dividends improperly paid out of capital have been made good out of subsequent profits, liability ceases to attach to the directors (*Boaler* v. *The Watchmakers' Alliance, and others*, 1903, Acct. L.R. 23).

The liability of the auditor in connection with the payment of dividends out of capital is fully dealt with in Chapter XII.

(F) SCRIP DIVIDENDS

Power is sometimes taken to pay dividends in kind, i.e. by the distribution of specific assets, but unless there is such power, dividends must be paid in cash (*Wood* v. *Odessa Water Works*

Co, 1889, 24 Ch. D. 636; *Hoole* v. *Great Western Railway Company*, 1867, 3 Ch. App. 262).

Power is sometimes taken by finance companies and others to pay dividends by the distribution of shares or debentures held by them in other companies, and such a distribution is known as a scrip dividend. The shares etc., should be distributed to the members of the company in the same proportion as that in which they are entitled to cash dividends. The distribution must be made free of income tax, and would thus represent to the shareholders a dividend of such an amount as, after deduction of income tax at the standard rate, would leave a net sum equal to the value of the scrip distributed. Power to pay scrip dividends is given by clause 120 of Table 'A'.

The process of capitalizing reserves by the distribution of a bonus, to be satisfied by either an issue of fully-paid shares, or to be applied in reduction of uncalled liability on shares already issued, has been dealt with in Chapter IX, § 14.

(G) VOUCHING DIVIDENDS

The auditor must examine the terms of the resolution of the directors or shareholders by which the dividend has been declared and satisfy himself that the dividend rights attaching to each class of shares, as defined by the articles, have been complied with. A representative number of the entries on the dividend list should be tested with the register of members, and a number of the calculations of gross and net dividends shown as payable to individual shareholders should also be checked. It must be seen that the total of the shareholdings shown by the list agrees with the total issued share capital of the class on which the dividend is payable, and that the totals of the columns for gross dividend, income tax and net dividend are in agreement with the dividend declared.

It is usual, in the case of public companies, for a separate banking account to be opened for each dividend declared, an amount equal to the total of the net dividend payable being transferred thereto from the main account. The bank statement should be checked or tested with the dividend list and the balance, representing dividends so far unclaimed, identified and also verified by banker's certificate. The auditor should vouch a number of the entries on the dividend list with the returned dividend warrants, seeing that the cheques were made payable to the shareholders concerned or in accordance with mandates given by them to the company authorizing payment to be made to bankers or others.

Where scrip dividends are issued, a schedule should be submitted to the auditor, showing the shares allotted or transferred to each member, which he should check with the receipts obtained from the members. Where no such receipts have been obtained, reference should be made to the secretary of the company whose shares have been distributed for verification of the schedule.

Under the *Finance Act 1965*, income tax deducted from dividends paid must be paid over to the Inland Revenue under Schedule F. The auditor should verify the payments so made and examine the entries in the company's income tax account relating thereto. The treatment of taxation has been fully dealt with at the close of Chapter IX.

(H) UNCLAIMED DIVIDENDS

Dividends are sometimes unclaimed, and where this is so, the amount should be shown as a liability on the balance sheet. If a separate banking account is utilized for the payment of dividends, the unclaimed dividends will appear as a balance on this account as against the corresponding liability.

Dividends constitute a specialty debt and as such do not become statute barred for twelve years.

Power may be taken in the articles to forfeit unclaimed dividends but this is unusual, since the London Stock Exchange will not grant an official quotation of the shares where the company has this power.

(I) RESERVES FOR THE EQUALIZATION OF DIVIDENDS

Where the profits of a company fluctuate considerably from year to year, it is sometimes found desirable to institute a reserve for the equalization of dividends, profits being transferred to the credit of this account in good years, and withdrawn subsequently should the current year's profits be insufficient to pay the rate of dividend desired.

If the circumstances of the company are such that the amounts so placed to the credit of the equalization reserve are liable to become locked up in the general assets of the company, and thus not readily available for the payment of cash dividends when required, it may be desirable that the amounts placed to the credit of the equalization reserve account should be represented by specific investments, which can be realized as occasion arises.

Equalization reserves will be shown in the balance sheet as revenue reserves.

CHAPTER XI

THE FORM OF ACCOUNTS

§ 1. The Form of Final Accounts

Although it is not the duty of the auditor to draft the accounts, he must see that the form in which they are presented is such as to exhibit a true and fair view of the state of the affairs of the undertaking, and, in the case of companies, that the accounts disclose all the information which is required by statute to be given therein. Certain companies are obliged by law to present their accounts in a prescribed form, and the auditor must see that the relevant requirements have been complied with. In other cases, any adequate form may be employed so long as the statutory information is given.

The final accounts of a concern will normally comprise a profit and loss (or income and expenditure) account and a balance sheet, and any associated schedules to be read in conjunction therewith.

§ 2. The Profit and Loss Account

The auditor is very often asked to prepare, in his capacity as accountant, the balance sheet and profit and loss account of an undertaking. In doing this, he should bear in mind that these accounts should afford his client as much information as possible, and he must take into consideration the ability of his client to understand formal accounts. For this reason it is sometimes advisable to prepare the profit and loss account in the form of a statement, rather than a ledger account, since the process of arriving at the net profit for the period is more readily grasped when the statement form is used.

The following is a condensed form of a profit and loss statement for the use of the management of a business:

TRADING AND PROFIT AND LOSS ACCOUNT FOR THE YEAR ENDED 31st DECEMBER 19..

	£	£	£
SALES			—
Less: COST OF SALES			
Opening Stock		—	
Purchases		—	
Carriage Inwards		—	
		—	
Less: Closing Stock		—	
		—	—
GROSS PROFIT ON SALES			—
Deduct:			
ADMINISTRATION			
Salaries and Wages	—		
Directors' Remuneration ..	—		
Rates and Insurances	—		
Printing and Stationery ..	—		
General Expenses	—		
Repairs and Renewals	—		
Depreciation	—		
		—	
SELLING			
Travellers' Salaries and Expenses	—		
Advertising	—		
Bad Debts	—		
		—	
FINANCE			
Debenture Interest	—		
Bank Interest	—		
Discount Allowed	—		
	—		
Less: Discount Received ..	—	—	
NET PROFIT FOR YEAR ..			—
Less:			
Preference Dividend	—		
Transfer to Reserve	—	—	
			—
UNAPPROPRIATED PROFIT FOR YEAR			—
Add: Balance brought forward ..			—
BALANCE CARRIED FORWARD ..			£ —

Of course, in practice, a statement such as the one shown above for the use of management, would include additional columns for comparative purposes, and for the purpose of expressing items of expenditure as a percentage of turnover. The precise design of the statement will in all cases be determined by the particular requirements of the management, and will, especially in the case of larger manufacturing organizations, afford a useful link with the costing and budgetary records.

Although the auditor is not responsible for the form of the profit and loss account, he is bound, in the case of companies, to satisfy himself that it contains all the information required by the Companies Acts to be given therein, as in his report to the members he must state whether in his opinion such account:

(a) has been properly prepared in accordance with the provisions of the Acts;

(b) gives a true and fair view of the company's profit or loss for its financial year.

The requirements of the Acts in this regard have been dealt with in detail in Chapter IX.

Many companies still present the profit and loss account in the conventional ledger account form, but an increasing number prepare the account in the form of a financial statement as shown below, as this is considered to be more intelligible to shareholders unversed in the science of accounting. It will be appreciated that the published profit and loss account of a public company cannot disclose the detailed information given in the accounts prepared for the use of the management, but the maximum possible information to shareholders should be furnished thereby, and the Companies Acts 1948 and 1967 ensure that the minimum essential information is given. The large increase in the amount of detailed information required to be disclosed under the amended Eighth Schedule, has resulted in the considerably extended use of schedules and notes accompanying the accounts, since this is the most intelligible (and convenient) way of presenting such extensive data.

A typical published profit and loss account, ignoring comparative figures, set out in this form is given below.

	Notes	£	£
TURNOVER	1		827,600
TRADING PROFIT	2		126,700
INCOME FROM INVESTMENTS	5		29,600
			156,300
INTEREST CHARGES	6		8,000
PROFIT BEFORE TAXATION			148,300
TAXATION	7		88,000
PROFIT AFTER TAXATION			60,300

APPROPRIATED AS FOLLOWS:

DIVIDENDS PAID AND PROPOSED
(GROSS)

6 per cent. Cumulative Redeemable Preference Shares	4,200	
7 per cent. Cumulative Preference Shares	5,600	
Ordinary Shares:		
Interim paid 9 per cent. ..	18,000	
Final proposed 11 per cent. ..	22,000	
	49,800	
TRANSFER TO CAPITAL REDEMPTION RESERVE	10,000	
		59,800
		500
BROUGHT FORWARD FROM PREVIOUS YEAR		21,200
		£21,700

NOTE 1 – TURNOVER

Turnover represents sales (less returns) to outside customers after deduction of trade discounts but includes duties and taxes chargeable to customers. In cases of hire purchase contracts, the cash price is included in sales at the time the contract is entered into.

NOTE 2 – TRADING PROFIT

The trading profit is disclosed after charging:

	£
Depreciation of fixed assets	28,500
Provision for renewal of fixed assets	11,200
Auditors' remuneration	500
Hire of plant and machinery	2,100
Provision for possible damages arising from pending legal actions	1,700

And after crediting:

Rents (less outgoings) from properties	3,500
Loan and other interest receivable	6,600
Additional profits arising on contracts completed in prior years	9,800
Exceptional income arising from change in basis of providing for unearned interest on hire purchase debts	700

NOTE 3 – DIRECTORS' EMOLUMENTS

	£
Fees as directors	5,500
Management remuneration	27,000
	32,500
Pensions to former directors	1,500
Compensation to former director for loss of office	4,700
	£38,700

Emoluments of the respective chairmen of the company during the year:

Mr L. Peters for the period January 1st to October 31st, 1969	4,200
Mr S. Michael for the period November 1st to December 31st, 1969	1,800
	£6,000
Emoluments of the highest paid director during the year ..	£16,700

	Number of directors
The emoluments of the directors fall into the following categories:	
Not more than £2,500	1
£2,501 – £5,000	2
£5,001 – £7,500	1
£15,001 – £17,500	1
Directors who discharged their duties wholly or mainly outside the United Kingdom	2
	7
Emoluments waived by two directors	£2,000

NOTE 4 – EMPLOYEES' EMOLUMENTS

	Number of Employees
The emoluments of certain employees of the company (other than those working wholly or mainly outside the United Kingdom) fall into the following categories:	
£10,000 to £12,500	2
£12,501 to £15,000	1

NOTE 5 – INCOME FROM INVESTMENTS

	£
Quoted:	26,900
Unquoted:	2,700
	£29,600

NOTE 6 – INTEREST CHARGES

		£
Interest on bank loans and overdrafts and on loans repayable within five years		5,500
Interest on other loans, including debenture stocks		2,500
		£8,000

NOTE 7 – TAXATION

The charge for taxation comprises:

	£
Corporation tax based on profit for the year, at 45 per cent. ..	68,000
Less: Double taxation relief	8,200
	59,800
Income tax on surplus franked investment income	12,000
Overseas taxes on profits for the year	4,800
Transfer to taxation equalization account	10,200
Adjustments relating to prior years	1,200
	£88,000

Surplus franked investment income of £8,200 is available to be carried forward and set off against future distributions by the company thereby relieving the liability to income tax thereon.

§ 3. The Balance Sheet

A balance sheet is a classified summary of the balances remaining in a set of books, after the profit and loss account has been prepared, and including the balance of that account. Except in the case of current assets whose market value at the relevant date is less than their cost, a balance sheet does not normally profess to disclose either the realizable or the 'going concern' value of the assets. What it does show is the capital employed in the business and the various sources from which such capital is derived, and, under appropriate headings, the expenditure incurred in the acquisition of assets used in the business to the extent that it has not been used up or written off. In other words, a balance sheet, on its own, is little more than a statement of unexpired or unexhausted expenditure. Although a balance sheet may afford useful information as to the nature of the security underlying the share capital, as to the adequacy or otherwise of the liquid resources, and as to the general financial

stability of the concern, it gives little indication of its income-
earning capacity, which is the principal factor to be considered
in estimating the proprietorship worth of a business.

Assets and liabilities should be properly grouped and arranged
in logical order, and separate sub-headings and sub-totals should
be shown of the various groups. All reserves and other balances
representing undistributed profits should be aggregated with the
issued share capital to show in one total the interest of the proprietors in the assets of the company. The *Companies Acts 1948
and 1967* lay down certain rules as to the information to be
afforded by the balance sheets of companies as well as to the
manner in which they are to be grouped. This matter has been
fully dealt with in Chapter IX.

Balance sheets are traditionally presented to show assets on
the right-hand side and capital, liabilities and reserves etc., on
the left-hand side. As in the case of the profit and loss account,
however, many companies present their balance sheets in the
form of a statement which reveals to a layman more clearly the
manner in which the company's capital has been invested.

The following is an example of a pro forma balance sheet and
annexed notes of a company without subsidiaries, which complies with the requirements of the Companies Acts.

PRO FORMA COMPANY LIMITED
Balance Sheet at 31st December, 1969

EMPLOYMENT OF CAPITAL	*Notes*	£
Goodwill, patents and trade marks at cost less amounts written off	—	—
Fixed assets	1	—
Other long term investments	2	—
Miscellaneous assets not realizable within a year ..	3	—
Current assets	4	—
		£—
Less: Current liabilities	5	—
Provisions..	6	—
		£—
		£—

CAPITAL EMPLOYED

Share capital	..	..	..	..	..	7	—
Reserves	..	..	..	..	..	8	—
Taxation equalization account	..	..	..	—	—
Loan capital	..	..	..	..	..	9	—

....⎫

                                 ⎬ *Directors*   £——

....⎭

Notes 1 – 12 attached form an integral part of this balance sheet.

NOTE 1 – FIXED ASSETS

	Freehold land and buildings £	Plant and other equipment £	Leasehold properties Long lease £	Leasehold properties Short lease £	Total £
Cost and valuations at January 1st, 1969	—	—	—	—	—
Additions during the year at cost (Investment grants receivable thereon)	(—)				(—)
Amount added on revaluation of certain freehold property ..					—
	—	—	—	—	—
Less:					
Cost of disposals and items scrapped during the year	(—)				(—)
Cost and valuations at December 31st, 1969	£——	£——	£——	£——	£——
Comprising:					
Valuation in 1962	—		—	—	—
Valuation in 1965			—		—
Valuation in 1969 (see (*i*) below)					—
	—	—	—	—	—
Deduct: Aggregate depreciation and amortization ..	—	—	—	—	—
Net book value at Dec. 31st, 1969	£——	£——	£——	£——	£——
Net book value at Dec. 31st, 1968	£——	£——	£——	£——	£——

(*i*) During the year a freehold factory was valued on the basis of current use by a firm of chartered surveyors at £—— which has been incorporated above.

(*ii*) No provision has been made for depreciation of freehold properties, which are included above at an amount of £——.

In addition to providing for depreciation of certain plant, included at a cost of £——, separate provision is also made towards its renewals (see note 6).

(*iii*) Particulars relating to future capital expenditure –
Amounts contracted for but not provided for in the accounts .. £——

Amounts authorized by the directors but not contracted for .. £——

NOTE 2 – INVESTMENTS

Quoted or dealt in on recognized stock exchanges in the United
Kingdom at cost –   £
Shares comprising 17% of the issued ordinary share capital of
Abstract Company Limited (registered in England)   ——
Other investments   ..   ..   ——

£—

Quoted abroad at cost –
Shares comprising 30% of the issued common shares and 15%
of the issued preference shares of Spek Company (Pty.) Ltd
(incorporated in South Africa) ..   ..   ——
Other investments   ..   ..   ——

£—

Total quoted investments ..   ..   £—

(Market value of quoted investments)   ..   ..   ..   (£—)

Unquoted investments
Investments for which a directors' valuation is given – at cost less   £
amounts written off   ..   ..   ——
(Directors' valuation)   ..   ..   (—)

Other unquoted investments
Non Participating Preference shares and debentures at cost ..   ——
Equity shares (see below) at cost   ..   ..   ..   ——

——

Less: Amounts written off   ..   ..   ——

Total unquoted investments   ..   ..   £—

Total investments   ..   ..   £—

The following information relates to the unquoted investments in equity shares for which no directors' valuation is given: £

Income from these investments included in the profit and loss account .. .. —

Proportion of net aggregate profits less losses of companies in which shares are held (as shown by the accounts of those companies received during the year) attributable to those shares – .. ..

before taxation .. .. —
after corporation tax .. .. —

Proportion of net aggregate undistributed profits less accumulated losses of companies in which shares are held, attributable to those shares for the respective periods since they were acquired .. .. —

Amounts written off unquoted investments in respect of losses of companies in which shares held – .. ..

in year to December 31st, 1969
in previous years .. .. —

NOTE 3 – MISCELLANEOUS INVESTMENTS NOT REALIZABLE WITHIN A YEAR

£

£— nominal of the company's 7% Debenture Stock 1985 .. —
Loans to trustees of employees' share purchase scheme .. —
Loans to officers of the company (including £— advanced by the company during the year)* .. .. —
Instalments on hire purchase debts repayable after one year (less provision for unearned interest) .. .. —

£—

*These loans were made in the ordinary course of the company's business.

NOTE 4 – CURRENT ASSETS

Stocks and work in progress valued at the lower of cost, including an appropriate proportion of manufacturing overheads, and net realizable value .. .. —
Trade and other debtors and payments in advance .. .. —
Bills receivable .. .. —
Instalments on hire purchase debts repayable within one year (less provision for unearned interest) .. .. —

Carried forward £—

Brought forward	£—

Investments:

Quoted or dealt in on recognized stock exchanges in the United Kingdom	—
(market value)	(—)
Quoted abroad	—
(market value)	(—)
Tax reserve certificates	—
Short term deposits with local authorities	—
Bank balances and cash on hand	—
	£—

NOTE 5 – CURRENT LIABILITIES

£

Bank loans and overdrafts (secured)	—
Interest accrued on loans and debenture stocks – secured	—
unsecured	—
Trade and other creditors ..	—
Bills payable	—
Taxation (including corporation tax based on the profit for the year, payable on January 1st, 1971)	—
Proposed ordinary dividend (gross) ..	—
	£—

NOTE 6 – PROVISIONS

Provision for deferred repairs (after deducting £— applied for other revenue purposes) ..	—
Provision for renewal of certain plant (see note 1 (*ii*))	—
	£—

NOTE 7 – SHARE CAPITAL

	Authorized £	Issued & fully paid £
6% Cumulative Redeemable Preference shares of £1 each	—	—
7% Cumulative Preference shares of £1 each	—	—
Ordinary shares of £1 each	—	—
	£—	£—

(*a*) The 6 per cent. Cumulative Redeemable Preference shares may be redeemed at a premium of 12½p per share at any time between January

1st, 1978, and December 31st, 1982, at the option of the company on giving twelve months notice and, if not so redeemed, the shares must be redeemed at par on January 1st, 1983.

(*b*) Options to subscribe for a total of —— ordinary shares of £1 each have been granted and are exercisable at any time up to December 31st, 1976 at a price of —*p* per share.

NOTE 8 – RESERVES

Share premiums (including £— on shares issued during the year)   £——

Capital redemption (including £— transferred from profit and loss
    account)   ..   ..   £—

Unrealized surplus on revaluation of fixed assets –
    At January 1st, 1969   ..   ..   £—
    Amount arising on revaluation during the year   ..   ..   —
    Less: Potential taxation liability thereon transferred to taxation
       equalization account   ..   ..   (—)

    At December 31st, 1969   ..   ..   £—

General reserve –
    At January 1st, 1969   ..   ..   £—
    Retained profit for the year, per profit and loss account   ..   —

At December 31st, 1969   ..   ..   £—

Total reserves at December 31st, 1969   ..   ..   ..   £—

NOTE 9 – LOAN CAPITAL

7 per cent. Debenture Stock 1985 secured by trust deed, repayable
    at par on July 1st, 1985   ..   ..   £—
Other loans carrying interest at rates varying between 6 per cent.
    and 8 per cent. per annum and repayable at par at various dates
    between 1973 and 1983 – secured   ..   ..   ..   —
                    unsecured   ..   ..   ..   —

Other loans repayable within five years   ..   ..   ..   —

                                                      £—

The company has the power to re-issue £— 8 per cent. Debenture Stock. previously redeemed.

NOTE 10 – CONTINGENT LIABILITIES

(*a*) There are contingent liabilities in respect of:

Partly paid shares held as investments	..	..	..	£—
Guarantees to third parties	..	..	..	—
Bills discounted	..	..	..	—
Pending litigation	..	..	..	—

(*b*) The company has guaranteed the borrowings of certain subsidiaries which amounted to £— at December 31st, 1969.

NOTE 11 – HOLDING COMPANY

The company is the partly owned subsidiary of The BBQ Finance Corporation Ltd, a company incorporated in the United Kingdom, which, in the opinion of the directors, is the company's ultimate holding company.

NOTE 12 – OVERSEAS ASSETS AND LIABILITIES

The values of assets and liabilities in foreign countries have been converted to sterling on the following bases:

Fixed assets and cost of long term investments – at rates of exchange ruling at respective dates of acquisition.

Current assets, market value of long term investments and liabilities – at rates of exchange ruling at December 31st, 1969.

§ 4. Group Accounts

Where at the end of its financial year a company has subsidiaries it must, in addition to its own accounts, lay before its members accounts or statements, called group accounts, which show the combined position of the company and such subsidiaries both as regards assets and liabilities and profit or loss (Section 150, *Companies Act 1948*).

A company is a subsidiary of another company if, but only if –

(*a*) the other company is either –

    (i) a member of it and controls the composition of its board of directors; or

    (ii) holds more than half in nominal value of its equity share capital; or

(*b*) the company is a subsidiary of any company which is the other company's subsidiary.

A company is deemed to control the composition of the board of directors of another company if it can, by the exercise of some power available to it, without the consent or concurrence of any other person, appoint or remove the holders of all or a majority of the directorships. The company of which another company is deemed to be a subsidiary is known as the holding company (Section 154, *Companies Act 1948*).

The obligation to lay group accounts before the members of the holding company does not apply where that company is, at the end of its financial year, the wholly-owned subsidiary of another body corporate incorporated in Great Britain; moreover, group accounts need not deal with a subsidiary if the directors of the holding company are of opinion that –

  (i) it is impracticable, or would be of no real value to members of the company, in view of the insignificant amounts involved, or would involve expense or delay out of proportion to the value to members of the company; or

 (ii) the result would be misleading, or harmful to the business of the company or any of its subsidiaries; or

(iii) the business of the holding company and that of the subsidiary are so different that they cannot reasonably be treated as a single undertaking.

If the directors are of such an opinion about each of the company's subsidiaries, group accounts are not required.

The approval of the Board of Trade is required for not dealing in group accounts with a subsidiary on the ground that the result would be harmful, or on the ground of the difference between the business of the holding company and that of the subsidiary (Section 150, *Companies Act 1948*).

For the above purposes a company is deemed to be the wholly-owned subsidiary of another if it has no members except that other and that other's wholly-owned subsidiaries and its or their nominees.

(A) THE FORM AND CONTENTS OF GROUP ACCOUNTS

Section 151, *Companies Act 1948*, provides for the form of group accounts as under:

(1) Subject to the next following subsection, the group accounts laid before a holding company shall be consolidated accounts comprising –

(*a*) a consolidated balance sheet dealing with the state of affairs of the company and all the subsidiaries to be dealt with in group accounts;

(*b*) a consolidated profit and loss account dealing with the profit or loss of the company and those subsidiaries.

(2) If the company's directors are of opinion that it is better for the purpose –

(*a*) of presenting the same or equivalent information about the state of affairs and profit or loss of the company and those subsidiaries; and

(*b*) of so presenting it that it may be readily appreciated by the company's members;

the group accounts may be prepared in a form other than that required by the foregoing subsection, and in particular may consist of more than one set of consolidated accounts dealing respectively with the company and one group of subsidiaries and with other groups of subsidiaries or of separate accounts dealing with each of the subsidiaries, or of statements expanding the information about the subsidiaries in the company's own accounts, or any combination of those forms.

(3) The group accounts may be wholly or partly incorporated in the company's own balance sheet and profit and loss account.

The group accounts must give a true and fair view of the state of the affairs and profit or loss of the holding company and its subsidiaries as a whole, so far as concerns members of the company and comply with the following requirements of the Eighth Schedule to the *Companies Act 1948*, now incorporated in the Second Schedule to the *Companies Act 1967*.

(*a*) The group accounts must combine the information contained in the separate balance sheets and profit and loss accounts of the holding company and of the subsidiaries dealt with by the consolidated accounts, but with such adjustments (if any) as the directors of the holding company think necessary.

(*b*) The consolidated accounts must, so far as is practicable, comply with the requirements of the Acts as if they were the accounts of an actual company.

A holding company need not publish a profit and loss account in addition to a consolidated profit and loss account provided the latter account shows how much of the consolidated profit or loss for the financial year is dealt with in the accounts of the holding company.

It is not, however, necessary to show in the consolidated accounts the information required by Sections 196 and 197 of the 1948 Act to be disclosed regarding directors' remuneration and loans to officers of the company; nor, in this connection, is it necessary to show the information required by Sections 4, 6, 7 and 8 of the 1967 Act. This information must be given in the separate accounts of the companies concerned. If, however, a holding company does not publish its own profit and loss account this information must either be given in the published consolidated profit and loss account or in a schedule or note annexed thereto.

Section 196 (5) of the 1948 Act requires that the information to be given in regard to directors' emoluments, pensions and compensation for loss of office shall include all relevant sums paid by or receivable from –

(i) the company; (ii) the company's subsidiaries; and (iii) any other person.

The *Companies Act 1967* extends these disclosure requirements to sums paid in respect of chairman's emoluments (and the emoluments of the highest paid director if he is not the chairman), and to the emoluments of all the directors for the purpose of determining in which brackets of £2,500 they should be included; contributions paid in respect of a director under any pension scheme are, however, excluded from emoluments for the purposes of Section 6 (Section 6 (3)). Such contributions must be *included* when determining whether the £7,500 criterion applies under Section 6 (6). Emoluments, as defined in Section 196 of the principal Act, are also to be taken into account in arriving at the aggregate amount of emoluments waived, if any (Section 7 (1) (*a*)).

In the opinion of counsel obtained by the Institute of Chartered Accountants the expression 'any other person' includes any body corporate, e.g. for the purpose of a subsidiary company's accounts, its holding company or any other company in the group or outside it. Accordingly, if a director of a holding company is also a director of a subsidiary and the whole of his emoluments are paid and borne by the holding company (such emoluments including emoluments paid to or receivable by him in respect of his services as director of the subsidiary), the whole of the sums received by the director from the holding company must, unless apportioned, be shown in a statement annexed to the subsidiary's accounts. If, for instance, a director is paid £1,000 by a holding company for services as a director of the holding company and four subsidiaries, and the sum is not apportioned by the directors of the holding company, then the holding company and each subsidiary would be bound to show this sum, either in its accounts or in a statement annexed thereto. Counsel further stated that in their opinion, provided that the directors of the subsidiary are not mere figureheads accepting the instructions of the holding company without regard to their duties as directors of the subsidiary, it could not be said that the holding company is a director of the subsidiary.

Where the financial year of a subsidiary does not coincide with that of the holding company, the group accounts must, unless the Board of Trade on the application or with the consent of the holding company's directors otherwise direct, deal with the subsidiary's state of affairs as at the end of its financial year ending last before that of the holding company, and with the subsidiary's profit or loss for that financial year (Section 152 (2). It is the duty of the holding company's directors, however, to arrange for the financial year of each subsidiary to coincide with the financial year of the holding company, unless in their opinion there are good reasons against such a procedure.

The opinion of counsel obtained by the Institute of Chartered Accountants on this matter is given below.

'In our opinion the accounts of a subsidiary dealt with in consolidated accounts need not have been formally adopted by the subsidiary in general meeting. But unless the Board of Trade, on the application or with the consent of the holding company's directors, otherwise directs, the group accounts must deal with the subsidiary's state of affairs as at the end of its financial year ending with or last before that of the holding company, and with the subsidiary's profit or loss for that financial year. If the Board of Trade makes a direction that the group accounts need not, as regards a particular subsidiary, comply with Section 152 (2) then in our opinion special accounts of the subsidiary would have to be made up to the date authorized by the direction.'

It will be observed that the directors of the holding company may, if they have good reasons for doing so, continue to allow the financial year of a subsidiary to end on a date other than the closing date for the accounts of the holding company. The directors also have power to exclude a subsidiary from the group accounts, and if they think that all subsidiaries should be excluded, then they may decide not to prepare group accounts. The Institute of Chartered Accountants obtained the opinion of counsel on these powers of the directors and the position of the auditor in relation thereto, and the opinion obtained is given hereunder.

'In our view the responsibility for giving the opinion that group accounts need not deal with a particular subsidiary or that there are good reaons against the financial year of any of the subsidiaries of a holding company coinciding with the holding company's own financial year is that of the directors of the holding company alone. If in giving their opinion the directors make statements of fact which are inconsistent with the accounts, the auditors will be bound to draw attention to this in their report. Where, however, the reasons given by the directors are matters of opinion, or matters of fact which are consistent with the accounts on which the auditors are reporting, the auditors in our opinion owe no duty to the shareholders to make any comment on the directors' reasons.'

As indicated in Chapter IX, where group accounts are not submitted the reason therefor must be given in a statement annexed to the balance sheet. This statement must also show –

(i) the net aggregate amount, so far as it concerns members of the holding company and is not dealt with in the company's accounts, of the subsidiaries' profits after deducting the subsidiaries' losses (or vice versa) –

> (*a*) for the respective financial years of the subsidiaries ending with or during the financial year of the company;
>
> and
>
> (*b*) for their previous financial years since they respectively became the holding company's subsidiary;

(ii) the net aggregate amount of the subsidiaries' profits after deducting the subsidiaries' losses (or vice versa) –

> (*a*) for the respective financial years of the subsidiaries ending with or during the financial year of the company;
>
> and
>
> (*b*) for their other financial years since they respectively became the holding company's subsidiary;
>
> in so far as those profits are dealt with, or provision is made for those losses, in the company's accounts.

The purpose of the above provisions is to ensure that where group accounts are not prepared, shareholders should be given information regarding their share of annual and accumulated profits, including revenue reserves, or losses of the group as a whole, equivalent to that which they would have been given in consolidated accounts. The information which would thereby

have been provided regarding the profits, less losses of subsidiaries, would have included the following:

(a) the amount thereof which has neither been dealt with in the
holding company's accounts of the year nor in its accounts of
any prior year; and

(b) the amount of profits, less losses, dealt with in the holding
company's accounts of the year, subdivided to distinguish
the amounts derived respectively from current and other results of the subsidiaries dealt with.

The wording of the provisions is, however, far from clear
because, in law, the references to 'accounts' of the holding company mean only the accounts of the year. Taken literally, therefore, the provisions call for the disclosure of figures of profits,
less losses, of subsidiaries for the whole period from the dates of
the acquisition of the shares therein, less only the amounts dealt
with in the holding company's accounts of the year and not after
deducting amounts dealt with in earlier accounts of the holding
company. This interpretation would result in much useless information being given to shareholders. In view of this the
Council of the Institute of Chartered Accountants invited the
Board of Trade to clarify the position and were authorized to
state that the Board of Trade would take no exception to the
requisite information being given on the lines indicated in (a) and
(b) above. The form of statement on these lines could be as under:

	Profits in respect of financial years of subsidiaries		
	Ending in 1969	Other years	Total
The net aggregate amount of the profits less losses (†) of the subsidiaries so far as it concerns the members of the company (‡) –			
(i) dealt with in this company's accounts for the year 1969 amounted (gross) to ..	£10,072	—	£10,072
Less: Income tax ..	3,903	—	3,903
	£6,169	§	£6,169
(ii) not dealt with in this company's accounts for the year 1969 or in prior years amounted, after charging taxation, to ..	£15,000	£10,000	£25,000

† Where applicable.

‡ Where one or more than one subsidiary is not wholly owned.

§ 'Other years' will normally be years of subsidiaries ending prior to the holding company's year 1969; but if an interim dividend were declared by a subsidiary out of profits for a year ending within the holding company's year 1970 and taken up in the holding company's accounts for 1969, the amount of such interim dividend would be included in this column.

(B) THE AUDIT OF GROUP ACCOUNTS

In the accounts of the holding company the shares held in and indebtedness to and by subsidiaries must be shown separately, and in order that he may report that the balance sheet shows a true and fair view of the affairs of the company, the auditor must take whatever steps may be necessary to satisfy himself as to the values placed upon these items. In this respect his duty differs in no way from that in relation to other assets and liabilities of the holding company

For the purpose of such verification the auditor should examine the last balance sheets and accounts of the subsidiary companies in order to form an opinion, as far as he is able, whether or not the shares held therein are worth the values placed upon them in the holding company's balance sheet. If it is found that any of the subsidiary companies have suffered losses, this might have the effect of reducing the value of the shares below their book value, and if such diminution in value has not been provided for in the accounts of the holding company, the auditor should consider the need to refer to this fact in his report.

Further, the balance sheets and profit and loss accounts of the subsidiaries should be consulted by the auditor of the holding company to enable him to verify to what extent the profits and/or losses of the subsidiary companies have been incorporated in the holding company's accounts. Furthermore, where a subsidiary company is indebted to its holding company, an examination of the balance sheet and accounts of that subsidiary by the auditor of the holding company is necessary to ascertain whether that subsidiary is apparently solvent, and whether or not some provision for possible loss in connection with that indebtedness should be made by the holding company.

The forms of audit report, under Section 14, *Companies Act 1967*, recommended by the Institute of Chartered Accountants are given in the Appendix and in Chapter VIII, § 5, to which reference should again be made. Where group accounts are prepared, the auditor of the holding company submitting such accounts must state in his report whether, in his opinion, the group accounts have been properly prepared in accordance with the Companies Acts so as to give a true and fair view of the state of affairs and profit or loss of the company and its subsidiaries so far as concerns members of the company (Section 14). Where such accounts are submitted in the form of consolidated accounts, the auditor's report should deal therewith in terms similar to the following:

'We have also examined the annexed consolidated balance sheet and consolidated profit and loss account of the company and its subsidiaries dealt with thereby with the audited accounts of those companies *certain of which have not been audited by us. Subject to the foregoing,* in our opinion such consolidated balance sheet and consolidated profit and loss account have been prepared in accordance with the provisions of the *Companies Acts 1948 and 1967,* so as to give a true and fair view respectively of the state of affairs and of the profit (or loss) of X Ltd, and its subsidiaries dealt with thereby, *and so far as is practicable having regard to the fact that accounts of some of the subsidiaries are made up to different dates and cover different periods from those of X Ltd.*'

The words given in italics will, of course, be included only where appropriate.

Where group accounts other than consolidated accounts are submitted, the auditor of the holding company should deal therewith in his report in the following terms:

'We have also examined the annexed group accounts, comprising . . . , with the audited accounts of the companies dealt with thereby, *certain of which have not been audited by us. Subject to the foregoing,* in our opinion the group accounts have been properly prepared in accordance with the provisions of the *Companies Acts 1948 and 1967,* so as to give, *in conjunction with the balance sheet and profit and loss account of X Ltd,* a true and fair view of the state of affairs and of the profit (or loss) of X Ltd, and its subsidiaries dealt with by such group accounts, so far as concerns members of X Ltd, *and so far as is practicable having regard to the fact that accounts of some of the subsidiaries are made up to different dates and cover different periods from those of X Ltd.*'

Once again, the words in italics will only be included where appropriate. The words 'in conjunction with the balance sheet and profit and loss account of X Ltd' will be deleted where the holding company's accounts are also incorporated in the group accounts.

In view of the fact that the auditor of a holding company must report on group accounts involving the accounts of companies of which he may not be the auditor, the Institute of Chartered Accountants obtained the opinion of counsel on the responsibility undertaken in this respect by the auditor, and have issued for the guidance of their members a statement which has the approval of counsel. This statement entitled 'Auditors' Reports on Group Accounts', is fully reproduced in the Appendix. It will be seen that the statement includes the following two extracts, which have given rise to a certain amount of controversy within the profession:

'The judgment which has to be exercised in forming an opinion on the group accounts is . . . that of the auditors of the holding company; it follows that the holding company's auditors must consider whether all material aspects of the group accounts have been subjected to an audit examination of which the nature and extent are in their own judgment adequate and reasonable for the purpose of forming an opinion on the group accounts.'

and:

'In the view of the Council there will be many cases in which it would not be reasonable for the auditors of a holding company to seek to duplicate or supplement the examination made of the accounts of a material subsidiary by its own independent external auditors, but cases may arise where this is necessary, for example where consultation with the auditors of a subsidiary leave the holding company's auditors in doubt about the adequacy in some significant respect of the audit examination as a basis for forming their own opinion on the group accounts . . .'

The Institute of Chartered Accountants in Scotland categorically dissented from certain of the views expressed in the statement, maintaining that these views of the obligations of the parent company auditor are not the only possible interpretation of present-day law; are 'impractical and in some ways anomalous; and are likely to have undesirable results.'

(C) THE CONSOLIDATION OF ACCOUNTS

In the large majority of cases the group accounts take the form of consolidated accounts, in which the whole group is regarded as one undertaking, and the whole of the assets and liabilities of all the companies in the group are incorporated in one balance sheet. Similarly, the income and expenditure of all the companies are combined in one profit and loss account. The members are thus able to form some opinion as to the security underlying their shares. It also makes it possible for them to see what surplus is available for dividend purposes and how much of the capital of the holding company is represented by payments for goodwill, or the cost of acquiring control of the subsidiaries.

On the other hand, consolidated accounts may be objected to on the ground that they do not show which of the constituent companies are earning profits, and which are making losses; nor do they show the proportions in which the assets of the group are held by the companies comprising the group. An analysis of profits and losses arising from the various companies in the group may be important where the bulk of the profits are earned by a company which has small capital commitments, whereas other companies which have heavy liabilities in the form of debentures etc., are making losses.

For the purpose of preparing consolidated accounts, regard must be had *inter alia* to the following:

(i) The balance sheets of all the companies must be made up to the same date, or proper adjustments made to enable the exact position at the date of consolidation to be ascertained.

(ii) All assets and liabilities must be classified and valued on similar bases, or proper adjustments made to bring them on to similar bases.

(iii) A consolidated balance sheet is merely the balance sheet of the holding company, in which the item 'Shares in Subsidiary Companies' is replaced by the actual assets and liabilities of the subsidiary companies, which represent such shares. Where, therefore, the price paid for the shares exceeds the book value of the actual net assets of the subsidiary as at the date of acquisition, such excess represents the price paid for goodwill, and must be shown as such in the consolidated balance sheet, the other assets and liabilities being shown under their respective headings.

(iv) If the holding company does not own the whole of the capital of the subsidiaries, the consolidated balance sheet must show as a liability the total interest of all outside shareholders in the subsidiaries.

(Alternatively, only the proportion of each separate asset and liability which is attributable to the capital in the subsidiary company held by the holding company may be included in the consolidated balance sheet, the interest of the outside shareholders being entirely eliminated. This latter method, however, may lead to complications, and is not to be recommended.)

(v) In the consolidated balance sheet it is usual to credit all reserves and profits of the subsidiary existing at the time of the acquisition of the controlling interest to a capital reserve, and then to transfer therefrom to the liability to outside shareholders the proportion of such pre-acquisition reserves attributable to their holding, the balance being deducted from the excess of the cost of the shares over their nominal value in order to compute goodwill. Where the shares in the subsidiary were acquired between two balance sheet dates of the subsidiary, the pre-acquisition profits will usually be found to consist of the balances brought forward on profit and loss account and/or reserves at the date of the balance sheet immediately preceding the acquisition, plus the proportion of the profit (or less the proportion of the loss) that has arisen between that date and the date of the acquisition, less any dividends paid during that period.

(vi) If the shares in the subsidiary were purchased at a discount (i.e. the price paid for the shares was less than the net book value of the assets represented thereby) the discount must be deducted from goodwill. (If this results in a credit balance, then, following general accounting principles, there will be a capital reserve.) If there was a deficiency of assets in the subsidiary (e.g. a profit and loss account debit balance) this must be added to the cost of goodwill, as the tangible assets are reduced by such deficiency.

(vii) Where the shares in the subsidiary were acquired some time prior to the date of the consolidated balance sheet, the reserves and profit and loss account balances of the subsidiary will probably include profits earned *since* the acquisition of the shares. Such profits are divisible between the holding company and the outside shareholders – the holding company's proportion being transferred to the consolidated profit and loss account, and the outside shareholders' proportion to the liability to outside share-holders, usually termed the minority interest. Only the reserves and profits in existence at the date of the acquisition are taken to capital reserve, all subsequent profits being properly taken to revenue.

(viii) If all or any of the preference shares in subsidiary companies are not held by the holding company, the nominal value of the preference shares not so held should be shown as a liability.

(ix) Inter-company indebtedness must be set off, and not included either as an asset or as a liability in the consolidated balance sheet.

(x) Inter-company profits included in stocks or other assets, should be deducted from consolidated profits, and from the appropriate assets, so as to reduce these items to their cost to the group. If, however, there are outside shareholders, only the holding company's proportion of such profit need be eliminated, since from the point of view of the outside shareholders, the profit has been realized, and to the extent that the profit is attributable to the shares held by outside shareholders it increases the cost of the goods to the combine. It should be added, however, that some accountants consider it more correct to eliminate the *whole* of the inter-company profit, on the ground that it should not be regarded as divisible, even to the minority interests, until it has been finally realized.

(xi) In the consolidated profit and loss account the proportion of the profit or loss attributable to outside shareholders must be deducted and included in the liability to outside shareholders in the consolidated balance sheet. Any inter-company dividends, purchases, sales, and expenses shown in the respective profit and loss accounts will form *contra* items in the consolidated profit and loss account, and will be eliminated therefrom.

For the purposes of his report on consolidated accounts the auditor should pay particular attention to the following matters:

(1) The computation of the amount shown under the heading of goodwill. This will consist of the amounts appearing as goodwill in the respective balance sheets plus the excess of the

cost of the parent company's holdings in the subsidiary companies over the value of the net assets represented by such holdings at the date of acquisition of the control, or less the excess of the net asset values over the cost of the holdings at the same date.

(2) The liability to minority interests in the subsidiary companies. This will be represented by the nominal amount of the shares held by outside shareholders of the subsidiary companies, plus their proportion of the reserves and profit and loss account balances of the subsidiaries as at the date on which the consolidated balance sheet is drawn up.

(3) The cancellation of any inter-company liabilities.

(4) The elimination of unrealized inter-company profits.

(5) If any of the assets of the subsidiary companies have been revalued for the purpose of the consolidated balance sheet, it should be seen that proper effect has been given to such revaluation in arriving at the amount of the goodwill and the liability to minority interests. It should also be ascertained that the charge to the consolidated profit and loss account for depreciation, by reference to such revaluation, has been adjusted correctly.

(6) In the consolidated profit and loss account it should be seen that proper adjustment has been made for dividends paid by the subsidiary company to the parent company. If any dividend has been paid out of pre-acquisition profits such dividend should be deducted from the purchase price of the shares in arriving at the value of goodwill, and should not appear in the consolidated profit and loss account. A holding company should not normally distribute any dividends received by it from subsidiaries which have been paid out of pre-acquisition profits. If the holding company has paid dividends out of the pre-acquisition profits of subsidiaries, this fact must be made clear to the shareholders.

(7) If the holding company is availing itself of the permission accorded by Section 149 of the *Companies Act 1948* of not publishing its own separate profit and loss account it must be seen that the consolidated profit and loss account shows how much of the consolidated profit or loss for the year is

deal with in the accounts of the company. For this purpose the auditor must check, by reference to the accounts of the subsidiaries, the amount deducted in the consolidated profit and loss account from the group profit for the year as representing the amount retained by the subsidiaries, in so far as it concerns the holding company. It must also be seen that the information required to be given by Section 196, *Companies Act 1948*, regarding the emoluments etc., of directors and past directors is correctly shown.

(8) Where the accounts which have been consolidated are made up to different dates, the adjustments (if any) which have been made must be carefully examined in order to ensure that the financial position and the profit or loss of the group, as shown by the consolidated accounts, are not distorted or misrepresented.

Adjustments may be necessary in the following circumstances:

(*a*) Where a substantial trading loss is known to have been sustained by a subsidiary between the end of its financial year and the date of the consolidated accounts;

(*b*) where the liquidity of the group has been materially changed by the transfer of cash or other assets from one member of the group to another, or where substantial capital expenditure has been incurred, in the interval between the balance sheet dates;

(*c*) for the purpose of reconciling the balances on inter-company accounts in respect of cash and other assets in transit.

(9) The conversion into sterling, for the purpose of the consolidated accounts, of the figures relating to foreign subsidiaries.

CHAPTER XII

THE LIABILITY OF AUDITORS

§ 1. The Sources of Liability

An auditor's liability, in relation to accounts which he has audited, may arise from any of the following sources:

(1) For negligence, under the Common Law.

(2) Under Statute.

    (*a*) Civil –
        Companies Act 1948.

    (*b*) Criminal –
        Companies Act 1948.
        Theft Act 1968.
        Prevention of Fraud (Investments) Act 1958.

§ 2. Liability for Negligence under the Common Law

Every agent is presumed to bring reasonable skill and diligence to bear upon the work which he is employed to do, and an auditor, who may be said to be an agent to the extent of his duties as auditor, is no exception to this rule. If, therefore, an auditor is guilty of negligence in the execution of his duty, he may be held liable to make good any damage resulting from that negligence.

This liability springs from the general principle of law that where a person is under a legal duty to take care, whether imposed by specific contract or otherwise, the failure to exercise a *reasonable standard* of care will make that person responsible for any resultant damage or loss to those to whom the duty is owed.

What conduct satisfies the standard of care required will, in any particular case, depend entirely upon the circumstances. The general degree of skill and diligence demanded of and attained by auditors today is unprecedented, and the question as to whether an auditor is or is not guilty of negligence in any particular case, is largely determined by reference to the standard to which contemporary members of the profession conform.

It will readily be appreciated that contemporary standards provide an ever-shifting criterion, and this has never been more true than at the present time, when judges are likely to place far less reliance than in previous years upon legal decisions reached when the professional standards and skills demanded of an auditor were, from both a statutory and a conventional viewpoint, far less exacting. This should be firmly borne in mind when considering the case decisions relating to the auditor's liability later in this chapter. Particular attention should accordingly be paid to the decisions which have been made in more recent years.

§ 3. Liability under Statute

(A) CIVIL

(1) *Companies Act 1948, Section 333.*

If in the course of the winding-up of a company it appears that the auditor has been guilty of any misfeasance or breach of trust in relation to the company, he may be held liable as an officer of the company. The Court, on the application of the official receiver, the liquidator, or any creditor or contributory, may examine his conduct, and compel him to contribute such sum to the assets of the company by way of compensation in respect of the misfeasance or breach of trust as the Court thinks just. Liability under this section can only arise on the winding-up of a company.

It is laid down by Section 448, however, that where in any proceedings for negligence, default, breach of duty, or breach of trust against an officer or an auditor, it appears to the Court hearing the case—

(*a*) that he is or may be liable;

(*b*) that he has acted honestly and reasonably;

(*c*) that, having regard to all the circumstances of the case, including those connected with his appointment, he ought fairly to be excused for the negligence etc.,

the Court may relieve him wholly or partly on such terms as it may see fit.

Where the auditor has reason to apprehend that any claim will, or might be made against him in respect of any negligence default, breach of duty or breach of trust, he may apply to the Court for relief without waiting for proceedings to be taken against him. The Court, on such an application, has the same power to relieve him as it would have had if it had been the Court before which proceedings against him for negligence etc., had been brought.

It is important to realize in this context that Section 333 does not specifically include the auditor within its scope: it refers to 'any person who has taken part in the formation or promotion of the company, or any past or present director, manager or liquidator, or any officer of the company . . .'. However, it was in this context that the auditor was regarded as an officer in the leading cases of the *Kingston Cotton Mill Co Ltd* (1896, 2 Ch. 279) and *London and General Bank* (No. 1, 1895, 2 Ch. 166), both of which are fully dealt with in this chapter. In this connection, reference should also be made to Chapter VIII, § 2 (B).

(B) CRIMINAL

(1) *Companies Act 1948, Section 438*

If an auditor in any report, certificate, balance sheet or other document wilfully makes a statement false in any material particular he may be criminally liable under Section 438. The maximum penalty in England or Scotland on summary conviction is imprisonment with or without hard labour for a period of four months, and a fine not exceeding £100 in lieu of or in addition to imprisonment. The reports, certificates etc., mentioned above are those required by or for the purposes of the Act and are specified in the Fifteenth Schedule thereto. The requirement in Section 14 (1) of the *Companies Act 1967* that the auditors shall make a report to the members on the accounts examined by them, is included within the scope of Section 438 and the Fifteenth Schedule to the principal Act. Similar consideration applies to Section 14 (5) of the 1967 Act, under which the auditor is entitled to require from the officers of the company such information and explanations as he deems necessary for the performance of his duties (Section 14 (8) (*b*), *Companies Act 1967*).

Conviction under Section 438 will not operate to relieve the auditor from liability for misfeasance under Section 333 of the principal Act.

(2) *The Theft Act 1968*

This Act, effective from 1st January 1969, repealed the *Larceny Acts 1861* and *1916*, and *Falsification of Accounts Act 1875*, and re-enacted many provisions contained in the earlier statutes.

Under Sections 17 and 18, an officer of a company may be imprisoned for up to seven years if he destroys, defaces, conceals or falsifies any account, record or document required for any accounting purpose; or, in furnishing information, produces or uses any account, record etc., which to his knowledge is or may be materially misleading, false or deceptive.

Section 15 (i) provides: 'A person who by any deception dishonestly obtains property belonging to another, with the intention of permanently depriving the other of it, shall on conviction or indictment be liable to imprisonment for a term not exceeding ten years.'

Section 16 (i) states: 'A person who by any deception dishonestly obtains for himself or another any pecuniary advantage shall on conviction or indictment be liable to imprisonment for a term not exceeding five years.'

Cases of pecuniary advantage arise where debts or charges are reduced, evaded or deferred; overdrafts and insurance policies are negotiated on improved terms; opportunity is given to earn greater remuneration or win money by betting (Section 16).

Offences under Sections 15, 16 and 17 are extended to officers of companies and members (where they manage the company's affairs) (Section 18).

Under Section 19 an officer may be imprisoned for up to seven years if shown to have published or concurred in publishing a written statement or account which to his knowledge is or may be materially misleading, false or deceptive, with intent to deceive members or creditors about the company's affairs. This section is very similar to Section 438 of the *Companies Act 1948*, except that offences under the latter section carry a maximum penalty of two years' imprisonment. Section 19 is also similar to Section 84 of the *Larceny Act 1861* (now repealed) under which Lord Kylsant was convicted (see *Rex* v. *Kylsant and Morland*, below). However, whereas Section 84 extended to cases involving fraudulent inducements to invest, e.g. mis-statements in prospectuses, Section 19, *Theft Act 1968*, is narrower in scope in that it applies to false circulars, accounts etc., sent to *existing* shareholders and creditors. This limitation does not mean that fraudulent prospectuses are outside the scope of the Act, since Section 15 is extremely wide in its application to all forms of fraud, and would cover cases of false inducements to invest. Under this section 'deception' means 'any deception (whether deliberate or reckless) by words or conduct as to fact or as to law, including a deception as to . . . present intentions'. Although it would appear that the attitude of mind in offences under Section 15 is thus the same as that required under *Prevention of Fraud (Investments) Act 1958* (see below) and *Protection of Depositors Act 1963*, 'recklessness' under Section 15 must carry some element of moral guilt since conviction is possible only if property is obtained 'dishonestly'.

Following the decision in *Regina* v. *Shacter* (see pages 217 and 440) it would appear that auditors would be included as officers under Sections 15 to 19, *Theft Act 1968.*

(3) *The Prevention of Fraud (Investments) Act 1958.*

This Act consolidated the *Prevention of Fraud (Investments) Act 1939* and certain provisions of the *Companies Act 1948.* Section 12 provides that:

'Any person who, by any statement, promise or forecast which he knows to be misleading, false or deceptive, or by any dishonest concealment of material facts, or by the reckless making of any statement, promise or forecast which is misleading, false or deceptive, induces or attempts to induce another person:

(*a*) to enter into, or offer to enter into—

    (*i*) any agreement for . . . acquiring, disposing of, subscribing for, or underwriting securities . . . .

shall be guilty of an offence and liable to penal servitude for a term not exceeding seven years . . . .'

The first successful prosecution of an auditor under the original section occurred in June 1954 (*Regina* v. *Wake and Stone* (Acct. October 30th, 1954)). As this case was concerned with the report given by the auditor for inclusion in a prospectus, it has been dealt with in more detail in Chapter XV. It should be noted that Section 12, quoted above, is worded extremely widely, and, unlike the Theft Act, is not restricted in its application to cases of dishonesty involving moral guilt. It has been held that the word 'reckless' 'must be left to bear its full meaning, and be constructed, therefore, as covering also the case where there is a high degree of negligence without dishonesty'. (Per Donovan, J., in *R.* v. *Bates* [1952], All E.R. 842). Reference should also be made to § 3, Chapter XV below.

§ 4. Major Legal Decisions

A summary of the major legal decisions of the past is given below, and a detailed consideration of these decisions, and others subsequent thereto, will follow in the next section.

(A) LEEDS ESTATE BUILDING AND INVESTMENT CO. V. SHEPHERD (1887 36 Ch. D. 787).

Held – THAT AN AUDITOR WHO FAILS TO SATISFY HIMSELF THAT TRANSACTIONS ARE *ULTRA VIRES* THE DIRECTORS IS NEGLIGENT.

This company was formed for the purpose of dealing in loans and lending money on mortgage; the remuneration of the directors was payable in proportion to the dividend paid, no dividend being payable except out of profits. No profit was made by the company during the whole period in which it carried on business, except in one year. The action was brought by the company against the directors, the manager, and the auditors, to make them liable in respect of certain sums paid out of capital for dividend, and the fees and bonuses of the directors and manager respectively. The balance sheets were false and misleading, and contained fictitious items, having been prepared with a view to the declaration of dividends.

The accounts were examined by the auditor, but he was not furnished with a copy of the articles, the provisions of which had not been complied with. The directors were not aware that dividends had been paid out of capital, or that the balance sheets were inaccurate.

In the course of his judgment, Stirling, J., said:

'It is the duty of the auditor not to confine himself merely to the task of ascertaining the arithmetical accuracy of the balance sheet, but to see that it is a true and accurate representation of the company's affairs. It was no excuse that the auditor had not seen the articles when he knew of their existence. The Statute of Limitations had been pleaded on his behalf, and the plea had not been resisted so that his liability would be limited to the dividends paid within six years of the commencement of the action.'

(B) IN RE LONDON AND GENERAL BANK (No. 2). (1895 2 Ch. 673.)

Held – THAT AN AUDITOR, WHO DOES NOT REPORT TO THE SHAREHOLDERS THE FACTS OF THE CASE WHEN THE

BALANCE SHEET IS NOT PROPERLY DRAWN UP, IS GUILTY OF MISFEASANCE.

This case was heard after it had been determined by the Court of Appeal that the auditor of the company was an officer of the company within the meaning of the *Companies (Winding-up) Act 1890 (in re London & General Bank* (No. 1), 1895 2 Ch. 166). So far as this point of view is concerned, the case has already been considered in Chapter VIII, § 2 (B).

This was an appeal by Mr Theobald, one of the auditors of the London & General Bank, which was being wound up, against an order made by Vaughan Williams, J., under Section 10 of the *Companies (Winding-up) Act 1890* (now Section 333 of the 1948 Act). By this order Mr Theobald and the directors of the bank were declared jointly and severally liable to pay to the Official Receiver of the company two sums of £5,946 12s and £8,486 11s, being respectively the amounts of dividends declared and paid by the bank for the years 1890 and 1891, with interest on those sums. The grounds on which this order was made on Mr Theobald were that these dividends were paid out of capital, and that such payment was made pursuant to resolutions of the shareholders, based upon the recommendations of the directors of the bank, and upon balance sheets prepared and reported on by Mr Theobald, which did not fully represent the financial position of the company.

The failure of the company was principally due to the fact that large sums had been advanced to customers on loan and current account, in respect of which the security lodged was entirely insufficient, and the dividends in question were paid out of sums taken to the credit of profit and loss account in respect of interest on such advances, which interest was never, as a fact, paid. Had proper provision been made for bad debts in respect of sums advanced, and interest accrued thereon, the accounts of the company would not have shown a profit, but a loss.

The Court held that the auditor was liable to refund, by way of damages, the amount of the second dividend, on the ground that he was aware of the critical position of affairs, and acted negligently in not reporting the facts to the shareholders, although he reported them to the directors. As regards the first dividend, the Court did not hold the auditor liable, as it was of opinion that the evidence was not sufficiently strong to establish a case of misfeasance against him, although it thought he was guilty of an error of judgment.

In the course of his judgment, Lindley, L.J., said (Acct. L.R. 1895, 173).

'It is no part of an auditor's duty to give advice either to directors or shareholders as to what they ought to do. An auditor has nothing to do with the prudence or imprudence of making loans with or without security. It is nothing to him whether the business of a company is being conducted prudently or imprudently, profitably or unprofitably; it is nothing to him whether dividends are properly or improperly declared, provided he discharges his own duty to the shareholders. His business is to ascertain and state the true financial position of the company at the time of the audit and his duty is confined to that. But then comes the question: How is he to ascertain such position? The answer is: By examining the books of the company. But he does not discharge his duty by doing this without enquiry, and without taking any trouble to see that the books of the company themselves show the company's true position. He must take reasonable care to ascertain that they do. Unless he does this, his duty will be worse than a farce. Assuming the books to be so kept as to show the true position of the company, the auditor has to frame a balance-sheet showing that position according to the books, and to certify that the balance-sheet presented is correct in that sense. But his first duty is to examine the books, not merely for the purpose of ascertaining what they do show, but also for the purpose of satisfying himself that they show the true financial position of the company. An auditor, however, is not bound to do more than exercise reasonable care and skill in making enquiries and investigations. He is not an insurer; he does not guarantee that the books do correctly show the true position of the company's affairs; he does not guarantee that his balance-sheet is accurate according to the books of the company. If he did, he would be responsible for an error on his part, even if he were himself deceived, without any want of reasonable care on his part – say by the fraudulent concealment of a book from him. His obligation is not so onerous as this.

'Such I take to be the duty of the auditor; he must be honest – that is, he must not certify what he does not believe to be true, and he must take reasonable care and skill before he believes that what he certifies is true.

'What is reasonable care in any particular case must depend upon the circumstances of that case. Where there is nothing to excite suspicion, very little enquiry will be reasonable and quite sufficient; and in practice, I believe, businessmen select a few cases haphazard, see that they are right, and assume that others like them are correct also. When suspicion is aroused, more care is obviously necessary; but still, an auditor is not bound to exercise more than reasonable care and skill, even in a case of suspicion; and he is perfectly justified in acting on the opinion of an expert where special knowledge is required. . . .

'A person whose duty it is to convey information to others does not discharge that duty by simply giving them so much information as is calculated to induce them, or some of them, to ask for more. Information and means of information are by no means equivalent terms. . . . An auditor who gives shareholders means of information, instead of information, in respect of a company's financial position, does so at his peril, and runs the very serious risk of being held, judicially, to have failed to discharge his duty.

'In this case I have no hesitation in saying that Mr Theobald did fail to discharge his duty to the shareholders, in certifying and laying before them the balance sheet of February, 1892, without any reference to the report which he laid before the directors, and with no other warning than is conveyed by the words, "The value of the assets as shown on the balance sheet is dependent upon realization. . . . " It is a mere truism to say that the value of loans and securities depends upon their realization. We are told that a statement to that effect is so unusual that the mere presence of those words is enough to excite suspicion. But, as already stated, the duty of an auditor is to convey information, not to arouse enquiry, and although an auditor might infer from an unusual statement that something was seriously wrong, it by no means follows that ordinary people would have their suspicions aroused by a similar statement if, as in this case, its language expresses no more than any ordinary person would infer without it.'

In the course of his judgment, Rigby, L.J., said:

'The words "as shown by the books of the company" seem to me to be introduced to relieve the auditors from any responsibility as to affairs of the company kept out of the books and concealed from them, but not to confine it to a mere statement of the correspondence of the balance sheet with the entries in the books. Now, a full and fair balance sheet must be such a balance sheet as to convey a truthful statement as to the company's position. It must not conceal any known cause of weakness in the financial position, or suggest anything which cannot be supported as fairly correct in a business point of view.'

(C) IN RE THE KINGSTON COTTON MILL CO., LIMITED (No. 2). (1896 2 Ch. 279).

Held – THAT IT IS NOT THE DUTY OF THE AUDITOR TO TAKE STOCK; AND THAT HE IS NOT GUILTY OF NEGLIGENCE IF HE ACCEPTS THE CERTIFICATE OF A RESPONSIBLE OFFICIAL IN THE ABSENCE OF SUSPICIOUS CIRCUMSTANCES.

This case was heard after it had been determined by the Court of Appeal that the auditors of the company were officers of the company within the meaning of the *Companies (Winding-up) Act 1890* (*In re Kingston Cotton Mill Company, Ltd* (No. 1),

1896 1 Ch. 6). So far as this point of view is concerned, the case has already been considered in Chapter VIII, § 2 (B).

This was an appeal by the auditors of the Kingston Cotton Mill Company, Ltd (then in liquidation), against an order made by Vaughan Williams, J., under Section 10, *Companies* (*Winding-up*) *Act 1890* (now Section 333 of the 1948 Act,) under which they were made liable to contribute to the assets of the company a sum equal to the amount improperly applied in payment of dividends on the faith of certain balance sheets examined by them. The profits of the company were increased fictitiously by deliberate manipulation of the quantities and values of the stock-in-trade, and the question was whether the auditors were guilty of negligence in accepting the certificate of the manager as to the correctness of the stock-in-trade without checking the stock in detail. The facts of the case appear sufficiently from the following extract from the judgment of Lindley, L.J., (Acct. L.R. 1896, 77).

'For several years frauds were committed by the manager, who in order to bolster up the company and make it appear flourishing when it was the reverse, deliberately exaggerated both the quantities and values of the cotton and yarn in the company's mills. . . . The auditors took the entry of the stock-in-trade at the beginning of the year from the last preceding balance sheet, and they took the values of the stock-in-trade at the end of the year from the stock journal. The book contained a series of accounts under various heads purporting to show the quantities and values of the company's stock-in-trade at the end of each year, and a summary of all the accounts showing the total value of such stock-in-trade. The summary was signed by the manager, and the value as shown by it was adopted by the auditors and was inserted as an asset in the balance sheet, but "as per manager's certificate". The summary always corresponded with the accounts summarized, and the auditors ascertained that this was the case. But they did not examine further into the accuracy of the accounts summarized. The auditors did not profess to guarantee the correctness of this item. They assumed no responsibility for it. They took the item from the manager, and the entry in the balance sheet showed that they did so. I confess I cannot see that their omission to check his returns was a breach of their duty to the company. It is no part of the auditor's duty to take stock. No one contends that it is. He must rely on other people for details of the stock-in-trade in hand. In the case of a cotton mill he must rely on some skilled person for the materials necessary to enable him to enter the stock-in-trade at its proper value in the balance sheet.'

Lopes, L.J., in the course of his judgment made the following remarks:

'It is the duty of an auditor to bring to bear on the work he has to perform that skill, care and caution which a reasonably competent, careful and cautious auditor would use. What is reasonable skill, care and caution must depend on the particular circumstances of each case. An auditor is not bound to be a detective, or, as was said, to approach his work with suspicion or with a foregone conclusion that there is something wrong. He is a watchdog, but not a bloodhound. He is justified in believing tried servants of the company in whom confidence is placed by the company. He is entitled to assume that they are honest, and to rely upon their representations, provided he takes reasonable care. If there is anything calculated to excite suspicion he should probe it to the bottom, but in the absence of anything of that kind, he is only bound to be reasonably cautious and careful. . . . The duties of auditors must not be rendered too onerous. Their work is responsible and laborious, and the remuneration moderate. I should be sorry to see the liability of auditors extended any further than in *In Re The London & General Bank* (*supra*), indeed, I only assented to that decision on account of the inconsistency of the statement made to the directors with the balance sheet certified by the auditors and presented to the shareholders. This satisfied my mind that the auditors deliberately concealed that from the shareholders which they had communicated to the directors. It would be difficult to say this was not a breach of duty. Auditors must not be made liable for not tracking out ingenious and carefully laid schemes of fraud, when there is nothing to arouse their suspicion and when those frauds are perpetrated by tried servants of the company and are undetected for years by the directors. So to hold would make the position of an auditor intolerable.'

(D) THE IRISH WOOLLEN CO, LIMITED, v. TYSON AND OTHERS (1900 Acct. L.R. 13.)

Held – THAT AN AUDITOR IS LIABLE FOR ANY DAMAGE SUSTAINED BY A COMPANY BY REASON OF FALSIFICATIONS WHICH MIGHT HAVE BEEN DISCOVERED BY THE EXERCISE OF REASONABLE CARE AND SKILL IN THE PERFORMANCE OF THE AUDIT.

This case was heard before the Irish Court of Appeal, and was an appeal by Mr Edward Kevans, the auditor, against the judgment of the lower Court, holding him responsible for the non-detection of the fraud. The appeal was dismissed.

The frauds were principally occasioned by the suppression of invoices outstanding at the date of the balance sheet, thus reducing the amount of purchases and the amount of creditors. The goods, however, were taken into stock and a fictitious profit was therefore shown to that extent. This amounted ultimately to £4,095.

The Court gave considerable weight to the fact that a special arrangement had been made between the company and the auditor, for a monthly audit to be conducted, which should lead up to the half-yearly audit. This monthly audit consisted merely in checking the current details and did not involve the preparation of monthly profit and loss accounts or balance sheets. The portion of the audit covering the year-end transactions and adjustments was not performed by the auditor himself, but by his clerks, and the Court stated that although the auditor is bound to employ reasonable care and skill, this can also be exercised by his deputy. At the same time, if the deputy fails in his duty, the responsibility falls upon the auditor; and where such failure is due to lack of supervision on the part of the auditor, in allowing the details of the audit to be carried out in a mechanical way by his clerks, he must suffer the consequences.

In the course of his judgment, Holmes, L.J., said:

'Mr Kevans seems to have done little of the actual work himself, and the evidence varies as to the nature of the supervision which he gave to it; the investigation of the books he deputed to his assistants . . . and it must be on the faith of their representations that he certified the balance sheets. I presume this course is not unusual, and that an accountant with a large business is not supposed to do everything himself. The auditor is bound to give reasonable care and skill, but this can also be exercised by his deputy. . . . There is no doubt that both the suppression and carrying over of invoices would have been detected if the auditor had called for the creditors' statements of account upon which payment was ordered, and compared them with the ledger. I should have thought this was part of the auditor's duty for many reasons; but . . . apart altogether from the statements of account and the monthly check, I do not understand how the carrying over of the invoices could have escaped detection by the accountant, who should have used due care and skill, and who was not a mere machine. The invoices carried over were ultimately posted to the ledger. If they were posted to their true dates, it would be at once apparent that they were not entered in at the proper time. If they were posted under false dates, why was this not detected when the ledger accounts were checked with the invoices? And when no invoices came into the books, it is admitted that this ought to have excited suspicion. For these reasons I am of opinion that if due care and skill had been exercised, the carrying over and the suppression of invoices would have been discovered, and the auditor is liable for any damage the company has sustained from the under-statement of liabilities in the balance sheet due to this cause since January 4th, 1892. I consider that not only are Mr Kevans and his assistants not free from blame for this, but also for the mechanical way the audit was carried out.'

The circumstances of the above two cases bear a certain resemblance to the more recent case of re *Thomas Gerrard and Son Ltd*, which is fully discussed later in this chapter, and to which reference should be made.

(E) THE LONDON OIL STORAGE CO LIMITED, V. SEEAR, HASLUCK & CO (1904, Acct. L.R. 30, 93.)

Held – THAT THE AUDITOR IS LIABLE FOR ANY DAMAGE SUSTAINED BY A COMPANY BY REASON OF HIS OMISSION TO VERIFY THE EXISTENCE OF ASSETS STATED IN THE BALANCE SHEET.

This was an action brought by the company for damages for alleged neglect by the auditor in omitting to verify the existence of a sum of £796, shown in the balance sheet as petty cash in hand. In fact, the balance in hand was only £30, the difference having been misappropriated by the secretary, who kept the petty cash book.

The auditor's clerk did not count the balance of cash in hand, but merely referred to the petty cash book, to see that the amount shown in that book agreed with the amount shown in the balance sheet.

This case was heard before Alverstone, C.J., and a special jury, with the result that the jury found that the auditor had committed a breach of duty, and assessed the damages at five guineas. The jury considered that the directors had been guilty of gross negligence in allowing such a large balance of cash to remain in the hands of the petty cashier, and it was owing to this fact that the damages given against the auditor were only nominal.

In the course of his summing-up, Alverstone, C.J., addressing the jury, said:

'The auditor most undoubtedly does undertake very considerable responsibilities, and is liable for the proper discharge of his duties, and if by the neglect of his duties, or by want of reasonable care, he neglects his duty, and damage is caused to the company as such, he is responsible for that damage. . . . The plaintiffs must satisfy you that the damage has been occasioned, to whatever extent you think it was occasioned, by the breach of duty on the part of the auditor. . . . The conduct of the directors is no answer to any breach of duty by the defendant, but it is a circumstance you must take into consideration, because if you are of opinion that the loss was occasioned by the man stealing the money in consequence of there being a want of proper control over him, then the fact of there being a breach of duty by the auditor is what we lawyers call a *causa causans*, which contributed to, but would not be the cause of, the loss. . . . Was he guilty of breach of duty, and, if so, what loss was occasioned to this company by that breach of duty? You must not put upon him the loss by reason of theft occurring afterwards or before, but you must put upon him such damages as you consider in your opinion were really caused by his not having fulfilled his duty as auditor of the company.'

The auditor had earlier contended that his duties ended when he had seen that the entries in the books created an asset, but the absurdity of such a contention is clearly manifest.

However, the decision of the jury to award nominal damages only is important, since it illustrates the point that the auditor is liable only for such damage as flows *directly* from the act of negligence complained of.

(F) ARTHUR E. GREEN & COMPANY, V. THE CENTRAL ADVANCE & DISCOUNT CORPORATION LTD (1920, Acct. L.R. LXIII, p. 1.)

Held – THAT AN AUDITOR IS GUILTY OF NEGLIGENCE WHEN HE ACCEPTS A SCHEDULE OF BAD DEBTS FURNISHED BY A RESPONSIBLE OFFICIAL, ALTHOUGH IT IS APPARENT THAT OTHER DEBTS NOT INCLUDED IN THE SCHEDULE ARE ALSO IRRECOVERABLE.

This case is of importance in that it shows that an auditor is not entitled to rely upon the statement of an official, however apparently trustworthy, where, but for the confidence reposed in him, it should be evident that his statement is inaccurate.

The defendant company were moneylenders against whom the auditors claimed the fees due to them. The defendants counter-claimed for negligence and were awarded damages.

The plaintiffs had audited the company's books for many years, and over a considerable period worthless debts to the value of nearly £19,000 had accumulated. Some of these debts had been outstanding for a number of years and a great proportion were actually statute-barred, and therefore should have been regarded for all practical purposes as irrecoverable.

The auditor accepted the figures supplied by the managing director and the board as to the amounts to be written-off for bad and doubtful debts each year. The managing director had explained his reason for allowing old debts to remain on the books by saying that in a moneylending business it did not matter how old the debts were, because people would come back and pay in order to be able to obtain further advances. Such an explanation, in the opinion of Shearman, J., was not a satisfactory one. On no occasion did the auditor, in his report to the members, refer to the state of the book debts.

His Lordship said that if there were circumstances which seemed to call for enquiry, the auditor must make the proper enquiry, and if he did not take the proper steps to have the matter sifted, he did not fulfil the duty he owed to the company as one of its officers.

(G) IN RE THE CITY EQUITABLE FIRE INSURANCE CO, LTD (1924, Acct. L.R. 53 and 81).

This was an action brought by the Official Receiver as liquidator of the company under Section 215, *Companies (Consolidation) Act 1908* (Section 333 of the 1948 Act), against the directors and auditors for damages arising out of misfeasance. The case was first heard before Mr Justice Romer in Chancery, who dismissed the action both against the directors and the auditors although, on one count, the auditors escaped liability only by virtue of an indemnity clause in the company's articles. Such clauses are now void (Section 205, *Companies Act 1948*). The Official Receiver did not proceed with any appeal so far as the directors were concerned, but took the case against the auditors to the Court of Appeal, where the judgment of the first Court was unanimously confirmed and the auditors were held not to be liable, although once again it was necessary to invoke the indemnity clause.

The City Equitable Fire Insurance Company Ltd carried on re-insurance business. The chairman was also the senior partner in the firm of Ellis & Company, the company's stockbrokers, who at all material times were very heavily indebted to the company.

The charges against the auditors were ultimately confined to the contention that they were guilty of negligence in respect of the audit by them of the balance sheets of the company for the years ended February 28th, 1919, 1920 and 1921 respectively, under the following three heads:

(1) Their misdescriptions in the balance sheets of the debts of Ellis & Co., and Mansell (the company's general manager)

by including them under 'Loans at call or short notice', or 'Loans', or in the case of part of Ellis & Co's debt, under the heading of 'Cash at Bank and in Hand', and their consequent failure to disclose to the shareholders the existence of those debts.

(2) Their failure to detect the fact that much larger sums were in the hands of Ellis & Co at the date of each of the balance sheets than were so included.

(3) Their failure to detect and report to the shareholders the fact that a number of the company's securities, which were in the custody of Ellis & Co, were being pledged by that firm to its customers.

In the course of his judgment Mr Justice Romer referred at some length to the duties of auditors as laid down by the judgments in *re London & General Bank* and *Leeds Estate Building and Investment Co* v. *Shepherd*, referred to above, and stated that, generally speaking, the auditors in this case had displayed great care, skill, and industry in the discharge of their duties. He added, however, that if, even in any one instance, the auditors had fallen short of their strict duty they could not be excused merely because in general they had displayed the highest degree of care and skill.

With regard to the first charge, the judge held that the sums in the hands of Ellis & Co ought not to have been described as 'Cash at Bank and in Hand', but that no damages flowed from this misdescription, as he considered it would have made no difference to anyone, in the circumstances of the case, had the item been included under the heading of 'Loans' or of 'Sundry Debtors'.

In dealing with the question of loans, he pointed out that if directors choose to lend monies to their brokers or their general manager, there is no reason why they should not do so, nor did he see any reason why the auditors should call the attention of the shareholders specifically to the fact of their having done so, although they must take care that they did not bring into the balance sheets at face value a debt that is not a good one. On this point he considered that on the evidence before them there were no grounds upon which the auditors were entitled to assume that at the time of the audit these debts were not good.

The second charge related to the fact that in consequence of the method of 'window dressing' employed, much larger sums were in the hands of Ellis & Co at the date of each balance sheet than appeared to be the case according to the books. This operation was effected by the nominal purchase of Treasury Bonds by Ellis & Co shortly before, and a nominal resale immediately after, the close of each financial year of the company. In fact, these securities were never in the hands of Ellis & Co, but were retained by the sellers as security for a loan against them to Ellis & Co. Similarly, in 1921, there was an alleged purchase and resale by Ellis & Co, of National War Bonds, both purchase and resale taking place a few days after the date of the company's balance sheet, although Ellis & Co sent a bought note to the company recording the purchase as having taken place on February 25th. (The company's financial year ended on February 28th.) Ellis & Co certified that they held these securities at the date of the balance sheet, and this certificate was accepted by the company's auditors.

The transactions were recorded in the company's books, and on examination in the light of after-events it was apparent that the operations were of a 'window dressing' character, but the judge held that the auditors had not been guilty of negligence in not detecting this from the books, having regard to the state of their knowledge at the date of each audit.

The third charge related to the failure of the auditors to detect and report to the shareholders the fact that a number of the company's securities in the custody of Ellis & Co were pledged by that firm. The auditors relied upon the certificates of Ellis & Co that these securities were held by them, and the question as to whether they were justified in accepting these certificates instead of inspecting the securities personally was dealt with at some length, and is of major importance.

In the course of his judgment Mr Justice Romer said:

'That it is the duty of a company's auditor in general to satisfy himself that the securities of the company in fact exist and are in safe custody cannot, I think, be gainsaid. If authority for the proposition be required, it may be found in the passage from Lord Justice Lindley's judgment in the *London & General Bank* case, which has already been referred to. The auditor in that case, amongst other things, "saw that the bills and securities entered in the books were held by the bank", and this the Lord Justice plainly treated as being part of an auditor's "legal standard of duty", though he did not of course mean that in all cases the bills and securities should be lodged with the bank. He meant "with the bank or in other proper custody". Nor is it at all clear whether the Lord Justice meant that in all cases the securities should be personally inspected by the auditor. For an auditor may "see" that the bank holds the securities in the sense that he satisfies himself of the fact. In the case of a responsible and reputable bank this, according to the evidence of Mr Van de Linde, would seem to be the custom of auditors. But I think that it is a pity that there should be any such custom. It would be an invidious task for an auditor to decide as to any particular bank whether its certificate should be accepted in lieu of personal inspection. The custom, too, at once raises the question, much debated in the course of the evidence before me, whether the courtesy of accepting a certificate should be extended to an insurance company or a safe deposit company. Indeed, if once it be admitted that, in lieu of inspecting the securities personally, the auditor may rely upon the certificate of the person in whose custody the securities have properly been placed, the auditor would be justified in accepting the certificate of any official of the company who happened to be in charge of the safe in which the securities are placed, supposing such official to be a reputable and responsible person. At some time or other it will, I think, have to be considered seriously whether it is not the duty of an auditor to make a personal inspection, in all cases where it is practicable for him to do so, whatever may be the standing and character of the person or company in whose possession the securities happen to be. I do not, however, propose to investigate this question further upon the present occasion. *For an auditor is not in my judgment ever justified in omitting to make personal inspection of securities that are in the custody of a person or company with whom it is not proper that they should be left.* Whenever such personal inspection is practicable, and whenever an auditor discovers that securities of the company are not in proper custody, it is his duty to require that the matter be put right at once, or, if his requirement be not complied with, to report the fact to the shareholders, and this whether he can or cannot make a personal inspection. The securities, retained in the hands of Ellis & Co for periods long beyond the few hours in which securities must necessarily be from time to time in the possession of the company's stockbrokers, were not in proper custody. That Ellis & Co were at all material times regarded, and reasonably regarded, by Mr Lepine as a firm of the highest integrity and financial standing is not to the point. *A company's brokers are not the proper people to have the custody of its securities, however respectable and responsible those brokers may be.* There are of course occasions when, for short periods, securities must of necessity be left with the brokers, but the moment the necessity ceases the securities should be lodged in the company's strong room or with its bank, or placed in other proper and usual safe-keeping. In my judgment, not only did Mr Lepine commit a breach of his duty in accepting, as he did from time to time, the certificate of Ellis & Co that they held large blocks of the company's securities, but he also committed a breach of his duty in not either insisting upon those securities being put in proper custody or in reporting the matter to the shareholders. This was negligence, and but for Article 150, it would be my duty so to declare and to order Messrs. Langton & Lepine to make compensation for all the damages that such negligence caused to the company, directing an inquiry to ascertain what those damages were. For it is settled by authorities that are binding upon me that an auditor is an officer of the company within the meaning of Section 215 of the *Companies (Consolidation) Act 1908*, though Mr Stuart Bevan, while admitting that it was not open to him to argue the contrary in this court, reserved to his clients the right to contest the point in a superior one. But Article 150 in express terms includes the auditors of the company in the protection that it gives, and it must be taken to be one of the terms upon which the auditors were employed and gave their services. They are therefore protected, unless the negligence of Mr Lepine in the matter was wilful. This it certainly was not, unless I am mistaken as to the true meaning of the phrase "wilful negligence". I have heard Mr Lepine's evidence in the witness box, and I have inspected many of the numerous documents prepared by him for the purposes of the audits that he conducted. I am convinced that throughout the audits that he conducted he honestly and carefully discharged what he conceived to be the whole of his duty to the company. If in certain matters he fell short of his real duty, it was because, in all good faith, he held a mistaken belief as to what that duty was. As against him and his partner, the application of the Official Receiver must accordingly be dismissed.'

By the company's articles the directors, auditors, secretary and other officers were to be indemnified against any liability attaching to them, unless the liability arose through their own *wilful* neglect or default. Auditors were removed from the protection of such an article by the *Companies Act 1929*, and such indemnification clauses are now altogether void under Section 205, *Companies Act 1948*.

The remarks of the Master of the Rolls, made when the case went to appeal, on the question of the custody of securities are of great interest and are therefore quoted verbatim below. He said:

'Now I come to the last point, part of which is contained in the third charge, and that is the failure to detect the fact that much larger sums were in the hands of Ellis & Co at the date of the balance sheet, and the failure to detect and report that the securities were in the hands of Ellis & Co. Now upon that matter I want to say a word or two about the evidence. In fact Mr Lepine inquired from the bank and got a certificate from the bank that a certain number of securities were there, and then he turned to Ellis & Co, and he got from Ellis & Co under the signature of Ellis & Co a certificate attached to the document, apparently not by Mr Bevan but by one of the partners, a certificate that a number of securities were in the hands of the stockbrokers. It is said it was quite wrong to accept the certificate of the brokers, and we are asked to accept the evidence of Mr

Cash and Mr Van de Linde as meaning this, that you may accept the certificate of a bank apparently in all cases, but you may never accept the certificate of stockbrokers. I cannot agree that the evidence is so to be read, or is intended by the witnesses to be so understood. What I think the witnesses meant to express was this: Banks in ordinary course do hold certificates of securities for their customers; it is part of their business, and therefore certificates in the hands of bankers are in their proper custody, and if then a bank is a reputable bank, a bank which holds a high position, you may legitimately accept the certificate of that bank because it is a business institution in whose custody you would expect both to find and to put securities, and also it is respectable, but the fact that it calls itself a bank does not seem to me to conclude the matter either one way or the other. On the other hand, it may be said that it is the duty of an auditor not to take a certificate as to possession of securities unless from a person who is not only respectable – I should prefer to use the word "trustworthy" – but also of that class of persons who in the ordinary course of their business do keep securities for their customers, and it may be said that a broker does not in the ordinary course of business keep securities for his customers, and therefore he is ruled out because the auditor ought not to accept from a person of that class, whether he be respectable or not, a certificate that he has got securities in his hands. Now, accepting the rule as stated, that it is right to find the securities in the hands of the bank whose business it is to hold securities, and applying the proviso that that bank must be one that is trustworthy, it seems to me that that rule may be a right rule to follow, and I think it is *prima facie*, but it is going too far to say that under no circumstances may you be satisfied with securities in the hands of a stockbroker, because it seems to me in the ordinary course of business you must from time to time, and you legitimately may, place in the hands of stockbrokers securities for the purpose of their dealing with them in the course of their business. With a large institution like the City Equitable Company, with a very considerable amount of investments to make and investments to sell, it may well be that for the purpose of the convenience of all parties it may have been a useful method of business even if it had been examined with the most exiguous care, for the directors to decide that they would in the interests of their business leave securities of a considerable amount in the hands of their stockbrokers, who, I suppose, at that time held a position not less trustworthy or respected than the City Equitable itself. I therefore do not wish in any way by anything that I say to discharge the auditors from their duties as laid down in the *Kingston Cotton Mill* case; far less do I wish to discharge them from their duty of seeing that securities are held and only accept the certificate that they are so held from a respectable, trustworthy and responsible person, be that person the bank or be it somebody else; but in applying my mind to the facts of this case I am not content to say that simply because a certificate was accepted otherwise than from a bank therefore there was necessarily so grave a dereliction of duty as to make Messrs. Langton & Lepine responsible. I think in the light of the evidence which has been given it is for the auditor to use his discretion and his judgment, and his discrimination as to who he shall trust; indeed I think that is the right way to put a greater responsibility on the auditors.

'If you merely discharge him by saying he accepted the certificate of a bank because it was a bank you might lighten his responsibility. I think he must take a certificate from a person who is in the habit of dealing with, and holding, securities, and who he, on reasonable grounds, rightly believes to be, in the exercise of the best judgment, a trustworthy person to give such a certificate. Therefore I by no means derogate from the responsibility of the auditor, I rather throw a greater burden upon him, but at the same time, I throw a burden upon him in respect of which the test of common sense can be applied, and common business habits can be applied, rather than a rigid rule which is not based on any principle either of business or common sense.'

The Master of the Rolls then confirmed the view held by the Chancery judge, Mr Justice Romer, that despite the auditor's mistaken view of what his duty was, and certain errors of judgment, there was no evidence whatever of wilful misconduct on his part; he was therefore protected by the company's own indemnity clause (which excluded liability arising from wilful neglect or default).

(H) REX V. KYLSANT AND MORLAND. (1931, Acct. p. 109 et seq.)

Criminal proceedings were taken against the chairman and the auditor of the Royal Mail Steam Packet Co, Ltd, under the *Larceny Act 1861*, the allegation being that the chairman had issued false annual reports to the shareholders *with intent to* deceive, and that the auditor had been guilty of aiding and abetting in the issue of such false reports. Both the chairman and the auditor were acquitted of this charge, but the chairman, on a further charge, was found guilty of publishing a prospectus which he knew to be false in a material particular.

For some years the Royal Mail Co had incurred actual trading losses, but their published accounts revealed considerable profits available for dividend. This position was largely brought about by the utilization of taxation and other reserves created in past years and no longer required for the purposes for which they were made. These reserves were secret reserves, inasmuch as they were not disclosed in the accounts, and the only indication of the fact that such reserves were being transferred to the profits of the years in question were the words 'after adjustment of taxation reserves' included in the omnibus item of income shown to the credit of the published profit and loss account. It was shown that during the years 1921-1927 no less than £5,000,000 taken by the company to the credit of its profit and loss accounts was the result of drawing upon secret reserves or taking credit for such non-recurring items as bonus shares received. It was alleged by the prosecution that the result of such adjustments was to cause shareholders to believe that the company was trading profitably, whereas in fact it was making losses.

In the course of his opening remarks the Attorney-General said that when an auditor signed accounts, and stated 'to the best of my information this balance sheet is properly drawn up so as to exhibit a true and correct view of the company's affairs as shown by its books' he was stating something upon which the ordinary investor was entitled to rely.

The auditor was charged under Section 84, *Larceny Act 1861*, with aiding and abetting in the circulation of a written statement or account which he knew to be false in a material particular. In this connection, Wright, J., said, in the course of his summing-up –

'What exactly does that mean? The conclusion I have arrived at is this – that it is not limited to a case where you point to a written statement or account and say, "Here are certain figures and words which are false". I think that is to narrow unduly the words "in any material particular". If it is true in that way it would shut out the type of fraud in connection with written documents and accounts which may be of the utmost importance – *the type of fraud where you have a document, not fraudulent in the sense of what it states, but in the sense of what it conceals or omits.*

'I think the language which is used means more than that. It will cover the case where you have a written statement or account which is false in no specific words or figures which it contains, but which is false in the way in which it may be formed.

'You may say, referring to every word and every figure, there is nothing false about this or that, but the document as a whole may be false, not because of what it states, but because of what it does *not* state and because of what it implies.

'Of course, that type of falsity, which is indeed the type of falsity in question here, is more difficult to establish than a case where you can point to a specific false word in a sentence. Where the falsity consists in fraudulent design to create a false impression you have got to show affirmatively that there was a deliberate attempt to create a false impression.

'If you have a definite falsehood then that speaks for itself.'

Mr Justice Wright pointed out that the section involved three things – a false written document, knowledge of the falsity by the person who put it forward, and intent to deceive.

Little was said at the trial about the balance sheet of the company, the main allegation being that the profit and loss account contained information which was false in that it included 'old' reserves without that fact being disclosed.

In his summing-up, Wright, J., made the following remarks in connection with secret reserves –

'We have heard a great deal about the keeping of secret reserves, and we have heard a great deal about the commercial troubles which may flow from that practice. We have heard a great deal about what is often done in practice, and it may be reasonably and properly done, but the question may arise some day, and possibly will arise, in some appropriate proceeding, in order to find out and elucidate these very special matters. It was said by a learned judge on one occasion, by way of observation and not by judgment, that a company, that is to say the shareholders, could not complain if the position of the finances of the company was better than the accounts disclosed. That has been quoted from time to time as a justification for this method of keeping reserves secret. But there may be very great evils if those who have the control and management of companies, and who control and manage companies for the benefit of the shareholders who entrust their moneys to companies, have very large portions of the company's assets left in the secret disposition of the managing authority. It may work very well in many cases; no doubt it does. It is a practice which is being followed, no doubt, by many concerns of the highest standing. On the other hand, it may be the subject of almost intolerable abuse. Such a system may be used to cover up negligences, irregularities and almost breaches of faith. It is said to be a matter of domestic concern between the company and the shareholders, but if shareholders do not know and cannot know what the position is, how can they form any view about it at all?'

With regard to the use of the words 'adjustment of taxation reserves' Mr Justice Wright said –

'Is this phrase sufficient? Is it a proper intimation to the shareholder in the year 1926 of what has been going on in the company's affairs, in order to produce year by year, not only debenture interest and the interest, discounts and other things, but the preference dividend and the ordinary dividend? . . . I am reminding you, although I am sure you have it in your minds, that it is my duty to remind you of what appears to me to be the first question you have to consider, granting all this, was it false and misleading in all the circumstances to put forward to all the shareholders in the balance sheet* merely these words "adjustment of taxation reserves", as a warning that these enormous sums were being drawn from these funds, the nature of which I must consider a little later?'

[*These words actually appeared in the profit and loss account, not in the balance sheet.]

In connection with the auditor's position in regard to secret reserves, the Judge said –

'If the accounts from which the dividends were being paid or the expenses were being met were being fed by undisclosed reserves, it seems very difficult to see how an auditor could discharge his duty of giving a true and accurate view of the correct state of the company's affairs without drawing attention to those facts, which were vitally important.

'No doubt an auditor in his important and delicate duties must use a certain amount of discretion, but whatever discretion he may feel justified in exercising, he must remember he is under statutory duty, and he may come under the penalties of law, if he fails in *that* duty. . .

, 'The auditor is not concerned with questions of policy, but if he sees that there is something in the accounts to which he ought to draw the attention of the shareholders it is his duty to do so. Either he will not sign the certificate at all or he will sign it with some qualifications such as circumstances require.

'The question is not whether the two defendants or either of them have committed any breach of duty to the company, either as chairman or auditor. If a breach of duty has been committed in connection with the accounts, if there has been any negligence, anything for which the directors or auditor may be liable to the company, then that is a matter directly and entirely beyond your purview and consideration.

'You are not here dealing with questions of civil liability. For civil liability the appropriate remedy is an action for damages.'

(1) IN RE THE WESTMINSTER ROAD CONSTRUCTION AND ENGINEERING CO, LTD (1932, Acct. February, 1932, pp. 203–204.)

Held – THAT AN AUDITOR IS GUILTY OF MISFEASANCE WHEN HE FAILS TO DETECT THE OMISSION OF LIABILITIES FROM THE BALANCE SHEET IN CIRCUMSTANCES WHERE THEIR OMISSION SHOULD HAVE BEEN APPARENT.

Held also – THAT AN AUDITOR IS GUILTY OF MISFEASANCE WHEN HE FAILS TO DETECT THE OVER-VALUATION OF WORK-IN-PROGRESS IN CIRCUMSTANCES WHERE AMPLE EVIDENCE IS AVAILABLE FOR THE PURPOSE OF CHECKING THE ACCURACY OF THE FIGURES GIVEN TO HIM.

This was an action brought by the liquidator of the company against the directors and auditors for the recovery of a dividend paid by the company. The dividend was paid for the year ended March 31st, 1928, the profits of that year being shown by the accounts to be £3,458. It was contended by the liquidator that there had been no profits out of which a dividend could be paid, and that the profit shown by the accounts was created by understating the company's liabilities and overstating the value of work-in-progress. The auditors had also acted as accountants to the company. No charge of dishonesty was made against any of the respondents, the allegation being that they had failed in the proper discharge of their duties.

The claim against the directors was dismissed on the grounds that they had all believed in the balance sheet reported upon by the auditors. The action against the auditors succeeded.

In the course of his judgment, Bennett, J., said –

'If the auditor found that a company in the course of its business was incurring liabilities of a particular kind, and that the creditors sent in their invoices after an interval and that liabilities of the kind in question must have been incurred during the accountancy period under audit, and that when he was making his audit a sufficient time had not elapsed for the invoices relating to such liabilities to have been received and recorded in the company's books, it became his duty to make specific enquiries as to the existence of such liabilities and also, before he signed a certificate as to the accuracy of the balance sheet, to go through the invoice files of the company in order to see that no invoices relating to liabilities had been omitted. The evidence has established to my satisfaction that no experienced auditor would have failed to ascertain the existence of the liabilities omitted from this balance sheet.'

With regard to the over-valuation of work-in-progress the expert evidence was that it was the duty of the auditor to check the value at which work-in-progress was shown in the balance sheet. The judge stated that he was satisfied that there was ample material in the possession of the company with which the auditor could have tested the accuracy of the figures given to him, and that he was guilty of negligence in failing to make use of such material.

§ 5. Consideration of Case Law affecting Auditors

(A) INTRODUCTION

A broad survey of the categories of legal liability of auditors, as decided in important cases, is given in this section. The cases described in the previous subsection will be given such further consideration as is appropriate, and other cases, up to the present time, will also be considered. It is most important to remember that the cases involving the liability of auditors which are settled out of court far outnumber those which are given a public hearing, and the comparative rarity of the latter category should not cause one to assume that involvement in litigation is a matter far from the auditor's concern – in fact, both in this country and in North America, the number of cases involving the liability of members of the auditing and accounting profession has shown an increase, and the insurance premiums payable by firms in respect of legal indemnity have been markedly raised in recent years, in both countries. The comparatively unsettled state of many aspects of the law governing the liability of auditors is partly responsible for this trend, and this coincides with the adoption in recent years of many advanced techniques in auditing procedures on a progressively increasing scale. Moreover, as mentioned previously, these factors have combined with the unprecedented demands now made upon the professional auditor: demands arising out of the need to conform to accounting principles which are themselves in serious need of standard expression and uniform interpretation; demands arising out of the need to reconcile auditing standards with the age of electronic technology, particularly in relation to data processing; demands made by ever-increasing complexity in legislation relating to companies and taxation; demands arising from the vastly escalating scale of commercial operations at a time when the tendency towards centralization has never been stronger, and the need nevertheless to maintain the traditional standards of skill and integrity in audit work; demands made by the advent of new situations, such as the requirement to investigate and report on profit forecasts made by company directors during take-over negotiations, new stock exchange requirements, etc.; and, finally, the demands made by the inexorable movement towards higher and higher professional standards, and the associated procedures which are thereby introduced, such as the requirement that auditors should physically observe stocktaking, as part of their normal audit work.

It should moreover be appreciated that auditing firms are naturally more inclined to settle disputes concerning the standard of work performed by them without recourse to litigation, since experience has shown that even where courts have found that no negligence was attributable to the professional work executed, the firms involved have suffered as a result of the adverse publicity which was associated with the suit. This fact has, to a degree, placed the auditor in a situation of which an unscrupulous client might seek to take advantage. In a leading article in *Fortune* an American (New York) legal firm reported that it was handling forty malpractice lawsuits at one time (all involving accountants and auditors), and the same firm estimated that as many suits were filed against auditors in the twelve months to April 1968 as in the previous twelve years!

(B) LIABILITY FOR NEGLIGENCE UNDER COMMON LAW

It has already been pointed out that it is extremely important for the auditor of a private firm to have a clear understanding with his clients as to the extent of his responsibility. This was illustrated in the case of *Wilde and Others* v. *Cape & Dalgleish* (1897, Acct. L.R. 81), where, owing to the auditors omitting to examine the pass book, frauds were not discovered. The defence in this case was that an audit of the cash transactions was not part of the original arrangement, but this could not be substantiated, and a settlement was arrived at.

A further instance of the auditor's liability in this connection is to be found in the case of *Smith* v. *Sheard* (1906, 34 Acct. L.R. 65). The defence in this case was that no agreement to perform an audit had ever been made, and that no audit was in fact conducted, with the result that defalcations were not discovered. The defence, however, was not substantiated, and the auditors were held liable, although no certificate was placed by them on the accounts. The absence of such certificate, therefore, though it may have an important bearing on the result, will not of itself be sufficient to free the auditor from liability.

In the case of *Chas. Fox & Son* v. *Morrish Grant & Co* (1918, 59 Acct. L.R. 29), the accountants were employed to check the books and prepare accounts, but they did not examine the pass book, and were held liable for damages in consequence of defalcations arising which would have been discovered had the pass book been examined. The defence was that no audit was undertaken, and that it was not necessary to examine the pass book in checking the mathematical accuracy of the books and preparing accounts. The Court held, however, that the checking of the books and the preparation of accounts in the circumstances in question, where 'Cash at Bank' was inserted in the balance sheet by the accountants, implied a duty on their part to see that this asset actually existed.

In the case of *Martin* v. *Isitt* (1898, Acct. L.R. 41), a similar fraud took place. One of the terms of the contract for the audit was that it should be a monthly one, but although the fraud commenced in November 1896, it was not discovered by the auditors until April 1897, thus enabling the defalcations to be continued during that period. The defence was that the delay was occasioned by the state of the books, and a settlement was ultimately arrived at.

In the case of *Maritime Insurance Co, Ltd* v. *William Fortune & Sons* (1931, Acct. L.R. pp. 44–51), a claim was made against accountants for the non-discovery of defalcations. The defendants had certified the monthly returns made by a branch of the plaintiffs, and had at no time qualified their certificate in any way. It was alleged that not one of these returns accorded with the true facts, and had the accountants applied at least one of a number of tests (in particular an examination of the counterfoil paying-in-slips) they would have discovered the fraud. The defendants contended that they had been employed not to audit the books of the branch but merely to see that the monthly returns were correctly made out from the books kept by the company's servant, and that, therefore, unless they had reason to be suspicious it was not their duty to impose tests upon the accuracy of the records kept. Mr Justice Roche stated in the course of his judgment that, in his view, according to the terms of the arrangements made between the accountant and the client, the defendant's duties were limited to examining the books, seeing that they corresponded with the books that had to be kept and in that sense seeing that they were adequately kept and seeing that they were adequately summarized in the return to the head office. His Lordship also stated that there was no doubt that had the accountants' suspicions been aroused, it would have been their duty to report upon the matter, but in his view there was nothing which excited or ought to have excited their suspicions, and the claim therefore failed.

Another case in which the charge of negligence against accountants was not substantiated was that of *Leech* v. *Stokes and others* (1937, 81 Acct. L.R. 87), in which a claim was made against a firm of chartered accountants for damages for alleged negligence and breach of duty. The facts in this case were that the accountants had failed to detect misappropriations by the cashier of a firm of solicitors, of considerable amounts of rents collected by them for clients. No proper books of account were kept, there being no cash book nor a clients' ledger. The only book available was a costs furnished book in which were entered particulars of the costs charged to clients and weekly summaries of the firm's expenses. From these particulars the accountants prepared profit and loss accounts, but no balance sheets. On behalf of the defendants it was alleged that they were merely instructed to prepare a return of profits of the firm for income tax purposes, and that no investigation of the books was necessary or required for that purpose. Accordingly, they did not verify the transactions, nor carry out anything in the nature of an audit, neither was it possible, from the material available, to prepare balance sheets. The first year's profit and loss account was certified by the accountants to be in accordance with the books 'subject to our report of this date,' which was in the following terms:

We have pleasure in enclosing profit and loss account for the year ended April 5th, 1928. Costs and Agency Fees: This total has been compiled from the costs furnished book, which, we are informed, includes all costs and fees furnished during the year. In accordance with your instructions, we have excluded the sum of £655 1s 7d as representing costs etc., earned prior to April 5th, 1927, the date of the commencement of the present partnership. Office Outlay: The total expenditure during the year as shown by the weekly summaries amounted to £1,235 18s 5d, of which the sum of £450 4s 2d represented sundry disbursements charged to clients. These latter have been deducted from the costs and agency fees as shown in your statements, leaving office expenditure amounting to £785 14s 3d. If you approve of the account, we shall be pleased to forward a copy to the Inspector of Taxes on hearing from you.

The plaintiffs claimed that, as auditors, the firm of accountants should have verified the records before preparing the profit and loss account, and should have prepared a balance sheet, and had they done so the defalcations would have been revealed.

In the course of his judgment, the judge stated that he was satisfied that a balance sheet could not have been prepared in the absence of a clients' ledger and cash book, and that if a balance sheet had been necessary, apart from being a reasonable and a desirable requirement, which might or might not have been dispensed with, it would have been necessary to write-up the cash book and a clients' ledger. The accountants advised their clients that proper books ought to be kept and a balance sheet prepared, and even provided a set of books in which they made the opening entries, but when they next attended, the clients' ledger had not been written-up, on the grounds that the cashier was overworked.

His Lordship found that 'the instructions given to the defendant firm were to prepare a report of profits for the Inspector of Taxes' and that 'in this case there was no proper book-keeping material available for the preparation of a balance sheet', and 'that there was no actionable negligence or breach of duty on the part of the defendants in any of the matters relied upon'.

In the case of *Armitage* v. *Brewer and Knott* (1932 Acct., p. 836), the auditors were found guilty of negligence consisting of their failure to detect defalcations perpetrated by manipulation of the wages records and petty cash vouchers. The case, which did not concern the audit of a limited company, turned very largely upon the exact arrangement made between the auditor and the client as to the work to be performed. In the course of his judgment Talbot, J., said:

'The documents at the beginning set out that the defendants would vouch all payments with receipts in petty cash, check calculations and additions of all wage sheets, check totals of wage sheets into wages book and check weekly totals, with other detailed provisions, and accountants undertaking duties of that kind could not be heard to excuse themselves on the ground that this or that was a small matter; they undertook a vigorous check, and they did so because that is what their client wanted.'

In the course of the hearing Talbot, J., declared 'that it was the duty of auditors to be suspicious, that was what they were there for. If everybody was honest and careful, there would be no need for auditors'. These remarks have been the subject of much comment in view of the judgment of Lindley, L.J., in *The Kingston Cotton Mill* case. It must, however, be remembered that a judgment must be read in conjunction with all the facts of the case; the plaintiff in the *Armitage* case was shown to have told the auditors at the time of their appointment that he wanted protection against petty frauds and the auditors undertook the work and gave the plaintiff the reassurances that he frequently asked for.

It is interesting to note that in this case the auditors were held responsible for the amount of the defalcations which arose subsequent to their failure to detect fraud with regard to petty cash in an earlier period. In a leading article in *The Accountant*, referring to the case, it was stated:

'As we have said, however, the case gives a footing disadvantageous to the profession for applying the principle of consequential damage to audit claims, and one of our correspondents has pointedly stated a case of pure consequential damage, which merits careful consideration. Thus, if an auditor omits to detect a defalcation by an employee and in the following year, before there is a chance of any further audit, the employee, emboldened by having escaped detection, embezzles a larger sum, is the auditor liable both for the original embezzlement which he failed to detect and for the subsequent loss to the employer as well?

'So far as we are aware there is no exact professional precedent . . . Addressing ourselves then, with such help as we can get, to the questions set to us, the answer to our minds depends upon the character of the initial error or omission. A mere mistake will not render a professional man liable for its consequence, but if the negligence was of the same type as was alleged in the case under discussion, i.e. omitting to detect a fraud which by the exercise of reasonable care an accountant would have detected, then we are inclined to think a jury would take into account the consequential loss in their award of damages . . .'

Much of the question in the above cases is as to the precise terms of the agreement, and unless the limitations of responsibility are very clearly defined between the parties, the accountant or auditor should regard himself as under as much responsibility as if he were conducting a complete audit.

The Council of the Institute of Chartered Accountants have issued the following statement to members on the subject of accountants' reports on the accounts of sole traders and partnerships:

1. Practising members of the Institute have clients, such as sole traders and partnerships, who are not subject to statutory requirements relating to the preparation and audit of accounts. There is considerable diversity of practice among members in regard to the manner in which they associate their names with accounts they prepare or audit for such clients. Some members issue accounts in folders bearing their name and qualification, but without giving any indication of the capacity in which they have acted or the nature of the duties undertaken. Other members give an indication by means of a statement on the face of the accounts or by a separate report to the client.

2. The work which a member does is dependent upon the terms of his appointment by the client who may, on the ground of expense or otherwise, have limited the scope of the work to be done; it is also dependent upon the adequacy of the records kept by the client. There is a great diversity of circumstances and therefore uniformity of practice is neither possible nor desirable.

3. Such diversity provides scope for misunderstanding as to the significance of the association of the member's name with the accounts and any serious misunderstanding may damage the interests of the client or the professional reputation of the member. Accordingly the Council considers it desirable to issue this statement for the guidance of members.

4. It is important that a client (including every partner in a partnership) should understand the degree of responsibility which the member accepts in relation to accounts or similar financial statements. Moreover, the accounts will normally be submitted, either by the client or on his behalf by the member, to the Inland Revenue and may be made available by the client to other third parties. It is desirable that anyone who sees the accounts should be aware of the nature of the responsibility which the member has undertaken towards his client.

5. The Council is therefore of the opinion that when a member allows his name to appear on, or be otherwise associated with, a balance sheet and profit and loss account, or similar financial statements, he should give a clear indication of the significance of the association of his name with the accounts. This indication may be given by means of a statement on the face of the accounts or by including thereon a reference to a separate report to the client.

6. The choice of method and the terms of the member's statement or report to the client are for him to determine in the circumstances relevant to each client. In reaching a decision the essential matters for the member to consider are:

(a) The capacity in which he has acted.

(b) Whether the records appear to be reliable and adequate in relation to the nature of the business.

(c) Whether he has been able to obtain necessary information and satisfactory explanations.

(d) Whether the effect of the client's instructions is to impose material limitations on the work to be undertaken; in particular whether the instructions involve the omission of work which the member would need to do in order to form an opinion as to whether the accounts show a true and fair view.

7. Where the member has been appointed as auditor, he should state that *he has audited the accounts and also state whether in his opinion they present a true and fair view subject to any reservations he may consider necessary.*

8. In the great majority of cases the member will not have been appointed as auditor, although he may often carry out considerable auditing work in preparing the accounts. For such clients he should state that *he has pre-*

pared the accounts and should then make such observations as will ensure that the association of his name with the accounts does not imply that they can be regarded as more reliable than the circumstances warrant. The following examples indicate how this general principle can be applied in three broad types of circumstance:

(*a*) If the member is able to do so, having carried out sufficient auditing work to his satisfaction, he could state that he has prepared the accounts and in his opinion they present a true and fair view, subject to any reservations he may make. Such an opinion should not be expressed if the reservations are so extensive as to vitiate the opinion.

(*b*) If the client's instructions involve the omission of work which the member would need to do in order to form an opinion as to whether the accounts show a true and fair view but the records are *prima facie* satisfactory, he could appropriately state that he has prepared the accounts from the records and other information supplied by the proprietor but without verification thereof (or without verification of specified matters).

(*c*) If, however, the records are materially inadequate or otherwise unsatisfactory the member should state that he has prepared the accounts from records and other information supplied by the proprietor and should then specify the matters in respect of which he has been unable to satisfy himself, making clear the significance thereof on the reliability of the accounts.

9. Where the member finds it necessary to make lengthy reservations it will normally be found convenient to do this by means of a separate report to the client with a reference thereto on the face of the accounts indicating that they are to be read in conjunction with that report. Where the member is able to make a short statement it will normally be more convenient and appropriate for this to appear on the face of the accounts.

10. If the accounts of a sole trader do not themselves sufficiently indicate that they are confined to dealing with the position and results of a particular business carried on by that person, the member's statement or report should contain such an indication.

The failure to detect defalcations was the occasion of the case of the *Astrachan Steamship Company Ltd and Others* v. *Harmood Banner & Son* (1900, Acct. L.R. 49), where an action was brought for damages for alleged negligence, which was ultimately settled in favour of the plaintiffs.

In the case of *Scarborough Harbour Commissioners* v. *Robinson, Coulson, Kirby & Co* (1934, Acct. L.R. 65), the Court of Appeal reversed the decision of the lower Court which had found the auditors guilty of negligence in failing to report to the Harbour Commissioners that a debt due to them appeared to be bad. It was shown that the auditors had reason to believe that the state of the debt in question was known to the Commissioners and that their policy was not to press immediately for payment. The Master of the Rolls in the course of his judgment laid emphasis on the fact that all the circumstances of the case must be considered, and said 'it is difficult to reconstruct the circumstances, but, having regard to all the facts of the case, it appears to me that the charge has not been made out'.

More recently, in the case of re Thomas Gerrard and Son Ltd (Chancery D: Pennycuick, J.: T.L.R. April 14th, 1967) six partners in a firm of Chartered Accountants were held to be guilty of, or liable for, negligence or breach of duty in respect of the audit of the company's accounts for the financial periods ended in March from 1957 to 1962, whereby the company paid dividends out of capital or otherwise irregularly to the extent of £26,254 (net of tax), and made payments of income tax and profits tax in excess of the company's liability to the extent of £56,659. The case was heard in the Chancery Division on a summons by the liquidator of the company.

The New Law Journal of May 18th, 1967, carried the following description of the case: 'The company was a private company of long standing. It carried on business as cotton spinners. Its accounts had for some years shown steady profits and a prosperous business. The managing director was a man of good repute. Each year the auditor's report had been satisfactory. One autumn the crash came. The company's financial position was investigated and it was found to be insolvent; in the recent years in which profits had been shown, there had not in fact been profits. The fault was falsifications by the managing director in relation to stock. He was prosecuted and convicted. In the creditors' winding-up the liquidator proceeded against him for misfeasance, and the sum of £7,100 was paid by him in settlement. In other misfeasance proceedings against the auditors, the liquidator claimed compensation for loss as a result of alleged breach of duty by the auditors in their audits. The apparent profits had been shown as the result of the manipulation of stock. Purchases at the end of an accounting period had not been brought into that period; this had continued increasingly over years. Sales or receipts had been wrongly attributed at the ends of periods. For these purposes dates on invoices had been altered and top copy invoices had been torn out of the invoice books by the managing director. The auditor conducting the audits had asked for an explanation and the managing director had said that these were end of period transactions and it was more convenient not to include them in the period in question. The auditors accepted that explanation.

Mr Justice Pennycuick found, however, that once the auditors had known that the invoice books had been altered, and that top copy invoices had been extracted, they were put on enquiry. Thereafter they should have made a complete examination of suppliers' statements, and, if necessary, should have enquired of the suppliers. They should have reported the result to the board and, if necessary, should have qualified their report. Accordingly the auditors were in breach of duty and were liable to make compensation. The measure of this compensation was the loss incurred by the payment of net dividends out of moneys not available for the purpose, because in fact the profits shown on the accounts had not been earned. So, too, the income tax and profits tax paid in respect of the apparent profits was a loss attributable to the negligence in audit and, though much of the tax had been recovered from the Revenue on appeal, the auditors were liable to make compensation to the extent that the tax had not been recovered. Against these liabilities they were entitled to be allowed credit for the amount recovered from the managing director.'

In addition to the manipulations of year-end purchases and sales invoices described above, the managing director had also caused the half-yearly stock valuations to be considerably inflated by the inclusion of non-existent stock. Accountants of high standing had given evidence on both sides concerning the conduct of an audit where suspicious circumstances had arisen, and as to what in fact constituted 'suspicious circumstances'. His Lordship reminded the Court that it had been laid down in re *Kingston Cotton Mill Co* that it was no part of an auditor's duty to take stock; nor was he bound to be suspicious where there was no cause for suspicion, and the case appeared at first sight, therefore, to be conclusively in favour of the defendants if the falsification of the stocks were taken in isolation, particularly as a certificate had been received from the managing director each year. However, the judge deliberately declined to comment on what decision the Court would have reached if there had been no altered invoices, as these constituted 'suspicious circumstances' in the sense referred to by the *Kingston Cotton Mill* judge. These circumstances ought to have been thoroughly investigated and reported on, and this the auditors had failed to do. No alternative was left but to find for the plaintiff. His Lordship did state, however, that the *Kingston Cotton Mill* case could be 'distinguished on the ground that standards were now more stringent'.

This comment is particularly interesting in the light of the subsequently issued recommendations of the Institute of Chartered Accountants entitled 'Auditors' Attendance at Stocktaking' (July 1968), the major burden of which is contained in paragraph two: 'Therefore, wherever it is practicable and stock-in-trade and work in progress is a material factor in the business, the auditors should satisfy themselves as to the effectiveness of the application of the client's stock-taking procedures *by observation on a test basis of these procedures whilst the stocktaking is in progress.*' The recommendations, which are fully reproduced in the Appendix, go on to describe the further procedures to be adopted in order to check the 'follow-through' of items on the inventory lists to the totals used for balance sheet purposes. These recommendations may be regarded as the long-awaited indication that the *Kingston Cotton Mill* decision should no longer be relied upon as a binding precedent in relation to the verification of stock-in-trade by auditors.

(C) CIVIL LIABILITY TO THIRD PARTIES UNDER COMMON
      LAW

The legal remedies available to third parties who have suffered physical injury through the negligence of persons with whom they have no contractual relationship, have been well established in the long series of cases concerning the tort of negligence, the most famous of which is probably *Donoghue* v. *Stevenson* (1932 A.C. 562) (the 'snail in the bottle' case). Unfortunately, however, the question of liability to third parties for financial injury arising from negligence has been confused for many years, mainly due to a series of conflicting legal decisions, the details of which are outside the scope of this volume. The present state of the law relating to this matter is therefore dealt with below, as arrived at through certain major decisions which have arisen within the latter half of this century.

The question as to whether an auditor sustains any civil liability in damages to third parties to whom approved or audited accounts have been submitted, such accounts having been relied upon by the third parties in granting loans or credits to the client, was considered in the case of *Candler* v. *Crane, Christmas and Company* (1950, 211, The Law Times, p. 96). In this case the managing director of a company had instructed the defendants, a firm of accountants and auditors, to prepare the company's accounts and it was known to the defendants that such accounts would be used to induce the plaintiff to invest money in the company. The draft accounts were shown to the plaintiff in the presence of the defendant's clerk and, relying on their accuracy, the plaintiff subscribed for shares in the company. The accounts in question had been prepared negligently by the defendants, but without fraud, and on the liquidation of the company the plaintiff lost the money he had invested. The plaintiff sought to recover damages from the defendants for negligence or, alternatively, for breach of their duty as the company's auditors to give the plaintiff, as a shareholder, accurate information. It was held by the Court of Appeal (Lord Denning dissenting) that there was no contractual or fiduciary relationship between the parties and that, therefore, the plaintiffs could not maintain an action for negligence against the defendants. It was further held that as the plaintiff had made his investment before the relationship of shareholder and auditor became operative no damage flowed from the breach of any such duty owed by the defendant to the plaintiff in that capacity.

The decision in the *Candler* case was also followed in the later case of *De Savary* v. *Holden, Howard & Co* (*The Times*, Law Report, January 11th, 1960). In this case the plaintiff was the managing director and virtual owner of three limited companies, all of which were heavily indebted to a bank. The bank was anxious to reduce this indebtedness, but the plaintiff wanted to extend his credit facilities. At the suggestion of the bank the plaintiff agreed to pay the cost of an independent investigation of his companies' affairs by the defendants, a well-established and reputable firm of accountants. The subsisting contract was between the bank and the accountants.

The defendants duly prepared accounts for the companies for the five months ended May 31st, 1950, and reported to the bank. The accounts showed that the companies had made a net profit during the period of about £14,000. The plaintiff, having himself subsequently relied upon the accounts and sustained a loss, contended that in preparing these accounts the defendants had been negligent in that the figures for stock and work-in-progress shown therein were grossly inflated, and the figure of profit was fictitious; in fact, the companies were trading at a loss, and he sued the accountants for damages arising out of negligence.

After considering the facts, Mr Justice Barry said that there was a complete lack of any evidence that the defendants were told that their accounts were to be used or relied on by the plaintiff for any purposes. The accountants took instructions only on behalf of the bank. They were the bank's accountants and acted in that capacity alone. The fact that the bank caused the plaintiff to pay for the defendants' services had nothing to do with it. Had the plaintiff not paid the defendants' fees the bank would have been responsible. In the absence of a contractual relationship between the plaintiff and the defendants his Lordship was bound by the judgment in the Court of Appeal in *Candler* v. *Crane Christmas & Co* (1951). A careless misstatement, acted on by another to his detriment, was not actionable in the absence of a contract or a fiduciary relationship. There was no such relationship here. It followed that the defendants owed no duty to the plaintiff and the negligence claim could not be sustained.

Although the issue of whether the defendants had been negligent was therefore immaterial, his Lordship thought it right to express his views on the point. The accounts contained a serious misstatement of the amount of the stock-in-hand and work-in-progress at two of the companies, and the plaintiff alleged that these errors were *prima facie* evidence of negligence. His Lordship said that was not so where much of the information upon which the accounts were based emanated from the books of the plaintiff's companies. To establish negligence it was necessary to show either that the accounts were carelessly prepared or that the accountants were under an obligation to satisfy themselves that the companies' books represented the true position of the companies. The trouble was that the records of the companies were in fact wrong and did not give a correct picture of the stock. It followed that no negligence had been established. (It will be appreciated that the accountants in this case were not acting as auditors.)

However, it was more recently held by the House of Lords in the case of *Hedley Byrne & Co* v. *Heller and Partners* (1963) that the *Candler* case had been wrongly decided. Although the *Hedley Byrne* case did not concern auditors (it concerned the issue, negligently, by a bank of a certificate of creditworthiness in respect of a customer) it is considered that, as a result of the decision, an auditor can no longer be regarded as immune from liability to make good losses sustained by third parties through relying on misstatements in accounts which had been negligently prepared or reported on by him.

In view of the uncertainty which prevailed after the *Hedley Byrne* decision, as to its scope as affecting auditors and accountants, the Institute of Chartered Accountants obtained counsel's advice and subsequently issued a statement in 1965 which sought to clarify the situation. This statement is given in the Appendix in its entirety. The position now appears to be that if a person gives information to another to whom he was under no contractual or fiduciary obligation to do so, but in such circumstances that it was reasonable to suppose that the skill or judgment of the person giving the information was being relied upon, a legal duty rests on him to exercise such skill and care as the circumstances require; and if, as a result of his omission to do so, the person relying upon the information sustains financial loss, the person giving it may be liable to him in damages unless, when giving the information, he expressly disclaimed responsibility.

The case relied upon by counsel in forming its opinion, *Ultramares Corporation* v. *Touche, Niven & Co* (1931), decided in the State of New York, is worthy of consideration, since the facts of the case bear a close resemblance to those of the *Candler* case, *supra*.

The defendants had been employed to audit the books of and prepare a balance sheet for a firm, Stern & Co. The defendants presumably knew that the statement supplied by them would be used as a representation of the firm's financial position in order to raise loans, but there was no specific mention of the plaintiffs in connection with the granting of such loans. The

balance sheet showed the firm to be financially sound when
in fact it was insolvent, the defendants through negligence failing
to discover falsifications and fictitious debtors. The plaintiffs
claimed that they had given credit on the strength of the statement and had thereby suffered loss. In the lower court the
action was dismissed on the ground that the defendants could
not be held responsible to third parties for damages for negligence, but this decision was reversed by the Appellate Division
Court. The Court of Appeals in turn reversed the decision of the
Appellate Division, it being held that the plaintiffs could not
recover on the ground of negligence for they were not parties to
the contract under which the auditors were employed, but that
they might have recovery in an action for deceit, and the case
was sent back for a new trial on that issue.

The danger was pointed out in the judgment of leaving
auditors liable for thoughtless slips or blunders or the failure
to detect theft or forgery *which might expose them to claims 'for
an indeterminate amount, for an indeterminate time, to an indeterminate class'*. The Chief Justice also stated that where there has
been an honest blunder, the ensuing liability for negligence is one
that is bounded by the contract, and is to be enforced only by
the parties by whom the contract has been made.

The case was subsequently settled out of court and to that
extent was inconclusive, but the words of the Chief Justice
quoted above appear to have had the effect of narrowing considerably the field of potential liability for misstatements relied
upon by third parties to those cases where:

(*a*) negligence is clearly established;

(*b*) the persons responsible for the issue of the statement or
document relied upon *knew or ought to have known* that it
was being prepared for the specific purpose which actually
gave rise to the loss;

(*c*) the persons responsible knew that the statement or document would be shown to and relied upon by the third party
concerned *in that particular connection.*

The *Hedley Byrne* decision was given recent support in the
Canadian case of *Myers* v. *Thompson & London Life Insurance
Co* (1967), in which an insurance agent failed to see that his
insurance company carried out the instructions of the plaintiff's

solicitor for surrender of the plaintiff's term policy and issue of a new one to his wife. Thus, when the plaintiff died shortly after, a part of the insurance proceeds was taxed in his estate. Following *Hedley Byrne*, the agent was held personally responsible, for he knew that reliance was being placed on him and his negligence caused the loss to the estate through his failure to exercise the implied duty of care.

(D) RELATIONSHIP BETWEEN RESPONSIBILITIES OF DIRECTORS AND AUDITORS

When considering whether there has been negligence on the part of an auditor, the following important statement made by the Council of the Institute of Chartered Accountants in 1961, should be borne in mind.

Responsibility for the accounts and financial control of a company rests upon the directors. Their statutory duties include responsibility for ensuring the maintenance of adequate records and the preparation of annual accounts showing the true and fair view required by the Act. They are responsible for safeguarding the assets of the company and *are not entitled to rely upon the auditors to protect them* from any shortcomings in carrying out their responsibilities.

Auditors have their own independent responsibility to form and express their professional opinion on the accounts to be presented by the directors to the shareholders. Auditors do not guarantee or certify the accounts but their responsibility is heavy and cannot be discharged without a full realization of the professional skill and judgment which need to be exercised in carrying out their duties. They must approach their work as auditors with an independent outlook and must do nothing which would impair that independence.

If the directors have carried out their duty properly the detailed checking by the auditors will be limited to appropriate tests which, if suitably planned, may extend to only a small proportion of the total transactions unless the company is a small organization in which the scope for internal control is limited. If on the other hand the directors have not carried out their duty properly this will have a material bearing on the terms of the auditors' report and may well involve the auditors in extensive checking, at the expense of the company; but it is not their function to act as a substitute for proper management control.

(E) CIVIL LIABILITY FOR MISFEASANCE UNDER THE COMPANIES ACT 1948

The term 'misfeasance' implies a breach of trust or duty. The auditor of a company, therefore, commits a misfeasance if he is negligent in the performance of his duties, but he cannot be made liable in damages under Section 333 of the *Companies Act 1948* in the event of winding-up, unless such misfeasance has directly resulted in damage to the company.

This section merely provides an expedient form of procedure and created no substantial new safeguard for the interests of the company. Proceedings under the Section must accordingly be founded upon circumstances which would give rise to a claim against the auditors at common law. It is to be noted that Section 333 relates to the liability of 'officers', and auditors have been held to be officers for the purposes of this section, in the leading cases mentioned below.

In the *London & General Bank* case (which was tried under a section of the *Companies (Winding-up) Act 1890* equivalent to Section 333) it was proved that the auditor was aware of the serious position of the company, owing to the fact that large sums advanced to customers on loan and current accounts were insufficiently secured, and he was also aware that interest on such advances was taken to the credit of the profit and loss account, although such interest had not been paid or provided against. He reported upon this state of affairs to the directors, but failed to induce them to make the necessary alterations in the accounts, or to refrain from paying a dividend. Lindley, L.J., said that taking the balance sheet, certificate, and report to the directors together, the auditor had stated the true financial position of the bank to the directors, and if this report had been laid before the shareholders he would completely have discharged his duty to them. The misfeasance in this instance consisted in not placing this information before the shareholders. It was pointed out by the learned judge that information, and means of information, are not equivalent terms, and that 'a person whose duty it is to convey information to others does not discharge that duty by simply giving them so much information as is calculated to induce them, or some of them, to ask for more. An auditor who adopts such a course as this does so at his peril, and runs a very serious risk of being held, judicially, to have failed to discharge his duty'. It is clearly the auditor's duty, therefore, in cases when the balance sheet is not in order, to report fully to the shareholders.

The auditor is not concerned whether the business of the company is prudently or imprudently conducted, and it is no part of his statutory duty to give advice either to directors or to shareholders. Whether dividends are properly or improperly declared is immaterial to the auditor, *provided he discharges his own duty to the shareholders.*

Lindley, L.J., went on to point out that the auditor's duty is not merely confined to verifying the arithmetical correctness of the balance sheet, and comparing it with the books. He must make proper enquiries to see that the books of the company themselves show the true position: at the same time, he is not bound to do more than exercise reasonable care and skill. He is not an insurer and he does not guarantee that the books do correctly show the true position of the company's affairs or that the balance sheet is accurate according to the books. The auditor 'must be honest, that is, he must not certify what he does not believe to be true, and he must exercise reasonable care and skill before he believes that what he certifies is true'.

In the case of *Re the Kingston Cotton Mill Co, Ltd*, No. 2 (*supra*), the stock-in-trade had been deliberately manipulated, and the auditors accepted the certificate of the manager as to the correctness thereof, without checking the stock in detail. The Court of Appeal held that they were not guilty of negligence in so doing; that it is not the duty of the auditor to take stock, and that he is entitled to rely upon other people for details of this nature. *In the absence of suspicious circumstances*, the auditor can rely upon the representations of trusted officials; he is justified in believing tried servants of the company, in whom confidence is placed by the company. Lopes, L.J., said that auditors must not be held liable for not tracking down ingenious and carefully-laid schemes of fraud, when there is nothing to arouse their suspicion, and when those frauds are perpetrated by tried servants of the company, and are undetected for years by the directors. In the light of the most recent recommendations of the Institute of Chartered Accountants on the auditor's attendance at stocktaking, and the judge's dicta in *Re Thomas Gerrard & Son Ltd* (*supra* (B)) this decision can no longer be regarded as a binding precedent.

It was nevertheless valuable as defining, to some extent, the liability of the auditor, but it has been observed that the question as to whether or not the auditor may be held to have been negligent will depend entirely upon the circumstances in each case;

that this is so is confirmed by the decision in *Henry Squire* (*Cash Chemists, Limited*) v. *Ball, Baker & Co*, and *Mead* v. *the same* (1911, Acct. L.R. 44, 25) and, in the Court of Appeal, *Mead* v. *Ball, Baker & Co* (1911, Acct. L.R. 45, 33).

It was shown in the course of the latter case that stock sheets had been falsified for years, and that they contained numerous alterations, which it was argued, should have caused suspicion. It was held, however, that the auditors had relied upon the certificate of a responsible official, and their suspicions had not been aroused in the course of their investigations, and that *in the given circumstances* there was nothing necessarily to arouse the suspicions of an auditor who had exercised the skill necessary in conducting the audit.

It has been shown clearly, however, in *Re The Westminster Road Construction and Engineering Co, Ltd*, that an auditor must make the fullest use of all material available to him, and although it has been decided that he is not a stocktaker, and presumably not a valuer of work-in-progress, he will be guilty of negligence if evidence is available from which the over-valuation of work-in-progress could be detected, and he fails to utilize such evidence.

It has already been pointed out that as a result of the disclosures in the American case of *McKesson and Robbins* (see Chapter VI) the accountancy profession in the U.S.A. has adopted as part of normal auditing practice, some form of test check of the actual physical stock. This procedure has now been recommended in this country, as reflecting the general standard of auditing which firms should adopt.

It is the duty of an auditor of a limited company to make himself acquainted with the articles of the company and this applies particularly to the passing of payments made by the directors *ultra vires*. Where such payments have been made, the auditor must be careful to refer to them in his report to the members, since if this is not done it might be held that the company had suffered loss by reason of its having been unable to recover the amounts improperly paid away.

In the case of *In re Bolivia Exploration Syndicate* (1913, 30 T.L.R. 146), where circumstances of this nature arose, but where the auditors had pointed out the facts or they had been disclosed on the face of the accounts, it was held that damage to the company had not been established and that the auditors had not been guilty of any breach of duty.

Again, in *Re S. P. Catterson & Sons Ltd* (1937, 81 Acct. L.R. 62) where considerable defalcations by a servant of the company had not been revealed by the audit, the auditors were acquitted of liability for negligence on the grounds that they had pointed out to the directors that the system of recording certain sales was unsatisfactory, and had recommended improvements, but these recommendations were not adopted. Mr Justice Bennett, in reviewing the responsibility of the auditors, stated that the primary responsibility for the accounts of a company is with the directors, and in this case they were not a satisfactory team. He stated, 'I have no doubt as to where the primary responsibility for finding out the defalcations of this man Spicer lies. It lies upon the shoulders of the man whose duty it was, as a director of this company, to collect from Spicer the cash that he received. If that man had done his duty in any degree at all, the frauds could not have been perpetrated in the way in which they were perpetrated'. The judge came to the conclusion that the auditor was an honest man trying to do his duty, and that in view of all the facts of the case and the audit notes, the applicant had quite failed to satisfy him that there was any negligence in respect of the matters charged.

The case of *In re The City Equitable Fire Insurance Co Ltd* (*supra*) is one of the most complicated and important cases which have yet been fought under what is now Section 333 of the *Companies Act 1948*, and the detailed judgments are worthy of close study. The Court of Appeal followed the principles laid down in earlier cases as to the duties of auditors, and, as full extracts from the judgments have already been given, there is no need to recapitulate the facts here.

The main point related to the auditors' duties in connection with the custody and inspection of securities. In this case the auditors did not inspect the securities which purported to be in the hands of the company's brokers, but accepted from the brokers certificates that they held them, though in fact the securities either did not exist or if they did exist had been pledged to other clients of the broking firm. At the time the certificates were given the auditors had no reason to doubt the integrity and standing of the brokers in question.

Considerable arguments arose on the question as to whether the auditors were entitled to accept a certificate from a 'reputable' bank, and also whether in any circumstances a certificate should be accepted from stockbrokers or other persons, in respect of assets held in safe custody.

The Court of Appeal declined to lay down any hard-and-fast rule, but indicated that the auditor is entitled, at his discretion, to accept a certificate from a person who is in the habit of dealing with and holding securities and who, in the exercise of his best judgment, he considers a trustworthy person to give such a certificate. If the auditor is not satisfied on these points, he should require the company at once to obtain delivery of the securities, and failing this he should report the matter to the members.

Notwithstanding this, it would appear to be desirable that the auditor should actually inspect the securities in the custody of third parties wherever this is practicable, and, where this is not done, *should state in his report that he has accepted a certificate.* Where a certificate is relied on, it should state that the securities are held free from any charge or encumbrance.

(F) CRIMINAL LIABILITY

There is no doubt that although the auditor of the *Royal Mail Steam Packet Co* was found not guilty of the charges brought against him, auditors were given serious warning of the dangers involved if full information was not given to the shareholders, of the utilization of secret reserves. The *Royal Mail Company* was a chartered company, but this did not affect the principle involved.

No doubt, however, any longer exists as to the information to be provided by the profit and loss account as the result of the passing of the *Companies Acts 1948* and *1967*.

As has been pointed out in (E) above, Section 333 of the *Companies Act 1948* is concerned with the civil liability of officers for misfeasance or breach of trust, and in the major cases of *London & General Bank, Kingston Cotton Mill Co*, and *City & Equitable Fire Insurance Co, Ltd*, auditors have been included within the term 'officer' for this purpose. The question remained, however, as to whether, for the purposes of the remaining winding-up penalty sections (328 to 332) of that Act, all of which involve *criminal* actions, the term 'officer' includes the 'auditor'. This was answered in the affirmative in the case of *Regina* v. *Shacter* (1960: 1 All E.R. 61). In 1953 the appellant was appointed auditor of a company and his appointment was continued from year to year thereafter. He was convicted as a 'public officer' of a public company of falsifying the company's books and publishing fraudulent statements contrary to Sections 83 and 84 of the *Larceny Act 1861*, and, *being 'an officer' of the company*, of making false entries, fraud and defaults contrary to Sections 328 (1) (*j*), 330 and 331 of the *Companies Act 1948*. On appeal on the ground that at the material time the appellant was not 'an officer' of the company, it was held that an auditor appointed to fill an office of a company was an officer, whereas an auditor appointed *ad hoc* for a limited purpose was not, and that the appellant was thus 'an officer' of the company and a 'public officer' within the meanings of the *Companies Act 1948* and the *Larceny Act 1861*, respectively. (It will be recalled that Section 159 of the 1948 Act refers to the 'office' of the auditor.)

§ 6. Unlawful Acts or Defaults by an Accountant's Clients

A professional accountant has access to much information of a private character and, on occasions, during the course of his duties, he may acquire knowledge which indicates that his client has, or may have been, guilty of some unlawful act or default.

In 1957 the Institute of Chartered Accountants in England and Wales issued a statement on this subject for the guidance of its members, and this was completely revised in November 1968, the previous guidance having become outdated through legislative change. Much of the original series of recommendations was based on the distinction between felonies and misdemeanours, but, as a result of Section 1 of the *Criminal Law Act 1967*, the distinction between felonies and misdemeanours has been abolished. This section reads as follows:

1. – (1) All distinctions between felony and misdemeanour are hereby abolished.

(2) Subject to the provisions of this Act, on all matters on which a distinction has previously been made between felony and misdemeanour, including mode of trial, the law and practice in relation to all offences cognisable under the law of England and Wales (including piracy) shall be the law and practice applicable at the commencement of this Act in relation to misdemeanour.

The law has thus been assimilated to that previously applicable to misdemeanour, and therefore all consequences peculiar to felony now lapse, with certain exceptions which are not relevant for present purposes. The particular offences of compounding a felony, misprision of felony, and being an accessory after the fact to felony, all lapse and the Act creates new, but substantially similar, offences in each case, although narrower in their application so that concealment through simply not reporting a crime (misprision) would not come within the scope of the new offences created. Although no offence equivalent to being an accessory after the fact to felony previously existed in relation to misdemeanour, the *Criminal Law Act 1967* has created a new offence for *actively* assisting an offender (Section 4 (1)).

The following extract from the Institute's latest recommendations on this matter is of major importance to practising accountants:

'Criminal offences may be classified as indictable offences, that is to say those which admit of trial by jury, and petty offences, that is to say those which are tried summarily by justices of the peace sitting without a jury. There used to be an important distinction between indictable offences which were felonies and indictable offences which were misdemeanours, but the *Criminal Law Act 1967* provides that on all matters on which a distinction was previously made between felony and misdemeanour the law and practice in relation to all offences shall be the law and practice applicable to misdemeanour. The Act, however, introduced a new distinction between 'arrestable offences' and other offences. Arrestable offences are stated in the Act to be 'offences for which the sentence is fixed by law or for which a person not previously convicted may under or by virtue of any enactment be sentenced to imprisonment for a term of five years', and 'attempts to commit any such offence'. The requirement that liability to five years' imprisonment be under or by virtue of any enactment excludes common law misdemeanours.

'A member would himself be guilty of a criminal offence:

(*a*) if he were to advise a client to commit any criminal offence, whether or not the client accepts his advice; or

(b) if he were to help or encourage a client in the planning or execution of any criminal offence; or

(c) if he were to agree with a client or anyone else to pervert or obstruct the course of public justice by concealing or destroying or fabricating evidence or by misleading the police by statements which he knew to be untrue; or

(d) where a client has committed an arrestable offence, if he (the member), knowing or believing the client to be guilty of the offence or of some other arrestable offence, were to do without lawful authority or reasonable excuse any act with intent to impede the apprehension or prosecution of the client; or

(e) where a client has committed an arrestable offence, if he (the member), knowing or believing that the offence or some other arrestable offence has been committed, and that he (the member) has information which might be of material assistance in securing the prosecution or conviction of the client for it, were to accept or agree to accept for not disclosing that information any consideration other than the making good of loss or injury caused by the offence, or the making of reasonable compensation for that loss or injury; or

(f) in a case of treason, if he knew that the client had committed a treason and failed to disclose what he knew to the proper authority.

'The offences dealt with in (d) and (e) above are offences created by the *Criminal Law Act 1967* and are punishable by imprisonment. With regard to their effect on a practising member's duty the Council is advised that:

(i) a member would have to do some positive act to assist a client to escape arrest or prosecution for an arrestable offence before he could be convicted of the offence of impeding the apprehension or prosecution of the client (see (d) above). If he did such a positive act, the mere fact that he was the client's accountant would not be a reasonable excuse. It is not doing an act to impede the apprehension or prosecution of a client if a member refuses to answer questions by the police about the client's affairs or to produce documents relating to the client's affairs without the client's consent;

(ii) a member who knows or believes a client to have committed an arrestable offence would not be guilty of the offence of accepting a consideration for not disclosing material information (see (e) above) merely because he accepted a reasonable fee for professional services rendered. Only if the fee were wholly or in part paid in consideration of the member not disclosing the information would he be guilty of an offence. The acceptance of an unusually large fee obviously might be used against a member as evidence that it must in part have been paid for not disclosing the information.

'Except in cases of treason, a member who acquires knowledge of the commission of a criminal offence (or of a default which is a civil wrong only) is under no legal obligation to disclose what he knows to a proper authority, and it is an implied term of a member's contract with his client that the member will not, as a general rule, disclose to other persons information about his client's affairs which he has obtained by virtue of his professional relationship with his client. There are, however, circumstances in which, while not obliged to do so, a member is contractually free to make a disclosure of his client's affairs if he so wishes. But this does not mean that in all cases in which he is contractually free to do so he should in fact make disclosure.

'The cases where there is no contractual ban on a member's disclosure of information can be classified as follows:

(i) where disclosure is authorized by the client either expressly or by implication;

(ii) where the disclosure is compelled by process of law;

(iii) where the member's interests require disclosure;

(iv) where the circumstances are such as to give rise to a public duty to disclose.

'The first head explains itself. Examples of the second head are where a member is ordered to give discovery of documents or to give evidence in the course of legal proceedings. The third head must be strictly interpreted. Examples are where a disclosure is necessary to enable a member to sue for his fees or to resist an action for negligence brought against him by his client or some third person or to clear himself of suspicion of a criminal offence or to defend himself against a criminal charge or to resist a claim for a penalty under Section 50 of the *Finance Act 1960*, if it is suggested that he has assisted his client to make an incorrect return.

'With regard to the fourth head, there is normally no contractual ban on disclosing information:

(*a*) as to an intended criminal offence whether it be serious or trivial;

(*b*) as to an intended civil wrong or breach of statutory duty if the damage to an individual is likely to be serious or if the wrong is likely to affect a large number of individuals;

(*c*) as to a past arrestable offence whatever its nature or even as to a past non-arrestable offence or civil wrong or breach of statutory duty if the non-disclosure is likely to cause public harm, for example by enabling the offence to be repeated with impunity or by enabling the perpetrator of some serious fraud to go unpunished.

'There may, however, be special circumstances particularly in regard to (*c*) above which would lead to a different result. If, for example, the client having committed, or having received information that he was about to be accused of an arrestable offence, were to consult the member on the question whether he had any defence to the charge or what should be his proper course of action, a Court would probably equate the member's position with that of a solicitor and hold that the information was not disclosable.

'Moreover, the fact that there may be no contractual ban on his doing so does not necessarily mean that a member should make disclosure. The relationship between client and member is a highly confidential one, in which candour on the part of the client is of great importance, and it is in the public interest that in general this confidence should be maintained. The very fact that clients, relying on the confidential relationship which exists, are frank with members of itself probably prevents a large number of offences, for members may point out that certain things which have been done or are contemplated are in fact offences with the result that such things are either not repeated or not done at all. If, although contractually free to do so, members were to make a practice of disclosing past serious offences and all intended offences the result might well be that the total number of offences would increase.

'The Council therefore recommends that members, albeit they may be contractually free to do so, should not disclose past or intended civil wrongs or crimes (except treason, which they are legally obliged to disclose) unless they feel that the damage to the public likely to arise from non-disclosure is of a very serious nature and that in any such case members should if time allows always take legal advice before making disclosure.**

'Although a member who obtains knowledge of the commission of an offence by a client has no duty, except in the case of treason, to act as an informer and would very seldom be justified in volunteering information against his client, he cannot merely ignore the situation:

(a) the member must ensure that he himself does not do anything actively to assist a client to commit any criminal offence or to escape the consequences;

(b) if the offence is being or was committed by an employee of a client, the member should consider the facts and, if appropriate, bring them to the notice of the client;

(c) the member should consider whether the possible consequences of the offence are such as to prevent accounts which he is engaged in preparing or auditing from giving a true or fair view unless appropriate disclosures are made in the accounts or appropriate qualifications are included in his report. Without presuming to anticipate any decision of the competent authorities whether or not to prosecute or initiate penalty proceedings or what fine or penalty to impose, the member should have regard to his own assessment of the materiality of the offence and the effect on the financial position of any potential money penalties;

(d) the member should consider whether in the light of the information he has acquired past accounts in respect of which he is acting or has acted in any way for the client were defective. If so, the member should not only bring the defect to the notice of his client but should also advise his client to make or authorize appropriate disclosures;

(e) the member should consider whether he is prepared to continue to act for the client. This is a matter on which the member must make his own decision. He may not wish to continue to be associated in any way with the client; but on the other hand he could (subject to (a) above) lawfully continue if he wished to do so, for example if he took the view that it was desirable for him to continue, including qualifications in his reports where necessary, rather than to give the client the opportunity of using the services of a less scrupulous person.

'If a member has reason to suspect, but has no actual knowledge, that a client has committed some offence within the scope of the matters on which the member acts for him then the member should make such enquiries as he thinks are likely to confirm or remove his suspicion. If it is confirmed, the case would then become one of actual knowledge and the member's conduct should be in accordance with the advice contained in this statement. If on the other hand his suspicion is removed, then no further point arises. If he finds no confirmation but his suspicion is still not removed, he may prefer no longer to act for the client, but he can properly continue to act if he so desires.'

Taxation frauds are one of the most likely offences to be encountered by the professional accountant in the course of his practice and the advice given on this subject by the Institute is summarized below:

(a) Where the accountant finds that accounts he has prepared or reported upon, and which have been submitted to the Inland Revenue, are defective because his client withheld information from him or otherwise deceived him, he should advise his client to make a complete disclosure to the Inland Revenue. If the client refuses to accept this advice, the accountant should inform him that he can no longer act for him and that it will be necessary to inform the Inland Revenue that accounts on which he has reported or which he has prepared have been shown from information subsequently obtained to be inaccurate. The accountant should also inform his client that he will at the same time advise the Inland Revenue that he has ceased to act for him but he is under no duty to furnish details of the reasons why the accounts are defective and it would be improper for him to do so without first obtaining the client's consent, except in the circumstances outlined above.

(b) If, during the course of preparing or auditing accounts, the accountant acquires knowledge of matters which would result in the Inland Revenue being defrauded if not dealt with properly in such accounts, he must:

(i) if preparing the accounts, see that they are drawn up correctly;

(ii) if auditing the accounts, qualify his report thereon if they are not amended to his satisfaction.

In such circumstances the accountant should not, without the client's authority, send the accounts to the Inland Revenue. Furthermore, the accountant should always bear in mind that: 'Any person who assists in or induces the making or delivery for any purposes of income tax of any return, accounts, statement or declaration which he knows to be incorrect shall be liable to a penalty not exceeding £500 (Section 50, *Finance Act 1960*.)

Where the accountant has not been engaged to deal with the client's taxation affairs, he should not make disclosure to the Revenue regarding inaccuracies in past accounts, except in the special circumstances mentioned in the recommendations quoted above. Enquiries addressed to him from the Revenue, concerning his client's taxation affairs, should be dealt with by simply replying to the effect that he is not handling that person's taxation matters, and all enquiries should be directed to the client himself.

(c) Where an accountant, in the course of preparing or auditing accounts for a new client, acquires knowledge indicating that accounts submitted to the Inland Revenue for previous years were defective, he should advise his client to make a complete disclosure to the Inland Revenue. The nature of the defects in the past accounts may be such that an adjustment therefor may be necessary in the accounts of the year now under review if these are to be correct, and if the client refuses to agree to such an adjustment, the accountant must qualify his report. If no such adjustment is required in the accounts now being prepared or audited and the client has refused to make a complete disclosure to the Inland Revenue, the accountant has no duty in the matter and may continue to act for the client but he may, in the circumstances, prefer to terminate the association.

Section 47 of the *Finance Act 1960* makes liable to penalties a person who fraudulently or negligently submits incorrect returns or accounts. It also provides that where incorrect returns or accounts are submitted by a person neither fraudulently nor negligently he may nevertheless be treated as having submitted them negligently unless the error is remedied without unreasonable delay after the error comes to his notice. Where there have been genuine mistakes through carelessness or ignorance and the client refuses to take appropriate steps to rectify the position, the member should follow the same course as if the client had knowingly defrauded the Inland Revenue.

The following are examples of other offences which the practising accountant may encounter in the course of his duties: the fraudulent conversion by trustees and others entrusted with the ownership of property for special purposes; frauds by directors and officers of companies; falsification of accounts; a bankrupt's failure to keep proper books of account; share pushing; fraudulent trading; obtaining property by false pretences; offences against control regulations governing prices, quotas and licences; offences in respect of purchase tax; the payment or receipt of bribes.

A practising accountant acting in a professional capacity has no responsibility to ascertain whether a client is conducting his affairs in an unlawful manner, but if he becomes aware that a client has committed offences of the kind mentioned in the preceding paragraph he must not, in the opinion of the Institute, do anything to assist the client to commit any criminal offence.

He should further consider:

(i) whether the possible consequences of the offence are such as to prevent the accounts which he is engaged in preparing or auditing from giving a true and fair view and, therefore, call for appropriate reservations in his report on such accounts;

(ii) whether in all the circumstances he is prepared to continue to act for the client.

Special considerations apply in connection with limited companies, as the auditor's 'client' is the company and not the directors. If, however, it becomes necessary for the auditor to make reservations in his report, the reservations should be in such terms as will indicate clearly the respects in which he is unable to satisfy himself on the matters which he is required to investigate and on which he is required to express an opinion under Section 14 of the *Companies Act 1967*, even though the result will be to disclose to the shareholders and others who may see the accounts the fact that an offence has been committed.

If a practising accountant has reason to suspect, but has no actual knowledge, that a client has committed some offence within the scope of the matters on which the accountant acts for him, he should make such enquiries as he thinks are likely either to confirm or remove his suspicions. If his suspicions are confirmed, the accountant must act in accordance with the advice outlined above, but if confirmation cannot be obtained but his suspicions remain, the accountant may feel that he would rather terminate his association with the client.

CHAPTER XIII

SPECIAL POINTS IN DIFFERENT CLASSES OF AUDITS

In addition to the general procedure which has been dealt with at length in preceding chapters, special points arise for consideration in each different class of audit. It is not possible, owing to the limits of space available, to deal with every kind of business, or to discuss in detail the various special matters that have to be considered. In the following pages the important points that require the auditor's attention in a representative number of cases are considered.

§ 1. Banks

In the case of a bank it is of the utmost importance that a complete system of internal check should be in operation, and the auditor should obtain a written statement thereof.

The detailed checking of a bank's records will be undertaken by the internal audit staff whose programmes of work should be examined by the independent auditors.

The auditor should attend at the close of business on the day of the balance sheet, and count and weigh the cash in hand. Certificates should be obtained for the balances at the Bank of England and other banks. The cash articles should be verified; these are cheques etc., received too late on the last day of the accounts to be cleared, and be vouched by seeing that they come through in due course within the next few days.

Money at call and at short notice is usually represented by advances to bill brokers on the deposit of bills from day to day and to stockbrokers on the deposit of securities from one account to the next. The bills should be examined, and the securities lodged by the stockbrokers checked with the schedules appended to the borrowing notes. Special deposits, if any, should be verified by certificate from the Bank of England.

The investments of the bank must be examined, special precautions being taken to prevent the same securities being produced twice. The schedule of investments should show the book value and the market price on the day of the balance sheet, and it should be seen that sufficient provision is made if the total book value is in excess of the market value.

Bills in hand should be examined, and it should be seen that proper provision is made for rebate, representing the proportion of discount not earned at the date of the balance sheet.

The securities deposited against loans and overdrafts should be examined, and it should be seen that sufficient margin has been provided in the case of all items examined. The ledger balances on current, deposit, and loan accounts should be checked, particular attention being paid to overdrawn accounts, and it should be seen that sufficient provision has been made for bad debts.

If the auditor is not instructed to visit the branches he should examine the certified returns, and see that they are properly incorporated in the head office books.

Banks usually possess large secret reserves, the composition of which should be checked and noted.

Foreign currency transactions should be tested, and profits and losses arising thereon should be checked.

§ 2. Building Societies

The *Building Societies Act 1960* (consolidated in the *Building Societies Act 1962*), introduced fundamental changes in the law governing the accounts of building societies and their audit.

Section 86 of the Act provides that no person shall be appointed as auditor of a building society unless he is a member of one of the bodies of accountants recognised by the Board of Trade as qualified to act as auditors of limited companies, provided, however, that a person who was the auditor of a building society at the commencement of the Act will still be qualified to continue as auditor of that society if he comes within the provisions of Section 161 (1) (*b*) *Companies Act 1948* (see Chapter VIII). Section 86 also provides that none of the following persons shall be appointed as auditor of a building society:

(*a*) An officer or servant of the society;

(*b*) A person who is a partner of or in the employment of, *or who employs*, an officer or servant of the society;

(*c*) a body corporate.

It will be appreciated that the words shown in italics in (*b*) above make this provision more stringent than the similar provision relating to an auditor of a limited company.

The auditors are required to report on the accounts examined by them (Section 87) and also on the annual return which the building society is required to make to the Chief Registrar of Friendly Societies (Section 91). Section 89 specifies the disclosure requirements regarding advances to officers, and stipulates that this information shall be given by the auditors in their report, as far as they are reasonably able to do so. This section is thus equivalent to Section 197 of the *Companies Act 1948*. The provisions of these three important sections are set out in detail below.

Section 87. (1) The auditors of a building society shall make a report to the members on the accounts examined by them, and on every balance sheet and every revenue and appropriation account laid before the society at the annual general meeting during their tenure of office.

(2) The auditors' report shall be read before the building society at the annual general meeting and shall be open to inspection by any member.

(3) The report shall state whether the balance sheet and revenue and appropriation account are properly drawn up in accordance with the requirements of this Act and the regulations made thereunder and whether, in the opinion of the auditors, they give a true and fair view:

(*a*) in the case of the balance sheet, of the state of the building society's affairs as at the end of its financial year; and

(*b*) in the case of the revenue and appropriation account of the income and expenditure of the building society for its financial year.

(4) It shall be the duty of the auditors of a building society in preparing this report under this section to carry out such investigations as will enable them to form an opinion as to the following matter, that is to say:

(*a*) whether the society has kept proper books of account and proper records of the matters referred to in sub-section (1) of Section twenty-seven of this Act;

(*b*) whether the society has maintained a satisfactory system of control over its transactions and records, and, in particular, whether the requirements of paragraph (b) of sub-section (1) and sub-section (3) of Section seventy-six of this Act have been complied with, and

(*c*) whether the balance sheet and revenue and appropriation account are in agreement with the books of account and records of the society,

and if the auditors are of opinion that the society has failed to keep proper books of account or proper records of the matters referred to in sub-section (1) of Section twenty-seven of this Act, or to maintain a satisfactory system of control over its transactions and records, or if the balance sheet and revenue and appropriation account are not in agreement with the books of account and records of the society, the auditors shall state that fact in their report.

(5) Every auditor of a building society:

(a) shall have a right of access at all times to the books, accounts, records and vouchers of the society and to all other documents relating to its affairs including the deeds relating to property mortgaged to the society; and

(b) shall be entitled to require from the officers of the society such information and explanations as he thinks necessary for the performance of the duties of the auditors.

(6) If the auditors fail to obtain all the information and explanations which, to the best of their knowledge and belief, are necessary for the purposes of their audit, they shall state that fact in their report.

(7) The auditors of a building society shall be entitled:

(a) to attend any general meeting of the society and to receive all notices of and other communications relating to any general meeting which any member of the building society is entitled to receive; and

(b) to be heard at any meeting which they attend on any part of the business of the meeting which concerns them as auditors.

Section 91. (1) The auditors of a building society shall make a report on the annual return which shall be annexed to the annual return made to the Chief Registrar.

(2) Regulations under Section eighty-six of this Act may provide that the auditors of a building society shall not be required in their report on the annual return to deal with such of the matters to be contained in the annual return as may be prescribed by the regulations for the purposes of this subsection.

(3) The auditors' report on the annual return shall (without prejudice to any provision of this Act requiring any other information to be contained therein) contain statements as to the following matters, that is to say:

(a) whether in their opinion the annual return is properly drawn up in accordance with the requirements of the Act and regulations made thereunder:

(b) whether the annual return gives a true and fair view of the matters to which it is to be addressed (other than those which the auditors are by virtue of regulations made in pursuance of the last preceding subsection, not required to deal), and

(c) whether the annual return is in agreement with the books of account and records of the society.

Section 89. (1) Every annual return shall contain particulars showing the amount of any advances made by the society during the relevant financial year:

(a) to any director or the manager or secretary of the society, or (*b*) to any person who, after the making of the advance, became a director or the manager or secretary of the building society in that year, or

(*c*) to a company or other body corporate in which, when the advance was made, or at any later time in the relevant financial year, a director or the manager or secretary of the society held (either directly or through a nominee) shares the nominal value of which exceeded two and a half per cent. of the total paid-up share capital of the company or other body corporate, or

(*d*) to a company or other body corporate of which, when the advance was made, or at any later time in the relevant financial year, a director or the manager or secretary of the society was a director, general manager, secretary or other similar officer.

and also, in the case of an advance falling within paragraph (*c*) of this subsection, particulars of the officer's shareholding.

(2) It shall be the duty of any director and the manager and the secretary of a building society to give notice in writing to the society of such matters relating to his employment by, or other interest in, any company or other body corporate as may be necessary for the purposes of the preceding subsection, and subject to the next following subsection, a person failing to comply with this subsection shall be liable on summary conviction to a fine not exceeding two hundred pounds.

(3) In any proceedings against a person in respect of an offence under the last preceding subsection it shall be a defence to prove that at the time of the alleged offence he did not know that the building society had made the advance to the body corporate in question and that at that time reasonable arrangements were in operation to bring to his notice any advance made by the society to any body corporate.

(4) If the requirements of subsection (1) of this section are not complied with, it shall be the duty of the auditors of the building society to include in their report, so far as they are reasonably able to do so, a statement giving the required particulars.

(5) In this section 'the relevant financial year' in relation to an annual return of a building society means the society's financial year to which the return relates.

In October 1962 the Institute of Chartered Accountants in England and Wales issued a statement for the guidance of members concerned with the audit of building societies. In a preface to this statement the Council emphasized that it was for guidance only and that 'auditors must exercise their professional skill and judgment in deciding for themselves the nature and extent of the tests and enquiries which they must make in order to discharge their statutory duties'. The major part of this statement is reproduced in the Appendix, to which reference should now be made.

§ 3. Estate Agents, Auctioneers, Surveyors etc.

Where considerable sums are received on behalf of clients, whether from auctions, deposits or otherwise, it is most desirable that a separate banking account should be opened for clients' money. Where, however, such a system is not in force, the auditor should check the credit balances shown in the client's ledger, representing money held on behalf of clients, and ascertain that there is sufficient cash on the general banking account to cover such balances, drawing special attention to the fact if this is not the case.

Care should be taken to see that adequate control is exercised over the collection and recording of rents collected on behalf of clients and over payments made thereout for rates, repairs etc.

Considerable expenditure is frequently incurred on behalf of clients, both in respect of advertising and otherwise, and it should be seen that there is a proper system in force for passing the invoices relating thereto and charging the expenses to the clients. Similar remarks apply to disbursements incurred through petty cash on behalf of clients. Where sums have been received from clients for the purpose of incurring such expenditure and the whole or part thereof remains unexpended at the date of the balance sheet, it should be seen that such balances are carried forward as liabilities.

A proportion of the charges made to clients for fees and commission should be tested. Where outstanding fees and charges, which have not been debited to the clients, are brought into account, a schedule thereof should be prepared and signed by the partners, but care should be taken to see that no items are included that have not been actually earned, as the majority of the fees and commissions will only be payable in the event of negotiations for selling or letting the properties concerned being successful.

§ 4. Executors' and Trustees' Accounts

An auditor is frequently appointed to audit the first year's accounts of an executor or for the period up to the ascertainment of the residuary estate. In such cases the auditor's first duty will be to examine the will and to note carefully any instructions contained therein as to the disposition of property, the payment of debts and expenses, the creation of trusts, the distribution of the residue, the investment of money belonging to the estate, and similar matters. He should examine the private books of account, copies of taxation returns, bank statements, and other documents of the deceased, consult bankers, solicitors, stockbrokers, accountants and other persons with whom the deceased had dealings and who might be able to give information as to the deceased's affairs. With the information thus obtained, it should be possible for the auditor to satisfy himself whether all assets and liabilities of the deceased have been included in the estate duty account and accounted for in the executorship accounts.

From this point it would be the auditor's concern to verify all the executor's dealings. The sale of investments should be verified by reference to brokers' sold notes and the sale of property with accounts of solicitors, auctioneers and other agents. In this connection the auditor should take care to ascertain that no assets of the estate have been purchased by the executor himself and that the executor has made no secret profit in dealing with the assets.

The auditor should verify the payment of estate duty by reference to probate of the will and receipted estate duty account, legacies with the paid cheques or receipts therefor and all other payments with the usual vouchers. It should be seen that provision is made for all outstanding and accrued expenditure.

All rents, interest and dividends received should be verified by examination of counterfoil receipts given for rents and counterfoils of dividend and interest warrants and it should be seen that proper apportionment of all such receipts in accordance with the *Apportionment Act 1870* has been made. Where the residue of the estate has been settled on persons in succession, unless the equitable apportionments are barred by the will, the auditor should ascertain that apportionment of all relevant receipts and payments in accordance with the appropriate equitable rules has been made, and where no power to retain or postpone conversion of unauthorized investments is given, that all such investments have been converted into cash and the proceeds invested in authorized securities.

In so far as the estate has not been fully distributed, the auditor should verify the assets held in the usual way, by inspecting the title deeds of property, the certificates for stocks and shares, banker's certificates in respect of bank balances etc. It should be seen that all investments are in accordance with the terms of the will or statute, and that no devastavit has been committed in respect of capital.

Where trusts are created by a will or by a deed of settlement the testator or settlor may have provided that the trust accounts shall be audited. As stated in Chapter I, § 4 (D), banking and insurance companies insist on this condition before agreeing to act as trustees. The following are the principal matters to which attention should be given by the auditor:

(a) Ascertain the precise terms of the trust and see that all conditions have been complied with and that the funds or investments comprising the settlement are fully accounted for.

(b) Ascertain that all advances to beneficiaries are in accordance with the terms of the trust and examine appropriate vouchers therefor. Vouch all expenditure incurred on the maintenance of infant beneficiaries and see that such expenditure is properly authorized.

(c) Vouch the receipt of all income in a usual manner.

(d) Vouch payments to beneficiaries and disbursements by the trustees and see that any remuneration paid to them is in accordance with the trust instrument.

(e) Ensure that all bonus shares receivable, provisional allotment letters for rights to new shares and similar matters arising from the investments held by the trustees have been properly dealt with.

(f) Verify in the usual manner all securities etc., held at the date of the balance sheet and obtain confirmation of bank balances by banker's certificates.

(g) Enquire into the reasons for any undue delay in the reinvestment of trust funds and, if necessary, draw attention to this matter in his report.

(h) Where investments in equities have been made by virtue of the provisions of the *Trustee Investments Act 1961*, see that the requirements of that Act have been complied with.

(i) Written confirmation of details of any advancements made during the testator's lifetime should be obtained from beneficiaries concerned. Similar considerations apply in the case of gifts *inter vivos*.

(*j*) Vouch all rents and interest received, by reference to estate agents' accounts, interest counterfoils and any other available evidence. See that due provision has been made for all income tax liabilities outstanding at the date of death including any under Schedule D in respect of excess rents and untaxed interest received, and for repairs and other outgoings in respect of the properties. Counterpart leases and tenancy agreements relating to the letting of properties should be inspected and it should be seen that all rents receivable thereunder have been accounted for. It should be seen that any liability to capital gains tax arising at the date of death has been paid by the executors, taking into account the exemption from chargeable gains of £5,000 (Section 24, *Finance Act 1965*).

(*k*) It should be seen that prior to the distribution of the estate due provision has been made for any capital gains tax liability. In this connection the auditor should ensure that any exemptions allowed by the Ninth Schedule to the *Finance Act 1965* in respect of certain classes of government securities have been fully taken into account. Furthermore, losses incurred during the period of administration, which are not available against profits, may be set off against gains which have arisen within the period of three years prior to the date of death, and any such computations should be carefully checked by the auditor.

The following is a form of certificate which an auditor should append to the accounts examined by him, subject to any qualification that may be necessary:

'In my opinion the above accounts exhibit a true view of the state of the affairs of the..Trust, and I certify that I have had the securities of the trust fund investments produced to me, and that I have verified the same.'

Under Section 13 of the *Public Trustee Act 1906*, the condition and accounts of any trust shall, on application being made and notice thereof given in the prescribed manner by any trustee or beneficiary, be investigated and audited by such solicitor or public accountant as may be agreed on by the applicant and the trustees, or in default of agreement, by the Public Trustee or some person appointed by him. The section provides than an audit shall not be performed more than once a year except with the leave of the Court (Section 13 (1)). A beneficiary of a trust that is not administered by the Public Trustee may make application under this section. The Public Trustee may require the applicant to make a deposit sufficient to cover the costs of the investigation.

The auditor is given the right of access to the books, accounts and vouchers of the trustees and to any securities and documents of title held by them on account of the trust, and may require from them such information and explanation as may be necessary for the purpose of his duties. Upon the completion of the investigation and audit the auditor must forward to the applicant and to every trustee a copy of the accounts, together with a report thereon and a certificate signed by him to the effect that the accounts exhibit a true view of the state of the affairs of the trust, and that he has had the securities of the trust funds and the investments produced to and verified by him, or (as the case may be) that such accounts are deficient in such respects as may be specified in such certificate (Section 13 (2)).

Copies of the report and certificate of the auditor together with the accounts and any other documents he may require must be sent to the Public Trustee, who will then make an order as to the expenses of the investigation.

If, in the course of the investigation, any person having the custody of any books or documents to which the auditor has a right of access, fails or refuses to allow him to have access thereto, or in any wise obstructs the investigation or audit, the auditor may apply to the Court, and thereupon the Court shall make such order as it thinks just (Section 13 (6)). Any application by the auditor under this section is made to the Chancery Division by an originating summons, and any order then made will be enforced by a subsequent application for leave to issue a writ of attachment, or for an order of committal for contempt of Court.

The remuneration of the auditor and the other expenses of the investigation and audit are to be determined by the Public Trustee who may refer the costs of any solicitor (being part of such expenses) for taxation.

Unless the Public Trustee otherwise directs, the auditor's remuneration and expenses will be borne by the estate; but he may order that such expenses shall be borne by the applicant or by the trustees personally, or partly by them and partly by the applicant (Section 13 (5)). The Public Trustee may in his absolute discretion, upon the application of any trustee or beneficiary, direct that the investigation and audit shall extend only to a specified period of time or to a specified part of the trust property, or shall be otherwise restricted.

The trustee cannot make terms before producing the necessary books or documents (*re Williams*, 1916, 26 T.L.R. 604). An appeal from the order of the Public Trustee in non-administrative matters may be made to the Court (*In re Oddy*, 1911, L.J. Ch. 404).

Under the *Judicial Trustees Act 1896* the accounts of every trust of which a judicial trustee has been appointed shall be audited once in every year, and a report thereon made to the Court by the prescribed persons. In all ordinary cases the accounts are then audited by an officer of the Court, but the Court can refer them to a professional accountant for report if it considers the accounts are likely to involve questions of difficulty.

Under the *Trustee Act 1925* (Section 22 (4)), trustees may at their absolute discretion employ an independent accountant to audit the accounts of the trust property, but not more than once in three years, unless the nature of the trust or any special dealings with the trust property render a more frequent audit desirable.

§ 5. Insurance Companies

The *Insurance Companies Act 1958* applies to all insurance companies, not being companies registered under the Acts relating to friendly societies or trade unions, which carry on the following classes of business within Great Britain:

(*a*) life assurance;

(*b*) industrial assurance;

(*c*) accident insurance;

(*d*) fire insurance;

(e) bond investment business;

(f) motor vehicle insurance;

(g) marine, aviation and transit insurance.

Section 59 of the *Companies Act 1967*, however, has extended the list of traditional insurance business to include the following:

(a) liability insurance (third party risks other than those arising from the use of motor vehicles etc.);

(b) pecuniary loss insurance (bad debts, guarantees etc.);

(c) property insurance.

It redefines other classes of insurance, and generally increases the scope of the *Insurance Companies Act 1958*, which remains the 'principal Act' for the purposes of the whole of Part II of the *Companies Act 1967*.

The immediate purpose of Part II of the 1967 Act is to establish more rigorous standards for the conduct of insurance business. As well as increased financial criteria, provision is made for closer supervision and powers of intervention by the Board of Trade. The qualifications for entry into the insurance business have been vastly extended, as compared with the 1958 Act.

The principal Act also applies to an insurance company which carries on employers' liability insurance business only, but in the case of a company carrying on one or more of the classes of business mentioned above and also employers' liability business, the Act does not apply to the employers' liability section of its activities. The principal Act does not apply to members of Lloyds or of any other association of underwriters approved by the Board of Trade.

Sections 71 to 77 of the *Companies Act 1967* introduce several important changes concerning the accounts and audit of insurance companies. Under Section 71, a profit and loss account is required from all insurance companies, as well as (as previously) an annual revenue account and balance sheet. The profit and loss account must contain such information, and be accompanied by such further documents, reports and certificates, as are prescribed by the Board of Trade, and be signed by the persons prescribed.

Section 72 provides that the accounts and balance sheets of all insurance companies are to be audited in the manner prescribed and by a person of prescribed description. Regulations made for the purposes of this section may apply the audit provisions of the *Companies Acts 1948* to *1967* to insurance companies, subject to such modifications and adaptations as may appear necessary.

Section 73 provides that the annual statement of business (previously required of accident insurance companies) is now extendable to any class of business (with powers of relaxation) by the Board of Trade.

Section 76 allows the Board of Trade to grant exemption from disclosure of confidential information in filed annual statements, where such disclosure might prove harmful.

Section 78 reduces the maximum interval between statutory actuarial valuations (required under Section 5 of the principal Act) from five years to three.

'Bond investment business' (see (*e*) above) means the business of issuing bonds or endowment certificates by which the company, in return for subscriptions payable at periodic intervals of less than six months, contracts to pay the bond holder a sum at some future date.

'Industrial assurance business' means the business of effecting assurances upon human life, premiums in respect of which are received by means of collectors at intervals of less than two months.

Where an assurance company under the *Insurance Companies Act 1958* carries on industrial assurance business, the provisions of that Act relating to life assurance business also apply to industrial assurance business. Where any expenses of management, or interest from investments, or sums on account of depreciation of securities, are apportioned between the industrial assurance business and any other business carried on by the company, the auditor must include in his report a special report as to the propriety or otherwise of the apportionment. A copy of every report of the auditor must be furnished to the Industrial Assurance Commissioner.

In the case of life assurance the auditor should vouch the premium income with the policy books, renewals register, lapsed policies etc., from which it should be possible to verify the premium income in total by taking the gross premium income receivable and deducting premiums on policies matured, surrendered, or lapsed.

The agents' commissions should be vouched with the receipts, agents' accounts etc., and it should be seen that provision has been made for any commission outstanding. Some of the accounts in the agents' ledger should be tested with the returns from the agents.

Claims should be tested with cancelled policies, death certificates, discharge notes etc., and it should be seen that all claims notified but not admitted are provided for.

Surrenders should be tested with indorsed policies and receipts for cash; payments to annuitants should be tested, and it should be seen that the proportion of annuities accrued to the date of the balance sheet is brought into account.

The re-insurances and re-insurance recoveries should be checked, and it should be ascertained that all outstandings on this account are provided for. It should be seen that the premium reserve carried forward is adequate. The verification of the securities, and the income derived therefrom, will follow the usual lines.

Similar considerations apply to fire, accident, and other departments. The claims should be tested with the papers relating thereto, and it should be seen that all claims notified but not admitted are provided for.

The adequacy of the premium reserve carried forward should be fully enquired into, having regard to the nature of the business transacted, and the past experience of the company.

In the case of re-insurance companies, the treatise with the ceding companies should be examined, with particular reference to any provisions under which the ceding company is entitled to retain funds as security for the fulfilment of the treaties. Where this is the case, certificates should be obtained from the companies concerned of the funds held by them, and they should appear separately in the balance sheet of the re-insurance company as 'Deposited as security under Treaties', with an indication as to whether the assets concerned are under the control of the ceding companies, or in joint names or otherwise.

The accounts of the ceding companies should be tested and the outstanding balances agreed; similarly, treaties made by the re-insurance company with other companies, under which they may concede a portion of the re-insurances received by them, should be examined, together with the accounts relative thereto.

The auditor must see that the accounts have been drawn up in the prescribed form. The balance sheet must state how the values of the stock exchange securities are arrived at, and a certificate must be appended signed by the same persons as signed the balance sheet, to the effect that in their belief the assets set forth in the balance sheet are in the aggregate fully of the value stated therein less any investment reserve fund taken into account.

Where separate funds are required to be kept, the certificate must be appended, signed by the same persons as signed the balance sheet, and by the auditor, to the effect that no part of any such fund has been applied directly or indirectly for any purpose other than the class of business to which it is applicable.

§ 6. Solicitors

The auditor must ascertain that the rules of the Council of the Law Society, for the time being in force, relating to dealings with clients' moneys have been complied with.

Section 29, *Solicitors Act 1957*, provides that the Council of the Law Society shall make rules as to the keeping by solicitors of banking accounts for clients' moneys and contains similar provisions regarding rules for banking accounts to be kept by a solicitor for trusts of which he is a sole trustee or where he is co-trustee only with a partner, clerk or servant of his. (In such circumstances the solicitor is termed a solicitor-trustee.)

The section also empowers the Council of the Law Society to take such action as may be necessary to enable them to ascertain whether or not the rules are being complied with.

If a solicitor fails to comply with any of the rules made under the above section, any person may make a complaint to the disciplinary committee in respect of that failure.

The rules at present in force are the Solicitors' Accounts Rules 1967, and the Solicitors' Trust Accounts Rules 1967.

The principal object of these rules is to make it virtually impossible for a solicitor who complies with them to confuse his clients' money with his own and thus to prevent the recurrence of cases where, without any original intention to defraud, a solicitor has found himself in financial difficulties through confusion in his accounts.

The following is a synopsis of the rules referred to. (The rules have been renumbered for the purpose of simplifying this extract):

(i) Every solicitor who holds or receives client's money, or money which under Rule (ii) hereof he is permitted and elects to pay into a client account, shall without delay pay such money into a client account. Any solicitor may keep one client account or as many such accounts as he thinks fit.

(ii) There may be paid into a client account –

   (*a*) trust money;

   (*b*) such money belonging to the solicitor as may be necessary for the purpose of opening or maintaining the account;

   (*c*) money to replace any sum which for any reason may have been drawn from the account in contravention of paragraph (2) of Rule (vi) of these Rules; and

   (*d*) a cheque or draft received by the solicitor which under paragraph (*b*) of Rule (iii) of these Rules he is entitled to split but which he does not split.

(iii) Where a solicitor holds or receives a cheque or draft which includes client's money or trust money of one or more trusts –

   (*a*) he may where practicable split such cheque or draft and, if he does so, he shall deal with each part thereof as if he had received a separate cheque or draft in respect of that part; or

   (*b*) if he does not split the cheque or draft, he shall, if any part thereof consists of client's money, and may, in any other case, pay the cheque or draft into a client account.

(iv) No money other than money which under the foregoing Rules a solicitor is required or permitted to pay into a client account shall be paid into a client account, and it shall be the duty of a solicitor into whose client account any money has been paid in contravention of this Rule to withdraw the same without delay on discovery.

(v) There may be drawn from a client account –

   (*a*) in the case of client's money –

      (i) money properly required for a payment to or on behalf of the client;

      (ii) money properly required for or towards payment of a debt due to the solicitor from the client or in reimbursement of money expended by the solicitor on behalf of the client;

      (iii) money drawn on the client's authority;

      (iv) money properly required for or towards payment of the solicitor's costs where there has been delivered to the client a bill of costs or other written intimation of the amount of the costs incurred and it has thereby or otherwise in writing been made clear to the client that money held for him is being or will be applied towards or in satisfaction of such costs; and

(v) money which is thereby transferred into another client account;

(*b*) in the case of trust money –

(i) money properly required for a payment in the execution of the particular trust; and

(ii) money to be transferred into a separate bank account kept solely for the money of the particular trust;

(*c*) Such money as may have been paid into the account under paragraph (*b*) of Rule (ii) or paragraph (*b*) of Rule (iii), or money which may have been paid into the account in contravention of Rule (iv);

provided that in any case under paragraph (*a*) or paragraph (*b*) of this Rule the money so drawn shall not exceed the total of the money held for the time being in such account on account of such client or trust.

(vi) (1) No money drawn from a client account under sub-paragraph (ii) or sub-paragraph (iv) of paragraph (*a*) or under paragraph (*c*) of rule (v) above shall be drawn except by:

(*a*) a cheque drawn in favour of the solicitor; or

(*b*) a transfer to a bank account in the name of the solicitor not being a client account.

(2) No money other than money permitted by Rule (v) to be drawn from a client account shall be so drawn unless the Council specifically authorize in writing its withdrawal upon application by the solicitor.

(vii) (1) Every solicitor shall at all times keep properly written up such accounts as may be necessary –

(*a*) to show all his dealings with –

(i) client money received, held or paid by him; and

(ii) any other money dealt with by him through a client account; and

(*b*) (i) to show separately in respect of each client all money of the categories specified in sub-paragraph (*a*) of this paragraph which is received, held or paid by him on account of that client; and

(ii) to distinguish all money of the said categories received, held or paid by him, from any other money received, held or paid by him.

(2) All dealings referred to in sub-paragraph (*a*) of paragraph (1) of this Rule shall be recorded as may be appropriate –

(i) (*a*) either in a clients' cash book, or a clients' column of a cash book; or

 (*b*) in a record of sums transferred from the ledger account of one client to that of another; and in addition –

(ii) in a clients' ledger, or a clients' column of a ledger;

and no other dealings shall be recorded in such clients' cash book and ledger or, as the case may be, in such clients' columns;

(3) In addition to the books, ledgers and records referred to in paragraph (2) of this Rule, every solicitor shall keep a record of all bills of costs (distinguishing between profit costs and disbursements) and of all written intimations under Rule (v) (*a*) (iv) of these Rules delivered or made by the solicitor to his clients, which record shall be contained in a bills delivered book or a file of copies of such bills and intimations.

(4) In this Rule the expressions 'accounts', 'books', 'ledgers' and 'records' shall be deemed to include loose-leaf books and such cards or other permanent documents or records as are necessary for the operation of any system of book-keeping, mechanical or otherwise.

(5) Every solicitor shall preserve for at least six years from the date of the last entry therein all accounts, books, ledgers and records kept by him under this Rule.

(viii) In order to ascertain whether these Rules have been complied with, the Council may require any solicitor to produce at a time and place to be fixed by the Council, his books of account, bank pass books, loose-leaf bank statements, statements of account, vouchers and any other necessary documents for the inspection of any person appointed by the Council and to supply to such person any necessary information and explanations and such person shall be directed to prepare for the information of the Council a report on the result of such inspection. Such report may be used as a basis for proceedings under the *Solicitors Acts 1957* and *1965*.

The following points in connection with these Rules are stated by the Law Society as matters to be noted:

(1) *Signature of Cheques* – The signature of cheques on a client bank account by a person other than a solicitor is deprecated by the Council. Only in exceptional circumstances, e.g. illness, or unavoidable absence on business or holiday, should solicitors depart from the practice of themselves signing cheques drawn on client account. The practice of signing cheques in blank and leaving them with an employee is clearly unwise and is also deprecated.

(2) *A solicitor must not treat himself as a client* – By virtue of the definition of clients' money contained in the Rules [not reproduced in the previous extract], a solicitor cannot treat himself as his own client for the purposes

of the Rules nor can a member of the firm of solicitors be treated as a client of that firm.

(3) *Money received by a solicitor as trustee may be paid into a client bank account* – Where a solicitor is a trustee of a trust and receives money subject to that trust, he may receive it either in the capacity of a solicitor or in the capacity of trustee. To decide in which capacity a solicitor receives the money may, in some cases, present difficulties and to prescribe means whereby the capacity could be determined would involve the introduction of extremely complicated Rules. Accordingly, the Solicitors' Accounts Rules provide that money subject to a trust of which the solicitor is a trustee, whether or not he is a solicitor-trustee in the limited sense used in the Rules, may be dealt with through a client account.

(4) *The financing of clients out of a solicitor's own money held in a client account is forbidden* – If a solicitor wishes to advance money to or on behalf of a client, he must do so out of his office or private account.

(5) *A solicitor can only withdraw his own money from a client bank account by transfer to his office bank account or a cheque in his own favour* – Rule (vi) [see extract above] of the Solicitors' Accounts Rules provides that where money is due to the solicitor from his client account he can only withdraw it by a cheque in his own favour or by a transfer to his own or office bank account. The Council recommend that withdrawals from client account should be only for specific sums which the solicitor is entitled to withdraw and not of round sums generally on account of costs or other money due to the solicitor.

It should be noted that notwithstanding delivery to a client of a bill or other written intimation of costs incurred and notwithstanding that the client has been notified that money held for him will be applied towards or in satisfaction of such costs the money so held will continue to belong to that client until it is withdrawn from client account in accordance with Rule (vi) (1).

(6) *Recording of cheques or drafts endorsed over in the ordinary course of business* – While a cheque or draft received on behalf of a client and endorsed over in the ordinary course of business would not pass through the solicitor's client bank account, it should nevertheless be recorded in the solicitor's books of account as a transaction conducted on behalf of the client. Similarly cash received and paid out on behalf of the client should also be appropriately recorded.

(7) *Drawing against a cheque before it is cleared* – Where a solicitor receives on behalf of a client a cheque or draft which he does not endorse over in the ordinary course of business to a third party or to the client he must deal with that cheque through his client account. Ordinarily his bankers will credit the account with the amount of the cheque before it has been cleared and will later debit the account if the cheque is not honoured. A solicitor should therefore use discretion in drawing against the cheque before it has been cleared and should only do so with the clear understanding that if the cheque is not in fact met and if the amount drawn from

the client account is in excess of the amount held for the particular client, other client's money will have been used to make the payment and the solicitor will have committed a breach of the Rules. Where the solicitor on discovery of the breach at once pays the appropriate amount from his own resources into client account, it will be for his own accountant to decide whether to qualify his report.

(8) *Money paid to a solicitor for costs which have been agreed or costs incurred in respect of which a bill or other intimation of the amount has been delivered* – When a solicitor receives money on account of costs he must, if the costs have been incurred and an intimation or bill of costs has been delivered, pay the money into his office account and not into a client account. Moreover, any payment of or on account of an agreed fee must also be paid into office account. Money received on account of costs in any other circumstances must be paid into a client account.

By Section 30 of the *Solicitors Act 1957*, as amended by Section 9 of the *Solicitors Act 1965*, every solicitor in practice is required to deliver to the Law Society every year a report signed by an accountant, stating whether the solicitor has complied or not with the above rules.

This section does not apply, however, if the solicitor satisfies the Council that owing to the circumstances of his case the delivery of an accountant's report is unnecessary, or that he is a 'public officer' who does not take out a practising certificate.

The accountant's report has to be delivered once during each practice year (i.e. between the 1st November and the following October 31st, both dates inclusive). The rules governing the report are known as the Accountant's Report Rules 1967. The principal rules are given below:

3. – (1) An accountant shall be qualified to give an Accountant's Report on behalf of a solicitor if –

(*a*) he is a member of –

    (i) The Institute of Chartered Accountants in England and Wales; or

    (ii) The Institute of Chartered Accountants of Scotland; or

    (iii) The Association of Certified and Corporate Accountants; or

    (iv) The Institue of Chartered Accountants in Ireland; and

(*b*) he has neither been at any time during the accounting period to which the Report relates, nor subsequently, before giving the Report, become, a partner, clerk or servant of such solicitor or of any partner of his; and

(*c*) he is not subject to notice of disqualification under paragraph (2) of this Rule.

(2) In either of the following cases, that is to say, where –

(a) the accountant has been found guilty by the Disciplinary Tribunal of his professional body of professional misconduct or discreditable conduct; or

(b) the Council are satisfied that a solicitor has not complied with the provisions of the Solicitors' Accounts Rules 1967, in respect of matters not specified in an Accountant's Report and that the accountant was negligent in giving such Report, whether or not an application be made for a grant out of the Compensation Fund,

the Council may, at their discretion, at any time notify the accountant concerned that he is not qualified to give an Accountant's Report, and they may give notice of such fact to any solicitor on whose behalf he may have given an Accountant's Report, or who may appear to the Council to be likely to employ such accountant for the purpose of giving an Accountant's Report; and after such accountant shall have been so notified, unless and until such notice of disqualification shall have been withdrawn by the Council, he shall not be qualified to give an Accountant's Report. Before coming to their decision the Council shall take into consideration any observations or explanations made or given by such accountant or on his behalf by the professional body of which he is a member.

4. – (1) For the purpose of giving an Accountant's Report, an accountant shall ascertain from the solicitor particulars of all bank accounts (excluding trust bank accounts) kept, maintained or operated by the solicitor in connection with his practice at any time during the accounting period to which his Report relates and subject to paragraph (2) of this Rule make the following examination of the books, accounts and other relevant documents of the solicitor –

(a) so examine the book-keeping system in every office of the solicitor as to enable the accountant to verify that such system complies with Rule 11 [*Rule (vii) in the extract given above*] of the Solicitors' Accounts Rules 1967, and is so designed that –

   (i) an appropriate ledger account is kept for each client;

   (ii) such ledger accounts show separately from other information particulars of all clients' money received, held or paid on account of each client; and

   (iii) transactions relating to clients' money and any other money dealt with through a client account are recorded in the solicitor's books so as to distinguish such transactions from transactions relating to any other moneys received, held or paid by the solicitor;

(b) make test checks of postings to clients' ledger accounts from records of receipts and payments of clients' money and make test checks of the casts of such accounts and records;

(c) compare a sample of lodgments into and payments from the client account as shown in bank statements with the solicitor's records of receipts and payments of clients' money;

(d) enquire into and test check the system of recording costs and of making withdrawals in respect of costs from the client account;

(e) make a test examination of such documents as he shall request the solicitor to produce to him with the object of ascertaining and confirming –

   (i) that the financial transactions (including those giving rise to transfers from one ledger account to another) evidenced by such documents, are in accordance with the Solicitors' Accounts Rules 1967; and

   (ii) that the entries in the clients' ledger accounts reflect those transactions in a manner complying with the Solicitors' Accounts Rules 1967;

(f) extract (or check extractions of balances on the clients' ledger accounts during the accounting period under review at not fewer than two dates selected by the accountant (one of which may be the last day of the accounting period), and at each such date –

   (i) compare the total as shown by such ledger accounts of the liabilities to the clients, including those for whom trust money is held in the client account, with the cash book balance on client account; and

   (ii) reconcile that cash book balance with the client account balance as confirmed direct to the accountant by the bank;

(g) make a test examination of the clients' ledger accounts in order to ascertain whether payments from the client account have been made on any individual account in excess of money held on behalf of that client;

(h) peruse such office ledger and cash accounts and bank statements as the solicitor maintains with a view to ascertaining whether any client's money has not been paid into a client account;

(i) ask for such information and explanations as he may require arising out of sub-paragraphs (a) to (h) of this paragraph.

   (2) Nothing in paragraph (1) of this Rule shall require the accountant –

(a) to extend his enquiries beyond the information contained in the relevant documents relating to any client's matter produced to him supplemented by such information and explanations as he may obtain from the solicitor;

(b) to enquire into the stocks, shares, other securities or documents of title held by the solicitor on behalf of his clients; or

(c) to consider whether the books of account of the solicitor have been properly written up in accordance with Rule 11 [Rule (vii) in above extract] of the Solicitors' Accounts Rules 1967, at any time other than the time as at which his examination of those books and accounts takes place.

   (3) If after making an examination in accordance with paragraphs (1) and (2) of this Rule it appears to the accountant that there is evidence that the Solicitors' Accounts Rules 1967, have not been complied with, he shall make such further examination as he considers necessary in order to complete his Report with or without qualification.

(4) Except where a client's money has been deposited in a separate designated account, nothing in these Rules shall apply to any matter arising under Section 8 of the *Solicitors Act 1965*, or the Solicitors' Accounts (Deposit Interest) Rules 1965, notwithstanding any payment into client account of a sum in lieu of interest.

(5) In this Rule the expression 'separate designated account' shall have the same meaning as in Rule 2 of the Solicitors' Accounts (Deposit Interest) Rules 1965. [These rules are reproduced below.]

5. Nothing in these Rules shall deprive a solicitor of the right on the grounds of privilege as between solicitor and client to decline to produce to the accountant any document which the accountant may consider it necessary for him to inspect for the purposes of his examination in accordance with Rule 4 of these Rules and where the solicitor so declines, the accountant shall qualify his Report to that effect setting out the circumstances.

6. An Accountant's Report delivered by a solicitor under these Rules shall be in the form set out in the Schedule to these Rules or in a form to the like effect approved by the Council.

9. – (2) In the case of a solicitor who has two or more places of business –

(*a*) separate accounting periods covered by separate Accountants' Reports may be adopted in respect of each such place of business, provided that the accounting periods comply with the requirements of subsection (2) of Section 30 of the *Solicitors Act 1957*, as amended by Section 9 of the *Solicitors Act 1965*, and with these Rules; and

(*b*) the Accountant's Report or the Accountant's Reports delivered by him to the Society in each practice year shall cover all client's money held or received by him.

The following form of the Accountant's Report is given as a Schedule to the Rules:

FORM OF ACCOUNTANT'S REPORT

NOTE: In the case of a firm with a number of partners, carbon copies of the Report may be delivered provided section 1 below is completed on each Report with the name of the individual solicitor.

1. Solicitor's Full Name (*a*)..

2. Firm(s) Name(s) and Address(es) (*b*)...

....

....

....

....

....

3. Whether practising alone..

    or in partnership...

4. Accounting Period(s) (c)

    Beginning..   Ending...

    Beginning..   Ending...

(a) BLOCK CAPITALS

(b) Note: *All addresses at which the Solicitor(s) practise(s) must be covered by an Accountant's Report or Reports. If an address is not so covered the reason must be stated.*

(c) Note: *The period(s) must comply with Section 30 (2) of the* Solicitors Act 1957, *as amended by Section 9 of the* Solicitors Act 1956, *and the Accountant's Report Rules 1967.*

ACCOUNTANT'S REPORT

In compliance with Section 30 of the *Solicitors Act 1957*, as amended by Section 9 of the *Solicitors Act 1965*, and the Accountant's Report Rules 1967, made thereunder, I have examined to the extent required by Rule 4 of the said Rules the books, accounts and documents produced to me in respect of the above practise(s) of the above-named solicitor.

1. In so far as an opinion can be based on this limited examination I am satisfied that during the above-mentioned period(s) he has complied with the provisions of the Solicitors' Accounts Rules 1967, except so far as concerns:

(a) certain trivial breaches due to clerical errors or mistakes in book-keeping, all of which were rectified on discovery and none of which, I am satisfied, resulted in any loss to any client;

(b) the matters set out in the First Section on the back hereof, in respect of which I have not been able to satisfy myself for the reasons therein stated;

(c) the matters set out in the Second Section on the back hereof, in respect of which it appears to me that the solicitor has not complied with the provisions of the Solicitors' Accounts Rules 1967.

Delete appropriate sub-paragraph(s)

2. The results of the comparisons required under Rule 4 (1) (f) of the Accountant's Report Rules 1967 at the dates selected by me were as follows:

(i) at ....

    (a) the figures were in agreement;

(*b*) there was a difference computed as follows:

£

Liabilities to clients as shown by client's ledger
accounts   ..   ..

Cash held in client account as verified by the bank
after allowance for outstanding cheques and
lodgments cleared after date ..   ..   ..

Delete (*a*) *or* (*b*) *as appropriate*   £

(ii) at ....

(*a*) the figures were in agreement;

(*b*) there was a difference computed as follows:

£

Liabilities to clients as shown by clients' ledger
accounts   ..   ..

Cash held in client account, as verified by the bank
after allowance for outstanding cheques and
lodgments cleared after date ..   ..   ..

Delete (*a*) *or* (*b*) *as appropriate*   £

3. (*a*) Having retired from active practice as a solicitor the said.......................

....

ceased to hold client's money on...

(*b*) Having ceased to practise under the style of.................................

....

the said ....

ceased to hold client's money under that style on....................................

....

Particulars of the accountant:

Full Name...

Qualifications...

Firm Name...

Address ....

Signature ....

Date ....

To: The Secretary,
       The Law Society,
          The Law Society's Hall,
             113 Chancery Lane, London WC2.

FIRST SECTION

Matters in respect of which the accountant has been unable to satisfy himself and the reasons for that inability:

[*To be printed on the reverse of the Report.*]

SECOND SECTION

Matters (other than trivial breaches) in respect of which it appears to the accountant that the solicitor has not complied with the provisions of the Solicitors' Accounts Rules 1967:

[*A list of such matters would be entered here by the accountant.*]

The following extracts from an explanatory memorandum issued by the Council of the Law Society indicate the general nature of the work to be performed by the accountant:

Nature of the Accountant's Examination

The Council have sought to clarify within the Accountant's Report Rules 1967, particularly Rules 4 and 5, certain points which were explained previously by way of notes in the Explanatory Memorandum attached to the former Rules, or were implicit in the Rules. Neither the Act nor the Accountant's Report Rules require a complete audit of a solicitor's accounts nor do they require the preparation of profit and loss accounts or balance sheets. A complete audit would in any event be impracticable. Accordingly provision is made for a test examination of a solicitor's accounts. The nature of this examination is prescribed by Rule 4 of the Accountant's Report Rules. The accountant is not in the normal case required to check and vouch each and every item in the books or bank statements. If the general examination and detailed tests disclose evidence that the Rules have not been complied with the accountant is required to pursue a more comprehensive investigation.

Form of Accountant's Report

The form of Accountant's Report prescribed in the Schedule to the Accountant's Report Rules is such that the Report will relate to an individual solicitor whether or not he be a member of a firm of solicitors. Accordingly in the case of a firm where there are several partners, the accountant will render a Report in respect of each partner. It is not sufficient to give a single Report in respect of the firm.

Points to Note

(i) *Place of Examination of Solicitor's Books of Account by his Accountant*
Save in exceptional circumstances the place for examination of the solicitor's books of account and relevant documents by the accountant should be the office of the solicitor and not the office of the accountant.

(ii) *Signature of Accountant's Report*
There is nothing (other than the approval of the solicitor concerned) to prevent any partner in a firm of accountants signing the Report provided he

is duly qualified to do so under Rule 3 of the Accountant's Report Rules. The Council will regard the accountant who signs the Report as having thereby accepted responsibility for its accuracy.

(iii) *Responsibility for delivery of the Accountant's Report*

Although the solicitor may agree with his accountant that the accountant shall forward his Accountant's Report to the Society, the responsibility for delivery of the Report to the Society is that of the solicitor.

(iv) *Solicitor's instructions to his Accountant in respect of tax and other accountancy matters not connected with the Accountant's Report*

As regards work other than that required to be done by the accountant for the purpose of giving an Accountant's Report, a solicitor is free to instruct that or any other accountant as he wishes although he may vary his instructions at will. It is, however, advisable in the interests of both the solicitor and the accountant concerned that those instructions should be given and accepted in writing. The accountant who accepts such instructions neither increases nor diminishes his duties in connection with the giving of the Accountant's Report.

In view of the provision in Rule 4 of The Solicitor's Accounts (Deposit Interest) Rules 1965 (reproduced below), that a client who feels aggrieved may require the solicitor to refer to the Law Society for adjudication, reporting accountants need not concern themselves with matters arising under these Rules, except that where it has been decided that a client is entitled to the deposit account interest, the accountant should ensure that the gross interest arising has been properly credited to the client concerned.

Pursuant to Section 8 of the *Solicitors Act 1965*, Rules have been made by the Council of the Law Society, approved by the Master of the Rolls, designed to deal with the special question of whether in individual circumstances the interest arising on a client's money held by the solicitor on deposit account, should properly be regarded as the property of the solicitor or the client. These Rules are known as The Solicitors' Accounts (Deposit Interest) Rules 1965, and are reproduced hereunder:

1. These Rules may be cited as the Solicitors' Accounts (Deposit Interest) Rules, 1965, and shall come into operation on the 1st day of September, 1965.

2. (1) Subject to Rule 5 of these Rules, when a solicitor holds or receives for or on account of a client money on which, having regard to all the circumstances (including the amount and the length of time for which the money is likely to be held), interest ought in fairness to the client to be earned for him, the solicitor shall either –

(a) deposit such money in a separate designated account and account to the client for any interest earned thereon; or

(b) pay to the client out of his own money a sum equivalent to the interest which would have accrued for the benefit of the client if the money had been deposited in a separate designated account under this Rule.

(2) In this Rule the expression 'a separate designated account' shall mean a deposit account at a bank in the name of the solicitor or his firm in the title of which the word 'client' appears and which is designated by reference to the identity of the client or matter concerned.

3. Without prejudice to the generality of Rule 2 of these Rules, it shall be deemed that interest ought in fairness to a client to be earned for him where a sum of money is received for or on account of the client which exceeds £500 and at the time of its receipt is unlikely within two months thereafter to be either wholly disbursed or reduced by payments to a sum less than £500.

4. Without prejudice to any other remedy which may be available to him, any client who feels aggrieved that interest or a sum equivalent thereto has not been paid to him under these Rules shall be entitled to require the solicitor to obtain a certificate from The Law Society as to whether or not interest ought to have been earned for him and, if so, the amount of such interest and upon the issue of such a certificate the sum certified to be due shall be payable by the solicitor to the client.

5. Nothing in these Rules shall –

(a) affect any arrangement in writing, whenever made, between a solicitor and his client as to the application of the client's money or interest thereon; or

(b) apply to money received by a solicitor being money subject to a trust of which the solicitor is a trustee.

When a complete audit is undertaken, apart from the requirements of the Solicitors' Account Rules, the auditor should deal with the following matters:

The system of dealing with petty cash disbursements should be examined, and it should be ascertained that all disbursements made on account of clients are duly charged up to their accounts. In the case of a large office there may be several petty cash accounts, the balances of which should be counted simultaneously.

In checking the clients' ledger, allowances to clients should be vouched, and it should be seen that amounts disallowed on taxation are properly adjusted.

Credit balances may be found representing moneys paid by clients on account of costs and disbursements which have not yet been debited. If a payment of this nature is wholly on account of disbursements which have not yet been made, the item will in effect be a liability; but where the whole, or a portion, is in respect of costs which have been earned, but which have not yet been debited to the client, owing to the fact that no bill has been rendered, the ledger account should be adjusted by passing an entry through the bills delivered book for the amount of fees earned to date.

In order to ascertain profits correctly, it is necessary that undelivered costs should be valued, and a schedule should be prepared from the draft bills of costs. The valuation should be made on a conservative basis, provision being made for allowances, whether voluntary or by taxation. All items which are in any way doubtful should be omitted. This schedule should be signed by the partners.

Many solicitors, however, prefer to leave out of account undelivered costs not debited to clients. In such cases it is advisable that a note should appear on the balance sheet stating that these items are not brought into account.

§ 7. Stockbrokers

The requirements concerning the accounts and balance sheets of members of the Stock Exchange, London, are dealt with in Stock Exchange Rule 79A which is reproduced hereunder, as revised in August 1966:

RULE 79a

(*Note:* 'Partners' shall include limited partners unless otherwise stated)

(1) Every Firm shall maintain records in sufficient detail to show particulars of:

(*a*) all moneys received or paid by the Firm;

(*b*) all purchases and sales of securities by the Firm and the charges and credits arising therefrom;

(*c*) all transactions by the Firm with or for the account of –

(i) clients, excluding partners in the Firm;

(ii) partners in the Firm;

(iii) Firms of The Stock Exchange, London (including bargains to be settled through the Settlement Office);

(iv) Firms of all other Stock Exchanges in Great Britain and Ireland;

(v) Associated Members, Attachés and employees;

(vi) other persons.

(d) all income from commissions, interest and other sources and all expenses, commissions and interest paid;

(e) all assets and liabilities, including contingent liabilities, of the Firm;

(f) all securities which are the property of the Firm, showing by whom they are held and whether, if held otherwise than by the Firm itself, they are so held as collateral against loans or advances;

(g) all securities which are not the property of the Firm but for which the Firm or any nominee company controlled by it is accountable, showing by whom and for whom they are held and:

(i) the extent to which they are held for safe custody in which case, with effect on and after January 1st, 1967, they must either be registered in the name of the client or of the Firm's nominee company or be deposited in a specially designated Safe Custody Account with the Firm's bankers;

(ii) the extent to which they are deposited with any third party as collateral against loans or advances to the Firm in which case such deposit must be authorized by the client or other person concerned. Such authority must be in writing and must specify the period to which it relates and be renewed annually.

(h) all purchases and sales of options by the Firm, fees (option moneys) arising therefrom, any related covering transactions and all declarations to exercise the options.

The provisions of this Clause shall in so far as they are relevant apply not not only to records in the United Kingdom, but also to those of any Overseas Branch Office and not only to the Firm itself, but also to any company owned or controlled thereby for the purpose of conducting the business of the Firm.

(2) Every Firm shall cause a balance sheet to be prepared from time to time showing in accordance with the provisions of this Rule the assets and liabilities of the Firm and the partners' capital therein. The assets and liabilities shall be brought into account in the said balance sheet at such amounts and shall be classified and described therein in such manner that the balance sheet gives a true and fair view of the state of affairs of the Firm, as at the Balance sheet date. The said balance sheet shall be signed by each and all of the partners in the Firm.

(3) Each such balance sheet shall be prepared as at a date which is not, without the consent of the Council, more than fifty-four weeks after the date as at which a balance sheet was last prepared under the provisions of Rule 79a, or, as the case may be, the date on which the Firm began to trade. A balance sheet shall be deemed to comply with this Rule notwithstanding that it does not take into account transactions in securities since the close of dealing for the last preceding Stock Exchange Account.

(4) (a) Without prior consent of the Council no Firm shall change its practice with regard to the date as at which the said balance sheet is prepared.

(b) Every new Firm shall within one month from the date of commencement of business, notify the Council of the date as at which its balance sheet will be prepared in each year.

(5) In addition to all other requirements of this Rule there shall be disclosed in the said balance sheet:

(a) (i) the balances at credit on the Capital account of –

    (a) each limited partner;

    (b) each general partner.

(ii) the balances at debit on the Capital account of each general partner.

(b) the balance due to or from each partner in respect of transactions in securities.

(c) (i) credit balances on current and all other accounts of –

    (a) each limited partner;

    (b) each general partner;

(ii) debit balances on current and all other accounts of each general partner.

(d) Amounts due to banker specifying the nature and market value of any security given and the fact, where applicable, that the security given is not the property of the Firm.

(e) any other liabilities which are secured, either by the deposit of securities or otherwise, specifying the nature and market value of the security at the date of the balance sheet and the fact, where applicable, that the security given is not the property of the Firm.

(f) by way of note, full particulars of any transactions in stocks or shares for the account of partners which have been closed at the end of the Stock Exchange Account immediately prior to the date of the balance sheet and opened for the immediately following Account. If there were no such transactions such fact must be stated.

(6) For the purpose of clause (14) of this Rule and without prejudice to the general requirement of clause (2) the said balance sheet:

(a) shall distinguish the following classes of assets from one another and from any other assets –

(i) money receivable in the ordinary course of business from –

    (a) clients, excluding partners in the Firm;

    (b) Associated Members, Attachés and employees;

    (c) Firms of any Stock Exchange in Great Britain and Ireland (including tickets receivable), excluding amounts relating to transactions in securities undertaken for the account of partners in the Firm;

    (d) other persons, exluding partners in the Firm.

(ii) securities in which dealings are permitted under Rule 163 (1), stating by way of note the aggregate market value of such securities.

   (iii) payments for or towards the purchase of securities for which a quotation is pending;

   (iv) treasury bills, defence bonds, national development bonds and tax reserve certificates;

   (v) money on deposit (other than with banks) which is encashable within six months after the balance sheet date;

   (vi) cash and stamps in hand and balances on current or deposit account with banks;

   (vii) such other assets as may be agreed with the Council for the purpose of clause (14);

(*b*) shall include among the liabilities a provision for income tax to the extent, whichever is the greater, of –

   (i) the total amount of the income tax (or a fair estimate thereof) outstanding in respect of all years of assessment ended on or before the balance sheet date and, where applicable, the accrued proportion for the year of assessment in which the balance sheet date falls, or

   (ii) the total amount of the income tax liability (or a fair estimate thereof) which would be outstanding if the Firm had ceased business at the balance sheet date;

(*c*) shall distinguish the following liabilities from one another and from all other liabilities

   (i) credit balances as defined in paragraphs (*a*), (*b*) and (*c*) of clause (5) of partners in the Firm;

   (ii) those liabilities, if any, to Firms of any Stock Exchange in Great Britain and Ireland (including tickets payable) which relate to transactions in securities undertaken for the account of partners in the Firm;

   (iii) any amount set aside for income tax in excess of the provision specified in paragraph (*b*) of this clause;

   (iv) such other liabilities as may be agreed with the Council for the purpose of clause (14).

(7) Without prejudice to the general requirements of clause (2) of this Rule, the said balance sheet shall include provision for, or a note of:

(*a*) the amount, if any, by which the sum at which securities in which dealings are permitted under Rule 163 (1) owned by the Firm are brought into account exceeds their aggregate market value;

(*b*) the amount, if any, by which bear positions in securities in which dealings are permitted under Rule 163 (1) are brought into account falls short of the aggregate market value of the securities comprised in the bear position;

(*c*) the amount of any loss which the Firm could incur in respect of options granted and outstanding calculated on the basis of market values;

(*d*) the amount of any accumulated losses, so far as they concern the Firm, of any Service Company of which the Firm is owner;

(*e*) the amount of any foreseeable losses from bad or doubtful debts or from any other causes;

and for the purpose of clause (14) the said amounts shall be taken into account as liabilities except to the extent that any provision for them has been applied in the balance sheet in reduction of the amounts at which related assets have been included. In relation to securities quoted on The Stock Exchange, London, market value means the market value at the balance sheet date as evidenced by the quotations in the Stock Exchange Daily Official List.

(8) The said balance sheet shall be submitted to an independent qualified Accountant to whom shall be made available all the books and records of the Firm and all such explanations and other information as he may require for the purpose of carrying out under this Rule such examination as will enable him to meet the requirements of clause (10) of this Rule.

(9) For the purpose of this Rule 'independent qualified Accountant' means a person who is:

(*a*) in public practice; and

(*b*) independent of the Firm; and

(*c*) a member, or a firm all of whose partners are members, of one or more of the following professional bodies –

> The Institute of Chartered Accountants in England and Wales
> The Institute of Chartered Accountants of Scotland
> The Association of Certified and Corporate Accountants
> The Institute of Chartered Accountants in Ireland.

(10) (*a*) The said independent qualified Accountant shall provide the Firm with three signed copies of a report addressed to the Council of The Stock Exchange stating:

(i) whether, subject to any reservations relating to the scope of his examination or to any other matters, he is of the opinion that –

(*a*) the Firm had at the balance sheet date records properly maintained which comply with the requirements of clause (1) of this Rule;

(*b*) the balance sheet is in accordance with those records;

(*c*) the balance sheet gives a true and fair view of the state of affairs of the Firm at the balance Sheet date;

(*d*) the balance sheet complies with the requirements of clauses (5), (6) and (7) of this Rule;

and whether or not at the balance sheet date securities referred to in clause (1) (*g*) (ii) of this Rule were deposited with any third party as collateral for loans or advances to the Firm and, if so, whether he has inspected the written authorizations referred to in the said clause;

(ii) whether, as shown by the Balance sheet and at the date thereof, the excess of assets over liabilities as defined by clause (14) of this Rule was not less than the minimum amount which that clause requires the Firm to maintain;

(iii) whether, in the case of a limited partnership, as shown by the balance sheet and at the date thereof, the aggregate of the balances on capital, current and all other accounts of the limited partners was within the limits prescribed by clause (15) of this Rule.

(b) In the case of Broker Firms engaged in Arbitrage business as Arbitrageurs on Joint Account or conducting option business as Option Dealers, the independent qualified Accountant shall also provide the Firm with three signed copies of a Report addressed to the Council of The Stock Exchange stating whether, subject to any reservations regarding the scope of his examination or to any other matter, he is of the opinion that the Firm had properly maintained records in compliance with the undertakings in Appendices 32 or 32c as may be applicable and, that on the basis of his examination, no business had been executed on behalf of any of its clients with the Firm's Arbitrage or Option Accounts.

(11) Where the assets of a Firm include the entire share capital of a Service Company operated under the provisions of Rule 30b, the provisions of this Rule may be applied as though a consolidated balance sheet of the Firm and the company were the balance sheet of the Firm.

(12) (a) Where the assets of a Firm include the share capital of an unlimited company which is operating as a Corporate Member under the provisions of Rule 57b, the provisions of clause (14) of this Rule shall be applied as though the balance sheet of the Firm and the balance sheet of the company were consolidated.

(b) Where the assets of a Firm include an interest in any Branch Office whether separately incorporated or not, the balance sheet required by this Rule –

(i) shall include the assets and liabilities of such Branch Office;

(ii) shall disclose the aggregate amount of such assets included in those classes of asset which are specified in clause (6) (a) of this Rule.

(13) The Firm shall forthwith submit one copy of the Accountant's Report referred to in sub-clause (10) (a) to the Council so as to be received by the Council not later than six months after the balance sheet date together with any report pursuant to sub-clause (10) (b) and shall at the same time submit a further copy of any such Reports together with the related balance sheet to the Exchange Accountant selected under clause (16) (b) (i), who shall receive them on behalf of the Council.

(14) The partners of the Firm shall at all times maintain collectively a balance on Capital Account of such amount that the assets specified in clause (6) (a) of this Rule and such assets of the individual general partners as may be agreed by the Council in the aggregate (but, except as may be agreed otherwise with the Council, excluding the amount specified in clause (12) (b) (ii) of this Rule) exceed the liabilities (excluding liabilities specified

in clause (6) (c) but including the amounts specified in clause (5) (c) (i) (à) and amounts falling to be treated as liabilities by virtue of clause (7)) by not less than the sum obtained by multiplying £5,000 by the number of partners in the Firm, provided that in the case of any Jobber Firm or in the case of a Broker Firm engaged in Arbitrage business on Joint Account or conducting option business as Option Dealers such sum shall not in any event be less than £15,000 and in the case of any Member continuing to carry on the business of a Broker on his own account pursuant to Rule 86, such sum shall not in any event be less than £10,000.

Where a Firm has Associated Members and/or Attachés and the number of such persons exceeds the number of the general partners in the Firm then for the purposes of this clause the excess number of such persons shall be regarded as partners of the Firm.

(15) In the case of a limited partnership the sum of the amounts specified in paragraphs (a) (i) (a) and (c) (i) (a) of clause (5) of this Rule shall not at any time exceed one half (or such larger proportion as the Council may agree) of the net aggregate credit balance represented by the sum of the amounts specified in paragraphs (a) (i) (b) and (c) (i) (b) of that clause less debit balances as specified in paragraphs (a) (ii) and (c) (ii) thereof.

(16) (a) The Council shall from time to time appoint one or more Firms of professional Accountants as Exchange Accountants (in this Rule referred to as Exchange Accountant) and shall notify Member Firms of the name and address of each Exchange Accountant so appointed.

(b) (i) Every Firm shall select the Exchange Accountant to which its balance sheet is to be submitted and shall inform the Council of its selection and shall not make any change therein without the consent of the Council.

(ii) An Exchange Accountant shall be deemed to be authorized by the Firm to obtain direct from the Accountants reporting on the balance sheet any information or explanation which he may consider necessary for the purpose of carrying out his duties under sub-clause (c).

(iii) The Exchange Accountant selected shall not be either the Firm's independent Accountant or the Firm's Tax Adviser.

(c) In any case where a balance sheet or the information obtained (under sub-clause (b)) or any other matter arising out of his enquiries leads an Exchange Accountant to consider that further information should be obtained by the Council regarding the Firm's state of affairs, he shall report accordingly to the Council. All such reports shall be deemed to have been authorized by the Member Firm concerned.

(d) All balance sheets and other documents lodged for inspection as above provided shall be retained by the Exchange Accountant and shall be regarded as confidential to him and no disclosure of information contained therein or derived therefrom shall be made by him to any body or person except as the Exchange Accountant may consider necessary for the purposes of any report he may make under sub-clause (c) above.

Note – Rule 79a (10) (*b*) refers to the undertakings contained in Appendices 32 and 32c. These undertakings are set out as follows:

APPENDIX 32

ARBITRAGE
(Rule 92 (1))

BROKER MEMBERS
(Joint Account)

....19......

To the Council of the Stock Exchange

Gentlemen,

We apply under Rule 92 (1) for authority to carry on Arbitrage on Joint Account until March 24th, 19   , with or between the arbitrage correspondent(s) whose name(s), address(es) and description(s) are set out in the Schedule to this form. We have sent a copy of Rule 92 (1) to our correspondent(s) and attach a letter from them intimating their acceptance of the conditions laid down so far as such conditions affect the correspondents.

We hereby undertake –

(*a*) to exclude from Arbitrage any order received from a non-Member; and that if we execute such an order with a firm which is also our Arbitrage correspondent we will act solely as Broker and Agent and issue a Contract Note containing a charge for commission at a rate not less than that laid down in the Commission Rules.

(*b*) to maintain separate records for our Broker and Arbitrage business respectively showing for whom and with whom bargains have been transacted in such a manner as readily to demonstrate compliance with this undertaking.

(*c*) to instruct our Firm's independent qualified Accountant appointed to report on the balance sheet also to examine and report on these records as required by Rule 79a (10) (*b*).

Yours faithfully,

SCHEDULE

Name of Arbitrage Correspondent	Address	Description of Business*
....	....	....
....	....	....
....	....	....

*The applicant must state whether the Arbitrage Correspondents are Members or otherwise of the Overseas Stock Exchange.

Regulation

Except in special circumstances permission will not be granted to a Broker to carry on Arbitrage on Joint Account with more than one correspondent in the same centre or to more than one Member Firm to carry on Arbitrage on Joint Account with the same correspondent.

APPENDIX 32C

OPTION DEALING
(Rule 94)

BROKER MEMBERS

....19.....

To the Council of the Stock Exchange

Gentlemen,

We apply under Rule 94 for authority to carry on business as Option Dealers until March 24th, 19..........

We hereby undertake:

(*a*) not to execute any Option business received from our clients with the Option Dealing side of our business.

(*b*) to maintain separate records for our Broker and Option Dealing respectively showing for whom and with whom bargains have been transacted in such a manner as readily to demonstrate compliance with this undertaking.

(*c*) to instruct our Firm's independent qualified Accountant appointed to report on the balance sheet also to examine and report on these records as required by Rule 79a (10) (*b*).

Yours faithfully,

The following further memorandum was issued in 1966 by the Council of The Stock Exchange with the approval of the Council of the Institute of Chartered Accountants in England and Wales, the Institute of Chartered Accountants of Scotland and the Association of Certified and Corporate Accountants.

NOTES FOR THE GUIDANCE OF
MEMBER FIRMS AND THEIR ACCOUNTANTS

(*Note:* 'Partners' includes limited Partners unless otherwise stated.)

(1) *Summary of Provisions*

The Rule provides for the following matters, *inter alia:*

(*a*) The maintenance of a collective balance on Capital Account sufficient to ensure the required Minimum Margin of Solvency (see paragraph 2 below).

(*b*) The extent to which limited Partners may participate in providing finance for the Firm (see paragraph 3 below).

(*c*) The manner in which clients' securities must be held and the authority necessary before such securities can be pledged.

(*d*) The keeping by the Firm of adequate records including records of all securities held whether the property of the Firm or not.

(*e*) The preparation by or on behalf of the Firm of a balance sheet (which must be signed by every Partner) showing a true and fair view of its state of affairs as at the date thereof.

(*f*) The classification and disclosure of assets and liabilities included in the balance sheet.

(*g*) The appointment by each Firm of an independent Accountant to examine its balance sheet and to prepare a report thereon addressed to the Council of The Stock Exchange.

(*h*) The submission by each Firm of a copy of its balance sheet and of the Accountant's report to an Exchange Accountant for examination on behalf of the Council of The Stock Exchange. The Exchange Accountant selected shall not be the Firm's independent Accountant.

(2) *Minimum Margin of Solvency*

The minimum margin of solvency must be maintained at all times and must not be less than £5,000 per Partner with a minimum of £15,000 for a Jobbing Firm and any Broking Firm engaged in arbitrage on joint account or option business. All principals whether full Partners or otherwise and irrespective of whether they receive part or all of their remuneration by share of profits, commission or salary must be regarded as Partners for the purpose of calculating the minimum margin of solvency. Also to be regarded as Partners but only for this purpose is any excess in the number of Associated Members and Attachés over the number of general Partners in a Firm. The inclusion of Attachés will become operative from January 1st, 1967. (Attachés are those people entered on the Register of Attachés kept by the Council under Rule 199 (2) (*c*).)

Clause (14) lays down the manner in which the margin is to be computed. Broadly speaking, only money receivable in the ordinary course of business and those assets which are readily realizable may be taken into account. All balances related to uncompleted transactions in securities undertaken by the Firm for the account of Partners individually are to be ignored, as are securities in which dealings have been suspended, unquoted securities, and amounts receivable otherwise than in the ordinary course of business, e.g. Loans to staff for housing. Apart from the liabilities specified in Clause (6) (*c*), which are excluded for the purpose of this margin, all liabilities must be taken into account. The Council of The Stock Exchange have powers on application by a Firm to approve the inclusion of other assets of the Firm and assets of individual Partners (Clauses (6) (*a*) (vii) and (14)).

(3) *Limited Partners*

Clause (15) restricts the extent of limited Partners' interests in a Firm. Reference should be made to the *Limited Partnerships Act 1970* for the statutory rights and obligations of such Partners.

(4) *Brokers acting as Joint Account Arbitrageurs and/or Option Dealers*

Brokers acting as Joint Account Arbitrageurs and/or Option Dealers have to apply annually to the Council of The Stock Exchange for permission under Rules 92 (i) (*f*) and 94 respectively and, when permission is given, it is subject to the condition that there shall be a segregation of the two sides of the business of the Broker Firm. Separate records for each side of the business have to be maintained and an undertaking given that such a Firm will not execute business on behalf of its clients with the other (non-Broker) side of the business (Appendices 32 and 32c). As evidence of compliance with this undertaking, the Firm is required to submit a report from its Accountants addressed to the Council of The Stock Exchange at the same time as the report on the balance sheet is provided (Clause (10) (*b*)).

(5) *Securities*

Particular attention is drawn to sub-clauses (*f*) and (*g*) of Clause I regarding securities. All movements of securities should be recorded in such a manner as to enable the security position of the Firm and of any third party for whom securities are held to be readily ascertained as at any particular date.

The provision contained in Clause (1) (*g*) (i) in so far as it relates to the specially designated safe custody account with the Firm's bankers will become operative on January 1st, 1967, and evidence of compliance at the balance sheet date with this and the other provisions of Clause (1) will be provided in the Accountant's report (Clause (10) (*a*) (i) (*a*)).

(6) *Defence Bonds and National Development Bonds*

It is understood that Defence Bonds and National Development Bonds cannot be held in the name of a Firm, but for the purpose of Clause (6) (*a*) (iv) they may be held in the name of a Nominee Company on the Firm's behalf.

(7) *Other Assets of the Firm*

Clause (6) (*a*) (vii) refers to assets of the Firm as distinct from the assets of individual Partners which are dealt with in Clause (14). Normally the Council of The Stock Exchange will only give permission under the former clause for the inclusion in the margin of solvency calculation of those assets of the Firm which are readily realizable.

(8) *Assets of Individual Partners*

An application under Clause (14) may be made by a Firm for permission to include securities belonging to individual general Partners (and therefore not appearing as assets in the Firm's balance sheet) in the calculation of the margin of solvency. The following conditions will be included in any grant of permission which may be made by the Council of The Stock Exchange:

(a) Such assets must be limited to the securities held from time to time by the individual general Partners of the Firm, such securities being registered in the name of the Nominee Company of the Firm's bank and held to the Firm's order. A separate note to the balance sheet must disclose the market value of such securities and the manner in which they are held.

(b) (i) The Firm must have adequate control over the securities to ensure that they are available at all times for its requirements; the withdrawal from deposit must be adequately controlled to ensure that an individual Partner cannot withdraw securities from deposit on his signature alone.

(ii) The Firm must have adequate control over the quantum of the securities deposited with the Firm's bank by each individual Partner.

(c) These conditions must be notified by the Firm to its Independent Accountant who must confirm that, in his opinion, the measure of control by the Firm over the custody and quantum of such securities is not less than would be required to satisfy him were the securities included in the balance sheet as assets of the Firm. Such confirmation must be made at the same time as the report required by Clause 10 and a copy thereof furnished both to the Council of The Stock Exchange and to the Exchange Accountant.

(d) The permission of the Council of The Stock Exchange must be renewed annually.

(9) *The Balance Sheet*

(a) The general provisions, including the date as at which a Firm's balance sheet must be prepared, are contained in Clauses (2), (3) and (4).

(b) It is essential that the balance sheet should be prepared as soon as possible after the end of the accounting year in order to give adequate time for the Accountant's examination and the making of his report to the Council of The Stock Exchange who will require strict compliance with the six months' time limit (Clause (13)).

(c) To assist Firms to appreciate the matters dealt with in the Rule there follows a *pro forma* balance sheet [*not reproduced in this extract*] of a Broker Firm cross-referenced to the relevant Clauses of the Rule. This *pro forma* balance sheet is adaptable for a Jobbing Firm, subject to differences in the nature and description of certain assets and liabilities and to the inclusion of any amounts required to be provided under Clause (7) (b).

(d) It is emphasized that the *pro forma* balance sheet is illustrative only, does not form part of the Rule and is not to be regarded as a prescribed form. Each Firm is free to prepare its balance sheet in whatever form and showing whatever information the Firm thinks fit, provided it complies with the Rule and in particular with the requirement to give a true and fair view of the state of affairs of the Firm.

(e) Where a Corporate Member is owned by a Firm the Rule requires the preparation of a consolidated balance sheet. If, in such a case, the balance sheet of the Corporate Member is not made up on the same date as that of the Firm, it will be necessary for one or other to prepare a special interim balance sheet for consolidation to comply with Clause (12) of the Rule.

(f) The method of valuing securities is laid down in Clause (7); where the security is not listed in the appropriate Stock Exchange Official List, the accepted practice of valuing such securities will be followed.

(g) The adequacy of the provision for any foreseeable losses from bad or doubtful debts or from other causes should be carefully considered by member Firms (see paragraph (10) (b) below).

(h) In accordance with normal accountancy practice, option money receivable by a Firm in respect of options granted for the put or call should not be included in the balance sheet as an asset until the option is exercised or abandoned.

(i) In the case of a Firm with many Partners, it may be convenient to show the balances of each Partner's Capital, Current and other Accounts in an annexed schedule transferring the totals (both credit and debit) of each type of account to the balance sheet, which should make suitable reference to the schedule. Balances of general Partners must be distinguished from those of limited Partners.

(10) *The Independent Accountant's Report*

In accordance with Clause (10), which also specifies its contents, the independent Accountant's report is to be addressed to the Council of The Stock Exchange.

While the full extent of the Accountant's examination will be a matter for arrangement between him and the Firm, it must, as a minimum, be sufficient to enable him to discharge his responsibilities to the Council of The Stock Exchange in accordance with Clause (10) and, if the Firm has made an application under Clause (14), to comply with the additional requirements set out in paragraph 8 above.

The Council of The Stock Exchange will place great reliance on the Accountant's report and his verification for that purpose of the assets and liabilities. It follows that he will need to do a considerable amount of auditing work and to base his examination of the books and records (including correspondence files) on a careful and critical review of the system of accounting and internal control.

Particular attention should be paid to:

(a) the soundness of the debts due to the Firm;

(b) the adequacy of the provisions made for liabilities and losses, including losses on collection of the debts;

(c) the system of control over securities held for safe custody;

(d) the provision of information called for by the Exchange Accountant under Clause 16 (b) (ii) particularly those matters referred to in paragraph 11 below.

It will be for the Accountant to consider in the circumstances of the particular Firm and in the light of his assessment of its system of accounting and internal control whether, and if so to what extent, he needs:

(i) to make spot checks at dates other than that of the balance sheet;

(ii) to obtain independent confirmation of debtor or creditor balances;

(iii) to make a test verification of securities held for safe custody.

In making his report the Accountant will, if necessary, include such reservations as he considers appropriate having regard to any limitations the Firm has imposed on the scope of his examination (for example, in relation to the matters set out above) or to any other matters.

In many cases the independent Accountant will also assist in the preparation of the balance sheet and there is nothing in the Rule to prohibit the same Accountant acting in this way. Nevertheless the Firm remains responsible for the balance sheet.

(11) *The Exchange Accountant*

Clauses (13) and (16) provide for the examination of the balance sheet and Accountant's Report by an Exchange Accountant on behalf of the Council of The Stock Exchange, who will not themselves receive a copy of the balance sheet. Clause (16) (*d*) provides for all balance sheets and other documents lodged with an Exchange Accountant to be treated as confidential.

In order to assist the Exchange Accountant and to minimize the number of questions which it may be necessary to ask, Firms should arrange for their Accountants to supply the following information in so far as it applies to them in schedules accompanying the balance sheet:

(*a*) Particulars, without names, of each client's debit balance in excess of £500, which was outstanding at the date of the balance sheet and not fully secured at that date and which had not been paid by 14 days prior to the date of the Accountant's report. The schedule should include against each item, notes as to the reason for non-payment and indicate the extent to which provision against non-recovery has been made.

(*b*) Similar information in respect of money receivable in the ordinary course of business from Associated Members, Attachés, employees and other persons distinguishing between Associated Members, Attachés, employees and other persons (Clause 6 (*a*) (i) (*b*) and (*d*)).

(*c*) The total value of securities lodged as collateral against loans or advances to the Firm distinguishing between those which are the property of the Firm, of the Partners and of clients respectively.

Where an Exchange Accountant has reason to believe that a Broker Firm is conducting 'margin business', he may require the Firm to submit additional information with regard to the adequacy of the cover provided by the individual clients.

Hereunder are the principal detailed matters to which the auditor should pay attention:

In checking the balances on a stockbroker's clients' ledgers, it should be seen that sufficient cover is held for all debit personal balances of importance. Similar remarks apply to the balances on the partners' accounts representing their private dealings. In checking the balances on the jobbers' ledgers, it should be ascertained that they have been properly agreed with the jobbers on the occasion of each account, when it is usual to settle for the balance so agreed. Any balances carried forward for a considerable time, without subsequent dealings, should be enquired into, as they may represent items in dispute. In this connection the splits account should be examined. This account is often utilized to adjust small differences, and any items of consequence passed through it should be investigated.

The tickets receivable book should be tested exhaustively by the auditor, who should ascertain that the amount outstanding at the close of each account is subsequently cleared off, and this should be confirmed by reference to the dates of subsequent delivery as shown in the transfer delivery books.

When registered stock is purchased by a broker on behalf of his client, he issues a ticket which is termed a 'ticket payable'. The auditor should test the tickets payable book, and ascertain that the balances outstanding are subsequently cleared off as above indicated.

The general ledger, which will contain accounts for commission, interest, and expenses, should be checked completely. The commission should be checked from the commission columns of the purchases, sales, and special settlement books, and it should be seen that all half-commissions payable have been duly provided for. The expense accounts should be vouched, and it should be seen that all outstanding liabilities are brought into account.

Commission received on underwriting should be checked with the underwriting book, should one be kept, or with any other evidence available. Stocks of contract stamps should be checked and agreed with the stamp accounts. The dividend account should be examined and outstanding balances agreed.

The firm's investment ledger, representing investments held by the firm, should be checked in detail.

The verification of the securities is the most important and difficult part of the audit. It is sometimes arranged for this to take place several times during the year, without notice being given to the stockbroker's staff. In this way a considerable moral check is exercised. In any event the verification must be performed for the purposes of the annual balance sheet. The securities will be of four classes:

(1) Securities held by the firm as investments, according to the balances in the investment ledger.

(2) Securities held as cover against loans made by the broker, or balances due from clients.

(3) Securities awaiting delivery against tickets receivable.

(4) Securities held for safe custody on behalf of clients.

The auditor should attend as soon after the close of the account as possible, in order to avoid the numerous adjustments that become necessary if the examination of the securities is delayed, and dealings therein have taken place. The securities should all be produced at the same time, and should be checked off by the auditor with the security book or schedules. The security book is a memorandum book, which is made up for each account, showing the total amount and value of securities held, the parties on whose account they are held, and to whom they have been pledged, if at all. If not pledged, they will be in what is called the 'box', i.e. either in the strong room of the firm, or in a box deposited with their bankers. This book will not contain particulars of the securities held for safe custody on behalf of clients, which should be recorded in a separate book. It must be seen that there is sufficient margin where stock is held as security, the making-up prices and calculations being checked for this purpose, and the clients' balances compared with the ledger accounts. Care must be taken to see that all securities held according to the books are recorded in these schedules, and certificates must be obtained from all banks and other parties to whom stocks have been pawned as cover for loans, stating the amount of the loan and the various stocks held. These certificates will be checked off, and will serve to verify the existence of the stocks mentioned in them. All remaining stocks should be in hand, and be examined by the auditor, the usual precautions being taken to prevent stocks being produced twice.

Securities held for safe custody on behalf of clients will not appear in the financial books. A special memorandum book should be kept to record these securities, but in many cases it is found very difficult to do this, and they are included in the general memoranda books referred to above. In any case, it is impossible for the auditor to prove that all securities held for safe custody are produced to him, and he should be careful to refer to this point in his report.

If the firm has been converted into an unlimited company the auditor must see that its accounts comply with the provisions of the Companies Acts.

§ 8. Stockjobbers

The accounts of a stockjobber or dealer, although in many respects similar to those of a broker, differ in some important essentials. The business of a jobber or dealer is to buy and sell as principal, whereas a broker merely buys and sells, as agent for his client, from or to the dealer. Consequently the profit of a broker is obtained from the commission charged by him for his services, whereas the profit of a jobber is derived from selling stock at a higher price than he gave for it, or buying stock at a lower price than that for which he has previously sold it.

The stock journal records the dealings in each particular stock for each account, and columns are provided for the quantities of stock dealt in as well as the money values. If the opening balance is a debit, it represents stock in the box at the commencement of the account; if a credit, it is termed 'name-over' or 'box-short', and represents stock which has been over-sold and cannot be delivered. Where the jobber has purchased more stock than he has sold, he is a 'bull' for the balance he holds; where he has sold more stock than he has purchased, he is a 'bear' for the balance. At the close of each account the balance of the quantity columns, whether bull or bear, is inserted at the making-up price, or otherwise, as the case may be, and this should cause the stock quantity columns to agree. The money columns, however, will not usually agree, and the difference will represent profit or loss on the dealings during the account, which should be transferred to a profit and loss book.

The auditor should check the opening and closing balances, both in quantity and value. Postings from the cash book for application and allotment money on stocks applied for, underwriting commission etc., should be checked to the various accounts; the postings from the jobbers' or brokers' ledgers should be tested; the stock columns cast and agreed, and the profits and losses checked to the profit and loss book. Joint books are frequently kept with other jobbers, the profits or losses being divided by mutual agreement, and the auditor should see that the necessary transfers have been made.

The balances on the stock journals should be agreed with the 'bull and bear' books kept by the partners or their authorized clerks, which are memoranda books recording the dealings from day to day of each stock in quantities and prices only. The auditor should examine these books and ascertain that the bull or bear agrees with the stock journals both as to quantity and price, the price being usually marked by the partners for balance sheet purposes in the bull and bear books. The auditor should also check the calculations of the values of the stocks, as any error in extending the values affects directly the profit or loss.

The dividend journal records the dividends receivable or payable. The auditor should ascertain when the various stocks became quoted *ex div*. If the jobber was bull of the stock at that date, the dividend thereon should be ultimately received; if he was bear of the stock the dividend in respect thereof will be payable by him. If the stock is 'even', any dividends received will be payable to other persons, and should be treated as a liability, if not paid over at the date of the balance sheet.

The verification of the securities should be carried out in a similar manner to that described in the case of stockbrokers, but the securities to be examined will be all of one nature, namely, those recorded as box balances in the stock journals. The schedule of these should, therefore, be checked with the journals as to quantities and verified in the usual manner, certificates being obtained from bankers and others where securities have been pledged for advances. In the case of registered securities, the evidence will take the form of certificates, balance certificates, transfers, transfer receipts etc., and great care must be exercised by the auditor to ascertain that the total balance of each stock held is duly vouched in one form or another in accordance with the principles set out in Chapter VI, § 3.

§ 9. Trust and Finance Companies

The purchase and sale of investments should be vouched by inspection of brokers' contract notes. It should be ascertained that all dividends and interest receivable have been received, and that all bonus shares etc., receivable have been properly accounted for. Securities should be verified in the usual manner, and the book value should be compared with the market value at the date of the balance sheet. It is not usual to adjust the value of each investment to market price, but to provide, if necessary, for the difference between the total book value and the total market value.

Where shares are not fully paid, the contingent liability in respect of calls not yet made should be stated on the balance sheet; but where calls have actually been made, but not yet paid by the company, the amount should be treated as a liability.

The correct treatment of profits and losses made on the sale of investments and of the reduction, if any, in the value of investments at the date of the balance sheet, will depend upon the nature of the company.

In the case of a trust company proper, i.e. a company whose object is to earn income from the ownership of investments, it has been held that its investments are fixed assets, and that, subject to the articles, the excess or current income over current expenditure can be divided without making good any fall in the value of the investments (*Verner* v. *General and Commercial Investment Trust Ltd*, 1894, 2 Ch. 266). This decision has been discussed at length in Chapter X. Losses on investments sold by such companies need not, therefore, legally be charged to revenue before arriving at profits available for dividend, but similarly made profits must likewise be treated as capital profits. Each case must, however, be determined by a true construction of the provisions of the company's memorandum and articles. Where depreciation or losses have not been provided for, the auditor must see that the balance sheet describes clearly the true position, and, where necessary, he should refer to the matter in his report to the members.

In the case of a finance company, whose primary object is not to hold investments for the purpose of earning income, but to buy and sell them at a profit, the investments so held cannot be regarded as fixed assets. They are, in effect, the equivalent of stock-in-trade and must be treated as current assets, and brought into account at the lower of cost or market value as at the date of the balance sheet. Losses made on the sale of investments must be charged to revenue, or to provision for depreciation of investments account, and profits on such sales may be credited to revenue.

It is sometimes a matter of some difficulty to arrive at a proper value to be placed on shares held in companies which have been promoted by the finance company. The only sound system to adopt is to treat such shares on a cost basis, making the necessary provision if they have depreciated below cost. It is not always possible to rely on market quotations in the case of newly-promoted companies, since such quotations are frequently merely nominal.

Where promotion profits have been received in the form of fully-paid shares, these should not be brought into account at their nominal value. If there is a cash profit on the promotion, apart from the shares, the latter should remain unvalued until realized, when the amount so realized can be treated as additional profit. If, on the other hand, there is a cash loss on the promotion account, this can be regarded as the cost of the shares acquired, which can be brought into account at this figure, subject to depreciation.

Where underwriting transactions have been entered into, and the finance company has been obliged to take up shares, the underwriting commission received should be set against the cost of the shares so taken up, and not treated as profit.

Generally speaking, it may be said that the safest method is to credit profit and loss account only with profits actually realized. Where the accounts are not prepared in this manner, but credit is taken for profit represented by shares unsold, the auditor should deal with the matter fully in his report to the members.

The auditor should ascertain what, if any, transactions are open on the Stock Exchange at the date of the balance sheet, since shares may have been purchased but not taken up, or sold but not delivered. Where the transactions have been closed subsequent to the balance sheet, and the result is a loss, this should be provided for; but no credit should be taken for profit.

Where, however, the transactions are still open at the date of the audit, a note should appear on the balance sheet, stating that there are contingent liabilities in respect of transactions open on the Stock Exchange, and if the auditor considers the matter to be of sufficient importance, he should deal with it in his report to the members.

All transactions with associated companies should be carefully examined, and it should be seen that no manipulations are effected near the close of the financial year for the purpose of 'window-dressing' the respective balance sheets.

§ 10. Unit Trusts

The Board of Trade has issued the following regulations under the *Prevention of Fraud* (*Investments*) *Act 1958*, relating to the accounts and audit of Unit Trusts.

Audit – The trust deed should provide for audit by accountants approved by the trustees of all accounts before circularization and for a certificate of audit to be appended to the accounts circulated. The audit certificate should declare that the accounts and statements attached thereto have been examined with the books and records of the trust and of the management company, in relation thereto, and that the auditors have obtained all the information and explanations they have required. The auditors should report whether the accounts are, in their opinion, properly drawn up in accordance with such books and records to disclose the profits or losses accruing to the managers from the trust.

Accounts – The trust deed should provide for the circulation of accounts to unit holders, not less frequently than once a year (but not more than six months after the end of the period to which they relate). Attached to these accounts there must be a statement certified by the auditor showing the amount and percentage gross profits (before any deductions) or losses made (1) from the sale of new units; (2) from the resale of units; and (3) from the sale of the underlying securities of liquidated units.

If in the aggregate the holding of securities before appropriation or after liquidation of units and the holding of units results in a loss the manager shall disclose such loss in each of the above statements. The manager may disclose any holding profit if he so desires.

The percentage of profit or loss from the sale of new units should be calculated on the proceeds in the period of the account of the sale of new units. The percentage profit or loss from the resale of units should be calculated on the proceeds in the period of the account of the resale of units, and the percentage profit or loss from the sale of underlying securities of liquidated units should be calculated on the proceeds in the period of the account of such sales. (The cost of the securities to the manager should be regarded as the price allowed in the purchase of the relevant unit.)

Note – Holding profits or losses shall be deemed to be profits or losses resulting from price variations of (*a*) units between the dates of creation or purchase and sale; (*b*) underlying securities between the time of purchase and appropriation and between the time of liquidation of units and sale of the underlying securities.

Capital and Income Distributions – The trust deed should also provide that as at the end of each distribution period there should be circulated two statements certified by the auditors. The first should show what percentage of the total value of the trust funds was at the end of the distribution period invested in each investment and the percentage represented by cash (other than cash to be distributed for that period), and appended to these statements there should be quoted the bid price of units (ex dividend) on the last day of the distribution period.

The second statement should show how the amounts distributed to unit holders are made up, setting out in respect of each distribution and related to some convenient number of units, the gross amount of all cash dividends, interest, income bonuses etc., the amount of income tax deducted therefrom, the amount of any cash of a capital nature which is distributed and its source and the amount of all deductions, whether by way of annual or semi-annual charge from income or capital, together with an indication of the provisions in the trust deed which authorize such deductions and state separately the amount included in respect of any dividends accrued before the purchase or vesting of the relevant securities. The statement in respect of capital distributions should be kept distinct from that in respect of income distributions.

CHAPTER XIV

THE AUDIT OF ACCOUNTS OF LOCAL AUTHORITIES

§ 1. The Classification of Auditors of Local Authorities

There are three recognized systems of audit for the accounts of local authorities in England and Wales, viz. –

(1) Borough audit conducted by borough auditors under the provisions of Sections 237 and 238 of the *Local Government Act 1933*.

(2) Professional audit in accordance with the provisions of Section 239 of the *Local Government Act 1933*.

(3) District audit conducted by district auditors appointed by the Minister of Housing and Local Government and paid by the Treasury from monies provided by Parliament, which are recovered from the local authorities by means of a stamp duty based on the total of the expenditure and income audited. The relevant statutory provisions are contained in Sections 219-236 of the *Local Government Act 1933*.

§ 2. Borough Audit

Borough auditors are three in number, two called elective auditors, being elected by the local government electors for the borough, and one, who is appointed by the mayor, called the mayor's auditor. An elective auditor must be qualified to be a councillor, but must not be a member or officer of the council. The mayor's auditor, on the other hand, must be a member of the council.

The provisions relating to a borough audit apply only to county boroughs and non-county boroughs, and certain accounts of those boroughs must be submitted to the district auditor. The appointment is for one year, but the retiring auditors may be re-elected to the office at the end of each year.

The system of borough audit has been severely criticized in the courts. There is no provision for the borough auditors to make a report or issue a certificate on the completion of their audit, but it is usual for such auditors to sign a certificate in a simple form.

§ 3. Professional Audit

Professional auditors may only be appointed in boroughs, in pursuance of a resolution passed in accordance with the provisions of Section 239 of the Act of 1933. A resolution must be passed by a majority consisting of not less than two-thirds of the members of the Council present and voting at a meeting specially called for the purpose, of which not less than one month's previous notice of the object of the meeting has been given to every member of the Council, and which must be confirmed by the Council at a regular meeting held not less than one month after the passing of the resolution.

When professional audit has been adopted, the Council cannot revert to a system of borough audit.

Section 239 (3) of the Act contains the following provisions which apply to the audit by professional auditors:

(*a*) An auditor or auditors shall be appointed in writing under the seal of the Council for such period and upon such terms as to remuneration or otherwise as the Council of the borough thinks fit.

(*b*) No person shall be qualified to be so appointed unless he is a member of one or more of the following bodies, viz:

The Institute of Chartered Accountants in England and Wales.

The Institute of Chartered Accountants of Scotland.

The Association of Certified and Corporate Accountants.

(*c*) Any auditor so appointed shall be entitled to require from any officer of the borough such books, deeds, contracts, accounts, vouchers, receipts and other documents, and such information and explanations as may be necessary for the performance of his duties.

(*d*) Any auditor so appointed shall include in, or annex to, any certificate given by him with respect to the accounts audited by him such observations and recommendations (if any) as he thinks necessary or expedient to make with resepct to the accounts or any matter arising thereout or in connection therewith.

The duties of a professional auditor are not otherwise defined and they do not have the powers of disallowance and surcharge as in the case of district audit. There are no specific statutory powers which would enable the auditor to criticize the actions of the Council in relation to the making and collection of rates etc., similar to those which are contained in Section 228 (2) of the *Local Government Act 1933*, which applies to district auditors.

The work of professional auditors is, to a large extent, based upon the contract of appointment, but it may be assumed to include the following matters:

(1) The certification of the balance sheets of the borough council after due verification of the several items shown therein.

(2) An examination of the revenue accounts, in order to ascertain that all the income of the Council has been brought into account and that all expenditure is duly vouched and is in accordance with the law.

(3) A report to the Finance Committee of the Council drawing attention to any particular points which it is considered to be necessary to report upon.

In addition, the professional auditor might give the Council the benefit of his varied experience by way of suggestions for the improvement of systems of accounts and the possibility of adopting modern methods of accountancy and the use of machines. It is advisable that the professional auditor, when entering into the contract of service with the Council, should have his duties and responsibilities clearly defined. The existence or otherwise of a good system of internal check and internal audit will make a considerable difference to the quantity of detailed work which he would be called upon to audit.

As an alternative to professional audit, Section 239 of the Act of 1933 empowers a borough council to adopt the system of district audit for the whole of their accounts. Such a resolution cannot be rescinded.

§ 4. District Audit

The district auditor is responsible for the audit of the accounts of the following local authorities:

(a) The accounts of the Greater London Council and of every London borough council, county council, urban district council, rural district council and parish council, and of every parish meeting for a rural parish not having a parish council.

(b) The accounts of any committee appointed by such council or parish meeting.

(c) The accounts of certain joint committees where the accounts of one or more of the constituent authorities are wholly subject to district audit.

(d) Any other accounts which are made subject to audit by a district auditor by virtue of any enactment cr statutory instrument or, in the case of the accounts of the council of a borough, in pursuance of a resolution adopting the system of district audit.

District audit also applies to the rate collection accounts of all boroughs and to the accounts (of county borough councils) under the following statutes: *Education Act 1944, National Health Service Act 1946, National Assistance Act 1948, Coast Protection Act 1949* (maritime boroughs), *Police Act 1964*, and statutes relating to the care of children, viz: *Children and Young Persons Acts 1933* to *1963, Children Acts 1948* and *1958* and *Adoption Act 1958* (except transactions relating to approved schools or remand homes).

§ 5. Regulations applying to District Audit

Local Government Act 1933 – Sections 219-236

(a) The Minister of Housing and Local Government may appoint such number of district auditors as he considers necessary and assign to them their duties and districts.

(b) Salaries and expenses of district auditors are paid by the Treasury, and local authorities are charged by way of stamp duty according to a scale fixed by the Treasury. The charge may be reduced on application of the local authority if the scale charge exceeds the cost of the audit.

(c) The local authority must prepare and submit a prescribed form of financial statement to the district auditor in duplicate; one copy is stamped and certified by the auditor, and sent by him to the Ministry of Housing and Local Government.

(d) The accounts made up and balanced yearly to March 31st must be deposited in the appropriate office of the authority and be open to inspection by any person interested for seven clear days before the audit.

(e) Any local government elector for the area may make objection to the accounts before the auditor.

(f) The auditor may require the production of all books, vouchers and documents.

(g) The auditor, within fourteen days after the completion of the audit, must report to the local authority.

(h) The auditor must disallow every item of account which is contrary to law; surcharge the amount of any expenditure disallowed upon the person responsible for incurring or authorizing the expenditure; surcharge any sum not duly brought into account upon the person by whom that sum ought to have been brought into account; surcharge the amount of any loss or deficiency upon any person by whose negligence or misconduct it has been incurred; and certify the amount due from any person upon whom he has made a surcharge. Provided that no expenses may be disallowed by the auditor if they have been sanctioned by the Minister of Housing and Local Government.

(i) An appeal against an auditor's decision lies to the High Court where the amount exceeds £500, and if less than that sum, to the High Court or the Minister of Housing and Local Government, as the applicant may desire. A person surcharged may apply to the Court or the Minister for a declaration that he acted reasonably or in the belief that his action was authorized by law; if such a declaration is made, the Court or Minister may relieve him either wholly or partly from personal liability in respect of the surcharge.

(j) Any sum due in respect of a surcharge, unless there is an appeal, must be paid within fourteen days after the auditor has certified it. If it is not paid, the amount is recoverable either summarily or otherwise as a civil debt.

(k) The Minister of Housing and Local Government may at any time direct the auditor to hold an extraordinary audit of any accounts which are subject to district audit.

Accounts (Payments into Bank) Order 1922

(*a*) Where money is received by an officer of a local authority for payment into a banking account of the local authority or of their treasurer, the local authority must secure that a paying-in book is provided for the use of the officer.

(*b*) Every paying-in book must contain a number of paying-in slips for entry of money paid into the bank, together with a counterfoil or duplicate of each slip.

(*c*) Every officer who pays money into a banking account of a local authority or of their treasurer must, unless the local authority otherwise directs, enter on a paying-in slip and on the counterfoil or duplicate particulars of such payments, including in the case of each cheque paid in –

  (i) the amount of such cheque;

  (ii) some reference (such as the number of any receipt given or the name of the debtor) which will connect the cheque with the debts discharged;

  (iii) where any cheque paid in was not received in discharge of a debt due to the local authority, the officer must note the fact on the counterfoil or duplicate of the paying-in slip.

(*d*) Any officer of a local authority by whom a paying-in book is kept must produce the book for examination as and when required by the local authority or at district audit.

Accounts (Boroughs and Metropolitan Boroughs) Regulations 1930

These regulations deal with the accounts to be kept by London borough councils, and borough councils so far as they are subject to district audit. They define the principles upon which the accounts are to be kept and the results to be attained. The form and method of the book-keeping applicable to the chief accounts of the council is defined, but the forms of primary records, statements and accounts, are left to each council to devise in view of the widely differing circumstances and conditions which apply in different parts of the country. The accounts have to be supported by vouchers and be kept and examined by such officers as the council, or the chief financial officer acting under the authority of the council, may direct.

Audit Regulations 1934

These regulations amplify the provisions of the *Local Government Act 1933*, and apply to the audit of accounts of local authorities which are subject to district audit. The matters dealt with include the form of financial statement and certificate of the district auditor; notice of audit; certificate of compliance; production of accounts for audit; the preparation of an abstract of accounts; advertisements in local newspapers; the auditor's report and financial statement; and auditor's certificate.

Audit Stamp Duty (*Local Authorities*) Order 1938

This order prescribes the scale of stamp duty payable by local authorities whose accounts are subject to audit by district auditors.

Financial Statement Orders 1938 and 1951

These orders prescribe the form of financial statement to be used by local authorities in respect of such of their accounts as are audited by the district auditor.

Rate-Accounts Regulations 1962

These regulations prescribe the books, forms and accounts which are to be kept in respect of rates by the councils of London boroughs, county boroughs, non-county boroughs, urban districts and rural districts, acting as rating authorities. They also set out the duties of certain officers concerned with the accounts.

§ 6. Internal Audit

An internal audit is the recognized arrangement for securing a continuous and thorough check upon the financial transactions of a local authority. It should be regarded as supplementary to, and not in substitution for, an independent annual audit. It should consist of a complete and comprehensive check of both the income and expenditure of the council, including control over the preparation of wages sheets, disbursement of wages, the control of blank cheques and receipt forms, the supervision of stores and materials, and the organization of a periodical stocktaking of consumable stores held in various depots.

Internal audit has been devised to enable the chief financial officer to be assured that all details in connection with the accounts are correct. Where there is in operation a proper internal audit conducted by the staff, this relieves the external auditor of the necessity of detailed checking up to a certain point. He should, however, exercise reasonable care by an examination of the scope of the internal audit, in order to see whether it properly covers the ground and is performed in an efficient manner.

The advantages claimed for an internal audit include –

(1) It acts as a moral influence on the staff and promotes efficiency by compelling the officers to keep the books of account entered up to date.

(2) Cash disbursements such as wages and salaries may be checked before they are made.

(3) Important matters of principle which may arise may be dealt with expeditiously.

(4) Errors in account-keeping which arise can be corrected whilst the points are fresh in the minds of the officers concerned.

(5) Constant examination of the books of account facilitates the improvement and modernization of the system of accounting.

(6) Frauds and peculations are more likely to be discovered in their early stages.

(7) A detailed examination of the final accounts submitted by contractors is facilitated.

The internal audit system, to be efficient and satisfactory, should be based on the following rules:

(1) It should be comprehensive in its range. No department, however self-contained it may consider itself to be, should be excluded. The internal audit should be wide enough to cover the checking of all classes of income from the primary entries up to the point where the cash is paid into the bank and the final records entered into the appropriate books.

(2) The internal audit staff should be wholly engaged on this work. They should be organized in such a way that they are recognized in all departments as part of the general organization for exercising financial control.

Where such a system of internal audit is in operation, the professional auditor should appraise it thoroughly in order to satisfy himself that he need not cover the same ground. The scope and quality of the internal audit organization has an important bearing upon the audit fee payable for a professional audit.

§ 7. Preparations for Audit

The success of an audit will be dependent upon the preparation of an audit programme, and a notebook summarizing the sources of information to which the audit clerk must necessarily refer during the course of the audit. The audit principles applying to the accounts of local authorities are similar to those which are involved in the examination of commercial accounts, e.g. vouching of transactions, obtaining certificates of investments, stock on hand, bank balances etc. Some aspects of local authority activities which have their counterpart in commercial accounts are referred to in other parts of this book, for example, house purchase on mortgage.

The audit programme must be prepared after taking into consideration the scope of the internal audit, if any, and the books kept. The adequacy or otherwise of the system of internal control will modify the extent of the detailed work to be performed. An important source of information will be the minutes of the committees and the council of the local authority, and it must be remembered that any expenditure incurred by the local authority must be in accordance with law, i.e. be within the statutory powers of the council. A useful record for the auditor is a list of all financial provisions contained in general statutes and in any local Acts applicable to the authority.

§ 8. Capital Accounts

The statutory method of raising capital moneys by a local authority, viz. by loan, makes it necessary for these transactions to be kept distinct from revenue transactions, and it is usual to find that the accounts are recorded on a modified double account system. There are statutory provisions which control borrowed money, and the following points should be observed when auditing the capital accounts:

(1) Practically all expenditure out of loan must be covered by a sanction from a government department. The auditor should examine the loan sanctions received in order to verify the amount sanctioned and the purpose.

(2) Expenditure chargeable to loan may include the wages of permanent workmen employed on capital projects. In general, the salaries of officers may not be so charged except those which can be identified to specific officers wholly engaged on capital works whose offices would be abolished if the capital programmes were completed or suspended.

(3) Considerable sums are advanced to purchasers of houses under the provisions of the Small Dwellings Acquisition Acts and the Housing Acts. The repayments by the borrowers are generally calculated on an annuity basis. The rate of interest on an advance is normally one quarter per cent above the rate of interest at which the local authority could borrow. The rate remains fixed for the period of the advance unless the local authority have adopted a scheme for variable rates of interest.

The title and mortgage deeds should be examined, and the audit should follow the lines suggested for building societies.

§ 9. Loan Indebtedness

Local authorities raise a large part of the money required for capital expenditure by mortgages or bonds secured on the general rate fund or by the issue of stock. Large sums are borrowed from the Public Works Loan Board, for which mortgage deeds are not issued.

Considerable amounts are also obtained in the form of temporary borrowing from the money market, other lenders or by bank overdraft.

A loan may be earmarked to a particular loan sanction and repayment spread (by instalments or annuities) over the sanctioned period. More usually, loans are for varying amounts and periods repayable in full at maturity. The amounts so raised are 'pooled', advances are made from the loans pool to the borrowing accounts in accordance with the relevant loan sanctions, and repayments to the pool must be made over the sanctioned periods.

The following points should be observed in the audit of such borrowed moneys:

(1) Examine the minutes of the local authority which authorized the borrowing.

(2) Check the entry in the mortgage or bond register which has to be kept by the clerk of the local authority.

(3) Verify the amounts in respect of each mortgage or bond with the entries in the cash book or bank pass book.

(4) Check the final repayment which discharges a loan with the returned cheque and cancelled mortgage deed or bond and see that a proper entry is recorded in the register.

(5) See that the proper contributions are made from the general rate fund and trading accounts in respect of the annual charges for interest and repayment of the loans.

The moneys which are raised by loan are, in effect, the capital of the local authority. Loans outstanding, plus the loans which have been redeemed, are the principal items which appear on the liabilities side of the balance sheet as *contras* to the capital assets. Where loan redemption is effected by means of sinking funds, the amount held in those funds will appear on the liabilities side of the balance sheet, and the sinking fund money in hand and invested will be shown on the assets side.

§ 10. Stock Issue

Where a local authority makes a public issue of stock the issue will be handled by the authority's bankers. The time and terms of issue must be approved by the Bank of England and the minimum issue allowed is £3 million.

The auditor should inspect the loan sanctions exercised and the consent to the issue. The issue must comply with the Local Authorities (Stock) Regulations 1934 to 1956, or the terms of any local Act under which it is made. The auditor should also scrutinize the resolution of the council creating the stock, and, from the minutes and advertisements of the issue, ascertain the date and price of issue, rate of interest, underwriting commission, commission to brokers, due dates of instalments, discount for advance payments etc.

The following further audit programme is appropriate where the bank receive applications, issue allotment letters, and receive sums due on allotment and subsequent instalments, but the treasurer of the local authority is the registrar of the stock:

(1) Inspect orders for and record of consecutively numbered forms of letters of allotment and stock certificates and see that all forms are accounted for.

(2) See that sums paid upon application (less cheques returned) and allotment and instalments are promptly paid into the authority's special banking account, as required by the Stock Regulations. (The advertisement should require cheques to be made payable to a specified bank, with a special crossing indicating the local authority and account concerned.)

(3) Examine the statement of issue submitted by the issuing bank and reconcile total cash received, after allowing for any discount for payments in advance and any instalments in arrear; verify such items individually.

(4) Verify investment in statutory securities of moneys not immediately required for borrowing purposes.

(5) Before the stock certificates are sealed, check them with the stock register, and see that fully paid allotment letters (or forms of indemnity) surrendered are cancelled.

(6) Vouch the expenses of issue, e.g. printing and stationery, advertising and underwriting commission.

Where the authority's bank acts as registrar of the stock, the auditor should see that the appropriate sums are promptly paid into the local authority's special banking account and reconcile them with stock certificates issued. He should also check compliance with the Stock Regulations.

Stock Regulations

The Local Authorities (Stock) Regulations 1934 to 1956 provide for:

(1) The consent of the Ministry of Housing and Local Government to the issue.

(2) A Stock (Interest) Account to be kept for each class of stock to which the contributions for interest on stock appropriated

to the various sanctions are to be carried and out of which the interest is to be paid.

(3) A Stock (Sinking Fund) Account to be established for each class of stock. To this account must be carried the annual contribution for the redemption of the sum appropriated to each sanction.

The amount of the sinking fund contribution is determined by the rate of accumulation (if any), which must not exceed five per cent. per annum, and the period of the loan sanction. The latter is quite distinct from the date when the stock itself must be redeemed under the terms of issue.

(4) The accumulations in the sinking fund to be invested in statutory securities, applied in redeeming the stock or used for any capital purposes.

§ 11. Consolidated Loans Fund

The *Local Government Act 1958*, by Section 55, authorizes the establishment of a consolidated loans fund by a local authority in accordance with a scheme approved by the Minister of Housing and Local Government, subject to the consent of the Minister, in the case of a county district with a population of less than 60,000.

A consolidated loans fund records all borrowed money (with certain exceptions), and acts as an intermediary between the persons from whom money is borrowed and the departments of the council which carry out capital works. The provisions made by the borrowing accounts for the repayment of debt are paid into the fund, and sinking funds are eliminated. The revenue section of the fund comprises all amounts received from borrowing accounts in respect of interest charges, financing and management expenses, together with details showing how those moneys have been disbursed. The local authority may transfer to the loans fund the uninvested balances of reserve, renewals, depreciation, insurance, superannuation and other special funds, with the proviso that when such funds require moneys for purposes for which they are established, the loans fund will repay to the lending fund the sums so required.

The accounts must be prepared in prescribed form and be audited by the auditors of the local authority. The auditor's certificate must be entered on the balance sheet, the auditor being required to certify –

(1) that the balance sheet presents a true and complete statement of the loan debt of the council on March 31st, and of the advances owing on that day to the Consolidated Loans Fund by the several borrowing accounts of the Council;

(2) that the said loan debt and advances are respectively within the statutory borrowing powers of the Council;

(3) that all conditions attaching to those borrowing powers in regard to repayment and provision for repayment have been duly observed by the Council;

(4) that during the year, all sums of money required by the scheme to be paid into the Consolidated Loans Fund have been so paid, and have been duly allocated to capital or revenue in accordance with the provisions of that scheme.

§ 12. Arrangements for handling Receipts and Payments

The *Local Government Act 1958*, Section 58, requires every local authority to make safe and efficient arrangements for the receipt of money paid to them and the issue of money payable by them. The arrangements must be carried out under the supervision of the treasurer. Financial regulations should ensure a system of financial control. It is essential, for the administration of a sound system of control, for the local authority to appoint a finance committee with clearly defined responsibilities for regulating and controlling the finances of the authority.

§ 13. The Audit of Revenue Income

The income of a local authority is received from many sources and may be collected in a number of departments. The professional auditor must assess the effectiveness of the internal audit and decide the extent to which he must himself examine the detailed records. The principles which underlie the examination of income are:

(1) that satisfactory arrangements are in existence for calculating and recording sums due to the council, and that those operations are performed independently of the staff charged with the duty of collection;

(2) that the standing orders, financial regulations or minutes of the authority include detailed instructions for the control of sums received by officers in the course of their official duties and the frequency with which they bank them;

(3) that the approval of the local authority or of a committee thereof should be obtained before any sums are written off;

(4) that regular reports of arrears of income should be submitted to the finance committee;

(5) that all income has been credited to the proper account;

(6) that all income received is paid into the bank promptly: any delay may be merely neglect on the part of the officers concerned or due to bad systems of accounting, but it may equally be connected with embezzlements and frauds;

(7) that all income which is receivable is duly collected and brought into account.

From an accounting standpoint the income of a local authority may be divided into two classes:

(1) *Credit income*, for which rentals or other form of debtors accounts are needed: examples are rates, water charges, house rents.

(2) *Cash income*, received when the transaction occurs such as omnibus fares, swimming baths receipts, games in parks, cash sales.

The audit of credit income should be directed to ensuring that each item of income falling due is promptly and correctly recorded, that receipts in respect of such debts are duly brought into account and banked, that unpaid debts are followed up and no amount written off without proper authority.

The audit of cash income should aim at verifying that the correct charges are made, and that an acknowledgement is issued for the exact amount paid, e.g. by means of a receipt, ticket, cash sales slip or cash register operation. Supplementary checks may be afforded by turnstiles, test-checks by inspectors, slot meters, automatic locks etc.

The main types of income are:

Income from Rates

The *General Rate Act 1967* places upon each rating authority the duties of making, levying and collecting rates in their area.

A local rate is levied at an amount in the £ on the rateable value of each property shown in the valuation list, prepared by the Valuation Officers appointed by the Board of Inland Revenue, and only one rate is usually necessary for all purposes, which is called the general rate.

The rate book or record used in place of a rate book contains particulars of each person assessed to the rate, the rateable value, the rate due, the amount collected, any amount written-off or carried forward as arrears. The rate collection accounts are subject to district audit.

The special points to be observed in the audit of the rate collection accounts are –

(1) that all properties which are liable to be rated are included in the valuation list and the rate book;

(2) that due account is taken of the sums received in lieu of rates in respect of properties occupied by the Crown, and for railway and canal hereditaments, and the rate income from gas and electricity hereditaments;

(3) that all deductions are in order, e.g. where allowances (called 'compounding allowances') are made to owners who are rated direct;

(4) that rate rebates and all amounts written-off as irrecoverable are duly authorized by a committee of the local authority. Exemptions on account of poverty will also require authorization by the committee, except those allowed by the Justices. Reductions on appeal should be verified with the directions received from the Valuation Officer. Amounts written-off in cases of bankruptcy, empty properties etc., should be certified by some person other than the collector who is responsible for the area.

(5) the collectors' payments into the bank should be checked. The government grant in respect of rate rebates and the domestic element of the rate support grant are also included in the rate income.

Government Grants

Over half of the revenue expenditure of local authorities is met by exchequer grants. The main grant is now the Rate Support Grant payable under the *Local Government Act 1966*.

It comprises a needs element (based on a formula which takes into account the population of the local authority and other factors such as the number of children under five years of age, number of persons over sixty-five, 'education units' etc.), a resources element (payable to an authority whose penny rate product is less than a prescribed standard), and a domestic element (to reduce the rates levied on dwelling houses).

Separate grants are payable in respect of new houses and certain specific services the chief of which is police. Capital grants are paid towards the construction or improvement of principal roads.

Where a specific grant is paid in respect of any service, the accounts of which come within the scope of the audit, the auditor should satisfy himself as to the accuracy of the basis and the calculation of the grant. A register of grants should be maintained by the chief financial officer of the local authority.

Rents of Council property

Local authorities have very large rent rolls and it should be ascertained that all properties which are or can be let are included in the rental. These items can be verified by reference to the minutes of the local authority and the official terrier of council property. Amounts written-off as irrecoverable should be authorized by the appropriate committee of the Council. Regard should be had to any system of differential rents or rent rebates, which the Council may be operating.

Income from Public Utility Undertakings

This may include income from transport undertakings, the supply of water, markets, swimming baths, restaurants, abbatoirs, cemeteries and crematoria.

Miscellaneous Receipts

These will include interest on investments, licences, fees, recoverable private street works and other such items, sale of old stores, and receipts from conveniences, parks, parking meters etc. Most of these items consist of cash receipts and should come within the scope of the internal audit. Statistics showing a comparison of the receipts for several accounting periods will be of assistance: variations should be examined, and unless a satisfactory explanation is given a detailed examination should be instituted. The auditor should know the items of income which should be found in the various funds and undertakings of a local authority.

If the authority publishes an annual abstract of accounts in detail it should be studied and compared with the abstract of a similar local authority. A list of the miscellaneous items of income compiled therefrom will assist the audit.

§ 14. Audit of Expenditure

The expenditure of a local authority is divided into capital expenditure out of loans (or from capital funds) and revenue expenditure, which must be correctly analysed to the rate fund services or trading undertakings. The examination of expenditure is important: the district auditor pays particular attention to it with a view to ascertaining whether the local authority is keeping within its powers.

Points requiring attention in the audit of expenditure are:

(1) that the procedure laid down in the authority's standing orders and financial regulations for the incurring of expenditure is duly observed; there may be a restriction on the amount of any liability which may be incurred without specific approval;

(2) the inspection of tenders for the supply of goods and services;

(3) the examination of the system of recording stocks and stores and the preparation of inventories where appropriate;

(4) the inclusion of each invoice in an accounts schedule submitted to a committee of the local authority and duly signed by the chairman and two members of the committee when the accounts have been passed for payment; the method of approving urgent payments between meetings; (alternatively, the financial regulations may provide for accounts to be paid by the treasurer and subsequently reported to the appropriate committee);

(5) the control of access to blank cheques and the preparation, signing and despatch of cheques; the examination of paid cheques; and the reconciliation of cash books with bank pass books or statements;

(6) the examination of vouchers in relation to the creditor's name, the date of the invoice, the nature of the payment, the certification by the officers responsible for ordering and receiving the goods and the account to which the expenditure is allocated;

(7) due regard should be given to the nature of the payment: this requires a knowledge of the powers and duties of local authorities, and of legal decisions affecting illegal expenditure;

(8) when checking the allocation of expenditure, it should be seen that each item relates to the account to which it is debited;

(9) the system for the preparation and payment of salaries and wages should be inspected, and attention devoted to deductions for national insurance, P.A.Y.E. and superannuation contributions.

§ 15. Bank Accounts

The council's banking arrangements, including the terms agreed for management, the number of accounts to be opened and the manner in which they are to be operated, together with the name or names in which they are to stand, should be noted on the audit papers. Bank accounts operated by officers should be designated as accounts of the officers of the council, e.g. petty cash accounts, wages imprest accounts etc., and not as the accounts of individuals. Overdrafts should only be permitted if specifically authorized by a council communication to the bank.

The banks have requested that any instructions given to them for the opening and operation of accounts should be authorized by resolution of the council and that a certified copy of such resolution be supplied to them. The auditor should inspect the file of correspondence with the bank affecting the period under audit and extract any relevant information for his working papers.

§ 16. The Balance Sheet

A local authority may prepare separate balance sheets for different services or undertakings, although legally all their receipts and payments are centred in the 'county fund' or 'general rate fund'. In their publication *The Form of Published*

Accounts of Local Authorities the Institute of Municipal Treasurers and Accountants state: '. . . the practice of publishing partial balance sheets is still widespread and will no doubt continue so long as these fulfil a useful purpose within the authority's administration. For example, separate balance sheets are invariably published for trading services, and . . . authorities differ in the services which they so regard. The operation of a consolidated loans fund will almost certainly call for a separate published balance sheet.'

The suggested form of published accounts compiled by the I.M.T.A. shows on the assets side of the balance sheet:

Fixed assets
  Capital outlay on land, buildings, plant etc., to be retained at cost until the asset is disposed of.
  Other long-term outlay on roads, sewers, sea defence works, dredging works and other expenditure which does not represent saleable assets, to be written out of the accounts as and when the loans have been fully repaid.

Current assets
  Stocks on hand, works in progress, debtors, investments, cash in hand.

Other balances
  Deferred charges and revenue account deficiency (if any).

The liabilities side of the balance sheet shows:

Long-term liabilities
  Consolidated loans fund, loans pool, stock, mortgages, bonds, internal loans.

Current liabilities
  Temporary borrowing, creditors, cash overdrawn.

Provisions
  For example, renewal and repairs funds.

Other balances
  Capital discharged, capital fund, capital receipts unapplied and fund balances.

Separate statements are prepared to support the items in the balance sheet and these include:

(a) Details of capital expended, analysed into capital outlay and other long-term outlay.

(b) Details of capital discharged, analysed into loans redeemed; proceeds of sales and other capital receipts applied; gratuities and bequests; grants; revenue contributions to capital outlay; and reserve and capital funds applied.

(c) Details of capital projects in progress.

(d) Details of completed capital works.

(e) Deferred charges, analysed into expenses of local Acts; financial adjustments; expenses of stock issues, discount on stock etc.

A statement appended to the balance sheet shows the division between capital and revenue of the amounts shown for cash (in hand or overdrawn), debtors, creditors, investments, stocks etc.

Depreciation

This item, which is common in commercial accounts, is seldom found in the accounts of local authorities. The method of financing capital expenditure by way of loan, and the repayment of those loans by provision made annually, give rise to a consideration which does not apply in commerce, viz. a local authority are under no necessity to provide money in advance for capital expenditure when it can be raised by loan, and that since the loan period sanctioned is linked to the probable effective life of the assets the provision for loan redemption over the period of the loan sanction is broadly equivalent to provision for depreciation.

Revenue Contributions to Capital Outlay

Revenue contributions to capital outlay arise in two ways:

(1) the charging of comparatively small items of expenditure in excess of the loan sanction to revenue account, and

(2) the defraying of capital expenditure out of revenue in substitution for financing the expenditure out of loan.

Special Funds

The *Local Government* (*Miscellaneous Provisions*) *Act 1953*, enables a local authority to establish a capital fund for defraying any expenditure of the authority to which capital is properly applicable, and also a renewals and repairs fund for defraying expenditure in repairing, maintaining, replacing and renewing any buildings, works, plant, equipment or articles belonging to the authority.

Verification of Assets and Liabilities

The verification of assets will include the examination of all relevant documents in connection with freehold property, leasehold property, buildings in course of construction, plant and machinery, inventories, loans issued by the local authority on mortgage of freehold or leasehold property, investments, loose tools, vehicles, stocks and stores, revenue debtors, and cash at bank and in hand. The examination of liabilities will include a perusal of the registers of mortgages, bonds, stock and other securities. The balances owing to sundry creditors may be vouched by reference to the invoices and statements.

Aggregate Balance Sheet

An aggregate or consolidated balance sheet, which summarizes the balances appearing in the separate balance sheets, must be entered in the ledger of the council. On consolidation inter-departmental balances are eliminated including internal borrowings from reserve, repair, capital etc., funds. Balances on superannuation and trust funds must not be consolidated since they are not moneys at the disposal of the authority.

§ 17. The Auditor's Report

The balance sheet should be signed by the auditor, who should also give a general report for publication, in which a reference may be made to the Finance Committee report, if any.

General Report

So far as the published accounts are concerned, it is suggested that a general report of a professional auditor be given somewhat in the following form:

'In accordance with the terms of our appointment we have examined the books and accounts of the Corporation for the year ended March 31st, 19 , and the aggregate balance sheet at that date.

'Incorporated in the aggregate balance sheet are the subsidiary balance sheets of the rate fund and the trading undertakings and the consolidated loans fund. We have not audited the rate accounts, or the accounts of the children's, education, health, watch and welfare committees which are subject to audit by the district auditor, but we have seen that the respective balance sheets have been properly incorporated in the aggregate balance sheet.

'As regards the accounts audited by us, we have verified the securities for the investments of the Corporation, and all documents of title in respect of properties acquired during the year and advances to house purchasers. We have also verified with the bankers the correctness of the bank balances as appearing in the books.

'All the information asked for by us has been furnished, and we have satisfied ourselves as to the system of internal audit operative in relation to the accounts audited by us. We consider that this internal audit, together with the test checks we have made, enable us to state that, in our opinion, the said aggregate balance sheet and subsidiary accounts as signed by us exhibit a true and fair view of the financial position of the Corporation, according to the best of our information and the explanations given to us and as shown by the books of the Corporation.'

The report will of course be modified where necessary to meet the circumstances of each particular case.

Report to the Finance Committee

The report addressed to the Finance Committee should have regard to the following points:

(1) The scope of the audit. For example, the auditors should call attention to the existence or otherwise of an internal audit system, and state how far that has modified their examination.

(2) It is within the province of the auditor to express whether he is satisfied or not with the methods of accounting, and to make any suggestions for their improvement.

(3) The general financial position. This involves a summing up of the surpluses and deficiencies on the various funds, and the general position with regard to reserve funds.

(4) The auditor should report upon all instances where the expenditure is in his opinion *ultra vires*.

An auditor is sometimes asked to make a special report on circumstances relating to fraud and embezzlement. Such a report would be private and confidential and only a reference need be made to it in the general report. The special report requires careful drafting. It should show definitely and concisely how the fraud took place, the sum involved, the period which it covered, the reasons why it was possible, and suggestions for its prevention in the future.

CHAPTER XV

INVESTIGATIONS

§ 1. The Nature of Investigations

The term 'investigation' implies an examination of accounts and records for some *special* purpose. It differs from a conventional audit inasmuch as it is not primarily carried out for the purpose of ascertaining whether the accounts are properly brawn up and disclose a true and fair view, but rather for the purpose of obtaining information of a particular nature required by a client or, in the case of an investigation of fraud, for the purpose of ascertaining its extent.

The following are the principal classes of investigation met with in practice:

(1) On behalf of an individual or a firm proposing to buy a business.

(2) For the purpose of preparing a report on profits for insertion on a prospectus.

(3) On behalf of a prospective ingoing partner.

(4) On behalf of a bank for credit purposes.

(5) On behalf of a person intending to invest in a private business, firm, or company.

(6) On behalf of the proprietors of a business where fraud is suspected or known to have taken place.

(7) Investigations under Sections 164 and 165 of the *Companies Act 1948*, as extended by Sections 32, 38, 39, 42, and Part III of the *Companies Act 1967*.

(8) In connection with taxation liabilities ('back duty').

When an accountant is asked to make an investigation, he should obtain written instructions from his clients as to the exact purpose for which the investigation is required and the period which is to be covered. The accountant is, of course, consulted as an expert and must himself decide, within the limits imposed by his instructions, the extent to which the investigation should be carried, having regard for the information which he considers will be of importance to his clients and the manner in which his certificate or report will be utilized.

The amount of detail work performed during an investigation is not usually as great as is the case during an audit, although in its application to certain records or transactions it may be much more intensive. It is essential that the investigating accountant should bear in mind throughout the progress of his work the *purpose* of the investigation as this will indicate to him the particular matters to which he must give special attention and the particular viewpoint from which they must be regarded.

Where the books and other records which are the subject of investigation have been properly kept and the annual accounts subjected to a professional audit, the work of the investigating accountant is naturally simplified as he is entitled to assume that the books are arithmetically correct. It must never be overlooked, however, that the investigating accountant's interest in such accounts is different from that of the accountant by whom they were prepared or audited. Thus, where an investigation is being made on behalf of a person proposing to purchase a business, the accounts of past years are examined because they are the main guide to the possible future profits of the business, assuming that the turnover and other similar factors remain unchanged. It might well be, however, that although the accounts are perfectly correct, they contain items of income or expenditure which, if not adjusted, would distort any view of future profits which is based thereon.

The investigating accountant should take the greatest care to preserve all his working papers and notes made during the course of the investigation. The working papers should link up the figures shown by the books of the business with the final figures produced by the accountant and should contain adequate notes of all essential interviews. It is imperative that before a report is signed, all schedules are completed as to casts, calculations etc., and essential figures reconciled. The temptation to submit a report without delay and to leave the 'tidying up' of working papers until a later date must be resisted. Irremediable damage could be caused by the inclusion in a report of erroneous statements which would have been shown to be incorrect had a reconciliation of essential figures been attempted. Certain types of investigation may give rise to legal actions and the investigating accountant may be called upon to give evidence in civil or criminal proceedings; in such cases he will find that full working papers are essential. Furthermore, in view of the present state of the law relating to liability to third parties who have acted on the advice of professional experts, the investigating accountant will naturally wish to take particular care, for his own protection, over the accuracy of information which is included in his investigation report and allied documents. This question has been fully dealt with in Chapter XII above.

In the course of his professional work, the accountant may be called upon to report on statements of figures and other information for the purposes of trade returns, statistics, claims for subsidies, grants etc., on behalf of his client companies or firms. Such information is frequently required by central and local government departments, professional and trade associations etc., and considerable investigation work may be necessary before the accountant feels himself to be in a position to give the required assurances regarding the figures submitted, and it should be appreciated that accountants can and should report only on matters within their professional function as accountants; there should thus be a clear understanding between the body or council calling for the accountant's statement, the client, and the accountant, as to their respective positions. The Institute of Chartered Accountants have given positive advice to their members in this connection, and their recommendation, entitled *Special Reports Required of Accountants*, is given in the Appendix.

§ 2. Investigation on behalf of an Individual or a Firm proposing to buy a Business

(A) THE EXTENT OF THE INVESTIGATION

The accountant undertaking such an investigation must bear in mind that a person proposing to purchase a business wishes to obtain as much information about that business as possible, in order that he may form an opinion as to whether or not it is worth buying and, if he decides to buy it, how much he should pay for it.

Where the books have been properly kept and audited, the work of the investigating accountant is simplified but where the accounts have not been audited, it may be necessary for records to be examined much more fully. The client will, undoubtedly, require information not only as to the assets and liabilities at the date of the purchase, but also as to the trend of sales and the gross and net profits over a number of years; it will therefore be necessary to examine the profit and loss accounts as well as the balance sheets, and to suitably analyse the accounts for the purpose of making comparison between respective financial periods.

Where necessary, the trading and profit and loss accounts for each year should be redrafted on a uniform basis, so that a true comparison may be made. When this has been done, the accounts should be set out in columnar form with the addition of a percentage column for each year in which should be entered the percentage to turnover of each item of expenditure. Any material variations in these percentages from year to year will indicate items to which particular attention must be paid, and will also reveal any special expenditure incurred in any year in excess of the normal – as, for instance, in the case of advertising. The balance sheets should also be set out in columnar form, and from a comparison of the figures much valuable information may be gleaned which will be of material assistance in the course of the investigation. Having obtained all the information available in this manner, the accountant will be able to decide on the extent of his examination.

In many investigations, where the purchaser is familiar with the type of undertaking and the locality, he is mainly concerned with obtaining reliable information in regard to turnover, since from experience he will be able to estimate the costs of production and the selling and administrative expenses which are normally incurred. The accountant should prepare a statement of sales, so that a comparison between years and months may be effected. The cause of abnormal fluctuations in turnover should be enquired into. In arriving at the figure of sales, returns should be deducted as well as trade discount and all allowances, in order to disclose the *effective* net sales. Where the purchaser has no experience of the type of business which he proposes to acquire or is unfamiliar with conditions in the particular locality, he will require, in addition to details of sales, information covering the whole of the trading and profit and loss account.

In examining the trading accounts it should be seen whether the percentages of the various items of expenditure to turnover are constant, or whether they are subject to variation. In this connection, care must be taken when redrafting the trading accounts, to set out the items in such a way that the actual cost of each element of expenditure is revealed, and the percentage thereof to turnover calculated. For example, in the case of stores and stocks the closing stock should be deducted from the sum of the opening stock and purchases, thus showing clearly the cost of the stores *actually consumed* or of the *goods actually sold*. It will readily be understood that the percentage of such cost to turnover may remain constant, whilst the percentages of opening and closing stocks and purchases to turnover, may individually vary. The causes of variations revealed by such percentages *must* be ascertained. They may be due to a rise or fall in the cost of materials, manufacturing expenses, sale prices, rates of wages, or to variations in the types of product sold etc., but the possibility that they are due to errors or inflations in the value of the stocks, fictitious sales or other manipulations of the accounts, must not be overlooked. The stocks at the end of each period should be compared and tested with the stock records, and the accountant should ascertain that the basis of valuation of stock has been uniform throughout. If there is a considerable increase in the valuation of the stock held, without a corresponding increase in trade or rise in the prices of materials, this may be due to incorrect inflation of values, which may be expected to cause a variation in the percentage of the cost of goods sold to turnover.

The detailed stock sheets for each year under review should be examined and a comparison made of the values placed on stocks of similar items year by year. Care should be taken to see whether there is any evidence of obsolete stocks continuing to be included in the stock sheets at their previous values or any other suggestion of over-valuation. All insurance policies relating to stocks should be examined and the values placed on stocks for accounting purposes compared with those for which they have been insured.

The trading accounts for the last few financial years, and the records for the period from the date of the last balance sheet to the date of the investigation must be examined in greater detail, particularly where the gross profit has increased as compared with former years, as it is possible that, with a view to the sale of the business, manipulations may have been carried out with the object of inflating the profits of these years. This would have the result of disclosing a more prosperous position than was actually the case and, since the price payable for goodwill is usually calculated on the basis of profits or turnover, it would also have the effect of increasing the purchase consideration. The most usual methods of inflating sales are by:

(i) Treating goods issued on sale or return or on consignment as if they were completed sales;

(ii) ante-dating copies of sales invoices relating to the period subsequent to that covered by the accounts;

(iii) including fictitious invoices for credit sales or increasing cash sales by payments into the business by the proprietor.

Inflation of gross profit may also be effected by inflating the value of closing stock, or by omitting purchases, wages, or other manufacturing expenses.

The figure of purchases may be artificially reduced by:

(i) entirely omitting certain purchase invoices;

(ii) post-dating invoices so that they do not appear as a charge against the profits for the period;

(iii) payment by the proprietor personally for cash purchases, so that these are totally excluded from the records.

It will be necessary, therefore, for the investigating accountant to test the sales with the stock records, the order book, the goods outwards book, or such other records as may be available. Where no stock records are kept, or where those in use are inadequate, the accountant must scrutinize the sales with great care, and should note whether they have fallen since the date of the last balance sheet, or the date to which the investigation is being taken. The period following the period under investigation should also be scanned closely for rebates, allowances, returns etc., which are applicable to the period under investigation, as if fictitious sales have been included in the last year, entries of this character will be necessary to eliminate the fictitious debts thus created.

In order to ascertain whether purchases have been omitted, the goods inwards book should be tested with the records of purchases, and such creditors' statements as are available tested exhaustively with the creditor's ledger or schedules of liabilities. Workers' time cards, job cards, national insurance cards etc., must be tested with the wages records in order to ascertain that all wages have been included in the accounts, and the reasons for any marked decrease in expenditure must be enquired into.

In making an analysis of the sales the accountant should exclude all unusual profits resulting, for example, from exceptional contracts, or where it has been found more profitable to re-sell raw material than to use it for the manufacture of goods. If it is considered that such items should be included, it is preferable that the profit thereon should be shown in the profit and loss account, and not in the trading account, in order that the rate of gross profit on normal trading operations is not obscured.

In a similar manner it will be necessary to make an analysis of the profit and loss account items. The accountant should investigate any items that show undue variation. The last year and the period following it should be examined in greater detail in order to see that there has been no manipulation to increase the net profit. Vouchers should be seen for all payments made after the close of the period under investigation, to ensure that all outstanding accounts have been provided for during that period. Manipulations of a subtler order may be effected by the omission of outstanding liabilities, by insufficient provision for bad debts or depreciation, by starving the business of necessary expenditure on repairs and renewals etc., or by paying business liabilities out of private funds. The basis upon which bad debts have been provided for should be ascertained, and the debtors' balances at the close of the period checked in detail with a view to ascertaining that sufficient provision has been made.

The opening balance sheet should be checked. The impersonal ledger should be examined, the postings thereto of all the totals from the subsidiary records should be checked and the cash postings tested. The postings of the nominal account balances should be checked at the end of each year to the profit and loss accounts. As regards vouching, it is not usually considered necessary to vouch the payments for routine items of expenditure, even where no audit has been previously performed.

The object of the investigation is to ascertain the profits, and to verify the existence and value of assets, and the accountant is not concerned with the manner in which such payments have been made, or whether they can be satisfactorily vouched. A certain amount of vouching would be necessary, however, if for any reason the accountant suspected that the records of expenditure had been manipulated with a view to distorting the profits for the period. It is, however, important that all capital expenditure should be vouched, in order to ascertain that no revenue expenditure has been capitalized and profits thus inflated. The asset accounts should be checked in detail, care being taken to see that all items are properly chargeable to capital, and are not items of expenditure in the form of repairs and renewals, which should have been charged to revenue. The existence of assets and their ownership must be verified in the usual manner, as detailed in Chapter VI above.

The closing balance sheet should be checked in detail. If there has been an independent valuation of the assets, the revised figures should be incorporated, otherwise it should be seen that adequate depreciation has been written-off. Any assets which are no longer effective or in general use should be shown separately, and it is often advantageous to show the assets in a 'statement of assets and liabilities' in the same groups and order as those in which the income derived therefrom is shown in the profit and loss account. Expenditure on advertising which has been carried forward should receive careful consideration, as in the majority of cases it should be written-off.

(B) THE USUAL ADJUSTMENTS NECESSARY

Assuming that the accountant has investigated the accounts as far as he considers necessary and is of the opinion that they are correct, a considerable number of adjustments will, normally, have to be made to arrive at the profits upon which his report must be based.

The object of the report is to afford the purchaser information as to the achievements of the business in the past, from which he may form an opinion as to its probable earning capacity in the future. For this reason, although the report should deal with past facts, it is necessary to adjust the past profits of the business to conform to the conditions that will obtain after the purchase, i.e. to show what the net profits *would have been* had the conditions of management, finance etc., been the same in past years as those which *will* prevail after the purchase.

It will usually be found necessary to add back to profits the following items:

(i) Interest on partners' capital and current accounts, and also partners' salaries to the extent that these exceed a fair remuneration for management;

(ii) interest on loans and overdrafts (if any), except the interest applicable to loans to be taken over by the purchaser. Otherwise, it is to be assumed that the purchaser will provide sufficient working capital, in which case such charges will not be incurred;

(iii) rent, if the purchaser is purchasing the trade premises hitherto rented by the vendor;

(iv) discount on purchases, in so far as the business has not been able to take advantage of all discounts owing to lack of working capital;

(v) exceptional losses such as those arising by reason of insufficient insurance, although in such cases the full insurance premium should be charged; costs and damages incurred by actions-at-law and other losses not arising in the ordinary course of business;

(vi) capital losses such as losses on sales of fixed assets or investments;

(vii) any additions or improvements of a capital nature that have been charged to profit and loss account;

(viii) any excessive provisions for bad debts or other contingencies;

(ix) excessive provisions for depreciation.

The following items should be deducted from the profits:

(i) Income from assets not being taken over by the purchaser;

(ii) rent, if no charge has been made for this in the profit and loss accounts, and the purchaser is not acquiring the freehold of the trade premises;

(iii) exceptional profits, such as compensation for compulsory removal of premises, speculative profits etc.;

(iv) capital profits, such as those arising from sales of investments or fixed assets;

 (v) adequate depreciation, where this has not been provided for;

(vi) a reasonable sum for management remuneration, if this has not been charged in the accounts.

The question of depreciation is a most difficult matter to deal with, but it is preferable for the profits to be stated after providing an adequate amount for depreciation. As the values upon which the purchaser will in future base the provision for depreciation will in most cases be different from those adopted by the vendor in the past, it is clear that unless the rates of depreciation are based upon the take-over values, the inclusion of charges for depreciation that may have been sufficient in the past will be misleading as a guide to future charges. In other cases, difficulty may be experienced in arriving at a proper rate of depreciation having regard to the nature of the assets. Where accurate provision cannot be made, the usual charges for depreciation should be added to the profits and the report should state clearly that no provision for depreciation has been made. This matter, in relation to companies, is considered further in § 3 of this chapter.

(C) THE REPORT

The report should be worded in a clear and unambiguous manner, and must state the precise period covered by the investigation. It should contain all information which may be of assistance to the purchaser, and the accountant should not confine himself only to figures. He should, however, be very careful to avoid any statement which might lead his client to regard his remarks as predictions or estimates for the future. Where the adjustments made are merely of an ordinary nature, it is sometimes thought sufficient to say that all adjustments necessary in the opinion of the accountant have been made; but all adjustments involving items of special importance should be referred to specifically. The report should set out the information which the client requiries in sufficient detail to enable him to comprehend the exact position of the undertaking. In order to do this a number of matters which will affect the future will have to be dealt with. For example, where, owing to insufficiency of working capital the business was not able to avail itself of all cash discounts, this should be pointed out, and the effect upon the past profits should be shown. The approximate number of times per annum the capital is turned over should be calculated, as this will vitally affect the amount of working capital required.

The business may be fortunate in the possession of an efficient manager, and his willingness to continue in that capacity is an item of information which is of value to an intending purchaser. Where the proprietor has managed the business, but no charge for his services has been made in the accounts, the accountant should make adequate provision for management salaries and state clearly in his report the amount which he has provided therefor. All open contracts which will affect the future of the business, such as agreements to sell goods at a future date at an agreed price, should be set out in full, and it should be indicated whether it would be possible to rescind them if desired. Any necessary provisions in respect of these items should be made.

Reference should also be made to the tenure on which the business premises are held. If the premises are held on a lease of which only a short term remains unexpired, the question as to whether any difficulty will be experienced in obtaining a renewal of the lease at a reasonable rent may have a vital bearing upon the desirability or otherwise of acquiring the business.

§ 3. Investigation on behalf of the promoters of a proposed Company – Reports in a Prospectus

Under the *Companies Act 1948*, any prospectus issued by or on behalf of a company or by or on behalf of any person who is, or has been, engaged or interested in the formation of a company, must set out the reports specified in Part II of the Fourth Schedule of that Act. (See Chapter IX, § 3.)

An accountant making an investigation of the accounts of a business proposed to be acquired by a company out of the proceeds of an issue of shares to the public, should remember that he is not only responsible to his clients for the work he performs, but also that he bears no small responsibility towards the public, since, on the faith of his report as an expert the public will be asked to subscribe for shares in the company. It is, therefore, important that the accountant should ascertain as far as he can the *bona fides* of all parties interested in the matter, since in the event of the new company proving unsuccessful and legal proceedings being taken he is likely to find himself involved.

Similar remarks apply to the auditor of such a company who is required to prepare and sign a report for inclusion in a prospectus.

The prosecution brought in 1950 under what is now Section 12 (1) of the *Prevention of Fraud (Investments) Act 1958*, against two of the directors of Richard Crittall & Co Ltd and a partner in the firm appointed as its auditors, is of interest. The accused were charged with making a misleading statement in the prospectus and with having done so recklessly. It was shown that the accountant had delegated to one of his partners the investigation of the matter in question. In the course of his judgment the learned judge said:

'It seems to me a very serious matter for your consideration whether you can possibly say that Mr Steven, having handed that matter over to his partner, and his partner having in fact made tests and satisfied himself, rightly or wrongly – as we now know, wrongly – but satisfied himself at the time as an honourable man, as an accountant, and a careful accountant, that that document was right – you can say that Mr Steven was reckless in accepting Mr Morton's (*the partner's*) explanation of that . . . – That is the one thing that is said to be against him. There is plenty of evidence that in other parts he took meticulous care in trying to ascertain whether the books of this company were reliable or whether they were not. But in this particular his evidence is: "I relied upon Mr Morton".'

The accountant and one of the directors were acquitted, but in his judgment the learned judge cast doubts upon the wisdom of appointing a firm as auditors and stated:

'I think it right to say this, that it does call for consideration by the authorities whether this system of appointing a firm of auditors is a satisfactory one . . . – It may be that this case has shown that it is not very satisfactory, because you do not get what everybody desires – the personal assurance of an individual who is an expert that this is right. It turns out that all you get is, instead of a personal assurance, that that expert, it may be, accepted somebody else's view. It is very difficult to fix responsibility in that case . . .'

It is difficult to see how the position discussed by the learned judge would be improved by the appointment of individuals instead of firms as auditors. It cannot be suggested that a busy practitioner could, or that it would be reasonable that he should, do all the work involved in a audit or investigation himself. Sections of the work must be delegated to staff upon whom the accountant is forced to rely. When a firm is appointed as auditors it is the responsibility of one partner to take charge of the case and, in practice, the conduct of the work would be unaffected if the partner receives the appointment personally.

The prosecution, brought under the same section in 1954 against the managing director and the auditor of Wake and Dean Ltd (*Regina* v. *Wake and Stone*, Acct., October 30th, 1954), was concerned primarily with the inflated value which had been placed on the company's stock and work-in-progress. In the prospectus issued by the company in 1951 the auditor's report included a statement that the stock and work-in-progress as valued by the company's officials *at the lower of cost or market value* as at June 30th, 1950, amounted to £641,607. It was admitted in court that this figure was 'false, deceptive and misleading' in that it was far too high. It was shown that timber had been taken at a flat rate and had been measured in such a way as to include all the air as well as the timber. The stock sheets did not show the manner in which the figures for work-in-progress and general stocks had been arrived at and the original valuations, amounting to £495,000 (already excessive) had been plainly altered by percentage additions which increased the already inflated value by a further £140,000. Although the auditor asked for an explanation of the alterations, he accepted, without any attempt at independent corroboration, the statement of the managing director that they had been made to correct errors in the original valuation.

The managing director, who had pleaded guilty to the charges brought against him, was sentenced to imprisonment. The auditor, who had pleaded not guilty, was convicted on one count, viz. that he had signed the report *recklessly* and was fined £200 (with the alternative of six months imprisonment).

The following remarks made by the learned judge in the course of his direction to the jury are of great interest:

'It is quite impossible . . . to lay down that an auditor is correct and not being careless if he accepts the explanations of a director to any question he may put to him . . . Quite clearly you must look at all the circumstances of the case, and taking into account all the circumstances, say to yourselves: "Would a reasonably careful auditor and accountant be satisfied with the director's answer or the director's entry in the book, or ought he as a reasonably careful auditor and accountant to have gone further and checked it in some way?" That is really the question. You cannot, of course, lay down strict rules as to what is care and what is not. You must take into account all the circumstances of the case and make up your minds about it. You may, of course, take it that if an auditor neglects to take the reasonable steps that you think he ought to have taken, then he is being careless; but if he is careless, in all the circumstances, to a high degree so as to be deserving of punishment, then you may take it as being reckless.'

Before imposing the fine, the judge addressed the following remarks to the auditor:

'You are an auditor and an accountant; one of a professional body of men to whom the public at large is entitled to look for careful and disinterested advice and help and guidance; and you have failed in your duty and you were so excessively careless as to be reckless. I cannot treat that offence as anything but one of considerable gravity . . .'

It is interesting to note the distinction between Section 12 of the *Prevention of Fraud (Investments) Act 1958* (under which the prosecution in the above case was brought) and Section 438 of the *Companies Act 1948*. As has been shown above, it is necessary merely to establish recklessness in order to gain a successful prosecution under the former statute, whereas Section 438 of the 1948 Act specifies that criminal liability will result only if it is shown that the return, report, certificate, balance sheet or other document (required for any of the purposes set out in the 15th Schedule to the Act) is false in a material particular, and the person making it did so wilfully, knowing it to be false. It is thus clear that liability under Section 438 is comparatively difficult to prove. On the other hand, it was held in one case (not involving auditors) that the establishment of a high degree of negligence was sufficient to gain a successful criminal prosecution under the *Prevention of Fraud (Investments) Act 1958*, such negligence being tantamount to recklessness (*R. v. Bates* (1952), All E.R. 842). This view has, however, been criticized as being too wide an interpretation of 'recklessness'. (Reference should again be made to §3 (B) (3) of Chap. XII and to Chap. IX, §3, where the recent American case of *Escott, et al. v. BarChris Construction Corporation, et al.* (U.S. District Court, Southern District, N.Y. 1968) is described, underlining once again the high degree of care which must be taken by investigating accountants when reporting on past results of companies for the purpose of inclusion in a prospectus.)

The *Companies Act 1948* requires the prospectus to disclose the profits or losses of five years, but it is very common for the accountant to be asked by the promoters to investigate and report upon the profits of a larger number of years. A minimum period of ten years (or from the date of incorporation if the company has not been in existence for ten years) is normally required by the council of the Stock Exchange, London, to be reported on as a condition of granting a quotation.

The object of the investigation is to arrive at the normal trading profits during the period, and the accountant should confine himself to ascertainable facts, and not indulge in calculations or problematical estimates of future operations. The routine to be followed and the points to be borne in mind have already been set out at length in the preceding section, but an investigation with a view to giving a report as to profits for publication in a prospectus is of narrower scope than an investigation on behalf of an intending purchaser. Only those matters directly affecting the figures of normal trading profits for the periods should be examined and reported upon.

As has been indicated in § 2 of this chapter, the accountant will normally find it necessary to make a number of adjustments in the recorded profits or losses, or assets and liabilities, in arriving at the figures to be included in his report. The *Companies Act 1948* requires that the report shall either indicate by way of a note the adjustments which, in the opinion of the person making the report, ought to be made or, alternatively, that the adjustments should be made and the report indicate this fact. The latter alternative is more frequently employed in practice and where this procedure is adopted there must be filed with the Registrar of Companies a written statement setting out the adjustments which have been made and the reasons therefor. If a Stock Exchange quotation is required a copy of the statement of adjustments is one of the documents which must be submitted to the Stock Exchange with the appropriate application for a quotation and permission to deal.

One of the most important of the matters which frequently require adjustment is the provision for depreciation of fixed assets. Although fixed assets normally appear in the books at cost, less accumulated provision for depreceiation, they are usually valued for prospectus purposes at their current values which, under existing conditions, may be far in excess of cost. In some cases the new values are incorporated in the company's books, but in others the book values remain unaltered, the revised values being merely noted in the prospectus.

Whichever method is adopted, however, it will be appreciated that:

(a) The actual provisions made for depreciation in the years covered by the report will, in all probability, not have been calculated on the enhanced values now placed on the assets concerned;

(b) the revised values will probably have been employed by the directors in calculating the assets cover for the issue;

(c) the public may be asked to pay for the shares a price which has regard for the *current* values of fixed assets, whereas the profits for the years covered by the report will have been arrived at after charging depreciation calculated on *original* book values.

Intending investors, therefore, might be misled by a valuation of fixed assets calculated on one basis and provisions for depreciation of such assets calculated on a different basis. The taxation aspect has also to be considered: if capital allowances for taxation purposes differ materially from the provisions made in the accounts for depreciation the recorded net profits may give a misleading impression of the figures on which taxation will be payable, and thus of the balance available for distribution as dividend.

The recommendations of the Council of the Institute of Chartered Accountants on these matters are reproduced in full in the Appendix, to which reference should now be made.

Far more demanding than the statutory requirements regarding information to be set out in a prospectus, are the requirements of the Council of the Stock Exchange, as detailed in their publication *Admission of Securities to Quotation*. Under these requirements all prospectuses are to include a report by qualified accountants on the company with respect to:

(a) its profits or losses in respect of each of the *ten* completed financial years immediately preceding the issue of the prospectus, or, if it has been incorporated less than ten years, in respect of each of the years since its incorporation, and stating the charge for depreciation for each year reported on;

(b) its assets and liabilities;

(c) the aggregate emoluments of its directors during the last financial year and a comparison with the amount which would have been paid under the arrangements in force at the date of the prospectus; and

(d) such other matters which appear to the accountants to be relevant.

A report which contained any significant qualification or reservation as to any of the profits or losses reported on or as to the assets and liabilities, would not be regarded by the Quotations Department of the Stock Exchange as acceptable.

The following further matters have also to be dealt with:

(1) There should be included, where appropriate, an explanation of the trend of profits as shown in the accountants' report, dealing in particular with the effects of changes in the financing of the company, borrowings and the structure of the share capital, and of the acquisition of subsidiaries etc.

(2) A similar report has to be furnished with respect to the profits, assets and liabilities etc. (but not directors' emoluments) of a business being acquired or of a company being acquired which will then become a subsidiary and no part of whose securities are already quoted. If the business or new subsidiary has not been in existence for ten years the period is restricted accordingly.

(3) In the case of groups of companies, the requirements envisage a statement of the company's net assets and a statement, usually in consolidated form, of profits and losses and assets and liabilities of the group.

(4) Where, in view of the materiality of such matters in relation to their report as a whole, the reporting accountants make reference to reports, confirmations or opinions of valuers

or other accountants, the names, addresses and professional qualifications of such other persons of firms should be stated in the report.

(5) It should be noted that the Council are not normally prepared to grant an initial quotation where the figures reported on are more than nine months old.

Computation of Profits

(6) Neither the Stock Exchange requirements nor the Companies Acts lay down the basis on which profits or losses are to be computed. It is the practice, however, for the accountants to indicate in the report the basis which has been adopted. This normally states that the profits or losses have been arrived at after charging all expenses, after dealing with such items as depreciation, amortization, directors' remuneration, interest etc., on defined bases and after making such adjustments as are appropriate.

Adjustments

(7) A written statement for submission to the Quotations Department, signed by the accountants, should set out the adjustments made by them in arriving at the figures shown in their report and give the reasons therefor. In order that the Quotations Department can obtain what is required in sufficient detail and on a reasonably uniform basis, the statement of adjustments as regards profits and losses should be divided into two sections as follows:

SECTION 'A'

This section should begin with the net increase or decrease in the balance at credit or debit of profit and loss account shown by comparison of the balance sheets at the beginning and end of each of the financial periods under review; the net increase or decrease in the balance on profit and loss account for each of the last two years should normally be capable of ascertainment from the accounts which are required to be made available for inspection. There should then be shown and added to or deducted from this amount –

    (i) The items which are required by the Companies Acts to be stated separately in the profit and loss account, notes being included to disclose any further information required by the Acts to be disclosed by way of note to the profit and loss account.

(ii) Interest charges, analysed under appropriate headings, in addition to those payable on loans required to be separately shown, as in (i) above.

(iii) Material revenue items which have been dealt with otherwise than through the profit and loss accounts.

The sum finally arrived at in this section would normally be the profit or loss for the year before taking account of interest and of items which the Acts require in any event to be stated separately.

SECTION 'B'

This section should commence with the final figure of profit or loss shown in Section 'A' and should show in detail the adjustments made thereto in arriving at the profits or losses shown in the accountants' report and giving the reasons therefor.

Amount of Assets and Liabilities

(8) As regards assets and liabilities, if the final total amount of the net assets in the report differs from the total amount of net assets dealt with in the latest audited balance sheet, and the relevant adjustments are not set out in the report, a statement should be submitted showing the adjustments made and reconciling these totals.

Holding Companies

(9) If the company is a holding company, the statements of adjustments may deal with the consolidated figures of the company and of its subsidiaries or with the figures of the separate companies or groups of companies comprising the holding company and its subsidiaries. In the latter case, a summary combining the figures so as to arrive at those shown in the accountants' report should be submitted.

Submission of Adjustments

(10) The statement of adjustments, a draft of which must be submitted at least ten days prior to the date on which it is proposed to publish the prospectus, should be accompanied by a

letter from the accountants to the Quotations Department which should confirm that all adjustments which are appropriate for the purposes of the report have been made to the profits and losses (in respect of each year under review) and to the net assets and that no other adjustments have been made.

Depreciation

(11) The report, and the statement of adjustments, should state the amount of the charge, in each period reported upon, for amortization, depreciation and obsolescence. (The Quotations Department will consider some adaptation of this requirement in cases which involve complex multi-column statements.)

If the circumstances appear to warrant it, the Department may ask for information about the basis on which the charges for depreciation have been calculated and, in special cases, for the inclusion of an appropriate explanatory statement in the report.

Letter to be submitted to the Quotations Department Concerning Certain Accounting Matters

(12) There should be submitted to the Department by the accountants a letter confirming the following three matters:

(i) Stocks and Work in Progress –

That, save as indicated in their report, they have obtained sufficient information about the stocktakings and have examined sufficient records and other evidence to enable them to form the opinion that throughout the period under review stocks and work in progress were properly ascertained and, in arriving at the reported profits and losses, were brought into account on bases in accordance with generally accepted accounting principles which were applied consistently.

(ii) Depreciation and Amortization –

That they have satisfied themselves that the provisions for depreciation and amortization charged in arriving at the reported profits and losses, considered in conjunction with any qualifications or notes included in their report are in their opinion reasonable having regard, *inter alia*, to:

(a) assets in respect of which it has been or will be the company's practice to make no provisions for depreciation or amortization (which policy would require to be referred to in their report); and

(b) any revaluation of fixed assets either already incorporated into the company's accounts or to be incorporated therein.

(iii) Equalization of Taxation –

That the net book value of the fixed assets appearing in the report in respect of which depreciation and/or amortization will require to be provided out of future profits does not exceed by a material amount the corresponding amounts on which capital allowances will be obtained for taxation purposes, or, in the event of there being a material difference, how this has been taken into account, unless it is apparent from the prospectus (e.g. by setting up a tax equalization account which is deducted in arriving at the net assets or by including a suitable explanation in the accountants' report or elsewhere in the prospectus and making an appropriate adjustment for the non-allowable proportion of depreciation in computing the tax payable on the profit figures included in any forecast future profits).

Period Covered by the Report

(13) Although the Report is required to deal with the profits or losses of each of the preceding ten financial years, application may be made to cover a shorter period where it is considered that inclusion of the earlier years may be irrelevant or misleading.

Overseas Interests

(14) Where a material proportion of the profits arises overseas or a material proportion of the assets are situated overseas, the report or the document should give the best practicable indication of the amount and situation or source of such assets and profits. In the case of businesses with overseas interests, the basis on which overseas currencies and overseas taxation have been dealt with should, if the accounting treatment of these matters is material, be set out in the report.

The Department would also normally require the prospectus to contain an adequate explanation with regard to any restrictions affecting the remittance of profits or repatriation of capital from the countries concerned.

Long Term Hire of Plant

(15) Where contracts exist for the hire of plant to the company for a period of over one year which are substantial in relation to the company's business, details should be supplied to the Department, who may require details to be disclosed in the document.

Directors' Emoluments

(16) The accountants are required to deal in their report with the aggregate emoluments of the directors of the company for whose securities a quotation is sought. The exact comparison to be given must depend on the circumstances of each case and the comparison should normally deal with the emoluments of any person who is a director at the time of the report. (The emoluments for this purpose should follow the definition contained in Section 196 of the *Companies Act 1948*.)

Additional Information

(17) For certain types of company the Department may require information to be given in the document additional to that which is normally provided. Examples would be:

(a) Building, contracting and similar companies engaged in carrying out contracts of a long term nature, where these form a substantial proportion of the business. In such cases the method of taking credit for profits and of arriving at the amounts at which stocks and work in progress were brought into account should be defined in the document.

In such cases the Department would require the letter from the accountants to state also that in their opinion the methods used are in accordance with generally accepted accounting principles which have been consistently applied.

(b) Hire purchase finance companies, where the methods of valuing debts and taking credit for profits should be defined in the document. In such cases the Department would require the letter from the accountants also to confirm that the valuation of hire purchase debts and the method of taking credit for profits have been on bases which in their opinion are in accordance with generally accepted accounting principles which have been consistently applied.

An appendix to *Admission of Securities to Quotation* specifies the detailed requirements regarding the contents of a prospectus. A report by the auditors of the company seeking a quotation for its shares, or a particular class of shares, for the first time must be included, although in practice such reports are frequently given jointly by the company's auditors and another firm of independently reporting accountants.

The detailed contents of the report are given hereunder. (Although figures of sales turnover are not mentioned, these do in fact have to be given in the prospectus, and for convenience are normally given in the auditor's report. These figures must be given in respect of the preceding three financial years, and should contain a reasonable breakdown between the more important trading activities. In the case of a group, internal sales should be excluded.)

(i) The profits or losses of the company in respect of each of the ten completed financial years immediately preceding the publication of the prospectus, or in respect of each of the years since the incorporation of the company, if this occurred less than ten years prior to such publication; and, if in respect of a period ending on a date earlier than three months before such publication no accounts have been made up, a statement of that fact;

(ii) in the case of an issue by a holding company, in lieu of the report in (i), a like report with respect to the profits or losses of the company and of its subsidiary companies, so far as such profits or losses can properly be regarded as attributable to the interests of the holding company;

(iii) the rate of dividend for each class of shares during each of the five financial years preceding the issue of the prospectus with details of any waiver of dividends in such years;

(iv) the assets and liabilities of the company and, in the case of an issue by a holding company, a like report with respect to the assets and liabilities of the company and of its subsidiary companies so far as such assets can properly be regarded as attributable to the interests of the company, including an explanation of the bases used for the valuations of fixed assets and a reasonably detailed indication of the nature of the tangible assets;

(v) the aggregate emoluments paid to the directors by the company during the last period for which the accounts have been made up and the amount (if any) by which such emoluments would differ from the amounts payable under the arrangements in force at the date of the prospectus;

(vi) with respect to any other matters which appear to the auditors to be relevant having regard to the purpose of the report.

In making such report the auditors shall make such adjustments (if any) as are in their opinion appropriate for the purposes of the prospectus.

If after the latest date to which the accounts of the company have been made up and audited the company or any of its subsidiaries has acquired or agreed to acquire or is proposing to acquire a business or shares in a company which will by reason of such acquisition become a subsidiary of the company or any of its subsidiaries and no part of the securities of that subsidiary is already quoted a report made by qualified accountants who shall be named in the prospectus shall be given with respect to the following matters:

(i) the profits or losses of the business or the profits or losses attributable to the interests acquired or being acquired in respect of each of the ten completed financial years immediately preceding the publication of the prospectus, or in respect of each of the years since the commencement of the business or the incorporation of such subsidiary company if this occurred less than ten years prior ts such publication; and if in respect of a period ending on a date earlier than three months before such publication no accounts have been made up, a statement of that fact:

Provided that where any such subsidiary is itself a holding company the report shall be extended to the profits

or losses of that company and its subsidiary companies
which shall be ascertained in the manner laid down in sub-
paragraph (ii) above;

(ii) the assets and liabilities of the business or of the subsidiary
and where such subsidiary is itself a holding company, the
report shall be extended to the assets and liabilities of that
company and of its subsidiary companies in the manner
laid down in sub-paragraph (iv) above;

(iii) any other matters which appear to the accountants to be
relevant having regard to the purpose of the report.

In making such report the accountants shall make such
adjustments (if any) as are in their opinion appropriate for the
purposes of the prospectus.

When, in the course of his investigation, the accountant ascertains that the company has entered into exceptional forward
commitments which may affect adversely the position of future
profits, he should refer thereto in his report (*Rex* v. *Bishirgian
and Others*, 1936, Acct. March 28th, 1936, p. 494 *et seq.*), although it would appear that there is no necessity to refer to
normal commitments of this nature. In the course of his judgment in this case the Lord Chief Justice said: 'the future commitments of a normal business are one thing; the future commitments of a colossal gamble are different, not merely in degree,
but in kind . . . the financing, as it is called, is different; the risks
are different, and to advertise a business as an ordinary business
seeking development, when money is really being asked for to
feed and supply an ambitious gamble is simply deceit.' This case
did not concern the auditors of the company, who were shown
to have no knowledge of the excessive commitments, but it is
clear that when a prospectus is issued by a company in such
circumstances, the non-disclosure of abnormal future commitments may render the document 'a cheat from beginning to end'.
An auditor who gave a report on profits for inclusion in such
a prospectus, *knowing of the non-disclosure*, might find himself
involved with the directors in a criminal charge.

The wording of the report should be clear, and the precise
periods covered by the investigation should be set out. The

profits for *each year* must be set out separately; a statement of average profits will not satisfy the provisions of the Act or the Stock Exchange requirements.

As has already been pointed out, it is essential that the accountant should retain a complete record of all material information, and of the manner in which he has arrived at the figures he ultimately reports upon, so that he may be in a position to substantiate his report if called upon to do so.

§ 4. The City Code on Take-overs and Mergers

The establishment early in 1968 of the City Code on Take-overs and Mergers was intended to lay down principles to be followed by all parties engaged in take-over, merger and similar proceedings. Paragraph 15 of the Code specified the need for a report by the auditors or consultant accountants on any profit forecasts compiled by the directors during the negotiations.

In view of the traditional reserve displayed by accountants in relation to anything in the nature of prediction, this requirement clearly created a need for recommendations on a uniform approach to be followed by accountants in reviewing profit forecasts, while at the same time fully recognizing the desirability to guard against the practice of elevating into 'profit forecasts' what is little better than wishful thinking or plain guesswork.

The problem of devising a uniform approach for the profession, and clearly stating for the benefit of the investing public at large, what the role of the reporting accountant in merger and take-over situations ought to be, was somewhat emphasized by the publication (in July 1968) of the results for the year ended December 31st, 1967, of Associated Electrical Industries Ltd. These showed a profit shortfall of some £14½ million compared with forecasts which were made less than three months earlier in October of the same year, when the take-over battle with General Electric Company was at its height. Moreover, the forecasts (which covered the years 1967, 1968 and 1969) were stated by the A.E.I. auditors to 'have been prepared on a fair and reasonable basis and in a manner consistent with the principles followed by the company in preparing recent published annual accounts'.

The financial press were quick to seize the point that this startling discrepancy indicated that A.E.I. shares were considerably overpriced at the time of take-over, but it will probably never be known to what extent the disclosed shortfall simply reflected differing management attitudes to, say, valuation of inventories and work-in-progress, valuation of fixed assets, obsolescence etc.

The recommendations of the Institute of Chartered Accountants, also issued in July 1968, entitled 'Accountants' Reports on Profit Forecasts' were therefore especially timely and valuable in that they clarified for the mutual benefit of the profession, the City, and laymen alike, the scope and necessary limitations of accountants' reports on profit forecasts in such situations.

The whole text of the Code was revised, however, in April 1969 in the light of the experience gained by the specially appointed Take-over Panel during their first year of office (when some three to four hundred cases of take-overs and mergers were investigated by them). Rule 15, as revised, now requires accountants' reports on forecasts to be published in the same documents which actually set out the forecasts, whereas the original Rule 15 merely required an accountants' report to be submitted to the board of the company issuing the forecast. Rule 15, as revised, reads as follows:

'Without in any way detracting from the imperative necessity of maintaining the highest standards of accuracy and fair presentation in all communications to shareholders in a take-over or merger transaction, attention is particularly drawn in this connection to profit forecasts and asset valuations.

'Notwithstanding the obvious hazard attached to the forecasting of profits, profit forecasts must be compiled with the greatest possible care by the Directors whose sole responsibility they are.

'When profit forecasts appear in any document addressed to shareholders in connection with an offer, the assumptions, including the commercial assumptions, upon which the Directors have based their profit forecasts, must be stated in the document.

'The accounting bases and calculations for the forecasts must be examined and reported on by the auditors or consultant accountants. Any Merchant Bank or other adviser mentioned in the document must also report on the forecasts. The accountants' report and, if there is an adviser, his report must be contained in such document and be accompanied by a statement that the accountants and, where relevant, the adviser, have given and not withdrawn their consent to publication.

'Wherever profit forecasts appear in relation to a period in which trading has already commenced, the latest unaudited profit figures which are available in respect of the expired portion of that trading period together with comparable figures for the preceding year must be stated. Alternatively, if no figures are available, that fact must also be stated.

'When revaluations of assets are given in connection with an offer the Board should be supported by the opinion of independent professional experts and the basis of valuation clearly stated.'

Prior to the requirement that accountants' reports on profit forecasts should be published together with the forecasts themselves, shareholders were often left with little or no idea of the exact basis on which the forecasts were prepared. This was justified on the grounds that forecasts are often based on information which in any event is not available to shareholders. Experience showed that such an approach was unsatisfactory, and did little to enhance the standard of forecasting or to protect the name of the reporting accountants. The fact that a firm was known to act as auditor to a particular company usually made it obvious who had in fact checked that company's forecasts.

A further reason for claiming that the previous practice was unsatisfactory is that directors were afforded ample opportunity of claiming that their forecasts had been passed by the investigating accountants, while neglecting to point out the full implications of any qualifications which the accountants may have included in their report to the board on the forecasts.

The Institute's recommendations were, of necessity, revised at the same time as the City Code itself was revised (in April 1969), and the latest version is reproduced in full in the Appendix. It should be noted that, except in special circumstances, instructions to report should not be accepted by accountants unless adequate time is available to enable them to obtain all the information they require so that they may exercise their professional judgment for the purpose of reporting. If for any reason, including time-restriction, all such information has not been obtainable suitable qualification should accordingly be made in the report. The form of report suggested in the recommendations should be noted. The effect of such reporting, together with such qualifications as may be appropriate, may well be to discourage directors from requesting accountants to endorse hastily made and unduly optimistic estimates, and it is to be hoped that this will, in turn, remedy the more blatant discrepancies between forecast and reality which have so often arisen in take-over battles in the past.

The recommendations retain certain important features previously included, e.g. accountants should confine their consideration of forecasts to the company's current year and the succeeding one (if the current year is well-advanced); the fact that forecasts are the sole responsibility of the directors and not of the accountants; and a reminder that truly professional opinions can be submitted only on the *accounting* basis of the information supplied to the accountants (and related calculations) and *not* on wider horizons involving the general trading outlook and the technicalities of innovation and management.

§ 5. Investigation on behalf of an incoming Partner

In addition to the examination which it is necessary to make on behalf of an intending purchaser, the accountant should include in his report to a prospective incoming partner all information which comes to his knowledge that may be of importance to his client in arriving at a decision as to whether he should continue the negotiations.

The accountant should obtain a draft copy of the proposed partnership agreement, so that he may be in a position to advise his client as to whether or not the terms thereof appear to be reasonable. Special attention should be paid to the values at which the various assets are to be brought into the new partnership's books, as if they are over-valued the capitals of the continuing partners will be inflated, and the incoming partner might be prejudiced in the event of a dissolution. If the proposed partnership is to take over the debtors and liabilities of the old partnership, special care must be taken to see that adequate provision has been made in respect of bad debts, or that if bad debts are incurred in respect of debtors existing prior to the commencement of the new partnership, the continuing partners will be responsible for them personally. Careful attention should be paid to the treatment and valuation of goodwill, and the amount which the incoming partner is required to pay for his share of this asset. The basis on which goodwill has been valued should be investigated and its reasonableness assessed.

The accountant should ascertain the reason why the firm wishes to admit a new partner, as this could be due to financial weakness. Should the accountant receive any indication that any of the continuing partners are involved personally in financial difficulties he should report this fact to his client. If it is proposed that for taxation purposes the firm is to claim to be treated as though there had been no change in the partnership and, therefore, is to be assessed on the 'previous year' basis, the taxation implications arising from such a claim must be made clear to the prospective partner.

§ 6. Investigation on behalf of a Bank for purposes of obtaining Credit

It is usual for banks, when a loan or overdraft has been asked for, to demand a copy of the customer's latest balance sheet, in order to ascertain what assets are available to afford security for the accommodation and the general financial condition of the business.

Sometimes, however, the bank requires more detailed information, and an accountant may be called in to carry out an investigation for this purpose. Bankers are interested to know the reason for the required overdraft or loan, as they are careful to see that in such cases the money is usefully employed. Further they wish to know to what extent the loan is liquid.

The accountant should prepare a statement of assets and liabilities, giving in particular the following analysed information:

(1) *Sundry Debtors and Bills Receivable*

(i) Amounts due from:
   trade debtors *within* the period of credit;
   trade debtors *beyond* the period of credit;
   partners, directors, officers and employees;
   branches or subsidiaries.

(ii) Amounts due on bills, divided into short bills and others.

(iii) Amount of provision to cover discounts and bad and doubtful debts.

(iv) Nature and amount of any debts or bills pledged or assigned.

(2) *Stock*

(i) Finished stock, stating method of pricing.

(ii) Work-in-progress, stating method of pricing.

(iii) Raw materials etc., stating method of pricing.

(iv) Amount of stock included above held under trust receipts.

 (v) Stock held on consignment, and whether it has been included above.

(vi) Amount of stock pledged as collateral for other loans or advances.

(3) *Real Property, Plant, Buildings, Fixtures and Fittings*

A full description should be given of each item, and the method of valuation used in each case clearly shown. Particulars should be given of the method of writing-off depreciation, and any recent valuations by an expert valuer should be set out. Full particulars and the amount of all charges on the property etc., should be detailed.

(4) *Investments*

A list should be given of the investments showing the nominal, book and market values. Where any investments have been pledged as security for loans or advances, full details should be given.

(5) *Secured Liabilities*

Details should be given of all debentures and other secured liabilities, showing the amount outstanding, the date repayable, and whether, in the case of debentures, they have been issued as collateral secutiry for an overdraft. Details should also be given of the assets charged, and particulars of the provision made for meeting the amounts due at maturity.

(6) *Insurance*

A schedule of all insurance policies, stating the risks covered, and the insured amounts and confirming that all premiums due have been paid. It should be borne in mind that where the business is entirely dependent for its existence on assets such as a factory, advances may more easily be secured if a Loss of Profits Policy exists.

The accountant should also examine the profit and loss account for the last period and, if required, for earlier years in order to ascertain the maintainable profits. The method of doing this has already been dealt with earlier in this chapter.

The report should state the method of collecting debts, and the period of credit and the terms upon which sales are made. Particulars should be given of all contingent liabilities and especially in respect of the following:

(1) Bills discounted.

(2) Accommodation bills.

(3) Guarantees.

(4) Contracts or agreements.

(5) Pending law suits and arbitrations.

(6) Shares and debentures of subsidiaries where the dividends or interest have been guaranteed.

Finally the accountant should state the reason given for requiring the loan etc., and whether in his opinion the amount asked for will be usefully employed and adequate for the purpose for which it is required.

§ 7. Investigation on behalf of a Person intending to Invest in a Private Business, a Firm, or a Company

An investigation for this purpose should cover the same ground as an examination on behalf of a bank for credit purposes, but as an investor does not require his investment to be as liquid as does a banker, greater attention must be given to the maintainable profits and the trends of business.

In the case of a private business or a firm, the accountant should scrutinize carefully the proposed agreement between the investor and the business or firm, and see that its terms are advantageous to his client and that reasonable security is afforded. In most cases of this nature the lender is well acquainted with the character of the proprietors of the business or the members of the firm, but where he is not familiar with them, the accountant should, if he thinks it desirable, inform his client of any facts which render it undesirable for the investment to be made. For example, if there is obvious dissension among the partners of a business, it is possible that the firm may be dissolved in the near future.

In the case of a loan to a company, the memorandum and articles should be scrutinized to see that the loan is within the borrowing powers of the company and of the directors. If it is *ultra vires* the directors a resolution should be passed by the company in general meeting authorizing them to borrow the money. If the money is to be invested in the business on the security of debentures the terms of the issue should be examined carefully, and it should be seen that adequate provision will be made for repayment at maturity. In addition to verifying the existence of any property charged by the debentures, the company's file at Companies House should be examined, in order to see that there are no charges entered in the register of charges which are not entered in the company's own register of charges.

Where it is proposed that an investment should be made in the preference shares of a private company, which carry the right to a fixed rate of dividend, the price to be paid for such shares will, in the main, be determined by the current level of interest rates. Due allowance must be made, however, for the risk factor and for the non-marketability of the shares. If the shares are redeemable, regard must be had for the date on which such redemption can be effected and the premium, if any, which will by paid by the company. In many cases no date is fixed for the redemption of redeemable preference shares, the terms of issue merely providing that the company has the right to redeem on or after a certain date; in such cases it must be borne in mind that the holder of such shares has no power to insist on their redemption.

If it is proposed that the investment should be in the ordinary shares of a private company, the following factors must be taken into consideration in determining the price to be paid:

(a) The extent of the assets 'cover' for the ordinary share capital.

(b) The amount of profits required for the payment of dividends on shares with preferential rights, and interest on long term loans and debentures.

(c) The extent of the anticipated future earnings 'cover' available to the ordinary shareholders after allowing for (b).

(d) The current 'yield' obtainable on quoted shares of companies engaged in the same industry. The yield required will be increased to allow for the relative non-marketability of the shares to be purchased, as compared with shares which are quoted on the Stock Exchange.

(e) The 'price/earnings' ratio, or the number of years it would take to repay the cost of the shares to the investor, from the sums *earned* by those shares.

(f) The restrictions, if any, imposed by the company's articles of association on the rate of dividend payable on the ordinary share capital and any other matters which will limit such rate, e.g. amounts agreed to be set aside annually to provide for the redemption of debentures, loans or preference shares.

(g) The estimated proportion of future profits which must be left in the business to provide the funds necessary for its expansion.

(h) The proportion of the total ordinary share capital which it is proposed to acquire. If a minority interest is to be purchased in a director-controlled company it must be remembered that profits available for dividend may be reduced by increases in directors' emoluments and that, for a variety of reasons (e.g. taxation), the directors may wish to limit the rate of dividend payable without regard for the interests of the minority.

(i) The basis upon which the shares have been valued. Where the company's net assets have provided the basis, considerable care must be taken in investigating the asset valuations, particularly where goodwill is concerned. (It is not within the scope of this work to deal with the many and various methods by which goodwill may be valued.) Where a controlling interest in the company is to be acquired, it may be preferable for the shares to be valued by reference to the company's earnings, rather than dividends paid, since otherwise an undervaluation of shares would result, in cases where the directors had followed a policy of 'ploughing back' most of the profits in the past. Minority interests would be more appropriately valued by reference to *distributable* profits. The valuations used should be checked against the details of any recent transfers of shares of that class, if available.

(j) The continued demand for the company's output, and its revenue earning capacity in general, as far as may be reasonably assessed.

(k) The possible effects of anticipated legislation on the company's prosperity, e.g. in the fields of taxation, tariffs, transport etc.

(l) The general condition of the investment market as regards availability of finance, and interest rates.

(m) The voting powers attached to the shares to be acquired.

In all cases the accountant should satisfy himself that the funds to be provided can be usefully employed and, where they are required for a specific purpose, will be adequate for that purpose.

Where an auditor values shares in a company as an expert under the provisions of the company's articles of association it would seem that he cannot be called upon to justify his valuation provided that he does not express the reasons which impelled him to his decision. If, however, the auditor offers an explanation of his valuation the court is not precluded from examining such explanation and if it is considered to be incorrect, of upsetting the valuation (*Dean* v. *Prince and Others*, 1953, 3 W.L.R. 271).

§ 8. Investigation for Fraud

It has been pointed out in Chapter I that fraud may be divided into two classes, viz. defalcations involving misappropriations either of money or goods, or the manipulation of accounts, not involving defalcations. The conduct of investigations where fraud is suspected or known to have taken place varies very much according to the circumstances of each case, and it is only possible to consider the matter here in the most general manner.

The fraudulent manipulation of accounts without corresponding defalcations has already been considered from time to time in the course of this work, and usually takes the form of the inflation of assets, or the omission of liabilities, for the purpose of making the position of a business appear to be better than it really is, or enabling dividends to be paid when profits have not been earned.

Defalcations involving misappropriations of stock vary so much according to the nature of the goods and the trade carried on that it is not practicable to discuss the subject here; but defalcations involving misappropriations of cash present many features in common, and it may be convenient to indicate the general course of procedure when an investigation of this nature is made, taking as an instance the case of a trading business where fraud is known to have been carried out by some individual in charge of the books and cash.

Full enquiries should be made as to the authority exercised by the defaulting official and the nature of his duties, as this will give some indication of the opportunities of which he may have taken advantage. Assuming that the official has been in general control of the books and has been subject to little or no supervision, the accountant would be compelled to make a complete investigation from a date arranged with the proprietors of the business.

The cash book should be cast and vouched in detail, and certificates of the opening and closing bank balances obtained from the bank. The cash book should be checked completely with the bank statement, particular attention being paid to the dates when the receipts were paid in, and to ascertaining that each day's receipts have been banked intact.

Where money received from debtors has been misappropriated, it is common to find that, in order to prevent the debtor's account appearing overdue, cash received subsequently from other debtors is placed to the credit of the debtor whose remittance was originally misappropriated, this process being continued indefinitely. This type of fraud is commonly known as 'teeming and lading'. In such cases it may become necessary for the cashier to divide certain remittances in order to obtain the exact amounts necessary for this purpose, and, where possible, one method of discovering whether this has been done is to examine the original paying-in slips *at the bank*, and to compare them with the counterfoils of the paying-in book. The slip presented to the bank will contain the correct record of the amount of each cheque, whereas the counterfoil will show any division that may have taken place. This also serves as a check upon the improper manipulation of discounts. All discounts of any consequence appearing in the cash book should be tested, in order to ascertain that they are in order.

Where counterfoil receipt books are used, the counterfoils should be checked with the cash book; and where rough cash books or cash diaries have been kept, these should be compared with the fair cash book.

It should be seen that the proceeds of all bills receivable have been duly received, and bills in hand should be examined.

The best method of verifying the balances due by customers where it is suspected that amounts have been misappropriated, is for the accountant to send out a circular to the debtors, stating the amount of the balance as shown in the books, and asking the debtors to communicate to him direct if they do not agree the amount stated. Permission to circularize in this way must, of course, be obtained from the proprietors or directors. The detailed procedures to be followed in the exercise have already been dealt with in the section on the verification of debtor balances.

As regards cash payments, special care should be taken, in examining the supporting invoices, to note any that appear to be irregular; and the cancelled cheques should be examined to see that the payees' names agree with those appearing on the invoices. If any vouchers for material amounts are missing, duplicates should be obtained. All amounts charged to the drawings accounts of partners or directors should be vouched by them as being correct.

The petty cash book should be vouched and cast. Special attention must be paid to salaries and wages, and the accountant should confirm with a partner or director the existence of all the employees named in the salaries and wages books, and the amounts payable to them.

Where the defaulting party has had access to all the books, it will be necessary for the whole of the postings to be checked, the books cast, and a trial balance prepared. In checking the sales ledgers special attention should be paid to all allowances and bad debts written-off, as entries of this nature may have been made for the purpose of concealing misappropriations of cash. Similar remarks apply to returns, and where necessary the receipt of the actual goods returned should be traced. In some cases it may be found that the defaulting party has omitted to record sales, so as to be able to appropriate the remittances received without the necessity of falsifying the books further. In order to ascertain whether this has been done, the order book should be tested with the day book or copies of sales invoices, to see that all orders that have been executed have been recorded, and reference should also be made to the goods outwards records in order to verify deliveries of goods sold. Where cash sales are made, these should be vouched in detail with whatever evidence may be available, although, unless the system employed is a good one, it may be very difficult to ascertain whether irregularities have occurred.

Invoices should be vouched with the bought journal, if any, in order to ascertain that none has been passed through twice, payment in respect of the original invoice being made to the creditor, but payment for the duplicate being misappropriated by the defaulting party. Duplicates should be obtained of missing invoices, and the creditors' statements compared with the balances as shown by the bought ledger or its equivalent, and the schedule of unpaid accounts. The goods inwards book or the order book should be checked with the bought journal or purchase invoices to ensure that all invoices relate to *bona fide* purchases.

§ 9. Investigations under the Companies Acts 1948 and 1967

The *Companies Act 1948* provides for the appointment of inspectors to investigate a company's affairs in certain circumstances.

Section 164 provides that the Board of Trade *may* make such an appointment on the application –

(*a*) in the case of a company having a share capital, either of not less than two hundred members or of members holding not less than one-tenth of the shares issued;

(*b*) in the case of a company not having a share capital, of not less than one-fifth in number of persons on the company's register of members.

Under Section 165 the Board of Trade *must* appoint inspectors to investigate a company's affairs if –

(*a*) the company by special resolution, or

(*b*) the Court by order

declares that the company's affairs ought to be investigated.

The Board of Trade may also make such an appointment if it appears to them that there are circumstances suggesting –

(i) that the company's business is being or has been conducted with intent to defraud its creditors or the creditors of any other person, or otherwise for a fraudulent or unlawful purpose, or in a manner oppressive to any part of its members, or that it was formed for any fraudulent or unlawful purpose; or

(ii) that persons concerned with the company's formation or the management of its affairs have in connection therewith been guilty of fraud, misfeasance or other misconduct towards it or towards its members; or

(iii) that the members of the company have not been given all the information with respect to its affairs which they might reasonably expect.

(Sub-paragraph (i) of paragraph (b) above was made retrospective by Section 38, *Companies Act 1967*.)

Inspectors appointed under either Section 164 or 165 have power to investigate the affairs of any other body corporate which is or has at any relevant time been the company's subsidiary or holding company or a subsidiary of its holding company or a holding company of its subsidiary.

The inspector has power to examine on oath all *past and present* officers and agents (including bankers, solicitors and auditors) of the company and it shall be their duty to attend before him when required to do so. If he wishes to examine on oath any person whom he has no power thus to examine, he may apply to the Court, who may order such person to attend before it and be examined on oath. If any such officer or agent refuses to produce any book or document or to answer any question put to him, the inspector may certify his refusal, whereupon the Court may enquire into the case, and, after hearing witnesses for and against the alleged offender, may punish him as for contempt of Court (Section 167, as extended by Section 39 of the 1967 Act). The inspector must report to the Board of Trade, who must forward a copy of the report to the company, and a further copy shall, in the case of an investigation under Section 164, at the request of the applicants, be delivered to them. Where the inspection is under Section 165, a copy of the report must be furnished to the Court. If the Board of Trade think fit they may furnish a copy of the report, on payment of the prescribed fee, to any other person who is a member of the company or of any body corporate dealt with in the report or whose interests as a creditor of the company or any other body corporate appear to the Board to be affected (Section 168).

Under Section 37 of the *Companies Act 1967*, if it appears to the Board of Trade, from any report made under Section 168 of the principal Act, that civil proceedings ought in the public interest to be brought by any body corporate, they may themselves bring such proceedings in the name and on behalf of that body corporate.

If it appears to the Board of Trade that by reason of any such circumstances as are referred to in sub-paragraph (i) or (ii) of paragraph (*b*) of Section 165 (*supra*), it is expedient to do so, the Board may present a petition for the winding-up of the company (Section 35, *Companies Act 1967*).

If, from the report, it appears that any body corporate dealt with by the report ought, in the public interest, to bring proceedings for the recovery of damages in respect of any fraud, misfeasance or other misconduct in connection with the promotion, formation or management of that body corporate, or for the recovery of any of its property which has been misapplied, the Board of Trade may bring proceedings for that purpose in the name of the body corporate (Section 37, *Companies Act 1967*).

Investigations under Section 165 are usually instituted when it is suspected that the company has been mismanaged or that the directors or officers of the company have been using the company's resources for their own purposes.

The procedure to be followed by the accountant appointed to conduct such an investigation must be determined by the terms of his instructions, but in most cases a very detailed examination of the company's books and records will be necessary. Particular attention must be paid to the verification of the existence of assets, the nature of the liabilities contracted by the company, dealings with subsidiaries, and the manner in which the profits or losses disclosed by the published accounts have been arrived at.

Under Section 172 of the principal Act, where it appears to the Board of Trade that there is good reason so to do, they may appoint one or more competent inspectors to investigate and report on the membership of any company and otherwise with respect to the company for the purpose of determining the true persons who are or have been financially interested in the success or failure (real or apparent) of the company or able to control or materially to influence the policy of the company.

An application for an investigation under this section may be made to the Board of Trade by members of the company in the same way as under Section 164.

The investigation powers of the Board of Trade were considerably extended by the *Companies Act 1967*. Under Section 32 of that Act, where it appears to the Board that contraventions may have occurred of the requirements regarding dealings by directors and their families in share options, or the obligation of directors to notify the company of interest in its shares, or the granting by directors to members of their families of the right to subscribe for shares or debentures of the company, they may appoint one or more inspectors to carry out such investigations as will enable them to discover whether such contraventions have taken place, and to report thereon to the Board. Officers and agents of bodies being investigated have a duty to assist the inspectors, who may make interim reports to the Board, and on the conclusion of their investigation, shall make a final report to the Board.

The investigation powers of the Board of Trade are further extended by Section 42, *Companies Act 1967*, to apply to all bodies corporate incorporated outside Great Britain which are carrying on business in Great Britain, or have at any time carried on business therein as if they were companies registered under the principal Act.

Part III of the 1967 Act is extremely far reaching, and is concerned with the inspection of companies' books and papers. Under Section 109, the Board of Trade, 'if they think there is good reason so to do', may require virtually any company formed or carrying on business in the United Kingdom to produce books or papers – or any person having possession of them to do so (but without prejudice to any lien they may have). The Board of Trade may take extracts and require explanations (a power extended to all investigations by Section 39), refusal being punishable by three months imprisonment and/or a £200 fine maximum, and such statements may be admitted in evidence against such officers. If hindrance is suspected, the Board of Trade may obtain a warrant to search premises and to take away or safeguard documents; anyone obstructing this is liable to the same penalty (Section 110). Such information, however, is to be kept confidential, unless the Board of Trade need to use it for civil or criminal proceedings, or for the institution of action under Part II of the Act, or winding-up action or for appropriate publication in an Inspector's report (Section 111). The standard penalties under the Act for summary conviction or conviction on indictment apply equally to improper disclosure of such information and the destruction or falsification of documents or false statements. Solicitors' privileged communications are safeguarded as is bankers' information, except in regard to the person being investigated.

§ 10. Investigations in connection with Taxation Liability

An investigation in connection with taxation liability is usually carried out at the behest of the Inland Revenue authorities, where they have reason to suspect that complete and accurate returns of income for taxation purposes have not been made. When the investigation is in respect of tax which would otherwise be out of date, it is described as a 'back duty' investigation.

It is not within the province of this work to describe in detail the conduct of such an investigation, nor is it possible to lay down hard-and-fast rules as to the procedure which must be followed. So much must depend upon the nature of the business carried on, the records available, and the opportunities afforded for the falsification of records for the purpose of evading taxation liability. The accountant must bring into play not only a high degree of technical skill, but a wide knowledge of human nature and much ingenuity to arrive at the truth.

After ascertaining the period over which the investigation is to extend, the accountant should first obtain from his client such of the following documents and data as are available:

(1) Books and audited accounts of the business.

(2) Bank pass books or statements, deposit receipts etc., in the name of the client or his wife or over which either had control at any time during the years under review, and certificates from bankers as to current balances.

(3) Statements of all private assets and liabilities at the beginning and end of the period covered by the investigation.

(4) Schedules of all investments held, showing the dates and cost of purchase and the names and addresses of the persons in whose names they were bought.

(5) Acknowledgments from nominees that they hold assets in their names on behalf of the client.

(6) Bought and sold notes and brokers' accounts in respect of all dealings in investments during the period.

(7) Details of any other non-business assets or property purchased and sold during the period.

(8) Particulars of any legacies, insurance maturities, or other capital receipts during the period.

(9) Particulars of any insurance policies taken out, and receipts for premiums paid thereon during the period.

(10) All interest and dividend counterfoils, and accounts of rents and outgoings of any property held.

(11) Estimates of living and other personal expenses, including cost of children's education, holidays, gifts and other abnormal expenditure.

(12) Copies (if available) of all income tax returns made during the period, and receipts for tax paid.

Where books have been kept and accounts prepared, the investigation will follow the lines discussed in § 2 of this chapter, special attention being paid to the possibility of sales being omitted, purchases and expenses being inflated, and stock being improperly valued with the object of reducing the profit disclosed by the accounts. The pass books or statements of all personal bank accounts kept must be obtained and analysed in the minutest detail, in order to trace the origin of all lodgments and the destination of all payments recorded therein. All cheques drawn by the business in favour of the partners or, in the case of companies, in favour of directors or other officials whose affairs are also the subject of investigation must be traced into their private banking accounts. In the case of any cheques which cannot be so traced, the cancelled cheques, if available, should be examined. If it is found that such cheques are crossed cheques, the names and addresses of the banks through which they were cleared should be noted and enquiries made of the payees as to the manner in which they disposed of the cheques in question. Enquiries on these lines may reveal the existence of banking accounts in the names of the taxpayers or their nominees which have not so far been disclosed to the accountant.

The exact nature of all payments from private banking accounts must be ascertained, even though the amounts involved may be small, as such payments may indicate the existence of assets which have not been disclosed, e.g. a safe deposit rental, a furrier's charge for storage of a fur coat etc. For the same reason the nature of the risks covered by all insurance premiums paid must be ascertained by examination of the relevant policies.

A total account for receipts and payments of cash, as distinct from cheques, must be prepared for each individual who is the subject of investigation, in order that the accountant may satisfy himself that the person concerned appears to have had sufficient cash to meet his normal household and living expenditure. This account will be compiled as follows:

Debit side

(a) Cash drawn from bank.

(b) Cash drawn from business.

(c) Any other cash receipts, e.g. rents collected.

Credit side

(a) Cash paid in to bank.

(b) Bank lodgments from unidentified sources which, therefore, are assumed to have represented cash.

(c) Payments which must have been made in cash because they were not discharged by cheque, e.g. rates or other known expenditure.

(d) Cash allowance, if any, to wife for household expenses and to children for pocket money.

(e) Any other known cash payments.

(f) Estimate of the taxpayer's personal cash expenditure.

If the account prepared in this way reveals an excess of expenditure over cash received, the accountant will be forced to conclude, subject to the accuracy of the estimates made, that the taxpayer has received cash from sources not disclosed by him. Exhaustive enquiries into this possibility must be made, it being impressed upon the taxpayer that a satisfactory report cannot be made to the Inland Revenue with such a discrepancy unexplained.

Where no books have been kept, it will be necessary to construct accounts by analysing bank statements, invoices, creditors' statements, receipts or invoices for expenditure and any other available documents and data. Unless all cash takings and receipts from debtors have been paid into the bank, it may be very difficult, if not impossible, to obtain a reliable estimate of the total amount of the sales; but if the total purchases have been ascertained, it may be possible to estimate the amount of the gross profit by reference to the percentage on purchases normally earned in the particular trade, or by adding to the bank lodgments an estimate of the amount of cash takings applied in paying for purchases and expenses, and drawn by the client for his private use.

Where the available information is so meagre that it is impossible to construct profit and loss accounts, the only method of estimating the profit will be by the preparation of statements of 'net worth' at the beginning and end of the period under investigation. For this purpose, exhaustive enquiry must be made to ascertain the assets and the liabilities of the client at each date. To any increase in net worth disclosed by such statements must be added the estimated amount of the client's living and personal expenses (which, of course, must be related to the style in which he lives), any losses on sale of investments, gambling losses and any other losses of a capital nature, the value of any assets which have been worn out or discarded during the period, and any other items by which the final net worth has been reduced. From the total so found will be deducted any legacies received, insurance maturities, gambling profits, profits on the sale of investments and other capital receipts, and the result may then be taken to represent the total income from all sources during the period of the investigation. From this amount must be deducted the total income from investments, property and other sources on which tax has been paid, and the balance may be regarded as the net profit from the business for the whole period. This amount must be apportioned over the years comprised in the period on such basis as may appear to be equitable, having regard to all the circumstances, and in particular to any information that may be available as to the trend of business over the years in question or the assets owned at intervening dates.

In his report the investigating accountant should indicate fully any deficiencies in the data at his disposal, or matters on which he has been unable to obtain satisfactory explanations, and the extent to which he is able to accept responsibility for the accuracy of the figures disclosed by the accounts.

APPENDIX

CONTENTS

		PAGE
PART A ; EXTRACTS FROM STATEMENTS ON AUDITING, ACCOUNTING PRINCIPLES AND OTHER TECHNICAL STATEMENTS* ..		571

Published by The Institute of Chartered Accountants in England and Wales

1.	General Principles of Auditing	571
2.	Internal Control [Including Field of Relationship between Independent and Internal Auditor] ..	578
3.	Stock-in-Trade and Work in Progress	585
4.	Attendance at Stocktaking ..	589
5.	Treatment of Stock-in-Trade and Work in Progress in Financial Accounts	592
6.	Mechanized Accounting and the Auditor ..	603
7.	Verification of Debtor Balances: Confirmation by Direct Communication	614
8.	Auditors' Reports on Group Accounts ..	616
9.	Auditors' Reports—Forms and Qualifications	619
10.	Accountants' Reports on Profit Forecasts ..	627
11.	Accountants' Reports for Prospectuses:	
	(a) Fixed Assets and Depreciation ..	632
	(b) Adjustments and Other Matters	634
	(c) Disclosure of Depreciation	641
12.	Special Reports Required of Accountants ..	642
13.	Interpretation of 'Material' in Relation to Accounts	646
14.	Depreciation of Fixed Assets ..	648
15.	Accounting in Relation to Changes in the Purchasing Power of Money	651
16.	Accountants' Liability to Third Parties—the *Hedley Byrne* Decision	654
17.	Audits of Building Societies ..	657
	PART B: EXTRACTS FROM INTERNAL CONTROL QUESTIONNAIRE ..	673

Note: It will be appreciated that certain of the statements etc. which are reproduced were prepared and issued prior to the passing of the *Companies Act 1967*, and, at the time of this edition going to press, had not been revised by the Institute. Although several references to the *Companies Act 1948* might therefore be inappropriate, it is nevertheless considered that the value of the statements reproduced, as clear and concise directives on auditing and accounting principles and problems, is in no way undermined thereby.

PART A

1. General Principles of Auditing (*Issued 16th August 1961*)

INTRODUCTION

Auditors under the *Companies Act 1948* have specific duties laid upon them and they have an obligation to acquaint themselves with those duties. Their statutory duties cannot be limited by agreement with the members or directors of the company; and Section 205 of the Act renders void any provisions, in the articles or otherwise, purporting to exempt an auditor from or indemnifying him against any liability which by virtue of any rule of law would otherwise attach to him in respect of any negligence, default, breach of duty or breach of trust in relation to the company. On the other hand, additional duties and responsibilities may be placed upon auditors by the articles of the company or by special agreement with the members or directors. This may be particularly important where the auditors carry out other work in addition to their statutory duties as auditors. These circumstances are referred to later.

As a general statement of the degree of professional competence required of an auditor, reliance can properly be placed on the observation made by Lord Justice Lopes in *In re Kingston Cotton Mill Co. Ltd** ([1896] 2 Ch. 279 at pages 288–90):

'It is the duty of an auditor to bring to bear on the work he has to perform that skill, care, and caution which a reasonably competent, careful, and cautious auditor would use. What is reasonable skill, care and caution must depend on the particular circumstances of each case. . . . If there is anything calculated to excite suspicion he should probe it to the bottom; but in the absence of anything of that kind he is only bound to be reasonably cautious and careful. . . . The duties of auditors must not be rendered too onerous. Their work is responsible and laborious, and the remuneration moderate. . . .'

* Certain of the rulings made by Lord Justice Lopes on the particular facts of the case before him in 1896 would now be inappropriate in the light of the statutory duties imposed by the *Companies Act 1948*.

In the previous year similar judicial guidance on the duty of an auditor had been given by Lord Justice Lindley in *In re London and General Bank* ([1895] 2 Ch. 673 at page 683):

'He must be honest—that is, he must not certify what he does not believe to be true and he must take reasonable care and skill before he believes that what he certifies is true. What is reasonable care in any particular case must depend upon the circumstances of that case.'

The foregoing comments on the auditors' position in law are a necessary background to any consideration of the duties of auditors, but this Statement is concerned essentially with the general principles of auditing as a professional assignment rather than with the consequences in law of a failure by auditors to discharge their duties. The Council's object in issuing this Statement is not to define the liability in law for such a failure. Its object is to assist members to improve the standards of auditing for the good of the profession and the benefit of their clients and the public.

Responsibility for the accounts and financial control of a company rests upon the directors. Their statutory duties include responsibility for ensuring the maintenance of adequate records and the preparation of annual accounts showing the true and fair view required by the Act. They are responsible for safeguarding the assets of the company and are not entitled to rely upon the auditors to protect them from any shortcomings in carrying out their responsibilities.

Auditors have their own independent responsibility to form and express their professional opinion on the accounts to be presented by the directors to the shareholders. Auditors do not guarantee or certify the accounts, but their responsibility is heavy and cannot be discharged without a full realization of the professional skill and judgment which need to be exercised in carrying out their duties. They must approach their work as auditors with an independent outlook and must do nothing which would impair that independence.

If the directors have carried out their duty properly the detailed checking by the auditors will be limited to appropriate tests which, if suitably planned, may extend to only a small proportion of the total transactions unless the company is a small organization in which the scope for internal control is limited. If on the other hand the directors have not carried out their duty properly this will have a material bearing on the terms of the auditors' report and may well involve the auditors in extensive checking, at the expense of the company; but it is not their function to act as a substitute for proper management control.

The essential features of an audit are:

(a) to make a critical review of the system of book-keeping, accounting and internal control;

(b) to make such tests and enquiries as the auditors consider necessary to form an opinion as to the reliability of the records as a basis for the preparation of accounts;

(c) to compare the profit and loss account and balance sheet with the underlying records in order to see whether they are in accordance therewith;

(d) to make a critical review of the profit and loss account and the balance sheet in order that a report may be made to the members stating whether, in the opinion of the auditors, the accounts are presented and the items are described in such a way that they show not only a true but also a fair view and give in the prescribed manner the information required by the Act.

The auditors should aim to reduce their detailed checking to the minimum consistent with the system of internal control and the state in which they find the records. If their enquiries and tests satisfy them that the system is sound in principle and is carried out in practice then no useful purpose is served by extensive detailed checking. If on the other hand the system is not sound or is not properly carried out then the auditors must first reach a conclusion as to the nature of the shortcomings before they can decide upon the nature and extent of the detailed checking which they should undertake. Auditors should therefore direct their attention in the first instance to the system of internal control.

INTERNAL CONTROL

Ascertaining the system

By 'internal control' is meant not only internal check and internal audit but the whole system of controls, financial and otherwise, established by the management in order to carry on the business of the company in an orderly manner, safeguard its assets and secure as far as possible the accuracy and reliability of its records.

Auditors will find it of great advantage to have before them an up-to-date record of the system of internal control. For this purpose they will normally need to make a study of the following matters:

(a) the characteristics of the company's business and its activities, involving possibly an inspection of its physical assets and operations;

(b) the system of book-keeping and accounting;

(c) the duties of the executive directors and staff and the division of responsibilities;

(d) the system of internal check, that is to say, the checks on the day-to-day transactions which operate continuously as part of the routine system whereby the work of one person is proved independently or is complementary to the work of another, the object being the prevention or early detection of errors and fraud; it includes matters such as the delegation and allocation of authority and the division of work, the method of recording transactions and the use of independently ascertained totals against which a large number of individual items can be proved;

(e) internal audit, if any; where there is an internal audit the auditors should have regard to the Council's *Statement on Auditing 'Internal Control'*.

On the first occasion this study of the system will require extensive enquiry and the auditors may find it helpful to prepare for this purpose a comprehensive questionnaire, the answers to which will provide them with a basis for their record.

Examining the system

An examination of the system of internal control will enable the auditors to decide whether they can regard it as satisfactory. Of particular importance is the extent to which the system ensures that the division of work and allocation of responsibility are such that each of the following aspects of the company's activities is sufficiently independent of the others:

(a) the transacting of business (that is to say, the creation of contractual obligations and of any original records thereof);

(b) the recording of those transactions in the books and records;

(c) the custody and handling of the assets involved in the transactions.

A large company should have a comprehensive system of internal control. A smaller company, having less opportunity for division of responsibilities and the institution of internal checks, may have a system which is less comprehensive without necessarily being unsatisfactory. This is a matter upon which the auditors must exercise their judgment. The directors of every company, irrespective of its size, have a duty to ensure that there is a proper system of control over the transactions and records and that proper arrangements are made for safeguarding the company's assets. There will usually be some respects in which the possible errors or losses to the business are not sufficiently material to justify the additional expense which would be incurred by extending the control system sufficiently to prevent them.

Apart from the work which the auditors should themselves do if they encounter weaknesses in the system of internal control (as indicated in later paragraphs) it is good practice for them to advise a director or appropriate executive, preferably in writing, with the object of assisting the directors in the discharge of their obligation to control and safeguard the assets of the company.

THE NATURE AND EXTENT OF THE TESTS TO BE APPLIED

Audit procedures should be based primarily on an appropriate series of tests designed to satisfy the auditors that the system of internal control is properly operated and is effective, so that the records can be regarded as a reliable basis for the preparation of accounts. Tests of the detailed transactions should be reduced to the minimum considered necessary by the auditor to achieve this purpose and unnecessary expenditure of time on the massive vouching of routine transactions and extensive verifications of postings and additions should be avoided.

The nature and extent of the tests which the auditors apply will vary according to the strength or weakness of the system of internal control and the nature of the internal checks which exist as well as according to the type of transaction or item which is the subject of examination. It is important to include examinations 'in depth' among the tests to be applied. Examination 'in depth' involves tracing a transaction through its various stages from origin to conclusion, examining at each stage to an appropriate extent the vouchers, records and authorities relating to that stage and observing the incidence of internal check and delegated authority. For example, verification of a payment to a creditor for goods supplied could be made by examination of a paid cheque which had been drawn in favour of the creditor and crossed 'Account payee only'. Complete verification of this transaction 'in depth' might involve the examination of the transaction at all stages including the following documents or records:

(a) the invoice and statement from the supplier;

(b) evidence that the goods had been recorded in the stock records;

(c) the goods received note and inspection certificate;

(d) a copy of the original order and the authority therefor.

It is sound practice to reduce progressively the number of transactions selected for examination as the depth of the examination increases. For example, it might, in a particular case, be appropriate for the auditors to select one hundred payments to creditors for goods supplied and verify them by examination of the paid cheques properly crossed and stamped by the paying bank; only a proportion of those one hundred payments would also be verified with the suppliers' invoices and statements; a still smaller proportion would be verified in addition by evidence that goods had been recorded in the stock records; and so on until a comparatively small proportion had been verified completely in depth.

For a small company the tests which the auditors make will normally cover a greater proportion of the transactions than is necessary for a larger company where a more comprehensive system of control can be and is operated. In selecting items for examination and deciding upon the extent of the work to be done the auditors should always consider to what extent the transactions under review are material in relation to the affairs of the company as a whole.

In addition to the normal annual audit procedures covering all activities it is also sound practice to select each year, for a more intensive review of the accounting procedures, one of the main aspects of the activities of the business: for example, sales, wages, receipts from customers, payments to suppliers. Such reviews can usefully be planned to ensure that over a period of years they cover all the main aspects.

Depending on the circumstances it may or may not be necessary for the auditors to extend their tests in certain areas because of deficiencies in the system of internal control. Where, however, the auditors are of opinion that the internal control is inadequate to the extent of casting doubt on the reliability of the records, they will be obliged to undertake a great deal more detailed checking than would otherwise have been necessary. If, even after extensive detailed checking, they have been unable to satisfy themselves that the records are sufficiently reliable to enable the balance sheet and profit and loss account to show the true and fair view required by law, it will be their duty to state in their report that in their opinion books of account have not been properly kept and to make such other reservations as may be necessary.

In exceptional cases, auditors may find that the records and the system of internal control are so seriously inadequate that no useful purpose could be served by embarking upon extensive detailed checking, because even the most exhaustive tests would not enable them to form an opinion on the balance sheet and profit and loss account. In that event their appropriate course will be to report to that effect to the shareholders and to inform the directors of the respects in which the records and system are deficient.

EXAMINATION OF THE PROFIT AND LOSS ACCOUNT AND BALANCE SHEET

The auditors will compare the profit and loss account and balance sheet with the books and records in order to see whether they are in accordance therewith.

In addition, the auditors will make a critical review of the profit and loss account and balance sheet in relation to the following matters:

(a) whether the accounts have been prepared on sound accounting principles consistent with those applied in the previous period; the distinction between capital and revenue is particularly important to prevent the overstatement of profits by charging revenue expenditure to capital or their understatement by charging capital expenditure to revenue;

(b) the items in the balance sheet, with particular reference to the basis on which and the amounts at which they are stated and:
   (i) the existence, ownership and proper custody of assets,
   (ii) the existence of liabilities,
   (iii) their relation to the corresponding items at the end of the previous year and, where necessary, earlier years,
   (iv) the suitability of the descriptions used,
   (v) an adequate disclosure of information;

(c) the items in the profit and loss account with particular reference to adequate description, disclosure of information and the significance of variations as compared with previous periods;

(d) compliance with the requirements of the Act.

The purpose of the work of the auditors is to enable them to express an opinion as to whether the accounts presented to the members show a true and fair view. The purpose should govern their whole approach to the audit, the planning of their tests and the matters to be noted in the audit papers as the work proceeds. If they find weaknesses or matters which arouse their suspicion they should make exhaustive enquiries and if in any material respects they are unable to satisfy themselves it will be their duty to include appropriate reservations in their report, to the extent, if necessary, of stating that they are not able to express the opinion that the accounts show a true and fair view.

FRAUD

Irregularities which arise in the conduct of the affairs of a company may be classified broadly into:

(a) acts or defaults by an employee or a director which are committed without the knowledge of the board of directors; it is the responsibility of the directors to take all reasonable care that the system will prevent such irregularities or bring about their early detection;

(b) acts or defaults by the directors which are designed to mislead or defraud the members;

(c) acts or defaults designed to defraud the Inland Revenue or other third parties (on which the Council has already issued its statement entitled *Unlawful Acts or Defaults by Clients of Members* [*the principal legal considerations concerned being reproduced in Chapter XII*]).

Material irregularities of the above character will normally be brought to light by sound audit procedures but there is nothing in the *Companies Act*

1948 which specifically places a duty upon auditors to search for them or to examine the books and accounts with the object of discovering whether there have been defalcations or other irregularities by directors or employees of the company. Lord Justice Lopes pointed out in the *Kingston Cotton Mill* case:

> 'Auditors must not be made liable for not tracking out ingenious and carefully laid schemes of fraud, when there is nothing to arouse their suspicion, and when those frauds are perpetrated by tried servants of the company and are undetected for years by the directors. So to hold would make the position of an auditor intolerable.'

Although there is no statutory obligation upon the auditors to search for irregularities, the possibility of their existence will be a factor governing the auditors' approach to their work as described in paragraph 9 and in discharging their statutory duties. In normal circumstances they are entitled to rely upon the honesty of the directors and employees of the company. But if, in the course of their examination, their suspicions are aroused they have a clear duty to probe the circumstances to the bottom and to report appropriately to the members.

AUDITOR'S REPORT

The auditors' report is governed by the requirements of the Ninth Schedule to the Act. They should express their opinion in clear and unequivocal terms. If they are unable to satisfy themselves on any of the matters referred to in the Ninth Schedule they must include appropriate reservations in their report to the members of the company. They are not relieved of this obligation by making a report to the directors even though the directors may comprise all the members of the company.

[N.B. The *Companies Act 1967* has repealed the Ninth Schedule to the principal Act, and these matters are now dealt with in Section 14 of the 1967 Act.]

OTHER DUTIES UNDERTAKEN BY AUDITORS

Accountants acting as auditors of a company frequently provide other professional services for the company. In particular they may draft for the directors the balance sheet and profit and loss account and sometimes assist with the underlying records; and they may at the request of the directors undertake detailed checking beyond that which is required to enable them to make their report to the shareholders, for example checking with the specific object of ascertaining whether there have been defalcations or other irregularities. In doing work of this kind they are not acting as auditors appointed under the Act but are rendering a separate professional service. Such additional services may facilitate their work in their capacity as auditors but do not extend or reduce the responsibilities placed upon them as auditors by the Act.

Where such additional services are rendered the following are important considerations:

(a) the accounts should not undertake services which would impair their independence as auditors;

(b) the duty to take all reasonable care that there is adequate internal control and to present accounts to the shareholders in compliance with the Act rests firmly on the directors and cannot be avoided by them;

(c) there should be a clear understanding with the directors as to the nature of the responsibility undertaken by the accountants outside their duty as auditors, so that there is no misunderstanding as to the extent to which the directors, in discharging their own responsibilities, are placing reliance upon the additional services provided by the accountants.

2. Internal Control

ESSENTIAL CHARACTERISTICS

The elements of internal control are:

(a) the plan of organization (with particular reference to the allocation of staff duties);

(b) authorization, recording and custody procedures (including internal check); and

(c) managerial supervision and reviews (including internal audit).

PLAN OF ORGANIZATION

There can be no effective internal control without an adequate plan of organization. This involves the separation of a company's operations into appropriate divisions and sub-divisions, the appointment of persons to assume responsibility therefor, the establishment of clear lines of responsibility between each division and sub-division and the board of directors, and overall co-ordination of the company's activities.

AUTHORIZATION, RECORDING AND CUSTODY PROCEDURES (INCLUDING INTERNAL CHECK)

The objects of financial and accounting control procedures are to ensure that the funds and property of the company are kept under proper custody and may not be improperly applied, either by error or intent; that expenditure may be incurred only after authorization, and is properly accounted for; and that all revenues are properly accounted for and received in due course.

The achievement of these objects involves a suitable division of duties, the establishment of an appropriate accounting system and the institution of forms of internal check. By internal check is meant the checks on day-to-day transactions which operate continuously as part of the routine system whereby the work of one person is proved independently or is complementary to the work of another, the object being the prevention or early detection of errors or fraud.

A first principle is that all transactions, either individually or in groups, should involve surveillance by at least two persons, so far as possible independent of each other. Surveillance may take two forms:

(*a*) participation by others, through the division of responsibilities, in the processes by which a transaction is authorized, conducted and recorded; and

(*b*) the subjection of the individual's work to prompt and regular independent verification, by such means as reconciliation with pre-ascertained totals or direct examination.

MANAGERIAL SUPERVISION AND REVIEWS (INCLUDING INTERNAL AUDIT)

An important feature of effective internal control is that directors should review the company's financial operations and position at regular and frequent intervals by means of interim accounts and reports, operating summaries and other appropriate financial and statistical information. Comparison with results for previous periods may indicate discrepancies that call for further examination or, where budgetary control is in use, attention will be drawn to material variances and explanations required. In addition to regular reviews of this nature management may from time to time call for special reviews of particular items such as stocks, or the operation of the wages department; these constitute yet another instrument of control. In smaller firms examinations of the nature indicated may be carried out by the owner or manager personally. Managerial supervision and reviews of this nature are an essential element in any effective internal control system.

Internal audit is a review of operations and records, sometimes continuous, undertaken within a business by specially assigned staff. The scope and objectives of the internal audit vary widely in different businesses and may, particularly in large organizations, extend to many matters which are not directly of an accounting nature. The internal auditors' duties on non-accounting matters would not normally be a matter for consideration by the independent auditors and they are therefore not considered further in this Statement. On accounting matters the main objective of an internal audit is to assure management that the internal check and the accounting system are effective in design and operation.

PRACTICAL APPLICATIONS

The system of internal control to be adopted, and the means by which it is to be communicated and implemented, vary according to the nature and circumstances of each business. Broadly it may be said that larger companies tend to find it desirable, if not essential, to define their organization and procedures in writing, while smaller companies which are subject to closer proprietorial control may adopt a more informal approach. It remains true in all circumstances, however, that staff should be clearly aware of the scope and the limitations of their responsibilities.

In considering these matters it should be borne in mind that there are no absolute standards of internal control. The circumstances and needs of businesses vary so greatly that no two are exactly alike. The most that may be said by way of generalization is that an adequate system of internal control is one that is both economic and effective having regard to the resources, size and nature of the business concerned. Particular procedures should therefore be weighed against the risks they are designed to check. The cost of operating a check on any particular activity should be viewed in relation to the possible loss if the check were removed. A company may for example recognize that the cost of close supervision of cash collection by salesmen (for example roundsmen) would be prohibitive. Similarly it may be considered that checking the extensions and casts of suppliers' invoices is of little value where small amounts are involved, and checking of invoices for sums below a stated amount may in consequence be abandoned or curtailed.

Although cash is the most readily convertible of assets and thus most vulnerable to misappropriation, it normally forms only part of an undertaking's total assets, and equal attention should be given to custody and control procedures involving other forms of property, such as stocks. In all these matters the importance of physical as well as documentary controls should be borne in mind.

Automatic data processing can contribute materially to the effectiveness of internal control. For example, mechanized accounting systems generally involve the employment of specialist staff, to whom the recording function is entrusted, with the consequence that division and limitation of duties is automatically ensured. Furthermore, mechanized systems permit the ready preparation of totals for checking purposes.

AUDIT PRACTICE IN RELATION TO INTERNAL CONTROL

In the audit of larger companies it is not the practice to scrutinize every transaction in detail but to select groups of transactions for close examination. In making this selection auditors have regard to the system of internal control.

The first step is to ascertain the prescribed system. Some companies have organization charts and procedures manuals to which auditors can refer; others possess little in the way of written instructions and the auditors must rely on inquiry and observation. In all circumstances it is essential that the auditors should prepare, and retain, a record of the system in use, which should be revised and brought up to date regularly. The techniques adopted to draw up these records vary from narrative based on informal questioning (often reinforced by the use of aides-mémoire or check lists) to the completion of comprehensive questionnaires.

The object of the auditors' examination of the system is to determine the nature and extent of the audit procedures to be applied in order to establish the reliability of the records as a basis for the preparation of accounts which will present a true and fair view.

The auditors' examination may be divided into three stages: ascertainment, testing and assessment. These are, however, integral parts of a single process, normally carried on concurrently. In practice the procedures described do not fall into such clearly marked separate stages.

Examination involves ascertaining not only the procedures prescribed but also those actually used in practice. Unless careful supervision is exercised by responsible officials procedures tend to be unofficially modified with the passing of time and changes of staff. A theoretically sound system may prove defective in operation because its rules are not properly observed, or because the circumstances of the business have changed. Auditors should therefore seek, by inquiry, observation and tests, to ascertain that the system is being properly and effectively operated by competent staff. On the results of these observations auditors base their opinion of the adequacy of the internal control system.

The normal procedure is to select representative sections of the company's records for examination in detail and testing in depth to ensure that transactions are properly authorized, evidenced and recorded. (The considerations involved in testing in depth are described in Statement on Auditing, *General Principles of Auditing*.)

Some aspects of an internal control system may be verified in operation by direct observation. For instance, auditors may consider that attendance at stock-taking or payment of wages would assist them in the performance of their duties, the object of such attendance being to observe the operation of the prescribed procedures.

Where the system of internal control is judged inadequate the auditors must decide whether, and if so how far, audit tests should be extended to cover the unsatisfactory aspects of the system. As in all their work, however, they should preserve a sense of proportion; the uncovering of petty irregularities in circumstances where the maximum possible loss is insignificant will not always necessarily warrant extensive examination.

It is in the interests of all concerned—shareholders, management, employees and auditors—that any defects in the system of internal control, or respects in which there is scope for improvement, should be reported to the appropriate persons and the facts placed on record. This is particularly important where the system of internal control is judged inadequate in material respects, since such circumstances must cast doubts on the basic reliability of the records presented to the auditors. The possibility of error and omission, whether deliberate or accidental, may be materially increased in such circumstances. As was stated in *General Principles of Auditing*:

'In exceptional cases, auditors may find that the records and the system of internal control are so seriously inadequate that no useful purpose could be served by embarking upon extensive detailed checking, because even the most exhaustive tests would not enable them to form an opinion on the balance sheet and profit and loss account. In that event their appropriate course will be to report to that effect to the shareholders and to inform the directors of the respects in which the records and system are deficient.'

Where an internal audit is carried out it is for the independent auditors to decide whether and to what extent, consistently with their statutory responsibilities, they can rely on the work of the internal auditors in order to reduce the extent of their own examination of detail. Their decision will depend upon their judgment on the facts of each case, having regard in particular to:

(a) the extent and efficiency of the internal audit. In order to assess these matters the independent auditors should examine the internal audit programmes, working papers and reports and should make such tests as they think fit of the work done by the internal auditor;

(b) the experience and qualifications of the internal auditors and their staff and the character of their reports;

(c) the authority vested in the internal auditors and the level of management to which they are directly responsible.

The independent auditors cannot in any circumstances divest themselves of the responsibilities laid on them by statute.

APPLICATION TO SMALLER COMPANIES

Internal control is of importance to small as well as to larger companies, although its method of operation will necessarily vary from that adopted in major concerns. Where the number of employees is too few to establish an adequate division of duties, additional importance attaches to proper supervision by the owner, manager or other responsible employee.

Special problems may arise in the circumstances of a small firm whose business is expanding. There is an intermediate stage when it is no longer practicable for the owner or manager to maintain his previous close supervision of all aspects of the business, while the staff remains numerically too small for the adequate division of responsibilities and institution of automatic checks which may be expected of larger firms. Often the owner or manager may be unaware that control is weakening and in such circumstances the company's administration may be vulnerable to serious loss in a number of directions. It is at this stage that professional guidance is particularly desirable if suitable safeguards and procedures are to be established. Much, however, will depend on the extent to which the owner or manager is able to continue effectively to supervise the operations of the business; the extent to which managerial control is practicable and can be made effective has to be judged in the light of the limitations inherent in the situation. The problem assumes special importance where the manager is also a director and sole beneficial shareholder and thus the effective owner of the business.

In some circumstances the auditors may form the view that the business is soundly controlled by the manager, but that ultimately the reliability of the records depends almost entirely on one person. The auditors should have regard to this factor when determining the nature and extent of the work they consider necessary to carry out. For example in the case of

'. . . a small company the tests which the auditors make will normally cover a greater proportion of the transactions than is necessary for a larger company where a more comprehensive system of control can be and is operated. In selecting items for examination and deciding upon the extent of the work to be done the auditors should always consider to what extent the transactions under review are material in relation to the affairs of the company as a whole.' (Statement on Auditing, *General Principles of Auditing*.)

The circumstances need careful weighing where the manager is not sole shareholder but acts in a position of trust on behalf of others who do not participate in the management of the business.

FIELD OF RELATIONSHIP BETWEEN INDEPENDENT AND INTERNAL AUDITOR

On accounting matters the internal auditor and the independent auditor operate largely in the same field and they have a common interest in ascertaining that there is:

(*a*) an effective system of internal check to prevent or detect errors and fraud and that it is operating satisfactorily;

(*b*) an adequate accounting system to provide the information necessary for preparing true and fair financial statements.

Although the two forms of audit have a common interest in the important matters mentioned in the preceding paragraph, there are some fundamental differences:

(*a*) *Scope.* The extent of the work undertaken by the internal auditor is determined by the management whereas that of the independent auditor arises from the responsibilities placed on him by statute;

(*b*) *Approach.* The internal auditor's approach is with a view to ensuring that the accounting system is efficient, so that the accounting information presented to management throughout the period is accurate and discloses material facts. The independent auditor's approach, however, is governed by his duty to satisfy himself that the accounts to be presented to the shareholders show a true and fair view of the profit or loss for the financial period and of the state of the company's affairs at the end of that period;

(*c*) *Responsibility.* The internal auditor's responsibility is to the management whereas the independent auditor is responsible directly to the shareholders. It follows that the internal auditor, being a servant of the company, does not have the independence of status which the independent auditor possesses.

Notwithstanding these important differences, the work of both the internal auditor and the independent auditor, on accounting matters, is carried out largely by similar means, such as:

(*a*) examination of the system of internal check, for both soundness in principle and effectiveness in operation;

(*b*) examination and checking of accounting records and statements;

(*c*) verification of assets and liabilities;

(*d*) observation, inquiry, the making of statistical comparisons and such other measures as may be judged necessary.

CO-OPERATION BETWEEN INDEPENDENT AND INTERNAL AUDITOR

It will be evident from the preceding paragraph that the similarity between the means by which the independent auditor and the internal auditor carry out their respective duties is such that without co-operation between them there could be unnecessary duplication of work.

Because of his experience acquired in public practice, the independent auditor may be of assistance in an advisory capacity in connection with the installation and subsequent operation of an internal audit; and in carrying out his duties he may derive much assistance from the internal auditor's intimate knowledge of the accounting system and technical knowledge of the business, particularly in connection with stock-in-trade, the physical existence of fixed assets, depreciation charges, the ascertainment of liabilities and the risks of fraud or misappropriation.

There also exists considerable scope for mutual assistance between the two auditors in the planning of their respective audits. Where the independent auditor is satisfied that the internal auditor has adequately covered part of the work which the independent auditor would otherwise do he may be able to reduce the extent of his examination of detail; and consultation between the two auditors may enable the internal auditor to refrain from carrying out work which he would otherwise do but which, having regard to the examination which the independent auditor considers he must make in any event, would result in duplication. Examples of specific ways in which the work of the two auditors may be co-ordinated are:

(a) the independent auditor may be able to rely to a large extent on the internal auditor in determining whether the system of internal check is operating satisfactorily and in assessing the general reliability of the accounting records;

(b) the programme of the internal auditor may include, by agreement, work which has the effect of giving direct assistance to the independent auditor by participating during the accounting period in matters such as cash counts and visits to branches, made either by the internal auditor alone or jointly with the independent auditor;

(c) the internal auditor may arrange his programme at the end of the accounting period so that assistance is given to the independent auditor in connection with matters such as the confirmation of customers' accounts, verification of assets such as stock-in-trade and the preparation of audit working schedules required by the independent auditor for his records.

The internal auditor's responsibility is to the management and he is in no sense a servant of the independent auditor. It follows therefore that the extent to which the internal auditor can so arrange his work as to be of specific assistance to the independent auditor will depend upon decisions of the management on the scope of the internal audit and the number of staff employed thereon. Consultation between the two auditors, and where necessary with the management, should however ensure that so far as is practicable the fullest possible assistance is available to the independent auditor.

3. Stock-in-trade and Work in Progress   [*Issued April 1969*]

GENERAL CONSIDERATIONS

(1) Stock-in-trade and work in progress generally constitutes one of the largest items in the balance sheets of manufacturing firms and relatively small errors in computing the amount at which stock is stated in the accounts can have a marked effect on reported profits.

(2) Auditors must satisfy themselves as to the validity of the amount attributed to stock. In order to reach an opinion they will have to ascertain and consider the soundness of the procedures adopted and to test the competence with which these procedures are carried out. The nature and extent of the audit tests are matters for the auditors' professional judgment. Where applicable, however, and having regard to the nature of the business, these tests will include examinations 'in depth' (see 'General Principles of Auditing').

(3) The responsibility for properly determining the quantity and value of stock rests with the management of the business. It is therefore the directors' responsibility to ensure that:

(*a*) the physical quantities owned by the company are properly ascertained and recorded and that the condition is properly assessed;

(*b*) the amount to be carried forward in the balance sheet has been properly determined on an appropriate basis or appropriate bases by suitable methods.

Auditors should arrange that the client's instructions for stock-taking and for evaluation of stock are available to them for examination before they are issued, with a view to changes being made to remove defects which may exist.

QUANTITIES AND CONDITION OF STOCK

Attendance at stock-taking

(4) In most circumstances, the best method by which the auditors can satisfy themselves as to the effectiveness of the application of the client's stock-taking procedures is by observation on a test basis of these procedures whilst the stock-taking is in progress. Considerations relating to clients' stock-taking procedures and suggested audit procedures regarding the ascertainment of quantities and conditions of stock are set out in Statement on Auditing 'Attendance at Stock-taking'.

Other audit procedures

(5) Additional audit procedures to enable auditors to satisfy themselves that stock has been properly ascertained will include such of the following as the auditors may consider appropriate:

(a) general scrutiny of the inventory or the stock records (and comparisons with the previous year) including attention to the possibility of material omissions or the inclusion of items such as loose tools which ought not to be included because they appear elsewhere in the accounts;

(b) where applicable, tests by reference to statistical information covering matters such as yields which may be expected from given quantities and normal losses or gains by evaporation or absorption of moisture.

(6) Where stock is defective or is obsolete or slow moving, these factors must be taken into account in determining the amount at which stock is stated in the balance sheet. Appropriate audit tests of the company's procedure for judging the physical condition will normally include:

(a) scrutiny of stock records during the tests referred to in paragraphs 4 and 5, to ascertain what information as to condition and slow-moving stocks has been recorded and what action has been taken on that information;

(b) comparison with the stock records relating to the previous balance sheet date;

(c) examination by reference to normal experience of wastage due to rejects and deterioration;

(d) examination of the relationship between stocks and turnover, including consideration of current trading conditions and any changes in sales or stockpiling policies;

(e) discussions with the management.

AMOUNT AT WHICH STOCK IS STATED

(7) Audit procedures will be designed to ascertain whether the amount at which stock-in-trade and work in progress is stated has been computed on a basis (or bases) and by methods which, consistently applied and having regard to the nature and circumstances of the business, will enable the accounts to show a true and fair view of the trading results and the financial position. The accounting principles involved are dealt with in the Recommendation 'Treatment of Stock-in-trade and Work in Progress in Financial Accounts' [reproduced below].

(8) After examining the principles adopted by the management, the audit procedure to test the application of those principles will normally include:

(a) test of the stock sheets or continuous stock records with relevant documents such as invoices, costing records and other sources for the ascertainment of 'cost';

(b) examination and testing of the treatment of overhead expenses;

(c) test of 'net realizable value' (or as the case may be, 'replacement price') (see 'Treatment of Stock-in-trade and Work in Progress in Financial Accounts');

(*d*) careful inquiry of responsible officials and examination of evidence supporting the assessment of net realizable value, with particular reference to defective, obsolete or slow-moving stock, and consideration of the reasonableness of the replies from officials to the inquiries made;

(*e*) tests of the arithmetical accuracy of the calculations;

(*f*) tests of the consistency, in principle and in detail, with which the amounts have been computed;

(*g*) consideration of the adequacy of the description applied to stock-in-trade and work in progress in the accounts.

(9) Net realizable value can be defined as the amount which it is estimated, as on the balance sheet date, will be realized from disposal of stock in the ordinary course of business, either in its existing condition or as incorporated in the product normally sold, after allowing for all expenditure to be incurred on or before disposal. In estimating this amount regard should be had to excess and obsolete stocks, the trend of the market and the prospects of disposal. It is normal to estimate net realizable value by reference to all available information, including changes in selling prices since the balance sheet date, so far as the information is of assistance in determining the realizable value of the stock at the balance sheet date.

(10) In many instances the estimation of net realizable value requires the exercise of judgment by officials of the company who are responsible for the sale or realization of the stock or work in progress. While, therefore the auditors' review of such estimates will include consideration of the explanations given by the responsible officials it will be necessary for the auditors to review and test supporting evidence available to them in order to form an opinion as to whether the estimates of realizable value are fair and reasonable.

Work in progress

(11) Appropriate audit tests in relation to work in progress will include examination and testing of available records including costing records and work tickets attached to unfinished articles and, where there are long-term contracts, examination of the relevant contracts including any modifications thereof and other information such as subsequent cost reports and estimates of costs to complete. Physical checking of work in progress (see paragraph 4) will often not be possible by methods similar to those adopted for stocks. Reference to costing records is frequently necessary and it may not be possible to seperate the question of physical quantity from the question of the amount to be attributed to the work in progress. Where it is not possible or practicable to identify the work in progress with either the components which have gone into it or the products which will emerge from it, the auditors will be particularly concerned to ascertain:

(*a*) the costing system from which the work in progress is ascertained;

(*b*) whether the costing system is reliable and in particular whether it is integrated with the financial accounting;

(c) the extent to which checks are made by reference to statistical information concerning outputs of main products and of by-products (if any) which ought to be obtained from materials used;

(d) the system of inspection and reporting thereon to enable allowance to be made in the costing records for scrapping and rectification;

(e) the basis on which overheads are dealt with in the costing records;

(f) any profit element included for which adjustments are required.

Overall tests

(12) Audit tests which may often be appropriate by way of overall assessment of the reliability of the records will include, according to circumstances:

(a) reconciliation of changes in stock quantities as between the beginning and end of the financial year with the records of purchases, production and sales;

(b) comparison of the quantities and amounts of stocks in the various categories with those included at the previous balance sheet date and with current sales and purchases;

(c) consideration of the gross profit ratio shown by the accounts and its comparison with the ratio shown in previous years;

(d) consideration of the rate of turnover of stocks and its comparison with previous years;

(e) consideration of the relationship of the quantities ready for sale and in course of production with the quantities shown in operating and sales budgets;

(f) where applicable, examination of standard costing records and consideration of the variances shown thereby and their treatment in the accounts.

OTHER MATTERS

Independent stocktakers

(13) In some trades it is a common practice to employ firms of independent surveyors and valuers. These stock-taking firms are specialists and provided the auditor is satisfied as to their independence and standing, it is usual to accept their stock counts as reliable. The auditors, however, normally ascertain direct with the stock-taking firm the basis of valuation used, and assure themselves that proper cut-off procedures were operated.

(14) Sometimes the circumstances are such that physical count and valuation are virtually one operation where it is not practicable for the auditors to make any independent test of the basis of appraisal, so that they will have to rely on the independent stocktaker. A case in point might be an inventory of precious stones but the situation may be met in a number of types of business. Nevertheless, the fact that auditors are obliged to rely on reports of independent stock-takers does not relieve them of

their responsibility for forming an opinion on the amount at which stock is stated in the balance sheet.

Inventory letters

(15) It is usual and desirable practice to obtain from a director or other responsible official of the company a written statement outlining in detail the method of ascertaining stock quantities and bases of valuation. This statement may take the form of a separate inventory letter or may be included in a comprehensive letter of financial representations. It in no way relieves the auditors of their responsibility for forming their opinion whether stock has been fairly reported and presented in the accounts. The significance of inventory letters is that they constitute a record of the action taken by management and a formal reminder and acknowledgment of management's responsibility and for this reason considerable importance attaches to these representations.

4. Attendance at Stock-taking   [*Issued July 1968*]

GENERAL CONSIDERATIONS

Although it is not the auditors' duty to take stock, they must satisfy themselves as to the validity of the amount attributed to this asset in the accounts which are the subject of the audit. In determining the nature and extent of the audit steps necessary for this purpose the auditors must examine the system of internal control in order to assess its effectiveness relative to the ascertainment and evaluation of stock and work in progress. An important element in this system is the client's procedures for ascertainment of the quantities of stocks on hand and their condition. In most circumstances the best method by which the auditors can satisfy themselves as to the effectiveness of the application of the client's stocktaking procedures is by observation of those procedures. Normally this will be done on a test basis and it will not be necessary for the auditors to observe the application of the stock-taking procedures to the whole of the stock or to the stock at all locations. The extent of the auditors' test observation will depend on their assessment of the soundness of the system prescribed by the client.

Therefore wherever it is practicable and stock-in-trade and work in progress is a material factor in the business, the auditors should satisfy themselves as to the effectiveness of the application of the client's stocktaking procedures by observation on a test basis of these procedures whilst the stock-taking is in progress.

The presence of auditors at stock-taking does not relieve the management in any way of their responsibilities; in order to avoid misunderstanding the auditors should make it clear to the management that the reason for their attendance is not to take stock but to satisfy themselves as to the effectiveness of the application of the client's procedures. The auditors are neither stock-takers nor valuers, nor have they any responsibility for supervising the stock-taking. Their presence is to enable them as auditors to consider the adequacy and effectiveness of the client's procedures. They will however, be ready to advise or make recommendations, just as they would on other matters when they consider that the system of internal control is weak or is not being properly carried out.

While it will not normally be necessary for the auditors to observe the application of the client's procedures in their entirety or at all locations, the auditors' tests should cover a representative selection of the stock and of the procedures. Where stock is held at a number of locations, the selection of the location or locations to be visited by the auditors may be planned so as to cover all significant locations over a period of years. The extent of their tests will be for them to decide. There may be instances where it is not practicable to test the client's procedures by attendance and observation of the stock-taking, for example because the stocks are situated at locations at which the auditors cannot readily attend.

Suggested audit procedures

The audit steps relating to observation of the stock-taking by the auditors will cover three stages: *before*, *during* and *after* the stock-taking. The procedures described below are intended to be a broad outline which will need adaptation to meet the circumstances of the client, for example where a client's stock-taking is based on records substantiated by continuous physical stock-takings.

BEFORE STOCK-TAKING

Before the stock-taking the auditors will need to study the client's stock-taking instructions (preferably before they are issued), to become familiar with the location of the stocks and to plan the work they are to undertake during the stocktaking. The work to be undertaken will depend on the auditors' evaluation of the client's procedures, as contained in the instructions and explanations given by the client. The auditors will be concerned to see that the client's procedures are adequate in the light of the circumstances. These circumstances will include the locations at which stock is held, the quantities on hand and the values of the stocks, the factors affecting the condition of stocks and the possibilities of the existence of obsolete or slow-moving stocks. Where these procedures are considered to be weak or defective they should be discussed with the client before the stocktaking instructions are issued with a view to changes being made to remove the defects.

DURING STOCK-TAKING

The main task during stock-taking will be to ascertain whether the client's employees are carrying out their instructions properly. It may be sufficient to watch the counting and recording as it is done by the client's employees, but it would usually be advisable for the auditors to test the efficiency of the counting by arranging for a count or a recount of selected items in their presence. In arranging for items to be counted or recounted in their presence it will be advisable for the auditors to select items from both the count records and the factory or warehouse floor for tracing from one to the other. The test selection should include a reasonable proportion of high value items.

Auditors should make such notes as they consider necessary during the course of their observation, for follow-up. These notes will normally include the following:

(a) details of items of stock selected by the auditors so that the particulars may be checked to the final stocksheets;

(b) lists of items actually counted in the auditors' presence;

(c) details of any stock noted by the auditors as being obviously defective, damaged or slow-moving;

(d) details of instances where the client's stock-taking procedures were not carried out.

Where serious inaccuracies or irregularities are revealed during the course of the auditors' observations it may be necessary to arrange for certain sections of, or the whole of, the stock to be recounted.

AFTER STOCK-TAKING

The information obtained by the auditors at the stock-taking should be followed up when finally reviewing the amount at which the stock is stated in the accounts. The steps taken to do this will include the following:

(a) a check of the 'cut-off', using the details of stock movements and of the last numbers of goods inwards and outwards notes;

(b) a test that the final stock-sheets have been properly prepared from the count records and include all stocks belonging to the company. The test will be made by reference to the details of the stock-sheet numbering noted by the client and also the notes made by the auditors;

(c) a follow-up of all outstanding queries.

Stocks belonging to the company but held by others should be shown as such in the stock-taking records. The auditors should examine the confirmations obtained by the company from the custodians, and where the amounts of such stocks are material, the auditors should independently obtain confirmations from the custodians in selected cases. They should also examine reports on any periodic inspections of the stock made by the company's own employees and should make enquiries as to the standing of the custodians where the circumstances warrant it.

IF ATTENDANCE DURING STOCK-TAKING IS NOT PRACTICABLE

As stated above, there may be occasions when it will not be practicable for the auditors to observe the client's stock-taking. In such cases they should carry out such additional procedures (distinct from and extra to those usually followed when forming an opinion on stocks) as in their judgment, as skilled professional men, are necessary in the circumstances to satisfy themselves that:

(a) the records of the stock-taking produced to them represent a substantially correct inventory of the stocks and work in progress owned by the company on the stock-taking date; and

(b) the condition of the stocks and work in progress has been properly assessed.

The additional procedures to be followed for this purpose will depend on the circumstances which make it impracticable for the auditors to attend for the purpose of observing the stock-taking. In some instances, such as where stock is held overseas, it may be possible for the auditors to arrange for a suitably qualified agent to attend the stock-taking on their behalf and for him to report to them.

In other instances auditors who have numerous client companies, which may have a common accounting date and which take stock on the date, may find that their resources in manpower are insufficient for them to attend on every client for the purpose of observing at least some part of the stock-taking. If auditors find that they cannot attend every year, this does not relieve them of their responsibilities. They will have to consider carefully whether the alternative procedures available to them will be sufficient to discharge those responsibilities in the circumstances of each of the clients concerned. Where the client has a well-developed system of internal control and of stock recording it will usually be possible for the auditors to substantiate to their satisfaction the validity of the stocktaking records. This can be done by arranging for the test counts of selected items to be made at an earlier or later date when a representative can attend and observe.

In the case of smaller businesses, however, the systems of internal control are necessarily more elementary and in many instances the records of the annual stock-taking are not supported by any continuous stock records. Sometimes it may be possible to arrange for the stock-taking to take place on a date close to the accounting date at a time when the auditors can attend and for records of movements of stocks in the intervening period to be maintained. These records must be in such a form that the auditors can satisfy themselves as to their reasonable accuracy.

If, however, the auditors are unable reasonably to satisfy themselves as to the reliability of the stocktaking, and stock is a material factor in the business, they will have no alternative but to make an appropriate qualification in their report on the accounts.

5. Treatment of Stock-in-Trade and Work in Progress in Financial Accounts

In the financial accounts of industrial and commercial undertakings few matters require more careful consideration than the amount to be attributed to stock-in-trade and work in progress. Circumstances vary so widely that no one basis of arriving at the amount is suitable for all types of business nor even for all undertakings within a particular trade or industry. Unless the basis adopted is appropriate to the circumstances of the particular undertaking and used consistently from period to period, the accounts will not give a true and fair view either of the state of affairs of the undertaking as on the balance sheet date or of the trend of its trading results from period to period. The need to give a true and fair view is the overriding consideration applicable in all circumstances.

In order to arrive at the amount to be carried forward, as on the balance sheet date, for stock-in-trade and work in progress it is necessary to ascertain (from stock-taking at the end of the period or from stock records maintained and verified during the period) the quantities on hand and to make a proper calculation of the amount. It cannot be emphasized too strongly that all stocks belonging to the business should be taken into account, whatever their location or nature. This recommendation does not deal with the methods of ascertaining the quantities on hand but is confined to an examination of the factors to be considered when computing the amount. The word 'stock' is used hereafter to embrace stock-in-trade and work in progress.

NORMAL BASIS

The basis normally used for the determination of the amount to be carried forward for stock is its cost less any part thereof which properly needs to be written off at the balance sheet date. It is in computing cost and the amount, if any, to be written off that practical difficulties arise.

COST

Elements of cost

The elements making up the cost of stock are:

(a) direct expenditure on the purchase of goods brought for resale, and of materials and components used in the manufacture of finished goods;

(b) other direct expenditure which can be identified specifically as having been incurred in acquiring the stock or bringing it to its existing condition and location; examples are direct labour, transport, processing and packaging;

(c) such part, if any, of the overhead expenditure as is properly carried forward in the circumstances of the business instead of being charged against the revenue of the period in which it was incurred.

TREATMENT OF OVERHEAD EXPENDITURE

Before deciding upon the method by which to compute 'cost' it is necessary to consider to what extent, if at all, the inclusion of overhead expenditure is appropriate to the particular business.

Overhead expenditure may be divided into (a) production expenses such as factory rent, rates, depreciation, insurance and supervision, and other indirect expenses of acquiring and producing stock; (b) administration expenses not attributable directly to the acquisition or production of stock or the bringing of it to a saleable condition and location; (c) selling expenses; (d) finance charges. Another classification (which can be applied also to each of the foregoing divisions) is to distinguish between 'fixed overheads', that is to say standing charges, such as rent and rates which accrue and expire wholly or largely on a time basis, and 'variable overheads', which vary in a greater or lesser degree with the level of activity in the undertaking or of the department concerned but are not so closely associated with production or the volume of production as to be classed as direct expenditure.

Opinions differ on the extent to which overhead expenditure should be included in computing the cost of stock, though it is generally agreed that it cannot properly include selling and finance and other expenses which do not relate to the bringing of stock to its existing condition and location. The following are some practices which reflect the differing views on this matter:

(a) in some businesses no overhead expenditure is included as an element in determining the cost of stock which is to be carried forward;

(b) in others only the 'marginal' cost of unsold stock is included, that is to say that part of the cost of production of the period which has been incurred only because the stock remaining on hand was acquired or produced; all other expenses, including depreciation, are dealt with as revenue charges of the period for which they are incurred, the ground being that they arise irrespective of the quantity of stock which remains on hand at the end of the period and therefore are not an element in its cost;

(c) in other business an appropriate proportion of the overhead expenditure relevant to the period of production is included on the ground that for the purpose of financial accounting any expense, whatever its characteristics, which is related even though indirectly to the acquisition or production of goods ought to be included in the cost of those goods and ought not to be charged against revenue until they are sold; an 'appropriate proportion' is determined by reference to a normal level of activity.

These differing views about the inclusion of overhead expenditure may be very important in their effect upon the amounts carried forward for stock and upon the profits disclosed in the accounts. No one method of dealing with overhead expenditure is suitable for all businesses. The method selected by the management needs to be clearly defined and must have regard to the nature and circumstances of the business so as to ensure that the trend of the trading results will be shown fairly. Once the method has been selected it needs to be used consistently from period to period regardless of the amount of profits available or losses sustained. A change of method is appropriate only if there is a change in the relevant circumstances of the business. If material, the effect of a change of method would need to be disclosed in the accounts.

In selecting a method of dealing with overhead expenditure the following are among the considerations which arise:

(a) *The nature of the business*

In deciding whether to include a proportion of the overheads as expenditure on stock and also in deciding which elements of expenses may properly be included for that purpose, it is necessary to have regard to the nature and the stage of development of the business, particularly factors such as the length of the production period, the probability of fluctuations in the level of production or the volume of sales, the risk of selling campaigns by competitors at reduced prices and the extent to which production is undertaken only to a customer's order or 'for stock' in expectation of sales. At one extreme a business may operate at widely differing levels of production and produce goods in quantity in a highly competitive and sensitive market; at the other extreme, a business may be engaged on a long-term single project contract such as building a ship, a bridge, a road or a heavy engineering installation.

(b) *The levels of production and sales*

Where the levels of production and sales are relatively stable and production and sales are kept in balance the inclusion of overhead expenditure in the amount attributed to stock may have little impact upon the incidence of profits as between the accounts of one period and those of another. Where, however, the levels are subject to material fluctuation and are not kept in balance it may be decided to exclude these expenses from stock on the ground that as they would be incurred whatever the levels of production or sales their inclusion in stock has the effect of relieving the profit and loss account in the period when they are incurred of expenses which it should fairly bear and of charging these expenses in a later period to which they do not properly relate.

(c) *Interruption or other exceptional curtailment of production*

If overhead expenditure is included in the amount attributed to stock an adjustment will be necessary in the event of disruption in production by events such as a strike, a fire, an abnormal falling off in orders, or temporary difficulties in obtaining materials, with the result that the volume of production is abnormally or unexpectedly low. In such circumstances the amount included in respect of overhead expenditure ought not to exceed an appropriate proportion on the basis of normal activity, the excess being treated as a charge against revenue in the period in which the expenditure was incurred. If the overhead expenditure is not related in this way to the normal, instead of the actual, level of production the effect may be to carry forward an excessive part of the expenditure of the period in which the disruption occurred. The profit and loss account of that period would thereby be relieved of charges which it ought to include and it would fail to reflect the adverse effects of the disruption during that period.

(d) *The risks of realization at a loss*

In businesses which are highly competitive or have a sensitive market for their products, overhead expenditure may properly be omitted in order to avoid carrying forward expenditure which may prove irrecoverable. Examples are businesses dealing in 'fashion' goods or those of a speciality character where the public taste may change quickly with the result that stocks can be realized only at a loss; businesses whose competitors may launch selling campaigns at short notice to get rid of stocks at reduced prices, sometimes at no more than the cost of the material and direct manufacturing expenditure; and businesses where new methods of production or improved designs may render existing stocks obsolete.

(e) *Maturing stocks*

In businesses which mature large stocks over long periods (for example, whisky, wine, timber) it is usual to exclude fixed overheads in order to avoid carrying forward large and increasing amounts of time-expired expenditure, the recovery of which in the ultimate selling price is uncertain.

(f) *Long-term contracts*

In businesses which undertake contracts extending over a period of years the normal tendency is to include overhead expenditure in work in progress except where it is considered to be irrecoverable. If overheads are not included in work in progress on such contracts the accounts for the early years may indicate losses, followed by unduly large profits in the years when the contracts are completed. This would be a wholly unrealistic presentation in relation to a contract showing a normal profit. The distinction between businesses of this type and those referred to in (e) above is that in a business with firm contracts the prices are normally known or can be calculated whereas in a business with maturing stocks the ultimate price at which unsold stocks will be realized in the ordinary course of business is unknown and uncertain.

(g) *The extent of the variation in fixed or standing charges*

The less the fixed or standing charges vary in amount with variations in the volume of output, and the more they accrue on a purely time basis, the greater is the justification for their exclusion.

After weighing all relevant considerations it is necessary to decide whether and if so to what extent overhead expenditure should be included.

METHODS OF COMPUTATION OF COST

Apart from the variations which occur in calculating the amount to be attributed to each of the elements of cost there are various methods of computing cost. In a small business one method only will normally be used but in a large composite business carrying on a variety of activities different methods may be used for different activities; once selected, however, the methods should be applied consistently to those activities from period to period. The following are the principal methods:

(a) '*Unit*' *cost*

The total cost of stock is computed by aggregating the individual costs of each article, batch, parcel or other unit. The method is not always capable of application, either because the individual units lose their identity (notably where stocks are bulked or pass through a number of processes) or because it would involve undue expense or complexity to keep individual records of cost particularly where these necessitate allocations of expense.

(b) *'First in, first out'*
Cost is computed on the assumption that goods sold or consumed are those which have been longest on hand and that those remaining in stock represent the latest purchases or production.

(c) *'Average' cost*
Cost is computed by averaging the amount at which stock is brought forward at the beginning of a period with the cost of stock acquired during the period; consumption in the period is then deducted at the average cost thus ascertained. The periodical rests for calculating the average are as frequent as the circumstances and nature of the business require and permit. In times of rising price levels this method tends to give a lower amount than the cost of unsold stock ascertained on a 'first in, first out' basis and in times of falling prices a higher amount.

(d) *'Standard' cost*
A predetermined or budgeted cost per unit is used. The method is particularly convenient where goods pass through a number of processes or are manufactured on mass production lines; but it will not result in a fair approximation to actual cost unless there is a regular review of the standards with appropriate adjustment and revision where necessary.

(e) *'Adjusted selling price'*
This method is used widely in retail businesses. The cost of stock is estimated by calculating it in the first instance at selling prices and then deducting an amount equal to the normal margin of gross profit on such stocks. It should be appreciated that where the selling prices have been reduced the calculation will bring out cost only if appropriate allowance for price reductions is included in fixing the margin to be deducted; if no such allowance is made it may bring out amounts which approximate to replacement price as defined below. The calculations under this method may be made for individual items or groups of items or by departments.

REDUCTION TO NET REALIZABLE VALUE

When the cost of the stock has been determined it is then necessary to establish whether any portion of the outlay on stock is irrecoverable; to that extent a provision for the loss needs to be made. This calculation may be made either (i) by considering each article separately, or (ii) by grouping articles in categories having regard to their similarity or interchangeability, or (iii) by considering the aggregate cost of the total stock in relation to its aggregate net realizable value. The third method involves setting foreseeable losses against expected but unrealized profits and would not normally be used in businesses which carry stocks which are large in relation to turnover.

The irrecoverable portion of the cost of the stock is the excess of its cost as computed by the method of cost ascertainment which is deemed appropriate for the business, over the net realizable value of the stock. 'Net realizable value' means the amount which it is estimated, as on the balance sheet date, will be realized from disposal of the stock in the ordinary course of business, either in its existing condition or as incorporated in the product normally sold, after allowing for all expenditure to be incurred on or before disposal.

'Net realizable value' is estimated by taking account of all available information, including changes in selling prices since the balance sheet date, so far as the information is of assistance in determining, as on the balance sheet date, the net realizable value of the stock in the ordinary course of business. This involves consideration of the prospects of disposal, having regard to the quantity and condition of the stock in relation to the expected demand (particular attention being given to obsolete or excessive stock) and to the expected effect, if any, on selling prices of any change which has taken place in buying prices of materials or goods.

In some circumstances the replacement price of stock (as defined below) may be considered to be the best available guide to its net realizable value.

REDUCTION TO REPLACEMENT PRICE

In many businesses it is important to have regard to the price at which stock can be replaced if such price is less than cost. The considerations which lead to the use of replacement price include the following:

(a) *Uncertainty as to net realizable value*

Where the volume of stock carried is large in relation to turnover or there is a long period between the purchase of raw material and its conversion into and disposal as finished goods, selling prices current at the balance sheet date for the volume of orders then available may afford an unreliable guide to the prospective net realizable value of the stock as a whole. Replacement price may be considered to be the best available guide for this purpose.

(b) *Selling prices based on current replacement prices*

In some businesses where selling prices are based on or reflect current replacement prices it may be considered that the trading results of a subsequent period will be prejudiced if they are burdened with any amount for stock which exceeds its replacement price; where this view is taken it is regarded as important in reporting the results of the activities of a period, as compared with those of its successor or predecessor, that the period in which a reduction in buying prices occurs should bear the diminution in profit rather than the period of disposal whose realizations will be adversely affected by the events of the previous period.

(c) *Recognition of uneconomic buying or production*

Skill in buying or efficiency in production are most important matters in many businesses; the inclusion of stock in the accounts on a replacement price basis (where lower than net realizable value and cost) may be considered to reflect inefficiency in these respects on the ground that it involves the writing down of stock by an amount which represents approximately the result of misjudged buying or inefficient production.

Where replacement price basis is adopted the stock is stated at the lowest of (a) cost, (b) net realizable value, (c) replacement price, with the effect that the profit and loss account is charged with any reductions necessitated by an excess of (a) over (b) or (c) as the case may be.

'Replacement price' for this purpose means an estimate of the amount for which, in the ordinary course of business, the stock could have been acquired or produced either at the balance sheet date or during the latest period up to and including that date. In a manufacturing business this estimate would be based on the replacement price of the raw material content plus other costs of the undertaking which are relevant to the condition of the stock on the balance sheet date. In all cases the prices used should be a fair reflection of the ordinary course of business; a depression which has passed before the accounts are completed would generally be disregarded.

In the same way as it is necessary to decide whether and if so to what extent overhead expenditure should be included in calculating cost, it is necessary in each business to determine whether replacement price shall be taken into account in computing the amount carried forward for stock. The basis selected by the management should be clearly defined and applied consistently from period to period regardless of the amount of profits available or the losses sustained, so as to enable the accounts to show a true and fair view of the trading results and the financial position. If the basis is changed, the effect on the accounts would need to be disclosed if material.

SPECIAL BASES USED IN SOME BUSINESSES

Stocks at Selling Prices

In some types of businesses, such as tea and rubber-producing companies and some mining companies, it is a recognized practice to bring stocks of products into account at the prices realized subsequent to the balance sheet date, less only selling costs. By this means the whole of the profit is shown in the period in which the crop is reaped or the minerals won. This basis has come to be accepted as customary in the industries concerned.

In manufacturing businesses which carry stocks of by-products the separate cost of which is not ascertainable these stocks are normally included at current selling price (or contract sale price where applicable) less any expenses to be incurred before disposal; the cost of the main product is reduced accordingly.

Long-term Contracts

In businesses which involve the acceptance and completion of long-term contracts it is often appropriate to spread over the period of the contracts, on a properly determined basis, the profits which are expected to be earned when the contracts are completed. This procedure takes up in each period during the performance of the contract a reasonable amount as representing the contribution of that period towards the eventual profit; it thus recognizes to a prudent extent the value of the work done in each period and restricts the distortion which would result from bringing in the whole of the profit in the period of completion. The principles which determine whether an element of profit is to be included are:

(a) profit should not be included until it is reasonably clear from the state of the work that a profit will ultimately be earned; it is therefore inappropriate to include any profit element where at the balance sheet date the contract has been in progress for a comparatively short time or to include an amount in excess of the profit element properly attributable to the work actually done;

(b) provision should be made for foreseeable losses and allowance should be made as far as practicable for penalties, guarantees and other contingencies;

(c) a clear basis for including a profit element should be established and adhered to consistently.

'Base Stock'

In some businesses the minimum quantity of raw materials or other goods, without which they cannot operate their plant or conduct their operations, is treated as being a fixed asset which is under constant renewal by charges to revenue; that part of their stock (the base stock) is therefore carried forward not at its cost at the date of the accounts but at the cost of the original quantity of stock with which the business commenced operation. In old established businesses the amount will be based on prices paid for stocks acquired many years previously and many times replaced.

'Last In, First Out'

The 'last in, first out' basis, which is in use in some overseas countries, assumes that the stocks sold or consumed in any period are those which were most recently acquired or made and therefore that the stocks whose cost is to be carried forward are those which were acquired, or made, earliest. The result is to charge consumption at prices approximating to current replacement prices and to carry forward stocks held at the close of the period at prices at which goods were purchased, or made, in earlier periods. When prices are falling this basis may result in showing the stock at an amount in excess of current prices in which event provision is made for the excess. During periods of rising prices, except in those instances where the physical movement of goods corresponds with the assumption that 'last in' is 'first out', the effect is to state the stock at less than its cost. The amount carried forward for stock may represent prices at which goods were acquired or produced several years earlier.

DESCRIPTION IN THE ANNUAL ACCOUNTS

In most businesses the amounts carried forward for stock from one period to another are material in their effect upon the presentation of the trading results and financial position. The differences which exist among the methods which are recognized as proper for the computation of those amounts are also so important that, unless an indication is given of the way in which the amounts are computed, the significance of the results and of the financial position shown by the accounts may be obscured. The following are illustrations of how such an indication might be given concisely where the circumstances make this appropriate:

(a) *Normal basis*

 'at cost';

 'at the lower of cost and net realizable value';

 'at the lowest of cost, net realizable value and replacement price';

 'at cost less provision to reduce to net realizable value' (or 'to the lower of net realizable value and replacement price').

 The expression 'market value' does not indicate whether it implies net realizable value or replacement price and is therefore not regarded as suitable.

(b) *Special bases*

 If one of the special bases mentioned above is used an appropriate description would be required.

Whether a concise indication on the lines of the illustrations given above will be adequate for an appreciation of the significance of the accounts will depend upon the circumstances of the undertaking. The use of the word 'cost' may be inadequate unless it is accompanied by an explanation of the extent to which overhead expenditure is included as cost; in that event the explanation might be as follows:

 'Cost is confined to materials, direct wages and direct expenses, no addition having been made for overhead expenditure.'

 'Cost includes an appropriate proportion of variable overhead expenditure but excludes fixed overhead expenditure.'

 'Cost includes an appropriate proportion of all production and administrative overhead expenditure.'

In some businesses the complex nature of the stock and the use of different bases and methods of computation for determining the amounts of the various sections of the stock, particularly in a large composite undertaking or a holding company with subsidiaries of different types, may mean that no concise indication is feasible. In such circumstances it is, however, important that those to whom the accounts are submitted should have a specific assurance that the amount included for stock has been determined for the whole of the stock at the balance sheet date on bases by methods of computation which are considered appropriate in the circumstances of the business and have been applied consistently.

The effect of any change of basis or method of computation should be disclosed if the effect of the change is material.

RECOMMENDATIONS

Having regard to the foregoing considerations, it is recommended that the following principles be applied by every industrial and commercial enterprise.

Appropriate amounts for all stock-in-trade (including raw materials and partly finished or finished stocks) and all work in progress, wherever situated and whatever their nature, should be included in the financial accounts and should be computed in accordance with the recommendations below. There is no justification for the omission of stock nor for stating stock at an amount which is higher or lower than the amount so computed; to use a higher amount would be to overstate profits (or understate losses) of the period and reduce the profits (or increase the losses) of the next period, whilst to use a lower amount would be to create a reserve which should be so described and disclosed and should not be treated as a charge against revenue.

A profit should not be anticipated unless this is justified by the special bases used in some businesses but provision should be made to the full extent of expected losses.

The amount carried forward for stock and work in progress should be computed on a basis which, having regard to the nature and circumstances of the business, will enable the accounts to show a true and fair view of the trading results and the financial position. In most businesses the basis should be the cost of the stock held, less any part thereof which properly needs to be written off at the balance sheet date.

The circumstances of each business should determine the basis which is appropriate and the method of computation which should be adopted in determining cost and the part thereof, if any, which should be written off. In most businesses the choice lies between writing-off any excess of cost over either (a) the net realizable value of the stock, or (b) the lower of net realizable value and replacement price, these terms having the meanings attributed to them below. In some businesses it may be appropriate to use special bases, including some which depart from the rule that profit should not be anticipated.

The basis adopted and the methods of computation should be used consistently from period to period. A change of basis or method should not normally be made unless the circumstances have changed in such a way that its continued use would prevent the accounts from showing a true and fair view of the position and results. When a change is made the effect, if material, should be disclosed as an exceptional item in the profit and loss account or by way of note.

The following are the meanings attributed to 'cost', 'net realizable value' and 'replacement price' in this Recommendation:

(a) 'cost' means all expenditure incurred directly in the purchase or manufacture of the stock and the bringing of it to its existing condition and location, together with such part, if any, of the overhead expenditure as is appropriately carried forward in the circumstances of the business instead of being charged against the revenue of the period in which it was incurred:

(b) 'net realizable value' means the amount which it is estimated, as on the balance sheet date, will be realized from disposal of the stock in the ordinary course of business, either in its existing condition or as incorporated in the product normally sold, after allowing for all expenditure to be incurred on or before disposal;

(c) 'replacement price' means an estimate of the amount for which in the ordinary course of business the stock could have been acquired or produced either at the balance sheet date or in the latest period up to and including that date. In a manufacturing business this estimate would be based on the replacement price of the raw material content plus other costs of the undertaking which are relevant to the condition of the stock on the balance sheet date.

The comparison between cost and net realizable value or replacement price may be made by considering each article separately, or by grouping articles in categories having regard to their similarity or interchangeability. or by considering the aggregate cost of the total stock in relation to its aggregate net realizable value or, as the case may be, aggregate replacement price. The aggregate method involves setting foreseeable losses against unrealized profits on stock and may not be suitable for businesses which carry stocks which are large in relation to turnover.

Where the amount carried forward for stock is material in relation to either the trading results or the financial position, the accounts should indicate concisely the manner in which the amount has been computed. If this is not practicable the accounts should contain a note to the effect that a concise statement of the bases and methods used is not practicable but that the amount has been determined for the whole of the stock at the balance sheet date on bases and by methods of computation which are considered appropriate in the circumstances of the business and have been used consistently. The use of the term 'market value' should be discontinued.

Goods purchased forward do not form part of the stock-in-trade or work in progress on the balance sheet date but where they are not covered by forward sales provision should be made in the accounts for the excess, if any, of the purchase price over the net realizable value (or over replacement price, where lower-than net realizable value, if stock is stated at the lowest of cost, net realizable value, and replacement price). Similarly, where goods have been sold forward and are not covered by stocks and forward purchases, provision should be made in the accounts for the excess, if any, of the expected cost over their net realizable value. Such provisions should not be deducted from the amount at which stock is stated.

6. Mechanized Accounting and the Auditor

Internal check and control

One of the major purposes of mechanization is to canalize the accounting processes into well-controlled channels so that, provided the control is sound in principle and effectively applied, the channels themselves become unimportant. The introduction of a mechanized system therefore provides an opportunity for a complete examination of the safeguards required. The internal check imposed should form an integral part of the control system as a whole. For the auditor this aspect of mechanization is the most important one. It enables emphasis to be placed on principle rather than detail. Audit checks should, more than ever, be directed to testing the principles of the accounting system (including the internal check) and its practical operation. If the principles are sound and applied effectively, the auditor will be able to dispense with a considerable amount of detailed routine checking. The soundness and efficiency of the control system are of much greater importance than the mechanical operation of the machine or the hole in a card. If it is established by means of test-checks that the control records do prove the arithmetical accuracy of the ledgers, then it becomes possible for the auditor to vouch, by means of code references, direct from prime documents to the ledgers instead of through the intermediary of a daybook. Direct vouching in this way has distinct auditing advantages, particularly in vouching the private and nominal ledgers.

It will be evident from the preceding paragraph that the canalizing of processes may often be as advantageous to the auditor as it is to the client. Suitable machines installed in consultation with the auditor and operated under the supervision of competent accountants will usually be sound in principle and of advantage in many ways to the auditor; such audit difficulties as do arise are frequently capable of being met easily and promptly by minor modification of the system or by the preparation of special information from time to time. Because the fact of specialization tends to subdivide clerical processes into recognized channels, the checking of records by means of sample tests is rendered more satisfactory by the comparative certainty that transactions recorded by the same processes will all have been treated alike and the treatment of the bulk will correspond entirely to the treatment of the sample. This result is rendered even more certain by the internal checks which usually are or can be carried out as part of the accounting system.

Any variations from prescribed procedure will require close study by the auditors so that their implications can be appreciated. Similarly, items which do not lend themselves to the normal routine and for which special arrangements have been laid down, will require more individual attention than the bulk processes. In this connection, the question of correcting errors may be noted. The correction of errors by operators can be dangerous and a recognized procedure for the purpose should be instituted and insisted upon. In general it will be found essential to forbid the correction of errors by the operators and to provide instead for the corrections to be dealt with through an adjustment journal, but if correction by operators is permitted it is essential that every corrected item must be verified immediately by a senior clerk or supervisor.

Considerable emphasis has been laid in the three preceding paragraphs on the value of the control system and the internal check as means of enabling the auditor to be satisfied as to the detailed records without extensive detailed checking. It is, however, essential that the auditor should be satisfied that all 'balancing', 'proving' or 'control' systems are sound in principle. The control system must genuinely be independent and not merely serve to prove the machine against itself. For example, to ensure that all transactions have been included in a given process it is usually essential to supplement the machine control with some other control entirely independent of the machine and its operator. An independent control might take the form of a calculation (made from prime documents prior to the machine operation) of totals against which the machine totals can be checked – a procedure usually known as 'pre-listing'.

Apart from the arithmetical accuracy, which can be ensured by an effective system of controls, it is important to realize that balancing with the controls is not proof of the accuracy of the ledgers. It has always been one of the tasks of the auditor to detect errors of principle which do not affect the arithmetical accuracy and the auditor must examine carefully the possibility of errors of this kind in any mechanized system. Mis-postings are not only more easily made by the class of clerical staff employed in machine work, but the reduction of posting indications to code symbols tends to encourage error. There is also a danger – one of the most serious dangers in any mechanized system – of prime documents or punched cards being mis-coded and resulting in the transaction being guided from the start through the wrong channel, a type of error which may be difficult to locate. In general, it will be found that an internal check must be imposed in some form on all or most of the postings, particularly in regard to allocation, but to a large extent this can be achieved by breaking down the controls into suitable subsections, thus narrowing the risk of errors remaining undetected.

Fraud

It is not infrequently suggested that one of the dangers of mechanization is to increase the possibility of fraud. Although the sub-committee considers that fraud is not necessarily either facilitated or hindered by mechanization, various safeguards against fraud may in fact accrue. Thus:

(*a*) In a well-designed system attention will have to be given to the whole question of internal check and control. Cases will arise, however, where over-enthusiasm for machine methods has led to the abandonment of normal safeguards; for example, it may happen in a small business that a 'general purpose' machine operated by one person is used to do work normally segregated to different persons. Any such weakness would be evident on first examination of the system of internal check, enabling immediate remedial steps to be taken.

(*b*) The alteration of a machine record is more difficult than the alteration of hand-written entries. It would usually involve the operation of the appropriate machine and the production of records covering considerably more items than those in question; for example, to alter a machine record of cash received may involve the reproduction of at least one entire machine cash sheet.

(*c*) An important feature of an efficient mechanized system is that emphasis is placed on the control and supervision of the two ends of the accounting process—the originating voucher and the final entry—relegating the intermediate processes to a mechanized routine. Fraud by the supervisors would normally involve collusion with machine operators, whilst machine operators could not perpetrate a fraud without a knowledge of and access to the whole system which they are unlikely to possess.

(*d*) To perpetrate fraud on a large scale by fabricating all the records necessary to stand the tests of internal check and of the auditor would require knowledge of the operating mechanism of the machines to an extent that would be exceptional for persons of the seniority likely to attempt fraud of this kind.

On the other hand, the auditor must bear in mind that the avenues for fraud that are available under a manual system (particularly where loose-leaf records are in use) are in principle equally available under a mechanized system. The method of perpetrating the same fraud will, however, vary as between the two systems. The insertion of an incorrect total or carry-forward figure in a manual system would take the form, under a mechanized system, of manipulation of the machine; for example, a machine may be made to print a figure without adding it in the total, or to include in the total a figure not printed, or to add in an item which the printed record indicates is a subtraction. Similarly the fabrication of a false document may be effected by inserting, in a carbon-copy record, a carbon-copy sheet which has every appearance of authenticity. In these and similar devices, however, the risks are only those which must be considered in every audit however the records may be kept. So far as the auditor is concerned, the important question is the soundness of the internal check in principle and the efficacy with which it is applied in practice. Scrutiny of vouchers and records and the follow-up of explanations of abnormal items remain the foundation of the audit procedure.

SPECIFIC AUDIT DIFFICULTIES

(*1*) *Absence of Primary Records*

The abandonment in whole or in part of daybooks and journals, in favour of the use of prime documents as direct posting media, is one of the commonest features of a mechanized system although in itself it is no more than a 'modern method' particularly suitable for adaptation to mechanization. This aspect of mechanization may present three main difficulties to the auditor:

(*a*) The totals (for example of sales) which normally would be provided by the columns of a daybook or journal may not be readily capable of verification. A similar position may arise in respect of the sub-totals normally provided by the analysis columns of a day book.

(*b*) Documents used for two or more purposes (for example, sales invoices required for posting to personal accounts in the sales ledger, and also for regional analyses or salesmen's commission) may have been re-sorted into the order required for a second process, thus presenting difficulty in vouching the totals for the first process.

(c) Where the business involves a great number of transactions of the same kind, large blocks of them may be dealt with in one total so that it becomes impracticable to limit test-checks to manageable proportions.

Remedies

In order to meet the foregoing difficulties it is suggested that the control of the accounting system should be tightened by a system of numbering prime documents and of breaking down the means of control to practicable proportions. This would normally be of no less benefit to the client than the auditor. The principal features of control in this way are given below; they involve the introduction of new types of primary records in the form of invoice registers, 'batch' registers, summary books and similar records which are integrated with the double-entry system.

(a) *Serial numbering of all prime documents in the order of first entry in the accounting records.* This ensures that a document is given a permanent identity immediately it takes its place in the records and thus makes possible adequate cross-referencing of prime documents to the various ultimate records; for example, if the ledger is being posted from original invoices the ledger account reference can easily be recorded on the invoice and the invoice reference number can be recorded in the ledger if the invoices have already been numbered. A decision as to what is the point of 'first entry' at which prime documents should be numbered will depend on the individual circumstances and is one of those matters which call for considerable skill in the design of an accounting system. The point at which a 'batch' of documents is prepared (as suggested below) may well be regarded as the 'first entry' in appropriate cases.

(b) *Collection of prime documents, before first entry, into batches of suitable classification and manageable size (for example 50 or 100 copy sales invoices) and the serial numbering of the batches.* This not only facilitates the subsequent tracing of prime documents and enables them to be filed in accessible manner, but is also of vital importance in maintaining an adequate control over operations. Thus, by means of appropriately-designed batch cover-sheets the various stages through which a batch of documents passes can be recorded and each batch is sufficiently small to enable a close control to be imposed at every stage on the monetary amount it represents.

(c) *Permanent filing of batches in batch-number order.* This is an essential conclusion to the handling of documents in batches as suggested in (b) above. To avoid risk of documents being lost through carelessness during subsequent reference and to facilitate the actual filing, it is advisable to secure each batch by wire stitching, stapling or similar permanent binding.

(d) *Maintenance, as an integral part of the accounting system, of records of the batch totals of quantities, monetary amounts and any other information (including analyses) which has gone into the accounts from the documents comprising the batch.* These records are normally necessary for self-balancing procedures in mechanized systems and it would be difficult to over-estimate the importance of controlling by batches as the most effective way of breaking down voluminous documents into quantities which can safely be handled at one operation and which facilitate audit procedures. A simple example will illustrate the value of a sound batching system. A business which has sold goods during a month to 20,000 customers may require to record those sales so as to ascertain:

    (i) the total sales;

    (ii) the totals for each type of article;

    (iii) the totals for each of twelve areas.

If the copy invoices are handled in 200 batches of 100 each, and the three types of analysis are made for each batch, then the batch record will not only provide the analysis totals required, but will also enable other figures in the accounts to be verified (for example, those arising from posting to the personal ledger accounts of the 20,000 customers). If the auditor is satisfied that the system laid down is properly applied he can impose tests on selected batches in the knowledge that what he finds in those batches will be representative of the whole mass of sales records.

(e) *Sectional balancing of ledgers on the basis of the batch records suggested in (d) above.* This is a logical development of the batch system and will normally be required for the client's own purposes of control. The principles of sectional balancing are well known and it will be evident that the most satisfactory way of achieving this form of control is to link the ledger sections with the batch records of prime documents.

Circumstances will arise in which the information required by the auditor, but not available because the client has dispensed with primary records, cannot be obtained from the normal accounting routine in the ways suggested above. Such cases may be due to the failure of the client to maintain an adequate control system, or to the desire of the auditor to impose an occasional test for which the material is not normally available. It then becomes necessary for the auditor to request the client to prepare special lists or analyses for audit purposes only. Where punched cards are in use special operations of this kind can often be undertaken after a considerable period has elapsed since the cards were first used, but it will usually be desirable for the auditor to make his requests promptly while the transactions are being recorded; for example, his request may be for proof sheets showing all postings made to a particular ledger during the day, or for a machine list of all the items in a particular selection of batches normally recorded in total only. It is necessary for the auditor to be careful and tactful in making such special requests, otherwise the object and scope of the proposed tests will be disclosed to the client's staff.

(2) Cross-references

Largely as a result of the direct posting system referred to under the previous heading, a possible source of considerable difficulty under a mechanized system may be the absence or inadequacy of cross-references between prime documents, primary records (day books or their equivalents) and secondary records (ledgers or their equivalents). The difficulties which can arise from this cause are mainly:

(a) In the analysis of nominal accounts; for example, items in the ledger may have no direct reference to the prime documents, such as invoices, from which they originated, a position which might arise where the invoices are filed under suppliers, the nominal totals having first been ascertained by calculating machine.

(b) In checking postings to personal accounts; for example, prime documents may be filed in batches without adequate references in the ledger to the batch numbers.

(c) In checking totals; for example, a tabulation of sales compiled from copy invoices may contain no reference numbers enabling the tabulation to be checked with the prime documents since filed under, say, areas or salesmen.

So far as secondary records are concerned, in the majority of systems they will normally be arranged in code number or alphabetical order, so that reference forward from prime documents or primary records may cause little or no difficulty. It is in connection with reference back from the secondary records that difficulties frequently present themselves unless an adequate cross-reference system is in force. For the auditor this presents a serious position, since the tendency in modern auditing practice is to substantiate the final records by breaking them down, rather than proof by building-up. The use of code numbers instead of names and narrative may aggravate the audit difficulties. On the other hand, code numbers can facilitate cross-reference if properly used and if the points dealt with below in the paragraph dealing with code numbers are observed.

Remedy

The only remedy for the above-mentioned difficulties is to institute an adequate cross-reference system so that the prime documents which support the entries in primary and secondary records are identifiable with reasonable speed and with certainty. This course should be recommended by the auditor in the client's own interests.

(3) Code numbers

Under any mechanized system, and inevitably with punched cards, code numbers will be used on an extensive scale to replace the names and descriptions which would be used under a normal manual system. The X Co Ltd becomes number 7619; cash received is described in that account by, say, the code number 4, discount by code number 5, goods supplied by various code numbers according to type of goods and so on for all items. Similarly, lists of purchases may have been prepared, classified under types of article, by sorting punched cards under the code number appropriate to each type and tabulating accordingly. The machine list itself may reveal only the code numbers on which the cards were sorted. Moreover, a series of code numbers, say from 1 to 9, may be used on one column of a card for one series of items whilst another column, for an entirely different series of items, may also employ the numbers 1 to 9. In producing lists the machines themselves cannot show which particular column is involved on each list.

For the auditor the use of code numbers for descriptions is a matter of particular difficulty because his client will not usually experience the same troubles. The client's staff is accustomed to the meaning of the various code numbers since they are in daily use; whereas the auditor (for whom each business is only a small part of his practice and who is usually in contact with a particular system at infrequent intervals only) cannot hope to recognize all the code numbers with which he is confronted. The difficulties confronting the auditor are mainly:

(a) In checking personal accounts and nominal accounts, there being no effective narrative explaining the nature of the individual items posted.

(b) In analysing the content of nominal accounts where (as frequently happens) an account is not confined to items of an identical character.

(c) In examining machine lists where the nature of the content of the lists is shown only by the code numbers; for example, sales may be listed under seven numbers representing types of goods but the machine list may show only the code number in each case.

Remedies

Code numbers are to a great extent one of the difficulties which the auditor is obliged to accept. They are necessary or particularly convenient to his clients and particularly inconvenient to himself. The difficulties can, however, be eased in the following ways:

(a) *Lists of code numbers and their meanings should be furnished to the auditor for his own use.* In most cases such lists will already exist for the clients' use; but if not their preparation for the auditor will benefit the client as well.

(b) *Wherever practicable code numbers should be translated into narrative form in making entries in nominal accounts.* This will usually carry advantages for the client both in the preparation of periodical accounts or financial statements and in reference back to accounts over a period of years.

(c) *Records for all standard transactions should be kept on specially designed stationery.* Thus, machine lists of items can easily be printed on paper having printed headings over the various columns in which code numbers appear. Similarly, sales invoices and copies thereof can be designed so that particular items appear in particular spaces and explanations of code numbers appear on the document itself. Devices of this kind will be regarded as essential for the business itself in any well-installed mechanized system.

If the recommendations in paragraph (1) above are adopted, the nature of the registers kept and the methods of filing documents will remove many of the auditor's difficulties in regard to code numbers in primary records.

(4) Composition of ledger balances

In all ledger accounts, but particularly in personal accounts, the absence of adequate correlation of debits and credits will cause considerable difficulty. If debit entries are not identified with the relative credit entries and vice versa, the current balance on an account may become incapable of analysis into the items of which it is composed, resulting in inability to prepare an accurate statement explaining the amount apparently outstanding. For the auditor the principal difficulties which arise are in connection with:

(a) Examination of the system of credit control. The task is rendered doubly difficult because the absence of proper correlation may indicate an ineffective credit control system; from which it follows that consideration by the auditor of the risk of loss through bad and doubtful debts is a tedious and uncertain procedure.

(b) Verification of debtor and creditor balances as representing sums genuinely due to or by the client. This necessarily involves not only the possibility of error but also that of manipulation.

(c) Analyses of nominal accounts containing considerable transfers in and out.

Proper correlation is fundamental to any system of accounting (whether mechanized or not) and the absence of good ledger-keeping has often been a cause of difficulty in a purely manual system. But with mechanization its importance is emphasized by the extensive use of code numbers and symbols instead of narrative and by the absence of manual balancing. A clerk posting to a handwritten ledger is more likely to clear debits with credits as part of his posting process than is a machine operator whose ledger is mechanically balanced (whether or not the entries are in the correct account) and therefore liable to be accepted as in order.

Remedies

Fortunately for the auditor, the available remedies are of even greater value to the client than to the auditor. Accounts, particularly personal accounts, kept in a slovenly manner will never improve operating efficiency and may, in extreme cases, result in serious financial loss through inability to support a dispute in a court of law. There are two remedies which should be recommended strongly to clients:

(a) *Where practicable and desirable, items posted to an account should be marked with a code or symbol indicating the relevant item(s) on the other side.*

(b) *The regular identification of the composition of outstanding balances should be part of the normal accounting system.*

In order to carry out the above suggestions special 'query' and 'credit control' staff should be employed, where the magnitude of the task warrants it, to keep the accounts under constant review. The need for this type of organization is usually more apparent under a mechanized system because businesses dealing in large numbers of transactions are those most suitable for extensive mechanization, whilst the reading of an account is rendered more difficult by the use of code numbers and of a running balance column.

(5) *Absence of ledger records*

It is the practice under some systems, not necessarily mechanized, to dispense with the traditional form of ledger account. This is done more frequently for purchases than for sales, payments to suppliers being authorized only on original invoices and precautions against duplicate payment being taken at the authorization stage through the ordering system. In some cases no attempt is made to maintain records on a personal basis; in others a quasi-ledger is maintained in the form of filed documents. The auditor's difficulty lies in the verification of balances due to and from the clients.

Remedies

The remedies available are again all as much in the interests of the client as of the auditor:

(a) *The filing of original documents (or copies of documents sent out) as a quasi-ledger record in suitably designed binders or files.* Subsequent reference may become impossible if this is not done.

(b) *The maintenance of effective total accounts and other controls, rendering the individual items of secondary importance.* In this connection reference should be made to paragraph (1). Without an effective control system the discovery, tracing and correction of errors is difficult even with orthodox ledgers; it is virtually impossible where ledgers are abandoned.

(c) *The introduction of ledger accounts on orthodox principles where the complexity and value of the transactions are considerable.*

(6) *Misuse of accounting terms*

Some abuses of accounting terminology are found in practice in the operation of mechanized systems. It cannot be suggested that this gives serious difficulty to the experienced auditor, since he is concerned primarily with the principles of the system rather than the expressions used to describe the records and processes. For example:

(a) The expression 'control account' is sometimes incorporated in the title of accounts which are not control accounts in the accepted sense of providing in total a counterpart to a number of individual accounts. 'Control' is freely used in mechanized systems to indicate records which do no more than prove the accuracy of a mechanical operation.

(b) The expressions '*Dr*' and '*Cr*' are often applied to items or balances which under orthodox methods would be described by '*Cr*' or '*Dr*' respectively. This position arises because mechanization is operated not on a 'debit and credit' basis but on a 'positive and negative' basis. A machine will frequently be operated without printing either '*Dr*' or '*Cr*' for the positive items (for example the debit balances in a list of sales ledger balances) but for the negative items (credit balances on the sales ledger) the machine may print '*Dr*' against those items if the use of that particular symbol is the easiest way of indicating the negative. It is obviously advantageous to run a machine in such a way that the normal items can be dealt with as positive, leaving only the exceptions to be distinguished as negative, even though in many instances this may result in credit items being described as '*Dr*'.

Remedy

Much can be achieved through consultation with auditors when a mechanized system is installed, but no real remedy exists. Any unnecessary misuse of accounting terms may be remedied by appropriate recommendations from the auditor, but in general this question will gradually cease to have any practical importance as the use of mechanization is extended and its peculiarities become commonplace or are overcome. The misuse of terms which now exists serves mainly to emphasize the importance to the auditor of a detailed explanation of the whole system and routine adopted by a particular client.

(7) Incorrect allocations

As indicated earlier, successful mechanization depends on the grouping of transactions so that each group contains a large number of transactions requiring similar entries. Unfortunately it is found in practice that over-enthusiasm for the use of machines may result in their being used for tasks to which they are not really suited. This gives rise to a tendency to classify together transactions of fundamentally diverse types. A similar tendency results from inexperienced or incompetent supervision of the operation of a system that is sound in principle. For the auditor the serious difficulty where large numbers of transactions are involved, is the risk of failure to detect incorrect allocations of material amounts resulting in improper description in the balance sheet and revenue account.

Remedies

To minimize the possibility of incorrect allocations attention should be directed to the two main principles involved:

(a) *Some transactions are not suited to mechanization and they should be segregated and dealt with separately by manual methods rather than be forced into the system operated for the general run of normal transactions.* To attempt to force unsuitable items through by some deviation from the normal mechanical routine is undesirable and productive of error.

(b) *An adequate and effectively supervised system of classification and coding of prime documents is essential.* Whilst mechanization provides a speedy and accurate method of passing transactions through the appropriate channels, it requires the highest degree of control over documents before the mechanical process is put into motion.

Where necessary the auditor should recommend to his client the adoption of any changes which the audit shows to be desirable in these respects.

The auditor will in any event need to apply various tests, as a normal part of his audit, to enable him to judge whether or not material errors of allocation are likely to exist. These tests lie mainly in the following directions:

(a) Exhaustive vouching of selected blocks of entries with the supporting prime documents to determine that transactions dealt with in a common manner are genuinely of one class.

(b) Exhaustive scrutiny of selected batches of prime documents to verify the coding.

(c) Detailed vouching direct from the ledger to the supporting prime documents in the case of the more material nominal accounts and all accounts (such as capital expenditure and repairs) which may contain 'border-line' items.

(d) Scrutiny of all special entries.

The extent of the tests required will (as in all audit tests) be determined by the auditor's own opinion of the efficacy of the system.

7. Verification of Debtor Balances: Confirmation by Direct Communication

The decision to request the client to carry out a test circularization of debtors should not be construed as an assumption by the auditors of the directors' duties. Circularization is essentially an act of the client, who alone can authorize third parties to divulge information to the auditors. If a suitable approach is made the client's agreement will generally be forthcoming. Should the client refuse this will inevitably lead the auditors to consider whether they should qualify their report, as they may not be able to satisfy themselves, by means of other audit checks, as to the validity and accuracy of the debtor balances. In general, the weaker the internal control the more important it is to obtain external confirmation of debtor balances. The circularizing of debtors on a test basis should not be regarded as replacing other normal audit checks, such as the testing in depth of sales transactions, but the results may influence the scope of such tests.

When circularization is undertaken the method of requesting information from the debtor may be either positive or negative. Under the positive method the debtor is requested to confirm the accuracy of the balance shown or state in what respect he is in disagreement. Under the negative method the debtor is requested to reply if the amount stated is disputed. In either case the debtor is requested to reply direct to the auditor. Both methods may be used in conjunction.

Weak internal control, the suspicion of irregularities or that amounts may be in dispute, or the existence of numerous book-keeping errors are circumstances which indicate that the positive method is preferable as it is designed to encourage definite replies from those circularized. However, it will almost certainly be found in practice that certain classes of debtors, e.g. overseas customers and government departments, either cannot or will not respond. Nevertheless it is desirable, where the auditors judge it appropriate, to attempt verification, preferably by the positive method, but this should always be carried out in conjunction with such other audit tests as may be appropriate.

Good internal control, with a large number of small accounts, would suggest the negative method as likely to be appropriate. However, in some circumstances, e.g. where there is a small number of large accounts and a large number of small accounts, a combination of both methods, as noted above, may be appropriate.

It is seldom desirable to circularize all debtors and it is therefore necessary to establish an adequate sample, but if this sample is to yield a meaningful result it must be based upon a complete list of all debtor accounts. In addition, when constructing the sample, the following classes of account should receive special attention:

(a) old unpaid accounts,

(b) accounts written-off during the period under review, and

(c) accounts with credit balances.

Similarly, the following should not be overlooked:

(d) accounts with nil balances, and

(e) accounts which have been paid by the date of the examination.

The request sent to debtors may be either a specially prepared form of letter or an attachment to the client's normal statement giving a copy of the debtor's ledger account for an appropriate period and, in the case of a 'positive' request, being accompanied by a pre-paid reply form.

Whilst companies may be expected to favour circularizing debtors for audit purposes on the form of statement normally in use, it is to be preferred that the debtor should be sent a copy of his ledger account for an appropriate period as shown in the client's books, as by this means it is more likely that errors and fraud will be detected. This can be particularly useful where running accounts are maintained, possibly involving large amounts and many entries, e.g. contracting work, or where there is evidence that accounts are in dispute or are not being settled in accordance with the client's terms of trade.

The statements will normally be prepared by the client's staff, from which point the auditors, as a safeguard against the possibility of fraudulent manipulation, must maintain strict control over the checking and despatch of the statements. Precautions must also be taken to ensure that undelivered items are returned, not to the client, but to the auditors' own office for follow up by them.

When the positive request method is used the auditors must follow up by all practicable means those debtors who fail to respond. After two, or even three, attempts to obtain confirmation, a list of the outstanding items will normally be passed to a responsible company official, preferably independent of the sales accounting department, who will arrange for them to be investigated; this does not of course absolve the auditors from satisfying themselves that the clearance procedure is properly carried out and from examining the results. Where there is any limitation in the follow up procedure it is all the more important to apply other auditing tests to establish that there existed a valid debt from a genuine customer at the date of the verification.

Whether there is a satisfactory rate of response or not, any inaccuracies revealed by the circularization or by the additional tests mentioned in the previous paragraph may have a bearing on other accounts not included in the original sample. In these circumstances the auditors will have to consider what further tests they can make in order to satisfy themselves as to the correctness of the customers' balances taken as a whole. A tabulation of the results of the test by number and by value may help the auditors to form a view as to the adequacy of the work already carried out.

8. Auditors' Reports on Group Accounts

The Ninth Schedule of the *Companies Act 1948* provides that in the case of a holding company submitting group accounts its auditors shall expressly state whether, in their opinion, the group accounts have been properly prepared in accordance with the provisions of the Act so as to give a true and fair view of the state of affairs or profit or loss of the company and its subsidiaries dealt with thereby, so far as concerns members of the company. [This duty is now specified in Section 14 of the *Companies Act 1967*.]

This duty presents special problems for the auditors of a holding company when the group accounts contain material amounts relating to subsidiaries which they have not themselves audited. A holding company's auditors are not relieved of responsibility for accepting information from accounts which have been audited by others. It is proper to take account of the nature and extent of any examination carried out by other external auditors just as it is proper to take account of the internal control; but, whether the group accounts are prepared in the form of consolidated accounts or in some other form, the opinion which is expressed on them is the opinion of the auditors of the holding company. While it is usually desirable for the holding company's auditors to include in their report, for the information of the shareholders, some such factual statement (where the amounts involved are material) as:

'The accounts of one (or some) of the subsidiaries have been audited by another firm (or other firms)'

this does not relieve them of their obligations. The responsibility for the opinion which they express is theirs and theirs alone, and it is their professional competence and reputation on which the shareholders who appointed them are relying. In the words of the opinion given by counsel in 1948 and re-affirmed by counsel in 1965:

'The auditors of the holding company must take responsibility for accepting for the purposes of group accounts the balance sheets and profit and loss accounts of subsidiaries. This may involve either relying upon the reports of the auditors of the subsidiaries or making such inquiries regarding the subsidiaries' accounts as they deem to be necessary. It is for the holding company's auditors to decide, as reasonable men, which course it is necessary for them to take for this purpose.'

Thus, while the context in which auditors report on group accounts embracing subsidiaries of which they are not themselves the duly appointed auditors differs from that in which they report as the duly appointed auditors of a particular company and accordingly gives rise to a difference in the character of their audit enquiries, the auditors of a holding company have a duty to form in that context an opinion of their own on the group accounts; this is a duty which cannot and should not be disclaimed and is not discharged by uninformed acceptance of the accounts of the constituent companies.

If the auditors of a holding company are to form their own opinion about amounts in the group accounts relating to subsidiaries not audited by them, they will need to be able to ascertain how these amounts have been arrived at and what assurance there is of their reliability. For this information they should look first to the holding company, whose officers have a statutory duty to supply it to them. The accounts of individual subsidiaries are the concern of the directors of such subsidiaries who may often have to consider the interests of minority shareholders or, if the companies are abroad, to comply with local laws. But the presentation of the group accounts is the responsibility of the directors of the holding company. This means that the holding company must have sufficient information, and sufficient assurance, about the amounts derived from the accounts of the subsidiaries to satisfy its board and its auditors that the group accounts give, so far as concerns the holding company's shareholders, a true and fair view.

If it is found that the holding company lacks information about any of its subsidiaries which is needed by the holding company's auditors to enable them to form their opinion, the auditors of the holding company should ask for the deficiency to be made good. This can normally be done by direct contact between the companies, but it is both convenient and helpful if the respective auditors are also authorized to confer with one another through arrangements made by the holding company with the directors of the subsidiaries and by the latter with the auditors of their own companies. Such liaison is particularly desirable if the report of the auditors of a subsidiary contains a reservation which may be material in relation to the group accounts. Authorization is necessary because of the professional duty of confidence which each auditing firm has to its own clients, but it is difficult to envisage circumstances in which direct contact between different professional firms of auditors within a group would be other than advantageous to the group or to the individual companies. Refusal of such authorization or lack of collaboration on the part of the subsidiary company's auditors would inevitably put the auditors of the holding company on enquiry.

It is necessary in any event that consultation between the respective auditors should be authorized because of another aspect of the matter which can properly be dealt with only by direct contact between them. This concerns the nature and extent of the examination carried out by subsidiaries' auditors in discharge of their own duties. The auditors of a company, having given their professional opinion, would not usually entertain, even from professional colleagues, questions about the manner in which they had reached it and might regard such questions as implying some doubt as to their professional care or competence. Special considerations arise, however, where in a group of companies under common control some of the companies have auditors who are not those of the holding company. In such circumstances the auditors who are reporting on the group accounts should have regard to the auditing which has been done by the other firms, but in doing so they need to bear in mind that the nature and extent of the audit examination carried out is a matter of professional judgment and that no two firms of whatever standing and competence will necessarily exercise their judgment identically. The judgment which has to be exercised in forming an opinion on the group accounts is, however, that of the auditors of the holding company; it follows that the holding company's auditors must consider whether all material aspects of the group accounts have been subjected to an audit examination of which the nature and extent are in their own judgment adequate and reasonable for the purpose of forming an opinion on the group accounts.

The extent of the enquiries which the holding company's auditors find it necessary to make in fulfilment of this obligation will depend on their experience of the other auditors, on the degree of materiality from the group standpoint of the amounts involved, and generally on the circumstances of the particular case. In the view of the Council there will be many cases in which it would not be reasonable for the auditors of a holding company to seek to duplicate or supplement the examination made of the accounts of a material subsidiary by its own independent external auditors, but cases may arise where this is necessary, for example where consultation with the auditors of a subsidiary leave the holding company's auditors in doubt about the adequacy in some significant respect of the audit examination as a basis for forming their own opinion on the group accounts, or where such consultations or other considerations suggest that it may be necessary to consider important matters which, while not calling for investigation by the auditors of a subsidiary as a part of their duties in relation to its accounts, nevertheless require investigation for the purpose of the group accounts (for example, the extent of inter-company profit included in the cost of stock purchased from other companies in the group and held by the subsidiary at its balance sheet date). Nevertheless, as stated in the opinion of counsel quoted above, it remains the responsibility of the auditors of the holding company to make a decision, as reasonable men, on this matter.

Bearing in mind the considerations discussed above, it will often be helpful to arrange that consultation between the auditors is not deferred until the work of the subsidiary's auditors has been completed but begins when this work is being planned.

If the auditors of the holding company are denied information or facilities which in their judgment are necessary to enable them to form their opinion on the group accounts, their duty is to state the facts in their report and to make whatever reservation may be appropriate in the expression of their opinion.

9. Auditors' Reports: Forms and Qualifications [*Issued August 1968*]

References throughout are to the *Companies Act 1967* unless otherwise indicated.

GENERAL CONSIDERATIONS

(1) Auditors are required by section 14 (3) to state expressly whether in their opinion the accounts on which they are reporting give a true and fair view and have been properly prepared in accordance with the provisions of the *Companies Acts 1948* and *1967*. If they are unable to report affirmatively in the required respects they must say so.

(2) In the case of a banking, discount, insurance or shipping company which is entitled to avail itself and has availed itself of any of the provisions of Part III of Schedule 2, the auditors are not required to report, whether in their opinion, the accounts give a true and fair view. This dispensation however, applies only to the consequences of the exemptions from disclosure which are permitted by Part III and does not extend to other matters (for example the overstatement of assets or the omission of liabilities) which, in the auditors' opinion, prevent the presentation of a true and fair view in the generally accepted sense. Therefore if the auditors are not so satisfied, their report must be qualified, because the absence of any comment is equivalent to a positive statement that the accounts show a true and fair view subject to those dispensations.

(3) Auditors are required also to form an opinion whether:

(*a*) proper books of account have been kept by the company;

(*b*) proper returns adequate for their audit have been received from branches not visited by them;

(*c*) the accounts are in agreement with the books of account and returns.

It is their duty to report on these matters only if, in their opinion, these requirements have not been complied with. **The absence of any comment in their report is therefore equivalent to a positive statement by the auditors that they have investigated and satisfied themselves on all these matters.** Likewise their report must state, if such is the case, the fact that they have not obtained all the information and explanations which to the best of their knowledge and belief, were necessary for the purposes of their audit.

(4) The auditors have a specific duty to include in their report statements giving the particulars required under certain sections of the Acts if the accounts themselves fail to do so. Such particulars, which are statements of fact rather than opinion, speak for themselves and are not dealt with in this Statement. The relevant sections are:

(a) *Companies Act 1948*

(i) Section 196 – Particulars in accounts of directors' salaries' pensions etc.

(ii) Section 197 – Particulars in accounts of loans to officers etc.

(b) *Companies Act 1967*

(i) Section 6 – Particulars in accounts of directors' emoluments.

(ii) Section 7 – Particulars in accounts of directors' emoluments the rights to receive which have been waived.

(iii) Section 8 – Particulars in accounts of salaries of employees receiving more than £10,000 a year.

(5) Some suggested forms of unqualified report are set out in paragraph 16 below.

CIRCUMSTANCES IN WHICH QUALIFICATION IS NECESSARY

(6) The circumstances which cause auditors to introduce qualifying statements into their reports, *where the matters at issue are material*, include the following:

(a) If the auditors are unable to obtain all the information and explanations they consider necessary for the purpose of their audit, for example if they are unable to obtain satisfactory evidence:

(i) of the existence or ownership of material assets, or of the amounts at which they have been stated on the basis adopted;

(ii) of the validity of payments;

(iii) that the books properly record all transactions of the business because the evidence has been lost or destroyed, or is otherwise not forthcoming or has never existed.

(b) If in the opinion of the auditors:

(i) proper books of account have not been kept in accordance with section 147 of the *Companies Act 1948*;

(ii) proper returns adequate for their audit have not been received from branches not visited by them;

(iii) the balance sheet and (unless it is framed as a consolidated profit and loss account) profit and loss account are not in agreement with the books of account and returns.

(c) If in the opinion of the auditors the accounts, though based on proper books of account, fail to give the information required by the Acts; for example, a failure to comply in material respects with any of the specific disclosure requirements of Schedule 2.

(d) If in the opinion of the auditors the accounts, though otherwise complying with the requirements of Schedule 2, fail to disclose a true and fair view, for example:

  (i) because in the auditors' opinion they do not conform to accounting principles appropriate to the circumstances and nature of the business;

  (ii) because they are prepared on principles inconsistent with those previously adopted and without adequate explanation and disclosure of the effects of the change;

  (iii) because the auditors are unable to agree with the amount at which an asset or liability is stated;

  (iv) because the auditors are unable to agree with the amount at which income or expenditure or profit is stated;

  (v) because the accounts do not disclose information which, though not specifically detailed in the Acts, is necessary for the presentation of a true and fair view;

  (vi) because additional information given in a note, or in the directors' report, materially alters the view otherwise given by the accounts.

  (Notes to the accounts form part of the accounts for the purposes of the Acts but disclosure of significant accounting information by way of note on the accounts or otherwise does not necessarily ensure the presentation of a true and fair view.)

(e) If, in the case of a holding company submitting group accounts, it is the opinion of the auditors that the group accounts have not been properly prepared in accordance with the provisions of the Acts so as to give a true and fair view of the state of affairs and profit or loss of the company and its subsidiaries so far as concerns members of the company.

(7) More than one of the circumstances in which qualification is necessary may be present in any particular case. For instance, where the auditors are of opinion that the internal control is inadequate to the extent of casting doubt on the reliability of the records, they may be unable to satisfy themselves that the records are sufficiently reliable to enable the balance sheet and profit and loss account to show the true and fair view required by law. It will then be the auditors' duty to state in their report to the shareholders that in their opinion books of account have not been properly kept, together with any other necessary reservations which may, in exceptional circumstances, be to the effect that they are unable to form an opinion on the balance sheet and profit and loss account.

PRINCIPLES OF QUALIFYING REPORTS

(8) A qualified report is not normally necessary unless the amounts at issue are material. If a qualified report is called for the auditors must decide:

(a) to which specific matters their reservations apply;

(b) whether they actively disagree, or on the other hand lack sufficient evidence to enable them to form an opinion, as regards material items in the accounts;

(c) whether, in either event, the matters in question are so material as to affect the presentation of a true and fair view.

If, for instance, the items in doubt or disagreement are limited, that is, not so material that doubt is cast on the view shown by the accounts as a whole; the auditors will be able to report that, in their opinion, subject to specific reservations or with specific exceptions, the accounts present a true and fair view. There may, however, be cases where the unsubstantiated items, or those in disagreement, are so material that the auditors must report, stating their reasons, either:

(i) that they are unable to form an opinion whether the accounts present a true and fair view; or

(ii) that in their opinion the accounts do not present a true and fair view. A qualification in these terms is made only in extreme circumstances.

(9) The Acts lay down no specific requirements as to the manner in which auditors should, where they judge it necessary, qualify their report. This can only be decided in the light of the circumstances of each particular case. It would be undesirable, and this Statement does not try, to suggest standard forms of wording that might be appropriate to the variety of circumstances in which it may be necessary for auditors to give a qualified report. But the guiding principle, that it is the duty of an auditor to convey information, not merely to arouse inquiry, is long-established.

(10) Before giving a qualified report auditors should discuss the accounts with the company's management and make their views clear, so that the directors may examine the matter at issue and, so far as they judge practicable and appropriate, take steps to provide any information which is lacking or to amend the accounts in such a way as will enable the auditors to give a report without qualification.

(11) A qualifying statement should be direct and informative. It should be so phrased as to leave the reader in no doubt as to its meaning or the view formed by the auditors or the implications for the accounts. It should:

(a) be as concise as is consistent with clarity;

(b) be specific as to the items and facts and as far as possible the amounts involved;

(c) within the limits of the information available to the auditors, make clear its effects on the accounts; and

(d) express the auditors' opinions without possibility of misinterpretation.

The object should be to give in clear and unequivocal terms, so far as circumstances permit, such information in augmentation of that provided by the accounts and notes thereto as will, in the auditors' opinion, provide the information required by the Acts and ensure that the accounts will then give a true and fair view.

(12) The fact that the auditors have qualified their report normally merits special attention on the part of shareholders and others who may place reliance on the accounts. Prominence may be given to a qualification by placing it at the beginning of the auditors' report, and this practice has been adopted in the examples which follow, but position is less important than substance and observance of the standard suggested in paragraph (11) above.

(13) It must be emphasized that the fact that auditors may judge it necessary to include qualifying statements in their report does not necessarily impugn the financial integrity of a company's directors, who are ultimately responsible for the form and presentation of the accounts and the information they contain. There may, for instance, be factors affecting certain assets or liabilities of the company which give rise to a difference of opinion between directors and auditors as to the amounts at which the relevant items may be fairly stated in the accounts. It is the duty of the auditors to exercise their independent judgment and express their opinion. The auditors' obligation is inescapable. It would be wholly inappropriate, for instance, for auditors to seek to avoid it by resigning before the expiry of their term of office because they are dissatisfied with the position disclosed by their audit.

CONSOLIDATED ACCOUNTS: SUBSIDIARIES' ACCOUNTS AUDITED BY OTHER FIRMS

(14) In accordance with the terms of section 14 (3), the auditors of a company submitting group accounts must report whether these have been properly prepared in accordance with the *Companies Acts 1948* and *1967* so as to give a true and fair view. The special problems which arise for the auditors of the parent company (who are responsible for reporting on group accounts) where the group accounts include material amounts relating to subsidiaries which they have not themselves audited are dealt with in Statement on Auditing 'Auditors' Reports on Group Accounts'.

CONSOLIDATED ACCOUNTS: QUALIFYING STATEMENTS CONTAINED IN THE AUDITORS' REPORTS ON THE ACCOUNTS OF SUBSIDIARY COMPANIES

(15) Paragraph 15 (4) (*d*) of Schedule 2 requires that where group accounts are not submitted any qualifications contained in auditors' reports on the accounts of subsidiaries should be disclosed in the statement attached to the balance sheet of the holding company. If consolidated accounts are prepared the auditors' report thereon should include a qualification in appropriate terms if material reservations have been expressed by other auditors in their reports on subsidiary companies, in so far as

such reservations are judged by the holding company's auditors to be material in relation to the consolidated accounts and appropriate adjustments have not been made on consolidation.

UNQUALIFIED REPORTS – [*see Chap. VIII, § 5.*]

QUALIFIED REPORTS – INTRODUCTORY

(16) Since qualifications must be expressed in terms chosen to fit the particular circumstances to which they relate, it is impracticable, and could be misleading, to suggest standard forms of qualification. The examples which follow are intended as practical illustrations of the principles described in the first part of this Statement and should be read with this in mind. *It is emphasized that they are not intended, and are not necessarily suitable, for adaptation to and use in other circumstances.* The examples are fictitious and deliberately simplified. In practice, if circumstances call for a qualified audit report they will often be far more complex than the illustrations given, and may necessitate explanation at length to make the position clear. For the purposes of the examples it is assumed throughout that the matters in question are judged to be material.

(17) Where the auditors have reason to consider that their report should be qualified, the nature and importance of the items at issue should be assessed in relation to the accounts as a whole so as to determine their significance in judging the truth and fairness of the view presented. Auditors are usually able to report that in spite of the qualifying statement the accounts give a true and fair view in other respects. In the last resort, however, the reservation may be so fundamental as to make it necessary for them to state either that they are unable to express an opinion, or, in extreme cases, that in their opinion the accounts do not present a true and fair view.

AUDITORS' REPORT THAT THE ACCOUNTS PRESENT A TRUE AND FAIR VIEW SUBJECT TO SPECIFIC RESERVATIONS

(18) The auditors may be unable to obtain all the information which they consider necessary. In such circumstances their report should set out the nature of the information which is lacking and its effect upon the accounts. The facts should be expressed in terms which give as clear an indication as is practicable of the uncertainty which arises from the inadequate information. If, for example some sections of the company's stock-taking records have been destroyed in error, and after studying such ancillary records and other corroborating evidence as is available the auditors are unable to form a view as to the amount properly to be attributed in the accounts to the stocks affected, their report might be as follows:

'Some of the detailed stock-taking sheets relating to stocks held at the balance sheet date have been destroyed. In their absence we have been unable to substantiate the basis of computation of stock amounting to £. . . . . . out of the total of £. . . . . . at which stock is shown in the balance sheet.

'Subject to the foregoing reservation the accounts set out on pages .. to .. in our opinion give a true and fair view. . . .' (followed by an appropriate form of wording).

(19) In addition there will be cases in which for reasons such as the lack of certain records it will not be possible for auditors wholly to satisfy themselves as to the truth and fairness of the accounts. In such cases it may be necessary for them specifically to refer to those limitations and their report might be as follows:

'In the absence of adequate analyses of factory wages we are unable to verify the charge for labour and overhead amounting to £. . . . . . included in the additions of £. . . . . . to plant and machinery during the year.

'Subject to the foregoing reservation the accounts set out on pages .. to .. in our opinion give a true and fair view. . . .' (followed by an appropriate form of wording).

AUDITORS' REPORT THAT THEY HAVE BEEN UNABLE TO FORM AN OPINION WHETHER THE ACCOUNTS PRESENT A TRUE AND FAIR VIEW

(20) Section 14 requires auditors to report whether the accounts on which they are reporting present a true and fair view. It does not appear to envisage circumstances in which the auditors are unable to form an opinion on the accounts as a whole, so that they cannot positively report one way or the other. Such a situation may arise where considerable uncertainty surrounds an item which is so significant as to affect the accounts as a whole, so that auditors may be obliged to qualify their report in this way. If, for instance, a company holds substantial stocks or other current assets overseas and these are sequestrated or frozen by action of the Government of the territory in question, so that their realizability and ultimate value are uncertain, the auditors may be unable to form an opinion whether the amount at which they are shown in the accounts presents a true and fair view. In such circumstances the auditors' report might read:

'Stocks stated at £. . . . . . are located in (name of territory) and are at present unrealizable because they appear to have been sequestrated by the provisional Government. It is uncertain whether they will be realizable by the company at the amounts stated, if at all, and for this reason we are unable to form an opinion whether the accounts set out on pages .. to .. give a true and fair view of the state of the Company's affairs at . . . . . . and of its loss for the year ended on that date. In our opinion the said accounts comply in all other respects with the *Companies Acts 1948* and *1967.*'

AUDITORS' REPORT THAT THE ACCOUNTS DO NOT PRESENT A TRUE AND FAIR VIEW

(21) If in the auditors' opinion the accounts as a whole fail to present a true and fair view, it is their duty to report accordingly, giving their

reasons. For example, if a company's assets consist wholly or mainly of shares in another company which is in liquidation, but the investment is shown at cost without provision for any estimated loss and without any other indication of the position, the auditors' report might read:

'The shares in PO Ltd, which is in liquidation, are shown in the balance sheet at their cost of £...... but the liquidator has stated that it is unlikely that the company will be able to pay its debts in full, with the consequence that the shares appear to be valueless. For this reason the accounts set out on pages .. to .. in our opinion do not give a true and fair view. . . .' (followed by an appropriate form of wording).

NOTES ON ACCOUNTS

(22) If a note to the accounts or a reference in the directors' report materially alters the view otherwise given by the accounts, it will be necessary for the auditors to make a detailed reference to the matter in their report. For example, if a note to the accounts indicates that debtors include at least £...... which it is not expected will be recovered but that pending ascertainment of the loss no provision has been made in the accounts, the auditors' report might read:

'The accounts make no provision for an expected loss of at least £...... on the debtors referred to in Note ... With this exception the accounts set out on pages .. to .. in our opinion give a true and fair view . . .' (followed by an appropriate form of wording).

If the item in question is so substantial that doubt is cast on the view shown by the accounts as a whole the second sentence of the above report might read as follows:

'. . . For this reason the accounts set out on pages .. to .. in our opinion do not give a true and fair view . . .' (followed by an appropriate form of wording).

CONSOLIDATED ACCOUNTS

(23) Circumstances may arise when in the auditors' opinion the consolidated accounts do not give a true and fair view as required by paragraph 18 of Schedule 2 which provides that the consolidated accounts shall comply so far as practicable with the requirements of the Acts as if they were the accounts of an actual company. Accordingly even though the separate accounts of the individual companies in the group do not by themselves call for any qualification of the auditors' reports, qualifying statements may be necessary in the auditors' report on the consolidated accounts if in their opinion appropriate adjustments have not been made. For example, if the parent company manufactures goods for sale by a subsidiary and the inter-company profit on stocks existing at the date of the balance sheet has not been eliminated, the auditors' report might read:

'Group profits are overstated by £...... by the inclusion of unrealized profits on products transferred at selling price between members of the group and remaining in stock at the date of the balance sheet.

With this exception the accounts set out on pages .. to .. in our opinion give a true and fair view . . .' (followed by an appropriate form of wording).

10. Accountants' Report on Profit Forecasts [*Issued April 1969*]

The Statement has been prepared with particular reference to the April 1969 edition of the City Code on Take-overs and Mergers ('the Code'), but the principles set out apply equally to any independent accountants' review of the accounting bases and calculations for profit forecasts.

The Statement has been prepared in consultation with the Council of the Institute of Chartered Accountants of Scotland and is issued after discussion with the Panel on Take-overs and Mergers.

INTRODUCTION

(1) In this Statement 'profit forecasts' means any estimate of financial results made (*a*) in advance of the completion of audited financial statements for an expired accounting period, (*b*) for a current (or unexpired) accounting period, or (*c*) for a future accounting period.

(2) Profit forecasts are normally prepared solely for internal use by the managements of companies, but there may be occasions when, for special reasons, they are disclosed to outsiders. In such circumstances auditors or consultant accountants (subsequently referred to collectively as 'reporting accountants') may be asked to review and report on forecasts to boards of directors.

(3) In so far as it concerns reporting accountants, the City Code on Take-overs and Mergers requires (*a*) that where profit forecasts are included in a circular, the accounting bases and calculations for them must be examined and reported on by the company's auditors or consultant accountants, and (*b*) that the circular must contain the accountants' report. The Code also requires the assumptions, including the commercial assumptions, upon which the directors have based their profit forecasts to be stated in the document, and these must be reported on by the company's merchant bank or other adviser, if any. Accountants may be retained to report in the latter connection as 'other advisers' under the Code, but this is not a requirement of the Code and would involve separate instructions and considerations with which this Statement is not concerned.

(4) It is emphasized that profit forecasts necessarily depend on subjective judgments and are, to a greater or less extent, according to the nature of the business, subject to numerous and substantial inherent uncertainties, which increase markedly the further forward in time the forecasts stretch.

(5) In consequence profit forecasts, as defined in paragraph (1) above, are not capable of confirmation and verification by reporting accountants in the same way as financial statements which present the final results of completed accounting periods and there is no question of their being

'audited', even though the reporting accountants may also be the company's auditors. It is important that reporting accountants should make this clear when they accept instructions to review the accounting bases and calculations for profit forecasts, and in the wording of their report they should take care to avoid giving any impression that they are in any way confirming, underwriting, guaranteeing or otherwise accepting responsibility for the ultimate accuracy and realization of forecasts. Moreover, bearing in mind their special status and authority, reporting accountants should do or say nothing to encourage directors, third parties or the public to place mistaken reliance on statements as to future profits the achievement of which must always be subject to uncertainty.

(6) Reporting accountants can, however, within limits which are further discussed below, properly undertake a critical and objective review of the accounting bases and calculations for profit forecasts, and can verify that the forecasts have been properly computed from the underlying assumptions and data and are presented on a consistent basis.

PRELIMINARY CONSIDERATIONS

(7) Reporting accountants are advised to reach agreement with directors on the following fundamental points before accepting instructions to report in connection with profit forecasts:

(a) The time within which the accountants' report is required should not be so severely restricted that, having regard to the company's circumstances, and not withstanding their best endeavours, it would be plainly impossible for the reporting accountants to obtain sufficient information to enable them properly to exercise their professional judgment for the purposes of reporting. (See also paragraphs (16) and (17).)

(b) It should be clearly established that the reporting accountants' instructions and responsibility for reporting under the Code are confined to the accounting bases and calculations for the profit forecasts, as distinct from the assumptions, including the commercial assumptions, upon which the directors have based their forecasts.

(c) Because profit forecasts are subject to increasing uncertainty the further forward they reach in time, reporting accountants should not normally undertake to review and report to directors on profit forecasts for more than the current accounting period, and, provided a sufficiently significant part of the current year has elapsed, the next following accounting year.

(d) Although reporting accountants can provide the board with some reassurance on the lines referred to in paragraph (6) above, they cannot relieve the directors of the responsibility for profit forecasts which are disclosed to and may be relied on by outsiders.

(8) Before accepting instructions from boards of directors to review and report in connection with profit forecasts the reporting accountants will also wish to establish the following main points:

(*a*) The purpose for which the forecasts have been prepared and the accountants' report is required.

(*b*) That the directors assume full responsibility for the forecasts under review (as required by the Code) and that they will signify such responsibility by formal adoption by the board and a statement to that effect in any relevant circular.

(*c*) The identities of the company's merchant bankers, advisers or other independent professional experts reporting in connection with the forecasts, with whom the reporting accountants will wish to consult and keep in touch. It will be recalled that in any document addressed to shareholders in connection with an offer the assumptions, including the commercial assumptions, upon which the directors have based their forecasts must be stated, and must be reported on by the company's merchant bank or other advisers, and revaluations of assets must be supported by the opinion of independent professional experts (Code, paragraph 15 – *See Chapter XV, § 4*).

MAIN POINTS TO BE CONSIDERED IN REPORTING ACCOUNTANTS' REVIEW

(9) In carrying out their review the main matters to which the reporting accountants will direct their attention are as follows:

(*a*) The nature and background of the company's business.

(*b*) The accounting practices normally followed by the company.

(*c*) The assumptions on which the forecasts are based.

(*d*) The procedures followed by the company for preparing forecasts.

THE NATURE AND BACKGROUND OF THE COMPANY'S BUSINESS

(10) The reporting accountants will wish to review the company's general character and recent history, with reference to such matters as the general nature of its activities and its main products, markets, customers, suppliers, divisions, locations, labour force and trend of results.

THE ACCOUNTING PRACTICES NORMALLY FOLLOWED BY THE COMPANY

(11) The reporting accountants will wish to establish the accounting practices followed by the company, so as to ensure that the principles normally adopted in annual financial statements are acceptable and have been consistently applied in the preparation of interim accounts and profit forecasts. Areas which may require particular attention include, for example:

(*a*) The methods followed, and the nature of overheads included in determining the amount to be carried forward for stock and work-in-progress, and the identification, judgment and accounting treatment of obsolete and slow moving items.

(*b*) The bases adopted for recognising profits and providing for losses on long term contracts.

(c) Bases for calculating depreciation charges.

(d) The accounting treatment of research and development expenditure.

(e) The accounting treatment, and adequacy of disclosure, of exceptional items.

(f) The accounting treatment of taxation and investment grants.

THE ASSUMPTIONS ON WHICH THE FORECASTS ARE BASED

(12) If a circular includes profit forecasts Rule 15 of the Code requires the assumptions, including the commercial assumptions, upon which the directors have based their profit forecasts to be stated. As noted in paragraph (3) above, it is not the responsibility of the accountants reporting on the accounting bases and calculations for profit forecasts to report on the underlying assumptions but the task of the company's merchant bank or other adviser, if any. However, it is fundamental that the reporting accountants should report whether or not the forecasts are consistent with the given assumptions, economic, commercial, marketing and financial, which underlie them.

THE PROCEDURES FOLLOWED BY THE COMPANY FOR PREPARING FORECASTS

(13) In carrying out their review of the accounting bases and calculations for forecasts, and the procedures followed by the company for preparing them, the main points which the reporting accountants will wish to consider include the following:

(a) Whether the profit forecasts under review are based on forecasts regularly prepared for the purpose of management, or whether they have been separately and specially prepared for the immediate purpose.

(b) Where profit forecasts are regularly prepared for management purposes, the degree of accuracy and reliability previously achieved, and the frequency and thoroughness with which estimates are revised.

(c) Whether the forecasts under review represent the management's best estimate of results which they reasonably believe can and will be achieved as distinct from targets which the management has set as desirable.

(d) The extent to which forecast results for expired periods are supported by reliable interim accounts.

(e) The extent to which the forecasts are built up from detailed forecasts in respect of the main divisions or lines of activity of the business, distinguishing where possible between those which may be regarded as showing a proved and consistent trend and those of a more irregular, volatile or unproved nature.

(f) How the forecasts take account of any material exceptional items, their nature, and how they are presented.

(g) Whether adequate provision is made for foreseeable losses and contingencies.

(h) Whether working capital appears adequate for requirements as shown by properly prepared cash flow forecasts; and where short-term finance is to be relied on, whether the necessary arrangements have been made and confirmed.

(i) Whether the forecasts have been prepared and presented on acceptable bases consistent with the accounting principles and practices adopted by the company in previous years, and if not, whether the fact and effects of any material change of basis are made clear.

MAIN MATTERS TO BE STATED IN ACCOUNTANTS' REPORT

(14) The accountants' report under the Code will be addressed to the directors and will normally include statements dealing with the following matters, so far as appropriate.

(a) The fact that the reporting accountants have carried out a review of the accounting bases and calculations on which the profit forecasts have been based.

(b) Specific identification of the forecasts and documents to which the report refers.

(c) If, as will usually be the case, the reporting accountants have not carried out an audit of estimated results for expired periods, a statement to that effect.

(d) Whether in the opinion of the reporting accountants the forecasts have been properly compiled on the basis of the assumptions made by the board of directors, as set out in the circular, and are presented on any basis consistent with the accounting practices normally adopted by the company.

(15) If the reporting accountants have reason for material reservations about the accounting bases and calculations for the forecasts, or if they have reason to consider them inconsistent with the stated assumptions, they should qualify their report accordingly.

REPORTING ACCOUNTANTS' RESERVATIONS CAUSED BY SUBSTANTIAL RESTRICTIONS OF TIME

(16) It has been noted (paragraph (7) (a) above) that before accepting instructions to report on the accounting bases and calculations for profit forecasts, reporting accountants should be satisfied that the time within which their report is required should not be so severely restricted that it would be plainly impossible for them to obtain the information they require to enable them properly to exercise their professional judgment for the purpose of reporting.

(17) If for any reason, including unduly restrictive time limits, the reporting accountants have not obtained all the information they consider necessary, they should qualify their report accordingly. If they consider they have insufficient information to enable them properly to exercise their

professional judgment for the purpose of giving a meaningful report, they should say so.

SPECIMEN REPORT

(18) An accountants' report on the accounting bases and calculations for profit forecasts might, in appropriate circumstances, where there are no grounds for qualifications, read as follows:

To the directors of X Ltd.

We have reviewed the accounting bases and calculations for the profit forecasts of X Ltd (for which the directors are solely responsible) for the periods . . . set out on pages . . . of this circular. The forecasts include results shown by unaudited interim accounts for the period . . . In our opinion the forecasts, so far as the accounting bases and calculations are concerned, have been properly compiled on the footing of the assumptions made by the Board set out on page . . . of this circular [and separately reported on by Messrs . . . * on page 7] and are presented on a basis consistent with the accounting practices normally adopted by the company.

* i.e. the merchant bank or other adviser, if any.

LETTER OF CONSENT

(19) Rule 15 of the Code requires that accountants' reports on the accounting bases and calculations for profit forecasts contained in circulars must be accompanied by a statement that the accountants have given and not withdrawn their consent to publication.

(20) Before giving their consent (which should be in writing) to publication of their report, the reporting accountants should require to see the whole text of the circular and should be satisfied that it is appropriate, and not misleading, for their report on the accounting bases and calculations for profit forecasts to appear in the form and context in which it is included.

11. Accountants' Reports for Prospectuses

(A) FIXED ASSETS AND DEPRECIATION

It is recommended that:

(1) If material to the presentation of the figures, the amounts charged for depreciation in the years under review should be stated in the report.

(2) Where there has been a change (whether of rates or by reason of a valuation) in the basis of depreciation during the period covered by the report, the effect of the change should be indicated in the report if the effect is material and cannot be dealt with appropriately in the adjustments made in arriving at the figures shown in the report.

(3) Where the allowances obtained for taxation purposes differ materially from the corresponding charges made for depreciation in arriving at the profits or losses shown in the report:

(*a*) If the difference is material in relation to the profits or losses shown, the report should indicate the fact and should state the amount of the difference (or give the relevant amounts) for the last year covered by the report or for such other period as may be appropriate;

(*b*) If the allowances obtained are substantially greater than the amounts charged, it is a matter for consideration whether adjustments should be made so as to substitute the amounts of the allowances for the depreciation charged.

(4) Where the amounts chargeable in future for depreciation are materially in excess of the allowances obtainable for taxation purposes (for example, because the assets include assets on which no allowance for taxation is obtainable, or because of a writing-up of assets on a revaluation, or because of the acquisition of a business on terms that the purchase price of depreciating assets is materially in excess of the amount on which allowances for taxation purposes are available to the purchaser):

(*a*) The report should indicate the extent of the excess of the depreciation chargeable over the taxation allowances obtainable for the year immediately subsequent to the period covered by the report;

(*b*) The report should also indicate that owing to the disallowance for taxation purposes of this excess, the sum required to cover it is the gross amount which after deduction of income tax and profits tax will leave a net amount equal to the excess.

(5) Where a valuation of fixed assets is adopted for the purposes of the books and accounts:

(*a*) It is not normally appropriate or practicable, in a report dealing with a period during which there have been material changes in price levels, to make consequential adjustments in the depreciation provisions for past years;

(*b*) The report should, however, indicate the approximate future annual provision computed on the basis of the valuation and should give a comparison thereof with the actual provision made in arriving at the profit or loss shown in the report for the last year covered thereby.

(6) Where a valuation of fixed assets is used by the directors in the prospectus in order to indicate the assets cover for the issue, but the valuation is not adopted for the purposes of the books and accounts:

(*a*) The report should not include figures based on, or a reference to, a valuation in excess of the amounts standing in the books;

(*b*) Before consenting (under Section 40, *Companies Act 1948*) to the inclusion of their report in the prospectus, the accountants should either:

(i) Ascertain from the directors that the directors' estimates of future profits available for dividend, as shown in the prospectus, have been arrived at after appropriate deductions have been made for the profits which it will be necessary to retain as reserves (including profits set aside for the redemption of preference shares or debentures) in order to maintain the assets cover indicated in the prospectus; or

(ii) If such deductions have not been made, satisfy themselves that the disclosure is sufficient to show how far the directors have taken this factor into account.

(7) In the case of a holding company effect should be given to the foregoing recommendations where either:

(a) The cost of its shares in subsidiaries is materially in excess of the amount at which the underlying net assets are carried in their books and a material part of the excess relates to fixed assets which are subject to depreciation; or

(b) There is used in the prospectus a valuation of the fixed assets of the subsidiaries which is materially in excess of the amount at which such assets are carried in their books or (in a case where the valuation has been adopted by the subsidiaries for the purposes of their books and accounts) were so carried immediately prior to their adoption of the valuation.

(8) In the foregoing recommendations references to 'allowances for taxation purposes' should normally be interpreted as the annual allowances (other than initial allowances, balancing allowances and similar items) obtained for income tax purposes for the fiscal years of which the financial years are the basis years. In some cases, however, it may be more appropriate to apply the allowances for profits tax purposes. The circumstances of companies differ greatly and each case should be examined on its merits. In order to obtain a fair basis of comparison it may, for example, be necessary in some cases to take into account, whether by way of spreading or otherwise, initial and balancing allowances and charges, particularly in respect of assets which have a short effective life or where the aggregate depreciation charges over a long period are being compared with the corresponding aggregate taxation allowances.

(B) ADJUSTMENTS AND OTHER MATTERS

It is recommended that:

(1) The figures relating to profits or losses should be set out in the report in columnar form, accompanied by appropriate definition of the bases on which the figures have been computed. A figure of 'average profits' should not be stated.

(2) The report should show for each year the profits (as defined in the report) before charging any United Kingdom taxation on profits. In the absence of exceptional circumstances, the report need not include figures showing excess profits tax, national defence contribution, profits tax, or excess profits levy.

(3) If in any particular case the accountants should consider that there are exceptional circumstances which make it desirable to show the amounts

of excess profits tax, national defence contribution, profits tax and excess profits levy, it will be for the accountants to decide whether also to show for each year the profits after deducting those taxes.

(4) Where there are material items of expenditure which are chargeable in arriving at profits but are not allowable for taxation purposes, the report should indicate the amount of such expenditure for the last year covered by the report or for such other period as may be appropriate; and should also indicate that the sum required to cover such expenditure is the gross amount which after deduction of taxation will leave a net amount equal to the expenditure which is not allowed.

(5) The reporting accountants should make such adjustments to the profits or losses as shown by the accounts as they consider appropriate and the report should state that this has been done. If the amount involved in any adjustment is of special importance in relation to the results disclosed, the nature of the adjustment should be stated. The accountants should consider whether the amount involved in any such adjustment should also be stated.

(6) In some cases it may be necessary to consider whether adjustments should be made where there are facts which should have been taken into account in preparing the profit and loss accounts for the various years covered by the report if those facts had been known at the time when the accounts were prepared. These adjustments may often consist of a re-allocation, between one year and another, of items such as provisions. Where the correct credit or charge for each year concerned can be ascertained with reasonable accuracy at the date of the report, a reallocation may be appropriate if the amounts are material. In particular:

(a) *Contract prices.* Where material amounts of income were provisional in that they were derived from government or other contracts which were subject to cost investigations, or which for other reasons were known at the time of making up the accounts to be liable to subsequent price adjustments, consideration should be given to the question of whether estimates should be adjusted, having regard to the most recent information.

(b) *Deferred repairs.* Owing to conditions arising out of the war many businesses have had to defer necessary expenditure on maintenance of their equipment. Where claims have been made for allowances for deferred repairs for excess profits tax purposes, or provisions therefor have been made in the accounts, these should be regarded as *prima facie* evidence of the existence of deferred maintenance at the relevant dates. The accountants should, where necessary, make adjustments to correct under- or over-provisions at previous balance sheet dates.

(c) *Bad or doubtful debts.* Adjustments should not normally be made, in the light of subsequent events, to provisions which were considered to be reasonably necessary in respect of bad or doubtful debts having regard to information available when the accounts of any year were made up. Exceptional cases do arise, however, where the amounts involved are very material and in such cases it is necessary to consider whether adjustments should be made.

(7) The method of valuing stock-in-trade (whether of raw materials, partly finished or finished stocks) should be reviewed and tested in relation to the fair presentation of the trend of profits. Where it is established that the amount included in the accounts at any particular year end should have been materially different a reallocation should be made. Where during the period covered by the report there has been a material change in the basis on which stock-in-trade was valued and it is not practicable to make an adjustment, because the relevant figures are not ascertainable, there should be an appropriate reservation in the report. The taxation implications of any matters arising on stock-in-trade also requires consideration. In some businesses, for example constructional engineers or public works contractors engaged on large contracts on which work may be in progress over a lengthy period, some profit element may have been included in the valuation of work in progress. In other businesses no profit element may have been included until the period in which the contract has been completed. The basis on which the valuation has been made should be examined from the standpoint of seeing how far the practice which has prevailed is consistent with that in force at the time of the report and of deciding whether it would be appropriate to make adjustments so as to apportion the profit over the period of the performance of the contract.

(8) It may be undesirable to make an adjustment merely because in the period covered by the report there were items of revenue expenditure which it is believed will not recur in the future. In many businesses special expenditure of one kind or another may be incurred from time to time and it will often be inappropriate to eliminate the particular items which arose in the period covered by the report.

(9) Where a loan of fixed amount is to be repaid out of the proceeds of the issue, or has been repaid out of the proceeds of an issue during the period covered by the report, an adjustment to eliminate or amend the interest charged in each year may be appropriate. If a material adjustment has been made the fact should be stated in the report. In the absence of special circumstances it is inappropriate to make an adjustment for interest where a bank overdraft is to be repaid or reduced out of proceeds of the issue. Where interest charges or loans or overdrafts are of material amount and no adjustment is made, the report should state the facts and, if several years are affected, this may conveniently be done by showing the relevant interest charges in a separate column in the report.

(10) Where in the period covered by the report there were material changes in the nature of the business or the sources of income, or there have been exceptional receipts, the circumstances of each case will require consideration in deciding whether any adjustment be made, but regard should be had to the following general principles:

(a) Where another business has been acquired by means of an issue of share or loan capital it may be appropriate to make an adjustment to include the profits of the acquired business in respect of the years prior to acquisition; and for this purpose a suitable method may be to show in a separate column the profits which have been so included (Where a business is to be acquired out of the proceeds of the new issue, a report on the profits of that business must be given in accordance with paragraph 20 of the Fourth Schedule to the *Companies Act 1948*.)

(b) Where, however, another business has been acquired out of existing resources, the profits of such business for the years prior to the acquisition should not in general be included, for the reason, amongst others, that for those years the profits of the acquiring business already include profits derived from the use of the resources which were later used to acquire the further business. Similar considerations apply where the acquired business had sustained losses prior to acquisition; but there may be circumstances which require different treatment or appropriate comment in the accountant's report, for example where the further business has a record of material losses and it was acquired towards the end of the period covered by the report.

(c) Where a distinct and material section of the business has been discontinued or sold, it would normally be appropriate to show separately, or to make an adjustment to exclude, the profits attributable to that section of the business where ascertainable. Consideration should, however, be given to the effect of such adjustments on the trend of results shown by the adjusted profits. If losses have been sustained in the discontinued or sold section of the business and an adjustment is made to exclude those losses, the report should indicate that such an adjustment has been made and state the amounts of the losses so excluded. If no adjustment is made to exclude losses and the discontinuance or sale of the section has had a material effect on the trend of results in the later years, the accountants should refer to the matter in their report.

(d) Consideration similar to those mentioned in (a), (b) and (c) above apply in the case of groups of companies where subsidiaries are acquired or disposed of.

(11) There will be cases where items of expenditure to be incurred in the future have not been borne in the past, or have in the past been materially different in amount. In particular, the charge in future for directors' emoluments may differ materially from that in the past. In view of the length of the period covered by the report and the changes which have occurred in the purchasing power of money, it is usually inappropriate to adjust the past profits or losses. The report should, however, indicate the facts, for example by way of comparison of the emoluments for the last year covered by the report with what those emoluments would have been under the arrangements in force at the time of making the report.

(12) If the amounts involved are material, management remuneration not covered by directors' emoluments should be dealt with in the manner indicated in the preceding paragraph.

(13) When an item which has been charged in the accounts has been disallowed for taxation purposes as being capital expenditure, it should not necessarily be adjusted. Moreover no adjustment should be made to write back, as being capital, expenditure which has been charged in the accounts and allowed for taxation purposes, even though some items may be of a kind which might have been regarded as of a capital nature if a different accounting practice had been followed. Where an adjustment is made, it is necessary to consider whether it has a significant effect on the provisions for depreciation.

(14) Where a material amount of development or similar expenditure is carried forward on the grounds that it is abnormal and has a continuing value to the business, the nature of the expenditure and the manner in which such expenditure has been dealt with in the past or is proposed to be dealt with in the future, together with the reasons for carrying it forward, should be investigated. The treatment in the report will necessarily depend on the circumstances of each case. If necessary, adjustments should be made so as to charge the expenditure against the revenue of the appropriate period. If expenditure is carried forward the report should indicate the nature and amount of the expenditure carried forward at the close of the period covered by the report and, in some cases, should also indicate the period over which it is to be written-off in future years. Adjustment is not usually required for amounts which represent normal annual expenditure on designs and prototypes of the following year's products of companies whose usual practice is to carry forward such expenditure as a charge against the revenue of the following year. Conversely, the accountants should consider whether the trend of results has been affected materially by charging against profits expenditure of abnormal amount which could properly have been carried forward to a period following that in which it was incurred.

(15) Adjustments should be made in respect of any items which affect the profit and loss account but have not been dealt with through that account.

(16) Where in the period covered by the report there has been a material change in the accounting principles applied, or the method of computing profits or losses has in any material respects not been in accordance with accepted accounting principles, the profits or losses should, if practicable, be adjusted so that they are computed in accordance with consistent and accepted principles, or if this cannot be done, the matter should be explained in the report.

(17) The reporting accountants should consider whether a report covering the minimum period required by law, or by a stock exchange, presents a fair view of the trend of results having regard to any exceptional circum-

stances during that period. It may be necessary to extend the period or make appropriate comments.

(18) The reporting accountants may have knowledge of events subsequent to the end of the last year covered by their report, or of other special circumstances not dealt with in the foregoing recommendations, which in their opinion have had or may have a material bearing on the statement of past profits or losses, or on the context in which that statement appears. In such circumstances the accountants should consider whether the facts should be stated in their report or whether this is rendered unnecessary by the manner in which the matter has been dealt with elsewhere in the prospectus.

(19) The statement of assets and liabilities should be so arranged that the liabilities are deducted from the assets, ending with the proprietorship interest.

(20) The report should make clear whether an amount has been set aside for future income tax and, if so, should specify the amount and the basis on which it has been computed.

(21) Where quoted investments are held the report should state the market value on the balance sheet date; and if the amount standing in the books is greater than the market value on that date, the statement of assets and liabilities should include the market value instead of the book amount.

(22) The report should incorporate all notes (such as those relating to market values, commitments, rates of exchange or arrears of dividends on cumulative preference shares) which appeared on the last balance sheet, so far as the notes are material to a proper appreciation of the position at the balance sheet date.

(23) The accountants' report deals with the assets and liabilities at the last balance sheet date and should therefore not include any addition in respect of the expected proceeds of the issue. This can appropriately be dealt with elsewhere in the prospectus.

(24) The reporting accountants may have knowledge of material events subsequent to the last balance sheet date, for example where there has been a material fall in the market value of investments or of stock-in-trade. In such cases and where the reporting accountants have knowledge of any other special circumstances, not dealt with in the foregoing recommendations, which in their opinion have had or may have a material bearing on the statement of assets and liabilities, they should consider whether the facts should be stated in their report or whether this is rendered unnecessary by the manner in which the matter has been dealt with elsewhere in the prospectus.

(25) Where the report involves subsidiaries or branches or overseas businesses, the circumstances are not usually such as to be suitable for the

application of any general recommendations. For example, where subsidiaries or branches have different accounting dates it may not be practicable or appropriate to apportion the figures of profits or losses so as to obtain aggregates for a common period and the appropriate treatment will be a matter for the accountants to decide in the circumstances of each case. Similarly, where a material part of the profits is derived from overseas branches or companies it will be for the accountants to decide whether it is desirable to show separately the amount of such profits, or of the overseas taxation thereon, or of both, and the manner of indicating the position where there are material exchange restrictions on the transfer of overseas profits. All these matters and many others which arise in relation to groups and overseas businesses require consideration of the circumstances in each case to ensure that the report will not be misunderstood. In all cases where a matter is material the report should state clearly what has been done. The accounts of some subsidiaries or branches may have been audited by accountants other than those who are reporting for prospectus purposes and it is then necessary for the reporting accountants to consider in the circumstances of each particular case whether they should examine the books and records of the subsidiaries or branches concerned, for which purpose it may be necessary to employ overseas agents. The reporting accountants should consider the desirability of communicating with the other auditors to ascertain whether they wish to draw attention to any matters which may be relevant to the report required for prospectus purposes.

(26) Before consenting (under Section 40, *Companies Act 1948*) to the inclusion of their report in the prospectus, the reporting accountants should have regard particularly to:

(*a*) The manner in which the directors, in their statement of estimated current and future profits, deal with figures shown in the accountants' report and with matters to which attention has been drawn in that report.

Note: The Quotations Department of the Stock Exchange, London, requires the company to furnish the department with an outline of the facts on which the estimate of profits is founded.

(*b*) Material facts of which they have knowledge in relation to the directors' estimates.

(*c*) The manner in which any special circumstances have been dealt with in the prospectus, where the accountants have decided that no reference thereto is necessary in their report. (See paragraphs 18 and 24.)

(27) In cases where their report deals with assets and liabilities of a company or business acquired or to be acquired, the reporting accountants should ascertain from the directors that the directors' estimates of future profits available for dividend, as shown in the prospectus, have been arrived at after appropriate deductions have been made in respect of pre-acquisition profits which will not be available to the acquiring company for distribution as dividend.

Addendum

Accountants' reports for prospectus purposes involve the investigation of accounts covering a long period, normally at least ten years. Where the records of the business in respect of the whole of the period have not been preserved such an investigation can be hindered and the reporting accountants may find it necessary to include reservations in their report.

Such reservations may reflect adversely upon the reliability of the figures given in the report. Moreover they may be embarrassing to the company's auditors where they were entirely satisfied, at the time when their audits were conducted, in regard to figures which cannot be verified during the investigation because the records are no longer available.

The Council therefore wishes to emphasize to members of the Institute the desirability of advising that important records should be retained for a long period, particularly where a business is such that there is a possibility that at some future date it may be necessary for a prospectus or similar document to be issued.

The need to retain important records applies particularly to stock inventories, including not only the fair copy summaries but also the rough stock sheets made out at the time when a physical count was taken in the works or storehouse.

(c) DISCLOSURE OF DEPRECIATION

The following is an extract from a statement, the terms of which were agreed with The Stock Exchange, issued in October 1965, for the guidance of members:

(*a*) The present obligations of and requirements for reporting accountants in relation to charges against revenue for depreciation and amortization may therefore be summarized as follows:

(1) The responsibility of reporting accountants include that of inquiring into the amounts charged against revenue for amortization, depreciation and obsolescence and, in the light of the information and explanations which they obtain, of forming their own opinion as to the amounts which ought to be charged in arriving at the profits or losses stated in their report.

(2) It follows that, if in their opinion the amounts provided in the accounts in any relevant year were inadequate (or conversely, excessive), the amounts involved and their effect, if material, on the trend of results will need to be the subject of appropriate adjustments or, failing this, of disclosure in a clearly stated reservation in their report.

(3) Consideration has also to be given to the bearing of the report on the other important features of the document in which the report is included, notably on any directors' estimate of future profits and dividend cover. For example, if, in consequence of an upward revaluation, which is to be incorporated in the books, of assets which are subject to amortization or depreciation the charges against revenue will in future need to be materially larger than

those in the period covered by the report, this fact and the amount or estimated amount of the additional annual provision should be stated in the report. Additionally, where the purchase of the share capital of a company is involved and the price payable includes a premium which can be directly related to underlying assets which are subject to depreciation or amortization, reference to the estimated amount of any additional annual provision required should be stated in the report.

(4) Similarly, the report should disclose, if material, the extent to which the provisions for amortization or depreciation are not the subject of corresponding tax reliefs.

(b) Before giving their consent to the issue of the document with the report included, the reporting accountants should satisfy themselves that in any estimates of prospective earnings and dividend cover given elsewhere in the context due allowance has been made for, among other things, the matters referred to in (3) and (4) above.

(c) If the document in which the report is to appear is governed by the requirements of The Stock Exchange, London, the reporting accountants must in any event:

(i) state in their report (as well as in the Statement of Adjustments) the amount of the charge in each period for amortization, depreciation and obsolescence.

(*Note:* The Quotations Department will consider some adaptation of this requirement in cases which involve complex multi-column statements);

(ii) include in their letter to the Quotations Department the information called for by sub-paragraphs (ii) and (iii) of paragraph 10 of The Stock Exchange's memorandum of October 29th, 1962. This information concerns statements to be made by the reporting accountants to the Quotations Department, to the effect that they are satisfied as to the adequacy of depreciation and amortization provisions charged in the past, and that there is no material difference between the written-down value of assets and the amount on which future taxation allowances will be calculated, or alternatively, if such material differences do exist, an explanation is to be provided as to how these have been dealt with in the past.

If circumstances appear to warrant it, the Quotations Department may also ask for information about the basis on which the charges for depreciation have been calculated and in special cases for the inclusion of an appropriate explanatory statement in the report.

12. Special Reports Required of Accountants   [*Issued October 1968*]

INTRODUCTION

(1) Central and local government departments, professional and trade associations and other bodies frequently require the report of an accountant

in support of a statement of figures or other information prepared by a client company or firm for purposes which include the following:

(a) claims for a subsidy, grant or rebate or for special trading terms or facilities;

(b) the determination of basis figures for the purpose of quotas, levies or subscriptions;

(c) as a basis for statistics;

(d) confirming to a professional or trade association that its rules as to 'solvency' or the existence of an excess of assets over liabilities as at a particular date have been complied with.

(2) Members of the Institute can report only on matters which are within, and in terms appropriate to, their professional function as accountants, and there should be a clear understanding between the body which calls for the statement, the client and the accountant as to their respective positions.

RESPONSIBILITIES

(3) The principles which generally govern the preparation and form of the statement are:

(i) primary responsibility for the contents of the statement should be accepted by the client, evidenced by a suitable declaration appearing on the form;

(ii) the duty of the accountant should not exceed the reporting of his opinion on the truth and fairness of the contents of the statement;

(iii) responsibility for the dispatch of the completed statement to the body which requires it should normally rest upon the client, especially where it is essential for him to comply with a prescribed time limit. It is therefore suggested that the statement be sent to the client for dispatch.

PRACTICAL DIFFICULTIES

(4) Many statements on which members are asked to report are based on an imperfect understanding of the function which the accountant can properly and economically perform. In consequence, some statements are unsuitable in one or more of the following respects:

(a) their scope extends to matters outside the professional function of an accountant (paragraph 5);

(b) the title of the statement may be inadequate or misleading as a description of its objective or the headings used may be ambiguous (paragraph 6);

(c) the accountant's report is drawn in a form which requires him to 'certify' the correctness of the information given – that is, to make a factual assertion – in circumstances in which it is not feasible for him to give more than his normal professional service of expressing an independent opinion (paragraph 7);

(*d*) the amount of work required of the accountant, and often of his client, may involve disproportionate expense.

(5) *Scope*. It is not within the scope of an accountant to report on such matters as:

(*a*) the intentions of his client, for example as to the purpose for which articles or commodities were acquired or the manner in which they are to be used or dealt with;

(*b*) the technical constitution or quality of a product;

(*c*) the anticipated sales or production of any particular product.

He can, however, properly report whether a statement (in suitable form) showing, as regards (*a*), the purchases made and the manner in which they have been used, or as regards (*b*), the ingredients which are stated to have been used in making the product, is in accordance with the accounting and other records he has examined. If he so reports he should of course have carried out appropriate tests and inquiries so as to satisfy himself on the reliability of those records.

(6) *Certainty of interpretation*. Neither the title to the form nor any of the descriptive captions used in it should be capable of misunderstanding. For example, the term 'sales' used alone may imply either amounts delivered and invoiced or the value of contracts for sales entered into for future delivery. Moreover, some organizations call for the completion by accountants of forms described as 'certificates of solvency' in which the accountant is called upon, *inter alia*, to confirm the 'solvency' of a member firm or individual. Apart from the difficulties in the case of partnerships and individuals of ensuring that all relevant liabilities are taken into account, the word 'solvency' may itself be ambiguous; it may be used in the sense of an excess of assets over liabilities or as implying an ability to meet current liabilities as they fall due. It is therefore important that, where ambiguities of this kind exist, the intentions of the body requiring the form should be ascertained at an early stage and any necessary amendments made to the statement so as to remove any uncertainty as to the information provided. In appropriate cases it may also be necessary for any prescribed form of accountants' report to be amended or amplified in order to make clear the nature of the information provided and the extent of the responsibility the accountant has assumed.

(7) *Form*. The word 'certificate' is not an appropriate title to the report of the accountant nor should the word 'certify' appear in its text as both imply a degree of factual certainty which no examination of records can normally provide. The words can therefore only be used in relation to matters of which the accountant has or can obtain first hand knowledge. He can certify that a given statement is in accordance with particular records or documents because this can be verified at first hand but he can rarely certify that the records themselves are correct for he cannot normally be sure that he has had access at first hand to all the facts behind them. Moreover, the records themselves may reflect apportionments and alloca-

tions which are matters of judgment or interpretation rather than of fact. The form of words to which the accountant attaches his signature should be described as a report and it should be made clear that he does no more than express his professional opinion.

PERSON TO WHOM THE REPORT SHOULD BE ADDRESSED

(8) An accountant who completes a report of the kind referred to in the preceding paragraphs does so on the instructions of his client by whom he is remunerated for the work involved and to whom he is primarily responsible. It is therefore appropriate in principle that the report should be regarded as being addressed to the client and not to the body which requires it. However, it would appear to follow from the decision in *Hedley Byrne & Co Ltd* v. *Heller & Partners Ltd* ((1963), 2 All E.R. 575) that an accountant may be held liable in damages although no contractual relationship existed between him and the body to which the report is sent, if it suffered financial loss through reliance on the form in circumstances where the accountant knew or ought to have known that the form was prepared for the specific purpose which gave rise to the loss and would be shown to and relied on by it in that particular connection.

CONCLUSIONS

(9) The Council therefore recommends that the following principles should normally be applied:

(*a*) a statement is not suitable for reporting on by an accountant unless:

(i) its subject matter is wholly within the province of the accountant and is unambiguous (paragraphs 5 and 6);

(ii) the wording of the report which the accountant is required to complete makes clear the extent of the responsibility which he assumes; in particular he should not 'certify' the correctness of matters on which he cannot do more than express his professional opinion (paragraph 7);

(*b*) the accountant should take reasonable steps to ensure that clients in respect of whom statements are required are not involved in disproportionate or unnecessary expense;

(*c*) accountants who are asked to report on statements which are unsuitable (see (*a*) above) should, with the client's consent, take up the matter with the body which requires the report; this will be necessary where there is need for the removal of ambiguity in the requirements or for an interpretation of technical trade expressions, or where there is need for significant modification of the scope or wording of the statement either because of its inherent unsuitability or to save disproportionate expense;

(*d*) the accountant should be prepared to make any necessary amendments in the wording of the report so as to conform to the principles suggested in this statement while still satisfying the purpose for which the report is required; failure to agree appropriate amendments with the body concerned should not deter the accountant from making them;

(e) the accountant's responsibility should be to report on the claim or statement made by his client; in principle therefore the information on which the accountant is to report should be set out in a declaration by the client, on which the accountant may then report in suitable terms;

(f) responsibility for the lodgment of a statement by a prescribed date should rest upon the client. It is therefore normally appropriate for the accountant after signing his report to send it to the client for dispatch to the body concerned.

13. Interpretation of 'Material' in Relation to Accounts
[Issued September 1968]

INTRODUCTION

(1) The principle of materiality is and has always been fundamental to the whole process of accountancy and is not therefore confined to the statutory requirements recorded in the preceding paragraph. The whole process of preparing accounts consists of the aggregation, classification and presentation of all the transactions in such a way as to give a true and fair view of the results for a period and of the position at a specified date. Each of these processes involves the application of the principle of materiality. Questions of materiality arise in simple receipts and payments accounts or detailed profit and loss accounts as they do in any other kind of accounts.

INTERPRETATION

(2) The interpretation of what is 'material' is a matter for the exercise of professional judgment based on experience and the requirement to give a true and fair view. Some general considerations are set out below but their application will depend upon the context in which a matter falls to be judged.

APPLICATION

(3) The question of materiality can arise in various circumstances, including whether or not:

(a) an item should be disclosed:
   (i) by description in an omnibus item,
   (ii) separately,
   (iii) as an important reservation or a matter of deliberate emphasis in presentation (e.g. profit of the year before deducting special loss);
(b) an error or oversight needs correction;
(c) a method of computation, basis or formula properly allows for relevant factors.

(4) The application of the term 'material' to any item will include consideration of:

(a) the amount itself, in relation to:

    (i) the overall view of the accounts,

    (ii) the total of which it forms or should form part,

    (iii) associated items (whether in the profit and loss account or in the balance sheet),

    (iv) the corresponding amount in previous years;

(b) the description, including questions of emphasis;

(c) the presentation and context; and

(d) any statutory requirements for disclosure.

(5) Materiality can only be considered in relative terms. In a small business £100 may be material whereas £1 million may not be material in classifying the expenditure of a very large undertaking, especially as too much elaboration could obscure the true and fair view. Those responsible for preparing and auditing accounts have to decide which, out of the many facts available to them, are the ones that have a real bearing on the true and fair view which the accounts must give. In some circumstances a difference of about 10 per cent. might be acceptable but in other circumstances a difference as low as 3 per cent. might be too much. While percentage comparisons can, properly used, constitute useful broad guides, it must be kept in mind that they are no more than rough rules of thumb, and should not be applied indiscriminately without regard to particular circumstances.

(6) An item may be material in either a general or a particular context. The general context refers to the true and fair view given by the statement as a whole. The particular context relates to the total of which an item forms or should form part and any directly associated items. If an item is not material in the general context, the degree of latitude acceptable in the particular context may depend upon its nature. There is an important distinction between cases where the amount at issue is arrived at on the basis of assumption and exercise of judgment and those where it is capable of precise and objective determination. On the one hand, there are items such as depreciation where some measure of arbitrary assessment may be inherent in determining the amount to be written off in any one year. A margin of error which is high in relation to the item itself might be acceptable, if it is acceptable when viewed in the context of the profit and of the associated balance sheet item. On the other hand, items such as directors' emoluments, audit fees and investment income may have a particular interest or importance to shareholders, so that an error which might be trivial in the general context, and indeed may not be large in relation to the item itself, might nevertheless be considered material. It is relevant to observe that these items are usually capable of precise measurement, so that any departure from the exact figure would call for some justification. Indeed, in the case of directors' emoluments, the directors' fiduciary relationship inhibits any latitude in this respect.

MISCELLANEOUS FACTORS

(7) (a) *Degree of approximation*. The degree of estimation or approximation which is unavoidably inherent in arriving at the amount of an item may be a factor in deciding on materiality. Examples include contingency provisions, stock and work-in-progress, and taxation provisions.

(b) *Losses or low profits*. The use of the profit figure as a point of comparison tends to be vitiated when the profits are abnormally low or where there is a loss; when judging the materiality of individual items in the profit and loss account in such cases, the more normal dimensions of the business have to be considered.

(c) *Critical points*. The view given by accounts may sometimes be affected by the trend of profit, or turnover, and of various expense items. An inaccuracy which might not otherwise be judged to be material could have the effect of reversing a trend, or turning a profit into a loss, or creating or eliminating the margin of solvency in a balance sheet. When an item affects such a critical point in accounts, then its materiality has to be viewed in that narrower context.

(d) *Disproportionate significance*. An item of small amount may, nevertheless, be of material significance in the context of a company's particular circumstances, especially if the context would lead the reader to expect the item to be of substantial amount. In general, the statute calls for specific disclosure of the type of item to which such circumstances are likely to apply, e.g. income from investments.

(e) *Offset and aggregation*. It frequently happens that two items, which might each be material taken separately, will be of opposite effect. Care should be taken before offsetting such items. For example, a profit arising as a result of a change in the basis of accounting should not be offset against a non-recurring loss. It may also be necessary, where there are a large number of small items, for them to be aggregated to ascertain if they are material in total.

14. Depreciation of Fixed Assets

Fixed assets, whatever be their nature or the type of business in which they are employed, have the fundamental characteristic that they are held with the object of earning revenue and not for the purpose of sale, in the ordinary course of business. The amount at which they are shown in the balance sheet does not purport to be their realizable value or their replacement value, but is normally an historical record of their cost less amounts provided in respect of depreciation, amortization or depletion.

Depreciation represents that part of the cost of a fixed asset to its owner which is not recoverable when the asset is finally put out of use by him. Provision against this loss of capital is an integral cost of conducting the business during the effective commercial life of the asset and is not dependent upon the amount of profit earned.

The assessment of depreciation involves the consideration of three factors: the cost of the asset, which is known, the probable value realizable on ultimate disposal, which can generally be estimated only within fairly wide limits, and the length of time during which the asset will be commercially useful to the undertaking. In most cases, this last factor is not susceptible of precise calculation. Provisions for depreciation are therefore in most cases matters of estimation, based upon the available experience and knowledge, rather than of accurate determination. They require adjustments from time to time in the light of changes in experience and knowledge, including prolongation of useful life due to exceptional maintenance expenditure, curtailment due to excessive use, or obsolescence not allowed for in the original estimate of the commercially useful life of the asset.

There are several methods of apportioning depreciation as between the several financial periods which constitute the anticipated useful life of the asset. Those most commonly employed in industrial and commercial concerns in this country are the straight-line method and the reducing balance method.

Subject to any periodic adjustment which may be necessary, the straight-line method (computed by providing each year a fixed proportion of the cost of the asset) spreads the provision equally over the period of anticipated use. It is used almost universally in the United States of America and Canada and to a large extent in this country. Though other methods may be appropriate in the case of some classes of assets, the balance of informed opinion now favours the straight-line method as being the most suitable for general application.

The reducing balance method, which spreads the provision by annual instalments of diminishing amount computed by taking a fixed percentage of the book value of the assets as reduced by previous provisions, is also largely used in this country. It involves relatively heavy charges in the earlier years of the life of an asset and relatively light charges in the later years. In order to provide depreciation under this method within any given period, the percentage applied needs to be from two to three times that applied under the straight-line method. This is a fact not generally realized, the consequence being that rates of depreciation fixed on this basis may tend to be inadequate.

A third method, known as the sinking fund method, which endeavours to take account of anticipated income from funds set aside for depreciation purposes, is not used to any great extent in industrial and commercial concerns, though in public utility undertakings, where special considerations arise, it is frequently met. Under this method, fixed annual instalments are provided and set aside, which with compound interest, will accumulate to the cost of the asset by the end of its useful life. Where the amounts set aside are invested outside the business, the validity of the calculations depends upon the realization of the anticipated net rate of interest, and each change in tax rates or interest involves recalculation. Where the amounts are retained as additional working capital, the effect is to make a growing charge in the periodic accounts for depreciation, because the fixed periodic instalment has to be supplemented in each period by an amount equivalent to interest on past provisions. Experience shows that, with the uncertainties inescapable in industrial and commercial enterprises, it is not prudent to place reliance upon the accrual of additional earnings to the extent required.

A fourth method, also not commonly used in industrial and commercial concerns, is the renewals reserve method, under which round sums, not necessarily computed by reference to the useful lives of the assets, and sometimes determined largely by the results of the year's trading, are provided and set aside as general provisions towards meeting the cost of future renewals. This method does not accord with a strict view of depreciation and may distort the annual charges to revenue.

The different natures of assets involve consideration in deciding on the method of depreciation appropriate in each case. Unless the methods adopted are applied consistently the usefulness of periodic accounts for the purpose of comparison of one period with another may be vitiated.

Whatever be the method adopted, the periodical revision of depreciation rates and the ascertainment of the residue of cost which has not been covered by depreciation provisions made up to any given date are greatly facilitated by, and often impracticable without, the maintenance of fixed asset registers showing the cost of each asset, the provisions for depreciation made thereon and the basis on which these have been calculated.

It is therefore recommended that—

(1) Provisions for depreciation, amortization and depletion of fixed assets should be applied on consistent bases from one period to another. If additional provisions prove to be necessary, they should be stated separately in the profit and loss account. Where practicable, fixed assets *in existence at the balance sheet date* should normally be shown in the balance sheet at cost and aggregate of the provisions for depreciation, amortization and depletion should appear as deductions therefrom. The extent to which these provisions are being kept liquid will then be ascertainable from the balance sheet as a whole.

(2) Such provisions should be computed on the basis mentioned below as being appropriate to the particular class of asset concerned:

(a) *Goodwill and Freehold Land.*
Depreciation does not arise through use in the business, except in the case of freehold land acquired for purposes such as are referred to in (d) below. Amounts set aside to provide for diminution in value do not constitute a normal charge against revenue and should be shown separately in the profit and loss account.

(b) *Freehold Buildings, Plant and Machinery, Tools and Equipment, Ships, Transport Vehicles and similar assets which are subject to depreciation by reason of their employment in the business.*
Provision for depreciation should, in general, be computed on the straight-line method. Assets of very short effective life, such as loose tools, jigs and patterns, may, however, frequently be dealt with more satisfactorily by other methods such as re-valuation, which in no case should exceed cost.

(c) *Leaseholds, Patents and other assets which become exhausted by the effluxion of time.*

Provision for amortization should be made on the straight-line basis, including, in the case of leaseholds, allowance for the estimated cost of dilapidations at the end of the lease or useful life of the asset if shorter. If a leasehold redemption policy is effected with an insurance company, the charge of the annual premiums to profit and loss account provides a satisfactory method of amortization if supplemented in respect of dilapidations.

(d) *Mines, Oil Wells, Quarries and similar assets of a wasting character which are consumed in the form of basic raw material or where the output is sold as such.*

Provision for depreciation and depletion should be made according to the estimated exhaustion of the asset concerned. In the case of an undertaking formed for the purpose of exploiting this particular class of asset, if the practice is to make no provision this should be made clear in the accounts so that shareholders may realize that dividends are, in part, a return of capital.

(3) Where a method different from that recommended has hitherto been followed and it is not considered practicable or desirable to make a change in the case of assets already in use, it is suggested that the methods recommended should be followed in cases of assets subsequently acquired.

(4) Details of all fixed assets should be kept (preferably in registers specially maintained) to show the cost of each asset, the provisions made for its depreciation and the basis of the provisions made.

(5) Amounts set aside out of profits for obsolescence which cannot be foreseen, or for a possible increase in the cost of replacement are matters of financial prudence. Neither can be estimated with any degree of accuracy. They are in the nature of reserves and should be treated as such in the accounts.

15. Accounting in Relation to Changes in the Purchasing Power of Money

The Council cannot emphasize too strongly that the significance of accounts prepared on the basis of historical cost is subject to limitations, not the least of which is that the monetary unit in which the accounts are prepared is not a stable unit of measurement. In consequence the results shown by accounts prepared on the basis of historical cost are not a measure of increase or decrease in wealth in terms of purchasing power; nor do the results necessarily represent the amount which can prudently be regarded as available for distribution, having regard to the financial requirements of the business. Similarly the results shown by such accounts are not necessarily suitable for purposes such as price fixing, wage negotiations and taxation, unless in using them for these purposes due regard is paid to the amount of profit which has been retained in the business for its maintenance.

On the other hand the alternatives to historical cost which have so far been suggested appear to have serious defects and their logical application would raise social and economic issues going far beyond the realm of accountancy. The Council is therefore unable to regard any of the suggestions so far made as being acceptable to the existing accounting principles based on historical cost.

Unless and until a practicable and generally acceptable alternative is available, the Council recommends that the accounting principles set out below should continue to be applied:

(a) Historical cost should continue to be the basis on which annual accounts should be prepared and, in consequence, the basis on which profits shown by such accounts are computed.

(b) Any amount set aside out of profits in recognition of the effects which changes in the purchasing power of money have had on the affairs of the business (including any amount to finance the increase in the cost of replacements, whether of fixed or current assets) should be treated as a transfer to reserve and not as a charge in arriving at profits. If such a transfer is shown in the profit and loss account as a deduction in arriving at the balance for the year, that balance should be described appropriately, since it is not the whole of the profits.

(c) In order to emphasize that as a matter of prudence the amount so set aside is, for the time being, regarded by directors as not available for distribution, it should normally be treated as a capital reserve.

(d) For balance sheet purposes fixed assets should not be written up, especially in the absence of monetary stability.

The Council also recommends to members who are directors or officers of companies or who are asked by clients for advice, that they should stress the limitations on the significance of profits computed on the basis of historical cost in periods of material changes in the purchasing power of money; and that they should draw attention to the desirability of:

(a) Setting amounts aside from profits to reserve in recognition of the effects which changes in the purchasing power of money have had upon the affairs of the business, particularly their effect on the amount of profit which, as a matter of policy, can prudently be regarded as available for distribution.

(b) Showing in the directors' report or otherwise the effects which changes in the purchasing power of money have had on the affairs of the business, including in particular the financial requirements for its maintenance and the directors' policy for meeting those requirements, either by setting aside to reserve or by raising new capital.

(c) Experimenting with methods of measuring the effects of changes in the purchasing power of money on profits and on financial requirements. If the results of such experiments are published as part of the documents accompanying the annual accounts, the basis used for the calculations and the significance of the figures in relation to the business concerned should be stated clearly.

[The following is an extract from the views on this subject, expressed by the Association of Certified and Corporate Accountants:

In dealing with depreciation we must for the sake of clarity and simplicity define the nature and purpose of depreciation.

For our purpose we take depreciation in the narrower sense as the diminution in value which a physical asset suffers through use and the effect of time and which cannot be made good by maintenance. We leave out of account the wider interpretation of depreciation which includes the loss of value of assets due also to changes in economic conditions, such as changes in consuming habits or methods and techniques of production, which is compendiously termed obsolescence. For present purposes we define depreciation in the narrower sense as the consumption of utility value spread over the life of the asset, which cannot be recovered by maintenance. The essence of this definition is that it is not dependent on replacement, although the measure of value that has been consumed can only be correctly ascertained by reference to the current cost of replacement. The physical deterioration of an asset is an expense incurred now, during the current accounting period, whether this asset will or will not be replaced at a later date. The purpose of the depreciation charge is not to provide for a fund for replacing the asset (although that may be its incidental and useful result) but for accounting as an expense the cost of using it up. Depreciation is first and foremost the recovery, spread over the life of the asset, of the prepaid cost incurred by its acquisition.

An annual charge which will do this is the minimum that must be charged against current operations during the useful life of the asset. But if – owing to the inflationary rise in prices – this charge is lower than it would be if it were calculated on the same cost basis as other items of expenditure, e.g. maintenance and repair, then expenses are understated and profits overstated. To remedy this the depreciation charge can be divided in two parts:

(a) the basic charge, calculated on recorded cost and designed to recover it over the useful life of the asset; and

(b) a supplementary charge for the difference by which the basic charge falls short of the amount which would appear as an expense if it were calculated on a basis homogeneous with maintenance, repair and other current expenses.

The practical application of this convention would not create great technical difficulties, nor would it cause a breach in the structure of accounting principles. In fact, the whole system of accounts would remain unchanged, up to and including the trading or manufacturing account, where the basic depreciation would be accounted for. The balance – the trading profit – could be brought to a depreciation adjustment account where the supplementary depreciation could be charged. The balance would be carried to the profit and loss account. The basic depreciation would continue to be deducted from the book value of the assets in the balance sheet and the supplementary depreciation brought to a special replacement provision account.

It must be admitted that the choice of the coefficient to be used for measuring the trend in the purchasing power of money as regards its application to the current value of fixed assets presents some difficulty, for there does not appear to be available an index of prices which is closely suitable. The cost-of-living index has the advantage that it is official and is perhaps the nearest approach towards measuring the *general* trend of the purchasing power of money, but it is doubtful whether it is satisfactory for the purpose of fixed assets. Here, it seems, a more specialized index, more heavily weighted for fluctuations of wholesale prices of raw materials and for movements in wages, would be more satisfactory. No such comprehensive or official index appears to exist.]

16. Accountants' Liability to Third Parties – the Hedley Byrne Decision

The decision of the House of Lords in the case of *Hedley Byrne & Co Ltd* v. *Heller & Partners Ltd* (*1963*) indicates that actions for professional negligence may arise if financial loss is suffered by third parties through their reliance on the professional skill and judgment of persons with whom they were not in contractual or fiduciary relationship.

Until the *Hedley Byrne* case it had been generally believed that an accountant could not be held liable for financial loss suffered through his professional negligence by a third party with whom he was not in a contractual or fiduciary relationship. In this connection reliance had been particularly placed on the decision of the Court of Appeal in *Candler* v. *Crane Christmas & Co* (*1951*). The *Hedley Byrne* case has, however, introduced new considerations.

The effect of the *Hedley Byrne* decision is that someone possessed of a special skill may, quite irrespective of contract, be considered to have undertaken to apply that skill for the assistance of another person and thereby to have accepted a duty of care to that person. A negligent though honest misrepresentation which causes financial loss to another may thus in certain circumstances give rise to an action for damages at the suit of a person with whom no contract exists.

The implications are of particular concern to practising accountants, an important part of whose work consists in preparing, examining or expressing an opinion on, financial statements of various kinds which may be relied on by persons other than those for whom they were originally prepared and for other purposes than those originally intended; but the implications should not be overlooked by any accountant who knows that his professional skill exercised in an independent capacity, whether gratuitously or not, will be relied on by others.

COUNSEL'S ADVICE

Counsel has advised that the *Hedley Byrne* decision is much more restricted in its effect than may first appear, and has drawn attention to the development of the law in this sphere overseas, referring particularly to the cases of *Ultramares Corporation* v. *Touche* (255 N.Y. 170) in the United States, and *Herschel* v. *Mrupi* (1954 S.A. 464) in South Africa. In this connection the *Ultramares* case is of particular interest. There the Court decided that auditors were not liable for negligence to a plaintiff who lent money on the strength of accounts on which the auditors had reported but which they did not know were required for the purpose of obtaining financial assistance or would be shown to the plaintiff. In so deciding the Court recognized that it would be quite wrong to expose the auditors to a potential liability 'in an indeterminate amount for an indefinite time to an indeterminate class'.

In Counsel's view third parties entitled to recover damages under the *Hedley Byrne* principle will be limited to those who by reason of accountants' negligence in preparing reports, accounts or financial statements on which the third parties place reliance suffer financial loss in circumstances where the accountants knew or ought to have known that the reports, accounts or financial statements in question were being prepared for the specific purpose or transaction which gave rise to the loss and that they would be shown to and relied on by third parties in that particular connection. There is no general principle that accountants may be liable for damages if a report or statement which proves to have been prepared negligently by them is shown casually or in the course of business to third parties who suffer loss through reliance on the report or statement.

PRACTICAL APPLICATIONS

The application of these principles may be illustrated by reference to some of the types of work commonly carried out by practising accountants.

(a) *The position of clients' creditors.* Clients commonly produce their financial accounts to third parties in support of requests for credit or loans. An action for damages by third parties if they suffer financial loss through reliance on the accountants' reports or statements would be likely to succeed only if it could be shown that the reports or statements were made negligently and that the accountant knew or ought to have known at the time he was preparing them that they were required for this purpose, e.g. of being shown to bankers or others in order to obtain credit or the continuance of existing credit facilities.

(b) *Auditors and shareholders.* In Counsel's view the object of annual accounts is to assist shareholders in exercising their control of the company by enabling them to judge how its affairs have been conducted. Hence a decision by the shareholders collectively taken on the basis of negligently prepared accounts and resulting in improper payments by or financial loss to the company could result in liability. No claim by an individual shareholder, however, would succeed in respect of loss suffered through his own investment decisions made on the strength of misleading company accounts supported by an auditors' report containing negligent misrepresentations, since the purpose for which annual accounts are normally prepared is not to enable individual shareholders to take investment decisions. But if the audited accounts comprised in effect part of a document of offer, and the auditors knew or ought to have known that the accounts were intended to be so used, they could be liable to third parties for financial loss suffered through reliance on a negligent auditors' report in connection with the offer.

(c) *Taxation.* Although they themselves may not be charged with the task of agreeing the assessment, practising accountants often know that the accounts they are preparing or reporting on will also be submitted to the Inland Revenue and form the basis of the client's assessment to tax. There would, in Counsel's view, be no grounds for action by the Revenue to recover any tax claimed to have been lost by reason of reliance on negligent mis-statements by the accountant, since in fact any ultimate loss suffered by the Revenue through failure to recover tax lost must be attributed to the death, decamping or insolvency of the taxpayer, not to the negligence of his accountant.

Where the accountant is instructed to agree his client's tax liability with the Inland Revenue he is in law the taxpayer's agent and the law relating to principal and agent applies to the exclusion of the *Hedley Byrne* principle.

CONCLUSION

The *Hedley Byrne* decision has modified the liability of accountants for professional negligence in an important, but limited, respect. It has not introduced a new concept of negligence: for an action in damages under the *Hedley Byrne* principle to succeed, negligence must first be shown. But accountants may now be held in law to owe a duty of care to persons other than those with whom they are in a contractual or fiduciary relationship and may be liable for neglect of that duty if, but only if, they know or ought to know that a financial report, account or statement prepared by them has been prepared for a specific purpose or transaction, will be shown to a particular person or class of persons, and may be relied on by that person or class of persons in that particular connection.

Accountants have always recognized that they have a responsibility to third parties in these circumstances, even if it was hitherto considered to be unenforceable in law, and it is recognized best practice that, in the interests of all concerned, the extent to which the accountant accepts responsibility should be made clear beyond possibility of misunderstanding. The *Hedley Byrne* decision underlines the importance of observing best practice; and Counsel has further advised that where an accountant specifically restricts the scope of his report or expresses appropriate reservations in a note attached to and referred to in the financial statements he has prepared or the report which he has made thereon, this can constitute a disclaimer which will be effective against any action for negligence brought against him by third parties.

17. Audits of Building Societies

The following extract deals with suggested audit procedures—

TESTING THE SYSTEM OF INTERNAL CONTROL

(1) By 'internal control' is meant not only internal check and internal audit but the whole system of controls, financial and otherwise, established by the management in order to carry on the business of the society in an orderly manner, safeguard its assets and secure as far as possible the accuracy and reliability of its records.

(2) The auditors should compile and maintain an up-to-date record of the system of internal control, obtaining copies of rules, standard forms, internal instructions and any publications showing terms of business. This record should cover each aspect of the society's activities (such as advances, shares, deposits, custody of assets, handling of cash) and should include:

(a) decisions of the board of directors laying down policy concerning such matters as advances, rates of interest and the investment of surplus funds;

(b) the delegation of powers to officials and staff, names of authorized officials and the extent of delegated authority;

(c) the duties of the staff of the society and the division of responsibility between them;

(d) any limitation of access imposed on officials of one department to records maintained by another;

(e) the system of internal check, that is to say the checks on the day-to-day transactions which operate continuously as part of the routine system whereby the work of one person is proved independently or is complementary to the work of another, the object being the prevention or early detection of errors and fraud; it includes matters such as the allocation of authorities and the division of work referred to in (b), (c) and (d) above and also the proper method of recording transactions and the use of independently ascertained totals against which a large number of individual entries can be proved;

(f) internal audit, if any; where there is an internal audit the statutory auditors should have regard to the Council's *Notes on the relation of the internal audit to the statutory audit.*

(3) On the occasion of the first audit, the auditors may consider it advisable, so far as the above matters are not already covered by board instructions, to seek the confirmation of the board to the record which the auditors have prepared.

(4) An examination of the system of internal control will enable the auditors to decide whether they can regard it as satisfactory. With large societies and those having branches and agencies, it is to be expected that the system of control would be comprehensive; with smaller societies, having less opportunity for the division of responsibilities and the institu-

tion of internal checks, the system of internal control could be less comprehensive without necessarily being unsatisfactory. This is a matter upon which the auditors must exercise their judgment. The directors of every society, irrespective of its size, have a statutory duty to ensure that there is a proper system of control over the records and transactions and the safeguarding of the society's assets.

(5) The nature and extent of the tests which the auditors apply will vary according to the strength or weakness of the system of internal control and the nature of the internal checks which exist as well as according to the type of transaction or item which is the subject of examination. It is important to include examinations 'in depth' among the tests to be applied. Examination 'in depth' involves tracing a transaction through its various stages from origin to conclusion, examining at each stage to an appropriate extent the vouchers, records and authorities relating to that stage and observing the incidence of internal check and delegated authority. It is sound practice to reduce progressively the number of transactions selected for examination as the depth of the examination increases.

(6) For a small society the tests which the auditors make will normally cover a greater proportion of the transaction than is necessary for a larger society where a more comprehensive system of control can be and is operated. In selecting items for examination and deciding upon the extent of the work to be done the auditors should always consider to what extent the transactions under review are material in relation to the affairs of the society as a whole.

(7) In addition to the normal annual audit procedures covering all activities, it is also sound practice to select each year, for a more intensive review of the accounting procedures, one of the main aspects of the activities of the society. Such reviews can usefully be planned to ensure that over a period of years they cover all the main aspects.

(8) Depending on the circumstances, it may or may not be necessary for the auditors to extend their tests in certain areas because of deficiencies in the system of internal control. In the event of minor breaches of the system the auditor should see that appropriate steps are taken to rectify them. Where, however, the auditors are of opinion that the internal control is inadequate to the extent of casting doubt on the reliability of the records, they will be obliged to undertake a great deal more detailed checking than would otherwise have been necessary. If, even after extensive detailed checking, they have been unable to satisfy themselves that the records are sufficiently reliable to enable the balance sheet and revenue and appropriation account to show the true and fair view required by law, or that a system adequate to ensure the safe custody of all documents of title belonging to the building society and of the deeds relating to property mortgaged to the society has been maintained, it will be their duty to state in their report that in their opinion books of account have not been properly kept and to make such other reservations as may be necessary.

MORTGAGE ADVANCES

(9) The auditors will have to decide upon the nature and extent of the tests which they should apply to the new advances on mortgage, including such tests 'in depth' as may be appropriate. Some may find it expedient to do this work during the year of account, concurrently with the transactions. The auditors' procedures will be governed by their assessment of the system in the light of the considerations referred to in the following paragraphs.

(10) The proper control of advances on mortgage is of fundamental importance in the operations of a building society. A sound and effective system of internal control is vital. The system must take into account the provisions of the Act relating to 'special advances'; these are defined in Section 21 and Section 22 (1) provides specifically that a society 'shall so conduct its business as to secure that special advances are not made by it except as authorized by this section'. When the Act of 1960 came into force an essential step for every building society was to identify existing advances which fall within the definition of 'special advances'.

(11) The rules and policy of the society may impose limitations (additional to the statutory restrictions on 'special advances' and the requirements of Part II of the Act) as to:

(a) types of property which may be accepted as security;

(b) proportion of the value of the security which may be advanced;

(c) overall limit on the amount which may be advanced either per property, per borrower or over a stated period;

(d) types of additional security which may be accepted and any special conditions;

(e) the competent persons who are eligible to value properties;

(f) advances on properties in course of erection;

(g) rates of interest and repayment terms.

(12) There will usually be a scheme of delegation by the board whereby the society's officials and agents are authorized to offer advances, subject to limits which may vary according to the status of the official.

(13) The records maintained by the society in respect of advances should include the following which are hereafter referred to as the 'advance records', irrespective of the form they may take in any particular society:

(a) offers of advances and by whom authorized;

(b) security for advances, survey report, solicitors' report on title, and status reports;

(c) name and address of borrower;

(d) terms;

(e) records of compliance with any conditions;

(f) board approval;

(g) acceptance or withdrawal of applications.

(14) The society should have an established procedure to ensure that it obtains from its solicitors, within a reasonable time, either notice of completion and the mortgage and title deeds or return of the society's funds. This is important as building societies are normally obliged to pay to their solicitors the amount of the advance some time before they can expect the deeds; moreover a proportion of approved advances is never completed. There will accordingly be a need for an active 'follow-up' procedure for the return of unused funds from the solicitors.

(15) The 'advance records' should be in such a form as will enable the society to comply with the statutory restrictions on 'special advances' and to give the prescribed information in the annual accounts and the annual return. Thus, in the balance sheet the amount outstanding on mortgages is required to be classified to show the amounts due from:

> bodies corporate;
>
> persons other than bodies corporate where the debt exceeds £5,000 [now £7,000];
>
> others

and any provision for anticipated losses must be shown separately as a deduction from the total. The same figures in the annual return are required to be supported by a Schedule No. 7 classifying the mortgages by reference to amount and also stating the amounts and numbers of mortgages under various categories of possession, arrears and receivership. These requirements all fall within the matters with which the auditors are required to deal in their report on the annual return.

(16) It will be evident that a society will need to organize its records and its system in order to ensure that separate advances to the same borrower (possibly made at different branches) are brought together in the records. In the 'Notes for Guidance' issued by the Chief Registrar of Friendly Societies in connection with the annual return it is stated that for the purpose of the classification under Schedule No. 7 any further advance(s) under the original mortgage should be aggregated with the original advance so that the total debt is taken for each mortgage.

(17) There are also further requirements in the annual return which will govern the manner in which a society maintains its 'advance records' and which are therefore of importance to the auditors, even though the auditors are not required to report on some of these parts of the annual return.

The requirements referred to are:

(a) *Schedule No. 1* which requires a summary of all amounts advanced during the financial year, analysed first by reference to the type of property on which the advances are secured and second by reference to amount (divided for each amount between bodies corporate and others) and distinguishing between new mortgages, second or subsequent advances on instalment mortgages and further advances on existing mortgages other than instalment mortgages. The auditors are not required to deal with this schedule, but its requirements (as amplified by the 'Notes for Guidance' issued by the Chief Registrar of Friendly Societies) will have an important bearing on the manner in which the society maintains its 'advance records';

(b) *Schedule No. 2*, of which Section A requires the 'special advances' made during the year to be summarized so as to show the total (analysed by amount) for persons other than bodies corporate, the total for bodies corporate and transfers of mortgages where no new advance is made but which rank as special advances under Section 21 (7) of this Act. Sections B and C of the schedule require lists with extensive details of the individual items making up these totals. The auditors are not required to deal with Sections B and C but Section A falls within the matters to be covered by their report on the annual return;

(c) *Schedule No. 3* setting out the details required by subsection (1) of Section 89 which relates to disclosure of advances to any director or the manager or secretary or to companies in which any such person is interested. This schedule falls within the matters to be covered by the auditors in their report on the annual return. Moreover, if the annual return does not show the required particulars the auditors have a statutory duty under subsection (4) to include in their report, so far as they are reasonably able to do so, a statement giving the required particulars.

SAFE CUSTODY OF DEEDS

(18) The directors must, in order to comply with subsections (3) and (4) of Section 76, establish and maintain a system to ensure the safe custody of all documents of title belonging to the building society and of the deeds relating to property mortgaged to the building society. Subsection (4) provides specifically that a society shall not be taken to have established a proper system unless, under the system, on each occasion on which any such document of title or deed is released from the custody of the officers of the society, the consent is obtained of the board of directors of the society, or of a person authorized by the board to give such consent.

(19) The auditors have a statutory duty (Section 87 (4)) to carry out such investigations as will enable them to form an opinion whether the foregoing requirement has been complied with. Particular points to consider in examining the system include:

(a) the procedure for checking deeds on receipt from the solicitors to see that they are complete, in accordance with the 'advance records', correctly executed and stamped;

(b) the maintenance of a record showing the location of all the deeds and the dates of any changes in the location of any of them;

(c) the procedure for ensuring that the deeds are received from the society's solicitors without undue delay; solicitors frequently need to submit documents to the Land Registry and as there is often a delay of some months at the Registry it is important that the society should have an established follow-up procedure, to ensure that the receipt of deeds from the solicitors is not delayed longer than is necessary for registration to be completed;

(d) the authority required for any temporary release of deeds from their normal custody and proper control for their prompt return;

(e) whether there is a continuous independent check (which some large societies maintain) of the deeds against the 'advance records' or the borrowers' ledger accounts;

(f) the necessity for satisfactory cross-references between the 'advance records', the cash-book, the borrowers' ledger accounts and the deeds;

(g) the procedure for release of deeds on redemption of a mortgage; on premature redemption the discharge of a mortgage will usually have to be completed by the society and passed, with the title deeds, to the society's solicitors some time before the redemption money is received and there should therefore be an established follow-up procedure.

(20) Prior to the Act of 1960 the auditors of a building society were required by law to examine all deeds relating to each property in mortgage to the society at the balance sheet date. This obligation has now been superseded by the more important obligation to form an opinion on the system of control throughout the year and on the view of the state of the society's affairs as presented in the annual accounts. The number of deeds to be examined is a matter for the judgment of the auditors of each society in the process of examining the soundness and effectiveness of the system. Deeds which are not available for inspection will call for special inquiries to be pursued until the auditors are satisfied with the explanation.

(21) When examining the deeds the auditors' purpose should be to ascertain whether:

(a) the mortgage is in the name shown in the 'advance records', unless it is a 'transfer of equity' in which case the mortgage would be in the name of the original mortgagor while the name in the 'advance records' should be that of the transferee in the new document of title;

(b) there is a document of title to the property under mortgage (see paragraph 22 below) and the society's solicitors have been satisfied as to the borrower's title;

(c) the amount of the advance as stated in the mortgage deed is not less than that shown on the 'advance records';

(d) the mortgage deed is stamped, properly signed and witnessed and is *prima facie* in order;

(e) the property is adequately insured, the premium is paid up to date and the society's interest as mortgagee is endorsed on the insurance policy.

(22) Auditors are not expert at examining titles, but they should satisfy themselves that *prima facie* the documents of title cover the mortgaged property. Although there are a number of exceptions, documents of title are generally of the following kinds:

(a) *Conveyances of freeholds.* As the society can only accept first charges on property, apart from the exception given by Section 32 (1) of the Act, the conveyance to the borrower must be in the custody of the society. The name of the borrower appearing in the mortgage deed should be the same as the name of the purchaser in the conveyance and the property should be similarly described in both documents.

(b) *Leaseholds.* If the borrower is an original lessee the lease constitutes the title; if the borrower is not the original lessee the title is constituted by the lease and an assignment of it to the borrower. These documents should normally be in the custody of the society. In some cases the borrower has taken an assignment of part only of the property comprised in an original lease in which event the original lease will normally be retained by the assignor; in such a case a copy or abstract of the original lease certified by the society's solicitors and an assignment to the borrower should be in the custody of the society. The name of the borrower in the mortgage deed should be the same as the name of the lessee in the lease or of the assignee in the assignment as the case may be.

(c) *Land Registry certificates.* The details of the property and name of the borrower as appearing on the Land Registry certificate should correspond with the details in the mortgage deed. With new building plots the best identification may be the title number, which is noted on the certificate and on the mortgage. Section (c) of the Land Registry certificate is termed 'Charges Register'; under this section there will appear the society's name as mortgagee and the date of the mortgage. The society's charge should come first on the charges register unless a note that a prior charge has been postponed in favour of the society is also registered.

(d) *Scottish titles.* The 'disposition' dispones the property to the society while the 'minute of agreement' between the society and the borrower provides that this disposition although apparently absolute in its terms is granted only in security of the loan. The name of the borrower, the amount of the loan and the description of the property should coincide in these documents and with the society's records (except that the amount of the loan will not appear in the disposition). The disposition should be recorded in the Register of Sasines and should bear the Registrar's stamp; there is considerable delay in recording and in new cases it may be necessary to verify that the disposition has been lodged for recording. For leasehold property the 'assignation' will assign the lease of the property to the society and should be accompanied by a minute of agreement similar to that referred to above.

(23) Where the borrower is a company the registration of the charge should be evidenced by a certificate from the Registrar of Companies if the company has its registered office in England or if property in England has been mortgaged by any company with an established place of business in England.

(24) Where an advance is made by instalments and the mortgage deed does not record the receipt of the full consideration, the separate receipts, making up the total amount of the advance, should be available.

(25) Where a life endowment policy is collateral security for a mortgage, the policy and notice of assignment to the society, duly acknowledged by the insurance company, should be available with the receipt for the current premium; particulars of the policy should be correctly stated in the mortgage deed. If there is other collateral security, the document of title to the security or of agreement between the society and the person giving the security should be in the possession of the society.

(26) There are, however, circumstances in which the society's advance may be regarded as properly secured without the society being in possession of the documents of title, provided all necessary precautions have been taken. The situation may arise in the case of land in England and Wales not registerable under the *Land Registration Act* when the mortgage is of part only of property held under one title, where it is sometimes agreed that the mortgagor may retain the title deeds. To protect the mortgage, however, the following steps should be taken:

(a) for land situated elsewhere than in Yorkshire:

    (i) a Class C (1) Land Charge should be registered under the *Land Charges Act 1925*, and the buff form issued by the Registry should be attached to the mortgage;

    (ii) a memorandum of the mortgage should be endorsed on the conveyance or conveyances to the mortgagor (retained in his possession) and a note should also be endorsed on the mortgage by the society's solicitors giving particulars of such memorandum and stating that it has been inspected by them;

    (iii) there should be a deed of acknowledgment by the mortgagor of the society's right to production of the documents of title retained by him and an undertaking for their safe custody; normally this acknowledgment will appear in the mortgage deed itself;

    (iv) an abstract of title certified by the society's solicitors should be placed with the mortgage.

(b) for land in Yorkshire:

    a memorial of the mortgage has to be registered in the Yorkshire Deeds Registry and the Registry's stamp should appear on the mortgage deed. This registration constitutes legal notice to any person dealing with the property and protects the society's mortgage whether or not the documents of title are in its possession. In addition there should be a deed of acknowledgment and an abstract of title as in (iii) and (iv) above.

If, notwithstanding that there is evidence that those steps have been taken, the auditors are nevertheless in doubt about any deeds which are not in the possession of the society, they should ask the society to exercise its right to production of the deeds and call for them for their inspection.

REPAYMENT OF ADVANCES BY INSTALMENTS

The matters mentioned below will need consideration by the auditors when they are assessing the system of control and deciding what tests they should apply in order to satisfy themselves on the records of instalment payments by borrowers.

(27) In addition to the routine work of ledger posting, the society should have an established procedure for the identification of arrears of instalments and the issue of reminders and for reports to responsible officials and eventually to the board so that legal action to obtain possession of the property may be sanctioned.

(28) A new advance to a borrower whose repayments are in arrear is a transaction calling for special examination to ascertain whether the advance has been properly authorized and the security is adequate.

(29) It is desirable for the society to have a procedure for the confirmation of entries. Where borrowers have repayment pass-books these may be retained at intervals during the year on a satisfactory test basis and agreed with ledgers. Other borrowers may be circularized with a statement of their account and asked to communicate with the society or the auditors if the entries as shown by the statement are in their view incorrect. Where these queries are not addressed direct to the auditors the society should have an appropriate procedure to ensure that the queries are promptly and fully investigated by an official of the society who is not concerned with the keeping of the accounts of borrowers or the handling of cash.

SHARES AND DEPOSITS

(30) An indication is given below of matters which the auditors will need to consider when assessing the system and deciding what tests they should apply in order to satisfy themselves on the records of shares and deposits. An effective confirmation of balances is a most important safeguard and the auditors should either carry out or supervise the carrying out of a test confirmation at least once a year.

(31) Shares may consist of subscription shares and paid-up shares; there are also term shares where the shareholder will not normally require repayment until after a specified period of years. Interest on shares or deposits may be credited to the account instead of being paid. The following should be covered by the society's system to ensure proper control:

(*a*) responsible custody of unused share and deposit pass-books, receipt forms and share certificates;

(*b*) instructions to the staff as to the making of entries in pass-books, and the issue of receipts;

(*c*) withdrawal terms, notice, specimen signatures;

(*d*) authorization of withdrawals by ledger department or against pass-book;

(*e*) records of deaths, marriages, powers of attorney and transmission of shares and deposits;

Direct transfers from one account to another should not be permitted. Transfers should be entered in a journal so that all such entries may be verified.

(*f*) comparison of the balance shown in the pass-book with that shown in the ledger account; this may be carried out continuously by retaining pass-books for comparison before return or by periodical circularization of depositors or shareholders requesting them to send in their pass-books for the purpose. It is desirable that the Society's system should provide for special arrangements to deal with withdrawals from accounts where correspondence has been returned unanswered or trace has otherwise been lost of depositors or shareholders.

(32) The records must be in such form as will enable the amount due to shareholders and depositors to be classified in the detail required by Schedule No. 6 of the annual return. The records must also provide the information required in Schedule No. 5 as to the normal rates of interest.

CASH

(33) The handling of cash is always accompanied by possibilities of error and misappropriation, concealed by 'teeming and lading', manipulation of dormant accounts and other devices. This problem is of special importance to auditors of building societies because of the large extent of the cash transactions, but it does not involve audit considerations which differ in principle from those encountered in many other businesses. In assessing the system and testing its effectiveness the auditors will need to apply rigorously their professional techniques. Discrepancies revealed by surprise cash accounts or by searching tests 'in depth' will call for exhaustive investigation.

INVESTMENTS

(34) The investment powers of building societies (including a prohibition against placing funds with a bank which has not been designated by the Chief Registrar of Friendly Societies) are governed by Sections 58 and 61. Under Section 58 the Chief Registrar of Friendly Societies has made the Building Societies (Authorized Investments) Order 1962 (S.I. 1962 No. 2044) which came into operation on 1st October, 1962. Audit procedures in relation to investments will not raise points peculiar to building societies

except that attention is drawn to the classification required under the prescribed form of balance sheet and the considerable further detail required in Schedule No. 4 and Schedule No. 8 of the annual return. These schedules fall within the scope of the auditors' report on the annual return. The investment records should be designed to enable these details to be readily available.

INTEREST AND OTHER AMOUNTS PAID BY BORROWERS

(35) The prescribed form of revenue and appropriation account requires separate disclosure of 'interest on mortgages' and 'other amounts paid by borrowers as consideration for advances'. The auditors will therefore need to satisfy themselves that the records are maintained in such a way that this important distinction is properly made in the revenue and appropriation account.

(36) Further detail is required in the annual return. Schedule No. 5 requires a statement of the normal rates of interest, the maximum interest rate charged on any mortgage during the year, and particulars of any charges made to borrowers as consideration for advances in addition to the normal interest charge. (The 'Notes for guidance' issued by the Chief Registrar of Friendly Societies state that the number of the society's rule under which such additional charges are made should be shown in the return.) This schedule does not fall within the scope of the auditors' report on the annual return but these requirements will need to be borne in mind in considering generally the adequacy of the society's records.

TAXATION

(37) Auditors will need to be conversant with the current publication setting out the special income tax arrangements for building societies and satisfy themselves that the form of the society's records makes the required information available.

TRUE AND FAIR VIEW

(38) When the auditors have completed their tests and inquiries in relation to the records and system and have ascertained that the balance sheet and revenue and appropriation account are in agreement with the records they will need to review the accounts in order to reach an opinion on whether they show the true and fair view required by the Act. This overriding requirement should govern their whole approach to the audit and the matters to be noted in the audit papers as the work proceeds. *If in any respects the auditors are not satisfied that the view presented is both true and fair it is their duty to state in their report the respects in which they are not satisfied.* Particular matters which will need consideration are referred to below.

PRESCRIBED REQUIREMENTS

(39) The following requirements have been prescribed in paragraphs 3, 4 and 5 of the Building Societies (Accounts) Regulations 1962 (S.I. 1962 No. 2042):

'3. There shall be included against every heading in:

(*a*) the revenue and appropriation account, the corresponding amounts for the immediately preceding financial year; and

(*b*) the balance sheet, the corresponding amounts at the end of the immediately preceding financial year.

'4. There shall, if it is not otherwise shown, be stated by way of note to the revenue and appropriation account every material respect in which any items shown therein are affected:

(*a*) by transactions of an exceptional or non-recurrent nature; or

(*b*) by any change in the basis of accounting.

'5. The following matters shall be stated by way of note to the balance sheet, or in a statement or report annexed thereto, if not otherwise shown:

(*a*) particulars of any moneys owing by the society in respect of deposits, loans and overdrafts which are wholly or partially secured;

(*b*) the general nature of any contingent liability not provided for, and where practicable, the estimated amount of that contingent liability if it is material;

(*c*) where practicable, the aggregate amount or estimated amount, if it is material, of contracts for capital expenditure, so far as not provided for;

(*d*) where the amounts of the separate reserves or provisions as compared with the amounts at the end of the immediately preceding financial year show any increases or decreases, the sources from which the increases have been derived and how the amounts of any decreases have been applied;

(*e*) the method of arriving at the amount at which any office premises are shown;

(*f*) the basis on which any item of income tax has been computed.'

PROVISION FOR MORTGAGE LOSSES

(40) The provision for anticipated losses on mortgages is required to be stated separately in the balance sheet as a deduction from the total amount outstanding on mortgages. The auditors will need to be satisfied that where repayments are in arrear a realistic provision is made if the security is not adequate; and even if the account is dormant interest should be accrued and the provision for mortgage losses augmented accordingly. Where arrears have been satisfied by the granting of additional advances the soundness of the debts will need special examination, including a review of transactions with those borrowers subsequent to the balance sheet date.

(41) In the 'Notes for guidance' issued by the Chief Registrar of Friendly Societies it is stated that 'the power of boards of directors to remit interest is, in many cases, limited and generally speaking arrears cannot be regarded as waived or the payment thereof postponed unless the borrower has been

so informed. The correct procedure is to show the full amount due and make separate provision for any anticipated losses. Such provision should be adequate to cover all discernible losses.'

INCOME AND EXPENDITURE

(42) It is important to note that the revenue and appropriation account is required to give a true and fair view of 'the *income and expenditure* of the society *for the financial year*'. The auditors are therefore concerned with the fair presentation of both the income and the expenditure, not merely with the resultant balance. Moreover, they are concerned with whether the items in the account relate to the financial year. In this connection special attention should be given to the following where the amounts are material:

(a) any amounts paid by borrowers, in addition to normal interest, as consideration for advances (these amounts are required to be shown in the account as a separate total);

(b) any survey fees, redemption fees or other charges which are of abnormally large amount and have been included in the items of income shown under 'Valuation fees and expenses', 'Other fees, fines, rules and pass-books' and 'Other income'.

(43) In examining such matters it is essential to consider not only their proper description (for which purpose the wording in the prescribed form of accounts may require extension or adaptation) but also whether they can properly be regarded as income 'for the financial year'.

'WINDOW DRESSING'

(44) Auditors should examine transactions which have the effect of showing as on the balance sheet date a state of affairs (particularly the society's liquidity) which is materially better than it was during the year and shortly after. Items requiring particular attention are:

(a) large deposits received shortly before the year end and repaid shortly after;

(b) large mortgage repayments received shortly before the year end and re-advanced on the same property shortly after;

(c) unusual delay until after the year end in making payments in accordance with applications received for withdrawals of shares or deposits;

(d) an abnormal year end accumulation of commitments for advances followed by the making of the advances shortly after the year end;

(e) the significance of the items in bank reconciliation statements.

OTHER MATTERS

(45) The auditors are no longer required, as they were under the previous legislation, to make the ambiguous statement that the accounts 'are in accordance with law'. They are, however, required to be satisfied and to

state in their report that the accounts are properly drawn up in accordance with the requirements of the Act and the regulations made thereunder. They will in addition need to consider all the provisions of the Act and the rules of the society which govern the operations of the society. Any failure by the directors to have regard to their fiduciary position and any acts or defaults which may render the society liable to penalties under the Act will need careful consideration by the auditors in deciding upon the terms of their report. (There is no special relationship entitling the auditors to consult or disclose information to the Chief Registrar of Friendly Societies.)

AUDITORS' REPORTS:
REPORT ON THE ANNUAL ACCOUNTS

(46) Section 81 provides that the revenue and appropriation account shall be annexed to the balance sheet to which the auditors' report shall be attached. It also provides that the revenue and appropriation account shall be approved by the board of directors before the balance sheet is signed on their behalf. Section 80 requires the balance sheet to be signed on behalf of the directors by two directors and by the manager or secretary. The auditors have no responsibility in relation to the directors' report required under Section 82; the Act contains no provision comparable with Section 163 of the *Companies Act 1948*, and accordingly information which is required to be given in the accounts is *not* permitted to be given instead in the directors' report.

(47) Where the auditors have no reservations to make in respect of any of the matters specified in Section 87 a suitable form of report would be:

Report of the auditors to the members of the . . . .
Building Society

The foregoing balance sheet and revenue and appropriation account are properly drawn up in accordance with the requirements of the *Building Societies Act 1962*, and the regulations made thereunder. In our opinion they give respectively a true and fair view of the state of the society's affairs as on . . . . and of its income and expenditure for the financial year ended on that date.

If the auditors are unable to report in those terms or find it necessary to report on any of the matters referred to in subsections (4) or (5) of Section 87 their report should be factual, specific and as brief as is consistent with conveying the essential points.

REPORT ON THE ANNUAL RETURN

(48) The annual return form prescribed by the Chief Registrar of Friendly Societies does not embody any form of wording for the auditors' report on the annual return. Their report thereon is governed by the requirements of Section 91 and it must be annexed to the annual return.

(49) Under the Building Societies (Annual Return etc.) Regulations 1962 (S.I. 1962, No. 2043) prescribing the form and content of the annual

return, paragraph 8 provides that the auditors shall not be required to deal in their report with what may conveniently be called the 'front page' or with Schedule No. 1, Sections B and C of Schedule No. 2, and Schedule No. 5. The remainder of the annual return, on which the auditors must report, consists mainly of accounts and schedules containing summarized information about which they should be able to satisfy themselves as a result of the audit procedures already suggested.

(50) Some difficulty is, however, presented by Schedule No. 3 containing the particulars required by Section 89 which relates to disclosure of advances to any director or the manager or secretary or to companies in which they are interested. The auditors will be obliged to rely upon the information given to the society by the directors and officers in accordance with the duty imposed by subsection (2) of Section 89 and it is desirable that the auditors should so indicate in their report.

(51) Where the auditors have no other reservations to make, a suitable form of report on the annual return would be:

> *Report of the auditors on the annual return of the........*
> *Building Society for the year ended.........*

In our opinion the foregoing annual return for the year ended ....(so far as we are required to report upon it) is properly drawn up in accordance with the requirements of the *Building Societies Act 1962*, and regulations made thereunder, is in agreement with the books of account and records of the society and gives a true and fair view of the matters to which it is addressed.

In relation to Section B of Schedule No. 3 we have no information other than that disclosed by the directors and officers in accordance with subsection (2) of Section 89 of the Act.[1]

We are not required to deal with the information appearing before Account No. 1 or with Schedule No. 1, Sections B and C of Schedule No 2 and Schedule No. 5 and accordingly our report does not cover those matters.

(52) If the auditors find it necessary to make other reservations their report should be factual, specific and as brief as is consistent with conveying the essential points.

(53) It is important to bear in mind that the revenue and appropriation account and the balance sheet are reproduced in the annual return as Accounts Numbers 5 and 6. If, therefore, the auditors have made any reservations in their report on the annual accounts (see above) it will be necessary for them to incorporate in their report on the annual return the terms of their report on the annual accounts.

---

1 This reservation regarding Schedule No. 3 will not be adequate if the schedule does not give all the particulars which, according to the information available to the auditors, should be given. In that event the auditors have a duty under subsection (4) of Section 89 to include in their report, so far as they are reasonably able to do so, a statement giving the required particulars.

(54) Subsection (3) of Section 14 provides that an application under the section shall be granted by the Chief Registrar of Friendly Societies if all the requirements set out in the Second Schedule are fulfilled. If all those requirements are fulfilled the Chief Registrar has no discretion to refuse. Paragraph 5 of the schedule requires the application to contain or be accompanied by the report by the auditors of the society. *The paragraph calls for a positive opinion. If therefore the auditors are not able to report in the terms required by the paragraph then they cannot give a report for the purpose of the Section 14 application.* In that event their procedure should be to inform the directors in writing that they are unable to express the opinion required under paragraph 5 of the Second Schedule.

(55) Where the auditors are satisfied that they are able to give the report it should be addressed to the society and the terms of the report should be precisely as required by the schedule:

*Report of the auditors to the.........Building Society
for the purpose of an application under Section 14 of
the Building Societies Act 1962*

In our opinion the balance of the revenue and appropriation account for the financial year ended.........represents a surplus after making any adjustments which in our opinion are necessary to provide for diminution in value of assets, or in respect of items of an exceptional or abnormal nature.

(56) The revenue and appropriation account to which the report must relate is that for the last financial year ending before the date of the application. The making of the report does not arise until after the accounts for that year have been audited. The adjustments referred to in the report are a matter for the judgment of the auditors alone.

(57) The report required by paragraph 5 of the Second Schedule is the only respect in which the auditors are concerned with an application under Section 14. There are no provisions requiring their consent to the context in which their report appears. Auditors should therefore make their report as an independent document which can accompany (as distinct from being part of) the application.

PART B
EXTRACT FROM INTERNAL CONTROL QUESTIONNAIRE

The following extract includes the most important questions appearing in the sections dealing with Personnel, Wages, Cash and Bank, and Stock in a typical Internal Control Questionnaire. It has been largely based upon a specimen questionnaire prepared by Mr. A. D. Paton, C.A., and published in *The Accountants Magazine* in 1961.

Strictly Private and Confidential – Internal Control Questionnaire

Name of Client:...

GENERAL INSTRUCTIONS

(1) Answers should be entered in columns as 'Yes', 'No', 'None', or Not Applicable ('N/A') from assistant's own tests or observations.

(2) A memorandum should be cross-referenced to this questionnaire to amplify the answer 'No' on each occasion that it appears. This cross reference should appear in the column headed 'Ref.'.

PERIODIC REVIEWS

Assistant in Charge		*Partner*	
Signature	Date	Signature	Date
....	....	....	....
....	....	....	

PERSONNEL	Year ended 19...... Yes No None N/A	Ref.	Comments
1. Does the client have an organization chart showing in outline the functions, authority and duties of executives?			
2. Have the detailed duties of the accounting staff and others in a position of trust been set out in writing?			
3. Do we have up to date copies of the documents noted in (1) and (2) above in our permanent file?			
4. Are you satisfied from your observations that the duties mentioned above are being carried out by the persons designated and are not being exceeded?			
5. When the accounting staff and other employees in a position of trust take their annual leave, do they hand over their duties completely?			

	Year ended 19......		
PERSONNEL *continued*	Yes No None N/A	Ref.	Comments

6. Are satisfactory references obtained and taken up in respect of employees appointed to positions of trust?

7. Are all employees in a position of trust covered by adequate fidelity insurance?

RECEIPTS
(i) *General*

1. Is opening of mail supervised by an official *other* than the cashier or sales ledger clerk?

2. If not already so crossed, are all cheques and postal orders immediately restrictively crossed to the client?

3. Is an abstract prepared by the person opening the mail showing –
   (*a*) cheques and postal orders received?
   (*b*) cash received?

4. (*a*) Is the abstract signed by the supervising official?
   (*b*) Is the abstract checked with the cash book by someone other than the cashier?

5. Are all monies received paid into the bank?

6. Are bank lodgments made daily?

7. Is the cashier precluded from making entries in books other than the cash book?

8. Are statements to customers issued monthly without intervention by cash department?

9. Are receipts from cash sales recorded in the cash book daily?

10. Is the entry in the cash book for cash sales supported by a clear breakdown of the sales?

| | Year ended 19...... | | | |
| | Yes No None N/A | Ref. | Comments |

RECEIPTS *continued*

11. Is there an adequate system of control over
    (*a*) receipts from rents, dividends etc.?
    (*b*) scrap, by-products etc.?
    (*c*) sales to employees?
Briefly describe the system in force.

(ii) *Cash Sales*

1. Are books of pre-numbered cash sale slips used?

2. Does the system provide for control of the issue, exchange and return of these books?

3. Is a copy of the cash sale slip given to –
    (*a*) cash desk?
    (*b*) customer?

4. Is the sales assistant who makes out the cash sale slip precluded from taking the cash from the customer?

5. Does the system provide for a check on –
    (*a*) pricing of goods?
    (*b*) prices shown on sale slips?
    (*c*) calculations and additions of sale slips?

6. Is there a proper system of recording and controlling the return or exchange of goods from customers?

7. Are sales assistants precluded from accepting goods returned?

8. Is there a central cash desk for all collections?

9. Does the customer deliver to cash desk –
    (*a*) cash sales slip?
    (*b*) cash?

10. Is a record made of cash received for every sale?

	Year ended 19......			
RECEIPTS *continued*	Yes No None N/A		Ref.	Comments

11. Are cash registers in use?
   (*a*) Do they have locked-in totals which can only be cleared by a supervisor?
   (*b*) Are the cash register rolls suitably filed in support of the total for cash sales each day?

12. Is there a set cash float for each cash office or desk?

13. Are these floats counted periodically by a supervisor? State approximate intervals between checks.

14. Are payments from the cash desks prohibited?

15. Are the cash desks cleared during business hours?

16. Is the total of cash collected reconciled daily with –
   (*a*) cash records?
   (*b*) sales records?

17. Are the reconciliations made by a person other than the cashier?

18. Is cash collected banked intact at least once per day?

19. Does the system ensure that all sale slips issued have been accounted for?

20. Is a record of 'shorts' and 'overs' kept?

21. Does the system provide for investigation of 'shorts' and 'overs'

22. Is cash received and not banked on the day of receipt –
   (*a*) kept in a safe overnight?
   (*b*) deposited in a night-safe at a bank?
   (*c*) adequately insured?

Note: Clarify any aspects of the system not covered by the above.

	Year ended 19......			
(iii) *Banking* RECEIPTS *continued*	Yes No None N/A	*Ref.*	*Comments*

(iii) *Banking*   RECEIPTS *continued*

1. Does the person who makes out the paying-in list also prepare the abstract of receipts?

2. Can the details on the counterfoil of the paying-in slip be checked against the individual entries in the cash book?

3. Is a bank reconciliation prepared monthly and filed?

4. Is the reconciliation prepared or checked by a person not concerned with the recording of bank transactions?

PAYMENTS

(i) *By Cheque*

1. Is the signing of blank cheques prohibited?

2. Is the signing of cheques restricted to the directors and secretary?

3. Do cheques require –
    (*a*) one signature?
    (*b*) two signatures?
    (*c*) more than two signatures?
    (State number and names of signatories.)

4. Is a duly authorized invoice, statement or other voucher produced in respect of each payment for which a cheque is being signed?

5. Excluding wages, national insurance, travelling and petty cash expenses, and other payments normally made by cash, are all payments made by cheque? State whether any exceptions.

6. Are all cheques (other than those for cash) suitably crossed?

7. Are 'paid' cheques returned from the bank monthly?

	Year ended 19......			
PAYMENTS *continued*	Yes No None N/A		Ref.	Comments
8. Are these cheques filed in the order in which they appear in the cash book?				
9. Are creditors' statements, advices, invoices or other vouchers of payments –				
(*a*) attached to the 'paid' cheques?				
(*b*) otherwise suitably filed to facilitate easy reference?				
(ii) *By Cash*				
1. Apart from salaries and wages, are all cash payments made from an imprest?				
2. Are vouchers or pay slips a necessary prerequisite for making cash payments?				
3. Are these vouchers and pay slips authorized by a party other than the cashier?				
4. Are these vouchers and pay slips filed in the order of payment?				
5. Is the expenditure appropriately analysed?				
6. Are refunds of expenses supported by detailed analyses with vouchers?				
7. Are these claims checked and authorized for payment by a responsible person other than the cashier or petty cashier?				
8. Is the expenditure incurred during the period of the imprest checked by the cashier before refunding the amount expended?				
9. Are checks made on the balance of cash in hand at random intervals by an independent official?				
STOCK				
1. Are all incoming goods initially received at a central depot?				

	Year ended 19......			
STOCK *continued*	Yes No None N/A	Ref.	Comments

2. Are details of all goods received recorded by the depot and advised to the –
   (*a*) department or store which ordered the goods?
   (*b*) central purchasing department?
   (*c*) warehousing and stores control department?

3. Does the system provide for the goods being checked as to quantity and quality by the ordering department, and deficiencies or surpluses, etc., advised to the stores control and central purchasing departments?

4. Are perpetual inventory records maintained for –
   (*a*) raw materials?
   (*b*) finished stock?

5. Are bin cards maintained by the stores control department?

6. Are all stock issues supported by duly authorized requisitions?

7. Are the recorded stocks regularly reconciled with the physical quantities?
   State how regularly such a check takes place.

8. Are all discrepancies discovered independently investigated?

9. Are stock records brought into line with actual quantities after discrepancies have been investigated?
   Briefly describe the procedure.

10. Is physical stock at the close of the accounting year taken by someone other than the storekeeper or persons responsible for the stock records?

11. Have we on our permanent file a copy of the staff stocktaking instructions?

	Year ended 19......			
STOCK *continued*	Yes No None N/A		Ref.	Comments

12. Do the cost records provide a check on the materials used in production?

13. Do production and sales records provide a check on quantities of finished stocks?

14. Does the system provide for the control of quantities and values of finished stock at branches, depots or departments by charging goods at selling price?

15. Do the stock records show purchase prices as well as quantities?

16. Is the stock adequately insured against loss from –
    (*a*) burglary?
    (*b*) fire?
    (*c*) storm and other risks?

17. Are records maintained of the loss of stock through wastage during production or otherwise?

18. Does the system incorporate safeguards against theft of stock by –
    (*a*) employees?
    (*b*) the public?

19. Is provision made for the writing-down of stock which has –
    (*a*) deteriorated in quality?
    (*b*) become obsolete?
    (*c*) become slow moving?
    Describe the system for detecting losses under (*a*), (*b*) and (*c*) above.

WAGES

(i) *Permanent Records*

1. Are detailed records maintained of staff engagements, resignations and dismissals?

2. Is there a scale of rates of remuneration to which reference may be made for the following rates –

	Year ended 19......			
WAGES *continued*	Yes No None N/A	Ref.	Comments	

(a) normal?
(b) bonus?
(c) overtime?

3. Is there a record of standard deductions from pay?

4. Is this record periodically checked by an independent official?

5. Is a weekly or monthly establishment roll maintained listing all members of staff?

6. Are all alterations in the roll authorized by the chief accountant or other official?

(ii) *Preparation of Payroll*

1. Are the wages of time-workers checked by reference to either –
   (a) time sheets? or
   (b) clock cards?

2. Are the wages of pieceworkers checked by reference to authorized output schedules?

3. Are bonus payments checked by reference to authorized bonus records?

4. Are the gross wages of, and deductions from, each employee independently checked by a person other than the clerk preparing the payroll?

5. Is each completed payroll examined by a senior official and authorized by him?

6. How is this authorization evidenced?

(iii) *Payment of Wages*

1. Is a cheque drawn for the exact amount of the net wages payable?

2. Are employees who have been engaged on the preparation of the payroll prevented from gaining access to the cash to be used for wages?

	Year ended 19......			
WAGES *continued*	Yes No None N/A		Ref.	Comments
3. Is cash drawn for payment of wages kept separate from other cash?				
4. Are the wages paid by a person other than those employed in the preparation of the payroll and the making up of the pay?				
5. Is the foreman present at the payout for the purpose of identifying employees?				
6. Do employees sign for their pay?				
7. Is the drawing by an employee of another's wages forbidden?				
(iv) *Unclaimed Wages*				
1. Are unclaimed wages immediately entered in a book maintained for this purpose?				
2. Is this book signed by –				
(a) the foreman present at the payout?				
(b) the clerk who was responsible for paying the wages?				
3. Does the employee or his representative sign when he eventually receives his wages?				
4. Describe the security arrangements in force regarding the holding of unclaimed wages in cash pending payment.				
(v) *General*				
1. Are advances of wages prohibited?				
2. Is such prohibition always effective?				
3. Are special deductions from wages in respect of savings etc., paid over to those in control of such funds? Describe the system.				
4. Are all such funds in the hands of employees subject to audit by us?				
5. Describe the system for payment to employees –				
(a) when they are off ill?				
(b) when they leave?				

	Year ended 19......			
WAGES *continued*	Yes No None N/A		Ref.	Comments

6. Is a surprise count ever made of cash in the hands of the wages staff, including –
    (*a*) unclaimed wages?
    (*b*) national insurance stamps?
    (*c*) employees' savings held in trust?
    (*d*) cash floats?
State how frequently such checks are carried out.

(vi) *National Insurance Contributions*

1. Is payment in respect of national insurance etc., made by –
    (*a*) bulk stamping system?
    (*b*) franking machine?
    (*c*) monthly cheque to the Ministry of Pensions and Social Security?

2. Are the national insurance cards stamped or franked regularly?

3. (*a*) Does a responsible official examine the cards periodically to see that they are all stamped up to date?
(*b*) How often does this examination take place?

4. Are there satisfactory arrangements for the stamping or franking of cards of –
    (*a*) employees on holiday?
    (*b*) employees on sick leave?
    (*c*) new employees?
    (*d*) employees who leave before pay day?
    (*e*) casual employees?

5. Is there a float of insurance stamps? (state amount).

6. Are the cards in current use insured against loss by fire and theft?

7. If a franking machine is used, is a record of machine usage kept?

| | Year ended 19...... | | | |
	Yes No None N/A	Ref.	Comments

WAGES *continued*

(vii) *P.A.Y.E. and Graduated Pension Scheme Contributions*

1. (*a*) Are standard Inland Revenue Cards used to record earnings and deductions for income tax and graduated pension contributions?
(*b*) Alternatively, has permission been received to use another system?

2. (*a*) Are payments to the Inland Revenue made monthly?
(*b*) If not, state how often payments are made.

3. Are the gross pay and tax deducted shown on tax deduction cards checked against the payroll each week?

4. Where tax deduction cards are used, are the weekly totals of the gross pay per the cards reconciled with the gross wage per the payroll?
(State whether this reconciliation is done weekly or cumulatively at the end of the year.)

5. Where tax deduction cards are used, are the weekly totals of tax deducted per the tax cards reconciled with the deductions per the payroll?
(State whether this reconciliation is done weekly or cumulatively at the end of the year.)

6. Are those responsible for preparing the reconciliations mentioned in (4) and (5) above independent of the payroll preparation?

7. Is a copy of the employer's annual return to the Inland Revenue retained for reference?

8. How does the system ensure that coding changes are notified to persons preparing the payroll?

INDEX

Account Sales, 81
Accountant,
auditor, distinguished from, 10, 17, 31, 233
prospectus, report of, in, 248, 534
unlawful acts by clients, and, 440
Accountants' Report Rules, 469 *et seq.*
Accounts, forms of, 367 *et seq.*
balance sheet, 367
capital accounts, 372, 508
holding companies, 379 *et seq.*
profit and loss account, 367
Advertising,
capital expenditure on, 148, 149
payments in advance, 146
Agent,
accounts of, 81 *et seq.*
commission, 43
stock held by, Appendix A.4
Allotment Letters,
renounceable, issue of, 322
Allowances, 86
Alterations to Plant, 148
American Auditing Procedures,
influence of, 176
Annual Accounts,
pro forma under the Companies Acts, 369 *et seq.*
Annual Return,
Building Societies Act 1962, under, 451 *et seq.*, Appendix A.17
Companies Act 1948, under, 306
Annual Statement of Business, 462
Appointment of Auditor, 206 *et seq.*
Board of Trade, by, 206
Building Societies Act 1962, under, 451 *et seq.*, Appendix A.17
Companies Act 1948, under, 206
considerations on, 232
limited company, of, 206, 232
local authorities, by, 500 *et seq.*
Public Trustee Act 1906, under, 458, qualification for, 207
Trustee Act 1925, under, 460
Apportionment,
expenditure between capital and revenue, between, 146
profit or loss prior to incorporation, to ascertain, 265
Arbitrage, 485
'Arrestable Offences'
under *Criminal Law Act 1967,* 441 *et seq.*
Articles of Association,
inspection of, by auditor, 233

Assets,
abroad, 186
balance sheet, treatment of, in, 281, 287, 372
current, 335
depreciation of, 335, 336
fixed, 157 *et seq.*, 294, Appendix A.14
local authorities, depreciation of, by, 543
neither fixed nor current, disclosure of, 289
outstanding, 144 *et seq.*
plant and machinery, 187
valuation of, 294, Appendix A.14
verification of, 156 *et seq.*
wasting, 162
Attendance at Stock-taking.
(*See* Stock-in-Trade)
Auctioneers' Accounts,
Audit of, 455
Audit,
advantages of, 10, 11, 12
balance sheet, 194 *et seq.*
cash transactions, of, 35 *et seq.*
classes of, 8
Companies Acts 1948 and *1967*
provisions as to, 10, 267
conduct of, 14
considerations on commencement of 18
continuous, 15
debentures, issue of, 253
definition of, 2
difficulties re mechanized accounting, Appendix A.6
E.D.P., of, 115
essential features of, 18
final or completed, 14
first, 18
group accounts, of, 385
impersonal ledger, of, 136 *et seq.*
interim, 15
internal, 31
limited company, of, 232
mechanized systems, 98 *et seq.*
method of work in, 30
nature and definition of, 2
objects of, 3
partial, 10
programmes, 28, 198
scope of, 18
share transfer, 243
shares, issue of, 239 *et seq.*
statutory, 8, 262 *et seq.*
trading transactions, of, 72 *et seq.*

685

Audit, (*continued*)
   working papers, 199, 230
Audit, Internal,
   duties of staff, 32
   internal check distinguished from, Appendix A.2
   recommendation of Institute of Chartered Accountants on, Appendix A.2
Audit Fee,
   basis of charge for, 232
   outstanding, 141
Audit Programme, 28 *et seq.*, 198
Audit Trail, 109, 110, 117, 124, 126, 127
Auditor,
   accountant, distinguished from, 10, 17, 31, 98, 209, 233
   agent of members, as, 216
   appointment of (*see* 'Appointment of Auditor')
   change of, 18, 235
   duties of (*see below*)
   indemnity for misfeasance by, 307
   inspection of books and documents by, 233
   joint, 215
   liability of (*See* 'Liability of Auditor)
   lien of, 229
   limited company of, 206, 232
   local, 215
   officer of company, as an, 216, 395, 396, 439, 440
   persons not qualified to act as, 206
   powers of, 218
   qualifications required of under:
      Building Societies Act, 451 *et seq.*, Appendix A.17
      Companies Acts, 206
      Solicitors Acts, 464
      stockbrokers' and stockjobbers', rules, 478
   qualities required of, 32
   removal of, 210
   remuneration of, under Companies Acts, 210, 232, 270
   remuneration of, under *Public Trustee Act 1906*, 459
   report of (*See* 'Auditor's Report')
   rights of, 218, 233
   status of, 216
   statutory and internal, 32, Appendix A.2
Auditor, duties of, 220 *et seq.*
   Companies Acts, under, 222
   directors' remuneration, relating to, 310
   legal decisions, as to, 222 *et seq.*, 399 *et seq.*

Auditor, (*continued*)
   loans to officers and directors, as to, 297
   members, to, 218, 432
   petty cash, 57
   prospectus, as to, 223, 534 *et seq.*
   secret reserves, as to, 414, 439
   statutory report, in regard to, 223, 262
   stock-in-trade, in relation to, 175
   third parties, to, 432
   wages, in relation to, 49
Auditors and Directors,
   difference of opinion between, 212 *et seq.*
Auditor's Report, 224, 227
   Counsel's opinion on, 386, Appendix A.8
   local audit, in cases of, 215
   sole traders and partnerships, 424
Auditor's Reports and Certificates, 220, 224
   Building Societies Act 1962, under 451 *et seq.*, Appendix A.17
   Companies Acts 1948 and *1967*, under, 220 *et seq.*, 268, 273
   debenture holders' right to copy of, 228
   general meeting, must be read at, 228
   group accounts, as to, 219, 387
   Judicial Trustees Act 1896, under, 460
   loans to directors, relating to, 305
   local authorities, 521
   members' right to copy of, 228
   prospectus, in, 248, 534 *et seq.*
   Public Trustee Act 1906, under, 458
   publication of, 227
   qualification of, 226
   sole traders and partnerships, 424 *et seq.*, Appendix A.9
   Solicitors Acts, under, 464
   trust accounts, 458
   underwriters' accounts, on, 497
   unit trusts, 498
Audits,
   special points, 450 *et seq.*

Back Duty,
   investigations in connection with, 565
'Back-up' Arrangements, 135
Bad and Doubtful Debts, 91 *et seq*
   auditor's liability in connection with, 407
   provision for, 93, 153
   vouching of dividends from, 53
Balance Sheet,
   and annual return, 306
   audit, 197 *et seq.*
   auditor's report on, 220, 224, 227
   banking company, of, 227

Balance Sheet, (*continued*)
contents of, 250
debenture holder's right to, 228
definition of, 372
events after date of, 192
form of, 372, 380
group accounts, 379
holding company, of, 286
investigation, examination of, in course of, 526
local authorities, of, 518
members' right to copy of, 227
provisions, in, 281, 282, 289
publication of, 228
relationship to profit and loss account, 196
signing of, by directors, 227, 280
statutory requirements as to, 280 *et seq.*
Balance Sheet Audit, 194 *et seq.*
Bank,
accounts, audit of, 450
deposit, interest on, 53
investigation on behalf of, 553
payments into, 54
payments out of, 55
statements, 54
Bank Balance,
reconciliation of, with cash book, 56
verification of, 56
Bank Charges and Commission,
vouching, 43
Bank Loans and Overdrafts,
disclosure of, 252
Bank Statements,
auditor's liability for omission to examine, 420
cash book, checking with, 54 *et seq.*
investigations, examinations in connection with, 559
reconciliation with cash book, 56
Banking Companies,
disclosure exemptions of, 221, 222, 225, 271, 293, 324
Bearer Securities,
issue of, 240
verification of, 171
Bills of Exchange,
(*See* Bills Payable)
(*See* Bills Receivable)
Bills Payable,
vouching, 44
Bills Receivable, 185
contingent liability on, 143, 186
discounted, 54, 94
dishonoured, 44, 54
verification of, 185
vouching of, 44, 54
Blank Transfers, 245
Block Diagram, 116

Bond Investment Business, 462
Bonus Shares,
capitalization of reserves for issue of 322
renounceable allotment letter, issue by means of, 322
verification, 170
Book Debts,
(*See* Bad and Doubtful Debts)
sale of business, treatment of, on, 265
verification of, 90
Books,
auditor's report to members upon, 220, 268
Companies Acts 1948 and *1967*, requirements as to, 267 *et seq.*
falsification, investigation in cases of, 558
list of, 18
of account, 267
shares, relating to, 243
Bought Day Book,
audit of, 72
bought ledger, posting to, 87
invoices, vouching by means of, 73, 74, 541
Bought Ledger,
audit of, 87
verification of balances on, 87
Bought Returns Books, 77, 87
Breach of Trust,
(*See* 'Liability of Auditors')
(*See* 'Liability of Directors')
British Standards Institute, 22
Brokerage,
shares, on placing of, 262
Building Societies,
accounts, audit of, 451 *et seq.*
auditor, qualifications of, 209, 451
Building Societies Act 1962, provisions of, 451
verification of shares and deposits, 172
Buildings,
verification of, 167
vouching expenditure on, 41

Calls,
bonus, discharged by means of, 321
paid in advance, 246
Capital (*and see* Shares),
alteration of, 247
classes of, 235
increase of, 248
interest paid out of, 247
local authorities, raising by, 509
losses of, 330 *et seq.*
reduction of, 248
stamp duty on, 259

Capital Expenditure,
    allocation of, 146
    commitments for, statement in
        balance sheet, of, 286
    definition of, 40, 146
    investigations, verification for pur-
        poses of, 531
    vouching, 40
Capital Expenditure Authorized,
    disclosure of, 296
Capital Gains Tax, 13, 458
Capital Profits,
    application of, 355
    division of, when permissible, 357
Capital Redemption Reserve Fund, 237
Capital Reserve
    (*See* 'Reserves and Reserve Funds')
Card Ledgers, 97
Carriage,
    vouching of expenditure on, 45
Case Law affecting Auditors, 418 *et seq.*
Cash Book,
    bank statements, reconciliation with,
        56
Cash Discount, 52, 76
Cash Sales, 52, 80
Cash Transactions, 35 *et seq.*
    audit of, 35
    cash balances, verification of, 56
    internal check in relation to, 35
    payments, 36
    petty, 56 *et seq.*
    receipts, 35
    sales, 52, 78
Certificate,
    accounts of branches not visited, 224
    assets deposited with bankers etc.,
        of, 157, 170
    bank balance, of, 57
    Building Societies Act 1962, statutory
        form of, under 452, Appendix A.17
    capital expenditure, of, 147
    inscribed stocks, as to, 171
    land registry, 168
    local authorities, suggested form
        of, for, 523
    mortgaged property, verification by,
        168
    pawned stocks, for, 494
    profits for insertion in prospectus,
        of, 533
    securities, verification by, 169
    Solicitors' Acts, form of, under,
        472 *et seq.*
    trust accounts, 458
Certified and Corporate Accountants,
    Association of,
    recommendations relating to changes
        in purchasing power, Appendix
        A.15

Charges,
    balance sheet, statement in, 285
    registration of, 252
Chartered Accountants,
    The Institute of, statements on,
        (for full list, *see* p. 570, Appendix
        A.)
    accounting principles, 280
    auditor and stock-in-trade, 175
    auditor's remuneration, 210
    balance sheet date, events after,
        192
    clients' unlawful acts, 440
    depreciation of fixed assets, 295
    directors' benefits, auditor's duty as
        to, 275
    internal audit, 31
    internal control, 22, Appendix A.2
    other duties of accountants, 209
    provisions, presentation of, in bal-
        ance sheet, 290
    report on accounts of sole traders or
        partnerships, 424
    valuation of investments, 173 *et seq.*
    working papers, 230
Check Digits, 123
Cheques
    unendorsed, as vouchers, 37
Circularization of Debtors, 91
City Code on Take-overs and Mergers,
    549 *et seq.*, 627 *et seq.*
**City of London Real Property Co.
    Ltd,** 212 *et seq.*
Clients' Unlawful Acts, 440
Code Napoleon, 87
Code Numbers, 137, Appendix A.6
Collateral Security,
    debentures as, 256
Commission,
    bank, 43
    consignment account, on, 81
    receivable, outstanding, 145
    share placing on, 260
    travellers, 43, 141
    underwriting, 259
Company Law Committee, 353, 357
Computer Audit Programs, 133 *et seq.*
Computers, 115 *et seq.*
Consignments,
    goods on, 81 *et seq.*
Consolidated Accounts,
    (*See* Group Accounts)
Consultants and Auditors,
    Relationship between, 214, 215
Containers,
    accounts for, 85
Contingent Liabilities,
    balance sheet, treatment in, 143,
        285
Continuous Audit, 14, 31

Contracts, 235
contingent liability, arising on, 143
forward, 77, 83
Control Accounts, 96
Copyright,
assignment of, 190
valuation of, 167
verification of, 193
Corporation Tax, 311, 324 *et seq.*, **335**
Corporation Tax,
future, 290
vouching payment of, 46
Credit Sales,
audit of, 51, 78
Creditors,
bought ledger, audit of, 87
total account, 96
Cumulative Preference Shares,
dividend, arrears of, requirements of
Companies Acts as to, 286
Currency Debasement and Inflation,
accounting for (*See* Purchasing
Power Accounting)
Current Assets, 162
Customs Duties,
vouching, 45
Cut-off Procedure, 75, 80

Debentures,
accounts, rights of debenture holders
to copy of, 228
collateral security for a loan, as 256
definition of, 251
discount, issued at, 255
interest on, paid out of capital, 247
irredeemable, 258
issue of, 253
perpetual, 258
premium, issued at, 255
premium, repayable at, 256
redemption of, 257
registration of, 253, 255
trustees for holders of, 253
vouching of, 253
Debtors,
bad and doubtful debts, 91 *et seq.*,
153, 407
balances, verification of, 90
circularization of, 91, Appendix A.7
total account, for, 96
Defalcations,
investigation of, 558
nature of, 3
Deferred Revenue Expenditure, 147
Deposits, Building Society, 172
Depreciation, 162, Appendix A.14
annuity system, 165
assets, current, 162
fixed, 157
wasting, 162

Depreciation, (*continued*)
assets of local authorities, 520
causes of, 164
copyrights, 167
definition of, 162
depletion unit system, 166
depreciation fund system, 166
excessive treatment of, 289
fixed instalment system, 165, 167
fluctuation, distinguished from, 164
freehold land and buildings, 288,
Appendix A.14
fund, 165
goodwill, Appendix A.14
inflation, effect of, on, 159 *et seq.*,
Appendix A.15
insurance policy system, 166
investments, 169
leasehold land and buildings, Appendix A.14
legal aspects of, 335 *et seq.*
legal decisions, affecting, 335
local authorities' accounts, treatment in, 520
machine hour system, 166
mines, oil wells and quarries, of, 164
obsolescence, 165
patents, plant and machinery, Appendix A.14
provision for, 165, *et seq.*
recommendations of Institute of
Chartered Accountants on, Appendix A.14
reducing instalment system, 165
revaluation, an alternative to, 166
statement of, in balance sheet, 294
straight line system, 165
tools, vehicles, etc., Appendix A.14
trust and finance companies, investments of, 496
Depth Checking (*See* Vouching in
Depth)
Dilapidations,
leasehold property, of, 167
Directors,
accounts, responsibility for, 341
age limit to appointment of, 314
auditors' duties in regard to remuneration of, 308
benefits, 272 *et seq.*
company, nature of relationship
with, 306
contract with company, interest in
to be disclosed, 306
disqualification of, 314
emoluments, disclosure of, 272 *et seq.*
indemnities for negligence by, 308
liabilities of, 306 *et seq.*, 341, 362
loans to, 297
loss of office, payments for, 314

Directors, (*continued*)
managing, 317
minute book, for meetings of, 318
misfeasance, liability for, 308
number, minimum of for company, 306
pensions, 272 *et seq.*
qualification, share holding of, 314
removal of, retirement etc., 314, 315
remuneration of, 272, 310, 319
report by, 302
remuneration of, counsel's opinion on, 382
secretary, sole director cannot be, 306, 318
service contracts with, 307
tax-free payments, 314
travelling expenses, of, 317
Directors' Emoluments Waived,
disclosure of, 313
Directors' interests in Shares and Debentures,
register of, 307
Directors' Report,
audit approach to, 304 *et seq.*
Discount,
bills receivable, on, 44
cash, 52, 76
debentures, on, 255
debts collected for vendor of business, on, 266
improper manipulation of, 90, 559
provision for, 153
receivable, 40
shares on, 242, 281
trade, 76
verification of, 90
Discount Companies,
disclosure exemptions, 221, 222, 225, 271, 293, 324
District Auditor,
appointment of, 502
duties of, 502 *et seq.*
Distringas,
notices in lieu of, 246
Dividends, 341 *et seq.*
arrears of, 285, 362
bad debts, on, 53
capital, in case of losses, of, 335 *et seq.*
capital paid out of, 362
capital profits, when available for, 355 *et seq.* 358
cumulative preference, 285, 362
final, 361
income tax, treatment of deductions of, 328
interim, 359
outstanding, 145
payment of, banking arrangements for, 364

Dividends, (*continued*)
preference, 343, 362
reserve for equalisation of, 365
revenue profits, when available for, 330 *et seq.*
scrip, 363
unclaimed, 365
vouching, 52, 53, 364
Dividends,
tax free, disclosure of, 362
Divisible profits, 330 *et seq.*
Documents of Title,
verification, by means of, 167 *et seq.*
Double Taxation Relief,
disclosure of, 325
Double Account System,
local authorities, use of by, 508
Duties of Directors and Auditors,
relationship between, 434
Electronic Data Processing, 115
controls, 118
Employees,
loans to, 184
Endowment Policies, 186
Errors,
clerical, 6
commission, of, 6
compensating, 8
detection of, 5
in preparation of wages sheets, 46
omission, of, 6
principle, of, 7
stocktaking, in connection with, 178
Estate Agents,
accounts, audit of, 535
Estimation Sampling (*See* Statistical Sampling Techniques)
Etiquette,
events occurring after balance sheet date, 192
professional, 28, 214, 215
'Exchange Accountant', 491
Executors,
accounts, audit of, 13, 455
Exempt Private Company,
repeal of status of, 208
Fees,
auditors, of, 210, 232, 270
directors, of, 272, 310, 319
transfer, 243
Felony (*See* Misdemeanour and Felony)
Finance Companies,
accounts, audit of, 496
Fixed Assets, 157, 294
Fixtures and Fittings,
depreciation of, 43
vouching, 43
Flow Charting,
21 *et seq.*, 29, 69, 101 *et seq.*, 114, 116

Forecasts (*See* Profit Forecasts, Reports on)

Foreign Assets,
verification of, 189

Foreign Businesses,
accounts, audit of, 297

Foreign Companies,
accounts of, 297

Foreign Currency Transactions, 451

Forged Transfers, 245

Form of accounts, 367 *et seq.*

Formation Expenses,
(*See* Preliminary Expenses)

Forward Purchases, 77

Forward Sales, 83

Fractions, 171

Fraud,
auditors' liability, for failure to discover, 402
classes of, 3
detection of, 3
in connection with:
  allowances, 86
  bad debt dividends, 94
  bank balance, 56
  cash, misappropriation of, 156
  improper inflation of values, 157
  investigation, in cases of, 558
  investments, 156
  ledger balances, 31
  loose leaf ledgers, 97
  machine accounting and, Appendix A.6
  petty cash, 57
  postage book, 61
  purchases, 561
  stock-in-trade, 399, 402
  substitution, by means of, 156
  teeming and lading, 514, 559
  wages, 47

Freehold Properties,
valuation of, 167
verification of, 167
vouching expenditure on, 41

Freight Accounts, 45

Freight and Carriage,
outstanding, 140
vouching, 45

Furniture,
verification of, 188
vouching, 43

General Ledger,
(*See* Impersonal Ledger)

General Meetings,
auditors' power to attend, 220

Goods,
loan on, 183
misappropriation of, 3
on consignment, 81

Goods, (*continued*)
on sale or return, 81
paid for in advance, 88
stock of (*See* Stock-in-trade)

Goods Inwards Book,
internal check, in connection with, 72
verification of bought invoices, by means of, 74, 530

Goodwill,
advertising, arising from, 148
adjustment of, 265, 266
group accounts, in 388, 390
verification of, 191

Gross Profit,
investigations, use of, in, 526
percentage of, on turnover, 360, Appendix A.3

Ground Rents,
verification of, 168

Group Accounts, 379 *et seq.*
audit of, 386
auditor's duty in relation to, 220, 386, 391
auditor's report, form of, 387
consolidation of, accounts for purpose of, 388
counsel's opinion on auditor's report, 383, 388
form and contents of, 380
preparation of, requirements relating to 389 *et seq.*

Guarantee,
loan secured by, verification of, 184

Hash Totals, 123

Hire-Purchase Contracts,
sales under, 83
vouching payments under, 42

Holding Company,
balance sheet of, 285
definition of, 379
group accounts of, 379
loans to subsidiaries, 185

Impersonal Accounts, 136

Impersonal Ledger, 136 *et seq.*
outstandings, methods of dealing with, 138 *et seq.*
postings to, 137

Imprest System
for petty cash, 58

Income and Expenditure,
account, use of, 367
local authorities, of, 513 *et seq.*

Income Tax,
dividends, deduction from, 328
profit and loss account, in 269
provision for, 328
treatment in accounts, 324 *et seq*, 458
vouching payment of, 46

Industrial Insurance Business, 462
Industrial Insurance Commissioner, 462
Inspectors,
  companies' affairs, statutory investigation of, by, 558
Institute of Chartered Accountants,
  (See Chartered Accountants)
Institute of Municipal Treasurers and Accountants, The, 519
Insurance,
  life policies as security for loans, 184
  paid in advance, 146
  policies, examination of, 188
  policy system of depreciation, Appendix A.14
  provision for advance premiums, 146
  vouching premiums, 43
Insurance Companies,
  accounts, audit of, 460
  disclosure exemptions, 271, 272, 293, 324
Interest,
  bank deposit, on, 53
  calls paid in advance, on, 247
  loans, on 53, 142
  outstanding, 145
  overdraft, on, 43
  payable, out of capital, 247
  purchase consideration, on, in lieu of profits, 265
  suspense account, 181
Internal Audit,
  (See Audit, Internal)
Internal Check,
  appraisal of system of, 18
  balance sheet audit and, 204
  definition of, 4, Appendix A.2
  in relation to:
    banks, 450
    building societies, 451
    cash, 35, 89
    credit sales, 78, 90
    invoices and statements, 38
    mechanised systems, 99
    payments, 36
    petty cash, 59
    purchases, 72
    purchases returns, 77
    receipts, 50
    sales ledger, 89
    sectional balancing, 96
    wages, 46
  internal audit distinguished from, Appendix A.2
Internal Control and Check, 99, Appendix A.2
re computers, 118
Internal Control Questionnaire,
  19 et seq., 27, 29, 35, 69, 127, 673 et seq.

Investigations, 524 et seq.
  bank, on behalf of, 553
  classes of, 524
  Companies Acts 1948 and 1967 under, 561
  company, promotors of, for, 534
  fraud, in connection with, 558
  investors, on behalf of, 516, 555
  nature of, 524
  partner, incoming for, 552
  purchaser of a business, for, 526
  recommendations of Institute of Chartered Accountants on, Appendix A.11
  shares for purpose of valuation of, 556
  taxation liability, in connection with, 565
  trusts, 459
Investments,
  balance sheet treatment in, 173, 286, 287
  disclosure of, 292, 293
  in respect of reserve funds, 151
  income from, 52
  loans, on verification of, 183
  provision for fall in value of, 152
  purchased 'cum div.', 53
  sale of, 54
  sold 'ex div.', 53
  valuation of, 173
  verification of, 169 et seq.
  verification of uncompleted transactions, 171
  vouching purchase of, 43
Invoice Book
  (See Bought Journal)
Invoices,
  fraud, by omission of, 404
  internal check in relation to, 39
  post dated, 74
  reference to Goods Inwards Book, 74
  vouching, 74
I O U's, 61

Jenkins Committee
  (See Company Law Committee)
Joint Auditors, 215
Journal,
  use of, 86, 137
  vouching, 86

Keyboard Accounting Machines, 105, Appendix A.6
  proof systems, 106
  types of error, 105

Land Registry Certificate,
  verification, by means of, 168, 169

Leasehold Property, 41, 173
Leases,
  redemption of, 186
  short and long, disclosure of, 294
Ledgers,
  bought, 87
  card, 97
  checking, 87
  fraud in connection with, 30
  impersonal, 136
  loose leaf, 97
  sales, 89
Legal Decisions,
  relating to:
    ascertainment of profits, 330
    capital profits distributed, 355 *et seq.*
    divisible profits, 332
    liability of auditors, 399
    losses of capital not made good, 336 *et seq.*
Legal Expenses,
  outstanding, 141
  vouching, 41
Liabilities,
  balance sheet, in 281, 389
  bills receivable discounted, in respect of, 186
  contingent, 143
  outstanding, 138 *et seq.*
  provision for, 150 *et seq.*
  sale of business, treatment of, 267
Liability of Auditor, 394 *et seq.*
  assets, for omission to verify, 61, 406
  bad and doubtful debts, 407
  civil, 395
  clients' unlawful acts, 440
  common law, under, 394, 420
  criminal, 395, 414, 440
  false statements in certificates, etc. for, 395, 396, 414
  for failure to report to shareholders, 399
  frauds, for non-detection of, 404, 420
  legal decisions, affecting, 399 *et seq.*
  members, as agent of, 216
  misfeasance for, 216, 399, 408, 417, 434
  negligence for, 394, 399, 406, 407, 420
  officer of the company, as 216
  petty cash, 406
  statute, under, 395
  stock-in-trade, as to, 402
  third parties, to, 429, 526
  work-in-progress, as to, 417
Liability of Directors,
  breach of trust, for, 306
  misfeasance, for, 306

Liability of Directors, (*continued*)
  statutory offences, for, 306
Lien,
  auditors', 229
Liquidation,
  treatment of surplus assets on, 322
Loans,
  bill of sale, on security, of, 183
  directors, to, 297
  employees to, 184
  goods on security of, 183
  interest on, 53, 143, 181
  investments, on security of, 183
  life policies, on, security of, 184
  local authorities, to, 173
  mortgage, on security of, 182
  officers to, 297
  personal guarantee, on security of, 184
  secured, 181
  subsidiaries, to, 185
  verification of, 182
  vouching, 42
Local Auditor,
  appointment of, 215
Local Authorities,
  Accounts and Audit of, 500 *et seq.*
  loans to, 173
Loose-Leaf Ledgers, 97
Loose Plant and Tools, 187
Loss of Office,
  payments of directors for, 314

Machinery,
  (*See* Plant and Machinery)
Materiality in Accounts, 300 *et seq.*
Mechanized and Electronic Data Processing Systems, 98 *et seq.*, Appendix A.6
  development of, 98
  internal control, 99
  keyboard systems, 105
  local authorities, use by, 496
  methods of proof, 105
  punched cards, 109
  purchases records, 102
Members,
  liability of, in cases of dividends paid out of capital, 362
  minute book, 319
  nature of relationship of auditor with, 216
  register of, 240
  rights of alteration of, 247
Memorandum of Association,
  inspection of, by auditor, 233
Minute Books,
  directors, of, 239, 318
  members, of, 319

Misappropriation,
goods and money, of, 3, 157
Misdemeanour and Felony,
abolition of distinction between, 441
Misfeasance,
auditor's liability for, 216, 399 *et seq.*, 420 *et seq.*
director's liability for, 306
Mortgaged Property,
verification of, 168
Mortgages,
balance sheet, disclosure in, 252
deeds, custody of, Appendix A.17
deeds, examination of, 42, 182, Appendix A.17
definition of, 251
interest on, 53
loans secured by, 42, 182, 510
registration of, 253
second, 183
Motor Vehicles, 189

National Insurance Cards,
examination of, 50
Negligence,
auditor's liability for, 394, 399, 406, 407, 420
Nominal Accounts, 136
Nominal Ledger
(*See* Impersonal Ledger)

Obsolescence,
depreciation, arising from, 155, 175 *et seq.*
'Off-line' Peripherals, 124
Office Furniture,
vouching of expenditure on, 43
'On-line' Input, 117
'On-line' Output, 135
Operational Research, 17
Option,
underwriters, for unissued shares, 260
Option Dealing, 486
Outstanding Liabilities and Assets, 138
Oversea Companies,
balance sheet and accounts of, 297
Ownership of Records, 229

Partner, Incoming,
investigation of behalf of, 552
Partners' Drawings,
vouching payment of, 46
Partnership,
audit of accounts of, 10
Pass Book,
(*See* Bank Statements)
Patents,
verification of, 42, 190

Payments,
internal check in relation to, 36
vouching, 37
Pension Scheme Contributions re Directors, disclosure of, 277, 382
Percentage Sampling
(*See* Statistical Sampling Techniques)
Personal Accounts, 136
Personal Ledgers,
internal check in relation to, 27
sectional balancing of, 96 *et seq.*
verification of balances on, 91
P.E.R.T.
(*See* Programme Evaluation and Review Technique)
Petty Cash, 57 *et seq.*
auditors' liability for omission to verify, 61, 406
cheques drawn for, 44
imprest system for, 58
internal check in relation to, 59
postage, and, 60
verification of balances of, 61, 406
vouching, 44, 61, 493
Plant and Machinery,
expenditure on alterations to, 148
sale of, 80
verification of, 187
vouching expenditure on, 41
Pledge,
loans secured by, 183, 410
Policies of Insurance,
debentures, for repayment of, 256
depreciation, system of, 166
loans on security of, 184
sinking fund, for redemption of debentures, 258
verification of, 188
Postage Book,
audit of, 60
Precedent,
doctrine of judicial, 331, 332, 394, 395
Preliminary Expenses,
balance sheet, to be specified in, 281
expenditure on, 149, 259
statutory report, to be stated in, 262
vouching, 261
shares, discharged by issue of, 241
writing off, 259
Premium,
debentures issued at, 255
debentures repayable at, 256
redemption of shares, on, 237
shares issued, at, 241
Price/Earnings Ratio, 557
Private Firm,
audit of accounts of, 11
Private Individuals,
audit of accounts of, 12

Private Ledger, 136
Profit and Loss Account,
  auditor's obligation to report on, 220, 280, 367, 436
  auditor's remuneration, in 210
  balance sheet, must be annexed to, 228
  form of, 367, 369
  statutory requirements as to contents of, 269 *et seq.*
Profit Forecasts, Reports on, 549 *et seq.*
Profits,
  ascertainment of, 330
  capital, 355
  divisible, 330 *et seq.*, 358
  inflation of, 167
  prior to incorporation, 264
  promotion, 497
Program,
  computer, 116
Programme,
  (*see* Audit)
  for balance sheet audit, 197
Programme Evaluation and Review Technique, 17, 18
Programming Languages, 134
Prospectus, 248
  examination of, 234
  reports in, 223, 248, 534 *et seq.*
  statement in lieu of, 248
Provisions, 152
  audit fee, 141
  auditor's duty and, 152
  bad debts, for, 93, 153
  definition of, 152, 290
  depreciation of fixed assets for, 290, Appendix A.14
  dilapidation claim for, 170
  discounts, for, 153
  investments, for fall in value of, 154
  loan interest, 142
  maintenance of plant, for, 150
  reserve, distinguished from, 151
  taxation, 142
  travellers' expenses and commission, 141
Public Trustee,
  audit of trust accounts by, 458
Punched Card Systems of Accounting, 109
  proving accuracy of input, 111
Purchase of Business, 264
  apportionment of profit or loss prior to incorporation, 265
  investigation re, 526
  receipts and payments on behalf of vendors, 266
Purchase Tax,
  disclosure of on invoices, 80

Purchases, 72 *et seq.*
  bought day book, 72
  forward, 77
  internal check as regards, 72
  investigations, examination of invoices in, 560
  outstandings, 139
  vouching, 75
Purchases Returns, 77
Purchasing-power Accounting, 159 *et seq.*

Quotations Department of Stock Exchange,
  requirements of, 540 *et seq.*

Rates,
  local authorities, income from, 514
  outstanding, 140
  payments in advance of, 145
'Reasonableness' Checks, 117, 118, 123, 133
Receipts,
  internal check in relation to, 35
  issue of, by travellers, 52
  spoilt, treatment of, 51
  vouching of, 50
Receipts and Payments Account,
  difference between and profit and loss account, 361
'Recklessness', Legal Interpretation of, 397, 398, 537
Redeemable Preference Shares, 237
Register,
  charges of, 252, 255
  deeds of, Appendix A.17
  large holdings of voting shares, of, 243
  members, of, 243, 244
  transfers, of, 243
Registered Stocks and Shares,
  verification of, 171
Rent,
  outstanding, 140
  paid in advance, 145
Rents Receivable,
  outstanding, 145
  vouching income from, 53
Repairs and Renewals,
  balance sheet, treatment of provision for, in, 296
  provision for, 149
  treatment of expenditure on, 149
  wages of own workmen on, 147
Replacement Costs, Accounting for,
  (*See* Purchasing-power Accounting)
Report,
  auditor, of (*See* Auditor's Report)
  directors', 302
  late auditor's, 235
  prospectus in (*See* Prospectus, Reports in)

Report, (*continued*)
  statutory, 262
Research Foundation of the Institute of Chartered Accountants, The, 160
Reserves and Reserve Funds,
    150 *et seq.*, 319 *et seq.*
  additions or withdrawals, treatment of, 290, 323
  auditor's duty and, 151
  balance sheet, in, 283, 290
  capital redemption reserve fund, 237
  capital reserve, definition of, 151
  capital reserve, non-disclosure and treatment of, 291, 292
  capital reserve account, 321
  capitalization of, 365
  disclosures of, 323
  dividends, equalization of, 365
  legal decisions, affecting, 222
  liquidation, treatment on, 322
  provisions, distinguished from, 150
  redemption funds for debentures, 257, 319
  reserve, definition of 150, 289
  reserve fund, definition of, 150, 319
  revenue, reserve, definition of, 150, 281
  revenue reserves, use of, 151
  secret, 222, 323, 414, 439
  taxation treatment of, 324 *et seq.*
Returned Cheques,
  bad and doubtful debts, in connection with, 94
  investigations for fraud, need to examine in cases of, 560
  record in cash book of, 55
  vouchers, as substitute for, 45
Returns,
  purchases, 77
  sales, 84
Revaluations,
  legal decisions affecting, 347, 353
  reserve arising thereon, 290
Revenue Expenditure,
  allocation as, 146
  deferred, 147
  definition of, 146
  local authorities, of, 517

Salaries,
  vouching of, 44
Sale or Return
  goods on, 80
Sales, 78 *et seq.*
  capital assets of, 86
  cash, 52, 80
  credit, 51, 78
  day book, 78
  fictitious, 529
  fraud by inflation of, 529

Sales, (*continued*)
  future delivery, for, 83
  goods on consignment, of, 81
  hire purchase, 83
  internal check in connection with, 78
  investigation, examination in cases of, 529
  ledger, 89 *et seq.*
  ledger not kept, 79
Sales Returns, 84
Sampling
  (*See* Statistical Sampling Techniques)
Scrip Dividends, 363
Secretary of Company,
  appointment of, 318
  statutory requirements as to, 306, 318
Sectional Balancing, 96
Securities,
  banks, of, 450
  building societies, of, 453
  finance companies of, 496
  legal decisions, relating to, 409, 438
  stockbrokers of, 488
  stockjobbers of, 494
  trust accounts, of, 451
  trust and finance companies of, 496
  verification of, 42
Securities and Exchange Commission
  (**S.E.C.**), 176
Security in E.D.P. System, 129 *et seq.*
'Separate Designated Account', 472 *et seq.*
Sequence checks, 123
Service Bureaux, Computer, 129
Share Premium Account,
  application of, 241
Share Transfer Audit, 243
Shareholders
  (*See* Members)
Shares
  alteration to members' rights, 247
  bearer warrants, 240
  blank transfers of, 245
  bonus issue of, 237, 241, 321
  books, 243
  calls paid in advance on, 246
  cash issued for, 239
  certificates, examination of, 170
  classes of, 235 *et seq.*
  commission on placing of, 260
  commission on underwriting, 260
  consideration other than cash, issued for, 240
  deferred, 238
  discount, issued at, 242
  distinguished from stock, 238
  finance company, treatment in accounts of, 496
  forged transfers of, 245

Shares, (*continued*)
founders', 238
issue of, 239 *et seq.*
management, 238
ordinary, 238
partly paid, liability in respect of, 144
preference, cumulative, 235
redeemable, 237
premium, issued at, 241
registered, 171
stock, conversion into, 238
stock, distinguished from, 238
subsidiary company in, 379
transfer of, 243
trust company, treatment in accounts of, 496
valuation of, 173, 497, 557
verification of, 169
warrants, 240
Shipping Companies, Disclosure Exemptions, 221, 222, 225, 272, 293, 324
Sinking Funds,
debenture redemption for, 186, 257, 320
Sleeping Partner,
audit on behalf of, 12
Software 'packages', 134
Solicitors,
accounts, audit of, 464 *et seq.*
Solicitors' Accounts (Deposit Interest) Rules, 472 *et seq.*
Solicitors' Accounts Rules, 464 *et seq.*
Solicitors' Trust Accounts Rules, 464 *et seq.*
Special Reports Required of Accountants, 526, Appendix A.12
Statement in Lieu of Prospectus, 248
Statistical Sampling Techniques, Use of, 63 *et seq.,* 103
Statutory Audit, 261
Statutory Meeting, 223
Statutory Report, 223
Stock Exchange,
contingent liability for speculative transactions on, 144
permission to deal on, 240, 538
requirements re prospectuses, 539 *et seq.*
share transfer audit, requirements as to, 243
Stock Exchange (London),
accounts, rules as to preparation of by members, 478
Stock-in-Trade, 175 *et seq.*
auditor's duty in relation to, 175 Appendix A.3
basis of valuation, 179
consignment, on, 81, Appendix A.3
customers, in hands of, 80

Stock-in-Trade, (*continued*)
cut-off procedure, Appendix A.3, A.4.
method of taking, 178, Appendix A.3, A.4.
professional valuation of, Appendix A.3
recommendations of Institute of Chartered Accountants as to valuation of, Appendix A.3, A.4
stores of fuel etc., 180
valuation of, 179
verification of, 175
Stockbrokers,
accounts, audit of, 478
Stockjobbers,
accounts, audit of, 478, 494
Stocktaking Procedures,
physical observation of, 175 *et seq.,* Appendix A.4
Subsidiary Companies,
(*See* Holding Company)
Subsidiary Companies, Investments in, 292, 293
Surveyors,
accounts, audit of, 455
Systems Analysts, 116

Tax Reserve Certificates,
verification of, 172
Taxation,
accounts, treatment in, 324 *et seq.*
auditor's duties as to, 325
charges, 327
Chartered Accountants, Institute of, recommendations of, 328
Companies Acts, requirements of, 286, 324
distributions, 326, 327
franked investment income, 327
investigation in connection with liability, 565
outstanding, 142
permanent set-off, 328
profits, 327
temporary set-off, 327
unfranked investment income, 327
'Test Pack', 132, 133
Testing in Depth
(*See* Vouching in Depth)
Third Parties,
auditor's duty to, 429
Title Deeds,
examination of, by auditor, 157, 182
Tolerance checks, 123
Total Accounts, 96
creditors', 96
debtors', 96
Trade Discount,
(*See* Discounts)

Trade Marks, 191
Trade Investments, 174
Transfer Journal,
  (See Journal)
Transfer of Shares,
  audit of, 243
  forged, 245
  register of, 243
Travellers,
  commission and expenses of, 43, 141
  debt collection by, 51
Travelling Expenses,
  directors, 317
  outstanding, 141
  vouching, 43, 141
Treasury Bills,
  verification of, 173
Trial Balance,
  use of, 138
Trust Accounts,
  audit of, 13, 455
Trust Companies,
  accounts, audit of, 496
  unit trust accounts, audit of, 488
Trust Deed,
  examination of, 253
  recommended, 257
Trustee,
  accounts, audit of, 455
  debenture holders, for, 253, 316
  judicial, 460
  public, 459
Turnover,
  investigations, comparison of annual results for purposes, of, 527

Underwriting Commission, 260
  balance sheet, disclosure in, 262, 281
  finance companies, accounts, 496
  prospectus, disclosure in, 260
  stockbrokers' accounts, in, 492
  vouching, payment of, 260
Unit Trusts,
  accounts, audit of, 498
Unlawful Acts by Clients, 440 et seq.

Valuation,
  assets, 157 et seq., 294, 330
  copyrights, 167
  current assets, 162, 331
  fixed assets, 157, 331
  freehold property, 167
  furniture etc., 188
  investments, 169
  loose plant and tools, 188
  motor vehicles, 189
  patents, 166, 190
  plant and machinery, 187
  professional valuers, by, 294
  returnable containers, of, 85

Valuation, (continued)
  shares, of, 554, 556
  stock and shares, 169
  stock-in-trade, 175 et seq., 529
  stock-in-trade, by professional valuer, 183
  wasting assets, 162
Vendors of a Business,
  accounts, adjustment of upon acquisition, 264
  receipts and payments, treatment on behalf of, 265
Verification of Assets, 156 et seq.
  abroad, 186
  bearer securities, 171
  bills receivable, 185
  book debts, 91, 186
  building society deposits and shares, 172
  buildings, 167
  cash at bank, 56
  cash in hand, 56
  copyrights, 190
  endowment policies, 186
  freehold property, 168
  furniture etc., 188
  goodwill, 191
  in depth (see Vouching in Depth)
  investments, 169, 173
  land, 167
  leasehold property, 169
  loans on investments, 183
  loans on mortgage, 182
  loans on security, 181, 183
  loans by a company, of, 181
  loans to employees, 184
  loans to local authorities, 173
  loans to subsidiary companies, 185
  loose tools, 188, Appendix A.14
  mortgaged property, 168
  motor vehicles, 189
  patents, 190
  petty cash, 57 et seq.
  plant and machinery, 187, 188
  policies of insurance, 186
  registered stocks and shares, 171
  stamps in hand, 60
  securities in stockbrokers' accounts, 479, 482, 492
  securities in stockjobbers' accounts, 479, 482, 492, 495
  securities of building societies, of, Appendix A.17
  share transactions, when not completed, of, 171
  stock-in-trade, 175 et seq.
  tax reserve certificates, 172
  trade investments, 174
  trade marks, 191
  treasury bills, 173

Vouchers,
auditor's right to examine, 218
cheques as substitute for, 37, 45
examination to detect alterations of, 60
examining, 37 *et seq.*
investigation, examination of, in connection with, 560
missing, 40

Vouching,
agents' commission, 43
bad debt dividends, 53
bank charges, 43
bills payable, 44
bills receivable, 54
bills receivable dishonoured, 44, 45
brokerage on placing shares, 262
buildings, 41
capital expenditure, 40, 41
cash book, 37 *et seq.*
cash sales, 52 *et seq.*
commission on placing shares, 261
counterfoil receipts, by means of, 51, 52
credit sales, 51 *et seq.*
customs duties, 45, 46
debentures, issue of, 253 *et seq.*
debentures, redemption of, 257 *et seq.*
definition of, 37
directors' fees and remuneration, 310 *et seq.*
directors' travelling expenses, 316, 317
discount allowed, 52
discount on bills, 44
dividends paid, 364
dividends received, 53
forward purchases, 77
freeholds, 41
freight and carriage, 45
hire-purchase and instalment agreements, 42
hire purchase, sales under, 83, 84
'in depth', 62, 63, 79, 204, 205
income from investments, 52, 53
income tax, 46
insurance premiums, 43
interest on bank deposit, 53
interest on loans, 53
investment income 52, 53
investments, purchase of, 42
investments, sale of, 54
invoices, by means of, 74 *et seq.*
journal, 86, 87
law costs, relating to capital assets, 41
leaseholds, 41
loans, 42
miscellaneous receipts, 54

Vouching, (*continued*)
office furniture, fixtures and fittings, 43
partners' drawings, 46
patents, 42
payments, general considerations as to, 37 *et seq.*
petty cash, receipts, 44
expenditure, 57 *et seq.*
plant and machinery, 41, 42
preliminary and formation expenses, 259, 260
premium income, 462
purchase tax, 46
purchases, 74 *et seq.*
receipt of cash, 50 *et seq.*
rents receivable, 53
salaries, 44
sales, 51, 52
share capital, issue of, 239 *et seq.*
special payments, 43 *et seq.*
special receipts, 52 *et seq.*
statutory report, 262 *et seq.*
stock issues, by local authorities, 510
surveyors' fees, 41
travellers' commission, 43
travelling expenses, 43
underwriting commission, 260 *et seq.*
wages, 46 *et seq.*

Wages,
auditors' duty as regards, 49, 50
capital expenditure in, 41, 147
fraud, precaution against in, 46 *et seq.*
fraud by means of dummy names, 50, 205
internal check in relation to, 46 *et seq.*
outstanding, 140
payment of, 48
piece work basis for, 48
preparation for payment of, 48
repairs and renewals, on, 147
sheets, 48, 49, 50
time records, basis for, 47, 48
vouching, 49, 50

Wasting Assets,
definition of, 162
depreciation of, 336
legal decisions affecting, 336 *et seq.*
valuation of, 162

Wear and Tear,
(*See* depreciation)

Winding-up of Company,
auditor's liability in cases of, 395

Work-in-Progress,
auditor's liability in connection with, 417, 437

Work-in-Progress, (*continued*)
    valuation of, 180, Appendix A.5
    verification of, Appendix A.3, A.4
Working Papers,
    balance sheet audit, 199 *et seq.*

Working Papers, (*continued*)
    investigations, in need for preservation of, 525
    prepared by accountant, ownership of, 230